D0221291

THE POE ENCYCLOPEDIA

THE POE ENCYCLOPEDIA

FREDERICK S. FRANK
and
ANTHONY MAGISTRALE

GREENWOOD PRESS
Westport, Connecticut • London

Library of Congress Cataloging-in-Publication Data

The Poe encyclopedia / Frederick S. Frank and Anthony Magistrale.
p. cm.
Includes bibliographical references and index.
ISBN 0–313–27768–0 (alk. paper)
1. Poe, Edgar Allan, 1809–1849—Encyclopedias. 2. Fantastic literature, American—Encyclopedias. I. Frank, Frederick S. II. Magistrale, Tony. III. Poe, Edgar Allan, 1809–1849.
PS2630.P58 1997
818'.309—dc20 96–22005

British Library Cataloguing in Publication Data is available.

Library of Congress Catalog Card Number: 96–22005
ISBN: 0–313–27768–0

First published in 1997

Greenwood Press, 88 Post Road West, Westport, CT 06881
An imprint of Greenwood Publishing Group, Inc.

Printed in the United States of America

The paper used in this book complies with the Permanent Paper Standard issued by the National Information Standards Organization (Z39.48–1984).

10 9 8 7 6 5 4 3 2 1

Copyright Acknowledgments

The author and publisher gratefully acknowledge permission for the use of the following material:

From *The Collected Works of Edgar Allan Poe*; Volume One, poems edited by Thomas Ollive Mabbott. Copyright © 1969 by the President and Fellows of Harvard College. Reprinted by permission of Harvard University Press.

To Our Wives

Jennifer Magistrale and Nancy Frank

For her this rhyme is penned, whose luminous eyes,
Brightly expressive as the twins of Loeda,
Shall find her own sweet name, that, nestling lies
Upon the page, enwrapped from every reader.

Poe, ''A Valentine''

Contents

Preface

Planned and compiled as an eclectic reference aid to Poe studies, the purpose of *The Poe Encyclopedia* is to serve the factual and critical needs of readers of Poe at every level. Like any encyclopedia, the volume is a concentration of information embracing every aspect of the subject. Professional researchers and Poe scholars may consult the *Encyclopedia* to verify facts and ascertain both current and historical trends in Poe criticism. General readers of Poe already familiar with the primary texts can use the *Encyclopedia* to go deeper into the man and his writings. Teachers of Poe and undergraduates encountering his work for the first time in an intellectual context may go to the *Encyclopedia* for critical and factual guidance as well as a source for new approaches and topics of inquiry.

The assumption is that everything Poe wrote or did has now been subjected to scholarly scrutiny. It is a false assumption, as a survey of the scant criticism on many of the tales and poems will reveal, for there are many biographical and interpretive areas that remain to be explored. Certainly, one of the most immediate audiences for the *Encyclopedia* is in several senses the most universally vital, and it is certainly the largest. The legions of readers of Poe in every nation and every language who attend his work in search of sheer pleasure and entertainment may find in the *Encyclopedia* a repository of data that will lead to further pleasures and discoveries. The scope of the *Encyclopedia*, then, reflects the magnitude of Poe's appeal to many types of users who read Poe for diverse reasons and motives.

The majority of users will opt to consult the *Encyclopedia* selectively in pursuit of data on a special area or sequence of themes. Before undertaking any systematic search, however, the user is urged to peruse the ''Chronology,'' which records the major events of Poe's life as well as his ceaseless travels from city to city and editorial position to editorial position. While scholars have often disagreed over the significance of the biography in the shaping of his art, most have concurred that the interaction of the two is the basis for understanding Poe. For readers who are new to Poe or readers well grounded in Poe texts, beginning with the ''Chronology'' will provide a perspective or frame for nearly every entry in the *Encyclopedia.*

The individual entries are organized in simple alphabetized format. With the exception of his letters, they cover everything that Poe wrote including his long and short fiction, verse, critical essays, reviews, brief notices, and anecdotal writing. Unsigned pieces, some of which are still being identified as Poe's by modern scholarship, are also included along with his juvenalia and unpublished verse. All of Poe's literary and personal acquaintances who could be traced form a large body of entries. His ancestry, family, editorial associations, and acrimonious aggregation of enemies are identified and itemized. Places where Poe lived, or is thought to have lived, are designated by street name. Books that he read or is believed to have read, authors to whom he referred, and people and animals with whom he had dealings or was associated complete the encyclopedic character of the entries. The aim of the compilers was to be as inclusive as possible, and we have applied this liberal criterion in our investigation of the sources. Some biographical facts, such as the possible secret marriage of Poe and Virginia or his alleged sojourn in Paris, remain elusive. Other biographical hypotheses, such as the suggestion that Poe himself was the Outis who defended Longfellow from Poe's accusations of plagiarism, remain in dispute and warrant additional research. A few hours devoted to the vast array of Poe's allusions to classical and contemporary literature will yield a profile of his omnivorous reading on subjects as diverse as cryptography and street paving. Poe's connections with other writers of his own day and his global influence on all the arts are addressed by the numerous entries pointing to the legacy of Poe in France, Russia, Spain, South America, Germany, and Eastern Europe. In short, the standard of selection imposed by the compilers required a compendious assemblage of all branches of Poe knowledge in rapidly accessible form.

With the exception of Poe's characters, all entries are escorted by selected bibliographies that direct the user to specific topics of research where such pertinent criticism exists. To ascertain what areas stand in need of further inquiry, the user may wish to note the absence or inadequacy of current scholarship on certain tales and poems and, by contrast, the excess of critical writing on others. Criticism on a major tale such as ''The Fall of the House of Usher'' or his single novel *The Narrative of Arthur Gordon Pym* is now approaching critical mass, while fascinating pieces such as ''King Pest,'' ''Bon-Bon,'' and ''The Thousand-and-Second Tale of Scheherazade'' attract little scholarly enthusiasm. The criticism collected under ''Research'' is current to 1994 and in some cases represents the historical shifts in changing interpretation and thematic emphasis.

Poe texts are identified throughout the *Encyclopedia* by the keyed source *CWP*, which stands for *The Complete Works of Edgar Allan Poe*, edited by James A. Harrison, and *MCW*, which indicates *Collected Works of Edgar Allan Poe*, edited by Thomas Ollive Mabbott. Harrison's "Virginia Edition" in seventeen volumes and Mabbott's three-volume edition are to be found in most public and academic libraries and are to be regarded as standard or authoritative texts, although the user should be aware that the completion and perfection of the Poe canon remains an ongoing task of modern scholarship. Although not listed as a keyed reference source, Burton R. Pollin's scholarly edition of *Collected Writings of Edgar Allan Poe* in four volumes should be consulted as scholarly and reliable in every aspect. Entries referring to *Pinakidia* and *Marginalia* are sometimes keyed to the abbreviation *BRE* or *The Brevities*, Pollin's superlatively detailed edition of these anecdotal works. The compilers have minimized the use of cross-references among the entries, using the "See" category only in those instances where an important interrelationship or critical link might be overlooked by the user or some fact of mutual significance missed. To avoid bibliographic redundancy, no title of criticism cited in the "Research" categories is repeated in the Bibliography.

Preparation of the *Encyclopedia* would have been impossible without the assistance of Burton R. Pollin's *Dictionary of Names and Titles in Poe's Collected Works* (*DNT*), an indispensable, computer-generated thesaurus to all names and titles in Poe's writings. A similar electronic version of such a concordance employing Pollin's format and procedures would be an invaluable asset to the modern Poe scholar. Additionally, preparation and arrangement of the entries would have been equally hazardous without the availability of *The Poe Log: A Documentary Life of Edgar Allan Poe* (*TPL*), compiled by Dwight Thomas and David Jackson, a minute and exhaustive daily chronological record. In fact, the prodigious scholarly example of *The Poe Log* served as a foundation and inspiration for *The Poe Encyclopedia.* Together with *The Poe Log*, biographical particulars have frequently been drawn from the two most recent accounts of Poe's life, Kenneth Silverman's *Edgar Allan Poe: Mournful and Never-Ending Remembrance* (*MNR*, 1991) and Jeffrey Meyers's *Edgar Allan Poe: His Life and Legacy* (*PLL*, 1993). Their portraits of Poe bear some resemblance to the balanced and corrective outlook on the man and his work assumed by Hervey Allen in a biography that retains its place as one of the best factual and critical chronicles of Poe's short but complex life, *Israfel: The Life and Times of Edgar Allan Poe* (*LTP*, 1934). Nearly 150 years after his death, myth, rumor, prevarication, distortion, and exaggeration continue to mar the image of Poe, whose authentic self remains a challenge to biographers. As E. F. Bleiler has written, "The achievement of Edgar Allan Poe is still controversial, for it must be admitted that many major critics have damned his work. . . . It is safe to say that as his work is better understood in its complexity, it is more highly esteemed."

All of the keyed reference sources mentioned throughout the entries are supplemented by the general and special references found in the Bibliography. For enhanced information on general subject areas such as Poe biographers and biographies or psychoanalytic interpretations of Poe's work or narrower and specialized topics such as Poe's combativeness as a reviewer or the reception of Poe in Norway and Sweden, the user may move from the entry section of the Bibliography to one or more of the later ones. ''Bibliographies, Concordances, Synopses, Catalogues, and Other Reference Sources'' has been appended to assist users who desire further guidance inside the crowded and busy house of Poe scholarship.

The Poe Encyclopedia offers three indexes whose function is explained by their titles. An ''Index of Critics, Editors, and Acquaintances'' provides a quick and convenient means of locating data on any Poe critic or editor, family member, associate, or casual acquaintance. An ''Index of Authors, Artists, and Titles'' enables the user to trace Poe's literary knowledge and known reading, his opinion of another literary artist, philosopher, historian, or scientist, or his reaction to certain books. An ''Index of Themes, Subjects, and Characters'' identifies all of the characters in Poe's tales and poems, the human, the inhuman, and the superhuman, and guides the researcher to Poe's explicit use of a theme, locale, myth, biblical allusion, folklore figure, or gothic motif.

Since *The Poe Encyclopedia* is the first reference book of its type, the compilers ask for any suggestions from users concerning flaws in organization or content, especially the omission of any entries obviously necessary for encyclopedic thoroughness and success. Our constant goal has been to produce a useful lens for the clarification and magnification of Poe's achievements.

Acknowledgments

As with previous projects, the staff of the Pelletier Library, Allegheny College, assisted the preparation of this book at every stage and in too many ways to document briefly. The reference librarians, Donald A. Vrabel and Jane F. Westenfeld, were especially supportive. The early stages of research were carried out at the Alderman Library of the University of Virginia. The staff of the Rare Book Department and Special Collections there provided both access to an infinity of Poe materials as well as one of the most intellectually congenial settings for pursuing Poe studies in the world. We also wish to acknowledge the assistance given by Dr. Craige Champion, Department of Classics, Allegheny College, for his translations of several of Poe's Latin quotations and explanations of several of Poe's more obscure allusions to the ancient authors. The fact that the work is dedicated to our wives, Jennifer Magistrale and Nancy Frank, should indicate to all users our deepest and most affectionate debt.

Abbreviations

BPB	Miller, John Carl. *Building Poe Biography.* Baton Rouge: Louisiana State University Press, 1977.
BRE	Pollin, Burton R., ed. *The Brevities: Pinakidia, Marginalia, Fifty Suggestions and Other Works.* New York: Gordian Press, 1985.
CWP	Harrison, James A., ed. *The Complete Works of Edgar Allan Poe.* 17 vols. New York: Thomas Y. Crowell, 1902; Rpt. New York: AMS Press, 1965.
DIP	Pollin, Burton R. *Discoveries in Poe.* Notre Dame, IN: Notre Dame University Press, 1970.
DNT	Pollin, Burton R. *Dictionary of Names and Titles in Poe's Collected Works.* New York: Da Capo Press, 1968.
LET	Ostrom, John Ward, ed. *The Letters of Edgar Allan Poe.* 2 vols. New York: Gordian Press, 1966.
LTP	Allen, Hervey. *Israfel: The Life and Times of Edgar Allan Poe.* 2nd ed. New York: Farrar & Rinehart, 1934.
MCW	Mabbott, Thomas Ollive, Eleanor D. Kewer, and Maureen C. Mabbott, eds. *Collected Works of Edgar Allan Poe; Poems* (volume I); *Tales and Sketches, 1831–1842* (volume II); *Tales and Sketches, 1843–1849* (volume III). Cambridge, MA: Belknap Press of Harvard University, 1969–1978.
MNR	Silverman, Kenneth. *Edgar A. Poe: Mournful and Never-Ending Remembrance.* New York: HarperCollins, 1991.

PEP	Stovall, Floyd, ed. *The Poems of Edgar Allan Poe*. Charlottesville: Virginia University Press, 1965.
PJC	Jacobs, Robert D. *Poe: Journalist and Critic*. Baton Rouge: Louisiana State University Press, 1969.
PLB	Moss, Sidney P. *Poe's Literary Battles: The Critic in the Context of His Literary Milieu*. Durham, NC: Duke University Press, 1963.
PLL	Meyers, Jeffrey. *Edgar Allan Poe: His Life and Legacy*. New York: Scribner's, 1993.
TPL	Thomas, Dwight, and David Jackson. *The Poe Log: A Documentary Life of Edgar Allan Poe*. Boston: G. K. Hall, 1987.

Chronology

1809	Poe born on 19 January in Boston in a rooming house at 62 Carver Street.
1811	Disappearance of David Poe, Poe's father, and death of Elizabeth Poe, his mother, on 8 December 1811. Poe taken into the home of John and Frances Allan as a ward but not legally adopted.
1812	Under Allan's legal guardianship, Poe lives with the Allans at the corner of Main and Thirteenth Streets, Richmond.
1815	On 23 June, the Allans sail from Norfolk to Liverpool, taking young Edgar "Allan" Poe with them.
1816	Poe attends various English boarding schools including the Academy of The Misses Dubourg in Chelsea.
1817	Poe continues his education in England.
1818	At age nine, Poe enters the Manor House School of Doctor Bransby at Stoke Newington.
1819	Poe continues his education in England. John Allan has monetary problems. He tells William Galt that "Edgar is in the Country at School, he is a very fine boy & a good scholar."
1820	On 20 June, Poe returns to the United States from England with the Allans.
1821–25	Poe leads a Richmond boyhood, is athletically active, and is attracted to contemporary Romantic literature. He falls

in love with Jane Stith Stanard and Sarah Elmira Royster, claiming ''engagement'' to the latter. Beginnings of conflict with John Allan over matters of money and career choices.

1826 Poe enters the University of Virginia at Charlottesville on 14 February but is compelled to withdraw by Allan in December because of gambling debts. Poe is then employed without salary in Allan's counting house.

1827 On 19 March, following a quarrel with Allan, Poe leaves Richmond and the Allan household to embark upon his own career, eventually making his way to Boston. He discovers that Sarah Elmira Royster is to marry another man. On 26 May, Poe enlists in the United States Army. *Tamerlane and Other Poems. By a Bostonian* is published in June.

1828 Poe has various postings while in the United States Army including Fortress Monroe, Fort Moultrie, and Fort Independence in Boston Harbor.

1829 On 1 January, Poe is promoted to regimental sergeant major. Upon the death of his foster mother, Frances Allan, on 28 February, Poe returns to Richmond to attempt a reconciliation with John Allan. Discharged from the army on 15 April, he takes up residence with his aunt, Mrs. Maria Clemm, in Baltimore. In December, he publishes *Al Aaraaf, Tamerlane, and Minor Poems* and struggles to launch a literary career.

1830–31 Further clashes in the spring with the remarried John Allan, who was able to secure an appointment for Poe to the Military Academy at West Point. Poe enters the United States Military Academy on 1 July, deliberately neglects his duties, and is court-martialed on 28 January for ''gross neglect'' and ''disobedience of orders'' and is discharged on 6 March, leaving the Academy and going to New York on 19 February. He moves on to Baltimore in April, again residing with Maria Clemm. Second edition of *Poems* published in New York. Begins writing and submitting stories to the Philadelphia *Saturday Courier*.

1832 A final and futile visit to Richmond ends Poe's relationship with John Allan, who then revises his will on 17 April, omitting Poe. Poe continues to submit stories to various newspapers and journals.

1833 On 12 October, Poe is awarded a prize of $100 by the *Baltimore Saturday Visiter* for ''MS. Found in a Bottle.'' While living in Baltimore, he begins to assemble *Tales of*

	the Folio Club and develops a friendship with John Pendleton Kennedy.
1834	In February, Poe visits Allan who is near death, dying on 27 March. Thomas H. Ellis reports that during this final visit "Mr. Allan raised his cane, & threatening to strike him if he came within his reach, ordered him out." John Pendleton Kennedy recommends Poe to Thomas W. White, editor of *The Southern Literary Messenger*.
1835	*The Southern Literary Messenger* publishes "Berenice," "Hans Pfaall," and several reviews by Poe. In August, Poe joins the staff of *The Messenger*. On 22 September, a marriage license of Edgar A. Poe and Virginia Clemm was issued by the Baltimore County Court, but no firm evidence for a ceremony at this time exists. In October, Poe is joined in Richmond by Mrs. Clemm and Virginia.
1836	Poe contributes abrasive reviews to *The Southern Literary Messenger* and publishes the "Autography" series and "Maelzel's Chess-Player." Poe and Virginia Clemm are married on 16 May 1836. Feeling unsuccessful and circumscribed by *The Messenger*, Poe quarrels with White and is dismissed. In December, he resolves to enter the literary world of New York City.
1837	*The Southern Literary Messenger* publishes several chapters of *The Narrative of Arthur Gordon Pym* in the January number. Poe resides in New York City, contributes reviews to various journals, makes the acquaintance of Columbia College professor of classics Charles Anthon, and experiments with short fiction.
1838	In July, Harper publishes *The Narrative of Arthur Gordon Pym*. In the summer, Poe, Virginia, and Mrs. Clemm move to Philadelphia. *Pym* receives mixed reviews. *The American Museum* for September publishes "Ligeia" and a utopian satire, "The Atlantis, a Southern World—Or a Wonderful Continent Discovered," which is sometimes attributed to Poe. He has no journal employment in the year 1838.
1839	Poe becomes coeditor with William Burton of *Burton's Gentleman's Magazine* in July. He writes essays on cryptography, publishes "The Fall of the House of Usher" in *Burton's* for September, and extends his reputation as an excoriating reviewer. In December, the Philadelphia house of Lea & Blanchard publishes *Tales of the Grotesque and Arabesque*.
1840	Poe begins, then aborts the long short story *The Journal of Julius Rodman* as his relationship with Burton grows

antagonistic. When Poe accuses Longfellow of plagiarism and promotes his own journal, *The Penn Magazine*, Burton discharges Poe on 30 May. Poe devotes the remainder of the year to the failed attempt to enlist subscribers and contributors. No issue of *The Penn Magazine* is forthcoming.

1841 Poe begins an editorial affiliation with *Graham's Magazine* in February, writing numerous reviews, continuing the ''Autography'' series, and contributing ''The Murders in the Rue Morgue.'' His attempt to obtain a customs house appointment in the Tyler administration fails. He corresponds with James Fenimore Cooper and meets anthologist and littérateur Rufus Wilmot Griswold. In December, warfare with critic Edwin P. Whipple begins when he assails Poe in *The Boston Notion* and *Daily Times*.

1842 Poe leaves his editorial position at *Graham's Magazine* in April, having published some of his best work here, including ''The Masque of the Red Death.'' Virginia Clemm's pulmonary disorder and Poe's heavy drinking mark a year of unemployment and financial distress. He conducts two interviews with Charles Dickens and is solicited for contributions by James Russell Lowell in establishing his literary journal *The Pioneer*.

1843 Poe continues the struggle to found a magazine of his own, now to be called *The Stylus*. ''The Tell-Tale Heart'' appears in Lowell's *Pioneer* for January. Periods of hard writing are interrupted by drinking and erratic endeavors to gain a customs house appointment. In June, the Philadelphia *Dollar Newspaper* grants Poe a $100 prize for ''The Gold-Bug,'' the award stirring controversy among Poe's enemies. Living in Philadelphia on North Seventh Street, he contributes reviews to *Graham's Magazine*, travels to Saratoga Springs, lectures on poetry, and publishes the comic piece ''Diddling'' in the Philadelphia *Saturday Courier*.

1844 Poe severs connections with *Graham's Magazine* and moves to New York City with Virginia and Mrs. Clemm in April. With Virginia's condition declining, Poe labors at hack writing, contributing to the New York *Evening Mirror* and arousing a sensation with a fake, big story, ''The Balloon Hoax.'' Nathaniel Parker Willis, editor of the New York *Evening Mirror*, befriends Poe and brings him on the staff in October.

1845 The New York *Evening Mirror* publishes ''The Raven'' dated 29 January. Poe enjoys literary acclaim with the literati of the city, gives lectures and readings, and in February, is contracted as an editor of the newly founded *Broadway Journal* in partnership with Charles F. Briggs. Battles with Thomas Dunn English and quarrels with Briggs, who attempts to recover sole control of the paper. Wiley and Putnam publishes *Tales By Edgar A. Poe* in June and *The Raven and Other Poems* in November.

1846 A year of destitution and literary battles. On 3 January, the *Broadway Journal* ceases publication. In May, Poe and the weakening Virginia move to a cottage in Fordham. Begins friendship with the poet Frances Sargent Osgood and composes a series of profiles, ''The Literati of New York City,'' in *Godey's Lady's Book*. ''The Philosophy of Composition'' and ''The Cask of Amontillado'' appear.

1847 Virginia Clemm Poe dies on 30 January 1847 at the Fordham cottage. In ''The Philosophy of Composition,'' Poe had written, ''The death, then, of a beautiful woman is, unquestionably, the most poetical topic in the world—and equally is it beyond doubt that the lips best suited for such a topic are those of a bereaved lover.'' In February, Poe brings a libel suit against the publishers of the *Evening Mirror*. ''Ulalume: A Ballad,'' unsigned and dedicated to an unknown, appears in the *American Review* for December.

1848 Poe lectures on the cosmos, later expanding the talk into *Eureka: A Prose Poem*, published in July. He launches sentimental liaisons with two ladies, Mrs. Annie Richmond of Lowell, Massachusetts, and Sarah Helen Whitman of Providence. Attempts suicide in November when the Whitman family objects to his suit. Continues to lecture, write poetry, and promote the *Stylus* scheme.

1849 In July, Poe returns to Richmond to renew his courtship of Sarah Elmira Royster Shelton, now widowed. More lectures, poetry readings, alcoholic hyperactivity, and periods of instability and hallucination. He delivers a lecture on ''The Poetic Principle'' in Richmond and Norfolk and in May composes ''Annabel Lee,'' his final poem. On 3 October, an election day in Baltimore, he is found in a delirious and semiconscious state in a street near a tavern. Taken to Washington College Hospital, Poe dies there on Sunday, 7 October, at 5:00 A.M. reportedly shouting for the polar explorer Reynolds and pronouncing his own epitaph: ''Lord help my poor soul.'' He is buried in the Presbyterian Cemetery in Baltimore on 8 October.

1850 Postmortem character assassination of Poe begins with Rufus W. Griswold's scurillous portrait attached to volume III of *The Works of the Late Edgar Allan Poe, with a Memoir by Rufus Wilmot Griswold and Notices of His Life and Genius by N.P. Willis and J.R. Lowell.*

THE POE ENCYCLOPEDIA

Introduction

Passionate readers of Poe come to him early in life perhaps by way of a school assignment or a literate relative given to reading aloud from "The Raven" or "The Tell-Tale Heart." For most readers, Poe is a childhood author in spite of the fact that he remains one of the more complex and challenging writers in all of American literature.

The general reader usually comes to Poe through his short tales of horror, but it was his verse that first attracted the French symbolists, who in turn rescued him from literary obscurity and defended him from the lies of Griswold. As a consequence, Poe was the first American writer profound and gifted enough to impress literary Europe. During his lifetime, he had established himself as America's preeminent arbiter of artistic standards and taste attacking dull didacticism in some of the most progressive literary criticism written in the nineteenth century.

Yet it is not Baudelaire's Poe or Poe, the critic and essayist, who has so thoroughly captured the world's imagination for the past century and a half. Few contemporary readers, with the exception of Poe scholars and ardent fans who are driven to read the total Poe, now concern themselves with his rancorous reviews or the metaphysical peregrinations of his philosophical treatises. Ultimately, it is Poe, the master of the short story, the genre he helped to define and perfect, who allures the average reader and to whom even professional researchers revert.

The short narratives of horror and suspense offer a compressed world populated by psyches out of control. Poe's unprecedented success at evoking intense psychological obsessiveness yielded a body of fiction that still manages to disconcert jaded modern audiences thoroughly acclimated to audiovisual violence and gore. By depicting unstable minds unable to discipline their darkest urges, Poe's tales thrust even the reluctant reader inside the demented psyches of his characters. James B. Twitchell, a critic of popular culture, claims that Poe's art was the first to make the teller of the tale into the invading monster. We now have the gothic story, not from the victim's point of view but from the victimizer's.[1] Such a significant shift in narrative perspective forces the reader into an uncomfortable intimacy with the characters that is somewhat analogous to the role occupied by the viewer of the horror film. Both audiences are shocked into an awareness of their essential passivity and vulnerability in a dark cosmos. Like the horror film, Poe's tales produce contradictory tensions: the desire to watch and participate in unspeakable acts versus the wish to be free from monstrous drives. Poe was the first writer to press the relationship between monster or criminal and the reader to the point where it became simultaneously unbearable and pleasurable. Perhaps this central tension of reader response explains why generations of audiences have reacted to Poe's characters and their situations with mixed revulsion and secret identification.

The intertextual tensions inherent in Poe's tales return us once again to the connection between Poe and adolescence. Bedeviled by questions of authority and identity, anxiety over social acceptance, and sexual confusion, the adolescent can immediately relate to the violent proclivities of such antiheroes as William Wilson and the Dostoevskian killer of "The Tell-Tale Heart." The release of repressed energy in the form of antisocial acts suggests the tempestuous nature of adolescence in a high-achievement culture. The impulse toward self-destruction or the destruction of others as a relief for social or sexual repression are the normal conditions of Poe's abnormal worlds, terrors, and conflicts highly familiar to the young. Warped sexuality and sublimated sexual response, yet another major theme of the tales, suggests yet a further link with the terrors and tensions of puberty. Considering the appeal of the Poe tale to the pubertal prisoner, one ambivalent reader of Poe, T. S. Eliot, observed: "The forms which his lively curiosity takes are those in which a pre-adolescent mentality delights: wonders of nature and mechanics and of the supernatural, cryptograms and cyphers, puzzles and labyrinths, mechanical chess-players and wild flights of speculation."[2] Ironically, as inimical readers such as Eliot recognized, Poe's most memorable work conveys us downward in a direction diametrically opposite to those zones of supernal beauty of which he was so fond and into the fatally erotic milieu of the adolescent. By taking Poe seriously, Eliot realized that his fellow American writer refused to be disowned. Poe had a profound capacity for dramatizing the darkest elements of human psychology, especially child psychology.

The paradigmatic Poe horror story displays several unifying traits, the most common of which is isolation or sequestration. "The Pit and the Pendulum," "Ligeia," "The Cask of Amontillado," "The Tell-Tale Heart," "The Masque of the Red Death," "Berenice," "The Imp of the Perverse," "The Fall of the

House of Usher,'' and ''The Black Cat'' all involve what Poe himself designated ''a close circumscription of space'' or a condition of isolation in which the characters are cut off from meaningful forms of social communication. Under such circumscribed circumstances, the characters develop peculiar missions or secret schemes to escape the imprisoning realities of time and space, but only one of the protagonists, the anonymous heretic-narrator of ''The Pit and the Pendulum,'' achieves salvation. In almost every case, these isolatoes are in rebellion against some restrictive moral or physical law that denies them their high poetic place in the universe. Hence, their rebellion often is concentrated upon a person or object associated with some notion of personalized restriction, a black cat, a vulturelike eye, a blond, blue-eyed wife. These icons of propriety must be destroyed if the narrator is to attain the sort of freedom he craves. Typically, the attempt to forge a new identity through crime is an exalting experience. After disposing of wife and cat, the narrator of ''The Black Cat'' exults, ''My happiness was supreme! The guilt of my dark deed disturbed me but little. . . . I looked upon my future felicity as secured.'' But from such pinnacles of momentary bliss, they descend into the lonely silence of the tomb, the jail, or the lunatic asylum.

The ubiquity of time in these clock-ridden stories, especially the convergence of the two hands of the clock at the midnight hour, represents a verticality related to the aspirations of the self, as the two-hands-become-one point the way to an ideality above the material world. Poe's characters would annihilate time in order to transcend the limitations of a conventionally regulated world. But as the clock's hands must necessarily separate, so too must the narrator fall backward into the clock-ruled pit of time. The imposition of temporal authority thwarts the creation of any self-enclosed ideality; as an objective signifier, time shatters the subjective realm imagined by the criminal. What Jean-Paul Weber has called the ''superpositions and the vertical structures''[3] cannot be sustained as the main characters come to realize that in destroying the symbols of the material world they are destroying themselves.

The irrational crimes and punishments of the homicidal fantasies find a counterpart in the rational crimes and punishments of the detective tales in which Poe elaborates upon the skill of the central character, C. Auguste Dupin, in employing the imagination of the poet and the analytic intelligence of the mathematician to solve insoluble crimes. To crack his cases, Dupin's mind entertains a perfect balance of analysis and speculative insight rendered all the more effective by his close identification with the criminal and his thought processes. Solving the crime is not a moral act at all but an intellectual and intuitive exercise, like the writing of a beautiful poem. Poe's detective and Poe's criminals are opposite sides of the same authorial consciousness, for like the anonymous murderers of ''The Black Cat'' and ''The Tell-Tale Heart,'' Dupin is by design self stimulated by the exotic and peculiar and acting according to a master plan. Juxtaposing Dupin's deliberate methods to the criminal behavior dramatized in the horror tales, we discover that the mental routine of Dupin has much in common with the inquisitive narrators of the homicidal fantasies. Completely self-contained and deigning to enter the social sphere only to exhibit his crime-solving prowess to the embarrassment of the authorities, the great detective operates on a plane above the forces of law and social convention. Because the moral implications of the crime never intrude upon the ideal solution, Dupin always succeeds where the moralists fail. Beautiful and perfect in conception and execution, his solutions are works of art as Dupin has attained the sort of ideality that the killers and madmen vainly seek.

Everything that Poe carried out in a serious vein in the homicidal and suicidal fantasies and the detective tales he also performed in a hilarious key in his comic pieces, which constitute a large segment of his short story output. Irony, parody, masquerades, posing, hoaxing, and burlesques of revenge and detection mark that other dimension of the Poe canon that has prompted one modern critic, Daniel Hoffman, to rechristen him "Hoaxiepoe."[4] Hoffman scandalized Poe scholarship by declaring, "Hoaxiepoe. That's one of the mirror images of horror-haunted Edgar. The one that laughs immoderately." Hoffman's argument fomented a rereading of Poe that is still in progress to test the assumption that Poe, the sardonic comedian, chose to mock all expressions of reality as a demonic deception and all existence as a brutal cosmic hoax. Whether or not this critical hypothesis is valid, it cannot be denied that tales such as "A Predicament," "The Devil in the Belfry," "Never Bet the Devil Your Head," "The System of Doctor Tarr and Professor Fether," "King Pest," and "Lionizing" are as essential to an understanding of his art as the serious horror tales. Emboldened by Hoffman's thesis, another critic, G. R. Thompson in *Poe's Fiction: Romantic Irony in the Gothic Tales*,[5] argues that everything Poe wrote is potentially ironic, delusive, and satiric in tone and substance. The lines of demarcation between horror and hilarity, between the grotesque and the sublime, and between reality and illusion are eradicated to the point where no reader can be absolutely sure of anything at all in Poe's absurdist universe. Humor arises in the comic pieces when the entrapped characters attempt to deal with the world in serious terms, as when the gradually decapitated Signora Psyche Zenobia tries to analyze her way out of the lethal situation in "A Predicament." Much of Poe's morbid and emetic comedy involves explicit parody of the typical magazine fiction of his day, but his merciless burlesqueing may also be a possible mockery of his own serious work. When read in an ironic context, "A Predicament" becomes a comic inversion of "The Pit and the Pendulum."

The gullibility and misperception of readers encouraged Poe to turn one of the most popular genres of his time, the explorer's narrative, into scientific hoaxes as he did in the hot air extravaganzas "The Balloon Hoax," "The Unparalleled Adventure of One Hans Pfaall," and "Mellonta Tauta." These fake big stories not only contributed to Poe's desire for public notoriety; they confirmed his opinion of the stupidity of the democratic masses. The hoaxes and the imaginary voyages underscore a major critical problem confronting the reader of any Poe tale: To what degree and for what purpose is Poe hoaxing or duping the reader and warping the facts for his own private ends?

No irony, no impulse to deceive or hoax, no satiric subtext infuses Poe's verse where the sole reality is an aesthetic ideality described in "Dream-Land" as lying "Out of SPACE,—Out of TIME." Many of the shorter poems are lyrics of irrecoverable loss, the loss of youth, the loss of love, while longer poems such as "Al Aaraaf" and "The Raven" are versified narratives. Poe theorizes on the ideal nature of poetry and often draws examples from his own verse to clarify his central concept that poetry is "*the rhythmical creation of Beauty.*" In a trio of essays, "The Philosophy of Composition," "The Poetic Principle," and "The Rationale of Verse," he repeated and demonstrated this proposition, arbitrarily asserting "that Beauty is the sole legitimate province of the poem." Any poem that was not readable at one sitting was, by definition, not a poem at all, for in giving up the immediate impact of one sitting, it surrended all "totality of effect." Although it does not always succeed, all of Poe's poetry undertakes to communicate such a "totality of effect" through rhythmic cadence, proportion, repetition, and metrical austerity.

The locales of the poems are often those idealized sites of beauty or Edens of imagination that elude his failed questers. Other poems reveal a deserted psychic terrain that combines elements of beauty and horror within a doomed world viewed at the brink of collapse in its final moments. "Dream-Land," "The City in the Sea," and "Israfel" are beautiful lyrics of poignant and permanent loss. "The Bells," its rhythms punctuated by the king ghoul who keeps "time, time, time in a sort of Runic rhyme," illustrates Poe's commitment to the mechanics of verse and his technical virtuosity in presenting the poem to the reader as a purely musical experience.

The poems further indicate Poe's faith in the Baconian aesthetic of a lovely distorted strangeness, lovely because distorted, an ultimate beauty that must incorporate the bizarre and the charnel in order to rank as beautiful. The suggestion in "Fifty Suggestions" that "An artist is only an artist by dint of his exquisite sense of Beauty—a sense affording him rapturous enjoyment, but at the same time implying, or involving, an equally exquisite sense of Deformity or disproportion"[6] finds fulfillment in the elegy "Ulalume."

Quite opposite to the disembodied Keatsian voice of the poetry is the harsh and occasionally vituperative voice of Poe, the reviewer and practicing journalist. The pages of *The Southern Literary Messenger*, *Graham's Magazine*, and *The Broadway Journal* are strewn with the literary corpses of novelists and poets slain by Poe's sarcastic pen. He often exploited his editorial positions to perform vivisections on books that would not be matched in savagery until the arrival of H. L. Mencken on the literary scene. Much of his spleen was directed at the sentimental and didactic tendencies of the age that Poe felt had debased the arts in general and pandered to the low tastes of an ignorant readership. Although lengthiness in a work of art was anathema, Poe could be fair to lengthy novels and poems so long as they met his structural and aesthetic standards. But in all too many cases where he disliked both the book and its author, Poe simply substituted a sneering synopsis for any equitable scrutiny or appraisal. Many commentators on Poe's reviewing techniques have noted that in his detailed explications he was the first of the ''New Critics,'' who, a century later, would formulate the methodology for examining and judging an individual work of art as a self-contained unit existing in a sphere of its own creation. Certainly, he was the first American to make literary criticism a rigorous discipline rather than the appreciative ruminations of a leisurely reader, and as a theorist of genre, he worked nearly alone in an untrodden field.

What is perhaps most impressive about Poe's reviewing and literary criticism is its range and breadth. Along with belles lettres and works of contemporary and classical literature, he reviewed books on nostrums and medicine, archeology, travel, biography, translations, grammar and philology, exploration, phrenology, technical works and economics, and a host of variegated subjects. Pressed by too many editorial assignments, Poe also sometimes reviewed books that he had merely skimmed or not read at all. On other occasions, he relied on clichés and formulaic phrases to praise or denounce a work. A novel or book of verse ''lacks true ideality,'' or a medical tract such as Lewis Durlacher's *Treatise on Corns, Bunions, the Diseases of Nails, and the General Management of the Feet* is vaguely recommended as a book that ''cannot fail to do a great deal of good.''[7]

Surveying the daily output of Poe the reviewer, it is remarkable that he found time to do any creative work of his own or to engage in the dissipations of alcohol. Perhaps the onus of reviewing so much all of the time explains the caustic tone of so many of the reviews. Economic desperation, exploitive editors, and incessant and inflexible deadlines, compounded by domestic crises and intellectual fatigue, were among the demons with which Poe was forced to contend on a daily basis.

Teller of macabre tales of horror, brilliant critic and literary theorist, humorist, hoaxer, and parodist, and poet of strange beauty, Poe is and shall remain a genius without peer in his chosen spheres of art.

Notes

1. James B. Twitchell, *Dreadful Pleasures: An Anatomy of Modern Horror* (New York: Oxford University Press, 1985), 46.

2. Thomas Stearns Eliot, ''From Poe to Valéry,'' *Hudson Review*, 2 (1949): 327–342; Rpt. in *The Recognition of Edgar Allan Poe: Selected Criticism since 1829*, ed. Eric W. Carlson (Ann Arbor: Michigan University Press, 1966), 212.

3. Jean-Paul Weber, ''Edgar Poe or the Theme of the Clock,'' *La Nouvelle Revue Française*, 68–69 (August–September 1958):301–311, 498–508; Rpt. in *Poe: A Collection of Critical Essays*, ed. Robert Regan (Englewood Cliffs, NJ: Prentice-Hall, 1967).

4. Daniel Hoffman, ''Dull Realities,'' in *Poe Poe Poe Poe Poe Poe Poe* (New York: Doubleday, 1972), 179–200.

5. G. R. Thompson, *Poe's Fiction: Romantic Irony in the Gothic Tales* (Madison: Wisconsin University Press, 1973).

6. Edgar Allan Poe, ''Fifty Suggestions XXII,'' in *The Brevities: Pinakidia, Marginalia, Fifty Suggestions, and Other Works*, ed. Burton R. Pollin (New York: Gordian Press, 1985), 488–489.

7. Kenneth Silverman, *Edgar A. Poe: Mournful and Never-Ending Remembrance* (New York: HarperCollins, 1991), 276.

A

Abel-Phittim. Character in the short story ''A Tale of Jerusalem.'' He is one of the Gizbarim or collectors of the offering in the Holy City. The name was spelled ''Abel-Shittim'' when the story was published in *The Southern Literary Messenger* for April 1836.

Abel-Shittim. Alternate name for the character Abel-Phittim in the short story ''A Tale of Jerusalem.'' *See:* Abel-Phittim. *Text: CWP,* II, 378.

Abernethy, Dr. John. (1764–1831). Eccentric British physician. He is referred to by Dupin in ''The Purloined Letter.'' When a patient asked Abernethy what he should take, the reply was: ''Take advice.'' *Text: CWP,* VI, 38.

"About Critics and Criticism: By the Late Edgar A. Poe." Essay by Poe not published in his lifetime. It appeared posthumously in *Graham's Magazine* for January 1850. Poe had sent the piece to John Priestley of *The American Review* in January 1849. Poe praised the analytic and stylistic abilities of Macaulay and urged, ''The true course to be pursued by our critics—justly sensible of Macaulay's excellences—is *not*, however, to be content with tamely following in his footsteps—but to outstrip him in his own path—a path not so much his as Nature's.'' Poe also held up Edwin Percy Whipple, a New England literary critic, as a negative example of timid and undiscriminating, hence worthless, criticism. *See:* Whipple, Edwin Percy. *Text: CWP,* XIII, 193–202. *Research: TPL,* 788–789.

"Achilles' Wrath." In *The Broadway Journal* of 19 April 1845, Poe responded to an irate note from W. Dinneford complaining about his review of *Antigone.* Dinneford informs Poe that his name is to be removed from the free list for theater tickets in New York. *Text: CWP,* XII, 135–139.

"An Acrostic." Unpublished acrostic poem in nine lines that appears in the album of Poe's cousin Elizabeth Rebecca Herring. Mabbott included it among the fugitive pieces in his edition and dated the poem circa 1829. The influence of Keats and Thomas Moore is evident in the closing lines: ''Endymion, recollect, when Luna tried/ To cure his love—was cured of all beside—/ His folly—pride—and passion—for he died.'' *Text: MCW,* I, 149–150.

Ada. Character appearing in the 403-line 1827 version of the poem ''Tamerlane.'' ''One noon of a bright summer's day/ I pass'd from out the matted bow'r/ Where in a deep still slumber lay/ My Ada.'' *Text: MCW,* I, 35–36; *CWP,* VII, 138.

Adams, John. (1773–1825). Mayor of Richmond. When the young Poe was a member of the Junior Volunteers, a paramilitary unit, he received arms from the mayor to be used in forming a bodyguard for Lafayette in his visit to the city. *Research: TPL,* xv, 62.

Adams, John Quincy. (1767–1848). Sixth president of the United States. Poe mentions him in his review of Griswold's *The Poets and Poetry of America* as one of the writers misclassified by Griswold under ''Various Authors,'' ''thereby throwing openly the charge of their incompetency to sustain the name of Poets.'' Under the guise of Joseph V. Miller, Poe included an analysis of his signature in ''Autography.'' *Text: CWP,* IX, 241; XV, 160; XV, 233.

Addison, Joseph. (1672–1719). English essayist and contributor to *The Spectator* and *The Tatler.* Poe credits him with an original and natural style and compares Addison's easy brilliance with Nathaniel Parker Willis's command of language. *See:* Cary, Henry. *Text: CWP,* XIII, 147; XV, 11. *Research: LTP*, 82, 355.

"Address Delivered at the Annual Commencement of Dickinson College, July 21, 1836, by S. A. Roszel." Poe reviewed the address by S. A. Roszel, principal of the Grammar School, in *The Southern Literary Messenger* for October 1836. He praises Roszel's remarks on tutorial pedagogy as a ''defense of the learned tongues from the encroachments of a misconceived utilitarianism.'' *Text: CWP,* IX, 158–159.

"Address Delivered before the Baltimore Lyceum, Athenæum Society, William Wirt Society, Washington Lyceum, Philo-Nomian Society and Franklin Association, Literary and Scientific Societies of Baltimore, on the 4th of July, 1836. By Z. Collins Lee." Poe briefly reviewed an address delivered by Zaccheus Collins Lee in the November 1836 issue of *The Southern Literary Messenger*, referring to its ''impassioned and scholar-like performance.'' Lee had known Poe at the University of Virginia and attended Poe's funeral. *Text: CWP,* IX, 206.

"Address Delivered before the Goethean and Diagnothian Societies of Marshall College." Poe favorably reviewed an address of 24 September 1839 by Joseph R. Chandler in the December 1839 issue of *Burton's Gentleman's Magazine* on the subject of ancient versus modern oratory, noting ''the vast superiority of the modern intellect.'' Chandler was the editor of *The United States Gazette*, a Philadelphia daily. *Text: CWP,* X, 57–59.

"An Address Delivered before the Students of William and Mary at the Opening of the College on Monday, October 10, 1836. By Thomas R. Dew." Review of the address by the president of William and Mary, appearing in *The Southern Literary Messenger* for October 1836. In point of fact, Poe did not review the contents of the address but gave instead a description of the curriculum and degrees granted by ''this venerable academy.'' *Text: CWP,* IX, 192–194.

"An Address on Education, as Connected with Permanence of Our Republican Institutions. Delivered before the Institute of Education of Hampden Sidney College, at Its Anniversary Meeting, September the 24th, 1835." Poe noticed an address by Lucian Minor at Hampden Sidney College in the December 1835 issue of *The Southern Literary Messenger*. Poe referred to Minor's subject of establishing district schools in Virginia as a stroke of ''brilliant eloquence.'' Minor corresponded with Poe during his editorship at *The Southern Literary Messenger*. *Text: CWP,* VIII, 118–120. *Research: PJC,* 85–89.

"Address on the Subject of a Surveying and Exploring Expedition to the Pacific Ocean and South Seas. Delivered in the Hall of Representatives on the Evening of April 3, 1836. By J. N. Reynolds." Poe reviewed the explorer's address in the January 1837 issue of *The Southern Literary Messenger*. Poe became a lifelong admirer of Reynolds's polar projects, saluting in the review ''his energy, his love of polite literature, his many and various attainments, and above all, his ardent and honorable enthusiasm.'' *See:* Reynolds, Jeremiah N., *The Narrative of Arthur Gordon Pym. Text: CWP,* IX, 306–314.

"Adventures of a Gentleman in Search of a Horse. By Caveat Emptor, Gent." Review of a book on horse buying appearing in *The Southern Literary Messenger* for August 1836. He ''advise[s] all amateurs to look well, and look quickly into the pages of Caveat Emptor.'' *Text: CWP,* IX, 82–83.

Æcetes. (fifth century B.C.). Ancient philosopher and geographer who proposed that the earth moves in an orbit. Poe mentions him in *Pinakidia* as ''contend[ing] for the existence of what is now called the new world.'' The name may be Poe's misspelling of ''Hicetas,'' a Syracusan thinker. *Text: CWP,* XIV, 43. *Research: BRE,* 17.

Æschylus. (525–456 B.C.). Ancient Greek dramatist. Poe applies the word ''genius'' to the playwright and ranks him above Sophocles and Euripides. In *Marginalia*, Poe asserts that ''Euripides and Sophocles were merely echoes of Æschylus.'' In *Pinakidia*, Poe calls *The Persians* one of the ''only historical tragedies by Grecian authors.'' *Text: CWP,* X, 43; XII, 4, 131; XIV, 62; XVI, 72; XVI, 138.

Agathos. Character in the dialogic short story ''The Power of Words.'' He is one of the cosmic voices or angelic intelligences and assumes the Socratic or instructive role in the philosophic dialogue.

Ainsworth, William Harrison. (1805–1882). English novelist. Poe made him a passenger on the trans-Atlantic voyage in the story ''The Balloon Hoax.'' Poe's opinion of Ainsworth's powers as a historical novelist was severely negative. *See:* ''Guy Fawkes; or, The Gunpowder Treason. An Historical Romance. By William Harrison Ainsworth.'' *Text: CWP,* V, 224–225; X, 207; XVI, 7.

Al Aaraaf. In *The Koran*, a region between heaven and hell. Also the name of a star discovered by the astronomer Tycho Brahe in 1572. Poe noted that this nova suddenly appeared, then vanished, never to be seen again. In Poe's poem, Al Aaraaf is a place of idealized fantasy, sleepy seraphs, and golden air ''whence sprang the 'Idea of Beauty' into birth'' and is presided over by the Angel Nesace.

"Al Aaraaf." A difficult and confused early poem in two parts first published in December 1829 in the volume *Al Aaraaf, Tamerlane, and Minor Poems*. The work's 264 lines make it Poe's lengthiest poem. The poem can be described as an abstract meditation on higher æsthetic experience with ideal beauty symbolized by the maiden Nesace who lives on the star Al Aaraaf. Incurring God's anger, she is commanded to leave her stellar paradise and is doomed to wander the cosmos thereafter. In Part II, Nesace comes to ''a pile of gorgeous columns on th' unburthened air,'' a type of celestial paradise. Nesace's song of bliss, '''Neath blue-bell or streamer—/ Or tufted wild spray/ That keeps, from the dreamer/ The moonbeam away,'' is perhaps the finest section of the poem and contains a reference to Ligeia, Poe's most famous ''posthumous heroine'': ''Ligeia! Ligeia! My beautiful one! Whose harshest idea will to melody run.'' Poe recited ''Al Aaraaf'' as ''The Messenger Star'' to an indifferent and puzzled Boston audience at the Odeon Theater on 16 October 1845. *See:* Al Aaraaf; ''Boston and the Bostonians. Editorial Miscellany.'' *Text: MCW,* I, 92–127; *CWP,* VII, 23–39. *Research:* Cairns, William B. ''Some Notes on Poe's 'Al Aaraaf,' '' *Modern Philology,* 13 (1915): 35–44; Stovall, Floyd. ''An Interpretation of Poe's 'Al Aaraaf,' '' *University of Texas Studies in English,* 11 (1929): 106–133; Pettigrew, Richard C., and Mary Morgan Pettigrew. ''A Reply to Floyd Stovall's Interpretation of 'Al Aaraaf.' '' *American Literature,* 8 (1937): 439–445; De Prospo, R. C. ''Poe's Alpha Poem: The Title of 'Al Aaraaf.' '' *Poe Studies,* 22, no. 2 (1989): 34–39.

Al Aaraaf, Tamerlane, and Minor Poems. Poe's second collection of poetry. The seventy-one-page work was published by Hatch & Dunning of Baltimore. Two hundred and fifty copies of this volume were issued in December 1829. *Text: Al Aaraaf, Tamerlane, and Minor Poems by Edgar A. Poe,* ed. Thomas Ollive Mabbott. New York: Columbia University Press, 1933.

Albert, Paul Martin. (1666–1729). Hebrew lexicographer. His Hebrew dictionary is mentioned in *Pinakidia.* Each definition ''pretends to discover in each word, in its root, in its letters, and in the manner of pronouncing them, the reason of its signification.'' *Text: CWP,* XIV, 70.

"Alciphron: A Poem." Written by Thomas Moore, Esq. the poem was reviewed in the January 1840 issue of *Burton's Gentleman's Magazine.* Poe comments favorably on ''the facility with which he recounts a poetical story in a prosaic way.'' Moore's style reflects a ''vivid fancy'' and ''epigrammatic spirit.'' *Text: CWP,* X, 60–71. *Research: LTP,* 382, 407; *LET,* I, 239; *PJC,* 234–242.

Alcoholism. *See:* Poe, Edgar Allan.

Alcott, Amos Bronson. (1799–1888). American educator, transcendentalist, and utopian thinker. He was the father of Louisa May Alcott, author of *Little Women.* Because he was a New Englander, a transcendentalist, and associated with *The Dial,* Poe had nothing praiseworthy to say about Alcott or his social reforms, referring to ''the Orphicism of Alcott. . . . The quips, quirks, and curt oracularities of the Emersons, Alcotts, and Fullers, are simply Lyly's Euphuisms revived.'' *Text: CWP,* IX, 15, 189; XIII, 195. *Research: MNR,* 317–318.

Aldrich, James. (1810–1856). American poet and editor. Poe accused him of plagiarizing his poem ''A Death-Bed'' from Thomas Hood's poem of the same title in the New York *Evening Mirror* of 13–14 January 1845 and in *The Broadway Journal* of 8 March 1845. In *Marginalia,* Poe repeated the charge by quoting Aldrich's poem ''Lines'' as an example of ''imitation.'' ''The fact is I thought, and still think, that Mr. A. has been guilty of plagiarism in the first degree. . . . Still, what I mean to say is, that Mr. Aldrich's *penchant* for imitation does not show him to be incapable of poetry.'' In his portrait of Aldrich in ''The Literati of New York City,'' Poe repeated the charge of plagiarism but also praised Aldrich's poem "Molly Gray." *Text: CWP,* XII, 65, 68; XV, 62–64; XVI, 96–97. *Research: PLB,* 156, 169, 172–173; *TPL,* 502–504, 510–511.

Alessandra. Character in the drama *Politian.*

Alexander, Charles W. (1796–1866). Philadelphia publisher of several Philadelphia newspapers and magazines, among them *Burton's Gentleman's Magazine, Alexander's Weekly Messenger,* and *The Daily Chronicle.* Poe published pieces on cryptography and cryptograms in *Alexander's Weekly Messenger. Research: MNR,* 152–153.

Alexander's Weekly Messenger. Philadelphia journal edited by John Frost. Upon his arrival there in 1838, Poe became acquainted with the magazine and published several articles on cryptograms and cryptography in this journal from 1839 to 1842. *See:* "Enigmatical and Conundrum-ical"; Alexander, Charles W. *Research: TPL,* 253–254, 268–270.

"Alfred Tennyson." A critical essay on Tennyson's poetry appearing in *The Broadway Journal* of 19 July 1845. Poe extracts passages from a British journal article on "Poets and Poetry of the Nineteenth Century" and proceeds to redress "the injustice done in America to the magnificent genius of Tennyson." "Examine his poetry minutely," Poe urges the reader, "and the wonderful artistic finish becomes evident. There are few authors who will bear the probe of analysis better." *Text: CWP,* XII, 180–184.

Alfriend, Edward M. Friend and confidante of Poe. His son, Edward Alfriend, an editor of *The Southern Literary Messenger,* recorded various bits of conversation between his father and Poe in "Unpublished Recollections of Edgar Allan Poe," *Literary Era* (Philadelphia), for August 1901. *Research: MCW,* I, 76, 83, 474.

"Alice Ray: A Romance in Rhyme. By Mrs. Sarah Josepha Hale." Review of a poetic romance that had been sent to Poe. Poe reviewed it favorably in the 1 November 1845 issue of *The Broadway Journal,* noting that he was pleasantly surprised by its "delicacy and fancy of conception and the truthful simplicity and grace of its manner. . . . We have read many of Mrs. Hale's poetical compositions, but were prepared for nothing so good." *Text: CWP,* XII, 259–262.

Allamistakeo, Count. The prematurely embalmed hero of Poe's tale "Some Words with a Mummy." The hieroglyphic cartouche on the sarcophagus indicates Allamistakeo is the mummy's name.

Allan, Agnes Nancy. One of John Allan's sisters. She married Allan Fowlds of Kilmarnock in 1799. *Research: TPL,* xvi.

Allan, Elizabeth Allan. One of John Allan's sisters. *Research: TPL,* xvi.

Allan, Frances Keeling Valentine. (1785–1829). Poe's foster mother and first wife of John Allan. Devoted to Poe during his childhood in the Allan household, she often took Poe's side in the quarrels between him and her husband. Poe maintained contact with her even after his departure from the Allan household and held her in great affection. Chronically ill and dying at age forty-four, she could offer the young Poe only a limited amount of the maternal security he so desperately required. *Research: LTP*, 53–56.

Allan, Jane. One of John Allan's sisters. *Research: TPL,* xvi.

Allan, John. (1779–1834). Poe's guardian and foster father. With his wife, Frances Keeling Valentine Allan, he assumed custodial care of Edgar Poe after his mother's death in 1811 but never legally adopted him. The Poe-Allan relationship is a saga of mounting mutual dislike that gradually deepened into permanent animosity with distinct overtones of violence. In Poe's case, the bitter resentment of authoritarian annoyances in his life extended beyond Allan's death to the point where Poe may well have recreated his foster father in his portrayals of dark fathers and judgmental authority figures such as the condemning inquisitors in "The Pit and the Pendulum." Allan was a Scotch immigrant and a Richmond merchant and mercantiler. With Charles Ellis, he established the Richmond firm of Ellis & Allan to market Virginia tobacco for European commodities. He was frugal, shrewd, financially discreet, and insistently pragmatic about his own life and the lives of others in his family care. His rigorous materialism is a possible subject for ridicule in Poe's short story "The Business Man." At first, Allan treated the foster child Poe kindly if not indulgently, although any real affection came from Allan's wife, Frances Keeling Valentine, not from the pater familias. As Poe entered adolescence, Allan became increasingly impatient and abrupt, thus signaling the nearly internecine conflict of temperaments that would mark their deteriorating relationship until Allan's death. Some accounts actually have Allan threatening the young Poe with a cudgel during one of their frequent quarrels over money and careers. Poe accused Allan of failing to provide sufficient financial support while he was at the University of Virginia and the Military Academy. Although there was a superficial reconciliation in February 1829 when Poe returned to Richmond for his foster mother's funeral, the severe father and the prodigal son were permanently estranged after Poe quit the Allan household in March 1827. Upon his death, Allan excluded Poe from his will by making no mention of him but did provide for two illegitimate twin sons born in 1830. In an antipatrimonial gesture of defiance, Poe always signed his name "Edgar A." rather than "Edgar Allan."

John Allan's psychological presence in Poe's troubled life is perhaps just as significant as the psychological stress created by David Poe's absence. An overbearing father figure and the missing father figure have quite naturally stimulated the many psychobiographic interpretations of the tales and poems. *See:* "The Business Man." *Research: TPL,* xv; *LTP*, 24, passim; *MNR,* 10, passim; *PLL,* 36–40, 48–50.

Allan, John, Jr. (b. 1831). Son of John Allan and Louisa Gabriella Patterson Allan. *Research: TPL,* xvi.

Allan, Louisa Gabriella Patterson. (1800–1881). John Allan's second wife. Married Allan on 5 October 1830, while Poe was a cadet at the United States Military Academy. The marriage probably precipitated Poe's decision to get himself court-martialed and dismissed from the Academy. Poe's hostility toward her arose from his fear that she would cut him off from any inheritance from Allan. *Research: LTP*, 162, 280, 287; *TPL,* xvi; *MNR,* 63, 97.

Allan, Mary. (d. 1850). Oldest sister of John Allan. She lived in the family's Bridegate House in Scotland. *Research: TPL,* xvi.

Allan, Patterson. (b. 1834). Son of John Allan and Louisa Gabriella Patterson Allan. *Research: TPL,* xvi.

Allan, William Galt. (b. 1832). Son of John and Louisa Gabriella Patterson Allan. Named after William Galt. *Research: LTP*, 273, 280; *TPL,* xvi.

Allen, Hervey. (1889–1949). Poe biographer and American novelist. Author of *Israfel: The Life and Times of Edgar Allan Poe*. With Thomas Ollive Mabbott, he collected and edited *Poe's Brother: The Poems of William Henry Leonard Poe* (New York: George H. Doran, 1926). *Research:* Wilson, James Southall. "Poe and the Biographers." *Virginia Quarterly Review*, 3 (1927): 313–320; Moore, Rayburn S. " 'Prophetic Sounds and Loud': Allen, Stovall, Mabbott and Other Recent Work on Poe." *Georgia Review*, 25 (1971): 481–488.

Allen, Paul. (1775–1826). American journalist and author of *Original Poems, Serious and Entertaining* (1801). He is mentioned by Poe in connection with plagiarism in the Outis letter of 22 March 1845: " 'Pray,' inquires Outis of Mr. Willis, 'did you ever think the worse of Dana because your friend John Neal charged him with pirating upon Paul Allen?" *Text: CWP,* XII, 66.

Allen, Robert T.P. (1813–1888). Fellow cadet at West Point. He entered the Academy with Poe in June 1830. *Research: TPL,* xvi.

Allen, William. Character in the novel *The Narrative of Arthur Gordon Pym*. He is one of the members of the cook's party aboard the *Jane Guy*.

Allen, Wilson. Character in the novel *The Narrative of Arthur Gordon Pym.* He is with Pym and Peters when they explore the fissure on the Island of Tsalal.

Allston, Washington. (1779–1843). American novelist, painter, and author of *Monaldi.* Poe includes an analysis of his signature in "Autography," commenting, "Of his paintings we have here nothing to say—except briefly, that the most noted of them are not to our taste. His poems are not all of a high order of merit; and, in truth the faults of his pencil and of his pen are identical. Yet every reader will remember his 'Spanish Maid' with pleasure." *Text: CWP,* XI, 136; XV, 253–254. *Research:* Omans, Glen A. "Poe and Washington Allston: Visionary Kin." In *Poe and His Times: The Artist and His Milieu,* ed. B. F. Fisher IV. Baltimore: Edgar Allan Poe Society, 1990, 1–29; Weston, Debra Faye. "Smashing the Monuments and Saving the Pedestals: Washington Allston and Edgar Allan Poe's Mandate for the American Artist." *Dissertation Abstracts International,* 53 (1993): 3532A–3533A (University of North Carolina–Greensboro).

"Alnwick Castle, with Other Poems. By Fitz-Greene Halleck." This collection of poems was reviewed by Poe in the April 1836 issue of *The Southern Literary Messenger.* The review is generally referred to in Poe criticism as "The Drake-Halleck Review." Poe and Halleck had a mutual respect for each other's literary skills, although "Alnwick Castle" could not escape Poe's critical scalpel. The mixing of ideality with low burlesque at the conclusion of the poem was particularly reprehensible to Poe because it "depriv[ed] the entire poem of all unity of effect." Poe's moderate praise of Halleck's verse—he found Drake a superior poet to Halleck—drew a wide response including an endorsement from Washington Irving in a letter of June 1836. "Your article on Drake and Halleck one of the finest pieces of criticism ever published in this country." *See:* "Drake-Halleck. The Culprit Fay, and Other Poems"; "Our Contributors, No. VIII.—Fitz-Greene Halleck." *Text: CWP,* VIII, 275–318. *Research: PJC,* 154.

"Alone." Untitled poem by Poe written in 1829 and placed in the album of Lucy Holmes sometime around 8 May. It was published in *Scribner's Monthly* for September 1875. The poem expresses the artist's credo and emphasizes aesthetic issues that will become important in his more mature work. Central to the poem is the poet's sense of isolation and estrangement from all others, of his apartness from how they think and feel: "From childhood's hour I have not been as others were—I have not seen as others saw—I could not bring my passions from a common spring." *Text: MCW,* I, 145–147; *CWP,* VII, 227. *Research:* Cauthen, I. B. " 'Alone': Its Background, Source, and Manuscript." *Studies in Bibliography: Papers of the Bibliographical Society of the University of Virginia,* 3 (1950): 284–291; Bandy, W. T. "Poe's 'Alone': The First Printing." *Papers of the Bibliographical Society of America,* 70 (1976): 405–406.

Alpha Lyra. Star in the constellation Lyra that seemed to obsess Poe. He refers to it in "Mellonta Tauta" and *Eureka.*

Ambler, Richard Carey. (1810–1877). One of Poe's boyhood friends. He recalled swimming with Poe and listening to him recite satiric verses about the members of a Richmond debating society. Ambler was a physican and a Virginian gentleman farmer. *Research: LTP*, 51–52; *TPL*, xvi.

"Amelia Welby." Favorable review of Amelia Welby's verse appearing in the *Democratic Review* for December 1844. Except for occasional tonal lapses and some want of originality, the poetry has qualities of "which nothing could be more pure, more natural, or more judicious. The perfect keeping of the various points is admirable—and the result is entire unity of impression, or effect." Poe compared her metrical successes with his own poem "Lenore." *Text: CWP*, XI, 275–281.

"America and the American People. By Frederick von Raumer." Poe noticed a translation of Frederick von Raumer's book in the 29 November 1845 issue of *The Broadway Journal.* Poe took exception to von Raumer's favorable opinion of Griswold's *The Poets and Poetry of America*, remarking, "If Dr. Griswold's book is really to be received as a fair representation of our poetical literature, then we are in a very lamentable—or rather in a very ridiculous condition indeed." *Text: CWP*, XIII, 13–16. *Research: PLB*, 203.

"American Almanac, and Repository of Useful Knowledge for the Year 1837." The eighth number of a year-and-fact book reviewed by Poe in *The Southern Literary Messenger* for October 1836. The book is recommended for its "perspecuity and brevity" and "worthy of the highest commendation." *Text: CWP*, IX, 160–162.

"The American Drama." Critical essay published in the *American Whig Review* for August 1845. Poe proposes in a series of papers "to take a somewhat deliberate survey of some few of the most noticeable American plays," among them Nathaniel Parker Willis's *Tortesa, the Usurer* and Longfellow's *The Spanish Student.* Poe judges Longfellow's play to be a failure because it confuses the genres and is a "hybrid and paradoxical composition," that is, a "dramatic poem." "Let a poem be a poem only; let a play be a play and nothing more." *Text: CWP*, XIII, 33–73. *Research: PLB*, 153–155.

American Hotel, Main Street, Richmond. Poe address in Richmond during July and August 1849. *Research: MNR*, 419.

"The American in England." Review of Lieutenant Alexander Slidell's book published in *The Southern Literary Messenger* for February 1836. Of the literary abilities of the traveler Poe remarks that he has "a fine eye for the picturesque" and has sketched his scenes "with all the spirit, vigor, raciness and illusion of a panorama." *Text: CWP*, VIII, 214–222.

American Monthly. Baltimore journal. Poe submitted his poem ''FairyLand'' to the editors. *Research: MNR,* 53–54.

The American Museum of Science, Literature, and the Arts. Baltimore journal that published some of Poe's work in 1839. *Research: MNR,* 137–138.

"American Parnassus." One of Poe's literary projects that never came to light. He had planned an evaluative compendium of American writers and asked Evert A. Duyckinck by letter on 26 June 1845 ''for an advance of $50 on the faith of the 'American Parnassus'—which I will finish as soon as possible.'' *Research: TPL,* 542.

"American Poetry." Public lecture delivered by Poe on 21 November 1843 in Philadelphia. Poe was critical of Griswold's anthology *The Poets and Poetry of America. Research: TPL,* 441.

"American Prose Writers. No. 2. N.P. Willis. New Views—Imagination—Fancy—Fantasy—Humor—Wit—Sarcasm—The Prose Style of Mr. Willis." A critical essay on Nathaniel Parker Willis appearing in *The Broadway Journal* of 18 January 1845. Poe finds ''innumerable merits'' in Willis's writing, but he categorizes Willis as fanciful rather than imaginative. ''Still, they are merits which he shares with other writers.'' Most of the essay is devoted to Poe's assertion of his shared position with Coleridge's distinction between fancy and imagination by citing Coleridge's remark that ''fancy combines—Imagination creates.'' Poe extends Coleridge's distinction by adding, ''The pure Imagination chooses, *from either beauty or deformity*, only the most combinable things hitherto uncombined.'' *Text: CWP,* XII, 36–40.

American Quarterly Review. Philadelphia periodical edited by Robert Walsh. Poe briefly noticed its contents in *The Southern Literary Messenger* for June 1835. *Research: TPL,* 160.

Ames Street. A Poe address in Lowell, Massachusetts, where Poe lodged with the Richmonds in October 1848.

Amity Street (number 3). A Poe address in Baltimore. Poe lived here briefly upon his return to Baltimore in May 1831. *Research:* Evans, Mary Garretson. ''Poe in Amity Street.'' *Maryland Historical Magazine*, 36 (December 1941): 363–388.

Amity Street (number 85), Washington Square. A Poe address in New York City. Poe resided here from September 1845 to February 1846.

Anacreon of Teos. (sixth century B.C.). Ancient Greek poet. His lyrics celebrate the virtues of wine, women, and song. Poe alludes to Anacreon in discussing ''[t]hat *indefinitiveness* which is, at least, *one* of the essentials of true music.'' And in the poem ''Romance'' (''Introduction''), he recalls his youthful reading of Anacreon somewhat sarcastically: ''For, being an idle boy lang syne,/ Who read Anacreon, and drank wine,/ I early found Anacreon rhymes/ Were almost passionate sometimes.'' *Text: MCW,* I, 157; *CWP,* X, 43; XVI, 138, 164.

Ana-Pest, Arch Duchess. Character in the short story ''King Pest.'' She is one of the six rotting relatives of King Pest's family court.

"Anastatic Printing." Essay by Poe published in the 12 April 1845 issue of *The Broadway Journal.* The article discusses at length a printing process whereby facsimiles of writings and drawings could be produced from zinc plates and then transformed into an unlimited number of copies at minimal cost. Poe believed that such a technological advance would reduce the importance of a magazine or book as mere material objects but greatly enhance the value of their literary content. ''It will be evident that the discovery of Anastatic Printing will not only obviate the necessity of copy-right laws, and of international law in especial, but will render this necessity more imperative and more apparent.'' *Text: CWP,* XIV, 153–159. *Research:* Campbell, Killis. ''Miscellaneous Notes on Poe.'' *Modern Language Notes,* 28 (1913): 65–69.

Anaxagoras. (b. 500 B.C.). Ancient Greek philosopher and cosmologist. His ideas probably influenced Poe's notion of negative creation in *Eureka.* His work *On Nature* attempted to unite and integrate the spiritual and material universes. Poe mentions Anaxagoras in the short story ''Loss of Breath'' and cites him in an odd context in *Pinakidia.* ''Anaxagoras of Clazomenæ is said to have prophesied that a stone would fall from the sun.'' *Text: CWP,* II, 154; XIV, 53.

Andreini, Giovanni Battista. (1579–1654). Actor, dramatist, and opera composer mentioned in *Pinakidia.* Poe credits him as furnishing the source for Milton's *Paradise Lost. Text: CWP,* XIV, 47.

"The Angel of the Odd. An Extravaganza." Short story published in the *Columbian Magazine* for October 1844. The tale might be called a dipsomaniac farce or drunkard's dream of doom. The narrator is one of Poe's rational skeptics, a man who subscribes to a tidy universe devoid of ''impossible probabilities,'' but he is also a drinker whose chambers abound in miscellaneous bottles. When the narrator asserts that he ''intends to believe nothing henceforward that has any thing of the 'singular' about it,'' the angel of the odd suddenly appears to set him straight about such foolish skepticism, especially when it is fortified by too much wine. With his torso consisting of kegs and puncheons, his limbs of bottles, and his head in the shape of a Hessian canteen topped by a funnel, the odd intruder is the very embodiment of the irrational spirit ''whose business it was to bring about the *odd accidents* which are continually astonishing the skeptic.'' Following his discourse with the angel, a series of irrational events and bizarre accidents befall the narrator. A clock hand gets stuck, and he fails to keep an appointment to renew his fire insurance. Shortly thereafter, his house burns, and he breaks his arm when a hog decides to scratch itself on the escape ladder he is descending. When the narrator attempts suicide by leaping into the river, he finds his suicide interrupted by a guide rope coming into his hands as it hangs down from a passing balloon piloted, of course, by the angel of the odd. '' 'Ave you pe got zober yet and come to your zenzes?' '' comes the query from the basket car above. But when the narrator stubbornly refuses to submit to the reality of the absurd, the pilot cuts the rope. The narrator then awakens at four in the morning amidst the rubble of his latest drunken binge. Amidst the shattered bottles and overturned jugs, the narrator can only revise his narrow philosophy of a reasonable universe. Having sobered up, the skeptic is forced to admit the existence of the other world of accident, unreason, and absurd probability. The relationship of alcohol to creativity and the antinomies within Poe's character, particularly the opposition of cold logic and doubt and high fantasy and untethered imagination, are all implied by the angel's visit. *Text: MCW,* III, 1098–1112; *CWP,* VI, 103–115. *Research:* Gerber, Gerald. ''Poe's Odd Angel.'' *Nineteenth Century Fiction,* 23 (1968): 88–93.

Angelo. Character in the poem ''Al Aaraaf.'' He is an angelic creature, a posthumous aesthete, and the lover of Ianthe. He leaves the earth of his own volition to seek a life of decadent sensuality with Ianthe on Al Aaraaf. '' 'The last spot of Earth's orb I trod upon/ Was a proud temple called the Parthenon—.''

"Animal and Vegetable Physiology, Considered with Reference to Natural Theology." Review of Peter Mark Roget's contribution to a series of scientific texts sponsored by the Royal Society appearing in *The Southern Literary Messenger* for January 1836. Poe calls Roget's book ''the best of the Bridgewater series'' because of its handling of ''difficulty of selection from an exuberance of materials.'' *Text: CWP,* VIII, 206–211.

Ann Street (number 4) and Fulton Street. Poe address in New York City where he lodged in 1845.

"Annabel Lee." Poem by Poe. This famous recitative set piece is Poe's final finished poem, composed in May 1849. It was published posthumously in *The Southern Literary Messenger* for November 1849 and *Sartain's Union Magazine* for January 1850. Griswold's 9 October 1849 obituary notice in the New York *Tribune* also prints the poem. Various women in Poe's life, including Sarah Anna Lewis, Helen Whitman, and Elmira Shelton, saw themselves in the poem's child heroine, but the poem is clearly a keepsake for Virginia Clemm Poe. The poem lyricizes issues common to many of Poe's works: the death of a beautiful woman, her interment, and the poet's undying love and deification of her memory. The power of the love that the narrator shares with the dead Annabel Lee is so exalted that it is coveted even by the angels and ''those who are older . . . / many far wiser than we.'' Poe's celebration of children in love is reminiscent of Wordsworth's and Blake's poems in which the eye of the child is superior to the adult. The narrator's bond with Annabel Lee transcends death and overcomes those forces, both human and cosmic, that endeavor to ''dissever my soul from the soul of the beautiful Annabel Lee.'' Poe's lifelong resentment of paternal authority may be heard in the lines ''So that her highborn kinsmen came and bore her away from me.'' *Text: MCW,* I, 468–481; *CWP,* VII, 117–118. *Research:* Booth, Bradford A. ''The Identity of 'Annabel Lee.' '' *College English,* 7 (October 1945): 17–19; Nagy, Deborah K. '' 'Annabel Lee': Poe's Ballad.'' *RE: Artes Liberales,* 3, no. 2 (1977): 29–34.

Annie (1). Character in Poe's Poem ''For Annie.'' She is the dying persona's beloved, a maternal figure who bathes him in caresses, puts out the light, and covers him gently.

Annie (2). Character in the architectural sketch ''Landor's Cottage.'' She is the hostess of the cottage. The intense ''expression of *romance*'' from her deep-set eyes renders her Poe's pen portrait of Annie Richmond.

"The Antediluvians, or the World Destroyed: A Narrative Poem, in Ten Books. By James McHenry, M.D." Review of a pretentious epic appearing in *Graham's Magazine* for February 1841. Poe attacked what he perceived to be McHenry's conceit in associating himself with Milton and denounced the melodramatic excesses of the poem. ''There are two marriages, a rescued maiden, one or more heroes, and many heroines, with an innumerable catalogue of minor incidents—in short, the materials of half a dozen bad novels woven into a worse poem.'' *Text: CWP,* X, 105–109. *Research: PJC,* 65.

Anthon, Charles. (1797–1867). Professor of Greek and Latin classics at Columbia College. He was an early supporter of *The Southern Literary Messenger.* Poe devoted a long entry to him in ''Autography'' and profiled him in ''The Literati of New York City,'' commenting upon the ''extensive erudition of his 'Classical Dictionary' '' as the work of ''the best classicist in America.'' From Anthon's signature in ''Autography'' Poe noted, ''[W]e may at once recognise in this chirography the scrupulous precision and finish—the love of elegance—together with the scorn of all superfluous embellishment, which so greatly distinguish the compilations of the writer.'' Poe noticed Anthon's ''Sallust's Jurguthine War'' in *The Southern Literary Messenger* for May 1836 and asked him by letter to translate several Hebrew phrases while preparing his review of Stephens's *Arabia Petræa. Text: CWP,* VIII, 104, 338; XV, 34–36, 169–170, 179–182. *Research:* ''Edgar Allan Poe on Professor Anthon.'' *Columbia University Quarterly,* 11 (March 1909): 207–208; Jackson, David Kelly. ''Poe Notes: 'Pinakidia' and 'Some

Ancient Greek Authors.' " *American Literature*, 5 (1933): 258–267; *LET*, I, 268–271; *MNR*, 120, 232.

"The Antigone at Palmo's." The revival of the tragic drama by Sophocles was indignantly reviewed by Poe in *The Broadway Journal* of 12 April 1845. Poe panned the contemporary rendition because it lacked sufficient attention to "the mode in which the Greeks wrote dramas and performed them." The current production is merely "an unintentional burlesque." *Text: CWP*, XII, 130–135. *Research: LTP*, 518; *PJC*, 378–379.

Apelles. (4th century B.C.). Ancient Greek painter during the age of Alexander. In *Marginalia* Poe alludes to "the crime imputed by Apelles to [his fellow painter] Protogenes—that of 'being too natural.' " *Text: CWP*, XVI, 173.

Aphrodite, Marquesa. Character in the short story "The Assignation." She is the beautiful woman who appears to have dropped her child into a canal.

Apollinaire, Guillaume. (1880–1918). French symbolist poet. Like Baudelaire and Valéry, he worshipped Poe, once calling him "the marvellous drunkard of Baltimore." *Research: PLL*, 328.

"An Appendix of Autographs." A supplementary article on autographs published in *Graham's Magazine* for January 1842. Poe analyzes nineteen signatures, among them those of Ralph Waldo Emerson, Doctor Oliver Wendell Holmes, and Washington Allston. *Text: CWP*, VIII, 304; XV, 246–261.

Apuleius. (b. ca. A.D. 125). Roman author and writer of *Asino Aureo* [The golden ass], a tale of bestial transformation, a subject of interest to Poe. He also accused the poet Thomas Moore of pilfering his line "woven snow" from Apuleius in his review of *Alciphron*. The line "*ventum textilum*" is also mentioned by the narrator in the short story "The Spectacles." *Text: CWP*, V, 180; X, 70.

Arago, Dominique François Jean. (1786–1853). The French astronomer and chemist Dominique François Jean Arago was the subject of one of the *Sketches of Conspicuous Living Characters of France* in a book of biographies translated by R. M. Walsh and reviewed by Poe. "The genius of Arago is finely painted, and the character of his quackery put in a true light." *Text: CWP*, VI, 253; X, 136, 138.

Arch Street (number 127). Poe address in Philadelphia. Poe resided here during the summer of 1838.

Archer, Robert. (1794–1877). Army surgeon. When Poe was ill with some sort of fever in January 1829, he was attended by Archer, a surgeon at the military hospital at Fortress Monroe, Virginia. To Dr. Archer, Poe revealed that he was serving in the army under an alias. *Research: TPL,* xvi, 88.

Archimedes. (287–212 B.C.). Ancient Greek scientist and author of *Incidentibus in Fluido*, a work referred to in "The Descent into the Maelström" for its description of the hydraulic law that a cylinder in a vortex offers resistance to suction. *Text: CWP,* II, 245.

Argensola, Bartolomé Leonardo de. (1562–1631). Spanish poet and historical writer. The translation of his *Mary Magdalen* is mentioned as a fine "specimen of versification" in Poe's review of the poems of William Cullen Bryant. *Text: CWP,* IX, 296.

Aristarchus. (d. 153 B.C.). Ancient Greek scholar of Homeric literature associated with the great library at Alexandria. Poe mentions his studious edition of *The Iliad* in *Pinakidia*. Aristarchus "published from a collection of all the copies then existing, a new edition, the text of which has finally prevailed." *Text: CWP,* XIV, 66. *Research: TPL,* 669.

Aristophanes. (ca. 446–385 B.C.). Ancient Greek comic dramatist. Poe refers to Aristophanes in several tales and critical pieces. The soul of Aristophanes tastes "racy" to the devil in "Bon-Bon." In *Marginalia*, Poe credited Aristophanes with the invention of rhyme. "It is very commonly supposed that rhyme, as it now ordinarily exists, is of modern invention—but see 'The Clouds' of Aristophanes." *Text: CWP,* II, 142, 359; VIII, 84; XIV, 64; XVI, 87.

Aristotle. (384–322 B.C.). Ancient Greek philosopher and writer on psychology, nature, logic, physics, metaphysics, and ethics. Poe's reading and interest in Aristotle is reflected in the numerous references in his fiction, poetry, and criticism. Poe comments on Artistotle in *Marginalia* and *Eureka* and associates his positions with the didactic or moral sense, the enemy of art and beauty, writing in *Marginalia*, "The fact is, that Aristotle's Treatise on Morals is next in succession to his Book on Physics, and this he supposes the rational order of study." In the short story "Bon-Bon" the devil disposes of Aristotle's philosophy as so much deductive and didactic nonsense. " 'There is only one solid truth in all that he has written, and for that I gave him the hint out of pure compassion for his absurdity. . . . Why it was I who told Aristotle that, by sneezing, men expelled superfluous ideas through the proboscis.' " *Text: CWP,* II, 142; VIII, 45; XI, 12, 70; XII, 15; XIV, 272–273; XVI, 25, 192. *Research:* Albee, John. "Poe and Aristotle." *The Dial*, 16 March 1903, 192; Pritchard, John Paul. "Aristotle's Influence upon American Criticism." *Proceedings of the American Philological Association*, 67 (1936): 341–362; *PJC,* 221–222.

Arnay, Jean Rodolphe D'. (ca. 1757). English historian and author of *De la Vie privée des Romains* [Private life of the Romans] (1764). In *Marginalia*, Poe criticizes Bulwer for failing to acknowledge his extensive use of this social study ''which he had so little scruple about incurring, during the composition of 'The Last Days of Pompeii.' '' *Text: CWP,* XVI, 31.

Arnold, Elizabeth. (?-1798?). Poe's maternal grandmother. Actress at the Theatre Royal, Covent Garden London. Emigrated to Boston, Massachusetts, with her daughter Eliza in January 1796.

Arnold, William Henry. (d.1790). Poe's maternal great-grandfather. He was a professional actor at Covent Garden Theatre, London. *Research: LTP*, 680.

Arthur, Timothy Shea. (1809–1885). American novelist, editor of *The Baltimore Athenæum and Young Men's Paper,* and author of the famous temperance tale *Ten Nights in a Barroom and What I Saw There* (1854). Arthur praised Poe's work as ''irresistably interesting,'' but Poe did not return the compliment. In his damning review of Lever's novel *Charles O'Malley*, Poe sneered at Arthur's tendency toward melodramatic moralizing. Examining Arthur's signature in ''Autography,'' Poe was even more excoriating: ''Mr. Arthur is not without a rich talent for description of scenes in low life, but is uneducated, and too fond of mere vulgarities to please a refined taste. . . . His hand is a commonplace clerk's hand, such as we might expect him to write.'' *Text: CWP,* XI, 90; XV, 240–241. *Research: LET,* I, 175.

Ashburton, Richard. Poet included by Griswold in his anthology *The Poets and Poetry of America.* In his review of Griswold's collection, Poe cites Ashburton as one of numerous examples of bad poets ''whose only merit is their wealth, and whose intellects rarely expand beyond the cut of a coat or the fashion of a mantilla.'' *Text: CWP,* XI, 239.

Asimov, Isaac. (1920–1992). American science fiction writer. In his autobiography, *Memory Yet Green: The Autobiography of Isaac Asimov* (1979), he recalls his childhood affection for Poe's tales of terror and detection. Among the many stories which demonstrate Asimov's feeling for Poe are ''The Brazen Locked Room'' and ''Flies.'' Asimov's novels *The Caves of Steel* (1954) and *The Naked Sun* (1957) contain stylistic and thematic reminders of Poe's poems and tales. *Research:* Wages, Jack D. ''Isaac Asimov's Debt to Edgar Allan Poe.'' *Poe Studies*, 6, no. 1 (1973): 29.

"The Assignation." Short story by Poe originally entitled ''The Visionary'' and first published under that title in *Godey's Lady's Book* (or *The Lady's Book*) for January 1834. When the story was reprinted in *The Southern Literary Messenger* for July 1835, it included the poem ''To One in Paradise.'' The title became "The Assignation" in a revised version published in *The Broadway Journal* of 7 June 1845. Set in Venice, the tale speculates upon the contrasting conditions of ideality and ordinary reality, with the former often preferable to the latter. The narrator comes upon an unfolding midnight tragedy. Marchesa Aphrodite, "[t]he adoration of all Venice—the gayest of the gay—the most lovely where all were beautiful," has accidentally dropped her child into the dark water of a canal. Horrible death is averted when a Byronic stranger appears and plunges into the canal to rescue the child. But no expression of joy and gratitude follows from the mother since the timely rescue uncovers a cryptic relationship between the Marquesa and the dark stranger. The final scene takes place in the stranger's rooms where the narrator discovers a painting of the Marquesa "beaming all over with smiles . . . inescapable from the fitful stain of melancholia which will ever be found inseparable from the perfection of the beautiful." The stranger is apparently no stranger to the Marquesa, for it seems that the two have planned a beautiful union in death that they could not attain in life. In Poe's version of *Romeo and Juliet* the two form a suicide pact to immortalize their unfulfilled passion. Like the "Ligeia" narrator, the stranger has surrounded himself with exotic furnishings and opulent decor in order to facilitate "the contemplation of the magnificent." The fatal pact enables him to complete his journey into "that realm of dreams." As the two die in unison by poison, they leave behind all mortal fetters and enter a paradise of imagination. A distinct side of Poe's character resides in the stranger's remark, "To dream has been the business of my life, I have therefore framed for myself a bower of dreams." *Epigraph:* "Stay for me there! I will not fail/ To meet thee in that hollow vale." Johann Goethe, "Das Veilschen." *See:* "To One in Paradise." *Text: MCW,* II, 148–169; *CWP,* II, 109–124. *Research:* Benton, Richard. "Is Poe's 'The Assignation' a Hoax?" *Nineteenth Century Fiction*, 28 (1963): 193–197; Pitcher, Edward W. "Poe's 'The Assignation': A Reconsideration." *Poe Studies*, 13 (1980): 1–4; Pahl, Dennis. "Recovering Byron: Poe's 'The Assignation.' " *Criticism*, 26 (1984): 211–229; Ketterer, David. "The Sexual Abyss: Consummation in 'The Assignation.' " *Poe Studies*, 19 (1986): 7–10; Zorzi, Rosella Mamoli. "The Text Is the City: The Representation of Venice in Two Tales by Irving and Poe and a Novel by Cooper." *Revista d'Studi Anglo-Americani*, 6 (1990): 285–300.

Astor, John Jacob. (1763–1848). American businessman, fur trader, and entrepeneur. In his review of Irving's *Astoria*, Poe gives an approving biography of Astor, traces the founding and growth of the American Fur Company, and describes his trading expeditions on the Columbia River, material that forms the basis for the novella *The Journal of Julius Rodman*. *Text: CWP,* IV, 19–20; IX, 207–222, 236, 242.

"Astoria; or, Anecdotes of an Enterprise beyond the Rocky Mountains. By Washington Irving." Favorable review of Irving's account of the founding of Astoria and John Jacob Astor's fur trading enterprises beyond the

Rocky Mountains published in *The Southern Literary Messenger* for January 1837. Irving's travelogue has a "masterly manner" as well as "fullness, comprehensiveness, and beauty, with which a long and entangled series of details, collected, necessarily, from a mass of vague and imperfect data, has been wrought into completeness and unity." *See: The Journal of Julius Rodman. Text: CWP,* IX, 207–243.

Atlantic Souvenir. Philadelphia journal. At the suggestion of Isaac Lea of the publishers Carey and Lea, Poe submitted several poems to this journal. *Research: LTP*, 199, 203.

"The Atlantis, A Southern World—Or a Wonderful Continent Discovered." This unsigned satiric fantasy piece appeared in *The American Museum* for September 1838 and has been attributed to Poe by the biographer, Arthur Hobson Quinn. *Research:* Quinn, Arthur Hobson. *Edgar Allan Poe: A Critical Biography*. New York: Appleton-Century-Crofts, 1941; Rpt. New York: Cooper Square Publishers, 1969, 757–761; *TPL,* 256.

Auden, W.[ystan] H.[ugh]. (1907–1973). Literary critic, English poet, and modern proponent of Poe's genius. Auden edited a modern edition of Poe's works (*Edgar Allan Poe: Selected Prose and Poetry*, 1950). The edition includes *The Narrative of Arthur Gordon Pym*, called by Auden "[o]ne of the finest adventure stories ever written . . . an object lesson in art." His reestimation of Poe's status as a writer signaled a renaissance in Poe studies and established Poe as the leading figure among American authors in international influence. "His portraits of abnormal or self-destructive states contributed much to Dostoevski, his ratiocinating hero is the ancestor of Sherlock Holmes and his many successors, his tales of the future lead to H. G. Wells, his adventure stories to Jules Verne and Stevenson." Auden's essay "The Guilty Vicarage" defines the narrative structure of detective fiction as a search for elusive truth marked by a puzzle and its proper solution. Beginning with a tranquil state of affairs before the eruption of the crime, Auden traces the process whereby the detective distinguishes false leads from an accurate perception of guilt. As he proceeds, the detective gains in stature by establishing control over initially chaotic circumstances. When the perpetrator is identified and the arrest is made, order and innocence are restored by the detective's salvational hand. *Research:* Auden, W. H. "Introduction to Edgar Allan Poe: Selected Prose and Poetry." In *The Recognition of Edgar Allan Poe*, ed. Eric Carlson. Ann Arbor: Michigan University Press, 1966, 220–230.

Auditor within the tomb. The unnamed character in the short story "Silence—A Fable," to whom the Demon tells his fable.

Augustine of Hippo, Saint. (354–430). Latin church father and author of *Confessiones* [The confessions] and *De Civitate Dei* [The city of God]. Saint Augustine is mentioned several times in Poe's fiction and criticism. Egaeus, the narrator of "Berenice," numbers *The City of God* among the books in his library. St. Augustine is quoted twice in *Marginalia*: "Si poficere cupis," says the great African bishop, "primo id verum puta quod sana mens omnium hominum attestatur" ["If you wish to progress, first consider as true the thing which the sound mind of all men corroborates"]. *Text: CWP,* II, 21; XIV, 90; XVI, 45, 166.

Austin, Gilbert. (ca. 1794). English clergyman. He was the author of the theological pamphlet *A Sermon on a Future State*, combating the opinion that "Death is an Eternal Sleep" (1774). Poe mentions him in *Marginalia* and rejects his speculations on the afterlife. "The pamphlet proves nothing, of course; its theorem is not to be proved." *Text: CWP,* XVI, 39.

"Autography." Poe showed a keen interest in deducing personality from signatures. He wrote a series of fictional letters on the subject in installments appearing in *The Southern Literary Messenger* for February and August 1836 and continuing in *Graham's Magazine* in December 1841 and January 1842. The series consisted of epistolary fabrications purportedly written and signed by contemporary literary figures including thirty-eight American writers. Poe appended fake or facsimile signatures for each writer, then analyzed the personality on the basis of the signature's autographic characteristics and penmanship. The series contains the signatures of James K. Paulding ("the writing is *formed*—that is to say, *decided*"), Mrs. Signourney ("Freedom, dignity, precision, and grace of thought"), Fitz-Greene Halleck ("a free, mercantile hand"), Washington Irving ("an eye deficient in a due sense of the *picturesque*"), John Neal ("One might suppose Mr. Neal's mind from his penmanship to be bold, excessively active, energetic, and irregular"), John Quincy Adams ("The chirography of the Ex-President is legible—but has an odd appearance"), Louis Godey ("gives evidence of a fine taste, combined with an indefatigability"), Jeremiah N. Reynolds ("His MS. is an ordinary clerk's hand, giving no indication of character"), Lambert A. Wilmer ("plainly indicates the cautious polish and terseness of his style"), William Burton ("scratchy and petite, betokening indecision and care or caution"), Mrs. E. Clementine Stedman ("Her chirography differs as materially from that of her sex in general as does her literary manner from the usual namby-pamby of our blue-stockings"), and other figures from politics, literature, and the professions. Poe's own literary prejudices often color his analytic comments. Of James Fenimore Cooper, he wrote: "Mr. Cooper's MS. is bad—very bad. There is no distinctive character about it, and it appears to be *unformed*." Of John Greenleaf Whittier: "His themes are *never* to our liking." The "Autography" series was attacked by Boston critic Edwin Percy Whipple in the Boston *Daily Times* and the Boston *Notion* of 18 December

1841. *See:* Miller, Joseph. *Text: MCW,* II, 259–291; *CWP,* XV, 139–261. *Research:* Mabbott, T. O. "Poe's Obscure Contemporaries." *American Notes & Queries*, 1 (February 1942): 166–167; Hammond, Alexander. "The Hidden Jew in Poe's 'Autography.' " *Poe Newsletter*, 2 (October 1969): 55–56.

Azrael. In Hebrew tradition, the angel of death. Poe refers to Azrael in describing the death throes of Ligeia. "I saw that she must die—and I struggled desperately in spirit with the grim Azrael."

B

B____, Madame. Character mentioned in the short story ''The Mystery of Marie Rogêt.'' She visits Madame Rogêt's house after the murder.

Baal-Zebub. Character in the short story ''Duc de L'Omelette.'' He is the devil who takes the Duc from his rosewood coffin and is defeated by the Duc at cards.

Bacon, Sir Francis. [Lord Verulam]. (1561–1626). English essayist and the philosopher of the new science. Poe refers to Bacon's concept of beauty in ''Ligeia,'' misquoting him slightly. Bacon's statement in his essay ''Of Beauty'' is: ''There is no excellent beauty that hath not some strangeness in the proportion.'' This is altered to: ''There is no exquisite beauty without some strangeness in the proportions.'' Poe's other references to Bacon and Bacon's inductive scientific method occur in reviews, critical essays, and the tales. In ''Mellonta Tauta,'' the reference to Bacon reveals Poe's view that both the inductive and deductive methods of seeking objective truth were too restrictive. Poe thought Bacon's methodology for attaining scientific truth faulty because it ''cultivat[ed] the natural sciences to the exclusion of Metaphysics, the Mathematics, and Logic.'' '' 'Baconian,' you must know, was an adjective invented as equivalent to Hog-ian and more euphonious and dignified.'' In *Marginalia*, Poe adds one more idol to Bacon's four idols or delusive beliefs. ''Here then is a subtle source of error which Lord Bacon has neglected. It is an Idol of the Wit. . . . the idol whose worship blinds man to truth by dazzling him with the *apposite*.'' *Text: CWP,* III, 336; VI, 202; X, 47; XIV, 133, 210; XVI, 31, 85, 129, 149, 169, 191.

Bacon, Roger. (1214–1294). English philosopher and proponent of experimental science. Poe mentions Bacon's antischolastic theory of science in *Marginalia*. *Text: CWP,* XVI, 118.

Bag. Character in the short story ''The Business Man.'' He is Peter Proffit's lawyer.

Baggesen, Jens. (1764–1826). Danish poet mentioned in Poe's discussion of taste in his review of Longfellow's *Ballads and Other Poems*. ''Taste itself, in short, is an arbitrary something, amenable to no law, and measurable by no definite rules.'' *Text: CWP,* XI, 65.

Baldazzar, Duke of Surrey. Character in Poe's drama *Politian*. He is a close friend of the hero.

"Ballads and Other Poems." Two reviews of Henry Wadsworth Longfellow's poetry appearing in the March and April 1842 numbers of *Graham's Magazine*. The first review is a detailed criticism of both Longfellow's work and his conception of poetry. In the second review, Poe continued to censure ''the obtrusive nature of [the poems'] didacticism'' and took issue with Longfellow's perceived need for poetry to have straightforward moral content, arguing that while poetry might concern itself with morality, it had no business advocating positions or decreeing moral absolutes. ''Much as we admire the genius of Mr. Longfellow, we are fully sensible of his many errors of affectation and imitation. His artistical skill is great, and his ideality high. But his conception of the *aims* of poesy *is all wrong*.'' Poe thought that by being overly didactic, Longfellow did ''violent wrong to his own high powers.'' Instead of ethical instruction, Poe insisted that art must serve the imagination first and that the primary purpose of poetry was ''the rhythmical creation of beauty,'' Poe's famous definition of the poetic ideal. Poe singles out several of the poems in the Longfellow collection, namely, ''The Village Blacksmith,'' ''The Wreck of the Hesperus,'' and ''The Skeleton in Armor,'' as fine specimens of rhymically created beauty. *Text: CWP,* XI, 64, 68. *Research: PJC,* 311–313.

"The Balloon Hoax." Short story first published in the New York *Sun* (*The Extra Sun*) of 13 April 1844 followed by a printing in the New York *Sunday Times* of 14 April 1844. The phony dispatch appeared under the fake headline ''Postscript: Astounding Intelligence by Private Express from Charleston via Norfolk!—The Atlantic Ocean Crossed in Three Days!!—Arrival at Sullivan's Island of a Steering Balloon Invented by Mr. Monck Mason!!'' The midday issue of the *Sun* carried the story as a one-page broadside. Written in the style of a ''scoop'' or ''big story'' journalism, the tale includes a detailed technical description of the balloon and its wicker basket car, transatlantic aerodynamics, and up-to-date dispatches from the journal of the balloonist Mr. Mason. The story temporarily duped New Yorkers into believing that the Atlantic had indeed been crossed by the balloon *Victoria* in seventy-five hours. Poe was guileful enough to have the balloon land not in New York but on Sullivan's Island near Charleston. Among the passengers was the novelist William Harrison Ainsworth, who is called upon to supply further particulars where the journal entries leave off. The quasi-scientific tone of the piece and the first-person reports contributed to the literary success of the hoax. *See:* "The Unparalleled Adventure of One Hans Pfaall." *Text: MCW,* III, 1063–1088; *CWP,* V, 224–240. *Research:* Scudder, H. H. "Poe's 'Balloon Hoax.' " *American Literature*, 21 (1949): 179–190; Wimsatt, William K., Jr. "A Further Note on Poe's 'Balloon Hoax.' " *American Literature*, 22 (1951): 491–492; Wilkinson, Ronald S. "Poe's 'Balloon Hoax' Once More." *American Literature*, 32 (1960): 313–317.

Baltimore Library Company. Circulating library often visited and used by Poe during his residencies in that city. *Research: LTP*, 267, 709, 710.

Baltimore Saturday Visiter. Perodical edited by Lambert Wilmer. The *Visiter* offered monetary prizes for the best poem and short story in June 1833, which prompted Poe to submit his work. *See:* "MS. Found in a Bottle." *Research: PLL,* 65.

Balzac, Honoré de. (1799–1850). French novelist quoted in "The Island of the Fay." Mabbott suggested that his story of the walling up of a victim "La Grande bretêche" is an analogue to "The Cask of Amontillado." Another writer, the essayist Jean-Louis Guez de Balzac (1597–1654) is mentioned in *Pinakidia and Marginalia. Text: CWP,* II, 125; IV, 196; XII, 11; XIV, 39, 59, 68; XVI, 30. *Research: MCW,* III, 1254; Eisenzweig, Uri. "L'Instance du policier dans le romanesque: Balzac, Poe et le mystère de la chambre close." *Poétique*, 12, no. 51 (1982): 279–302; BRE, 95.

Bancroft, George. (1800–1891). American statesman and historian. He was the author of *History of the United States.* In "Fifty Suggestions" Poe refers somewhat disparagingly to Bancroft's "painstaking precision. . . . Bancroft is a philosophical historian; but no amount of philosophy has yet taught him to despise a minute accuracy in point of fact." *Text: CWP,* VIII, 243–244; XIV, 180. *Research: LET,* I, 179.

Banim, John. (1798–1842). Irish novelist and dramatist. In his review of "Rienzi, the Last of the Tribunes" Poe compares him with Bulwer, stating that "Banim is a better sketcher of character." *Text: CWP,* VIII, 223.

Bank and 12th Streets, Capitol Square. A Poe address in Richmond. Poe resided here with the Clemms at the Yarrington Boarding House in October 1835. *Research:* Sheldon, Lynn W. Jr., J. B. Barnett, and Jeanne K. Hanson. "The Days of Edgar Allan Poe." *Historic Traveler: The Guide to Great Historic Destinations*, October–November 1995, 36–41.

Barbour, John Strode. (1790–1855). Virginia politician. He endorsed Poe's appointment to the U.S. Military Academy at West Point. *Research: TPL,* xvi.

Baretti, Giuseppe Marco Antonio. (1719–1789). Italian lexicographer and music historian mentioned in *Pinakidia* for his collection of 4,000 dramas, "of which the greater part were comedies—many of a high order." *Text: CWP,* XIV, 46.

"The Bargain Lost." First title and draft version of the short story "Bon-Bon" appearing in the Philadelphia *Saturday Courier* of 1 December 1832. The piece includes a translation of a couplet from Luigi Pulci (1432–1484) that Mabbott believed to be Poe's own: "Brethren, I come from lands afar/ To show you all what fools you are." *See:* "Bon-Bon."

Barker, James Nelson. (1784–1858). American poet and playwright included by Griswold in his anthology *The Poets and Poetry of America* under the heading "Various Authors." In his review of Griswold's anthology, Poe objected to Griswold's categorization implying that Barker and others were "only occasional scribblers." *Text: CWP,* XI, 241.

Barlow, Joel. (1754–1812). American epic poet and author of *The Columbiad* (1807). In "The Angel of the Odd," the narrator has been reading *The Columbiad* prior to the visit of the odd angel. Barlow's plan for a national university is also mentioned in Poe's review of Walsh's *Didactics—Social, Literary, and Political. Text: CWP,* VI, 103; VIII, 322.

"Barnaby Rudge." Two long, extremely laudatory reviews by Poe of Charles Dickens's novel appeared in the Philadelphia *Saturday Evening Post* for 1 May 1841 and *Graham's Magazine* for February 1842. Poe reviewed the novel while its serial installments were in progress, predicting that "Barnaby, the idiot, is the murderer's own son." Some critics have also pointed out that Dickens's verbose raven, Grip, is a source for Poe's avian commentator in his poem "The Raven." In March 1842, Poe sent these reviews to Dickens and requested an interview with the English novelist, who was currently on tour in the United States. Poe summarizes the novel in lengthy detail and criticizes Dickens for the novel's central structural weakness of inventing the plot as it went along instead of carefully constructing the novel from the artistic vantage point of a preconceived effect. But Poe praises Dickens as a masterful "delineator of character." Poe concludes that Dickens "has done this thing well, to be sure—he would do anything well in comparison with the herd of his contemporaries—but he has not done it so thoroughly well as his high and just reputation would demand. We think that the whole book has been an effort to him—solely through the nature of its design." *Text: CWP,* XI, 38. *Research:* Baker, Harry T. "A Source of 'The Raven.' " *Nation*, December 22, 1910, 601–602; Whitty, James Howard.

"Did Poe Solve the Plot of *Barnaby Rudge*?" *New York Times*, 11 May 1913, 287; Stewart, Charles D. "A Pilfering by Poe." *Atlantic Monthly*, December 1958, 67–68; *PJC,* 289–291; Westburg, Barry. "How Poe Solved the Mystery of *Barnaby Rudge*." *Dickens Studies Newsletter*, 5 (1974): 38–40; Rice, Thomas J. "Dickens, Poe, and the Time Scheme of *Barnaby Rudge*." *Dickens Studies Newsletter*, 7 (1976): 34–38.

Barnard, Augustus. Character in the novel *The Narrative of Arthur Gordon Pym*. He accompanies Pym in a drunken frolic aboard the sailboat *Ariel*, sails with him on the *Grampus*, and later becomes a reluctant cannibal along with Pym when they are forced to eat the corpse of seaman Richard Parker. Augustus dies at sea and is thrown to the sharks.

Barnard, Captain. Character in the novel *The Narrative of Arthur Gordon Pym*. He is Augustus Barnard's father and captain of the *Grampus*, the vessel on which Pym stows away.

Barnes, Joshua. (1654–1712). English antiquary and Greek scholar. Poe mentions him in *Pinakidia* as having "attribut[ed] the authorship of the Iliad to Solomon" and repeats this absurdity in *Marginalia*. "For my part I agree with Joshua Barnes:—nobody but Solomon could have written the Iliad." *Text: CWP,* XIV, 67; XVI, 37.

Barrett, Elizabeth Barrett [Browning]. (1806–1861). English poet and wife of Robert Browning. Her poem "Lady Geraldine's Courtship" influenced "The Raven." Poe dedicated his edition of *The Raven and Other Poems* to her. Poe contributed a long, double review of her poetry to *The Broadway Journal* of 4 January 1845 and 12 January 1845. *See:* "The Drama of Exile, and Other Poems." *Text: CWP,* XIII, 200–202; XVI, 136. *Research:* Varner, John Grier. "Poe and Miss Barrett of Wimpole Street." *Four Arts* (Richmond), 2 (January–February 1935): 4–5, 14–15, 17; Dedmond, Francis B. "Poe and the Brownings." *American Transcendental Quarterly*, 1 (1987): 111–122.

Barry, Lyttleton. Pen name used by Poe for the story "King Pest" appearing in *The Broadway Journal* of 18 October 1845. The pseudonym was also used for the short stories "Loss of Breath," "Duc de L'Omelette," "Mystification," and "Why the Little Frenchman Wears His Hand in a Sling." *Research:* Gerber, Gerald E. "Poe's Littleton Barry and Isaac D'Israeli's Littleton." *Poe Studies*, 14, no. 2 (1981): 32; *TPL,* 580.

Barthélemy, Jean-Jacques Abbé. (1716–1795). In his review of Mrs. Child's *Philothea: A Romance*, Barthélemy's *Voyage du jeune Anacharsis en Gréce* (1788) is mentioned twice to highlight the literary virtues of *Philothea*. *Text: CWP,* IX, 146, 155.

Bas-Bleu, Miss. (1). Character in the short story "The Man That Was Used Up." She is one of the guests at Mrs. Kathleen O'Trump's party. When she interrupts, the narrator informs her that Byron's drama is entitled "Man-Friday," not "Man-Fred."

Bas-Bleu, Miss. (2). Character in the short story "Lionizing" designated "big" Miss Bas-Bleu.

Bas-Bleu, Miss. (3). Character in the short story "Lionizing" designated "little" Miss Bas-Bleu.

Bas-Bleu, Mrs. Character in the short story "Lionizing." She is an appreciator of the eminent nosologist Robert Jones.

Basompière, François de. (1579–1646). French soldier and diplomat. Poe had read his Bastille memoirs. In *Pinakidia*, Poe quotes his anagram upon being released from the Bastille: "France, je sors de ma prison." *Text: CWP,* XIV, 60.

Bassett, Margaret. Poe wrote the poem "To Margaret" for the album of this Baltimore lady sometime in 1827 and signed it "E.A.P." *See:* "To Margaret." *Research: MCW,* I, 14–15; *TPL,* 82.

Baudelaire, Charles. (1821–1867). French poet and early critical defender of Poe's genius. He also translated Poe's stories and published several critically appreciative essays on Poe after his death. Baudelaire spent much of his later life translating Poe's work into French. Like Mallarmé and many other French symbolist poets, Baudelaire found in Poe the supreme example of the tortured artist who flouted all conventions and whose dissolute brilliance was a proper response to the oppressive strictures of bourgeois morality and taste. In the essays on Poe in the collection *The Painter of Modern Life* (1863), Baudelaire recognized and saluted what set Poe apart from the naive optimism of his age and culture. "This writer, the product of a self-infatuated age, the child of a nation more self-infatuated than any other, has clearly seen and dispassionately asserted the natural wickedness of man." Baudelaire bonded with Poe, finding in him an aesthetic kinsman and brother artist. *Research:* Baudelaire, Charles. *Baudelaire on Poe*, trans. Lois and Francis Hyslop, Jr. State College, PA: Bald Eagle Press, 1952; Rohmann, Gerd. "Der Dichter als Dandy: Vergleichende Betrachtungen zur äesthetischen und zum Künstlerideal bei Edgar Allan Poe und Charles Baudelaire." *Germanisch-romanische Monatschrift, Neue Folge*, 25 (1975): 199–213; Block, Haskell M. "Poe, Baudelaire, Mallarmé, and the Problem of the Untranslatable." In *Translation Perspectives, Selected Papers, 1982–1983*, ed. Marilyn Gaddis Rose. Binghamton, NY: TR. Research & Instruction Program, SUNY at Binghamton, 1984, 104–112; Culler, Jonathan. "Baudelaire and Poe." *Zeitschrift für Französische Sprache und Literatur*, 100 (1990): 61–73; Harner, Gary Wayne. "Edgar Allan Poe in France: Baudelaire's Labor of Love.'' In *Poe and His Times: The Artist and His Milieu*, ed. B. F. Fisher IV. Baltimore: Edgar Allan Poe Society, 1990, 218–225.

Beardsley, Aubrey Vincent. (1872–1898). English decadent artist and illustrator. Beardsley's medium was pen and ink; his style, black on white with the elongation of the human body and the grotesque enlargement of the genitalia, especially the female, and hermaphroditic figures. Beardley illustrated several Poe stories including ''The Fall of the House of Usher'' and ''The Masque of the Red Death.'' *Research:* Beardsley, Aubrey Vincent. *Four Illustrations for the Tales of Edgar Allan Poe*. Chicago: H. S. Stone, 1901.

Beauchamp-Sharp Murder Case. This 1825 celebrated crime of passion also known as ''The Kentucky Tragedy'' furnished Poe with a real-life source for his drama *Politian*. The woman in the case was Ann Cook of Frankfort, Kentucky, who was seduced by Solomon P. Sharp, the solicitor general of Kentucky. After bearing Sharp's child, Ann Cook agreed to marry Jeroboam O. Beauchamp in 1824 if he would promise to carry out her revenge on Sharp by killing him. Beauchamp stabbed Sharp to death on 5 November 1825, and a long and sensational trial followed, with Beauchamp pleading not guilty. Convicted of murder, he was joined by Ann Cook in his cell on the eve of his execution where the pair attempted double suicide. Ann Cook died of laudanum and stab wounds, while Beauchamp survived to be hanged on 7 July 1826. In Poe's time, the case inspired William Gilmore Simms's novel *Beauchampe* (1842) and and Thomas Holley Chivers's *Conrad and Eudora* (1834). Poe's drama relocates the elements of this plot to sixteenth-century Rome. *See: Politian*; Chivers, Thomas Holley. *Research:* Jillson, Willard Rouse. ''The Beauchamp-Sharp Tragedy in American Literature.'' *Kentucky State Historical Society Register*, 36 (January 1938): 54–60; Kimball, William J. ''Poe's *Politian* and the Beauchamp-Sharp Tragedy.'' *Poe Studies*, 4, no. 2 (1971): 25–27; Goldhurst, William. ''The New Revenge Tragedy: Treatments of the Beauchamp Case.'' *Southern Literary Journal*, 22 (1989): 117–127; Ryan, Steven T. ''World Enough and Time: A Refutation of Poe's History as Tragedy.'' *Southern Quarterly*, 31 (1993): 86–94.

Beauvais, Monsieur. Character in the short story ''The Mystery of Marie Rogêt.'' He identifies the corpse of Marie Rogêt and in doing so runs the risk of implicating himself in her murder.

Beckford, William. (1759–1844). English author of the oriental gothic fantasy *Vathek; An Arabian Tale* and builder of Fonthill Abbey. It is probable that Poe found partial inspiration for many of his exotic settings and themes from his reading of *Vathek*. The tale is mentioned in several of Poe's works including ''The Premature Burial'' (''The imagination of man is no Carathis''), ''The Domain of Arnheim,'' ''Landor's Cottage'' (''On this peninsula stood a dwelling house . . . like the infernal terrace seen by Vathek''), *Pinakidia*, and '' 'Thou

Art the Man.' '' In *Marginalia*, Poe makes a metaphorical reference to Vathek's infernal mother to describe the descent of the imagination into its own private hells. ''There are moments when, even to the sober eye of Reason, the world of our sad humanity must assume the aspect of Hell; but the Imagination of Man is no Carathis, to explore with impunity its every cavern.'' *Text: CWP,* V, 273, 299; VI, 190, 264; VII, 8; XIV, 69; XVI, 167. *Research: MCW,* II, 971–972; Tintner, Adeline R. ''Fire of the Heart in 'Al Aaraaf': Beckford and Byron as Source.'' *Poe Studies*, 22 (1989): 47–48; Graham, Kenneth W. '' 'Inconnue dans les annales de la terre': Beckford's Benign and Demonic Influence on Poe.'' In *Vathek & the Escape from Time: Bicentenary Revaluations*. New York: AMS Press, 1990, 201–223.

Bedloe, Augustus. Character in the short story ''A Tale of the Ragged Mountains.'' He is killed when a poisonous sangsue (an asp) is applied to his forehead by mistake instead of a leech.

Belial. Character in the short story ''Duc de L'Omelette.'' He is one of the devil's assistants who conveys the Duc to hell.

Bellow, Saul. (1915–). American novelist. His early novel *Dangling Man* (1944) and *Humboldt's Gift* respond to the situation of Poe as artist in permanent isolation. Bellow observed bitterly: ''Edgar Allan Poe, picked out of the Baltimore Gutter. And Hart Crane over the side of a ship. . . . The country is proud of its dead poets.'' *Research: PLL,* 278.

"The Bells." Poem by Poe written in May 1848 and published posthumously in *Sartain's Union Magazine* for December 1849. Poe submitted three versions of the poem to Sartain, each version longer than the former. An eighteen-line version of the poem had appeared in the *Home Journal* for April 1849. Poe received inspirational assistance from Marie Louise Shew who had attended the Poes during Virginia's terminal illness. Cast in the form of an irregular ode, ''The Bells'' is divided into four sections or movements, each of which enjoins the reader through onomatopoeic devices to attend to the different variations of the bells' language. Each of the four types of bells, the wedding bells, alarm bells, silver bells, and iron bells, resonates with its own unique voice and mood. To secure its sonic range of effects, the poem relies heavily on alliteration, assonantal rhyme, and monosyllabic rhyme to attain the preconceived effect of musical richness. Thus, the king of the ghouls in the finale (section IV) is heard ''Keeping time, time, time, In a sort of Runic rhyme.'' *Text: MCW,* I, 429–441; *CWP,* VII, 119–122. *Research:* DuBois, Arthur E. ''The Jazz Bells of Poe.'' *College English*, 3 (1940): 230–244; Dedmond, Francis B. ''The word 'Tintinnabulation' and a Source for Poe's 'The Bells.' '' *Notes & Queries*, 196 (24 November 1951): 520–521; Fusco, Richard. ''An Alternative Reading of Poe's 'The Bells.' '' *University of Mississippi Studies in English*, 1 (1980): 121–124.

"The Beloved Physician." Unpublished poetic fragment written for his benefactor Marie Louise Shew. T. O. Mabbott dated the composition at April 1847. The text of the poem appears in an 1875 letter from her to Poe's biographer John Ingram in which she partially quoted the poem. Poe had also mentioned the poem's title in 1848 correspondence with her. Ingram published the fragment in the January 1909 number of New York *Bookman.* The fragment reads: ''The pulse beats ten and intermits./ God nerve the soul that ne'er forgets/ In calm or storm, by night or day,/ Its steady toil, its loyalty. . . . The pulse beats ten and intermits./ God shield the soul that ne'er forgets. . . . so tired, so weary. . . . The soft head bows, the sweet eyes close;/ The faithful heart yields to repose.'' *See:* Shew, Marie Louise [Houghton]. *Text: MCW,* I, 401–404. *Research: LET,* II, 374.

Benjamin, Park. (1809–1864). Editor of the New York weekly *The New World* from October 1839 to March 1844. An article sometimes attributed to Poe, ''Our Magazine Literature,'' was published in the 11 March 1843 issue. *The New World* reprinted Poe's essay ''Autography'' and defended Poe's art in the issue of 4 June 1842 where Benjamin comments that Poe ''is one of the best writers now living. . . . [I]n whatever sphere he moves, he will surely be distinguished.'' In ''A Chapter on Autography'' in *Graham's Magazine* for November 1841, Poe wrote, ''He is a warm friend, and a bitter, but not implacable enemy. His judgment in literary matters should not be questioned, but there is some difficulty in getting at his real opinion.'' *See:* ''Our Magazine Literature.'' *Text: CWP,* XV, 183–184. *Research: LET,* I, 126, 193; *PLB,* 33, 84, 94, 95; *TPL,* xvii.

Bentham, Jeremy. (1748–1832). English philosopher and exponent of utilitarian socialism. He is mentioned in a satiric context in Poe's mock treatise ''Diddling Considered as One of the Exact Sciences'' as one of the Jeremys who ''wrote a Jeremiad about usury, and was called Jeremy Bentham.'' Poe reacts to Bentham's philosophy of material goodness for the greatest number in the first entry of *Marginalia* by insisting upon the value of idle pleasure in his marginal musings and useless literature. ''In getting my books, I have been always solicitous of an ample margin; . . . it may be not only a very hackneyed, but a very idle practice;—yet I persist in it still; and it affords me pleasure; which is profit, in despite of Mr. Bentham, with Mr. Mill on his back.'' *Text: CWP,* V, 204; VIII, 85; XI, 148; XIV, 104; XVI, 1, 27, 38, 193.

Béranger, Pierre-Jean de. (1780–1857). French poet and song writer. As a chansonnier, Béranger was esteemed by Poe who often compared his lyrics with the lyrics of poets he was reviewing. In *Marginalia,* in his discussion of ''*indefinitiveness* which is, at least, *one* of the essentials of true music,'' he cites the songs of Béranger as models. ''Coming down to our own times, it is the vital principle of de Béranger.'' *Text: CWP,* VIII, 139; X, 43–44, 198; XI, 107, 151–

152; XVI, 138–139, 165; *Research:* Pollin, Burton. ''Béranger in the Works of Poe.'' *DIP*, 54–74.

Berard, Claudius. Professor of modern languages at West Point. Through Berard's classes, Poe again came into contact with Le Sage's picaresque novel *Gil Blas. Research: PLL,* 45.

"Berenice." Short story by Poe published in *The Southern Literary Messenger* for March 1835. The tale has connections with two other love stories, ''Morella'' and ''Ligeia,'' these three stories forming Poe's marriage group. Markedly present in ''Berenice'' is a theme to which Poe would return in ''Ligeia,'' the narrator's obsession with a uniquely beautiful woman whose beauty is enhanced because she is dying. But unlike the ''Ligeia'' narrator who speaks in terms of the entire influence of the woman, her prodigious intellect as well as her physical beauty, the protagonist of ''Berenice'' is manically selective in defining his aesthetic fetish: ''In the multiplied objects of the external world I had no thoughts but for [her] teeth. For these I longed with a frenzied desire.'' Because of the dental idée fixe, some students of Poe have seen the tale as his subtle parody of the bizarre and outré themes of his own work and, more particularly, the obsessive masculine aggressiveness that surfaces throughout the Poe canon. Other Poe scholars contend that the narrator's gruesome extraction of this symbol of Berenice's beauty is nothing more than a mordant satire of gothic violence and, more specifically, the central brutal and unspeakable domestic atrocities of the most lurid gothic novels such as M. G. Lewis's *The Monk.* The Freudian reading of the tale sees the narrator's assault as a vaginal violation and destruction of the mother in the narrator's symbolic mutilation of the entrance to the womb. Whatever Poe's intentions, the narrator's treatment of women in ''Berenice'' stands out as one of Poe's most shocking and repulsive depictions of disturbed behavior. It is clear that the narrator's erotic fascination with Berenice increases in proportion to the debilitating influence of epilepsy upon her body. As the atrophy progresses, he becomes more conscious of her teeth and their powerful attraction, convincing him that only possessing them separately from Berenice's diseased body ''could alone ever restore me to peace, in giving me back to reason.'' ''They alone were present to the mental eye'' further suggests the division that the narrator makes between the dying individual and the vitality represented by the teeth that he ''covets so madly.'' This dissociation of all other parts of her anatomy from the teeth leads him finally to pull the teeth from the corpse even though the ''piercing shriek of a female voice'' rings in his ears during the thirty-two-step operation. Berenice's agonized screams and the imprint of female fingernails leave no doubt as to the true nature of the deed and intensify the horror to an almost emetic level of response. The concluding paragraphs of the story constitute a realization, if not a confession, of his gruesome deed by the narrator. A neighbor who has heard shrieks in the night and seen the violated grave containing a still-living orally mutilated victim brings the narrator back to reality if not to sanity. As the narrator fumbles to get at the trophies of his distorted affection, the box containing Berenice's teeth spills like dragonseed across his library floor. *Epigraph:* "Dicibant mihi sodales, si sepulchrum amicæ visitarum, curas meas aliquantulum fore levatas." Latin source unknown (Poe attributed to Ben Zaïat of Baghdad). *Text: MCW,* II, 207–221; *CWP,* II, 16. *Research: LET,* I, 57–58; Forclaz, Roger. "A Source for 'Berenice' and a Note on Poe's Reading." *Poe Newsletter*, 1 (October 1968): 25–27; Sloan, David E. E. "Gothic Romanticism and Rational Empiricism in Poe's "Berenice.' " *American Transcendental Quarterly*, 19 (summer 1973): 19–26; Ziolkowski, Theodore. "The Telltale Teeth: Psychodontia to Sociodontia." *Publications of the Modern Language Association*, 91 (1976): 9–22; Blythe, Hal, and Charlie Sweet. "Poe's Satiric Use of Vampirism in 'Berenice.' " *Poe Studies*, 14, no. 2 (1981): 23–24; Dayan, Joan. "The Identity of Berenice, Poe's Idol of the Mind." *Studies in Romanticism*, 23 (1984): 491–513.

Bergerac, Cyrano de. (1616–1655). French soldier, poet, and dramatist. Poe refers to his *Voyage to the Moon* in "The Unparalleled Adventure of One Hans Pfaall." *Text: CWP,* II, 48.

Berlifitzing, Count Wilhelm. Character in the short story "Metzengerstein." He perishes in a stable fire, but his spirit reinhabits the body of a horse to become an agent of supernatural revenge.

Bernadin de St. Pierre, Jacques Henri. (1734–1814). French author of the Rousseauistic novel *Paul and Virginia.* He is mentioned in the short story "Loss of Breath" and credited by Poe with fixing in the language "two significance words, viz.; *bienfaisance*, and the diminutive, *la gloriole*." *Text: CWP,* II, 359; VII, 25; XIV, 45. *Research:* Pollin, Burton R. "Poe's Use of Material from Bernadin de St. Pierre's *Études*." *Romance Notes*, 12 (1971): 331–338.

Berri, Duchesse Marie de. (1798–1870). Poe's interest in her arose out of her use of epistolary ciphers and her essay "The Secrets of the Alphabet." In his essay "Secret Writing," he mentions that the French minister, M. Berryer, "displayed the highest ingenuity in the solution of a cipher addressed by the Duchess of Berri to the legitimists of Paris, but of which she had neglected to furnish the key." *Text: CWP,* X, 135–136; XIV, 135.

Berryer, Pierre Antoine. (1790–1868). French politician, essayist, and adept cryptographer. He is mentioned in *Marginalia* as " 'the man in whose description is the greatest possible consumption of antithesis.' " *Text: CWP,* XIV, 123, 135; XVI, 83.

Bessel, Friedrich W. (1784–1846). German astronomer mentioned in *Eureka.* "Bessel, not long ago deceased, has lately succeeded in determining the distance of six or seven stars; among others, that of the star numbered 61 in the constellation of the Swan." *Text: CWP,* XVI, 288. *Research: LET,* II, 408.

Betjman, John. (1906–1984). English poet. His "Indoor Games Near Newberry" is a modernized version of Poe's "Annabel Lee." *Research: PLL,* 331.

Bewick, William. (1753–1828). English illustrator and engraver. He made engravings for Æsop's fables. Poe comments on his portrait of William Hazlitt in his review of the "Literary Remains of the Late William Hazlitt." *Text: CWP,* IX, 140.

The Bible, Poe's Use of. Poe's knowledge of scripture and his use of the Bible in his poetry and tales is extensive, indeed, almost pervasive. The Bible's influence may be found in his choice of epigraphs, character naming, apocalyptic style, prophetic and catastrophic climaxes, and philosophic revelations. T. O. Mabbott's index to the tales identifies and connects Biblical allusions in the short stories to the books of Genesis, Exodus, Leviticus, Numbers, Deuteronomy, Joshua, Judges, I Samuel, II Samuel, II Kings, Ezra, Esther, Joab, Psalms, Proverbs, Ecclesiastes, Isaiah, Jeremiah, Lamentations, Ezekiel, Daniel, Hosea, Joel, Jonah, Micah, St. Matthew, St. Mark, St. Luke, St. John, Acts, Romans, I Corinthians, II Corinthians, Philippians, I Thessalonians, I Peter, II Peter, Jude, Revelation, and Maccabees. Biblical passages sometimes served as a source for various poems. "The City in the Sea," for example, may derive its disastrous situation from Poe's memory of Revelation 16: 18–19; "And there were voices, and thunders, and lightnings,; and there was a great earthquake, such as was not since men were upon the earth, so mighty an earthquake and so great. And the great city was divided into three parts, and the cities of the nations fell." In a similar apocalyptic vein, Poe appears to have inserted the prophetic words of Ezekiel 43: 2, "and his voice was like a noise of many waters," in the final sentence of "The Fall of the House of Usher" with the reference to "a long tumultuous shouting like the voice of a thousand waters." Poe's *Eureka* occupies a place in his canon similar to the final book of the New Testament, The Revelation of Saint John the Divine. *Research: MCW,* III, 1414; Smith, Charles Alfonso. "Poe and the Bible." *Biblical Review*, 5 (July 1920): 354–365; Forrest, William Mentzel. *Biblical Allusions in Poe*. New York: Macmillan, 1928; Campbell, Killis. "Poe's Knowledge of the Bible." *Studies in Philology*, 27 (1930): 546–551.

Biddle, Nicholas. (1786–1844). Philadelphia financier and president of the United Bank. In 1840, Poe appealed to Biddle to fund *The Penn Magazine*. *Research: TPL,* xvii.

Bielfeld, Baron de. (1717–1770). German author who wrote in French *Les premiers traits de l'erudition universelle* (1768), a learned work of criticism cited several times by Poe for its profound insights. His definition of poetry, "L'art de exprimer les pensées par la fiction," impressed Poe and was quoted in *Marginalia* and *Pinakidia*. In *Eureka*, Poe quoted Baron de Bielfeld on the nature of God: "We know absolutely nothing of the nature or essence of God:

—in order to comprehend what he is, we should have to be God ourselves'' [Poe's translation]. *See:* ''Bon-Bon.'' *Text: CWP,* X, 47, 62; XI, 74; XIV, 67; XVI, 91, 130. *Research:* Griggs, Earl Leslie. ''The Sources of Edgar Allan Poe's 'Pinakidia.' '' *American Literature*, 1 (1929): 196–199; Mabbott, Thomas Ollive. ''Que tous ses pas.'' *American Notes & Queries*, 1 (April 1941): 11–12; Pollin, Burton R. ''Empedocles in Poe: A Contribution of Bielfeld.'' *Poe Studies*, 13 (1980): 8–9.

"Big Abel and the Little Manhattan." Novel by Cornelius Mathews reviewed favorably by Poe in *The Broadway Journal* of 27 September 1845. A lengthened version of the notice of Mathews's historical fantasy appeared in *Godey's Lady's Book* for November 1845. The novel concerns two claimants to the island of Manhattan and is ''an ingenious, an original, and altogether, an excellent book. . . . Its chief defect is a very gross indefiniteness, not of conception, but of execution.'' *Text: CWP,* XII, 73. *Research: PLB,* 105.

"The Biography and Poetical Remains of the Late Margaret Miller Davidson. By Washington Irving." Review of Irving's biography of the child poet Margaret Miller Davidson appearing in *Graham's Magazine* for August 1841. Poe was particularly interested in her 2,000-line poem ''Lenore'' and credits her with ''occasional bursts of the truest poetic fire.'' He further singled out two other poems for high praise, ''To Mamma'' and ''My Native Lake.'' *Text: CWP,* X, 174.

Bird, Robert Montgomery. (1806–1854). American novelist remembered for his novel *Nick of the Woods; or, The Jibbenainosay* (1837). Poe reviewed several of his books for *The Southern Literary Messenger* including *Calavar,* ''by far the best of them, and beyond doubt one of the best of American novels,'' and included a character reading of his signature in ''Autography,'' noting from its ''degree of nervousness'' that ''a restless and vivid imagination might be deduced from this MS.'' *See:* ''The Hawks of Hawk-Hollow.'' *Text: CWP,* XV, 156, 203–204. *Research:* Campbell, Killis. ''The Source of Poe's 'Some Words with a Mummy.' '' *Nation*, 23 June 1910, 625–626.

Bird. William. Character in the short story ''The Murders in the Rue Morgue.'' He is an English tailor who deposes that the voice of the murderer belonged to a German.

Bisco, John. Poe's partner for a brief period in 1845 at *The Broadway Journal.* He sold the magazine to Poe for $50 in October 1845, Poe paying him with a loan from Horace Greeley. *Research: LET,* II, 325; *TPL,* xvii.

Blab. Character in the short story ''Loss of Breath'' whose incessant conversation with Wind-enough causes the latter's epileptic attack.

"The Black Cat." Short story by Poe originally published on page one of the Philadelphia *Saturday Evening Post* of 19 August 1843. The narrator is a man whose kindly temperament is warped by ''the spirit of perverseness'' that compels him to commit vile acts precisely because he knows they are depraved and perverse. The story centers on the narrator's relationship to two cats. One night in a drunken rage, he mutilates and then murders Pluto, an entirely black cat, the deed causing a mixture of pleasure with ''the bitterest remorse at heart'' and terrible self-loathing. But when his wife replaces Pluto with a second cat, also entirely black except for a single splotch of white on its breast, his aggression is rekindled with a corresponding elevation of guilty desire to perform acts of even more loathsome perversity. Gradually the white splotch assumes the shape of a gallows in the diseased eye of the narrator. When his wife attempts to protect the new cat, the narrator axes her to death while attempting to bludgeon the cat and inters her in a false chimney in the cellar with ''a glee at heart [that] was too strong to be restrained.'' The narrator then caps his perverse crimes by inviting the police to search the cellar for the corpse, but his perverse plan is foiled when strange inhuman shrieks and howls are heard coming from behind the wall. When the wife's body is unwalled by the police, the narrator beholds his accuser, the detested cat, adorning the gore-clotted corpse's head. The cat that condemns him to the hangman is the containing symbol of his egotism and rage at the same time that it symbolizes the narrator's culminating perverse urge toward self-destruction and violent retribution for his crimes. In its stark dramatization of Poe's theory of human perversity, the tale is linked with another psychometric exercise in self-contempt, ''The Imp of the Perverse.'' *Text: MCW,* III, 847–860; *CWP,* V, 143–154. *Research:* Bonaparte, Marie. '' 'The Black Cat,' '' trans. John Rodker, *Partisan Review*, 17 (1950): 834–860; Gargano, James W. '' 'The Black Cat': Perverseness Reconsidered.'' *Texas Studies in Literature and Language*, 2 (1960): 172–178; Anderson, Gayle Dennington. ''Demonology in 'The Black Cat.' '' *Poe Studies*, 10 (1977): 43–44; Crisman, William. '' 'Mere Household Events' in Poe's 'The Black Cat.' '' *Studies in American Fiction*, 12 (1984): 87–90; Heller, Terry. ''The Pure Fantastic Tale of Terror.'' In *The Delights of Terror: An Aesthetics of the Tale of Terror*. Urbana: Illinois University Press, 1987, 100–107; Weaver, Aubrey Maurice. ''And Then My Heart with Pleasure Fills . . .'' *Journal of Evolutionary Psychology*, 9 (1988): 317–320; Cleman, John. ''Irresistible Impulses: Edgar Allan Poe and the Insanity Defense.'' *American Literature*, 63 (1991): 623–640; Badenhausen, Richard. ''Fear and Trembling in the Literature of the Fantastic: Edgar Allan Poe's 'The Black Cat.' '' *Studies in Short Fiction*, 29 (1992): 487–498; Benfey, Christopher. ''Poe and the Unreadable 'Black Cat' and 'Tell-Tale Heart.' '' In *New Essays on Poe's Major Tales*, ed. Kenneth Silverman. Cambridge: Cambridge University Press, 1993, 27–44; Madden, Fred. ''Poe's 'The Black Cat' and Freud's 'The Uncanny.' '' *Literature & Psychology*, 39, nos. 1–2 (1993): 52–62.

Blackbeard. Book briefly noticed by Poe in *The Southern Literary Messenger* for June 1835. *Research: TPL,* 160.

Blackwell, Anna. Woman physician and amateur poet. She attended the Poes at Fordham cottage in October 1847. *Research:* Miller, John C. ''Poe and Miss Anna Blackwell.'' *Poe Studies*, 12 (1979): 28–29; *TPL,* xvii; *MNR,* 351–354, 359.

Blackwood, William. (1776–1834). Authentic editorial personality who appears as a character in several Poe short stories involving sensational journalism. He was the founder and editor of *Blackwood's Edinburgh Magazine*, which abounded in stories of garish psychological states and tales of solitary victims in lethal predicaments. In the short story ''How to Write a Blackwood Article'' he interviews Signora Psyche Zenobia and advises her that an author who wishes to be published should use real experiences embellished by foreign phrases. Blackwood also appears in the short stories ''Lionizing'' and ''A Predicament.'' *Research:* Daughrity, Kenneth L. ''Notes: Poe and *Blackwood's*.'' *American Literature*, 2 (1930): 289–292.

Blackwood's Magazine. Scottish literary periodical whose gothic and sensational content influenced Poe and was sometimes imitated by him. Poe's article ''The Buried Alive'' appeared in the October 1821 issue. *See:* Blackwood, William. *Research:* Dameron, J. Lasley. ''Poe and Blackwood's on the Art of Reviewing.'' *Emerson Society Quarterly*, 31 (2nd Q 1963): 29–30.

Blaettermann, George. Professor of modern languages at the University of Virginia during Poe's residency. Poe's proficiency in Italian earned Blaettermann's praise. *Research: LTP*, 122; *PLL,* 23.

Blair, Hugh. (1718–1800). Scottish rhetorician and author of *Lectures on Rhetoric*. In a composite review of books (''Exordium'') in *Graham's Magazine* for January 1842, Poe defended the theoretical views of the rationalist critics of the eighteenth century ''for the principles of these artists will not fail until Nature herself expires.'' *Text: CWP,* XI, 5. *Research: PJC,* 277.

Blair, Robert. (1699–1746). English poet and member of the ''Graveyard School.'' Poe cites Blair's lines 588–589 from his poem ''The Grave''—''Its visits like those of angels, short and far between''—in *Marginalia* and in *Pinakidia* to prove a plagiarism by Thomas Campbell. *Text: CWP,* XIV, 47; XVI, 75.

Bless-My-Soul, Duchess of. Character in the short story ''Lionizing.'' She is sitting for her portrait when Robert Jones enters the artist's studio.

Bliss, Elam. Publisher of Poe's third volume of poetry in 1831.

Block, Captain E. T. V. Character in the novel *The Narrative of Arthur Gordon Pym.* He is the captain of the *Penguin*, the whaler that runs down the sailboat *Ariel.*

Bluddennuff, Elector of. Character in the short story ''Lionizing.'' His nose is shot off in a duel with Robert Jones.

Blunderbuzzard. Character mentioned in the short story ''The Devil in the Belfry.'' He is cited as the author of *De Derivationibus* as a name source for the borough of Vondervotteimittiss.

Bob, the devil. Printer's devil in the short story ''X-ing a Paragrab.''

Bob, Thingum. Character in the short story ''The Literary Life of Thingum Bob, Esq.'' He is a mysterious author who explains how he attained literary success.

Bob, Thomas, esq. Character in the short story ''The Literary Life of Thingum Bob, Esq.'' He is the father of the narrator, Thingum Bob.

Bobby. Character in the short story ''Three Sundays in a Week.'' He is the narrator and the nephew of the curmudgeonly granduncle Rumgudgeon.

Boccalini, Trajano. (1556–1613). Italian poet and political satirist. Poe recites an anecdote from Boccalini in his review of Dickens's *Barnaby Rudge* on the proper duty of the critic. ''Boccalini, in his 'Advertisements from Parnassus,' tells us that a critic once presented Apollo with a severe censure upon an excellent poem. The God asked him for the beauties of the work. He replied that he only troubled himself about the errors. Apollo presented him with a sack of unwinnowed wheat, and bade him pick out all the chaff for his pains.'' *Text: CWP,* XI, 41.

Bogart, Elizabeth. [pseud. Estelle]. (1806–?). Minor poet sketched by Poe in ''The Literati of New York City.'' ''Miss Bogart has not yet collected her writings in volume form. Her fugitive pieces have usually been signed 'Estelle.' They are noticeable for nerve, dignity, and finish.'' *Text: CWP,* XV, 107.

Boileau. [Nicolas Boileau-Despréaux]. (1636–1711). French satirist, literary critic, and author of the important treatise *L'Art poétique*. Poe had read Boileau's *The Art of Poetry* and quotes from his verse several times in *Marginalia. Text: CWP,* XIV, 56, 58, 182; XVI, 47, 77.

Bolingbroke, Lord. [Henry St. John]. (1678–1751). English politician and historian. Poe mentions his erudition in *Pinakidia* and *Marginalia*. *Text: CWP,* X, 47; XIV, 39; XVI, 30.

Bolton, Richard. In ''Secret Writing,'' Poe mentions Mr. Richard Bolton of Pontotoc, Mississippi, to be the ''only one [who] has succeeded in solving the cryptograph of Dr. Frailey.'' *Text: CWP,* XIV, 149.

Bonaparte, Marie. (1882–1962). Poe biographer, student of Freud, and literary psychoanalyst. She was the author of *Edgar Poe, sa vie—son oeuvre: Étude analytique* [The life and works of Edgar Allan Poe: a psychoanalytic interpretation] (1933), with a foreword by Sigmund Freud. Madame Bonaparte conducted a Freudian inquiry into Poe's lifelong fixation on women as mother surrogates and the specific effects of this obsession on his fiction and poetry. Bonaparte believed that Poe was impotent, that his marriage to his cousin Virginia Clemm was never consummated, and that Poe's writings furnish overwhelming evidence of his sexual maladjustment. In ''The Black Cat,'' for example, Bonaparte reads the hanged cat not as a general symbol of progressive psychosis but as a specific symbol of the penis of the impotent Poe. Never willing to separate Poe the artist from the characters and episodes of his fiction, she concluded from her case studies that he was psychotically disturbed and maternally ambivalent as well as deeply guilty over his sexual inadequacy. Furthermore, she identified Poe's characters with real people in his life: the husband/narrator of ''Ligeia'' is Poe himself; Ligeia is the dead mother, Elizabeth Arnold Poe; and the second wife is Virginia Clemm. Bonaparte's theories advanced earlier psychoanalytic readings such as Lorine Pruette's essay ''A Psychoanalytic Study of E. A. Poe'' appearing in the *American Journal of Psychology*, 31 (1920), and opened up a main vein of Poe criticism that would interpret his works through the lens of Freudian psychobiography. *Research:* Bonaparte, Marie. *Le Sphinx, et autres contes bizarres, by Poe*, trans. Matilda C. Ghyka and Maurice Sachs. Paris: Gallimard, 1934; Bruss, Neal. ''The Discourse of Pym and Marie Bonaparte's Analysis of Poe.'' *Rackham Literary Studies*, 2 (1972): 51–59; Forclaz, Roger. ''Psychoanalysis and Edgar Allan Poe: A Critique of the Bonaparte Thesis.'' In *Critical Essays on Edgar Allan Poe*, ed. Eric W. Carlson. Boston: G. K. Hall, 1987, 187–195.

"Bon-Bon." Short story by Poe first published in draft form under the title ''The Bargain Lost'' in the Philadelphia *Saturday Courier* for 1 December 1832 and later published under the title ''Bon-Bon—A Tale'' in *The Southern Literary Messenger* for August 1835. Each version of the story had its own epigraph. Part farce and part intellectual satire, this early tale is typical of Poe's witty stories concerning comic demonic encounters. The restaurateur and chef, Pierre Bon-Bon, whose superb omelettes are exceeded only by his masterful philosophical acumen, receives a visit from the archfiend one nasty winter night.

Both a metaphysical genius and a gourmet (''It is to Bon-Bon that Kant himself is indebted for his metaphysics''), Bon-Bon draws great satisfaction from mixing the pleasures of the palate with ''the diablerie of his German studies.'' As he imbibes deeply of books and bottles of Chambertin, Bon-Bon suddenly becomes aware of Satan's presence in his apartments. Bon-Bon's demonic guest is a vampiric figure with a ''set of jagged, fang-like teeth,'' a savage laugh, and most notably, ''no eyes whatsoever, . . . simply a dead level of flesh.'' With urbane nonchalance, the devil recites the large roster of intellectual worthies who have fallen to his infernal care and who have been roasted, fricaseed, parboiled, sauteed, and souffléed down in hell's kitchens. To Bon-Bon's desperate question, ''What is the soul?'' the devil equivocates by describing the flavor of those great intellects he has tasted. In a clever reversal of the Faustian pact, the devil turns down Bon-Bon when the distraught philosopher offers him his soul. '' 'I'll let you have it—hiccup!—a bargain.' '' '' 'Couldn't think of such a thing,' said the latter calmly. The metaphysician stared. 'Am supplied at present. Have no funds on hand.' '' The conversation of the two characters, the drunken gibberish of the tipsy Bon-Bon set against the suave and solicitous ironies of the devil, anticipate the colloquy of dunce and demonic genius in the underground of ''The Cask of Amontillado.'' *Epigraphs:* ''The heathen philosopher, when he had a mind to eat a grape, would open his lips when he put it into his mouth, meaning thereby that grapes were made to eat and lips to open.'' Shakespeare, *As You Like It*; ''Quand un bon vin meuble mon estomac,/ Je suis plus savant que Balzac—/ Plus sage qu Pibrac;/ Mon bras seul faisant l'attaque/ De la nation Cosaque,/ La mettroit au sac:/ De Charon je passerois le lac,/ En dormant dans son bac;/ J'irois au fier Eac,/ Sans que mon coeur fit tic ni tac,/ Présenter du tabac.'' Passage quoted in Bielfeld's *Érudition Universelle*. *Text: MCW,* II, 83–117; *CWP,* II, 125–146. *Research:* Lynch, James J. ''The Devil in the Writings of Irving, Hawthorne, and Poe.'' *New York Folklore Quarterly*, 8 (1952): 111–113; Christie, James W. ''Poe's 'Diabolical' Humor: Revisions in 'Bon-Bon.' '' *Library Chronicle*, 41 (1976): 44–55; Galloway, David. Introduction to *The Other Poe: Comedies and Satires*. Harmondsworth, United Kingdom: Penguin, 1983, 7–22.

Bon-Bon, Pierre. Character in the short story ''Bon-Bon.'' He attempts to bargain away his soul to the devil but is refused.

Bonner, Jim. Character in the novel *The Narrative of Arthur Gordon Pym*. A sailor aboard the *Grampus*, he is thrown off the deck during an argument.

Bonneville, Captain Benjamin Louis Eulalie de. (1796–1878). American army officer and explorer of the Rocky Mountain region. Irving's *Adventures of Captain Bonneville, U.S.A.* was known to Poe. Bonneville's expeditions are mentioned in *The Journal of Julius Rodman*. *Text: CWP,* IV, 20–21, 48.

"The Book of Gems. The Poets and Artists of Great Britain." Poe reviewed an anthology by S. C. Hall in *The Southern Literary Messenger* for

August 1836. A second version of the review was published in *The Broadway Journal* of 17 May 1845. Poe is harshly critical about some of the selections, saying, "There are long passages now before us, of the most despicable trash, with no merit whatsoever, beyond that of their antiquity." He cites Andrew Marvell's "Maiden Lamenting for Her Fawn" as truly superlative verse. *See:* "Old English Poetry.—The Book of Gems. Edited by S. C. Hall." *Text: CWP,* IX, 91. *Research: PJC,* 168–171.

Borges, Jorge Luis. (1899–1986). Argentinian poet, novelist, and critic. The example of Poe played an important part in his own fiction even though he downgraded the poetry, calling him a "mediocre poet, a sort of miniature Tennyson." In a literary interview, Borges stated that "Poe's importance is considerable if we judge it historically." His stories "Death and the Compass," "The Immortals," and the pieces in the collection *Labyrinths* suggest the impact of Poe on Borges's imagination. *Research:* Lima, Robert. "A Borges Poem on Poe." *Poe Studies*, 6, no. 1 (1973): 29–30; Fulton, Patricia Teague. "Borges, Hawthorne, and Poe: A Study of Significant Parallels in Their Theories and Methods of Short Story Writing." *Dissertation Abstracts International*, 40 (1980): 5461A; Bennett, Maurice J. "The Detective Fiction of Poe and Borges." *Comparative Literature*, 35 (1983): 266–275.

Borlase, William. (1695–1772). Antiquarian and writer on Stonehenge, the druids, and *Cornish Antiquities* (1754). His view that "[t]he work of Stonehenge must have been that of a great and powerful nation, not of a limited community of priests" is cited by Poe in his essay on the construction of Stonehenge in *Burton's Gentleman's Magazine* for June 1840. *Text: CWP,* XIV, 113.

Bossuet, Julien. Character in "The Premature Burial." He exhumes and embraces his beloved who has been prematurely buried.

"Boston and the Bostonians. Editorial Miscellany." Two essays by Poe appearing in *The Broadway Journal* of 1 November 1845 and 22 November 1845, in which he defended himself against the strictures of Cornelia Walter against his insulting choice of "Al Aaraaf" for the reading and berated the boorish Boston audience "who evinced characteristic discrimination in understanding, and especially applauding, all those knotty passages which we ourselves have not yet been able to understand." Walter, the editor of the Boston *Evening Transcript*, had also found fault with Poe's inclusion of "The Raven," a "composition better appreciated by its author than by his auditory." In the 1 November piece, Poe cites a review of his Boston Lyceum reading of "The Messenger Star" from the *Sunday Times and Messenger* of 26 October 1845 and accuses the Boston audience of lacking soul. "They have always evinced towards us individually the basest ingratitude for the services we rendered them in enlightening them about the originality of Mr. Longfellow." Poe opens the second piece by quoting a review of his poetry from the Charleston *Patriot* and replies acidly to the ''abuse'' of his work and Lyceum lectures by the Bostonians and Frogpondians. ''We knew that write what we would they would swear it to be worthless. . . . The Frogpondians may as well spare us their abuse. We despise them and defy them (the transcendental vagabonds!) and they may all go to the devil together.'' *See:* ''Al Aaraaf,'' Frogpondians; Walter, Cornelia Wells. *Text: CWP,* XIII, 1–13.

Boston Lyceum. Poe gave poetry readings here. Biographer Jeffrey Meyers remarks that ''Boston, for Poe, was enemy territory. But he entered it with reckless audacity.'' *Research:* Casale, Ottavio M. ''The Battle of Boston: A Revaluation of Poe's Lyceum Appearance.'' *American Literature*, 45 (1973): 423–428; *PLL,* 180–183.

Boswell, James. (1740–1795). English diarist, essayist, and conversationalist. He wrote a *Life of Samuel Johnson, LL.D.* In *Marginalia*, Poe names Boswell ''the best historiographer of true talk ever to record conversations.'' *Text: CWP,* XVI, 60. *Research:* Whitty, James Howard. ''Poe's Relationship to Boswell.'' *Nation*, 21 August 1918, 227–228.

Boteler, Captain Thomas. (fl. 1825). Author of the travel saga *A Voyage of Discovery to Africa and Arabia, Performed in His Majesty's Ships Leven and Barracouta, from 1822 to 1826, under the command of Captain F. W. W. Owen, R.N.* Poe mentions the book in his summary of reviews appearing in the *Edinburgh Review* for July 1835. *Text: CWP,* VIII, 84.

Boucicault, Dion. (1820–1890). English playwright and play adapter. In his review of ''The New Comedy by Mrs. Mowatt,'' Poe refers to Boucicault's *London Assurance* as ''that most inane and utterly despicable of all modern comedies.'' *Text: CWP,* XII, 120; XV, 30.

Boullard. Character in the short story ''The System of Doctor Tarr and Professor Fether.'' He thinks he is a top and spins constantly.

Bowen, Charles. (fl. 1830). Boston publisher. His house published *The American Almanac*, which Poe had reviewed in *The Southern Literary Messenger* for October 1836. *Text: CWP,* IX, 162.

Bowen, Eli. (1824–1868). Editor of *The Columbia Spy*, Columbia, Pennsylvania, in 1843–1844. Poe published seven New York dispatches in Bowen's journal between May and July 1844. *Research: TPL,* 17.

Bowen, Walter G. One of Poe's journalistic pseudonyms. *See:* ''A Reviewer Reviewed.''

Bowler Cocke Plantation. At Turkey Island, Henrico County, Virginia. The Allans took the young Poe here for Christmas 1811. *Research: TPL,* 16.

Bradstreet, Ann. (ca. 1612–1672). American poet and author of *The Tenth Muse Lately Sprung Up in America.* Poe mentions that she was the first poet represented in Griswold's anthology *The Female Poets of America*, but he does not evaluate her work. *Text: CWP,* XI, 159.

Brady, Mathew B. (1823–1896). Famous American photographer. He made one daguerreotype of Poe in 1849. *Research: TPL,* xvii.

Brahe, Tycho. (1546–1601). Danish astronomer whose celestial discoveries influenced Poe. In 1572, Brahe discovered and named the star "Al Aaraaf." In a letter to the publisher Isaac Lea, Poe informed him that "I have placed this 'Al Aaraaf' in the celebrated star discovered by Tycho Brahe which appeared & disappeared so suddenly." *Text: MCW,* I, 93, 96, 115; *CWP,* VII, 23. *Research: LET,* I, 18, 33; *PLL,* 41.

Bransby, Reverend Dr. Character in the short story "William Wilson." He is young William Wilson's schoolmaster.

Bransby, Reverend John. (1784–1857). Master of the Manor House School at Stoke Newington where Poe was a student in 1818–1820. Bransby regarded his pupil Edgar Allan as "a quick and clever boy and would have been a very good boy if he had not been spoilt by his parents. Allan was intelligent, wayward, and wilful." Poe included him among the characters in "William Wilson." *Research:* Chase, Lewis. "John Bransby, Poe's Schoolmaster." *Athenæum*, 4605 (May 1916): 221–222; *TPL,* xvii.

Breton, André. (1896–1966). French surrealist poet and proponent of the surreal movement in art. His attitude toward Poe, unlike most French poets, was mixed. "Let us spit in passing on Edgar Poe." *Research:* Richard, Claude. "André Breton et Edgar Poe." *Nouvelle Revue Française*, 172 (April 1967): 926–936; *PLL,* 329.

"Bridal Ballad." Poem by Poe. This youthful composition in seven six-line stanzas was first published under the title "Ballad" in *The Southern Literary Messenger* for January 1837. A second version of the poem now called "Bridal Ballad" appeared in the *Saturday Evening Post* of 31 July 1841. It was one of the selections included by Poe in *The Raven and Other Poems* in 1845 in which the title "Bridal Ballad" was used. The ballad is told or sung from the point of view of the bride. Just after her marriage to another man, she laments her lover "who fell/ In the battle down the dell,/ And who is happy now." She awakens in the arms of a rescuer and comforter and feels obliged to remain faithfully married to him even though her "plighted vow" probably means that her dead lover will suffer her breaking of faith to him while in his grave. "For I dream I know not how,/ And my soul is sorely shaken/ Lest an evil step be taken,—/ Lest the dead who is forsaken/ May not be happy now." *Text: MCW,* I, 304–310; *CWP,* VII, 81.

Briggs, Charles F. [Harry Franco]. (1804–1877). Author and editor of *The Broadway Journal.* He admired Poe's work and found him a compatible coeditor but objected to his drinking sprees. In July 1845, Briggs left *The Broadway Journal* feeling that Poe had betrayed him professionally. "He cannot conceive of anybody's doing anything, except for his own personal advantage. He knows that I am possessed of the secret of his real character and he no doubt hates me for it." Briggs assailed Poe's character in an unsigned piece in the *Evening Mirror* of 26 May 1846 and published an additional scurillous portrait long after Poe's death, "The Personality of Poe," in *The Independent* of 13 December 1877. Poe is broadly caricatured in his novel *The Trippings of Tom Pepper* (1847). From his adversarial perspective, Briggs discerned a psychological fact about Poe's character that cannot be disputed: "One of the strange parts of his strange nature was to entertain a spirit of revenge towards all who did him service." Poe's profile of Briggs in "The Literati of New York City" is not completely unflattering. "He has much warmth of feeling, and is not a person to be disliked, although very apt to irritate and annoy." *Text: CWP,* XII, 44; XV, 20–23, 67, 75. *Research: LTP,* 509–511; Ehrlich, Heyward. "Briggs' Dilemma and Poe's Strategy." *Bulletin of the New York Public Library,* 73 (1969): 74–93; *TPL,* xvii-xviii; *MNR,* 243–245, 272–273.

Briscoe, Captain John. American whaling captain and navigator mentioned in chapter sixteen of *The Narrative of Arthur Gordon Pym.* He discovered Enderby Land in 1831. *Text: CWP,* III, 170–171.

Bristed, John. (1778–1855). English barrister. He wrote *America and Her Resources* (1818). Poe alludes to Bristed's book in *Marginalia. Text: CWP,* XVI, 43.

Broadway and 84th Street. Poe address in New York City. Poe resided at a boarding house here in the summer of 1844.

The Broadway Journal. Magazine operated in partnership with Poe by a former schoolteacher, John Bisco. Poe began writing for the magazine in December 1844 at $1 per column and assumed editorial duties in February 1845. Poe republished many revised versions of his tales in *The Broadway Journal* including "Ligeia," "William Wilson," and "The Tell-Tale Heart." After buying out John Bisco, Poe became sole owner and editor on 24 October 1845. Under Poe's management, the magazine was defunct by December 1845. Poe did realize his dream of a journal of his own, but only for three months. It ceased publication on 3 January 1846, with Poe, in his final editorial, ''bid[ding] farewell—as cordially to foes as to friends.'' *Research: LTP*, 530–533; Golden, Alan. ''Edgar Allan Poe at *The Broadway Journal*.'' *Poe Messenger* (Richmond Poe Museum), 12 (summer 1982): 1–6; *MNR*, 243–252, 268–270.

"The Broken Vow and Other Poems. By Amanda M. Edmond." A negative review of a volume of verse appearing in *The Broadway Journal* of 11 October 1845. Poe objected to the ''abolition topics'' of some of the poems. ''In the virtues of the muse—in the loftier and distinctive attributes, we are pained to say that she is totally wanting.'' *Text: CWP*, XII, 250.

Bronson, Cotesworth P. (fl. 1840). American elocutionist and lecturer. He requested a recitable poem from Poe to be used in his lectures on elocution. Poe responded with one of his most sonorous productions, ''Ulalume.'' *Research: TPL*, xviii.

Bronson, Mary Elizabeth. Cotesworth Bronson's daughter. She wrote a reminiscence of the Poes for the New York *Home Journal* of 21 July 1860. *Research: TPL*, xviii.

Brontë, Charlotte. (1816–1855). English novelist. Poe refers to her in *Marginalia*, calling Bulwer's work inferior to ''the author of 'Jane Eyre.' '' The other Brontë sisters, Emily and Anne, are not mentioned by Poe in his criticism or fiction. *Text: CWP*, XVI, 157. *Research:* Friesner, Donald Neil. ''Ellis Bell and Israfel.'' *Brontë Society Transactions*, 14, no. 4 (1964): 11–18.

"Brook Farm." Poe wrote an editorial commentary about the Brook Farm weekly magazine *Harbinger* in the 13 December 1845 issue of *The Broadway Journal*, calling the publication ''the most reputable organ of the crazyites.'' Poe's editorial is in part a response to John S. Dwight's condescending review of *The Raven and Other Poems* published in the 6 December 1845 issue of *The Harbinger*. Poe referred to the Brook Farmers as ''The Snook Farm Phalanx'' and hoped that in the future they ''will never have any opinion at all of us.'' *Text: CWP*, XIII, 27.

Brooks, James Gordon. (1801–1841). Minor American poet. He was an editor of *Minerva; or Literary Entertaining and Scientific Journal*. Poe said of him in ''Autography'' that he possessed ''nervous common sense, without tinsel or artificiality, and a straightforward directness of composition.'' *Text: CWP*, XV, 160, 238.

Brooks, Mrs. Maria Gowen. [Maria del Occidente or Maria of the West]. (1794–1845). American poet and author of the epic *Zóphiël* singled out by Poe as possessing ''that peculiar spirit of *abandon*.'' Poe considered her verse to be marked by "bold and rich imagination," her work exhibiting a "glowing, vigorous, and *sustained* ideality." *Text: CWP,* XI, 159; XIII, 18, 125, 192, 224–225.

Brooks, Nathan Covington. (1810–1873). Editor of the Baltimore journal *The American Museum.* He knew Poe in Baltimore in the 1830s and solicited Poe for contributions in the summer of 1838. His signature is included in "Autography": "His serious prose is often very good—is always well-worded—but in his comic attempts he fails, with appearing to be aware of his failure." *Text: CWP,* XV, 225. *Research: TPL,* xviii.

Brown, Charles Brockden. (1771–1810). American novelist of the early Republic. Four of his six novels—(1) *Wieland; or, The Transformation,* (2) *Arthur Mervyn; or, The Memoirs of the Year 1793,* (3) *Ormond; or, The Secret Witness,* and (4) *Edgar Huntly; or, The Memoirs of a Sleep-Walker*—are regarded as specimens of the American gothic romance. Their violent and preternatural content and pathological extremes of behavior anticipate many of the conditions, settings, and actions of Poe's tales of terror. There are three references to Brown's work in Poe's criticism, each one respectful and deferential. In his review of Cooper's *Wyandotté,* Poe numbers Brown "[a]mong American writers of the less generally circulated, but more worthy and more artistical fictions." Discussing William Gilmore Simms in *Marginalia,* Poe ranks Brown with Hawthorne as a novelist of the highest merit in comparing them with Simms. "Nevertheless, leaving out of the question Brockden Brown and Hawthorne, (who are each a *genus,*) [Simms] is immeasurably the best writer of fiction in America." In his essay "Tale Writers" published in *The Daily National Intelligencer* of 30 August 1845, Rufus Griswold wrote that "Mr. POE resembles BROCKDEN BROWN in his intimacy with mental pathology, but surpasses that author in delineation." *Text: CWP,* XI, 206; XII, 224; XVI, 41. *Research:* Kerlin, R. T. "Wieland and 'The Raven.' " *Modern Language Notes,* 31 (1916): 503–505; Clark, David Lee. "Sources of Poe's 'The Pit and the Pendulum.' " *Modern Language Notes,* 44 (1929): 349–356; Carter, Boyd. "Poe's Debt to Charles Brockden Brown." *Prairie Schooner,* 27 (1953): 190–196; *TPL,* 565; Stern, Julia Ann. "Parsing the First Person Plural: Transformations of Gender and Voice in the Fiction of Charles Brockden Brown and Edgar Allan Poe." *Dissertation Abstracts International,* 52 (1992): 2926A (Columbia University).

Brown, David Paul. (1795–1872). Philadelphia lawyer and amateur playwright. He may have been one of Poe's legal advisers in the libel suit against Francis H. Duffee. According to the "Autography" signature, "As a dramatic writer he has met with much success." *Text: CWP,* XV, 245. *Research: TPL,* 121, 124, 424.

Brown, Goold. (1791–1857). American writer and author of *Institutes of English Grammar* (1823), cited by Poe in "The Rationale of Verse" for his definition of versification. " 'Versification is the art of arranging words into lines of correspondent length, so as to produce harmony by the regular alternation of syllables differing in quantity.' " *Text: CWP,* XI, 225; XIV, 212.

Brown, Thomas. (1663–1704). English satirist. Poe knew his *Amusements Serious and Comical* (1700) and cited a ludicrous example from Brown's gallery of foolery in *Marginalia.* "Brown, in his 'Amusements,' speaks of having transfused the blood of an ass into the veins of an astrological quack—and there can be no doubt that one of Hugo's progenitors was the man." *Text: CWP,* XVI, 91.

Brown, Thomas Dunn. Poe's name for his enemy Dr. Thomas Dunn English in "The Literati of New York City." *See:* English, Dr. Thomas Dunn.

Browne, Hablot Knight. (1815–1882). English engraver and illustrator. He illustrated several Dickens novels. Poe objected to the maudlin religious sentimentalism of his drawings for the final page of *The Old Curiosity Shop.* "The designs by Cattermole and Browne are many of them excellent; some of them outrageously bad. . . . We must enter our solemn protest against the final page full of little angels in small frocks, or dimity chemises." *Text: CWP,* X, 155; XI, 38.

Browne, Sir Thomas. (1605–1682). English author. His *Hydriotaphia* [Urn Burial] left its imprint on Poe's spirited morbidity. Poe refers to Browne in his review "The Quacks of Helicon" by repeating the epigraph he had used for "The Murders in the Rue Morgue": "What song the Syrens sang, or what name Achilles assumed when he hid himself among women." He added: "[B]ut it would puzzle Sir Thomas, backed by Achilles and all the Syrens in Heathendom, to say, in nine cases out of ten, *what is the object* of a thorough-going Quarterly Reviewer?" *Text: CWP,* X, 189; XVI, 90.

Browne, William Hand. (1828–1912). American critic and early defender of Poe's personal and artistic reputation. He encouraged and assisted John H. Ingram in his work on Poe's life. In his review of Ingram's biography of Poe in the *Southern Monthly–New Eclectic Magazine* for June 1875, he agreed with Ingram's corrective portrait of Poe's character. *See:* Ingram, John Henry. *Research:* Miller, John Carl. "William Hand Browne Becomes a Loyal Ally." *BPB*, 65–87.

Browning, Robert. (1812–1889). English poet and husband of Elizabeth Barrett. Through his wife, Browning was aware of Poe's work. The "Madhouse Cell" poems, "Porphyria's Lover," and "Johannes Agricola in Meditation" in *Dramatic Lyrics* have a commonality of theme and atmosphere with Poe's tales. Browning's word *losel* for the lost selves of his dramatic monologues fits many of the narrators in Poe's monologic tales. *Research:* Melchiori, Barbara. ''The Tapestry Horse: 'Childe Roland' and 'Metzengerstein.' '' *English Miscellany*, 14 (1963): 185–193; Whitla, William. ''Sources for Browning in Byron, Blake, and Poe.'' *Studies in Browning and His Circle*, 2, no. 1 (1974): 7–16.

Brownson, Orestes Augustus. (1803–1876). American clergyman associated with transcendentalism and liberal causes. His moralistic novel *Charles Elwood; or, The Infidel Converted* (1840) is closely studied by the narrator of ''Mesmeric Revelation'' who finds it ''logical, but the portions which were not *merely* logical were unhappily the initial arguments of the disbelieving hero of the book.'' In ''Autography'' Poe declared that Brownson's signature showed that ''the writer has not altogether succeeded in convincing himself of those important truths which he is so anxious to impress upon his readers.'' *Text: CWP,* V, 243; XV, 194.

Brun, Johann Nordahl. (1745–1816). Danish author mentioned in Poe's review of Longfellow's *Ballads and Other Poems. Text: CWP,* XI, 65.

Bryan, Daniel. (1790–1866). A poet who exchanged letters with Poe in the summer of 1842. Poe included an analysis of his signature in ''Autography.'' ''Mr. Bryan has written some excellent poetry. . . . He is fond of underscoring his sentences; a habit exactly parallel with the argumentative nature of some of his best poems.'' *Text: CWP,* XV, 218. *Research: LTP*, 386, 426–427; Binns, Elizabeth. ''Daniel Bryan: Poe's Poet of the 'Good Old Goldsmith School.' '' *William and Mary Quarterly*, 23 (1943): 465–473; *TPL,* 371–376; Cash, Jean W. ''Edgar Allan Poe and Daniel Bryan: A Brief Correspondence.'' *Studies in the American Renaissance*, (1990): 107–118.

Bryant, Jacob. (1715–1804). English author and mythographer. Dupin refers to his *New System, or, an Analysis of Ancient Mythology* in ''The Purloined Letter.'' Poe admired the erudition of Bryant's *New System* and called attention to its value in *Pinakidia* and *Eureka*. ''Mr. Bryant, in his learned 'Mythology,' says that although the Pagan fables are not believed, yet we forget ourselves continually and make inferences from them as existing realities.'' *Text: CWP,* VI, 45; XIV, 53, 113; XVI, 217. *Research:* Griggs, Earl Leslie. ''Five Sources of Edgar Allan Poe's 'Pinakidia.' '' *American Literature*, 1 (1929): 196–199; Levine, Susan, and Stuart Levine. ''Poe's Use of Jacob Bryant in 'Metzengerstein.' '' *Poe Studies*, 9 (1976): 53.

Bryant, William Cullen. (1794–1878). American poet and editor of *The New York Evening Post*. Poe and Bryant met once in 1845. Poe wrote several favorable notices of Bryant's poetry, for example, ''Poems, by William Cullen Bryant.'' Poe's general view of Bryant was laudatory, although he sometimes took exception to Bryant's diction as in his careful dissection of the poem ''The Past.'' In ''The Poetic Principle,'' Poe quoted a portion of the poem ''June'' as a salient example of ''the rhymical creation of beauty,'' adding enthusiastically, ''The rhythmical flow, here, is even voluptuous—nothing could be more melodious. . . . The intense melancholy which seems to well up, perforce, to the surface of all the poet's cheerful sayings about his grave, we find thrilling us to the soul—while there is the truest poetic elevation in the thrill. . . . The impression left is one of a pleasurable sadness.'' In ''Autography'' Poe found no trace of the poet in Bryant's pedestrian signature. *Text: CWP,* XI, 68, 149–150, 192–195, 223, 241, 280; XIII, 170; XIV, 182–183, 258, 278–279; XV, 49–50, 115, 189, 239, 254. *Research:* McDowell, Tremaine. ''Edgar Allan Poe and William Cullen Bryant.'' *Philological Quarterly*, 16 (1937): 83–84; Brown, Charles H. *William Cullen Bryant.* New York: Charles Scribner's Sons, 1971, 244–245, 319–322; Bryant, William Cullen, II. ''Bryant and Poe: A Reacquaintance.'' *Studies in the American Renaissance*, (1993): 147–152.

"Bubbles from the Brunnens of Nassau, by Francis Head." Review of travel sketches and stories based on his visits to various mineral springs and spas appearing in *The Southern Literary Messenger* for April 1836. Poe judged the book to be pleasant reading, its style ''an agreeable mixture of Charles Lamb's and Washington Irving's.'' *Text: CWP,* VIII, 319.

Buckingham, Mr. Silk. Character in the short story ''Some Words with a Mummy.'' He takes cover under the table when the mummy's eyelids move.

Buffon, Comte Georges Louis Leclerc de. (1707–1788). French naturalist. Buffon's equating of genius with perseverence and diligence is cited approvingly by Thingum Bob near the end of ''The Literary Life of Thingum Bob, Esq.'' *Text: CWP,* VI, 26; X, 122.

Bulgakov, Mihail Afanas'evich. (1891–1940). Russian novelist. Living in exile in 1938 he wrote *Edgar Poe: Drama in Five Acts and Seven Scenes. Research: PLL,* 329.

Bullet-head, Mr. Touch-and-go. Character in ''X-ing a Paragrab.'' Fiery editor of the Alexander-the-Great-o-nopolis *Tea-Pot.*

Bulwer, Edward Lytton. *See:* Lytton, Edward George Earle Lytton Bulwer.

Burckhardt, Dr. John Lewis. (1784–1817). Eastern traveler and explorer mentioned in *Marginalia.* Poe had read his *Travels in Arabia* (1829). *Text: CWP,* XIV, 83–84; XVI, 63.

"The Buried Alive." Anonymous short story appearing in *Blackwood's Magazine* for October 1821 and probably read by Poe whose interest in the situation can be seen in the short stories "The Premature Burial" and "Loss of Breath." *Research: PLL,* 157–158.

Burke, Edmund. (1729–1797). Irish statesman, parliamentarian, orator, and philosopher. Poe was familiar with Burke's aesthetic of fear set forth in his *A Philosophical Inquiry into the Origin of Our Ideas of the Sublime and Beautiful* (1757) which he called an "inimitable treatise on that subject." *Text: CWP,* IX, 31; XI, 97. *Research:* Ljungquist, Kent. "Burke's *Enquiry* and the Æsthetics of 'The Pit and the Pendulum.' " *Poe Studies,* 11 (1978): 28–29; Howes, Craig. "Burke, Poe, and 'Usher': The Sublime and Rising Woman." *ESQ: A Journal of the American Renaissance,* 31 (3rd Q 1985): 173–189; Voller, Jack G. "The Power of Terror: Burke, Kant, and the House of Usher." *Poe Studies,* 21, no. 2 (1988): 27–35.

Burke, William. Master of the Richmond boys' seminary where Poe studied classical subjects and languages in the spring of 1823. *Research: TPL,* xviii.

Burling, Ebenezer. (d. 1832). Childhood friend of Poe with whom Poe left Richmond after the March 1826 quarrel with Allan. Burling is a possible model for the character Augustus Barnard in *The Narrative of Arthur Gordon Pym. Research: LTP,* 77–79.

Burnet, Thomas. (1635–1715). English clergyman and cosmographer. Poe was acquainted with his "The Sacred Theory of the Earth" ("Theoria Sacra"), which is mentioned in his review, "Edinburgh Review, No. CXXIV, for July 1835," in *The Southern Literary Messenger* for December 1835. *Text: CWP,* VIII, 83.

Burney, Fanny [Frances, Madame D'Arblay]. (1752–1840). English novelist. The author of *Evelina* is mentioned once by Poe in *Marginalia* in a discussion of the merits and demerits of Bulwer Lytton. "As a novelist, then, Bulwer is far more than respectable; although generally inferior to Scott, Godwin, D'Israeli, Miss Burney, Sue, Dumas, [and] Dickens." *Text: CWP,* XVI, 157.

Burns, Robert. (1759–1796). Scottish poet. Poe cited Burns's "Tam O'Shanter" as an example of "entire poems of purest ideality" in the "Drake-Halleck" review. Elsewhere, Poe was less enthusiastic about Burns, designating him "a man whose merits at least have been more grossly—more preposterously exaggerated (through a series of purely adventitious circumstances) than those of any man that ever lived upon the earth." *Text: CWP,* VIII, 299; IX, 203; XII, 240–241.

Burr, Charles Chauncey. (1815–1883). He provided Poe with financial assistance during his July 1849 visit to Philadelphia and later defended Poe's character in an article in the *Nineteenth Century* for February 1852. *Research:*

LTP, 649; Hubbell, Jay B. '' Charles Chauncey Burr: Friend of Poe.'' *Publications of the Modern Language Association*, 69 (1954): 833–840; *TPL*, xviii.

Burton, William E. (1802–1860). Owner and editor of *Burton's Gentleman's Magazine*, which began publication in July 1837. In May 1839 he hired Poe as an all-purpose assistant editor. Poe was expected to perform a variety of editorial tasks, many of them trivial or prosaic, to proofread, and to contribute occasional reviews. On several occasions, Burton refused to publish Poe's inflammatory reviews. Their strained relationship was terminated in May 1840. Burton's signature in ''Autography'' ''is scratchy or petite, betokening indecision and care or caution.'' *Text: CWP*, XV, 236. *Research:* Thomas, Dwight. ''William E. Burton and His Premium Scheme: New Light on Poe Biography.'' *University of Mississippi Studies in English*, 3 (1982): 68–80; *TPL*, xviii-xix; *MNR*, 142–144, 155–158.

Burwell, William McCreery. (1809–1888). Editor of *De Bow's Review*. He had known Poe in his student days at the University of Virginia and published his reminiscences in the New Orleans's *Times-Democrat* of 18 May 1884. *Research: TPL*, xix.

Bush, George. (1796–1859). A professor of Hebrew at the University of New York, his profile is included in ''The Literati of New York City'' in which Poe describes him as ''a Mesmerist and a Swedenborgian—has lately been engaged in editing Swedenborg's works, publishing them in numbers.'' *Text: CWP*, XV, 6–7; XVI, 97–98. *Research: TPL*, xix.

"The Business Man." Short story by Poe published in *The Broadway Journal* of 2 August 1845. An earlier version of the story under the title ''Peter Pendulum'' had appeared in *Burton's Gentleman's Magazine* for February 1840. Narrated by Peter Proffit, a man who prides himself on his ''general habits of accuracy and punctuality,'' the story reflects Poe's stressful relationship with his foster father, John Allan, as well as the tensions felt by Poe between writing for art's sake and writing for money. The businessman's smug self-evaluation of the means and methods of his rise discloses the egotism at the heart of commercial success. The story contains a mock account collectible served upon Mssrs. Cut and Comeagain and selected entries from the businessman's diary, each involving bill collecting. The businessman's ethics are legal but only marginally so, as indicated in his description of profits gained in ''the eyesore trade,'' a slum building scheme to drive down real estate prices, and the ''Assault and Battery Business.'' Similar shady dealings such as the businessman's ''cat-growing'' scheme coupled with Poe's use of names such as Peter Proffit give the story an air of harsh satire on the values of the Franklinesque hero and, later, the Barnumesque success legend in American life. The story's opening sentences, ''I am a business man. I am a methodical man,'' bear comparison with Melville's portrait of a pragmatic man of business in ''Bartleby the Scrivener.'' *Epigraph:* ''Method is the soul of business.'' Similar to a remark in Lord Chesterfield's correspondence. *Text: MCW,* II, 480–493; *CWP,* IV, 122–133. *Research:* Lemay, J. A. Leo. ''Poe's 'The Business Man': Its Contexts and Satire of Franklin's *Autobiography.*'' *Poe Studies*, 15, no. 2 (1982): 29–37.

Butler, Samuel. (1612–1680). English poet, satirist, and author of *Hudibras* (1663–1664). Poe enjoyed Butler's flaying sense of humor and quoted from his poetry in *Pinakidia* and *Marginalia.* ''Samuel Butler, of Hudibrastic memory, must have had a prophetic eye to the American Congress when he defined a rabble as—'A congregation of assembly of the States-General. . . . They meet only to quarrel.' '' *Text: CWP,* XIV, 57–58; XVI, 38, 75–76, 160.

Butterfield, Eliza Jane. (1828–1892). One of the women in Poe's life. She was a Lowell, Massachusetts, school mistress. Poe knew her in May and June of 1849 and apparently engaged in a brief flirtation with her. *Research:* Freeman, Fred B., Jr. ''The Identity of Poe's 'Miss B.' '' *American Literature*, 39 (1967): 389–391; *TPL,* xix.

Buzi-Ben-Levi. Character in the short story ''A Tale of Jerusalem.'' He is one of the collectors of the offering in the holy city.

"Byron and Miss Chaworth." An article with an engraving of Byron and Mary Chaworth, his youthful sweetheart, appearing in the *Columbian Magazine* for December 1844. Of Byron's passion for her, Poe observes, ''It was born of the hour, and of the youthful necessity to love. . . . It had no peculiar regard to the person, or to the character, or to the reciprocating affection of Mary Chaworth. . . . The result was not merely natural or merely probable, it was as inevitable as destiny itself.'' *Text: MCW,* III, 1120–1124; *CWP,* XIV, 150–152.

Byron, George Gordon Lord. (1788–1824). English poet and notorious socialite much appreciated by Poe for both his poetry and his rebellious stances. Poe was fond of reciting Byron's poetry during his public recitations. The influence of the Byronic personality and attitudes on Poe's work can be documented in letters, poems, and several tales. Several Poe characters are direct transcriptions of the Byronic physiognomy and personality. For example, the nameless suicidal stranger in ''The Assignation'' has ''the mouth and chin of a deity,—singular, wild, full liquid eyes—and a profusion of curling black hair, from which a forehead of unusual breadth gleamed forth at intervals all light and ivory,'' while the face of Byron is also recalled in the countenance of Roderick Usher. Poe's link to the immoral cult of Byron was abhorred by John Allan, who blamed Byron for much of Poe's profligate behavior. *See:* ''The

Assignation.'' *Research:* Campbell, Killis. ''Poe's Indebtedness to Byron.'' *Nation*, 11 March 1909, 248–249; Pollin, Burton. ''The Role of Byron and Mary Shelley in Poe's 'Masque.' '' *DIP*, 75–90; Soule, George H., Jr. ''Byronism in Poe's 'Metzengerstein' and 'William Wilson.' '' *Emerson Society Quarterly*, 24 (1978): 152–162.

C

Cabell, Julia Mayo. (1800–1860). Relative of John Allan's second wife, Louisa G. Patterson. She was friendly to Poe. *Research: TPL,* xix.

"Cabs." Short unsigned piece on the introduction of cabs and cabdrivers to New York City appearing in *Alexander's Weekly Messenger* of 1 April 1840 and attributed to Poe by Clarence S. Brigham. "The cab-introduction will bring among us a peculiar race of people—the cabman. . . . They bear a droll kind of resemblance to the human species—but their faces are all fashioned of brass, and they carry both their brains and their souls in their pockets." *Text: MCW,* II, 493–494. *Research:* Brigham, Clarence Saunders. "Edgar Allan Poe's Contributions to *Alexander's Weekly Messenger.*" *Proceedings of the American Antiquarian Society*, new series, 52 (April 1942): 45–124.

Cadmus of Miletus. (sixth century B.C.). Ancient Greek logographer (historian) mentioned in *Pinakidia.* "The Greeks had no historian prior to Cadmus Milesias." *Text: CWP,* XIV, 51.

Calderón de la Barca, Pedro. (1600–1681). Spanish dramatist. Poe paraphrases Calderón's remark that "a man who has never seen the sun cannot be blamed for thinking that no glory can exceed that of the moon" in his discussion of the critic's task "to soar so that he shall see *the sun.*" *Text: CWP,* XIII, 43; XVI, 81.

Calvert, George H. (1803–1899). An editor of the *Baltimore American* where he had been critical of Poe's work. In ''Autography,'' he is denounced as ''a feeble and common-place writer of poetry, although his prose compositions have a certain degree of merit.'' *Text: CWP,* XV, 221–222. *Research: TPL,* 157.

Calvin, John. (1509–1564). French religious reformer. A satiric reference to Calvin occurs in ''Never Bet the Devil Your Head'' and is repeated in *Pinakidia.* According to Jacobus Hugo, ''by Euenis, Homer meant to insinuate John Calvin.'' *Text: CWP,* IV, 214; XIV, 66.

Camden, William. (1551–1663). English antiquary. Poe dismisses Camden's description of Stonehenge as not ''entitled to notice.'' *Text: CWP,* XIV, 112.

Camden Street, Baltimore. The residence of ''General'' David Poe, Sr., and Elizabeth Cairnes Poe. When Poe was five weeks old, he was left with his grandparents by his itinerant parents. *Research: TPL,* 5.

Campbell, Thomas. (1777–1844). English poet and author of *Gertrude of Wyoming* (1809). Thomas Gibson, Poe's West Point roommate, recalled that Poe sneered at Campbell's verse as plagiarized, a charge that Poe later repeated against Campbell in *Pinakidia* and elsewhere. ''In the meantime Campbell, in 'Gertrude of Wyoming,' has the words '—the hunter and the deer a shade.' Campbell stole the idea from our own Freneau.'' *Text: CWP,* XI, 23, 35; XII, 201; XIV, 41, 47; XV, 38; XVI, 39, 75, 77, 146. *Research: TPL,* 108, 339.

"Camperdown; or, News from Our Neighborhood." Review of Mary Griffith's collection of six tales appearing in *The Southern Literary Messenger* for July 1836. Poe found the stories ''The Little Couple'' and ''The Thread and Needle Store'' full of ''originality of thought and manner'' and several others ''sufficiently outré.'' *Text: CWP,* IX, 71.

Canning, Sir Launcelot. Character mentioned in the short story ''The Fall of the House of Usher.'' He is the author of *The Mad Trist.* Canning also appears in Poe's motto for *The Stylus,* his magazine scheme. ''Prospectus for The Stylus'' appeared in the Philadelphia *Saturday Museum* of 25 February with a three-line poem signed by ''Launcelot Canning'': ''——— unbending that all men/ Of thy firm TRUTH may say—'Lo! this is writ/ With the antique iron pen.'' Mabbott placed the motto among Poe's poems in his edition of the poems. *Text: MCW,* I, 328.

"Canons of Good Breeding, or the Handbook of the Man of Fashion." Review of a courtesy book appearing in *Burton's Gentleman's Magazine* for November 1839. Poe finds that ''the volume abounds in good things,'' among them its "grouping together of fine things from the greatest multiplicity of the rarest works." *Text: CWP,* X, 45.

Canova, Antonio. (1757–1822). Italian sculptor whose *Venus* is mentioned in "The Assignation" and in several other places in Poe's works. The Byronic stranger prefers his Venus to the Venus di Medici. *Text: CWP,* II, 118; VIII, 52, 190; XIII, 34.

Capote, Truman. (1924–1984). American novelist and short story writer. Various critics have pointed out the influence of Poe on Capote's presentation of the theme of the divided or opposing self. *Other Voices, Other Rooms* and *In Cold Blood* establish further parallels with Poe. *Research:* West, Ray. *The Short Story in America.* Chicago: Henry Regnery, 1952, 110–111; *PLL,* 352.

Capricornutti, Count. Character in the short story "Lionizing." He is a guest at Almack's and witnesses Robert Jones's challenge to the Elector of Bludden-uff.

Carew, Thomas. (1598–1639). English poet and song writer. Poe refers to his "fervid, hearty, and free-spoken songs" in *Marginalia. Text: CWP,* X, 44; XVI, 139.

Carey [Edward L.] and [Abraham] Hart. Philadelphia publishing house on Chestnut and Fourth Streets. This house also published an annual, *The Gift,* in which "The Pit and the Pendulum," "William Wilson," and several other Poe stories appeared. *Research:* Thorp, Willard. "Two Poe Letters at Princeton." *Princeton University Library Chronicle,* 10 (1949): 91–94; *TPL,* xix, 181–192, 363–364.

Carey, Mathew. (1760–1839). Philadelphia bookseller and publisher. Poe includes an analysis of his signature in "Autography." *Text: CWP,* XV, 161. *Research: TPL,* xix.

Carling, James. (fl. 1870). Victorian artist. In the 1880s he illustrated Poe's poem "The Raven." *Research:* Schubert, Leland. "James William Carling: Expressionist Illustrator of 'The Raven.' " *Southern Literary Messenger,* 4 (1942): 173–181.

Carlyle, Thomas. (1795–1881). English essayist, literary critic, and social historian. Because of his connections with transcendental ideas, Poe was usually inimical to Carlyle's writings, mocking the transcendental leap of intuition in "Never Bet the Devil Your Head" and referring to "Carlyle's hyper-ridiculous elisions in prose." He began his *Marginalia* entry on Carlyle with this forthright opinion: "I have not the slightest faith in Carlyle. In ten years—possibly in five—he will be remembered only as a butt for sarcasm." *Text: CWP,* IV, 218; XI, 22, 99, 114–115; XV, 78; XVI, 16, 99–101, 122, 167, 175. *Research: PLB,* 97;

Ware, Tracy. ''A Note on Poe and Carlyle's German Romance.'' *Notes & Queries*, 36 (1989): 181.

Carmine Street (number 113). A Poe address in New York City near Washington Square where Poe lived in the spring of 1837.

Carson, John. Character in *The Narrative of Arthur Gordon Pym*. He is a member of the *Jane Guy* crew and killed by savages.

Carver, Captain Jonathan. (1710–1780). English explorer of the western Great Lakes and author of *Travels Through the Interior Part of North America* (1778). Poe devotes several passages to him in *The Journal of Julius Rodman* and in ''Astoria'' took note of Carver's attempt to find a northwest passage. ''In 1763 shortly after acquisition of the Canadas by Great Britain, this gentleman projected a journey across the continent, between the forty-third and forty-sixth degrees of northern latitude, to the shores of the Pacific.'' *Text: CWP,* IV, 15–16; IX, 211–212.

Carver Street (number 62), Boston. Address of Poe's parents, David and Elizabeth, at the time of his birth on 19 January 1809. *Research: TPL,* 3.

Cary, Alice. (1820–1871). American poet. Poe complimented Griswold for including her work along with her sister Phoebe's poems in *The Female Poets of America*, ''show[ing] him to be a man not more of taste than—shall we say it?—of courage.'' *Text: CWP,* XI, 157–158.

Cary, Henry. (1804–1870). American poet and translator of Dante. In *Marginalia*, Poe favorably compared his vigorous style to that of Addison in *The Spectator* but undercut this compliment in portraying Cary in ''The Literati of New York City.'' ''The truth seems to be that Mr. Cary is a vivacious, fanciful, entertaining essayist—a fifth or sixth rate one—with a style that . . . may be termed respectable and no more.'' *Text: CWP,* XV, 67–68; XVI, 94.

Cary, Phoebe. (1824–1871). American poet. She was the sister and poetic collaborator of Alice Cary. *See:* Cary, Alice.

"The Cask of Amontillado." Short story by Poe first published in *Godey's Lady's Book* for November 1846. The tale of revenge as a fine art may embody certain autobiographical features insofar as it reflects Poe's desire to punish the anonymous author of the 26 May 1846 article in the New York *Evening Mirror* assailing him for ''creating a great sensation [of disgust] throughout the country.'' The author, later revealed to be Charles F. Briggs, editor of *The Broadway Journal*, had censured Poe's drinking and slandered his physical appearance, noting that Poe had ''a chin narrow and pointed, which gives his head upon the whole, a balloonish appearance which may account for his supposed light-headedness.'' ''The Cask of Amontillado'' remains one of Poe's most popular short stories and a frequent performance piece. As a dramatic monologue, it has a brilliance of aesthetic construction that reveals a total mastery of his material in the conjunction of plot, theme, and ''preconceived effect.'' The principals in Poe's subterranean comedy of revenge are the sober and methodical Montresor and the inebriated and careless Fortunato. Planning his revenge with consummate skill, Montresor lures Fortunato ever deeper into the family wine vault to pay him back for the thousand injuries and one insult suffered at Fortunato's hands. When the drunkard cannot recall Montresor's family coat-of-arms as they descend, he perhaps commits the thousand and first injury, which seals his doom. Given several opportunities to foresee his fate and to comprehend his danger and turn back, Fortunato insists upon walking or staggering into his own tomb, his foolishness savored in stages by Montresor like a fine wine sipped on the fiftieth anniversary of his enemy's premature burial. When Fortunato enters the cryptic niche that holds the Amontillado, he finds himself fettered to the wall while his host demonstrates his masonic prowess by building a wall across the narrow recess. Now sobered up, Fortunato pleads for his life with the pitiful outcry from within the drunkard's horrible shrine, '' 'For the love of God, Montresor.' '' But because fools deserve to die, Montresor politely reminds Fortunato of the justice of his sentence even as he completes the wall and inserts the final stone like a cork being rammed into his well-preserved cask of well-aged revenge. Montresor's conversational skills are amusingly ironic throughout the descent, reaching a climax in his mock epitaph, ''Yes, for the love of God.'' Although some readers might want to attach a confessional moral or a remorseful admission to Montresor's fifty-year memoir, it seems clear that after the passage of fifty years Montresor can still rest in peace, comforted by his pleasant and almost ritualized memorial reenactment of the ''immolation'' of his drunken rival. The mock requiem of the jingling of the bells at the tale's finale is yet another indication of Montresor's desire to recreate every detail of the final hours of the drunken dunce. By this interpretation, the Latin epitaph ''In pace requiescat'' applies only with gruesome irony to Fortunato and stands as Montresor's reassurance to himself that he has fully enjoyed fifty years of freedom and peace from the annoyances of a fool. Whether ''The Cask of Amontillado's'' final scene is read as a confessional or a triumphant recollection, the story's influence on the modern gothic tale of elaborate revenge cannot be denied. Stephen King's short story ''Dolan's Cadillac'' is but one example of Poe's artful tour de force of revenge modernized. *See:* Balzac, Honoré de. *Text: MCW,* III, 1252–1266; *CWP,* VI, 167–175. *Research:* Gargano, James W. '' 'The Cask of Amontillado': A Masquerade of Motive and Identity.'' *Studies in Short Fiction*, 4 (1967): 119–126; Harris, Kathryn Montgomery. ''Ironic Revenge in Poe's 'The Cask of Amontillado.' '' *Studies in Short Fiction*, 6 (1969): 333–336; Strepp, Walter. ''The Ironic Double in Poe's 'The Cask of Amontillado.' '' *Studies in Short Fiction*, 13 (1976): 447–453; Engel, Leonard W. ''Victim and Victimizer: Poe's 'The Cask of Amontillado.' '' *Interpretations*, 15 (1983): 26–30;

Sorenson, Peter J. ''William Morgan, Free Masonry, and 'The Cask of Amontillado.' '' *Poe Studies*, 22, no. 2 (1989): 45–47; White, Patrick. '' 'The Cask of Amontillado': The Case for the Defense.'' *Studies in Short Fiction*, 26 (1989): 550–555; Cervo, Nathan. ''Poe's 'Cask of Amontillado.' '' *Explicator*, 51, no. 3 (1993): 155–156.

Cass, Lewis. (1782–1866). Secretary of war under President Jackson and literary scholar. An analysis of his signature in ''Autography'' mentions ''excellent papers'' contributed to *The Southern Literary Messenger* which Poe had solicited while editor. *Text: CWP,* XV, 238. *Research: TPL,* 214.

Cassini, Giovanni Domenico. (1625–1712). Italian astronomer whose observations on the comet of 1680 and the terrestrial planisphere attracted Poe. He is cited in *Pinakidia*: ''The peculiar zodiac of comets . . . comprised in three verses of Cassini:—'Antinous, Pegasusque, Andromeda, Taurus, Orion./ Procyon, atque Hydrus, Centaurus, Scorpius, Arcus.' '' *Text: CWP,* II, 97; XIV, 41; XVI, 352.

Castiglione. Character in Poe's drama *Politian*. He is the rakish and cowardly son of the Duke di Broglio and seduces Lady Lalage but refuses to duel with Politian when challenged.

Castiglione, Baldassare. (1478–1529). Italian humanist and author of *Il Cortegiano* [*The book of the courtier*] (1528). In *Pinakidia*, Poe called the book ''the first attempt at periodical moral Essay with which we are acquainted'' and repeated this claim in *Marginalia* in correcting Macaulay. ''The first periodical moral essay! Mr Macaulay forgets the 'Courtier of Baldazzar Castiglione—1528.' '' *Text:* CWP, XIV, 48; XVI, 37.

Castle Island. Site of a United States Army military installation in Boston Harbor, Fort Independence. Poe entered the army here in May 1827. The fort is a possible source locale for the tale of live burial, ''The Cask of Amontillado.'' *Research: LTP*, 167, 168; Snow, Edward Rowe. ''The Facts behind 'The Cask of Amontillado.' '' *Mysterious New England.* Boston: Yankee, 1971, 204–205.

Catalini, Angelica. (1780–1849). Opera singer mentioned by Dupin in ''The Purloined Letter.''

Caterrina. Bright black cat owned by Poe. In his essay ''Instinct VS Reason—A Black Cat,'' Poe speculates that feline intuition is in many instances superior to human reason, offering as evidence Caterrina's ability to unlock door latches with her cunning paws. Poe also kept a tortoiseshell cat while residing at the Fordham cottage and was especially fond of feline companionship while writing. Poe's lifelong fond association with cats is first documented in 1812 when Rosanna Dixon, Frances Allan's niece, writes to tell him of the welfare of her cat

Tib. No reader of Poe should confuse the feline sadism of the narrator of ''The Black Cat'' with Poe's deep and genuine affection for these animals and his need for their presence in his life. *See:* ''Desultory Notes on Cats.'' *Research:* Weiss, Miriam. ''Poe's Catterina.'' *Mississippi Quarterly*, 19 (winter 1965–1966): 29–33; *LET,* I, 251, 252, II, 373.

"A Catholic Hymn." Poem incorporated into the text of the first periodical printings of the short story ''Morella.'' *Research: TPL,* 274–275.

Catullus. [Gaius Valerius]. (ca. 84–54 B.C.) Roman poet and epigrammatist. Poe refers to Catullus twice in ''Bon-Bon,'' where he is one of the poets ''toasted'' by the devil, and again in *Marginalia. Text: CWP,* II, 128, 142; XI, 33; XVI, 172. *Research:* Weston, Arthur Harold. ''The 'Nicean Barks' of Edgar Allan Poe.'' *Classical Journal*, 29 (1933): 213–215.

Cayley, George. (1774–1857). British scientist and aeronautical pioneer. Poe refers to his experiments with ellipsoid balloons in ''The Balloon Hoax.'' *Text: CWP,* V, 225–227.

Cedar and Greenwich (number 130) Streets. A Poe address in New York City. He resided in a boarding house here in April 1844. *Research: PLL,* 150–151.

Cervantes Saavedra, Miguel de. (1547–1616). Spanish novelist and author of *Don Quixote*. Although there is no direct reference to *Don Quixote* in Poe's writings, there are many instances of Quixotic comedy as in the fake verses on Martin Van Buren that the narrator attributes to Cervantes in ''A Predicament'' and ''How to Write a Blackwood Article.'' Other mentionings of Cervantes indicate Poe's familiarity with his dramas. *Text: CWP,* II, 279, 292; VIII, 77, 234; X, 116; XIII, 43, 60, 70. *Research: PJC,* 156, 157.

Chambers, Robert. (1802–1871). Author of *Vestiges of Creation*, a cosmological work that some of Poe's contemporaries thought had exerted a strong influence on Poe's *Eureka*. In the Boston *Evening Transcript* of 20 July 1848, the critic Epes Sargent mentions that *Eureka* reminded him ''of that remarkable work 'The Vestiges of Creation' by the character and tendency of the author's scientific romancing.'' *See:* Sargent, Epes.

Chamfort, Sebastian Roch Nicholas. (1741–1794). French writer of maxims. Dupin quotes from his *Maximes et pensées* in ''The Purloined Letter'' and in *Marginalia*: ''Il y a à parier que tout idée publique, toute convention retue, est une sottise, car elle a convenue au plus grand nombre.'' *Text: CWP,* VI, 44; X, 140; XVI, 166.

Chandler, Joseph R. (1792–1880). Editor of the Philadelphia *United States Gazette*. In his praise of *Tales of the Grotesque and Arabesque*, he noted that Poe could ''do other things in literature equally well. He is capable of much.'' There is a vague entry in ''Autography'' describing him as ''the editor of one of the best daily papers in the country.'' *Text: CWP,* XV, 216. *Research: TPL,* xix-xx, 278–279.

Channing, William Ellery. (1818–1901). Nephew of the eminent clergyman poet William Ellery Channing. Although Channing ranked high in literary circles and numbered among his friends Emerson, Hawthorne, and Thoreau, he himself was an undistinguished poet and essayist. Poe lampooned Channing's verse in *Graham's Magazine*. Channing's poetry is mentioned in a satiric context in the short story ''How to Write a Blackwood Article.'' In *Marginalia*, Poe accused an anonymous author in *The Monthly Magazine* of plagiarizing Channing's essay on Bonaparte. Channing's signature is included in ''Autography,'' where Poe places him ''at the head of our moral and didactic writers.'' *See:* ''Our Amateur Poets, No. III: William Ellery Channing.'' *Text: CWP,* II, 276; X, 156; XII, 107, 165; XV, 162, 226–227; XVI, 132–134. *Research: PJC,* 337.

Chantilly. Character mentioned in the short story ''The Murders in the Rue Morgue.'' He ''was a *quondam* cobbler in the Rue St. Denis, who, becoming stage-mad, had attempted the role of Xerxes, in Crébillon's tragedy.''

Chapman, George. (1559–1634). English dramatist. His tragedy *Bussy D'Ambois* is quoted by the narrator in the short story ''The Assignation.'' ''He is up/ There like a Roman statue! He will stand/ Till death hath made him marble.'' *Text: CWP,* II, 122.

"A Chapter of Suggestions." The New York annual *The Opal* published this essay by Poe in November 1845. *The Opal* was edited by Nathaniel Parker Willis. The piece consists of eleven paragraphs, each containing ''suggestions'' about the metaphysical life, the reliability of intuition, the power of the imagination, the steps by which a work of art is brought from conception to formal fact, the nature of true genius, and the necessity of precision and clarity in matters of logic. The exercise of intuition is especially important to Poe. He sums up its intellectual value by the apothegm: ''Great intellects *guess* well. The laws of Kepler were, professedly, *guesses*.'' *Text: CWP,* XIV, 186–192.

"A Chapter on Autography." Poe analyzed the fabricated handwriting and signatures of more literary personalities in a three-part series in *Graham's Magazine* for November 1841, December 1841, and January 1842. *See:* ''Autography.'' *Text: CWP,* XV, 175–261.

"A Chapter on Field Sports and Many Pastimes." Article on gymnastics appearing in *Burton's Gentleman's Magazine* for September 1839. *Research: LET,* I, 120; *TPL,* 267.

"Charles O'Malley, The Irish Dragoon." Review of a novel by Charles James Lever appearing in *Graham's Magazine* for March 1842. The review admits the novel's huge popularity but bitterly complains that popularity cannot be equated with literary skill, which the novel entirely lacks. The plot is meager with "more absurdities than we have patience to enumerate," and the style is "exceedingly rough, clumsy, and inartistical, just so much vulgar balderdash." *Text: CWP,* XI, 85. *Research:* Mabbott, T. O. "Evidence That Poe Knew Greek." *Notes & Queries*, 185 (July 1943): 39–40; *PJC,* 294–295.

Charmion. Character in the short story "The Conversation of Eiros and Charmion." The character is a celestial specter who has "passed into Night through the grave."

Chateaubriand, François-Auguste, Viscount of. (1768–1848). French Romantic writer. Poe disapproved of his "exaggerated sentimentality." There are additional comments on Chateaubriand in Poe's review of R. M. Walsh's *Sketches of Conspicuous Living Characters of France*. *Text: CWP,* X, 25, 133–134, 136–137. *Research:* Engstrom, Alfred G. "Chateaubriand's *Itinéraire de Paris à Jerusalem* and Poe's 'The Assignation.' " *Modern Language Notes*, 69 (1954): 506–507.

"A Chaunt of Life and Other Poems, with Sketches and Essays. By Rev. Ralph Hoyt." Favorable review of a collection of poetry and incidental writings published in *The Broadway Journal* of 26 July 1845. "The Chaunt of Life" itself is quite fine, but some of the other poems are marred by missing feet or "peculiarities of metre." *Text: CWP,* XII, 193.

Cheever, George B. (1807–1890). American religious writer. He was the editor of *The Commonplace Book of American Poetry*, an anthology attacked by Poe as unrepresentative of American verse. He described the collection as "a work which has the merit of not belying its title, and is exceedingly commonplace. . . . The selections appear to me exceedingly injudicious, and have all a marked leaning to the didactic." Poe included a profile of Cheever in "The Literati of New York City." *Text: CWP,* XI, 149–150; XV, 32–33.

Chénier, André Marie. (1762–1794). French poet executed during the French Revolution. In *Pinakidia*, Poe quotes a verse written in prison and adds that while he composed, "[a]t this instant André Chénier was interrupted by the officials of the guillotine." *Text: CWP,* XIV, 52.

Chesterfield, Lord. [Philip Dormer Stanhope]. (1694–1773). Eminent epistolarian famous for his letters of advice to his son. Poe mentions his wit and erudition in these model letters in his review of "The Canons of Good Breeding, or The Handbook of the Man of Fashion." *Text: CWP,* VIII, 91; IX, 104; X, 47.

Child, Lydia Maria. (1802–1880). Poet, abolilitionist, and crusader for the rights of women. In his sketch of her character in "The Literati of New York City," Poe described her as of "a fervid and fanciful nature" and quoted her poem "Marius amid the Ruins of Carthage" to illustrate the excellence of her shorter compositions. *Text: CWP,* XV, 105–107.

"The Child of the Sea, and Other Poems. By S. Anna Lewis." Review of her poems published in *The Southern Literary Messenger* for September 1848. The *Democratic Review* for August 1848 also notices her poetry favorably. Poe's praise for her verse was his way of repaying her for the financial and emotional assistance she gave him after Virginia's death. "All critical opinion must agree in assigning her a high, if not the very highest rank among the poetesses of her land." *See:* Lewis, Sarah Anna. *Text: CWP,* XIII, 155–165.

Chiponchipino. Character in the short story "The Man That Was Used Up." He is a sculptor and friend of the narrator.

Chippendale, Mr. An actor who appeared in Mrs. Mowatt's comedy *Fashion* and earned Poe's praise.

Chivers, Thomas Holley. (1809–1858). Georgia poet and Poe biographer. He met Poe in 1845. He wrote *Life of Poe.* (1852; Rpt. *Chivers' Life of Poe* [1952]). Chivers also authored *Conrad and Eudora* (1834), basing his story on the same material Poe had used for the drama *Politian.* He attributed to Poe "an uncompromising independence of spirit. . . . Yet no man living loved the praises of others better than he did." Chivers offered Poe a permanent home in Georgia, but Poe refused. He detested Poe's alcoholism but nonetheless maintained their friendship. In "Autography," Poe wrote of his signature that it suggested "one of the best and one of the worst poets in America. His productions affect one as a wild dream—strange, incongruous, full of images of more than arabesque monstrosity, and snatches of sweet unsustained song." *Text: CWP,* XII, 201–206; XV, 241–242. *Research:* Campbell, Killis. "A Bit of Chiversian Mystification." *University of Texas Studies in English,* 10 (1930): 152–155; Watts, Charles. "Poe and Chivers." In *Thomas Holly Chivers.* Athens: Georgia University Press, 1956, 138–169; *PLB,* 101; Rosenfeld, Alvin H. "The Poe-Chivers Controversy." *Books at Brown,* 23 (1969): 89–93.

"The Christian Florist; Containing the English and Botanical Names of Different Plants, with Their Properties Delineated and Ex-

plained." Book noticed by Poe in *The Southern Literary Messenger* for January 1836. He believes the volume to be "well adapted for a Christmas present." *Text: CWP,* VIII, 177–178.

Chubbuck, Emily [Judson]. (1817–1854). Minor American poet. Her "vivacious" poems are mentioned twice by Poe in "The Literati of New York City." *Text: CWP,* XV, 90, 113.

Church, Albert. Professor of mathematics at the United States Military Academy at West Point. For Poe, he embodied the harsh essence of the institution, "an old mathematical cinder, bereft of all natural feeling." *Research: PLL,* 45.

Churchill, Charles. (1731–1764). English author and political satirist. Poe refers to his sharp satiric abilities in "The Quacks of Helicon." *Text: CWP,* X, 184.

Cibber, Colley. (1671–1757). English poet and dramatist. Poe refers to his dramatic revisions of Shakespeare in a review of Mrs. Mowatt's performance in "Katherine and Petruchio." *Text: CWP,* XII, 211.

Cicero, Marcus Tullius. (106–43 B.C.). Roman statesman, orator, and writer on rhetoric. Poe cited his writings as examples of oratorical eloquence and raised a point of Latin grammar in *Pinakidia*: "Cicero makes *finis* masculine, Vergil feminine." *Text: CWP,* XII, 155; XIV, 43; XVI, 168. *Research:* McLuhan, Herbert M. "Edgar Poe's Tradition." *Sewanee Review*, 52 (1944): 24–33.

Cist, Lewis Jacob. (1818–1885). Amateur American poet. He offered his poem "Bachelor Philosophy" for publication in Poe's projected *Penn Magazine*. His signature in "Autography" suggested that his poems were "at times disfigured by false metaphor, and by meretricious straining after effect." *Text: CWP,* XV, 240; *TPL,* xx. *Research:* Mabbott, T. O. "An Unpublished Poe Letter." *American Literature*, 26 (1955): 560–561.

"The City in the Sea." Poem first published under this title in the *American Review* for April 1845. An earlier version of the poem under the title "The Doomed City" had appeared in 1831 in *Poems*. Poe's Atlantian fantasy is one of his most romantic poems and was much admired by the English pre-Raphaelite poets and the French symbolists. Swinburne found in the lines "Whose wreathed friezes intertwine/ The viol, the violet, and the vine" a perfect embodiment of his belief that poetry should be a synthesis of sensual sound and sensuous imagery contained within a lyrical unified structure. Poe's visionary meditation centers on an underwater necropolis where the buildings and streets "Resemble nothing that is ours" and are illumined from beneath rather than above. Thus, instead of any contact with "rays from the holy heaven" the city draws its light from infernal energy beneath its foundation. Death resides in and presides over a city without populace, without sound, without movement, and without spiritual hope. Poe has written an inversion of the *Civitate Dei*, the heavenly city of the philosophers, and has given death the place of God. At the very center of the poem, death surveys with satisfaction his authority and handiwork: ''While from a proud tower in the town/ Death looks gigantically down.'' To some extent the poem also can be read aloud as a dark ode to the city of Venice in wintertime, its famous ''towers thrust aside,/ In slightly sinking, the dull tide.'' *Text: MCW,* I, 196–204; *CWP,* VII, 49–50. *Research:* Stockton, Eric W. ''Celestial Inferno: Poe's 'The City in the Sea.' '' *Tennessee Studies in Literature*, 8 (1963): 99–106; Clough, Wilson O. ''Poe's 'The City in the Sea' Revisited.'' In *Essays in American Literature in Honor of Jay B. Hubbell*, ed. Clarence Gohdes. Durham, NC: Duke University Press, 1967, 77–89; Thorpe, Dwayne. ''Poe's 'The City in the Sea': Source and Interpretation.'' *American Literature*, 51 (1979): 394–399; Leonard, Douglas Norvich. ''Poe's 'The City in the Sea.' '' *Explicator*, 43, no. 1 (1984): 30–32; Dameron, J. Lasley. ''Another Source for Poe's 'The City in the Sea.' '' *Poe Studies*, 22, no.2 (1989): 43–44; Garrison, Joseph M., Jr. ''Poe's 'City in the Sea.' '' *Explicator*, 48, no. 3 (1990): 185–188.

Clark, Lewis Gaylord. (1808–1873). Editor of the *Knickerbocker Magazine*. His severe criticism of *Pym* made him one of Poe's numerous literary enemies. Clark also frequently assailed Poe in his ''Editor's Table'' column. The two men feuded in print and in person in 1845 when Poe attempted to assault Clark on a New York street. Poe had to be restrained by Thomas Holley Chivers. Poe inserted a vindictive sketch of Clark's editorial character in ''The Literati of New York City.'' As an editor he ''has no precise character''; thus, the magazine he edits ''can have none.'' As a literary man, he ''has about him no determinateness, no distinctiveness, no saliency of point. . . . He is noticeable for nothing in the world except for the markedness by which he is noticeable for nothing.'' *See:* ''The Literary Life of Thingum Bob, Esq.'' *Text: CWP,* XV, 114–116. *Research:* Spivey, Herman E. ''Poe and Lewis Gaylord Clark.'' *Publications of the Modern Language Association*, 54 (1939): 1124–1132; Moss, Sydney P. ''Poe and His Nemesis—Lewis Gaylord Clark.'' *American Literature*, 28 (1956): 30–49.

Clark, Captain William. (1770–1838). American soldier, explorer, and co-commander of the Lewis and Clark Expedition. The explorations are referred to in *The Journal of Julius Rodman* and the review of Irving's ''Astoria; or, Anecdotes of an Enterprise beyond the Rocky Mountains.'' *Text: CWP,* IV, 18–19; IX, 212, 228.

Clarke, Anne E. C. Thomas Cottrell Clarke's daughter. She wrote a profile of Poe that was included in John Sartain's *Reminiscences of a Very Old Man* (1899). *See:* Clarke, Thomas Cottrell. *Research: TPL,* xx.

Clarke, Colin. (1792–1881). Virginia lawyer and gentleman farmer mentioned in a letter from Poe to John Pendleton Kennedy of 11 February 1836. *Research: TPL,* xx.

Clarke, Joseph Hanson. (1790–1885). Richmond schoolmaster and classical scholar who instructed the young Poe to give up the writing of verses. Poe was enrolled in Clarke's school in the fall of 1820 after returning from England. Clarke remembered Poe as a young man whose "imaginative powers seemed to take precedence of all his other faculties." *Research: LTP,* 81–83; Jackson, David K. "A Joseph H. Clarke Manuscript and Something about a Mr. Persico." *Poe Studies,* 9 (1976): 22; *TPL,* xx.

Clarke, Thomas Cottrell. (1801–1874). Philadelphia publisher of the *Saturday Museum.* He was a potential backer for Poe's *Stylus,* the projected magazine, but withdrew his support probably because of Poe's drinking. Poe reacted contemptuously to Clarke's withdrawal of support. "My magazine scheme has exploded, or, at least, I have been deprived, through the imbecility, or rather through the idiocy of my partner, of all means of prosecuting it for the present." *Research: TPL,* xx; *MNR,* 193–195; Kopley, Richard. "Thomas Cottrell Clarke's Poe Collection: New Documents." *Poe Studies,* 25, nos. 1–2 (1992): 1–5.

"The Classical Family Library, Numbers XV, XVI, and XVII. EURIPIDES Translated by the Reverend R. Potter." Review of Potter's translations of the plays of Euripides appearing in *The Southern Literary Messenger* for September 1835. These three volumes in Harper's Classical Family Library demonstrate the inferiority of Euripides to Æschylus and Sophocles. Euripides "falls immeasurably below his immediate predecessors." *Text: CWP,* VIII, 43–47.

Claudel, Paul-Louis-Charles-Marie. (1868–1955). French poet and critic. In 1892 and 1903, Claudel praised Poe's genius in letters to André Gide, commenting, "I only know two critics who deserve the name—Baudelaire and Poe." He credited Baudelaire with introducing him to Poe and singled out *Eureka* as a "magnificent" work. *Research:* Brunel, Pierre. "Claudel et Edgar Poe." *La Revue des Lettres Modernes,* 103 (1964): 99–130.

Clemm, Harriet Poe. (1785–1815). First wife of William Clemm, Jr. She was also Maria Poe Clemm's first cousin. She had five children by William Clemm, Jr.: William Eichelberger, Josephine Emily, Georgianna Maria, Catherine, and Harriet. *See:* Clemm, William, Jr. *Research: TPL,* xx.

Clemm, Maria Poe. (1790–1871). Poe's aunt, the sister of David Poe. She gave her support to Poe's literary genius and backed his efforts to publish his early stories. She married widower William Clemm, Jr., on 13 July 1817 and had three children by this marriage: Henry, Virginia Sarah, and Eliza. Extremely devoted to Poe, she offered him physical and mental support as well as emotional assistance throughout his career. Her nickname within the family was "Muddy." *Research:* Miller, John Carl. "Maria Poe Clemm Mourns Her Lost 'Eddie.' " *BPB*, 19–57; *MNR*, 81–82, 95–96, 107–109.

Clemm, Reverend William T.D. Methodist minister and Virginia Poe's cousin. He perfomed Poe's funeral rites on 8 October 1849. *Research: MNR,* 436; *PLL,* 256.

Clemm, William Jr. (1779–1826). Husband of Maria Clemm and William Clemm's second wife. William had previously been married to Harriet Poe Clemm, Maria Clemm Poe's first cousin. *See:* Clemm, Harriet Poe.

Climax. Character mentioned in the short story "The Man That Was Used Up." The narrator sees "that fine tragedian" playing Iago at the Rantipole Theatre.

Cline, Herr. A tightrope walker who performed at Castle Garden in New York. Poe mentioned the wonders of his act in a review of New York drama in *The Broadway Journal* of 2 August 1845. *Text: CWP,* XII, 212.

"Clinton Bradshaw; or the Adventures of a Lawyer." Review of F. W. Thomas's novel published in *The Southern Literary Messenger* for December 1835. Poe dismisses the novel as "the very worst species of imitation. . . . We dislike the novel considered *as a novel*" since it compares unfavorably with its obvious English source, Bulwer-Lytton's *Pelham, or The Adventures of a Gentleman* (1828). *Text: CWP,* VIII, 109–110. *Research: LET,* I, 101, 148.

Coates, Dr. Reynell. (1802–1886). Physician, amateur man of letters, and editor of the annual *Leaflets of Memory for 1850* which published Poe's sonnet "To My Mother." *Text: CWP,* XI, 224. *Research: TPL,* 349, 816.

Coates Street (number 2502). Poe address in northwestern Philadelphia where he lived in 1841.

Cobbett, William. (1763–1835). English political writer and pamphleteer. He also wrote an English grammar that Poe commented on in *Marginalia. Text:* CWP, VI, 21; XVI, 3.

Cocke, John Hartwell. (1780–1866). Virginia planter and planner who assisted Jefferson in the creation of the University of Virginia. He was an acquaintance of the Allans who took the two-year-old Poe to Cocke's plantation for the Christmas holidays in 1811. *Research: TPL,* xxi.

Cockton, Henry. (1807–1853). Minor English novelist. Poe remarked of his *Stanley Thorn* that the book "not only demands no reflection, but repels it, or dissipates it." Cockton also wrote *Valentine Vox, the Ventriloquist* (1841). *Text: CWP,* XI, 10, 90.

Cognoscenti, Arabella. Character in the short story "The Man That Was Used Up." She converses with the narrator during the play at the Rantipole Theatre.

Cognoscenti, Miranda. Character in the short story "The Man That Was Used Up." Her conversation with the narrator during the play is interrupted.

Coleridge, Samuel Taylor. (1772–1834). English poet and author of "The Rime of the Ancient Mariner," "Christabel," "Kubla Khan," and *Biographia Literaria.* Poe's intense admiration for Coleridge both as critical theorist and as poet appears in "Letter to B——." and elsewhere. "Of Coleridge I cannot speak but with reverence. His towering intellect! His gigantic power!" Poe appropriated almost verbatim Coleridge's definition of poetry when he declared in "Letter to Mr. ——," that "A poem, in my opinion, is opposed to a work of science by having, for its immediate object, pleasure, not truth." Poe also alludes to Coleridge's "Christabel" in "Drake-Halleck." *Text: CWP,* II, 273, 277–278, 286; IV, 106, 218; VIII, 93, 123, 285, 309; IX, 51–52; X, 61; XI, 65, 99, 255–256; XII, 33, 37, 140; XIII, 149; XIV, 191, 236–238, 245, 282; XVI, 72–73, 128, 150. *Research:* Baker, Harry T. "Coleridge's Influence on Poe's Poetry." *Modern Language Notes,* 25 (1910): 94–95; Stovall, Floyd. "Poe's Debt to Coleridge." *University of Texas Studies in English,* 10 (1930): 70–127; Abel, Darrel. "Coleridge's 'Life-in-Death' and Poe's 'Death-in-Life.' " *Notes & Queries,* 200 (May 1955): 218–220; *PLB,* 79, 82; Joost, Nicholas. "Coleridge, Poe, Baudelaire: Albatross and Poet Once Again." *Sou'wester* (Edwardsville, IL), 6, no. 1 (1978): 127–133.

"The Coliseum." Poem by Poe first published in the Baltimore *Saturday Visiter* of 26 October 1833. The poem is a Byronic meditation in which the poet reflects on the "grandeur, gloom, and glory" that shadow Rome's past and present. As he conjures up the doomed fame of ancient Rome, the poet hears sounds emerging "from all ruin" and the stones of the Coliseum speak their stern message: "We are not impotent—we pallid stones/ Not all our power is gone—not all our fame." The poet must believe that the essence of ancient Rome's greatness must still live in his imagination and in the quest of those who strive to achieve pomp and power. Mabbott believed that the poem was "atypical of Poe's work" and could have been written for a poetry contest in one of the journals. The poem also appears in the final scene of Poe's play *Politian. Text: MCW,* I, 226–231; *CWP,* VII, 56–57. *Research: LET,* I, 161, 258; Ljungquist, Kent. " 'The Coliseum': A Dialogue on Ruins." *Poe Studies,* 16, no. 2 (1983): 32–33.

Collections of Poe Papers, Letters, and Manuscripts. The major collections are the Rufus Griswold Collection in the Boston Public Library, the Richard Gimbel Collection in the Philadelphia Free Library, the Henry W. and Albert A. Berg Collection in the New York Public Library, the Tucker-Coleman Papers in the Earl G. Swem Library of the College of William and Mary, and the John H. Ingram Poe Collection in the Alderman Library of the University of Virginia. *See:* Correspondence and Correspondents. *Research:* Heartman, Charles F. and Kenneth Rede. *A Census of First Editions and Source Materials by or Relating to Edgar Allan Poe in American Public and Private Collections.* Metuchen, NJ: American Book Collector, 1932; Quinn, Arthur Hobson, and Richard H. Hart. *Edgar Allan Poe: Letters and Documents in the Enoch Pratt Free Library.* New York: Scholars' Facsimiles and Reprints, 1941; Gordan, John D. ''Edgar Allan Poe: An Exhibition on the Centenary of His Death, October 7, 1849; A Catalogue of the First Editions, Manuscripts, Autograph Letters from the Berg Collection.'' *Bulletin of the New York Public Library*, 53 (1949): 471–491; Gimbel, Richard. '' 'Quoth the Raven': A Catalogue of the Exhibition.'' *Yale University Library Gazette*, 33 (1959): 139–189; Jones, Joseph. *American Literary Manuscripts: A Checklist of Holdings in Academic, Historical and Public Libraries in the United States.* Austin: Texas University Press, 1960, 298–299; Miller, John Carl. *John Henry Ingram's Poe Collection at the University of Virginia: A Calendar.* Charlottesville: Virginia University Press, 1960; Randall, David A. *The J. K. Lilly Collection of Edgar Allan Poe: An Account of Its Formation.* Bloomington: Lilly Library of the University of Indiana, 1964; Hoffman, Paul Phillips. *Guide to Microfilm Edition of John Henry Ingram's Poe Collection.* Charlottesville: University of Virginia Library, 1967; Moldenhauer, Joseph J. *A Descriptive Catalogue of Edgar Allan Poe Manuscripts in the Humanities Research Center Library.* Austin: Texas at Austin University Press, 1973; Ostrom, John W. ''Fourth Supplement to *The Letters of Poe*.'' *American Literature*, 45 (1974): 513–536; Ostrom, John Ward. ''Revised Checklist of the Correspondence of Edgar Allan Poe.'' *Studies in the American Renaissance*, (1981): 169–255.

"The Colloquy of Monos and Una." Short story by Poe published in *Graham's Magazine* for August 1841. The story also appeared in the second volume of Poe's *Tales* in 1845. The story takes the form of a celestial dialogue between two posthumous lovers, Monos and Una. Reunited centuries after their burial, the two look back upon the condition of civilization to see nature ruined by industrial progress and society perverted by ''an omni-prevalent Democracy.'' Una tells Monos of the processes of death, decay, and alteration of consciousness in the postmortem state and the operation of a sixth sense expressed by ''the intemporal soul upon the threshold of temporal Eternity.'' The piece concludes with Una's vivid recollection of her own burial. Her self-resurrection is necessary, because she longs not only for a reunion after death with Monos but also ''for the redeemed, regenerated, blissful, and now immortal, but still for the *material* man.'' The names Monos and Una express a return to primal unity, one of the key concepts of the cosmological treatise *Eureka*. Poe's fascination with reversion to a primal oneness involves the crossing of temporal and spatial barriers as well as the psychic and mental barriers separating life from death.

Epigraph: ''These things are in the future [in Greek, Poe's translation].'' Sophocles, *Antigone. Text: MCW,* II, 607–619; *CWP,* IV, 200–212. *Research:* Varner, Cornelia. ''Notes on Poe's Use of Contemporary Materials in Certain of His Stories.'' *Journal of English and Germanic Philology,* 32 (1933): 77–80; *PJC,* 308–310, 406–410.

Colton, Charles Caleb. (1780–1882). American poet and author of *The Conflagration of Moscow* (1822) included by Griswold in his anthology *The Poets and Poetry of America.* His *Lacon* is mentioned several times by Poe as an example of gross imitation. *Text: CWP,* XI, 224; XIV, 39.

Colton, George Hooker. (1818–1847). Editor of *The American Review.* In February 1845, he bought Poe's poem ''The Raven'' for less than $20 and wrote of the poem in an editorial that it was ''one of the most felicitous specimens of unique rhyming which has for some time met our eye.'' Poe included a profile of him in ''The Literati of New York City.'' *Text: CWP,* XV, 7–9. *Research:* Colton, Cullen B. ''George Hooker Colton and the Publication of 'The Raven.' '' *American Literature,* 10 (1938): 319–330; *TPL,* 496.

Combe, George. (1788–1858). Scottish phrenologist and author of *The Constitution of Man Considered in Relation to External Objects* (1828). In ''Autography'' Poe says of Orestes Brownson that he ''reasons with the calm and convincing force of a Combe'' to demonstrate his point that ''the style of the profound thinker is never closely logical.'' *Text: CWP,* VIII, 252; XII, 165; XV, 194. *Research: PJC,* 140–141.

"The Coming of the Mammoth—The Funeral of Time, and Other Poems, by Henry B. Hirst." Review appearing in the 12 July 1845 issue of *The Broadway Journal* of a poetry collection by Philadelphia lawyer Henry B. Hirst. Hirst had presented Poe with a copy of his poems in June 1845. Poe responded with a rave review in which he paid tribute to Hirst's ''commendable poems.'' ''His versification is superior to that of any American poet.'' '' 'Isabelle' is the finest ballad ever written in this country.'' Even the mythological allegory ''The Burial of Eros'' attracts Poe's praise even though ''*all* allegories are contemptible'' with the exception of *The Pilgrim's Progress* and the *Færie Queene.* Griswold printed Poe's essay ''Henry B. Hirst,'' a revision of Hirst's poetic abilities in which Poe answered Hirst's claim that he had taken some lines for ''Ulalume'' from Hirst's ''Endymion'' and countered by suggesting that Hirst had stolen lines from ''Lenore'' in composing his ''The Penance of Roland.'' *Text: CWP,* XII, 166–180.

The Conchologist's First Book; or, A System of Testaceous Malacology [Shell-Covered Mollusks], Arranged Expressly for the Use of Schools. Illustrated textbook published in April 1839. It was a cheap edition of Thomas Wyatt's *Manual of Conchology* published by Harper in 1838. Professor Thomas Wyatt, a British scientific author and lecturer, paid Poe $50 to write the preface and introduction for a low-priced edition of his scientific textbook. Published by Haswell, Barrington, and Haswell, Poe's name appears on the title page of Wyatt's work. Poe's name on the publication enabled Wyatt to circumvent copyright restrictions that prohibited the production and sale of abridgements of the volume's Harper printing. *See:* "Preface and Introduction to 'The Conchologist's First Book.' " *Research:* Teall, Gardner. "Poe's Venture in Conchology." *New York Times Book Review*, 3 December 1922, 7; "Presentation Copy of the Second Edition of Poe's Conchologist." *American Transcendental Quarterly*, 14 (spring 1972): 87.

Condorcet, Jean Antoine Nicolas Caritat, Marquis de. (1743–1794). French physiocratic thinker mentioned in the short stories "Lionizing," "Bon-Bon," and "The Domain of Arnheim." *Text: CWP,* II, 38, 140; IV, 259; VI, 176.

Confession. Novel by William Gilmore Simms reviewed by Poe in *Graham's Magazine* for December 1841. *Research: TPL,* 351.

"Confessions of a Poet." Negative review of a novel by Laughton Osborn in *The Southern Literary Messenger* for April 1835. "The most remarkable feature in this production is the bad paper on which it is printed, and the typographical ingenuity with which matter barely enough for one volume has been spread over the pages of two." Poe also denigrated Osborn's satire *The Vision of Rubeta* (1838). These harsh rejections of his work were particularly affronting to Osborn since his estimation of Poe's work was high. Osborn told Poe: "With what sadness this is said you may conceive, when I assure you without the least reluctance, that had I the choice, of all the literary men of my country there is none whose friendship I should have preferred to yours." *Text: CWP,* VIII, 2–3. *Research: PLB,* 70–71, 75; *PJC,* 75–76, 78, 97.

"The Confessions of Emilia Harrington." A review of Lambert A. Wilmer's book published in the February 1836 issue of *The Southern Literary Messenger*. Poe is "satisfied of the author's genius from the simple verisimilitude of his narrative. Yet, unhappily, books thus written are not the books by which men acquire a contemporaneous reputation." *Text: CWP,* VIII, 234–237. *Research: PJC,* 126–127.

"The Conqueror Worm." Poem published separately and originally in *Graham's Magazine* for January 1843, then incorporated into the text of "Ligeia" when the story appeared in *The Broadway Journal*. To a certain extent, the poem needs to be read in the context of "Ligeia," as it is the creation of the tale's heroine. Ligeia's feeling for "Horror, the soul of the plot," reveals her anxiety over the menace of bodily decay as well as her desire to escape the ravages of physical death. But the hero, or perhaps the hero-villain, of the dark drama of life is the thing that devours the body in its cadaverous state. Like actors on a stage who are forced to conform to a repellent script, Ligeia's metaphor of human life consumed in the theater of death depicts "the blood-red thing['s]" triumph in the tragedy called "Man." Man is ultimately abandoned to the worm even by the angels who exit the theater "pallid and wan." *See: "Ligeia." Text: MCW,* I, 323, 328; *CWP,* VII, 87–88. *Research:* Swanson, Donald R. "Poe's 'The Conqueror Worm.' " *Explicator*, 19 (April 1961): item 52; Lubbers, Klaus. "Poe's 'The Conqueror Worm.' " *American Literature*, 39 (1967): 375–379; Tritt, Michael. " 'Ligeia' and 'The Conqueror Worm.' " *Poe Studies*, 9 (1976): 21–22; Pollin, Burton R. "Poe's 'The Conqueror Worm.' " *Explicator*, 40, no. 3 (1982): 25–28; Howard, Brad. " 'The Conqueror Worm': Dramatizing Æsthetics in 'Ligeia.' " *Poe Studies*, 21, no.2 (1988): 36–43.

"The Conquest of Florida, by Hernando de Soto; by Theodore Irving." Review of Theodore Irving's edition of de Soto's account appearing in *The Southern Literary Messenger* for July 1835. "Mr. Irving's work is one of great interest. . . . De Soto was doomed to prove that the golden dreams of wealth with which the unexplored regions of Florida had been invested, were baseless illusions. But his adventures and achievements afford a rich mine of romantic incidents which Mr. Irving has presented in a most attractive form." *Text: CWP,* VIII, 37–39.

Conrad, Joseph. (1857–1924). English novelist. Conrad had a high regard for Poe and praised in particular his maritime fantasy, "MS. Found in a Bottle" as "a very fine piece of work and so authentic in detail that it must have been told by a sailor of a sombre and poetical genius in the invention of the phantastic." One of many Conrad tales that displays the effect of Poe on his imagination is "The Inn of the Two Witches." *Research:* Amur, G. S. "*Heart of Darkness* and 'The Fall of the House of Usher': The Tale as Discovery." *Literary Criterion* (University of Mysore, India), 9, no. 4 (1971): 59–70.

Conrad, Robert Taylor. (1810–1858). American jurist, poet, and playwright included in Griswold's anthology. Poe refers to him as "one of the sweetest poets of the time." Conrad had chaired the committee that awarded the $100 prize to Poe for "The Gold-Bug." Appraising his character in "Autography," Poe remarks that "Judge Conrad occupies, perhaps, the first place among our Philadelphia *literati.*" *Text: CWP,* XI, 223–224, 242; XV, 232–233. *Research: TPL,* xxi, 442–443, 703–704.

Constantine VII, Porphyrogenitus. (912–959). Byzantine emperor who wrote *On the Ceremonies of the Court at Constantinople*, a treatise that Poe called "a pompous and silly volume." There is also an oblique reference to the emperor in the word "Porphyrogene" in the poem "The Haunted Palace." *Text: CWP,* VII, 83; XIV, 91.

"Conti, the Discarded, with Other Tales and Fancies, by Henry F. Chorley." Review of a collection of essays and tales published in *The Southern Literary Messenger* for February 1836. The work consists of eight tales and essays ''all of which papers evince literary powers of a high order.'' Poe compared the titular story, ''Conti, the Discarded'' to The *Bride of Lammermoor*, ''the master novel of Scott.'' *Text: CWP,* VIII, 229–234.

"A Continuation of the Voluminous History of the Little Longfellow War—Mr. Poe's Further Reply to the Letter of Outis." The New York *Evening Mirror* of 1 March 1845 contains a lengthy letter from a reader who calls himself ''Outis,'' the Greek word for ''nobody.'' Outis berates Poe for statements made about Longfellow's verse in his address for the Society Library on 28 February 1845. Poe had acknowledged Longfellow's genius in his lecture but severely criticized his ''fatal alacrity at imitation,'' thus renewing his earlier charges of plagiarism. Objecting to Poe's judgment, Outis concludes the letter by parodying ''The Raven'' and wondering if Poe himself might not be guilty of plagiarism in his borrowings from the anonymous poem ''The Bird of the Dream.'' The *Broadway Journal* for 8 March 1845 contains the first of five replies that Poe would make on the subject of plagiarism in literature. *See:* ''A Reply to Outis''; ''Imitation—Plagiarism—Mr. Poe's Reply to the Letter of Outis.'' *Text: CWP,* XII, 57–66.

"Contributions of the Ecclesiastical History of the United States of America—Virginia. A Narrative of Events Connected with the Rise and Progress of the Protestant Episcopal Church in Virginia. By the Reverend Francis L. Hawks." Review of a historical study published in *The Southern Literary Messenger* for March 1836. Poe criticized the historian George Bancroft for intimating that the Virginia colony had exhibited disloyalty during the protectorate of Oliver Cromwell, a remark that he later retracted in the April 1836 *Southern Literary Messenger.* An ''injustice'' has been done to Mr. Bancroft, ''not only by ourselves, but by Dr. Hawks and others.'' *Text: CWP,* VIII, 239–251.

"The Conversation of Eiros and Charmion." Short story by Poe first published in *Tales of the Grotesque and Arabesque* in December 1839 and *Burton's Gentleman's Magazine* for December 1839. The piece was reprinted in the Philadelphia *Saturday Museum* for 1 April 1843 under the title ''The Destruction of the World.'' The story is an apocalyptic dialogue between the two characters concerning the adjustments they must make in ''their perception of *the new.*'' Now long dead, they seek to understand their new condition existing posthumously as they now do in a strange nether realm more heavenly than infernal that appears to be like Poe's other paradise in ''Dream-Land'' that is ''[o]ut of space, out of time.'' Much of the tale is devoted to Eiros's description of events preceding the earth's destruction by collision with a comet. The tale's epigraph from Euripides suggests the fiery holocaust described by Eiros that ''[t]hus ended all.'' *Epigraph:* ''I will bring fire to thee'' [in Greek, translated by Poe]. Euripides, *Andromache*. *Text: MCW,* 451–462; *CWP,* IV, 1–8. *Research:* Robinson, Douglas. ''Poe's Mini-Apocalypse: 'The Conversation of Eiros and Charmion.' '' *Studies in Short Fiction*, 19 (1982): 329–337; Kock, Christian. ''The Irony of Oxygen in Poe's 'Eiros and Charmion.' '' *Studies in Short Fiction*, 22 (1985): 317–321.

"Conversations with Some Old Poets." Review of a book by James Russell Lowell appearing in the New York *Evening Mirror* of 11 January 1845 and reprinted in the *Weekly Mirror* of 18 January 1845. Poe deferred to Lowell's critical acuity and taste but disagreed sharply with Lowell's view that natural simplicity is always superior to artifice in poetic composition. The aesthetic debate was continued in Poe's editorial ''Nature and Art.'' *See:* ''Nature and Art.'' *Research: PJC,* 353.

Converse, The Reverend Amasa. Clergyman who perfomed the wedding ceremony for Poe and Virginia Clemm. *Research: TPL,* 207.

Cook, Captain James. (1728–1779). English navigator, Pacific ocean explorer, and author. Poe refers to Cook's voyages in *The Narrative of Arthur Gordon Pym* and *The Journal of Julius Rodman*. In his circumnavigation of the South Pole while sailing the *Resolution*, Cook had reached latitude seventy-one degrees ten minutes. Arthur Gordon Pym gives an account of Cook's polar voyage at the beginning of chapter sixteen of the novel. *Text: CWP,* III, 152, 165–166; IV, 17.

Cooke, Philip Pendleton. (1816–1850). Virginia poet and occasional Poe correspondent. Cooke admired and praised the gruesome verisimilitude of Poe's tales. Of ''The Facts in the Case of M. Valdemar,'' he wrote that ''that gelatinous, viscous sound of man's voice! There never was such an idea before.'' In an essay in *The Southern Literary Messenger* for January 1848, Cooke asserted that Poe ''dissects monomania, exhibits convulsions of soul.'' In ''Autography'' Poe spoke of Cooke's ''numerous excellent contributions to 'The Southern Literary Messenger.' He has written some of the finest poetry of which America can boast.'' *Text: CWP,* XV, 234. *Research: PJC,* 9–16, 63–65.

Cooper, James Fenimore. (1789–1851). American novelist and author of the *Leatherstocking Tales*. Poe wrote several reviews of the prominent American novelist, mostly sneering and condescending in tone. Burton objected to Poe's savage criticism of America's most revered author—but to no effect, as Poe continued his diatribes, excoriating Cooper's fiction at one point as ''a flashy succession of ill-conceived and miserably executed productions, each more silly than its predecessor. . . . [Cooper's books] had taught the public to suspect a radical taint in the intellect, an absolute and irreparable mental leprosy.'' Of

Cooper's handwriting in "Autography" Poe wrote: "Mr. Cooper's MS. is bad—very bad. There is no distinctive character about it and it appears to be *unformed*." *Text: CWP,* IX, 16, 162–164, 205–220, 223; XV, 51, 148–149, 205; XVI, 41. *Research: PJC,* 220; Jacobs, Edward Craney. "A Possible Debt to Cooper." *Poe Studies*, 9 (1976): 23.

Cooper, Joab Goldsmith. (fl. 1830). A grammarian and orthographer mentioned in the treatise on metrics and scansion, "The Rationale of Verse." He was a compiler of the *North American Spelling Book* (1830). Poe objected to his vagueness in defining versification. "Cooper, whose grammar is extensively used, defines it to be 'The arrangement of a certain number of syllables according to certain laws,' yet lays down no laws for its government, but drops the subject, fearful of burning his fingers." *Text: CWP,* XI, 225; XIV, 212.

Corbet, Richard of Norwich. (1582–1635). Minor English poet. His "Farewell Rewards and Fairies" from *The Fairies' Farewell* is quoted by Poe in his review of "The Book of Gems. The Poets and Artists of Great Britain." *Text: CWP,* IX, 98–100; XII, 143.

Corinnos. Character mentioned in the short story "Shadow—A Parable." He is the Greek artisan who created the brass door.

Corneille, Pierre. (1606–1684). French tragic dramatist. Poe cites Corneille's tragedies twice in *Pinakidia* and translates two lines from *Le Cid*: "Weep, weep my eyes! It is no time to laugh/ For half myself has buried the other half." These lines also furnished the epigraph for "The Man That Was Used Up." *Text: CWP,* III, 259, XIV, 41, 44.

Cornwallis, Lord Charles. (1738–1805). British general who surrendered to Washington at Yorktown. Poe uses him as a figure of fun at the conclusion of "Mellonta Tauta" in Pundit's translation of an inscription commemorating the surrender. "As to *where*, it was Yorktown (wherever that was), and as to *what*, it was General Cornwallis (no doubt some wealthy dealer in corn)." *Text: CWP,* VI, 215–217.

Correspondence and Correspondents. Poe's letters, many of which contain references to his reading, sources, and artistic aims, were collected by John Ward Ostrom. Other letters are in private collections or continue to turn up. *Research:* Campbell, Otis. "Poe's Documents in the Library of Congress," *Modern Language Notes*, 25 (1910): 127–128; Stanard, Mary Newton. *Edgar Allan Poe Letters Till Now Unpublished, in the Valentine Museum, Richmond, Virginia*. Philadelphia: J. B. Lippincott, 1925; Ostrom, John Ward. *A Checklist of Letters to and from Poe*. Charlottesville: University of Virginia Bibliographical Series Number 4; Alderman Library of the University of Virginia, 1941; Ostrom, John Ward. *The Letters of Edgar Allan Poe*. New York: Gordian Press, 1966; Ostrom, John Ward. "Revised Check List of the Correspondence of Edgar Allan Poe.'' In *Studies in the American Renaissance: 1981*, ed. Joel Myerson. Boston: Twayne, 1981, 169–255.

"Corse de Leon: Or the Brigand. A Romance, by G. P. R. James." Review of a historical romance of the times of Henry II appearing in *Graham's Magazine* for June 1841. To Poe, the book is just barely readable but both plot and characterization are ''commonplace. . . . Corse de Leon, the principal character, talks philosophy like Bulwer's heroes and is altogether a plagiarism from that bombastic, unnatural, cut-throat school.'' *Text: CWP,* X, 160–162.

Cottle, Joseph. (1770–1853). English bookseller and biographer. His *Reminiscences of Coleridge and Robert Southey* (1837) is described in ''Fifty Suggestions'' as a book that ''damns its perpetrator forever in the opinion of every gentleman who reads it.'' Burton Pollin points out that ''Poe's statement is either meaningless or based on error—perhaps on real ignorance of the volume itself.'' *Text: CWP,* XIV, 172. *Research: BRE*, 481.

Cousin, Victor. (1792–1867). French philosopher and translator. The narrator in ''Mesmeric Revelation'' has been advised to study Cousin. A second significant reference occurs in Poe's review of Horne's ''Orion,'' where he connects the thought of Cousin with ''that divine sixth sense which is yet so faintly understood—that sense which phrenology has attempted to embody in its organ of *ideality*.'' *Text: CWP,* V, 243; XI, 256.

Cowley, Abraham. (1618–1667). English poet. Poe groups Cowley with Donne and Carew and states that ''the 'metaphysical verse' of Cowley is no more than evidence of the straightforward simplicity and single-heartedness of the man.'' Poe was also attracted to Cowley's line in his poem ''Creation''—''An unshaped kind of something first appeared''—and quoted it several times. *Text: CWP*, VII, 133; IX, 95; X, 44; XII, 140; XIV, 49; XV, 69; XVI, 41, 139. *Research: PJC,* 168–169.

Cowley, Malcolm. (1898–1989). American critic and poet. His refusal to grant Poe a shaping role in American literature ignited scholarly controversy over his reputation. Cowley's essays ''The Edgar Allan Poe Tradition'' (*Outlook*, July 1928) and ''Aidgarpo'' located Poe outside the mainstream of American letters and identified his main failing as a writer to be ''his lack of visualization; his inability to see, or to make the reader see.'' *Research:* Cowley, Malcolm. ''Aidgarpo.'' *New Republic*, 5 November 1945, 607–610; Bak, Hans. ''Malcolm Cowley and Edgar Allan Poe.'' *Horns of Plenty: Malcolm Cowley and His Generation*, 2, no.2 (1989): 18–35.

Cowper, William. (1731–1800). English poet and author of the gloomy poem ''The Castaway.'' Poe used Cowper's lines from ''Tirocinium'' as an epigraph for *Tamerlane and Other Poems*. Poe apparently praised Cowper's style in *Marginalia:* "The more prosaic a poetical style is, the better. Through this species of prosaicism, Cowper, with scarely one of the higher poetical elements, came very near making his age fancy him the equal of Pope." *Text: CWP,* IX, 305; X, 68; XVI, 154.

Coxe, Reverend Arthur Cleveland. (1818–1896). *See:* "Coxe's Saul." *Text: CWP,* XII, 243–244; XVI, 154.

"Coxe's Saul." A brief review of the Reverend Arthur Coxe's *Saul, A Mystery* appearing in *The Broadway Journal* of 6 September 1845. Poe admits, "As yet we have not found time to read the poem—which, to say the truth, is an unconscionably long one." Poe archly denied that he had condemned Coxe's work, writing in *Marginalia*, "Latterly I have read 'Saul,' and agree with the epigrammatist, that it 'will do'—whoever attempts to wade through it. . . . The author is right in calling it 'A Mystery':—for a most unfathomable mystery it is." *Text: CWP,* XII, 243–244; XVI, 154.

Crab, Mr. Character in the short story "The Literary Life of Thingum Bob, Esq." He is the editor of the magazine *Lollipop*.

Crabbe, George. (1754–1832). English poet. As the narrator in "Loss of Breath" investigates the "numerous coffins," he remarks of one waddling carcass that "[h]is studies have been confined to the poetry of Crabbe." Poe also used the poetic example of Crabbe to demonstrate that beauty, not truth, is poetry's highest end: "If truth is the highest aim of either Painting or Poesy, then Jan Steen was a greater artist than Angelo, and Crabbe is a more noble poet than Milton." *Text: CWP,* II, 162; XI, 84.

Cranch, Christopher Pearse. (1813–1892). American poet and, as Poe described him in his profile in "The Literati of New York City," "one of the least intolerable of the school of Boston transcendentalists." There is a metrical analysis and scansion of some Cranch lines—"Many are the thoughts that come to me"—in "The Rationale of Verse." *Text: CWP,* XII, 239–240; XIV, 248–252; XV, 69–72. *Research: LET,* II, 316, 317.

Crane, Alexander. (1829–?). Office clerk who knew Poe at *The Broadway Journal*. *Research:* Isani, Mukhtar Ali. "A Further Word on Poe and Alexander Crane." *Poe Studies*, 7 (1974): 48; *TPL,* xxi.

Crane, Hart. (1899–1932). American poet whose own life was falling to pieces in the late 1920s when he composed his epic poem *The Bridge*. Crane's manic fluctuations of mood, his defensiveness about his art, his progressive alcoholism, and his psychic disintegration and suicide afford all-too-many parallels with

Poe's life. It is hardly surprising that Crane placed a powerful picture of Poe's final days and death in Baltimore on 7 October 1849 in "The Bridge." In fact, Poe's presence in "The Bridge" darkly balances Crane's Whitmanesque mysticism. Attracted as much to Poe's descents of no return as he was to Whitman's transcendences, Crane saw Poe's life as a foreshadowing of his own doomed art. His invocation to Poe expresses the deep personal alienation both poets experienced toward their respective Americas. Crane's bond of sympathy with Poe's isolated imagination climaxes in the pastiche and terrible tribute to his predecessor: "And Death aloft,—gigantically down/ Probing through you—and toward me, O evermore!" *Research:* Martin, Robert K. "Crane's *The Bridge*: 'The Tunnel,' [lines] 58–60." *Explicator*, 34 (1975): item 16.

Cratinus. (520–423 B.C.). Ancient Greek satiric playwright. In "Bon-Bon," the devil reports that the taste of Cratinus's soul was "passable" but perhaps not as tasty as his contemporary Aristophanes. *Text: CWP,* II, 142.

"The Crayon Miscellany. By the Author of the Sketch Book No.3." Review of Washington Irving's anthology of selections appearing in *The Southern Literary Messenger* for December 1835. Poe approves of the matter and "beauty of style" and singles out one sketch as more beautiful than the rest, "The Story of the Marvelous and Portentous Tower." *Text: CWP,* VIII, 91–92. *Research: PJC,* 174, 176, 214, 267.

"The Crayon Miscellany, No. II. Containing Abbotsford and Newstead Abbey." Laudatory review of the Irving work on Sir Walter Scott and Lord Byron appearing in *The Southern Literary Messenger* for July 1835. "He has given us a familiar (yet how beautiful!) picture of Abbotsford and its presiding genius; but the relics of Newstead, which his pensive muse has collected and thrown together, brightening every fragment by the lustre of his own genius, are perhaps even more attractive." *Text: CWP,* VIII, 40–41. *Research: PJC,* 174, 176, 214, 267.

Crébillon, Prosper Jolyot de. (1674–1762). French dramatist. Some lines from his 1707 revenge tragedy *Atrée* [*Atreus*] are cited by Dupin at the end of "The Purloined Letter." In *Marginalia,* Poe also cites the characterization of Crébillon by the Jesuits: "clever boy, but outstanding scamp." *Text: CWP,* II, 203; IV, 153; VI, 52; X, 206; XIV, 63; XVI, 12.

Cribalittle, Mademoiselle. Character mentioned in the short story "The Literary Life of Thingum Bob, Esq." She is one of the contributors to the *Lollipop.*

Crichton, James. (1560–1585). Soldier, poet, and man of many talents. He was called the "Admirable Crichton" and served as a symbol for many-sided genius. Poe mentions him as a symbol of false genius and showy erudition in

Marginalia and several reviews. "We have no faith in admirable Crichtons, and this merely because we *have* implicit faith in Nature and her laws." *Text:* CWP, X, 190, 214; XI, 99; XVI, 142, 158.

Crisp, Mr. W. H. American actor who appeared as the Count in Mrs. Mowatt's *Fashion.* Poe found his performance "a little too gentlemanly in the Count—he has *subdued* the part, we think, a trifle too much." *Text: CWP,* XII, 128, 185, 192.

"Critical and Miscellaneous Essays. By T. Babington Macaulay." Review of Thomas Babington Macaulay's collection of essays appearing in the June 1841 issue of *Graham's Magazine.* Poe approved of "the terseness and simple vigour of Macaulay's style" but was disturbed by "his exceeding *closeness* of logic . . . and the tendency of mere logic in general—to concentrate force upon minutiae, at the expense of a subject as a whole." Of Macaulay's overlogicality, Poe concludes that "he has forgotten that anagoligical evidence cannot, at all times, be discoursed of as if identical with proof direct." *Text: CWP,* X, 156–160. *Research: PJC,* 262–263.

"Critical and Miscellaneous Writings of Henry Lord Brougham." Review of miscellaneous selections from the writings of Henry Lord Brougham appearing in the March 1842 number of *Graham's Magazine.* Among the papers in the collection, Poe was attracted to Brougham's "Discourse on the Objects, Pleasures and Advantages of Science," a well-written essay but abounding in misstatements and contendable facts. "Its style, too, in its minor points, is unusually bad. The strangest grammatical errors abound . . . and the whole is singularly deficient in that precision which should characterise a scientific discourse." Poe was further amused by Brougham's paper on the identity of the eighteenth-century author Junius. *Text: CWP,* XI, 98–101.

"Critical and Miscellaneous Writings of Sir Edward Lytton Bulwer." Review of various selections from the writings of Sir Edward Lytton Bulwer published in *Graham's Magazine* for November 1841. Poe praised two of Bulwer's papers in particular, "Literature Considered as a Profession" and "Upon the Spirit of True Criticism." But his general view of Bulwer remained dismissive. "Mr. Bulwer is *never* lucid, and seldom profound. His intellect seems to be rather well balanced than lofty; rather comprehensive than penetrative." *Text: CWP,* X, 212–214.

Croissart, Madame. Character mentioned in the short story "The Spectacles." She is the wife of the French banker. Also referred to by her maiden name as Mademoiselle Croissart.

Cromwell, Oliver. (1599–1658). English politician, statesman, military leader, and Lord Protector of the Commonwealth. Although Cromwell is mentioned several times by Poe, his view of him is vague. In *Marginalia*, Poe notes bitterly that "Words—printed ones especially are murderous things. Keats did (or did not) die of a criticism, Cromwell, of Titus' [Oates] pamphlet 'Killing No Murder.' " *Text: CWP,* VIII, 23, 245–249; IX, 35; XV, 113; XVI, 74.

Crooks, Ramsey. Scottish trader and explorer mentioned in Poe's review of Irving's "Astoria." *Text: CWP,* IX, 224–226, 229, 235, 237.

Cryptography. Poe maintained a lifelong interest in codes, ciphers, and cryptograms, frequently reviewing books on these subjects and introducing cryptographic motifs into his tales. *See:* "The Gold-Bug." *Research:* "Edgar Allan Poe on Cryptography." *Bookman*, 17 (March 1903): 4–5, 7; Dredd, Firman. "Poe and Secret Writing." *Bookman*, 28 (January 1909): 450–451; Whitty, J. H. "A New Poe Letter: Hitherto Unpublished Note Deals with Strange Cryptogram." *Richmond Times-Dispatch*, 21 July 1935, 15; Friedman, William F. "Edgar Allan Poe, Cryptographer." *American Literature*, 8 (1936): 266–280; Wimsatt, William K., Jr. "What Poe Knew About Cryptography." *Publications of the Modern Language Association*, 58 (1943): 754–779; Rosenheim, Shawn. " 'The King of "Secret Readers' ": Edgar Poe, Cryptography, and the Origins of the Detective Story." *ELH: Journal of English Literary History*, 56 (1989): 375–400; Hodgson, John A. "Decoding Poe? Poe, W. P. Tyler, and Cryptography." *Journal of English and Germanic Philology*, 92 (1993): 523–534; Whalen, Terence. "The Code for Gold: Edgar Allan Poe and Cryptography." *Representations*, 46 (1994): 35–57.

Cullum, George Washington. Fellow cadet with Poe at West Point. He later recalled Poe as "slovenly, heedless, and eccentric, and more inclined to the making of verses than the solving of equations." *Research: TPL,* 115; *PLL,* 46.

Cunningham, Allan. (1784–1842). Scottish poet and song writer. Poe knew and admired his *Traditional Tales of the English and Scottish Peasantry* (1822). Poe mentions Cunningham's songs in several reviews and alludes to "the fervid, hearty, free-spoken songs of Cowley and of Donne—more especially of Cunningham, of Harrington and of Carew." *Text: CWP,* X, 44, 207; XVI, 139.

Curio, Cælius Secundus. (1503–1569). Italian theological writer. His book *De amplitudine beati regni dei* is one of the books in Egaeus's library in "Berenice." *Text: CWP,* II, 20.

Curran, John Philpot. (1750–1817). English politician and orator. In *Marginalia*, there is a somewhat sarcastic reference to his public speaking. "How overpowering a style is that of Curran! I use 'overpowering' in the sense of the English exquisite. I can imagine nothing more distressing than the extent of his eloquence." *Text: CWP,* XIII, 203; XVI, 48.

Curtis, Mrs. Adelaide, of Albany. Character mentioned in the short story "The Oblong Box." She is the artist's mother-in-law to whom the mysterious box is addressed.

Cushing, Caleb. (1800–1879). Boston orator. He once shared a lecture program with Poe at the Lyceum's Odeon Theater lecture series on 16 October 1845, where he preceded Poe on the program by delivering a long and tedious lecture on Great Britain, followed by Poe's reading of "Al Aaraaf," which he had retitled "The Messenger Star" for the occasion. In "Boston and the Bostonians" Poe recalled the occasion. "Mr. Poe committed another error in consenting to address an audience in verse, who, for three mortal hours, had been compelled to sit and hear Mr. Caleb Cushing in prose. The attempt to speak after this, in poetry, and fanciful poetry, too, was sheer madness." *Text: CWP,* XIII, 3, 5, 10. *Research: PLB,* 191–193; *TPL,* xxi, 577–579.

Cutter, William. (1801–1867). Amateur historian and poet of Portland, Maine, mentioned in "Autography." He wrote a *Life of Lafayette*. His "numerous compositions . . . prove him to be possessed of the true fire. He is, moreover, a fine scholar, and a prose writer of distinguished merit." *Text: CWP,* XV, 244.

D

D_____, Minister. Character in the short story "The Purloined Letter." He possesses the stolen letter and attempts to "hide" it in the obvious place so that it will be overlooked during a search.

Dacre, Lady. [Barbarina Ogle Brand]. (1757–1854). English author and editor of *Recollections of a Chaperon* (1833), written by her daughter, Arabella Jane Sullivan (1797–1839). Poe's estimation of both mother and daughter was high. Discussing Lady Georgiana Fullerton's *Ellen Middleton*, Poe added: "Who is that Countess of Dacre, who edited 'Ellen Wareham,'—the most passionate of fictions—approached, only in some particulars of passion, by this?" *Text: CWP,* VIII, 74–75, 223; XVI, 34, 157. *Research:* Pollin, Burton. "Poe and the 'Magic Tale' of *Ellen Wareham.*" *DIP*, 128–143.

Daguerreotypes of Poe. *See:* Portraits and Daguerreotypes of Poe.

Daily Forum. This Philadelphia newspaper was sued by Poe for libel over its accusation of collusion with the judges in the matter of the "Gold-Bug" prize. The editor, Frances Duffee, retracted the charge, and the suit was dropped. *Research: TPL,* 419–425, 429–430.

Dammit, Toby. Character in the short story "Never Bet the Devil Your Head." He loses the bet when his head collides with a bridge support.

"The Damsel of Darien." Review of a historical romance of Balboa and Panama by William Gilmore Simms appearing in *Burton's Gentleman's Magazine* for November 1839. Poe approves of the novel but not too enthusiastically: "The defects of the 'Damsel of Darien' are few and seldom radical. The leading sin is the sin of imitation—the entire absence of originality." *Text: CWP,* X, 49–56. *Research: PJC,* 229–230.

Dana, Charles. (1815–1882). American author and editor. He reviewed the 1845 edition of Poe's *Tales* in *The Harbinger*, observing acidly that they "are clumsily contrived, unnatural, and every way in bad taste. There is still a kind of power in them; it is the power of disease." *Research: PLL,* 178.

Dana, Richard Henry, Jr. (1815–1882). American author of *Two Years Before the Mast* (1840) and an influential essay on "Cruelty to Seamen." Poe reviewed Dana's *The Seaman's Friend* in *Graham's Magazine* for December 1841. *Research: TPL,* 351.

Dana, Richard Henry, Sr. (1787–1879). American poet, journalist, and founder of *The North American Review*. In reviewing a Poe lecture on American poets and poetry, Nathaniel P. Willis commented that "Mr. Poe thought his meter harsh and awkward, his narrative ill-managed, and his conceptions eggs from other people's nests." In his reply to Outis of 22 March 1845, Poe suggested that Dana's poem "The Dying Raven" had been pirated from Paul Allen. In "Autography," Poe summed up Dana's literary character: "He has high qualities, undoubtedly, but his defects are many and great." *Text: CWP,* XI, 223; XII, 66; XV, 49–50, 224; XVI, 175. *Research: PLB,* 164, 167; *LET,* 333; *TPL,* 447, 499, 509–510.

"The Danger of Premature Interment, Proved From Many Remarkable Instances of People Who Have Recovered After Being Laid Out." Treatise by Joseph Taylor published in 1816. Taylor's treatise exposed lethal errors in medical diagnoses and funeral practices that often led to live burial. The subject held such morbid fascination for the public that one year before Poe's tale "The Premature Burial" was published in 1844, Nathaniel Willis wrote an article for the *New York Mirror* that discussed a new life-preserving coffin that opened automatically if the occupant moved during or after interment. *Research: PLL,* 156, 157.

Daniel, John Moncure. (1825–1865). Editor of the Richmond *Semi-Weekly Examiner*. Poe challenged him to a duel in August 1848. No duel took place, and the two men were reconciled in 1849. Although the two men were enemies, Daniel recognized Poe's literary genius, praising "the complexity of his intellect, its incalculable resources, and his masterly control." His article in *The*

Southern Literary Messenger for March 1850 acknowledges Poe's literary brilliance. *Research: LTP,* 613–615; *TPL,* 825–828, 841–843.

Daniel, Peter Vivian. (1784–1860). One of the three members of the Virginia State Council whose aid Poe and the Junior Volunteers solicited in retaining the arms issued to them for Lafayette's visit to Richmond in October 1824. *Research: TPL,* xxi.

Dante [Alighieri]. (1265–1321). Italian poet and author of *The Divine Comedy.* In "The Literary Life of Thingum Bob, Esq.," Thingum Bob believes that he is every bit the equal of "Mr. Dante." There are also references to Dante in the criticism, although *The Divine Comedy* itself is not mentioned. *Text: CWP,* VI, 8; VIII, 163–164; XII, 16; XIV, 43. *Research:* Belden, Henry M. "Poe's 'The City in the Sea' and Dante's 'City of Dis.' " *American Literature,* 7 (1935): 332–334; Mathews, Joseph Chesley. "Did Poe Read Dante?" *University of Texas Studies in English,* 18 (1938): 123–136; Semark, Douglas Lee. "The Visionary Tradition: The Ancients, Dante, and Poe." *Dissertation Abstracts International,* 48 (1988): 1764A (Case Western Reserve University).

Darío, Rubén. [Félix Rubén García-Sarmiento]. (1867–1916). Spanish poet. He admired Poe deeply but could not understand his materialism and skepticism. In Darío's essay collection *Los Raros* (1905), he devoted a chapter to Poe, calling him "the father of the decadents. . . . Philosophical speculation stood between him and the faith he should have had as a great poet. . . . He didn't believe in the supernatural." *Research:* Johnston, Marjorie C. "Rubén Darío's Acquaintance with Poe." *Hispania,* 17 (1934): 271–278; Castro, Humbetto de. "Whitman y Poe en la poesía de Rubén Darío." *Boletín Cultural y Bibliográfico* (Bogota), 10 (1967): 90–104; Anderson-Imbert, Enrique. "Rubén Darío and the Fantastic Element in Literature." In *Rubén Darío Centennial Studies,* ed. Miguel Gonzalez-Gerth and George D. Schade. Austin: Latin American Studies, Texas University Press, 1970, 97–117.

Darley, Felix O. C. (1822–1888). Illustrator who provides the drawings for the first edition of "The Gold-Bug." *Research: TPL,* xxii, 395–396, 413–414.

Darley, George. (1795–1846). Irish mathematician and poet. Poe refers to his *Lillian of the Vale* in his review of Moore's *Alciphron. Text: CWP,* X, 63.

Darwin, Erasmus. (1731–1802). English physician, botanist, and poet. There are references to him in *Marginalia* and *Pinakidia. Text: CWP,* XIV, 53; XVI, 11.

"Dashes at Life with a Free Pencil. By N. P. Willis. Part III. Loiterings of Travel." Favorable review of Nathaniel Parker Willis's book appearing in the 23 August 1845 issue of *The Broadway Journal.* "We look upon Mr. Willis as one of the *truest* men of letters in America. About him there is no particle of *pretence*. His works show his fine genius as *it is*.'' *Text: CWP,* XII, 234–235. *Research: PJC,* 365–373.

Davidson, Lucretia Maria. (1808–1825). American child poet. Her poem *Amir Khan* (1829) contains a reference to ''Israfil'' which may have provided Poe with an idea for his poem ''Israfel.'' *See:* ''Poetical Remains of the Late Lucretia Maria Davidson.'' *Research: MCW,* I, 173.

Davis, Andrew Jackson. (1826–1910). American spiritualist. He was involved in mesmerism and composition while under a trance. Also known as ''the Seer of Poughkeepsie,'' he compiled *Principles of Nature, Her Divine Revelations, and a Voice of Mankind* (1847), a publication that may have influenced *Eureka*. *Text: CWP,* XIV, 173.

Davy, Sir Humphrey. (1778–1829). English scientist and experimenter. In Poe's ''Von Kempelen and His Discovery'' the narrator cites the ''Diary'' of Sir Humphrey Davy to demonstrate Von Kempelen's debt to the British scientist for his discovery. *Text: CWP,* VI, 645–648; XIV, 65.

Dawes, Rufus. (1803–1859). Baltimore poet and editor. He was the subject of a devastating critique in *Graham's Magazine* for October 1842. Poe's scathing review exacted literary revenge for the abuse received for ''Al Aaraaf'' when it was reviewed in Dawes's Baltimore *Minerva and Herald*. In ''Autography'' Poe repeated his rejection of Dawes's verse. ''His longer poems, however, will not bear examination. 'Athenia of Damascus' is pompous nonsense, and 'Geraldine' a most ridiculous imitation of 'Don Juan,' in which the beauties of the original have been sedulously avoided, as the blemishes have been blunderingly culled.'' *See:* ''The Poetry of Rufus Dawes—A Retrospective Criticism.'' *Text: CWP,* XV, 190–191. *Research: PJC,* 218, 331–333; *TPL,* xxii.

Day, John. One of the exploring party mentioned in *Astoria*. *Text: CWP,* IX, 235–237.

De Grand, P. P. F. Editor and owner of the Boston commercial newspaper the *Weekly Report*. He employed Poe as a reporter in the spring of 1827. *Research: PLL,* 32.

De Grät. Character mentioned in the unfinished short story ''The Light-House.'' He has asked the narrator to keep a journal while at the lighthouse.

De Kock, Monsieur. Character in the short story ''The System of Doctor Tarr and Professor Fether.'' He kicks Mademoiselle Laplace under the table to demonstrate the behavior of a patient who believes himself to be a donkey.

De la Mare, Walter. (1873–1956). English poet and short story writer. His ghost and horror stories, particularly ''Seaton's Aunt'' and ''All Hallows,'' register his interest in Poe's single preconceived effect. Such poems as ''The Listeners'' and ''The Riddle'' show the moods and sonorous qualities of Poe's verse. *Research:* Reid, Forrest. *Walter de la Mare: A Critical Study*. New York: Henry Holt, 1970, 221, 152–58.

De Quincey, Thomas. (1785–1859). English author and writer of *Confessions of an English Opium Eater*. Although De Quincey is mentioned by name only once in Poe's works in ''How to Write a Blackwood Article,'' the opium dream and psychedelic experience indicate De Quincey's influence. Tales such as ''The Island of the Fay'' and poems such as ''Dream-Land'' evoke De Quincey's *Confessions*. The narrator in ''The Fall of the House of Usher'' makes a telling reference ''to the after-dream of the reveller upon opium'' in the opening paragraph of the story. *Text: CWP,* II, 273. *Research:* Wilt, Napier. ''Poe's Attitude toward His Tales: A New Document.'' *Modern Philology*, 25 (1927): 101–105; O'Sullivan, Vincent. ''Edgar Poe, O'Brien, et Thomas De Quincey.'' *Mercure de France*, 1 June 1935, 445–448; *LET,* I, 58; Snyder, Robert Lance. ''A De Quinceyan Source for Poe's 'The Masque of the Red Death.' '' *Studies in Short Fiction*, 21 (1984): 103–110.

De Vere, Guy. Character in the poem ''Lenore.'' He is her grieving lover. *Research:* Pollin, Burton R. ''Poe's Use of the Name De Vere in 'Lenore.' '' *Names*, 23 (1975): 1–5.

Debussy, Claude. (1862–1918). French composer. He wrote two operas based on Poe stories, *La Chute de la maison Usher* [''The Fall of the House of Usher''] and *Le Diable dans le beffroi* [''The Devil in the Belfry''] and often declared Poe's profound effect upon his musical moods. *Research:* Lockspeiser, Edward. ''Debussy and Edgar Allan Poe.'' *Listener*, 68 (18 October 1962): 609–610; Brunel, Pierre. ''Claude Debussy interpréte d'Edgar Poe: *La Chute de la maison Usher.*'' *Revue de Littérature Comparée*, 61 (1987): 359–368; Sullivan, Jack. ''New Worlds of Terror: The Legacy of Poe in Debussy and Ravel.'' *Lit: Literature Interpretation Theory*, 5 (1994): 83–93.

"A Decided Loss." Original title for the short story ''Loss of Breath: A Tale Neither in nor Out of 'Blackwood.' '' *See:* ''Loss of Breath: A Tale Neither in nor Out of 'Blackwood.' ''

Dee, Doctor Dubble L. Character in the short story ''Three Sundays in a Week.'' He does not appear directly in the story but figures as an authority on ''the extraordinary concurrence of events.''

"Deep in Earth." Unpublished two-line poem first printed in the *Bulletin of the New York Public Library*, 18 (December 1914): 1462. The poem was written in Poe's hand on the manuscript of ''Eulalie'' and included by Mabbott in his edition of the poems with the comment that " 'Deep in Earth' was presumably written soon after the funeral of the poet's wife on February 2, 1847." The lines read: "Deep in earth my love is lying/ And I must weep alone." *Text: MCW,* I, 396.

Defoe, Daniel. (1659–1731). English novelist and author of *Robinson Crusoe* (1719). Poe read Defoe while at the Manor House School and commented admiringly on Defoe's power of verisimiltude, especially "the faculty of identification—that dominion exercised by volition over imagination which enables the mind to lose its own . . . individuality." *Text: CWP,* III, 267; VIII, 169–173, 235; X, 218; XI, 41. *Research: LET,* I, 224, II, 433; *PJC,* 120, 127; Pollin, Burton R. "Poe and Daniel Defoe: A Significant Relationship." *Topic* (Washington and Jefferson College), 16, no. 30 (1976): 3–22.

D'elormie. Character in the poem "Bridal Ballad." The woman's first love, he dies in battle and his memory keeps her from giving herself completely to a new husband.

Deluc, Madame. Character in the short story "The Mystery of Marie Rogêt." She owns the restaurant in which the corpse of Marie Rogêt is discovered.

The Demon. Character in the short story "Silence—A Fable." He narrates the tale.

Demosthenes. (384–322 B.C.). Ancient Athenian orator. Using the oratorical eloquence of Demosthenes as his example, Poe states in *Marginalia,* "We may safely grant that the effects of the oratory of Demosthenes were vaster than those wrought by any modern, and yet not controvert the idea that the modern eloquence, itself, is superior to that of the Greek." *Text: CWP,* II, 115; X, 58; XVI, 62.

Denner, Balthazar. (1685–1749). German realistic painter. In *Marginalia,* probably because of Denner's absolute attention to photographic detail, Poe calls him "no artist." *Text: CWP,* XVI, 164.

Dennis, John. (1657–1734). English dramatist and critic. In "A Chapter of Suggestions," Poe cites Dennis as an example of critical small-mindedness. "What names excite, in mankind, the most unspeakable—the most insufferable disgust? The Dennises, the Frérons, the Desfontaines. Their littleness is measured by the greatness of those whom they have reviled." *Text: CWP,* XIV, 189.

"A Descent into the Maelström." Short story first published in the April 1841 issue of *Graham's Magazine.* The tale begins with an indirect homage to Coleridge's "Rime of the Ancient Mariner" since the white-haired sailor who has made the descent feels compelled to relate the circumstances of this singular event that has transformed his life. His fateful experience has yielded a sort of visionary enlightenment since his submarine journey into a funnel ''vast in circumference, prodigious in depth'' has resulted in both a miraculous survival and an intensification of his understanding of the laws of the universe. Spinning inside the maelström, the narrator is both terrified and imaginatively inspired to the point of relinquishing all hope of survival to concentrate on the aesthetic opportunity of the descent, ''so wonderful a manifestation of God's power.'' ''Never shall I forget the sensations of awe, horror, and admiration with which I gazed about me.'' As he draws ever closer to annihilation, the ''old'' fisherman passes beyond terror to a contemplation of the omnipotent beauty of nature in one of its deadliest aspects. Suspended on the ''pathway between Time and Eternity,'' his hair instantaneously turns from black to white, thus affirming the mystical nature of the experience. He is saved through the application of his newly gained Dupin-like powers of ratiocination when he is able to intuit a hidden law of fluid dynamics from the other objects he observes in orbit around him. His incredible salvation and the profundity of the experience link the narrator to the speaker in ''The Pit and the Pendulum'' insofar as both victims bring a certain level of detached self-control to a terrifying situation that would cause lesser minds to succumb to hysteria or madness. The narrator's emergence from the whirlpool in possession of both life and knowledge will be paralleled a decade later by Melville in the final scene of *Moby Dick*. *Epigraph:* ''The ways of God in Nature, as in Providence, are not *our* ways; nor are the models that we frame any way commensurate to the vastness, profundity, and unsearchableness of His works, *which have a depth in them greater that the well of Democritus.*'' Joseph Glanvill, ''Against Confidence in Philosophy and Matters of Speculation,'' *Essays on Several Important Subjects*. *Text: MCW*, II, 574–597; *CWP*, II, 225–247. *Research:* Turner, Arlin. ''Sources of Poe's 'A Descent into the Maelström.' '' *Journal of English and Germanic Philology*, 46 (1947): 298–301; Yonce, Margaret, ''The Spiritual Descent into the Maelström.'' *Poe Newsletter*, 2 (April 1969): 26–29; Finholt, Richard D. ''The Vision at the Brink of the Abyss: 'A Descent into the Maelström' in the Light of Poe's Cosmology.'' *Georgia Review*, 27 (1973): 356–366; Murphy, Christina. ''The Philosophical Pattern of 'A Descent into the Maelström.' '' *Poe Studies*, 6 (June 1973): 25–26; Frank, Frederick S. ''The Aqua-Gothic Voyage of 'A Descent into the Maelström.'' *American Transcendental Quarterly*, 29 (1976): 85–93; Engel, Leonard W. ''Edgar Allan Poe's Use of the Enclosure Device in 'A Descent into the Maelström.' '' *Essays in Arts and Sciences*, 8 (1979): 21–26; Egan, Kenneth V., Jr. ''Descent to an Ascent: Poe's Use of Perspective in 'A Descent into the Maelström.' '' *Studies in Short Fiction*, 19 (1982): 157–162; Seaman, Robert E. ''Lacan, Poe, and the Descent of the Self.'' *Texas Studies in Language and Literature*, 31 (1989): 196–214; Ware, Tracy. '' 'A Descent into the Maelström': The Status of Scientific Rhetoric in a Perverse Romance.'' *Studies in Short Fiction*, 29 (1992): 77–84.

Desfontaine, Pierre François Guydot. (1685–1745). French critic mentioned for his pettiness in ''A Chapter of Suggestions.'' *Text: CWP*, XIV, 189.

"Desultory Notes on Cats." The third of three unsigned sketches appearing in the Philadelphia *Public Ledger* of 19 July 1844. The three pieces were accepted by T. O. Mabbott as from Poe's hand and printed in his edition of the *Tales and Sketches.* Poe commences his little nonsensical history of cats with the observation that ''[c]ats were first invented in the garden of Eden'' and closes with a note on feline value and fashion. ''The serenading cat makes a noise like an infant with the cholic, for which it is often mistaken. Both sexes of cats sport whiskers and moustaches; whether the actual she cats will ever change the fashion, as it applies to them, after it has so long prevailed, is doubtful.'' Mabbott notes Poe's affection for cats as well as the feline presence in the casts of several stories. *See:* Catterina. *Text: MCW,* III, 1095–1098.

The Devil. Character in the short story ''Bon-Bon.'' The devil visits Pierre Bon-Bon for the purpose of snaring his soul but rejects it.

"The Devil in the Belfry." Short story by Poe first published in the Philadelphia *Saturday Chronicle* of 18 May 1839. The satiric sketch in the Irvingesque mode is Poe's version of a Knickerbocker history of the Dutch borough of Vondervotteimittiss, a place of precision, order, neatness, uniformity, and punctuality where ''[t]he buildings themselves are so precisely alike that one can in no manner be distinguished from the other'' and where every single house is decorated with the same carvings of cabbages and timepieces. If the houses are all exactly alike, so are the citizens who are all perfect replicas of one another. The symbol of civic pride and punctuality is the seven-faced town clock which the burghers worship as a paragon of timely perfection. Into this precise and homogeneous world comes a mysterious stranger, ''a very diminutive foreign-looking man,'' who proceeds to disrupt the clockwork serenity of this smug paradise by invading the belfry and causing the town clock to chime thirteen strokes at high noon. Moreover, every clock in town then insists upon striking thirteen in devilish harmony with the bedeviled great clock in the belfry. Since chronometrical perfection is the burghers' source of civic pride, the little devil's disordering of the mechanical rationality that sustains the village is the knell of doom for the town's tidy reputation. Until the little devil in the belfry can be evicted, the borough of Vondervotteimittiss will never know the correct time again, and the cabbage will continue to taste sour. In comic terms, the tale might be seen as a variation of the theme of too much time keeping and reliance on rationality, threats that Poe handles humorously in ''A Predicament'' and melodramatically in ''The Pit and the Pendulum.'' *Epigraph:* ''What o'clock is it?'' Poe identified as an ''Old Saying.'' *Texts: MCW,* II, 362–375; *CWP,* III, 247–257. *Research:* Weber, Jean-Paul. ''Edgar Poe on the Theme of the Clock.'' *La Nouvelle Revue Français*, 68–69 (August-September, 1958): 301–311, 498–508; Claude Richard and Robert Regan Forbes, trans. *Poe: A Collection of Critical Essays*. Englewood Cliffs, NJ: Prentice-Hall, 1967, 80–93; Forbes, J. Christopher. ''Satire of Irving's *A History of New York* in Poe's 'The Devil in the Belfry.' '' *Studies in American Fiction*, 10 (1982): 93–

100; Bachinger, Katrina E. "The Æsthetics of (Not) Keeping in Step: Reading the Consumer Mobocracy of Poe's 'The Devil in the Belfry' against Peacock." *Modern Language Quarterly*, 51 (1990): 513–533.

Dew, Thomas Roderick. (1802–1846). Poe correspondent and frequent contributor to *The Southern Literary Messenger.* In "Autography," Poe comments that Dew's work has qualities of "*boldness* and *weight*. . . . He is remarkably lucid." Both his signature and his work "are heavy, massive, unornamented and *diffuse* in the extreme." *Text: CWP,* IX, 192–194; XV, 166–167. *Research: TPL,* xxii.

Di Broglio. Character in *Politian.* He is Castiglione's father.

Di Broglio, The Duke and Duchess. Characters in the short story "William Wilson." The Duchess is seduced by Wilson in Rome.

Diana. Canine character in the short stories "A Predicament" and "How to Write a Blackwood Article." She is the poodle of Signora Psyche Zenobia.

Dick, Dr. John. (1764–1833). English divine and author of *Dick's Christian Philosopher.* Poe used the title on several occasions to demonstrate that the public popularity of a book is often at odds with its true artistic value. *Text: CWP,* XI, 40; XV, 134.

Dickens, Charles. (1812–1870). English novelist. Poe met and conducted two interviews with Dickens at the United States Hotel in Philadelphia on 7 March 1842 during Dickens's first American visit. Poe also favorably reviewed several Dickens novels. Upon his return to England in 1842, Dickens endeavored unsuccessfully to obtain a London publisher for Poe's short stories. In the early 1840s, Dickens was briefly associated with the *Daily News.* When Poe asked Dickens by letter in 1846 to become the journal's American correspondent, Dickens replied that he was no longer connected with the journal. *See:* "Barnaby Rudge"; "Old Curiosity Shop." *Research:* Mason, Leo. "More about Poe and Dickens." *Dickensian,* 39 (winter 1942–1943): 21–28; Grubb, Gerald C. "The Personal and Literary Relationships of Dickens and Poe." *Nineteenth Century Fiction,* 5 (1950): 209–221; Nisbet, Ada. "New Light on the Dickens-Poe Relationship." *Nineteenth Century Fiction,* 5 (1951): 295–302; Senelick, Laurence. "Charles Dickens and 'The Tell-Tale Heart.' " *Poe Studies,* 6, no. 1 (1973): 12–14; Bracher, Peter. "Poe as a Critic of Dickens." *Dickens Studies Newsletter,* 9 (1978): 109–111; Moss, Sidney P. "Poe's 'Two Long Interviews' with Dickens." *Poe Studies,* 11 (June 1978): 10–12; Tintner, Adeline R. "A Possible Source in Dickens for Poe's 'Imp of the Perverse.' " *Poe Studies,* 18, no. 2 (1985): 25.

"A Dictionary of Greek and Roman Antiquities. Edited by William Smith. By Charles Anthon." Favorable review of the third American edition of Dr. Charles Anthon's classical compendium appearing in *The Broadway Journal* of 12 April 1845. ''In every respect this work is the most valuable of its class—or rather it is a class by itself.'' *Text: CWP,* XII, 129–130. *Research: PJC,* 160.

"Didactics—Social, Literary, and Political. By Robert Walsh." Review and critical notice of a collection of papers on education published in *The Southern Literary Messenger* for May 1836. Poe refers to Walsh as ''one of the finest writers, one of the most accomplished scholars, and when not in too great a hurry, one of the most accurate thinkers in the country.'' Poe objected to the paper on phrenology because it belittled this legitimate metaphysical science. *Text: CWP,* VIII, 321–329. *Research: PJC,* 78, 209.

"Diddling Considered as One of the Exact Sciences." Short story by Poe first published under the title ''Raising the Wind; or, Diddling Considered as One of the Exact Sciences'' in the Philadelphia *Saturday Courier* of 14 October 1843 and reprinted in *The Broadway Journal* of 13 September 1845. The piece is a mock treatise in the manner of Swift as a reference to Brobingnag indicates. Poe's straightfaced tract discusses manifold methods of diddling or stealing, swindling, and petty larceny. The elements of successful diddling are ''minuteness, interest, perseverence, ingenuity, audacity, *nonchalance*, originality, impertinence, and *grin*.'' Various instructive examples of diddling are offered such as obtaining free tobacco by confusing the shopkeeper about the change. Poe apparently felt little sympathy for the victims of diddling since the diddlers emerge as the admirable characters of his case studies of how to diddle for fun and profit. The scientific paper ends with a demonstration of how to compose a phony advertisement requiring those who answer it to make a $50 deposit. Thematically, the satiric sketch of good business is related to ''The Business Man'' and reveals Poe's fascination with hoaxing and duping of any kind in his taking of great delight at the unfolding of successful chicanery. *Epigraph:* ''Hey, diddle diddle,/ The cat and the fiddle.'' Mother Goose nursery rhyme. *Text: MCW,* III, 867–882; *CWP,* V, 210–216. *Research:* Richard, Claude. ''Poe and the Yankee Hero: An Interpretation of 'Diddling Considered as One of the Exact Sciences.' '' *Mississippi Quarterly*, 21 (1968): 93–109; Pollin, Burton. ''Poe's 'Diddling': The Source of Title and Tale.'' *Southern Literary Journal*, 2, no. 1 (1969): 106–111; Reilly, John E. ''Poe's 'Diddling': Still Another Possible Source and Date of Composition.'' *Poe Studies*, 25, nos. 1–2 (1992): 6–9; Whalen, Terrence. ''Poe's 'Diddling' and the Depression: Notes on the Sources of Swindling.'' *Studies in American Fiction*, 23 (1995): 195–201.

Didier, Eugene. (1838–1913). Early Poe biographer and editor. He wrote ''The Life of Edgar Poe,'' a preface to *The Life and Poems of Edgar Allan Poe* (1877) and defended Poe's character in ''Poe: Real and Reputed,'' a piece written for *Godey's Magazine* for April 1894.

Diodorus Siculus. (first century B.C.). Greek historian and author of the *Bibliotheca*, a thousand-year universal history to 60 B.C. He is mentioned in "Loss of Breath." Poe remarks in *Pinakidia* that "the fullest account of the Amazons is to be found in Diodorus Siculus." *Text: CWP,* II, 151; XIV, 42, 113.

"Disinterment." Little-known essay by Poe published in *Alexander's Weekly Messenger* in 1840. Poe defended the medical necessity of the scientific dissection of cadavers and exhumation when necessary. The essay was not included by Harrison in the *Collected Works. Research:* Brigham, Clarence. "Edgar Poe's Contribution to *Alexander's Weekly Messenger.*" *Proceedings of the American Antiquarian Society*, 52 (April 1942): 107; *PLL,* 160.

Disraeli, Benjamin. (1804–1881). English politician and novelist. He was the author of *Vivian Grey*. Poe's friend Lambert Wilmer cited Disraeli's writings as a strong influence in an article on Poe in the Baltimore *Daily Commercial* of 23 May 1866. Wilmer recalled that Poe had spoken admiringly about Tennyson's poetry and Disraeli's prose. "Among prose authors, Ben. Disraeli was his model." *Text: CWP,* II, 156, 168, 181, 202, 223; X, 47, 132; XVI, 157.

D'Israeli, Isaac. (1766–1848). English author remembered for *Curiosities of Literature*, a work well known to Poe. *Text: CWP,* VIII, 204–205; XIV, 56; XVI, 110–111. *Research:* Hudson, Ruth L. "Poe and D'Israeli." *American Literature*, 8 (1931): 402–416; West, Muriel. "Poe's 'Ligeia' and Isaac D'Israeli." *Comparative Literature*, 16 (1964): 19–28.

"Dissertation on the Importance of Physical Signs in the Various Diseases of the Abdomen and Thorax. By Robert W. Haxall, M.D." Review of a 108-page medical pamphlet appearing in *The Southern Literary Messenger* for October 1836. Poe judges the work "nearly faultless." "The most important and altogether the most original portion of the essay is that relating to the fever called *Typhoid*." *Text: CWP,* IX, 164–166.

"The Divine Right of Kings." Poem signed "P." appearing in *Graham's Magazine* for October 1845. J. H. Whitty speculated that the poem was written by Poe to Mrs. Frances Sargent Osgood. Mabbott included the poem in his edition of Poe's verse and further speculated that "Ellen King," the lady to whom the poem is addressed, was Mrs. Osgood. The poem has three quatrain stanzas and puns seriously on "King" and subject vassal. "O! would she deign to rule my fate,/ I'd worship Kings and kingly state,/ And hold this maxim all life long,/ The King—*my* King—can do no wrong." *Text: MCW,* I, 382–384. *Research:* Whitty, James Howard. "Discoveries in the Uncollected Poems of Edgar Allan Poe." *Nation*, 27 January 1916, 105–106.

Doane, Bishop George Washington. (1799–1859). American churchman and poet discussed briefly in "Autography." "Bishop Doane of New Jersey is somewhat more extensively known in his clerical than in a literary capacity, but has accomplished much more than sufficient in the world of books to entitle him to a place among the most noted of our living men of letters." *Text: CWP,* XIII, 16; XV, 256–257.

"The Doctor." A critical notice of a biography of Dr. Daniel Dove appearing in *The Southern Literary Messenger* for July 1836. Poe's review is severe as he inquires into the book's possible multiple authorship. He is "of the opinion that The Doctor is precisely—nothing . . . a tissue of bizarre and disjointed rhapsodies whose general meaning no person can fathom." Its "typographical queerity" suggests a madman or Laurence Sterne. *Text: CWP,* IX, 66–69.

Doctor D____. Character in the short story "The Facts in the Case of M. Valdemar." He attends the dying Valdemar.

Doctor F____. Character in the short story "The Facts in the Case of M. Valdemar." He attends the dying Valdemar.

Dodson, Richard W. Minor American poet. His "A Christmas Carol" is quoted by Poe in *Marginalia* as a blatant example of plagiarism from Felicia Hemans. *Text: CWP,* XVI, 141–142.

D'Oliva, Mademoiselle. Parisian actress. She bore a resemblance to Queen Marie Antoinette. In his review of N. W. Wraxall's *Posthumous Memoirs*, Poe recites the anecdote of this lady being bribed to impersonate Her Majesty to dupe Cardinal de Rohan. *Text: CWP,* IX, 181–183.

Dollar Newspaper. Philadelphia newspaper that awarded a prize of $100 for "The Gold-Bug" and published the story in installments beginning on 21 June 1843. *See:* "The Gold-Bug."

"The Domain of Arnheim, or the Landscape Garden." Sketch first published in the *Columbian Lady's and Gentleman's Magazine* for March 1847. The story is an enlarged version of "The Landscape Garden." The tale features evocative descriptions of a misty and mysterious landscape, a panorama of strange and exotic beauty created by the narrator's wealthy and artistic friend Ellison, Poe's paragon aesthete. Ellison is a man not unlike one side of Edgar Allan Poe who is "profoundly enamored of music and poetry" and who applies his wealth and talents to the construction of a picturesque and private paradise "which still is nature in the sense of the handiwork of the angels that hover between man and God." Ellison's name for his romantic domain is Arnheim, a physical and sensuous Eden reminiscent of Coleridge's Xanadu "upspringing confusedly from amid all, a mass of semi-Gothic, semi-Saracenic architecture, sustaining itself by miracle in mid-air.'' The story contains references to Madame de Staël and William Beckford, creator of *Vathek* and the opulent fantasy world of Fonthill Abbey. The vision of pleasure evoked by Ellison's domain strongly influenced the writing of J. K. Huymans's novel of self-induced paradise, *À Rebours* [Against the grain]. *Epigraph:* Giles Fletcher, ''Christ's Victorie on Earth.'' (Poe used the same epigraph for ''The Landscape Garden.''). *See:* ''The Landscape Garden.'' *Text: MCW,* III, 1266–1285; *CWP,* VI, 176–186. *Research:* Hess, Jeffry A. ''Sources and Æsthetics of Poe's Landscape Fiction.'' *American Quarterly*, 22 (1970): 177–189; Mize, George E. ''The Matter of Taste in Poe's 'Domain of Arnheim' and 'Landor's Cottage.' '' *Connecticut Review*, 6, no. 1 (1972): 93–99; Kehler, Joel R. ''New Light on the Genesis and Progress of Poe's Landscape Fiction.'' *American Literature*, 47 (1975): 173–183; Horn, Andrew. '' 'A Refined Thebaid': Wealth and Social Disengagement in Poe's 'The Domain of Arnheim.' '' *ESQ: A Journal of the American Renaissance*, 27 (1981): 191–197.

Don Quixote. A 1605 novel by Miguel de Cervantes. Poe received a gift copy from John Allan. Poe's adversary Thomas Dunn English published *The Adventures of Don Key Haughty* in 1848. In this Cervantian satire, Don Key Haughty has a jail encounter with an unnamed poet, ''a melancholy-looking little man, in a rusty suit of black,'' obviously a profile of Poe. *See:* Cervantes, Miguel Saavedra de.

Donne, John. (1571–1631). English metaphysical poet. Poe's attitude toward Donne's verse regards it as stylistically marred and overdidactic. In discussing Christopher Pearse Cranch, he criticizes the conceits of Donne and Cowley as ''[e]uphuisms beyond redemption—flat, irremediable, self-contented nonsensicalities.'' Elsewhere, in his review ''Old English Poetry,'' he comments, ''No general error evinces a more thorough confusion of ideas than the error of supposing Donne and Cowley metaphysical in the sense wherein Wordsworth and Coleridge are so. With the two former ethics were the end—with the two latter the means.'' *Text: CWP,* X, 44; XII, 140; XV, 69; XVI, 139. *Research: PJC,* 169–170.

The Doom of the Drinker. Novel by Poe's adversary Thomas Dunn English, published in 1843. The novel portrays Poe as a drunken critic and berates his plagiaristic habits: ''He made no ceremony in appropriating the ideas of others when it suited his turn; and as a man, was the very incarnation of treachery and falsehood.'' *See:* English, Dr. Thomas Dunn.

Doré, Gustav. (1832–1883). French artist and illustrator. He illustrated ''The Raven.''

Dostoevsky, Feodor. (1821–1881). Russian novelist. He was fascinated by Poe, especially his tales involving crimes of inexplicable perversity and double personalities at war with themselves. Such works as *Crime and Punishment* (1866), *The Insulted and the Injured* (1867), *The Double* (1846), and *Notes from the Underground* (1864) exhibit Dostoevsky's creative debt to Poe. Calling Poe "an enormously talented writer," Dostoevsky brought him to the attention of the Russian reading public by publishing critical articles on him in the journal *Wremia*, where he lauded Poe's power to persuade the reader to believe in the most extraordinary events through the use of ordinary details. Dostoevsky's own most memorable characters, such as the young murderer Raskolnikov in *Crime and Punishment* are Poe-esque portrayals of self-contradition, tormented pride, and dangerous antisocial behavior. Dostoevsky studied Poe's artful and artless murderers, noting particularly his ability to create physical environments that reflected their warped psychologies. As Poe had done before him, Dostoevsky would often define a character in terms of the circumscribed physical space he inhabits. Thus, Roderick Usher's confining and decaying mansion is mirrored in the decrepit one-room garret of Raskolnikov. Dostoevsky's shrewd and almost compassionate detective Porfiry Petrovitch, the inspector of police in *Crime and Punishment*, is endowed with the intellectual acuity of C. Auguste Dupin to which Dostoevsky adds a highly developed moral consciousness. *Research:* Astrov, Vladimir. "Dostoievsky on Edgar Allan Poe." *American Literature*, 14 (1942): 70–74; Estrada, Ezequiel M. "Balzac, Poe y Dostoiewsky." *Revista do Livro*, 7 (September 1957): 23–28; Purdy, S. B. "Poe and Dostoyevsky." *Studies in Short Fiction*, 4 (1967): 169–171; Harap, Louis. "Poe and Dostoevsky: A Case of Affinities." In *Weapons of Criticism: Marxism in America and the Literary Tradition*, ed. Norman Rudich. Palo Alto, CA: Ramparts Press, 1976, 271–285; Burnett, Leon. "Dostoevsky, Poe, and the Discovery of Fantastic Realism." In *F. M. Dostoevsky (1821–1881): A Centenary Collection*. Colchester, United Kingdom: University of Essex, 1981, 58–86.

Doucet, Father Edward. Jesuit priest. St. John's College (now Fordham University) was near the Poe cottage. Doucet allowed Poe the use of the college library. *Research: PLL,* 194.

Dow, Jesse Erskine. (1809–1850). Casual acquaintance of Poe and a writer of sea tales. He had been aboard the USS *Constitution* as a naval officer and wrote "Sketches from the Log of Old Ironsides" for *Burton's Gentleman's Magazine* in 1839 during Poe's editorship. Poe included his signature in "Autography," acknowledging "a fine imagination, which as yet is undisciplined, and leads him into occasional bombast." *Text: TPL,* xxii-xxiii; 295–297, 345–347.

Downes, Commodore John. American naval officer. Poe quoted from Downes's correspondence in which he gave his support to Reynolds's plans for an expedition to the South Seas. Poe agreed with Downes that, "It is our *duty*, holding as we do a high rank in the scale of nations, to contribute a large share to that aggregate of useful knowledge, which is common property of all.'' *See:* ''Report of the Committee on Naval Affairs, to Whom Were Referred Memorials from Sundry Citizens of Connecticut Interested in the Whale Fishing.''

Downing, Jack. Pseudonym for Seba Smith, the rustic Yankee writer of letters from ''Major Jack Downing.'' Poe recorded his signature in ''Autography'' but did not comment on it. *See:* Smith, Seba. *Text: CWP,* XV, 172.

Dowson, Ernest. (1867–1900). English poet. His estimation of Poe was high since Poe seemed far ahead of his overdidactic age in his art for art's sake aesthetics. He stated that a line from Poe's poem ''The City in the Sea,'' ''the viol, the violet, and the vine,'' was the most euphonious in all of English poetry. *Research:* Flower, Newman. ''Three Interesting Sinners.'' *Bookman*, 64 (October 1926): 148–155.

Doyle, Sir Arthur Conan. (1859–1930). English novelist, first writer of the modern detective story, and creator of Sherlock Holmes, an immediate descendant of Poe's C. Auguste Dupin. Doyle remarked of Poe's stories that ''each is a root from which a whole literature has developed. . . . Where was the detective story until Poe breathed the breath of life into it?'' Doyle modeled many of Holmes's character traits on Dupin including their tacit denigration of fumbling police methods of investigation and solution, their reliance on superreason or ratiocination, their eccentric and somewhat solitary personalities, and their peculiar attachment to loyal—albeit pedestrian—associates who document the successes of their brilliant mentors. *Research:* ''The Poe Centenary.'' London *Times*, 2 March 1909, 10; Cochran, William R. ''Rummaging Through the Empty House.'' *Baker Street Journal: An Irregular Quarterly of Sherlockiana*, 30 (1980): 212–215; Fleisser, R. P. ''Poe's C. Auguste Dupin and Sherlock Holmes's Initial Again.'' *Baker Street Journal*, 41 (1991): 226–229; Fleissner, Robert F. ''The Cask in the Catacomb: Poe and Conan Doyle Again.'' *ACD: The Journal of the Arthur Conan Doyle Society*, 3 (1992): 116–122.

Draco. (ca. 620 B.C.). Ancient Greek lawmaker noted for the severity of his decrees. He is mentioned in ''William Wilson'' and *Pinakidia*. The Greeks had no ''public inscription of which we can be certified before the laws of Draco.'' *Text: CWP,* III, 302; XIV, 51.

Drake, Joseph Rodman. (1795–1820). American poet who collaborated with his friend Fitz-Greene Halleck on *The Culprit Fay and Other Poems*. *See:* ''Drake-Halleck. The Culprit Fay, and Other Poems, by Joseph Rodman Drake.'' *Text: CWP,* X, 62–64; XI, 17–18, 21, 191; XV, 51–52.

"Drake-Halleck. The Culprit Fay, and Other Poems, by Joseph Rodman Drake." Poe noticed Drake's collection of poetry in *The Southern Literary Messenger* for April 1836. A second review of Fitz-Greene Halleck's *Alnwick*

Castle, with Other Poems also appeared in this same number of *The Southern Literary Messenger*. Hence, the double article is usually referred to as ''The Drake-Halleck Review.'' Poe dissented from the high public opinion that had accorded to both of these poets ''a very brilliant rank in the empire of Poesy.'' ''The Culprit Fay'' falls short of the Ideality attained by Shelley in his fairy poem ''Queen Mab'' and ''is utterly destitute of any imagination whatsoever.'' Poe's review commences with his thoughts on poetry and the current state of literary criticism in America and contains a definition of poetry that is exclusively aesthetic. ''Poesy is the sentiment of Intellectual Happiness here, and the Hope of a higher Intellectual Happiness hereafter.'' The review also contains a satiric poem mocking Drake's style and was printed in part by Mabbott in his edition of the poems as ''Parody on Drake.'' *See:* ''Alnwick Castle, with Other Poems''; ''A Few Words about Brainard.'' *Text: CWP,* VIII, 275–318. *Research: MCW,* I, 301–302; *PLB,* 49–50; *PJC,* 138–154.

"The Drama." (1). Two laudatory reviews of the acting of Anna Cora Mowatt in two productions, Tobin's *The Honeymoon* and *The Bride of Lammermoor,* appearing in *The Broadway Journal* of 19 July 1845 and 26 July 1845. Mowatt's ''noble acting'' was the sole worthy thing about *The Honeymoon,* a play that Poe labels ''a wretched affair [, a] palpable plagiarism of the worst demerits of 'The Taming of the Shrew.' '' As Lucy Ashton in this inferior dramatization of the Scott novel, Poe finds Mowatt to be intense and graceful. *See:* Mowatt, Anna Cora. *Text: CWP,* XII, 184–192. *Research: PJC,* 377–378.

"The Drama." (2). A dramatic notice appearing in *The Broadway Journal* of 2 August 1845. Poe reviewed the acting successes of Mrs. Anna Cora Mowatt as the Duchess in *Faint Heart Never Won Fair Lady* and as Katherine in *Katherine and Petruchio.* Poe asserted that ''she is destined to attain a very high theatrical rank. With the one exception of mere physical force, she has all the elements of a great actress.'' But he also displayed his distaste for Shakespeare's marriage farce, *The Taming of the Shrew*, writing of the skit *Katherine and Petruchio* that it was ''absolutely beneath contempt—a mere jumble of unmeaning rant, fuss, whip-smacking, crockery-cracking, and other Tom-Foolery.'' *Text: CWP,* XII, 210–212. *Research:* Fagin, N. Bryllion. ''Poe—Drama Critic.'' *Theatre Annual* (1946): 23–28.

"The Drama." (3). An unsigned humorous news item about rats infesting a New York theater appearing in the column ''The Drama'' in *The Broadway Journal* of 1 November 1845. Because Poe was then the sole editor, Mabbott assigned the paragraph to him. ''The well-known company of rats at the Park Theatre understand, it is said, their cue perfectly. . . . By long training they know precisely the time when the curtain rises, and the exact degree in which the audience is spellbound by what is going on. At the sound of the bell they sally out; scouring the pit for chance peanuts and orange-peel.'' *Text: MCW,* III, 1244–1245.

"The Drama of Exile and Other Poems: By Elizabeth Barrett Barrett." Poe's enthusiastic review of Elizabeth Barrett's collected poems was published in two installments in *The Broadway Journal* of 4 and 11 January 1845. Poe attributed ''Homeric force'' to her story of Adam and Eve. With her poem ''The Vision of Poets,'' Poe objected to its length and ''the didacticism of its design.'' Generally, her poems confirm that ''[h]er sense of art is pure in itself.'' In the 11 January segment of the review, Poe inserted four lines of his own composition by rewriting one of Miss Barrett's quatrains, a five-line imitation included in Mabbott's edition of the poems: ''Hear the far generations, how they crash/ From crag to crag down the precipitous Time,/ In multitudinous thunders that upstartle/ Aghast, the echoes from their cavernous lairs/ In the visionary hills!'' *Text: CWP,* XII, 1–35; *MCW,* I, 377–378. *Research: PJC,* 356–364; Boos, Florence and William Boos. ''A Source for the Rimes of Poe's 'The Raven': Elizabeth Barrett Browning's 'A Drama of Exile.' '' *Mary Wollstonecraft Journal,* 2, no. 2 (1974): 30–31.

Drayton, William. (1776–1846). Philadelphia judge and casual acquaintance who occasionally aided and encouraged Poe. Poe's *Tales of the Grotesque and Arabesque* are dedicated to Drayton. *Research: TPL,* xxiii.

"A Dream." Lyric poem in four quatrains first published in 1827 in *Tamerlane and Other Poems* and in the collection *Al Aaraaf, Tamerlane, and Minor Poems* in 1829. Because the poet is haunted by memories of ''a dream of joy departed,'' the poem is similar in theme to ''The Raven.'' Entrapped within his reverie, the poet cannot discover the distinction between the dream and the reality; his faculties are clouded ''with a ray/ Turned back upon the past.'' The poet-critic Richard Wilbur identified the source as Byron's lyric ''I Would I Were a Careless Child.'' *Text: MCW,* I, 79–80; *CWP,* VII, 19. *Research:* Wilbur, Richard. *Poe: Complete Poems.* New York: Dell, 1959, 122–123.

"The Dream, and Other Poems. By the Hon. Mrs. Norton." Review of a collection of poetry appearing in *Graham's Magazine* for January 1841. Poe sees Mrs. Norton as the successor to Felicia Hemans. ''Mrs. Norton is unquestionably—since the death of Mrs. Hemans—the Queen of English song. . . . If Mrs. Norton had written nothing before, this volume would have established her claim to be the first of living poetesses.'' *Text: CWP,* X, 100–105.

"A Dream within a Dream." Poem by Poe first published in *The Flag of Our Union* of 31 March 1849. The poet speculates about the extreme difficulty—perhaps the impossibility—of distinguishing between the dream and the reality. The first stanza terminates in a statement of resolution: ''*All* that we see or seem/ Is but a dream within a dream.'' The second stanza expresses this same assertion as an unresolved question: ''Is *all* that we see or seem/ But a dream within a dream?'' *Text: MCW,* I, 450–452; *CWP,* VII, 16. *Research:* Pollin, Burton R. ''Poe in Clavell's *Shogun: A Novel of Japan.*'' *Poe Studies,* 16 (1983): 13.

"Dream-Land." Lyric poem in five stanzas first published in the June 1844 issue of *Graham's Magazine* and again in *The Broadway Journal* of 28 June 1845. The opening and closing stanzas are identical, thus implying the poet's arrival and decision to remain in ''Dream-Land.'' The dream-voyager has reached an extraterrestrial place ''[w]here an Eidolon named Night'' reigns over a realm somewhere beyond time and space. He beholds a forsaken landscape of restless seas, chasms and caves, enormous forests, and ''mountains toppling evermore/ Into seas without a shore.'' The psychic terrain is struck through with gothic imagery: ghouls dwelling by dismal tarns and pools, shapes of dark memory, a general sense of loss and anguish. Like ''The City in the Sea,'' ''Dream-Land'' is about the final moment of perception of a world on the edge of collapse. Yet the voyage the poet has made has brought him to a perception of the beauty within the horror, ''a peaceful, soothing region . . . an Eldorado'' that can never be apprehended by the rational restraints of the waking state. ''Never its mysteries are exposed/ To the weak human eye unclosed.'' *Text: MWC,* I, 342–347; *CWP,* VII, 89–90. *Research:* Bailey, James O. ''The Geography of Poe's 'Dreamland' and 'Ulalume.' '' *Studies in Philology,* 45 (1948): 512–523; Reece, James B. ''Poe's 'Dream-Land' and the Imagery of Opium Dreams.'' *Poe Studies,* 8 (1975): 24; Postema, James. ''Edgar Allan Poe's Control of Readers: Formal Pressures in Poe's Dream Poems.'' *Essays in Literature,* 18 (1991): 68–75.

"Dreams." Poem first published by Poe's brother, Henry Poe, in *The North American, or, Weekly Journal of Politics, Science, and Literature* of 19 May 1827. The poem sadly acknowledges the chasm that separates the pleasures of the dream life from the pain of ''cold reality.'' The poet concludes that he can only be happy when he enters into the dream world: ''*I have been* happy, though in a dream./ I have been happy—and I love the theme.'' Moreover, such happiness exists because the dreamscape transforms reality by endowing it with a ''vivid coloring of life.'' *Text: MCW,* I, 67–69; *CWP,* VII, 11.

Dreiser, Theodore. (1871–1945). American novelist and author of *An American Tragedy* (1925). Several critics have persuasively argued that Dreiser kept the example of Poe in mind in writing the murder scene in the novel. *Research:* Kehl, Del G. ''*An American Tragedy* and Dreiser's Cousin, Mr. Poe.'' *Rocky Mountain Review of Language and Literature,* 32 (1978): 211–221; Riggio, Thomas P. ''American Gothic: Poe and *An American Tragedy.*'' *American Literature,* 49 (1978): 515–532.

Drummummupp, Rev. Doctor. Character in the short story ''The Man That Was Used Up.'' He is minister of the church where the narrator encounters Miss Tabitha T.

Dryden, John. (1631–1700). English poet and dramatist. The savage force of his satire impressed Poe who referred to "the bold, vigorous, and sonorous verse, the biting sarcasm, the pungent epigrammatism, the unscrupulous directness" of Dryden's lines in "The Quacks of Helicon—A Satire." *Text: CWP,* II, 374; VIII, 323; IX, 91; X, 183–184; XIV, 48, 58; XVI, 47, 76. *Research: LET,* I, 175.

Du Bartas, Guillaume Salluste. (1544–1590). French sonneteer and soldier. In his "Mr. Griswold and the Poets" Poe refers to him as "the once world-renowned Du Bartas—him of the 'nonsense verses' " and mentions Du Bartas's nonsense poetry in his laudatory review of R. H. Horne's *Orion. Text: CWP,* XI, 159, 259.

Du Solle, John Stevenson. (1810–1876). Editor of the Philadelphia *Spirit of the Times* and casual friend of Poe. Of Poe's savage skills as a reviewer, Stevenson commented: "If Mr. P. had not been gifted with considerable gall, he would have been devoured long ago by the host of enemies his genius has created." His signature in "Autography" suggests that Stevenson was a poet of talent. "As a poet, he is entitled to higher consideration. Some of his Pindaric pieces are unusually good, and it may be doubted if we have a better *versifier* in America." *Text: CWP,* XV, 219. *Research: PLB,* 198, 230; *TPL,* xxiii; *MNR,* 211.

Duane, William, Jr. (1808–1882). Poe correspondent and contributor to *The Southern Literary Messenger* during Poe's editorship. On 15 October 1844, Duane wrote an irate letter to Poe berating him for failing to return a borrowed issue of *The Southern Literary Messenger. Research:* Bandy, W. T. "Poe, Duane, and Duffee." *University of Mississippi Studies in English,* 3 (1982): 81–95; *TPL,* xxiii, 474–475.

Dubourg, The Misses. Poe's London boarding school tutors while residing in England in 1815. Their school was located at 146 Sloane Street, Chelsea. *Research:* Chase, Lewis. "Poe's School in Chelsea." *Times Literary Supplement,* 27 April 1916, 201–202. *Research: LTP,* 61–64; *MNR,* 17–18.

Dubourg, Pauline. Character in the short story "The Murders in the Rue Morgue." She is a laundress who gives testimony about the victims.

"The Duc de L'Omelette." Short story originally entitled "The Duke de L'Omelette" and first published in the Philadelphia *Saturday Courier* of 3 March 1832. The story is one of several Poe tales of the horrors and wonders of gourmet dining that leads the diner to a Satanic encounter. In this respect, the story is related to "Bon-Bon." Supping alone on a rare delicacy of ortolan or bobolink, the Duc dies and finds himself in the presence of his satanic majesty who orders him to strip. Upon arriving in hell, he finds it to be a lavish apartment filled with statuary and sumptuous paintings, but a single uncurtained window curbs the Duc's palate with a lurid vista of the hellfires just beyond the pleasure chamber. And seated on an ottoman in the apartment is Satan himself. To avoid the damnation that awaits just outside the window, the Duc plays a game of cards with the devil and cheats the fiend by slipping a card. *Epigraph:* ''And stepped at once into a cooler clime.'' William Cowper's *The Task*. *Text: MCW,* II, 31–41; *CWP,* II, 197–202. *Research:* Hirsch, David H. ''Another Source for Poe's 'The Duc de L'Omelette.' '' *American Literature*, 38 (1937): 532–536; Carson, David L. ''Ortolans and Geese: Origin of Poe's 'Duc de L'Omelette.' '' *College Language Association Journal*, 8 (1965): 277–283; Hirsch, David H. '' 'The Duc de L'Omelette' as Anti-Visionary Tale.'' *Poe Studies*, 10 (1978): 36–39; Clifton, Michael. ''Down Hecate's Chain: Infernal Inspiration in Three of Poe's Tales.'' *Nineteenth Century Fiction*, 41 (1986): 217–227.

Duffee, Francis Harold. Philadelphia businessman and amateur author. He accused Poe of collusion with the prize committee in the awarding of $100 for ''The Gold-Bug.'' In the Philadelphia *Daily Forum* of 27 June 1843, Duffee referred to the story as ''A Decided Humbug.'' *Research: TPL,* 419–424; 431–432.

"The Duke de L'Omelette." Original title of the short story ''The Duc de L'Omelette.'' *See:* ''The Duc de L'Omelette.''

Dumas, Alexandre. (1803–1870). French novelist of adventure books and author of *Comte de Monte-Cristo*. Dumas claimed that Poe had met him in Paris in 1832 and taken up residence in his house. *Text: CWP,* XVI, 157. *Research:* DeTernant, Andrew. ''Edgar Allan Poe and Alexandre Dumas.'' *Notes & Queries*, 162 (28 December 1929): 456; Roberts, W. ''A Dumas Manuscript. Did Edgar Allan Poe Visit Paris?'' *Times Literary Supplement*, 21 November 1929, 978; Mabbott, Thomas Ollive. ''Dumas and Poe.'' *Times Literary Supplement*, 2 January 1930, 12; MacPherson, H. D. ''Poe and Dumas Again.'' *Saturday Review of Literature*, 22 February 1930, 760.

Dumas, Paul. Character in the short story ''The Murders in the Rue Morgue.'' He is a physican who gives medical evidence as to the cause of death in the double murder.

Dundergutz. Character mentioned in the short story ''The Devil in the Belfry.'' He is the bogus author of the treatise *Oratiunculæ de Rebus Præter-Veteris*.

Dunderheads. Members of the Folio Club and contributing authors to the collection of tales. Poe observed that, ''The Folio Club is, I am sorry to say, a mere Junto of *Dunderheadism*. I think too the members are quite as ill-looking as they are stupid. I also believe it is their settled attention to abolish literature, subvert the Press, and overturn the Government of Nouns and Pronouns.'' Poe's roster of imaginary members of this imaginary literary society included Mr. Snap, the President, and nine other members as follows: Mr. Convolvulus Gondola, De Rerum Naturâ, Esqr., Mr. Solomon Seadrift, Mr. Horribile Dictû, Mr.

Blackwood Blackwood, Mr. Rouge-et-Noir, and two unnamed Dunderheads, ''a very little man in a black coat with very black eyes'' and ''a stout gentleman who admired Sir Walter Scott.'' *See:* ''The Folio Club;'' *Tales of the Folio Club.*

Dupin, André-Marie-Jean-Jacques. (1783–1865). French orator described by Poe in *Marginalia* as one who '' 'spoke, as nobody else, the language of everybody;' and thus his manner seems to be exactly conversed in that of the Frogpondian Euphuists.'' Poe thus berated the belabored style of Bostonian transcendentalists. The name of the clear-headed French orator furnished Poe with the name of his lucid detective, Monsieur Dupin. *Text: CWP,* X, 134; XVI, 172.

Dupin, C. Auguste. Poe's detective and ratiocinating crime-solver. He is the major character in the short stories ''The Purloined Letter,'' ''The Murders in the Rue Morgue,'' and the ''Mystery of Marie Rogêt.'' He resides at No. 33 Rue Dunôt, Faubourg St. Germain. Had Poe only written these tales of the master sleuth, he would have carved a place for himself in literary history. Dupin is part logician, part romantic poet, and part metaphysician, but his supreme crime-solving gift is his imagination, which enables him to identify with the criminal mind. He is a recluse who takes refuge in the exotic and the peculiar but also possesses a certain level of involved consciousness that allows him to enter freely into the mundane and the practical to crack cases that baffle everyone else including the police. His sharpest mental weapon is ''ratiocination,'' a higher form of reasoning that permits Dupin to detect what others have overlooked or dismissed as unimportant. Dupin shares this ''wild fervor and vivid freshness of imagination'' with a host of fictional detectives from Dostoevsky's Porfiry Petrovitch to Conan Doyle's Sherlock Holmes to Will Graham in Thomas Harris's 1981 novel *Red Dragon. Research:* Bandy, William T. ''Who Was Monsieur Dupin?'' *Publications of the Modern Language Association*, 79 (1964): 509–510; Brophy, Brigid. ''Detective Fiction: A Modern Myth of Violence?'' *Hudson Review*, 18 (1965): 11–30; Jones, Buford, and Kent Ljungquist. ''Monsieur Dupin: Further Details on the Reality behind the Legend.'' *Southern Literary Journal*, 9, no. 1 (1976): 70–77; Propp, William W. ''A Study in Similarity: Mycroft Holmes and C. Auguste Dupin.'' *The Baker Street Journal: An Irregular Quarterly of Sherlockiana*, 28 (1978): 32–35; Dameron, J. Lasley. ''Poe's Auguste Dupin.'' In *No Fairer Land: Studies in Southern Literature before 1900*, ed. J. Lasley Dameron and James W. Mathews. Troy, NY: Whitston, 1986, 159–171; Van Leer, David. ''Detecting Truth: The World of the Dupin Tales.'' In *New Essays on Poe's Major Tales*, ed. Kenneth Silverman. Cambridge: Cambridge University Press, 1993, 65–91.

Durand, Asher Brown. (1796–1886). American landscape painter and member of the ''Hudson River School.'' Poe refers to his ''exquisite picture, 'An Old Man's Recollections' '' in his review of Hoyt's ''A Chaunt of Life, and Other Poems.'' *Text: CWP,* XII, 195; XV, 37.

Duval, Henry. Character in the short story "The Murders in the Rue Morgue." He is a silversmith who testifies that the voice he heard was Italian.

Duyckinck, Evert Augustus. (1816–1878). New York litterateur and editor at Wiley & Putnam's publishing house. His editorial tasks kept him in constant contact with Poe, Hawthorne, Melville, and many other important authors. He made the selections for the edition of Poe's *Tales* published in 1845. Despite its critical success, Poe was irked by Duyckinck's story choices. Poe felt that the latter's emphasis on the ratiocinative works inadequately represented his full virtuosity. In his portrait of Duyckinck in "The Literati of New York City," Poe remarked, "In character he is remarkable, distinguished for the bonhomie of his manner, his simplicity, and single-mindedness, his active beneficence, his hatred of wrong done even to any enemy, and especially for an almost Quixotic fidelity to his friends." *Text: CWP,* XIII, 142; XIV, 73; XV, 58–61, 264. *Research:* Wells, Daniel A. " 'Bartleby the Scrivener': Poe and the Duyckinck Circle." *Emerson Society Quarterly*, 21 (1975): 35–39.

E

Eames, Charles. (1812–1867). Editor of the New York weekly journal, the *New York World*. He printed the revised version of ''Ligeia.'' *Research: TPL,* xxiii; 502–503.

Earle, Pliny. (1809–1892). Physician and amateur poet. He offered a poem to Poe's *Penn Magazine*. Poe included his signature in ''Autography'' with a brief praise of his work as a writer who ''has not only distinguished himself by several works of medical and general science, but has become well known to the literary world, of late, by a volume of very fine poems.'' *Text: CWP,* XV, 230.

"Early Naval History of England." Review of Southey's historical study published in *The Southern Literary Messenger* for September 1835. The review reflects Poe's high opinion of Southey as a writer. ''Southey is a writer who has few equals anywhere, either in purity of English prose, or in melody of immortal verse. He is great in every department of Literature which he has attempted.'' *Text: CWP,* VIII, 48–49.

East Broadway (number 195). Poe address in New York City. Poe resided here in May 1845.

Eaton, Major John Henry. (1790–1856). Secretary of war under Andrew Jackson. Poe saw him in Washington in July 1829 and was also casually acquainted with Cadet John Eaton Henderson at West Point. *Research: MNR,* 48–49.

Edgeworth, Maria. (1767–1849). English novelist. She is quoted in ''Fifty Suggestions'' and compared with Catherine M. Sedgwick in ''The Literati of New York City.'' ''Miss Edgeworth is the more acute, the more inventive and the more rigid. Miss Sedgwick is the more womanly.'' *Text: CWP,* VIII, 261; XIV, 184; XV, 109.

"The Edinburgh Review, No. CXXIV, for July 1835." Poe reviewed the contents of the American edition in *The Southern Literary Messenger* for December 1835. He covered nine articles on a variety of subjects including poetry, history, politics, and travel and showed some interest in Article III by Captain Thomas Boteler, Royal Navy, on ''A Voyage of Discovery to Africa and Arabia, Performed in His Majesty's Ships Leven and Barracouta.'' *Text: CWP,* VIII, 82–89.

"Editorial Miscellany." A brief peevish note appearing in *The Broadway Journal* of 9 August 1845. Poe responded to a note appearing in the *New York Morning Express* from the New York correspondent of the *Cincinatti Gazette*. The correspondent had called attention to ''a flare-up in *The Broadway Journal*, which prevented the appearance of one number a week or two since.'' Poe's rejoinder: ''What does he mean by his pet phrase, 'a flare-up'? There has been *no* flare-up.'' *Text: CWP,* XII, 224–225.

Edmunds. Character mentioned in *The Narrative of Arthur Gordon Pym*. Near Edmunds's well, Pym accidentally encounters his grandfather just before going to sea.

Egaeus. Character in and narrator of the short story ''Berenice.'' He becomes madly desirous of possessing Berenice's teeth and pries them from her mouth before burying her alive.

***Eighteen Forty Four.* (numeric title: *1844*).** Novel published in serial form in the New York *Evening Mirror* in September and October 1844 by Dr. Thomas Dunn English, Poe's bitter enemy. A novel of political intrigue, the book is also a savage caricature of Poe who is satirized in the main character, Marmaduke Hammerhead. He is a talentless hack writer who plagiarizes, pontificates, and drinks heavily. Hammerhead's career ends in the Utica insane asylum for ''confirmed madmen'' where he babbles about his literary fame and threatens to kill everyone in the institution. *Research:* Hurley, Leonard B. ''A New Note on the War of the Literati.'' *American Literature*, 7 (1936): 376–394; *PLB,* 237–238; *PLL,* 200.

Eiros. Character in the short story ''The Conversation of Eiros and Charmion.'' He gives Charmion an account of the end of the world.

"Eldorado." Poem first published in *The Flag of Our Union* of 21 April 1849. The poem is a four-stanza ballad with each stanza containing six staccato lines perfectly accenting a journey on horseback. The questing knight, the pilgrim shadow, and the unfinished search and task to which the knight, now grown old, has dedicated himself are in the medieval Arthurian tradition. But Poe's knight seeks neither the grail nor a guardian dragon nor a distressed maiden but a fabulous place. The name *Eldorado* means "gilded one," and the knight's quest is for the golden man in his city of gold. But the quest has cost him both youth and enthusiasm and has now brought him to the rim of mortality. The true nature of the quest may lie in the heroic striving rather than any arrival or attainment. Thus, the shade encourages the knight to press on "Over the Mountains of the Moon,/ Down the Valley of the Shadow" beyond all earthly limits. Although Poe disliked allegory, the poem invites allegorical interpretation if the knight can be said to represent the artist and his solitary quest for absolute and ideal beauty. *Text: MCW,* I, 461–465; *CWP,* VII, 123. *Research:* Coad, Oral. "The Meaning of Poe's 'El Dorado.' " *Modern Language Notes*, 59 (1944): 59–61; Pollin, Burton R. "Poe's 'Eldorado' Viewed as a Song of the West." *Prairie Schooner*, 46 (1972): 228–235.

"Eleonora." Short story first published in Carey and Hart's annual *The Gift: A Christmas and New Year's Present for 1842* and again in *The Broadway Journal* of 24 May 1845. Like the other narrators of Poe's "love" stories, the first-person voice of the tale is obsessed with the strange beauty of a dying woman, in this case, his cousin Eleonora. For fifteen years the two have lived together innocently and alone in the Valley of Many-Colored Glass. When they finally acknowledge their passion for one another, Eleonora dies, leaving the narrator only with his pledge of deathless love. As the years pass, he is drawn to a second woman, Ermengarde, whom he marries despite the fact that his vow to Eleonora that "[he] would never bind [him]self in marriage to any daughter of Earth" is broken. In the end, soothing voices absolve him of his choice to remarry and assure him that all will be explained in heaven. "Eleonora" shares some themes and situations with "Berenice" and "Ligeia" but lacks the first story's gothic violence and the second story's cadaverous climax. The conclusion to "Eleonora" poses a problem since it is never clear why the protagonist should be granted a dispensation from his violated vow. If Eleonora forgives him, then the only plausible explanation must be that her desire for his happiness transcends any feeling of betrayal. This idealized conception of love that will later be manifested to the narrator in heaven has apparently already been given to Eleonora in death. *Epigraph:* "Sub conservatione formæ specificæ salva anima" [Under the protection of a specific form, the soul is safe] in Victor Hugo's *Notre-Dame de Paris* (attributed by Poe to Raymond Lully). *Text: MCW,* II, 635–647; *CWP,* IV, 236–244. *Research:* Baskett, Sam S. "A Damsel with a Dulcimer: An Interpretation of Poe's 'Eleonora.' " *Modern Language Notes*, 78 (1958): 332–338; Snow, Sinclair. "The Similarity of Poe's 'Eleonora' to Bernadin de Saint-Pierre's *Paul et Virginie*." *Romance*

Notes, 5 (1963): 40–44; Pollin, Burton. ''The Motto of Poe's 'Eleonora': Its Source and Significance.'' *DIP*, 38–53; Robinson, E. Arthur. ''Cosmic Vision in Poe's 'Eleonora.' '' *Poe Studies*, 9 (1976): 44–46; Bachinger, K. E. ''How Sherwood Forest Became the Valley of Many-Colored Grass: Peacock's *Maid Marian* as a Source for Poe's 'Eleonora.' '' *American Notes & Queries*, 24, nos. 5–6 (1986): 72–75.

Eleonora. Character in the short story ''Eleonora.'' She is the narrator's first wife, and like other Poe heroines, ''she had been made perfect in loveliness only to die.''

Eliot, Thomas Stearns. (1888–1965). American poet and critic. Perhaps as a result of the influence of Freudian theory, Eliot held a divided opinion of Poe and his debatable achievement. Somewhat sarcastically, Eliot declared that Poe had ''the intellect of a highly gifted young person before puberty.'' Eliot saw in Poe an example of the artist without sufficient awareness of the culture and tradition necessary to the nurturing of the individual talent. He also saw in Poe an extreme case of confusion between the events of art and the travails of life. Because ''the symbolism of nightmare has its reference in the psychological ailment of Poe,'' his tales and poems are wholly lacking in the ''objective correlative'' or proper artistic expression of the emotion through artistic distancing. On the other hand, Poe's use of images and symbols to suggest rather than to define is a technique that anticipates Eliot's dream imagery in ''The Wasteland.'' Finally, Poe's willingness to borrow and transform other poets' work seems to anticipate Eliot's dictum: ''Immature poets imitate; mature poets steal.'' *Research:* Eliot, T. S. ''From Poe to Valéry.'' *Hudson Review*, 2 (1949): 327–342; McElderry, B. R., Jr. ''T. S. Eliot on Poe.'' *Poe Newsletter*, 1–2 (1969): 32–33; Osowski, Judith. ''T. S. Eliot on 'Poe the Detective.' '' *Poe Newsletter*, 3 (December 1970): 39; Auerbach, Gunter. ''Von Poe zu Eliot.'' In *Zur Aktualität T. S. Eliots*, ed. Helmut Viebrock and Armin Paul Frank. Frankfort: Suhrkamp, 1975, 56–91; Smith, Grover. ''Eliot and the Ghost of Poe.'' In *T. S. Eliot: A Voice Descanting: Centenary Essays*, ed. Shyamal Bagchee. London: Macmillan, 1990, 149–163.

"Elizabeth." Unpublished acrostic poem that appears in the album of Elizabeth Rebecca Herring, Poe's cousin. Mabbott dated the poem circa 1829. The poem contains the adage '' 'Always write first things uppermost in the heart,' '' an echo of the advice that Sir Philip Sidney gives to himself in the opening sonnet of *Astrophil and Stella*, '' 'Fool,' said my muse to me, 'look in thy heart and write.' '' *Text: MCW*, I, 147–149.

"Elizabeth Frieze Ellet[t]." Poetic profile included in Griswold's *The Female Poets of America*. She was ''the writer of 'Teresa Contarini,' a five-act tragedy, which had considerable merit, but was withdrawn after its first night of representation at the Park.'' In ''Autography,'' Poe commended her abilities as a translator. ''As a translator from the Italian, she has acquired an enviable reputation.'' *See:* Ellet, Elizabeth Fries. *Text: CWP,* XIII, 214; XV, 207; *PLB,* 211–217.

"The Elk." Travel essay and landscape sketch published in the annual *The Opal: A Pure Gift for the Holy Days* for 1844. Poe describes the beauties of the Wissahiccon, a brook that runs into the Schuylkill River near Philadelphia. ''Flowing in England, it would be the theme of every bard.'' He observes of American rural tourism in general, ''The Edens of the land lie far away from the track of our own most deliberate tourists.'' *See:* ''Morning on the Wissahiccon.'' *Text: MCW,* III, 860–867; *CWP,* V, 156–162. *Research: LET,* I, 253, 254.

"Elkswatawa; or the Prophet of the West. A Tale of the Frontier." Critical review of James French's novel appearing in *The Southern Literary Messenger* for August 1836. Poe gives a lengthy synopsis or a ''dry compendium,'' as he calls it, of this romance of Tecumseh and his brother Elkswatawa. Although their portraits ''appear to us well drawn,'' the novel as a whole is too imitative of Cooper and Scott to please Poe totally. *Text: CWP,* IX, 116–126.

Ellet, Elizabeth Fries. (1818–1877). Poet, translator, and New York bluestocking socialite. She was in love with Poe, but love turned to hate when he rejected her advances and returned her passionate letters. Poe's opinion of Ellet late in life forcefully states the relationship: ''The most malignant and pertinacious of all fiends—a woman whose loathsome love I could do nothing but repel with scorn.'' As leader of a bluestocking coterie, she continued to plague Poe in life and after death. After his rejection by Sarah Helen Whitman, an embittered Poe condemned ''the pestilential society of literary women. They are a heartless, unnatural, venomous, dishonorable set.'' Griswold printed Poe's opinion of her tragedy ''Teresa Contarini'' and her magazine articles that seemed to be ''hashed up for just so much money as they [would] bring.'' *See:* ''Elizabeth Fries Ellet[t]''; ''Frances Sargent Osgood.'' *Text: CWP,* VIII, 138–142; XI, 159–160. *Research:* Reece, James B. ''A Reexamination of a Poe Date: Mrs. Ellet's Letters.'' *American Literature*, 42 (1970): 157–164.

Ellis, Powhatan. (1790–1863). Brother of Charles Ellis, John Allan's business partner. As U.S. senator from Mississippi, he recommended Poe's appointment to the U.S. Military Academy on 13 March 1830. *Research: TPL,* xxiv.

Ellis, Thomas. The son of John Allan's business partner, Charles Ellis. Ellis was a boyhood friend of Poe who was much drawn to Poe's pranks and escapades. Ellis recalled that Poe ''once saved me from drowning'' after throwing young Ellis ''into the falls headlong.'' He estimated Poe's gambling debts at the University of Virginia to be in excess of $2,500. He authored a reminiscence of Poe for the *Richmond Standard* of 7 May 1881. *Research: TPL,* xxiv, 26–27, 49–50; *MNR,* 24.

Ellis & Allan. The Richmond business firm in which Poe's guardian, John Allan, was a partner with Charles Ellis. *Research: TPL,* xv, 41–43.

Ellison. Character in the short story "The Domain of Arnheim." He is the narrator's friend and a wealthy aesthete who has devoted himself to creating the ideal landscape plot as his private domain of beauty.

Ellison, Mr. Seabright. Character mentioned in the short story "The Domain of Arnheim." He is the rich ancestor of the narrator's friend who has insisted that his estate accumulate interest for a full century.

Ellsler, Fanny. (1810–1884). American ballerina and amateur poet. In Poe's opinion, her reputation was based on wealth. Although "Fanny Ellsler has been lauded ad infinitum, she can scarcely be compared with a poet of real talent such as Frances Sargent Osgood." *Text: CWP,* XI, 239; XIII, 114, 181.

Embury, Emma C. (1806–1863). Minor New York poet and novelist who wrote under the nom de plume "Ianthe." In his sketch of her in "The Literati of New York City," Poe called her "one of the most meritorious of our female *litterateurs*." Her handwriting in "Autography" told Poe that "[s]he is one of the most nervous of our female writers, and is not destitute of originality—that rarest of all qualities in a woman, and especially in an American woman." *Text: CWP,* XV, 90–91, 197–198. *Research: TPL,* 349, 351, 359, 606, 657.

Emerson, Ralph Waldo. (1803–1882). American essayist and philosopher of transcendentalism. In a literary conversation with William Dean Howells, he disparagingly referred to the poet Poe as "the jingle man" and found Poe's lack of "moral principles" unacceptable. Poe disliked Emerson's nebulous metaphysics and transcendental pontifications, declaring at one point, "His present role seems to be the out-Carlyling of Carlyle." Gleefully referring to all transcendentalists as "Frogpondians," Poe claimed that the transcendental party's chief trait was confusion. "They could not define their own position and it cannot be expected that I can define them exactly." In spite of Poe's fascination with the "transcendental unity" of the cosmos as depicted in *Eureka*, he would find himself at odds with Emerson's metaphysics, although, in actuality, Poe had only limited exposure to the major documents of the transcendentalist credo. Poe included an analysis of Emerson's signature in "Autography," declaring that "Mr. Ralph Waldo Emerson belongs to a class of gentlemen with whom we have no patience whatever—the mystics for mysticism's sake. . . . The best answer to his twaddle is *cui bono*? . . . To whom is it a benefit? If not to Mr. Emerson individually, then surely to no man living." *Text: CWP,* IV, 218; XI, 15, 189; XIV, 179; XV, 260; XVI, 100; XVI, 122. *Research:* Mabbott, T. O. "Poe and Emerson." *Notes & Queries*, 197 (December 1952): 566; Griffith, Clark. " 'Emersonianism' and 'Poeism': Some Versions of the Romantic Sensibility." *Modern Language*

Quarterly, 22 (1961): 125–134; Mulqueen, James E. "The Poetics of Emerson and Poe." *Emerson Society Quarterly*, 55 (1969): 5–11; Garner, Stanton. "Emerson, Thoreau, and Poe's 'Double Dupin.' " In *Poe and His Times: The Artist and His Milieu*, ed. B. F. Fisher IV. Baltimore: Edgar Allan Poe Society, 1990, 130–145; *PLL*, 264–265.

Emmons, William. (1792–?). American orator who excelled in patriotic subjects. In "Autography," we have the vague description that "the orator is bold, dashing, and chivalrous." *Text: CWP*, XV, 163.

Empedocles. (490–430 B.C.). Greek philosopher. He is supposed to have died by hurling himself into the crater of the volcano Mount Ætna. In *Pinakidia*, Poe explains his two principles of *principium amicitiæ* and *principium contentionis* as attraction and repulsion. Poe may have associated the Empedoclean fatal leap with the universal return to nothingness in *Eureka*. *Text: CWP*, XIV, 67. *Research:* Ketterer, David. "Empedocles in *Eureka*: Addenda." *Poe Studies*, 18, no. 2 (1985): 24–25.

"England in 1835. Being a Series of Letters Written to Friends in Germany, During a Residence in London and Excursions into the Provinces. By Frederick Von Raumer." A favorable review of a historical study appearing in *The Southern Literary Messenger* for July 1836. "Let this book of Von Raumer's be read with attention, as a study, and *as a whole*. . . . The book is the most valuable addition to our stock of knowledge about England and her institutions which America has ever received." *Text: CWP*, IX, 53–64.

English, Dr. Thomas Dunn. (1819–1902). First an ardent friend, then an ardent foe, of Poe, English was a doctor and an amateur poet. He edited the New York monthly *The Aristidean* in which he reviewed Poe's work. Mutual animosity began in 1843 when Poe mocked English's poems in public, and English sought revenge by featuring Poe in his novel *The Doom of the Drinker* (1843). Poe and English quarreled violently and came to blows in 1846, then waged unrestricted literary war when Poe published a scurrilous sketch of English in *Godey's Lady's Book* for July 1846 and held him up to mild ridicule in "The Literati of New York City," remarking in his sketch of English, "No spectacle can be more pitiable than that of a man without the commonest school education busying himself in attempts to instruct mankind on topics of polite literature." Poe sued English for libel and defamation of character on 23 July 1846 after English had retaliated with a fiery "Reply" in the New York *Evening Mirror*. In the opinion of the biographer Hervey Allen, it was "the English controversy more than any other which tarnished Poe's good name. Had it not been for that, we should now hear very much less about Poe's drinking." English would continue to excoriate Poe in his writings for the remainder of his life. *Text: CWP*, XV, 64–66. *Research:* Dedmond, Francis B. "Poe's Libel Suit against T. D. English." *Boston Public Library Quarterly*, 5 (January 1953): 31–37; *PLB*, 231–

233; Gravely, William H., Jr. ''Poe and Thomas Dunn English: More Light on a Probable Reason for Poe's Failure to Receive a Custom-House Appointment.'' In *Papers on Poe: Essays in Honor of John Ward Ostrom*, ed. Richard P. Veler. Springfield, OH: Chantry Music Press at Wittenberg University, 1972, 165–193; Thomas, Dwight. ''Poe, English, and *The Doom of the Drinker*: A Mystery Resolved.'' *Princeton University Library Chronicle*, 40 (1979): 257–268.

"An Enigma." Riddling poem first published in the *Union Magazine of Literature and Art* for March 1848 under the title ''Sonnet'' and retitled by Griswold ''An Enigma.'' The poem is a light and humorous sonnet with an odd rhyme scheme (ABABBCCB CDDBDD), which may be a structural lampoon of the English sonnet's terminal couplet and Italian sonnet's two-part octave-sestet construction. The sonnet is also a name puzzle containing a concealed anagram of Poe's poet friend at the Fordham cottage, Sarah Anna Lewis. Poe made a gift of the sonnet to Mrs. Lewis in a letter of 27 November 1847. Since the subject of the sonnet is a comic lament over the superficiality of periodical poetry, ''Trash of all trash!'' and ''The Owl-downy nonsense that the faintest puff/ Twirls into trunk-paper the while you con it,'' the mocking reference to ''Petrarchan stuff'' is appropriate to the light mood and anagrammatic game-playing. *See:* Lewis, Sarah Anna; ''For the Baltimore Visiter,'' *Text: MCW,* I, 424–426; *CWP,* VII, 110. *Research:*; Bandy, William T. ''Poe's 'An Enigma (or Sonnet), IV.' '' *Explicator*, 20 (December 1961): item 35; *LET,* II, 353.

"Enigmatical and Conundrum-ical." Article by Poe on cryptographic solutions published in *Alexander's Weekly Messenger* of 18 December 1839. Poe challenged readers to submit any cryptograms to him for decipherment.

Enslen, Carl Georg. (1792–1866). German optical scientist mentioned in *Pinakidia* and *Marginalia* for his creation of special spectral effects in *Macbeth. Text: CWP,* XIV, 42; XVI, 35.

Epicurus. (342–268 B.C.). Greek philosopher who taught that pleasure should be the end of all existence. Poe refers to Epicurus in ''Bon-Bon'' and *The Journal of Julius Rodman*. The Devil informs the astonished Pierre Bon-Bon that he is Epicurus himself. *Text: CWP,* II, 140; IV, 16; XVI, 166. *Research:* Basore, John W. ''Poe as an Epicurean.'' *Modern Language Notes*, 25 (1910): 86–87.

"Epigram for Wall Street." Eight lines of light verse attributed to Poe by the scholar T. O. Mabbott and included in his edition of the *Poems*. The verse appeared unsigned in the New York *Evening Mirror* of 23 January 1845. As the first four lines demonstrate, Poe was a capable punster: ''I'll tell you a plan for gaining wealth,/ Better than banking, trade or leases—/ Take a bank note and fold it up,/ And then you will find your money in *creases*!'' *Text: MCW,* I, 378. *Research:* Mabbott, T. O. ''Newly Found Verses Ascribed to Poe.'' *Notes & Queries*, 201 (March 1956): 122.

Epigraphs. More than thirty-five Poe stories and two poems, ''In Youth I Have Known One'' and ''Israfel,'' begin with mottos or epigraphs ranging from nursery rhymes to the Greek and Roman classics. Some epigraphs are obscure or spurious. Poe did not always indicate the specific source in an author's works as is the case with the fictitious epigraph to ''Ligeia'' from Joseph Glanvill. *See* individual tales and poems for the epigraphs and their sources.

Epimanes, Antiochus. Character in the short story ''Four Beasts in One.'' The word is a nickname for ''Antiochus the Madman.'' *See:* ''King Pest.''

The Equerry. Unnamed character in the short story ''Metzengerstein.'' He catches the strange horse ''all smoking and foaming with rage'' and brings the steed to Baron Metzengerstein.

Erasmus, Desiderius. (1466–1536). Dutch humanist and author of *Moriæ Encomium* [The praise of folly] (1516). Several of Poe's reviews refer to the careful Latin of Erasmus. *Text: CWP,* VIII, 49, 104.

"Erato." A notice of William Davis Gallagher's book of verse published in the *The Southern Literary Messenger* for July 1836. Poe praises many of the poems but finds the whole collection ''exceedingly unequal.'' Some poems such as the lengthy ''Wreck of the Hornet'' are tasteless and unmetrical but offer occasional moments of ''the loftiest beauty'' as in the ballad ''They Told Me Not to Love Him.'' *Text: CWP,* IX, 73–75.

Ermengarde. Character in the short story ''Eleonora.'' She is the narrator's ethereal and seraphic second wife.

Esling, Catherine H. *See:* Waterman, Catherine Harbeson. *Text: CWP,* XI, 241–242.

Espy, James Pollard. (1785–1860). American meteorologist and author of *Philosophy of Storms* (1841). Espy propounded a theory of rainmaking to which Poe refers in *Marginalia.* ''The chief portion of Espy's theory has been anticipated by Roger Bacon.'' *Text: CWP,* XI, 163; XVI, 118.

"Estelle Anna Lewis." Poetic profile by Poe included in Griswold's *The Female Poets of America.* ''In summing up the autorial merits of Mrs. Lewis, all critical opinion must agree in assigning her a high, if not the very highest rank among the poetesses of her land.'' *See:* ''The Child of the Sea, and Other Poems.'' *Text: CWP,* XIII, 215–225.

Ethelred. Character in the short story "The Fall of the House of Usher." He is the knight champion who appears in the inset story "The Mad Trist" of Sir Launcelot Canning.

Ethix, Æstheticus. Character in the short story "Lionizing." "He spoke of fire, unity, and atoms; bipart and pre-existent soul; affinity and discord; primitive intelligence and homoomeria."

Etienne, Alexandre. Character in the short story "The Murders in the Rue Morgue." He is a Parisian surgeon who corroborates the testimony of Doctor Paul Dumas as to the cause of death.

"Ettore Fieramosca, or the Challenge of Barletta, An Historical Romance of the Times of the Medici, by Massimo D'Azeglio. Translated from the Italian by C. Edwards Lester." An unenthusiastic review of an English translation of Massimo D'Azeglio's historical romance appearing in *The Broadway Journal* of 9 August 1845. Although it has vivacity and excited movement, the book is "defective in having little of what we understand by the 'autorial comment'—that which adds so deep a charm to the novels of Scott, of Bulwer, or of D'Israeli—most especially to the works of Godwin and Brockden Brown." *Text: CWP,* XII, 223–224.

"Eulalie." Poem first published in *The American Review* for July 1845 and again in *The Broadway Journal* of 9 August 1845. The poem is a bridal song describing how the poet's marriage to "the yellow-haired young Eulalie" brought him consolation from loneliness and "a world of moan." Eulalie derives her beautiful strength from the celestial goddess Astarte to whom Eulalie turns "her violet eye." *Text: MCW,* I, 347–350; *CWP,* VII, 206. *Research:* "The Manuscript of Poe's 'Eulalie.' " *Bulletin of the New York Public Library*, 18 (December 1914): 1461–1463.

Eureka: An Essay on the Material and Spiritual Universe. Cosmological treatise completed in January 1848 and published by the firm of George P. Putnam on 11 July 1848 as *Eureka: A Prose Poem.* A lecture version of the essay's ideas called "The Universe" was delivered on 3 February 1848 at the Society Library in New York. Running to nearly 40,000 words, it is the longest of Poe's nonfictional work. In his preface, Poe singled out as his audience "the dreamers and those who put faith in dreams as the only reality" and dedicated the work "to those who feel rather than . . . those who think." Relying upon the cosmological philosophers and astronomers of his time, especially Pierre Simon Marquis de Laplace (1749–1827) and Friedrich Heinrich Alexander Baron von Humboldt (1769–1859), author of *The Cosmos*, Poe constructed a cosmological synthesis based on mathematics, poetics, and intuition. Poe's universe was a unitary system imagined into existence by a godlike artist and moving inward toward a beautiful last moment of primal nothingness. If Einstein's cosmos is ever expanding and governed by immutable physical laws, Poe's cosmos is ever contracting and governed by sublimely immutable poetic laws. In Poe's view, the poetic imagination is a form of energy similar to gravitational force in the scientific universe. His poetic cosmos is a divine configuration of a single effect tending ever toward a sublime oneness at a point where the spiritual and the material are negatively syncretized. As his general proposition, Poe states: "In the Original Unity of the First Thing lies the Secondary Cause of All Things with the Germ of their Inevitable Annihilation." *Eureka* attempts to establish logical and intuitive connections between the individual soul and the mind of God whose cosmic masterpiece, the universe itself, is held to be "a plot of God." Thematically, the work is also related to Poe's lifelong effort to transcend the limits of death, to eternize the experience of beauty, and to "reach these lands but newly from some ultimate dim Thule." Philosophically, *Eureka* is, in part, an acknowledgment of such matters of faith with Poe as Ligeia's belief in the potency of the divine will to overcome death and the corruption of the flesh. In fact, various passages in *Eureka* sound like quotations from those characters in the poems and short stories who penetrate death's barrier to find the beautiful truth of some great beyond. "Guiding our imaginations by that omniprevalent law of laws, the law of periodicity, are we not, indeed, indulging a hope—that the process we have ventured to contemplate will be renewed forever, and forever, and forever?" In the rhythmical and cyclical creation and destruction of the universe, Poe set forth his concept of highest beauty in final and highest form. In February 1849, *Eureka* was attacked point by point in *The Indicator*, a journal published at Amherst College. *See:* Reynolds, Jeremiah. *Text: CWP,* XVI, 185–354. Harrison's edition of *The Complete Works* included "Poe's Notes to 'Eureka,' " Poe's 'Addenda' to 'Eureka.' " and "Poe's Unpublished Notes Apparently to 'Eureka' "; Benton, Richard P., ed. *Eureka: A Prose Poem by Edgar Allan Poe. New Edition with Line Numbers, Exploratory Essay, and Bibliographical Guide.* Hartford, CT: Transcendental Books, 1973. *Research:* Benton, Richard P., ed. *Poe as Literary Cosmologer: Studies on Eureka: A Symposium.* Hartford, CT: Transcendental Books, 1975; Brooks, Curtis M. "The Cosmic God: Science and the Creative Imagination in *Eureka.*" *American Transcendental Quarterly*, 26 (1975): 60–68; *TPL,* 789; Cantalupo, Barbara. " 'Of or Pertaining to a Higher Power': Involution in *Eureka.*" *American Transcendental Quarterly*, 4, no. 2 (1990): 81–90; *MNR,* 338; Welsch, Susan. "The Value of Analogical Evidence: Poe's *Eureka* in the Context of a Scientific Debate." *Modern Language Studies*, 21, no. 4 (1991): 3–15; Hume, Beverly A. "Poe's Mad Narrator in *Eureka.*" *Essays in Arts and Sciences*, 22 (1993): 51–65.

Euripides. (480–405 B.C.). Ancient Greek tragic dramatist. In his review of Potter's translation of Euripides's dramas, Poe expressed this view of the playwright: "Ardent admirers of Hellenic Literature, we have still no passion for Euripides. Truly great when compared with many of the moderns, he falls immeasurably below his immediate predecessors." Among other shortcomings, Poe called attention to his misuse of the chorus in Greek tragedy. "But the

Chorus of Euripides was not the true and unadulterated Chorus of the purer Greek tragedy. . . . In some instances . . . a female Chorus is permitted by him to make use of grammatical inflexions proper only for males.'' *Text: CWP,* VIII, 43–47; XII, 4, 131; XIV, 62, 65; XVI, 72.

Eveleth, George W. Casual Poe correspondent from 1845 on. He gave his correspondence with Poe to John H. Ingram, Poe's English biographer. He succinctly summed up the argument of *Eureka* by saying, ''Because nothing was, therefore all things are.'' *Research:* Mabbott, Thomas O. ''The Letters from George W. Eveleth to Edgar Allan Poe.'' *Bulletin of the New York Public Library*, 26 (March 1922): 171–195; Wilson, James Southall. ''The Letters of Edgar A. Poe to George W. Eveleth.'' *University of Virginia Alumni Bulletin*, 27 (January 1924): 34–59; Ostrom, John W. ''Two 'Lost' Poe Letters.'' *American Notes & Queries*, 1 (August 1941): 68–69; Miller, John Carl. ''George W. Eveleth Adds His 'Mite.' '' *BPB*, 195–234; TPL, xxiv, 632–633, 672–673, 679–684.

Evening Mirror. New York City newspaper. Poe began his work here as a paragrapher in 1844. On 26 May 1847, the *Evening Mirror* ran an excoriation of Poe's character by Charles Briggs containing strong insinuations of Poe's insanity. *See:* Briggs, Charles F.

"Evening Star." Poem by Poe first published in the collection *Tamerlane and Other Poems* (1827). The lyric ballad is addressed to a distant star. As the poet gazes at the star's ''cold smile,'' he finds it ''Too cold—too cold for me,'' but further contemplation brings him joy since he comes to recognize that the star establishes its illuminated place by a ''distant fire'' that is far more admirable than its cold light. The poem bears some comparison with Keats's sonnet ''Bright Star'' and Thomas Moore's ''While Gazing on the Moon's Light.'' *Text: MCW,* I, 73–74; *CWP,* VII, 15. *Research:* Kilburn, Patrick. ''Poe's 'Evening Star.' '' *Explicator*, 28 (May 1970): item 76.

Everett, Edward. (1794–1865). Distinguished American orator and editor of *The North American Review*. In ''Autography'' Poe wrote of Everett, ''The man who writes thus will never grossly err in judgment or otherwise. We may venture to say, however, that he will not attain the loftiest pinnacles of renown.'' *Text: CWP,* XV, 152–153, 203. *Research: LET,* II, 316, 317.

"Exordium." A group review of various books and authors previously reviewed by Poe appearing in *Graham's Magazine* for January 1842. Poe comments on the work of Cooper, Paulding, Macaulay, and other writers previously noticed, but ''Exordium,'' in the main, is Poe's manifesto on criticism that he refers to as an important science. He insists that literary criticism should be an exact art and protests against ''the frantic spirit of generalization. . . . Our views of literature in general have expanded, we begin to demand the use—to inquire into the offices and provinces of criticism—to regard it more as an art based immoveably in nature, less as a mere system of fluctuating and conventional dogmas.'' *Text: CWP,* XI, 1–8.

F

A Fable for Critics. Book of satiric portraits of various literary personalities by James Russell Lowell and published anonymously in October 1848 by George P. Putnam. It contains the following often-quoted caricature of Poe, a mixture of genius and schmalz. ''There comes Poe, with his raven, like Barnaby Rudge,/ Three-fifths of him genius, and two-fifths sheer fudge,/ Who talks like a book of iambs and pentameters,/ In a way to make people of common sense damn meters,/ Who has written some things quite the best of their kind,/ But the heart somehow seems all squeezed out by the mind.'' Injured by Lowell's derision, Poe, in turn, responded angrily to Lowell's satire in an unsigned review in *The Southern Literary Messenger* for March 1849 by ignoring whatever accuracies were present in the portrait and defending his erudite concern for metrics and scansion. Poe dismissed Lowell's book as ''at once so ambitious and so feeble—so malevolent in design and so harmless in execution.'' *Research: PJC,* 396–397.

"A Fable for the Critics." Lowell's satiric portraits of American authors was reviewed by Poe in *The Southern Literary Messenger* for March 1849. While with *Graham's Magazine*, Poe had received a letter from Lowell in March 1844 prompting him to write a biographical sketch of Lowell for the ''Our Contributors'' series in *Graham's Magazine*. His less-than-cordial review of Lowell's ''Fable'' is Poe's retaliatory response to Lowell's clever characterization of Poe as ''three-fifths of him genius, and two-fifths sheer fudge.'' Poe attacked Lowell's command of metrics, control of structure, and rough versification as well as his pro-abolitionist politics. ''His prejudices on the topic of slavery break out everywhere in his present book. Mr. L. has not the common honesty to speak well, even in a literary sense, of any man who is not a ranting abolitionist.'' *See:* ''Poems by James Russell Lowell'' *Text: CWP,* XIII, 165–175.

Fabricius, John Albert. (1668–1736). German classical scholar whose *Bibliotheca Græca,* ''in which his sole object is to render an account of the *Greek* authors *extant,*'' is mentioned once in *Pinakidia. Text: CWP,* XIV, 68.

"The Facts in the Case of M. Valdemar." Short story published in *The American Review: A Whig Journal* for December 1845 and in *The Broadway Journal* of 20 December 1845. With its emetic climax, the story is one of Poe's most visceral tales and belongs to the tradition of gore-gothic. The story is narrated as the factual case history by a professional mesmerist, ''P——,'' who has conducted a hypnotic experiment on a dying friend, M. Ernest Valdemar. In order to determine if the mesmeric process can forestall death and decomposition, the mesmerist places the moribund Valdemar in a trance just as he is about to expire. Although Valdemar becomes *in articulo mortis,* it is soon clear to the mesmerist that he has succeeded only in delaying the inevitable by seven months, for to awaken Valdemar or bring him out of the trance ''would be merely to insure his instant, or at least, his speedy dissolution.'' Nevertheless, and for reasons that the narrator does not clarify, the decision is made to awaken Valdemar. As his eyes close in death, there is a ''profuse outflowing of a yellowish ichor (from beneath the lids) of a pungent and highly offensive odor.'' Instantaneous decomposition now follows as the body of M. Valdemar ''absolutely rotted away beneath my hands.'' Unlike Hawthorne's treatment of perverse scientific experimentation on human subjects, there is no moral closure in Poe's tale, simply the sickening odor of ''detestable putrescence.'' A letter to *The Broadway Journal* of 1 February 1845 from Dr. A. Sidney Doane describing surgery performed on a patient during ''a magnetic sleep'' provided Poe with a factual source for the tale. *See:* Mesmerism. *Text: MCW,* III, 1228–1244; *CWP,* VI, 154–166. *Research:* Falk, Doris V. ''Poe and the Power of Animal Magnetism.'' *Publications of the Modern Language Association,* 84 (1969): 536–546; Carter, Steve. ''A Possible Source for 'The Facts in the Case of M. Valdemar.' '' *Poe Studies,* 12 (1979): 36; Ware, Tracy. ''The 'Salutary Discomfort' in the Case of M. Valdemar.'' *Studies in Short Fiction,* 31 (1994): 471–480.

"Fairy Land." The full version of this poem in forty-six lines was first published in *Al Aaraaf, Tamerlane, and Minor Poems* in December 1829. Fourteen lines from the poem had appeared in *The Yankee and Boston Literary Gazette* for November 1829. When ''Fairy Land'' was reprinted in the 1831 volume *Poems of Edgar A. Poe,* it had sixty-four lines. The lyric contrasts the eerie beauty of a moonlit landscape filled with ''forms we can't discover'' with the daylight when in ''a labyrinth of light'' these same lunar visions appear mundane and uninspired. ''They use that moon no more/ For the same end as before—.'' The 1831 version is literally a new and different poem addressed to a woman named Isabel. Here, the menacing moons descend upon the pair to blot out the inspiration of starlit ''Fairy Land.'' ''Huge moons—see! wax and wane/ Again—again-again—/ Every moment of the night—/ Forever changing places!/ How they put out the starlight/ With the breath from their pale faces!'' *Text: MCW,* I, 138–142; I, 161–163; *CWP,* VII, 44–45.

"The Fall of the House of Usher." Short story first published in the September 1839 volume of *Burton's Gentleman's Magazine.* The plot of the story is starkly simple and almost elemental like a young hero's journey of initiation or a mysterious visit to the grail castle that holds the secrets of life and death. The unnamed narrator approaches the decaying Usher mansion through a wasteland. He has been summoned to the House of Usher by its master, Roderick Usher, who abides within with his dying twin sister, Madeline. The house itself stands astride a mountain lake or tarn and is made particularly foreboding by the vacant stare of its windows and a nearly invisible crack or fissure that scars the facade. The narrator's sojourn with the Ushers involves him in a series of bizarre and supernatural events for which he has no scientific explanation. He has a conversation with Usher on the total ''sentience of all vegetable things'' and assists Usher with Madeline's ''temporary entombment'' after her apparent death. During a night of violent weather, the narrator reads aloud to Usher from a favorite medieval romance, the ''Mad Trist'' of Sir Launcelot Canning. As he reads, the storm rises—and so does Madeline from her copper-lined coffin in the subterranean burial vaults. At the zenith of the terrible tempest, Usher informs his guest that they have buried her alive and that she now ''*stands without the door.*'' Usher also calls the narrator a ''MADMAN,'' even though the narrator's conduct throughout his residency within the walls of the House of Usher has been consummately rationalistic. The narrator is now made to witness the primal horror as Madeline's walking cadaver falls atop her brother and bears ''him to the floor a corpse, and a victim to the terrors he had anticipated.'' As the sister falls atop the brother, the house itself begins to crumble and collapse on the pair, causing the narrator to flee aghast before he, too, is consumed by the final fall of this fallen world. Barely escaping with his life, the narrator gazes in horrified wonder as ''the deep and dank tarn at [his] feet closed sullenly and silently over the fragments of the *House of Usher.*'' The tale has been the object of diverse interpretation ranging from latent autobiographical and psychographic readings to claims that the story has no profound subtext whatsoever but is simply Poe's ingenious condensation of a gothic horror novel such as Walpole's *The Castle of Otranto*, which also features an architectural collapse at its climax. Because of Usher's loneliness, sensitivity, alienation, his immersion in painting, literature, and music, his secret guilt, and his apparent damnation by forces beyond his control, some critics have argued that the events and characters of the story are intended as parallels with Poe's own acute internal torments, a semiotic parable of the deadly relationship between the artist and his art. Roderick Usher's singular and vaguely incestuous bond with his sister Madeline has also suggested to some readers Poe's maternal and sexual ambivalence that involved him fatally in the search for an ideal woman who would share his private notions of beauty and fulfill all that was missing from his life. Cut off from all external reality and menaced by the enclosing mansion, Usher, the dying artist, lives a parasitic existence—feeding upon himself, his tenuous artistic creations, and finally his sister's very being. Many critical questions remain for those who would probe beyond the gothic surfaces of this tale. What is the "oppressive secret" between brother and sister that the narrator detects but cannot articulate, and why should Usher, himself the victim of progressive madness, refer to the narrator as a "MADMAN"? When Madeline emerges from the tomb, has she become a vampire in some form of the reanimated corpse? Or is her purpose to save or to doom her brother? Or is she just very accomplished at holding her breath? But the most provocative mystery of the house concerns the curse that is causing the mansion's steady decay. Has the narrator been summoned to the dying house to somehow forestall this process of ruination as the grail knight is required to seek out the grail castle to ask the proper question that will heal the maimed king and regenerate the wasteland? Profoundly aware of his dying condition, perhaps Usher has summoned his friend in a desperate attempt to pass on the secret legacy of the precarious palace of art to another living consciousness. Watching the insular universe of Usher collapse upon itself, the narrator may be something more than just a last gothic survivor since he is transformed as well as spared the doom of this fated family; he is, after all, the artist who recalls and retells the saga of the Ushers. The text of the story also contains the first version of the poem, "The Haunted Palace." In his edition of Poe's poems, Mabbott included the couplet written on the brass shield among Poe's poems. *Epigraph:* "Son coeur est un luth suspendu;/ Sitôt qu'on le touche il résonne" [His heart is a suspended lute; as soon as it is touched, it responds]. Pierre-Jean de Béranger, "Le Refus." *See:* "The Haunted Palace." *Text: MCW,* II, 392–422; *CWP,* III, 273–287. *Research:* Abel, Darrel. "A Key to the House of Usher." *University of Toronto Quarterly*, 18 (1949): 176–185; Olson, Bruce. "Poe's Strategy in 'The Fall of the House of Usher.' " *Modern Language Notes*, 75 (1960): 556–559; Bailey, J. O. "What Happens in 'The Fall of the House of Usher'?" *American Literature*, 35 (1964): 445–466; Hoffman, Michael J. "The House of Usher and Negative Romanticism." *Studies in Romanticism*, 4 (1965): 158–168; Butler, David W. "Usher's Hypochondriasis: Mental Alienation and Romantic Idealism in Poe's Gothic Tale." *American Literature*, 48 (1976): 1–12; Frank, Frederick S. "Poe's House of the Seven Gothics: The Fall of the Narrator in 'The Fall of the House of Usher.' " *Orbis Litterarum*, 34 (1979): 331–351; Thompson, G. R. "Poe and the Paradox of Terror: Structures of Heightened Consciousness in 'The Fall of the House of Usher.' " In *Ruined Eden of the Present: Hawthorne, Poe, Melville*. West Lafayette, IN: Purdue University Press, 1981, 313–340; Gargano, James W. " 'The Fall of the House of Usher': An Apocalypse of Vision." *University of Mississippi Studies in English*, 3 (1982): 53–63; Hoeveler, Diane. "The Hidden God and the Abjected Woman in 'The Fall of the House of Usher.' " *Studies in Short Fiction*, 29 (1992): 385–395; Kaplan, Louise J. "The Perverse Strategy in 'The Fall of the House of Usher.' '' In *New Essays on Poe's Major Tales*, ed. Kenneth Silverman. Cambridge: Cambridge University Press, 1993, 45–64; May, Leila S. '' 'Sympathies of a Scarcely Intelligible Nature': The Brother-Sister Bond in Poe's 'The Fall of the House of Usher.' '' *Studies in Short Fiction*, 30 (1993): 387–396.

"Fanny." A three-stanza eighteen-line poem signed ''Tamerlane'' included in Mabbott's edition of the poetry and first published in the *Baltimore Saturday Visiter* of 18 May 1833. The ''Fanny'' of the title has not been positively identified, but the passionate regret of the third stanza suggests an early love, perhaps Sarah Elmira Royster. ''Let memory the boy recall/ Who laid his heart upon thy shrine,/ When far away his footsteps fall,/ Think that he deemed thy charms divine.'' *Text: MCW,* I, 225–226. *Research:* French, John C. ''Poe and the *Baltimore Saturday Visiter*.'' *Modern Language Notes*, 33 (1918): 257–267.

Fatquack, Mr. Character mentioned in short story ''The Literary Life of Thingum Bob, Esq.'' He received sixty-two and a half cents for his domestic novelette the ''Dish-Clout.'' The character is associated with James Fenimore Cooper.

Faulkner, William. (1897–1962). American novelist and short story writer. Both his novels, especially the thriller *Sanctuary*, and his short fiction, tales such as ''Dry September'' and ''A Rose for Emily,'' show the mark of Poe on his imaginative design. *Research:* Stone, Edward. ''Usher, Poquelin, and Miss Emily: The Progress of Southern Gothic.'' *Georgia Review*, 14 (1960): 433–443. Edwards, C. Hines, Jr. ''Three Literary Parallels to Faulkner's 'A Rose for Emily.' '' *Notes on Mississippi Writers*, 7 (1974): 21–25.

The Fay. Silent character in the short story ''The Island of the Fay.'' She is seen by the narrator as she pilots her boat ''into the region of the ebony flood'' and is apparently the last ''of the few gentle Fays who remain from the wreck of the race.''

Fay, Theodore Sedgwick. (1807–1898). Author of the novel *Norman Leslie*, a book repeatedly puffed and praised by the New York *Mirror* and condemned by Poe. In ''Autography,'' Poe's Joseph Y. Z. Miller found Fay's signature ''has an air of swagger about it. There are too many dashes—and the tails of the long letters are too long. . . . It has a wavering, finicky, and over-delicate air, without pretension to either grace or force.'' *See:* ''Norman Leslie. A Tale of the Present Times.'' *Text: CWP,* XV, 173–174, 220. *Research:* Moss, Sidney P. ''Poe and the *Norman Leslie* Incident.'' *American Literature*, 25 (1953): 293–306; *PJC,* 95, 97–98.

Feltspar, Ferdinand Fitz Fossillus. Character in the short story "Lionizing." He is one of the guests at the Prince of Wales' literary banquet and an expert on rocks.

"Female Poets of America." Unsigned review of Rufus W. Griswold's anthology appearing in *The Southern Literary Messenger* for February 1849. The review is possibly, but not certainly, by Poe, and its authorship has been contested as more likely from the pen of Griswold's sycophantic friend John R. Thompson. To elevate the reputation and the sales of his book, Griswold forged a Poe letter that verified Poe's authorship of this favorable review. *Text: CWP,* XI, 156–160.

"Festus: A Poem by Philip James Bailey." Review of a narrative poem published in *The Broadway Journal* of 6 September 1845. Although "we have read it only in snatches," it is "beyond question, a poem of the most remarkable *power* . . . a Vesuvius-cone at least—if not an Ætna—in the literary cosmos." *Text: CWP,* XII, 241–243. *Research: PJC,* 339.

"A Few Words about Brainard." A review of the poetry of John G. C. Brainard appearing in *Graham's Magazine* for February 1842. The review also contains intermittent commentary on the state of American literature and the dubious poetical standing of Joseph Rodman Drake's "The Culprit Fay." Poe believes that "the general merit of our national Muse has been estimated too highly, and that the author of 'The Connecticut River' has, individually, shared in the exaggeration." As an example of second-rate poetry, Poe quotes and dismantles Brainard's "The Fall of Niagara," whose "monstrous assemblages of false imagery" mar a collection holding some very competent poems. *Text: CWP,* XI, 15–24. *Research: PJC,* 281–283.

"A Few Words on Secret Writing." An essay on crytography published in *Graham's Magazine* for July 1841. Poe discusses codes and code breaking in ancient times, the methods of enciphering and deciphering, prints several letters to *Graham's* containing cryptograms from subscribers, and shows a thorough knowledge of the history of cryptography in his references to treatises on the subject by Trithemius, Porta, Vigenere, and P. Nicéron. It is Poe's view "that human ingenuity cannot concoct a cipher which human ingenuity cannot resolve." *See:* "Secret Writing" [three entries]. *Text: CWP,* XIV, 114–149. *Research:* Rosenheim, Shawn James. "The King of the Secret Readers: Edgar Allan Poe and the Cryptographic Imagination." *Dissertation Abstracts International*, 54 (1993): 180A–181A (Yale University).

Fibalittle, Mrs. Character mentioned in the short story "The Literary Life of Thingum Bob, Esq." She is one of the contributors to the *Lollipop*.

Field, Joseph M. (1810–1856). Editor of the *St. Louis Daily Reveillé*. In the issue of 30 June 1846, he defended Poe against Charles F. Briggs's savage cartoon of Poe's face, remarking that his ''features are not only intellectual, but handsome.'' *Research: TPL,* xxiv, 645–646.

Field, Maunsell Bradhurst. (1822–1875). New York lawyer. He heard Poe's lecture ''The Universe'' on 3 February 1848 and remembered it as ''a rhapsody of most intense brilliancy.'' *Research: TPL,* xxiv.

Fielding, Henry. (1707–1754). English novelist and author of *Tom Jones. Tom Jones* is mentioned in Poe's negative reviews of the novels *Paul Ulric* and *Charles O'Malley, The Irish Dragoon.* Poe appears to have disliked the eighteenth-century picaresque novelists, ranking Dickens superior to the Fielding school and asserting that ''for one Dickens there are five million Smolletts, Fieldings, Marryatts, Arthurs, Cocktons, Bocktons, and Frogtons.'' *Text: CWP,* VIII, 186; XI, 14, 90.

"Fifth Despatch to The Spy." *The Spy* (Columbia, Pennsylvania) of 12 June 1844 contains a dispatch by Poe on street paving using chemically treated wood. *Research: TPL,* 465.

"Fifty Suggestions." Fifty brief, highly epigrammatic observations by Poe done in the style of *Marginalia* and touching a variety of subjects from publishing to politics. The piece was published in *Graham's Magazine* in two parts for May and June 1845. The tone is often vitriolic and cynical. On publishers: ''K——, the publisher, trying to be critical, talks about books pretty much as a washerwoman would about Niagara Falls or a poulterer about a phoenix'' [Suggestion XXIX]. On friendship, Poe wrote mordantly: ''As far as I can understand the 'loving our enemies,' it implies the hating our friends.'' *Text: The Brevities: Fifty Suggestions,* ed. Burton R. Pollin. New York: Gordian Press, 1985, 475–507; *CWP,* XIV, 170–185. *Research:* Hatvary, George. ''The Whereabouts of Poe's 'Fifty Suggestions.' '' *Poe Studies,* 4, no. 2 (1971): 47.

Fisher, E. Burke. (1799–1859). Editor of the Pittsburgh *Literary Examiner.* Poe was a contributor until Fisher offended him by making editorial changes to his work. *Research: LTP,* 361; *TPL,* xxiv.

Fitzgerald, F. Scott. (1896–1940). Poe is present in ''The Diamond as Big as the Ritz'' and in the character of Amory Blaine in *This Side of Paradise.* According to A. Robert Lee, ''Poe, like Fitzgerald later, was noted for—could be said to have originated a tradition of—fictions of women within a literary culture understood to be inimical to them.'' *Research:* Tuttleton, James W. ''The Presence of Poe in *This Side of Paradise.*'' *English Language Notes,* 3 (1966): 284–289; Aldrich, Elizabeth Kaspar. '' 'The Most Poetical Topic in the World': Women in the

Novels of F. Scott Fitzgerald.'' In *Scott Fitzgerald: The Promises of Life*, ed. A. Robert Lee. London: Vision Press, 1989; New York: St. Martin's Press, 1989, 131–136; Meyers, Jeffrey. ''Poe and Fitzgerald.'' *London Magazine*, August–September 1991, 67–73.

The Flag of Our Union. Boston weekly journal owned by Frederick Gleason. Among other pieces, it printed Poe's poem ''For Annie'' in the March 1849 number. The newspaper announced in April 1849 that it could no longer pay for whatever articles and poetry it published. *Research: TPL,* 793–802.

Flaminius, M. Antonius. [Marcantonio Flaminio]. (1498–1550). Italian poet whose Latin verse is quoted as an example of the ''concord of sound and sense'' in *Pinakidia* and *Marginalia*. *Text: CWP,* XIV, 61; XVI, 38. *Research: BRE,* 75.

Flaxman, John. (1755–1826). English sculptor and artist. Discussing mimesis in art, Poe cites the work of Flaxman as a demonstration of how ''[a]n outline frequently stirs the spirit more pleasantly than the most elaborate picture.'' *Text: CWP,* IX, 201; XI, 84. *Research: LET,* I, 221.

"Flora and Thalia: Or Gems of Flowers and Poetry. Being an Alphabetical Arrangement of Flowers, with Appropriate Poetical Illustrations." Appreciative review of a floral book of the hours ''By a Lady'' appearing in *The Southern Literary Messenger* for June 1836. The poems accompanying the floral illustrations are all ''above mediocrity.'' Poe also liked the format of the book in which flowers ''supply the place of a watch or clock.'' *Text: CWP,* IX, 43–44.

Folio Club. *See:* Dunderheads; *Tales of the Folio Club.*

"The Folio Club." Poe's unpublished introduction to the formation of the imaginary literary society and its membership. Mabbott included the 1833 piece in manuscript in his edition of the tales. *See:* Dunderheads. *Text: CWP,* II, xxxvi–xxxix; *MCW,* II, 200–206.

"For Annie." Poem by Poe first published in *The Flag of Our Union* of 28 April 1849 and in the *Home Journal* of 28 April 1849. Written to Annie Richmond on his conquest at last of ''the fever called 'Living.' '' the poem has autobiographical content in its allusions to Annie's pledge to attend Poe's deathbed. In addition, Annie's presence in the poem is tenderly maternal, comforting Poe with a gentle and protective embrace: ''She tenderly kissed me,/ She fondly caressed,/ And then I fell gently/ To sleep on her breast.'' *Text: MCW,* I, 452–461; *CWP,* VII, 111. *Research:* Hogue, L. Lynn. ''Eroticism in Poe's 'For Annie.' '' *Poe Symposium, Emerson Society Quarterly*, 60 (1970): 85–87; Armistead, J. M. ''Poe and Lyric Conventions: The Example of 'For Annie.' '' *Poe Studies*, 8 (1975): 1–5;

Bachinger, Katrina. ''Poe's 'For Annie.' '' *Explicator*, 43, no. 1 (1984): 33–35; Robbins, J. Albert. ''A New Manuscript of Poe's 'For Annie.' '' *Studies in Bibliography: Papers of the Bibliographical Society of the University of Virginia*, 39 (1986): 261–265; *TPL*, 798–804; *MNR*, 400–401.

"For the Baltimore Visiter." A sixteen-line riddling poem signed ''P.'' and published in the *Baltimore Saturday Visiter* of 2 February 1833. The poem was attributed to Poe by T. O. Mabbott in his edition of the *Poems* and given the title ''Enigma.'' Each line of the poem poses a question about a particular author. Thus, line 1, ''The noblest name in Allegory's page,'' yields Spenser; line 2, ''The hand that traced inexorable rage,'' yields Homer; and so on. Also in the questions list are Euripides, Shelley, Pope, and Shakespeare ''[i]n boldness of design surpassing all.'' *See:* ''An Enigma.'' *Text: MCW*, I, 220–222.

Forgues, Emile Daurand. (1813–1889). Early Poe translator. He translated ''A Descent into the Maelström'' in *Revue Britannique* for September 1846 and ''The Murders in the Rue Morgue'' for *Le Commerce* of 12 October 1846 and published an appreciative essay on Poe in October 1846. *Research:* Moss, Sidney P. ''Poe as Probabalist in Forgues' Critique of the *Tales*.'' *Poe Symposium, Emerson Society Quarterly*, 60 (1970): 4–13.

Fort Independence. Military post on Castle Island in Boston Harbor. Poe was stationed here from 26 May 1827 to the end of October 1827 with Battery H, First Artillery, when he entered the United States Army. *Research:* Snow, Edward Rowe. ''The Facts behind 'The Cask of Amontillado.' '' *Mysterious New England*. Boston: Yankee, Inc., 1971, 204–205.

Fort Moultrie. Military installation located on Sullivan's Island in the harbor of Charleston, South Carolina. Poe was posted here with Battery H, First Artillery, in November 1827. The Fort Moultrie-Fort Sumter area furnished detail for several of Poe's tales, especially ''The Gold-Bug.'' *See:* Military Service.

Fortress Monroe. United States Army military installation located at Old Point Comfort, Hampton, Virginia. Poe arrived here with Battery H in December 1828. *See:* Military Service.

Fortunato. Character in the short story ''The Cask of Amontillado.'' He is the victim of the story and a drunken fool.

"The Fortune Hunter; or, The Adventures of a Man About Town. A Novel of New York Society. By Mrs. Anna Cora Mowatt." Review of a novel appearing in *The Broadway Journal* of 2 August 1845. Poe quotes the whole of the novel's chapter four and promises a fuller notice at a later date. *Text: CWP*, XII, 207–210.

Foscolo, Ugo. (1778–1827). Italian poet whose *I Sepolcri* [Sepulchres] is mentioned in connection with Mrs. Ellet's verse. *Text: CWP,* VIII, 138–139.

Foster, George G. (?-1850). Amateur poet and travel writer characterized in "Autography" as "evincing a keen sense of the beautiful. . . . It seems, however, to be somewhat deficient in force." Foster was an editor of the satiric magazine *The John-Donkey*. *Text: CWP,* XV, 237. *Research: TPL,* 710.

Foster, Jane Frances. (1823–1911). She attended the wedding of Poe and Virginia on 16 May 1836 while at the Yarrington boarding house. *Research: TPL,* xxv.

Foster, Theodore. New York periodical editor who reprinted British magazines in the United States "for eight dollars any four of the British periodicals for a year." This exploitive practice is mentioned in Poe's exposé "Some Secrets of the Magazine Prison-House." He was also the author of *Practical Phrenology Simplified* (1838). *Text: CWP,* XIV, 160.

Fouqué, Baron Friedrich de la Motte. (1777–1843). German romance writer and author of *Undine* (1811) whose republication Poe reviewed in *Graham's Magazine* for September 1839. Poe rhapsodized on the beauties of the poem, calling it "the finest possible example of the purely ideal. There is little of fancy here, and everything of imagination." The water sprite heroine herself is described in Ligeian terms: "What can be more divine than the character of the soulless Undine?—What more august than her transition into the soul-possessing wife? What can be more intensely beautiful than the whole book?" *Text: CWP,* X, 30–39, 66; XI, 89, 247; XIII, 149; XVI, 48–51, 115–117.

"Four Beasts in One; The Homo-Cameleopard." Short story whose final and revised version was published in one of the final issues of *The Broadway Journal* of 6 December 1845. Poe's first title for the story is "Epimanes," and the first version was published under this title in *The Southern Literary Messenger* for March 1836 and appeared under this title again in *The Tales of the Grotesque and Arabesque* in 1839. The narrator is some sort of historian of antiquity who sets the tale in the Syrian city of Antioch in the year 3830 and guides the reader there to witness some rare spectacle. When they arrive, the streets of Antioch are swarming with wild beasts "entirely without restraint," for leopards, tigers, and lions have been so domesticated that they roam freely through this future world. But the strangest form of bestial behavior is that assumed by King Antiochus who is seen "ensconced in the hide of a beast and doing his best to play the part of a cameleopard," a four-part animal with the head of a man and the tail of a baboon "held aloft by his two principal concubines." So offensively grotesque is the appearance of the cameleopard to the natural animals that they turn on and attack the citizens of Antioch, who in turn pursue the royal four-part beast to the Hippodrome, where he will either be wreathed the victor for his agility of foot or devoured by his furious subjects. Poe's futuristic fantasy has connections with the man-into-ape transformations of the short story ''Hop-Frog'' and the riotous animal absurdities of ''A Tale of Jerusalem.'' The tale contains the mock Latin warsong ''Mille, mille, mille.'' *Epigraph:* ''Chacun a ses vertus'' [Everyone has good qualities]. Prosper Jolyot de Crébillon's *Xerxes*. *Texts: MCW,* II, 117–130; *CWP,* II, 203–213. *Research:* Lecompte, C. '' 'The Homeo-Cameleopard' ou la mort de Dieu.'' *Delta: Revue de Centre d'Études et le Recherche sur les Ecrivains du Sud aux Etats-Unis*, 1 (1975): 83–94; Itoh, Shoko. ''Urbanity in Poe.'' *Chu-Shikoku Studies in American Literature*, 22 (1986): 5–13.

Fourier, François Marie Charles. (1772–1837). French utopian social philosopher and communistic thinker. Poe showed his dispproval of ''the rant and cant'' of ''Fourier-izing'' by referring to such utopian schemes as a form of madness. In ''Fifty Suggestions,'' he so dismissed Fourierism: ''The world is infested, just now, by a new sect of philosophers. . . . Let us call it Insanity at once, and be done with it.'' *Text: CWP,* VI, 199; XIV, 172, 179; XVI, 100.

Fox, Charles James. (1749–1806). English politician and man of letters. Poe recognized his political and oratorical abilities but disparaged Fox's literary skills. ''Mr. Fox with a pen in his hand, and Sir James [Macintosh] on his legs in the House of Commons were, we think, each out of his proper element. We could never read a page of Mr. Fox's writings . . . without feeling that there was a constant effort, a tug uphill.'' *Text: CWP,* VIII, 82–83; IX, 175, 179.

"Fragment of a Campaign Song." Unsigned four lines of patriotic verse attributed to Poe by T. O. Mabbott and published in the *New York Times Saturday Review* of 4 March 1899 by Poe's friend the actor Gabriel Harrison. Mabbott suggests that Poe wrote the song for the presidential campaign of 1844. ''See the White Eagle soaring aloft to the sky,/ Wakening the broad welkin with his loud battle cry;/ Then here's the White Eagle, full daring is he,/ As he sails on his pinions o'er valley and sea.'' *Text: MCW,* I, 340–342.

Frailey, Dr. Charles S. He devised a cypher that Poe published in the second installment of ''Secret Writing'' in *Graham's Magazine* for August 1841 as part of a cryptograph contest. Poe published the solution in *Graham's Magazine* for October 1841. *Text: CWP,* XIV, 135–136, 138–140, 149. *Research: LET,* I, 172–173, 188–189; *TPL,* 333–334.

"Frances Sargent Osgood." Complimentary critical essay on the lady poet appearing in *The Southern Literary Messenger* for August 1849. Poe sees her as ''a worshipper of beauty,'' and because she is so, her verse is graceful, charming, and metrically sound. ''Her imagery is often mixed;—indeed it is rarely otherwise. The epigrammatism of her conclusions gives to her poems, as wholes, the air of being more skilfully constructed than they really are. On the other hand, we look in vain throughout her works for an offense against the finer taste, or against decorum—for a low thought or a platitude.'' *See:* Osgood, Frances [Fanny] Sargent. *Text: CWP,* XIII, 175–193.

Francis, John Wakefield. (1789–1861). Physician who attended the Poes from 1844–1846. There is a sketch of Francis in ''The Literati of New York City.'' ''His professional services and his purse are always at the command of the needy; few of our wealthiest men have ever contributed to the relief of distress so bountifully.'' *Text: CWP,* XV, 25–27. *Research: LTP,* 542, 563, 582; *MNR,* 238, 343.

Frauenhofer, Joseph von. (1787–1826). German astronomer mentioned in Poe's notes to *Eureka.* ''He recently announced that he had discovered a lunar edifice, resembling a fortification, together with several lines of roads.'' *Text: CWP,* XVI, 348.

Freeman, Dr. New York doctor who attended the Poes at the Fordham cottage. *Research: TPL,* xxv.

French, James Strange. (1807–1886). American novelist. Discussing his signature in ''Autography,'' Poe recalled that ''a denunciatory review of [his novel *Elkswatawa*] in the 'Southern Literary Messenger,' some years ago, deterred him from further literary attempts.'' The review was by Poe himself. *Text: CWP,* XV, 219–220. *Research: TPL,* 231–232.

Freneau, Philip. (1752–1832). American poet sometimes called ''The Poet of the Revolution.'' Although Poe refers to Freneau's verse in several reviews, he never expresses any definite opinion about its worth. When Freneau is mentioned, Poe usually uses the reference to accuse others of plagiarism as when Poe charged Thomas Campbell of stealing from Freneau in certain lines of *Gertrude of Wyoming.* *Text: CWP,* XI, 35, 124, 154; XIV, 41; XVI, 77.

Fréron, Elie Catherine. (1719–1776). French literary critic and foe of Voltaire mentioned in ''A Chapter of Suggestions.'' His name evokes ''insufferable disgust'' because of the ''littleness'' of his criticism that can only be ''measured by the greatness of those whom [he] has reviled.'' *Text: CWP,* XIV, 189.

Fricassee. Character in the short story ''Lionizing.'' He is a gourmet and a guest at the Prince of Wales's literary banquet.

Frogpondians. Poe's derogatory name for the New England and Boston literati. Boston itself was ''the Frogpond.'' *Text: CWP,* VI, 231; XVI, 172; Casale,

Ottavio M. ''Poe on Transcendentalism.'' *Emerson Society Quarterly*, 50 (1st Q 1968): 85–97.

Froissart, Monsieur. Character mentioned in the short story ''The Spectacles.'' He is Napoleon Buonaparte Simpson's father.

Froissart, Napoleon Buonaparte. Patronymic name of a character in the short story ''The Spectacles.'' The character traces his descent ''from the immortal author of the 'Chronicles.' '' *See:* Simpson, Napoleon Buonaparte.

Frost, John. (1800–1859). Editor of *Alexander's Weekly Messenger* in Philadelphia and compiler of *The Young People's Book.* He also wrote historical fiction. His journal published several favorable reviews of Poe's tales. The signature in ''Autography'' manifests ''fine taste, sound scholarship, and great general ability.'' *Text: CWP,* XV, 242–243. *Research: TPL,* xxv, 274–275; 282–283.

Frost, Robert. (1874–1963). American poet. He did not exactly dislike Poe, but did sometimes denigrate him as in his judgment that ''Poe was not truly great, his chief feeling was that derived from throwing stones at a tomb.'' Although the two poets are stylistically antithetical, Frost's own poems of terror are not without a certain grotesque element that is reminiscent of Poe. The ominous landscape of ''Desert Places'' and the ghostly tale in verse ''The Witch of Coös'' demonstrate the influence of Poe. *Research:* Dendinger, Lloyd N. ''The Ghoul-Haunted Woodland of Robert Frost.'' *South Atlantic Bulletin*, 38 (1973): 87–94; Angyal, Andrew J., and Kent Ljungquist. ''Some Early Frost Imitations of Poe.'' *Poe Studies*, 9 (1976): 14–16.

"Fugitive Pieces." General title for several poems in *Tamerlane and Other Poems*. Under this heading Poe included all the poems in the volume with the exception of ''Tamerlane.'' *See: Tamerlane and Other Poems.*

Fuller, Frances A., and Metta Fuller. (1826–1902 and 1831–1885, respectively). Poet sisters included by Griswold in his *Female Poets of America*. Poe compliments Griswold on their inclusion, especially because they ''have not had the good fortune to be born in the North.'' *Text: CWP,* XI, 157, 159.

Fuller, Hiram. (1814–1880). Editor of the New York *Evening Mirror*. Fuller sided with Poe's literary enemies Charles Briggs and Dr. Thomas Dunn English when he published their attacks on Poe in the *Evening Mirror* of 26 May 1846 and New York *Morning Telegraph* for 23 June 1846. *See:* ''Reply to Mr. Poe.'' *Text: CWP,* XV, 264. *Research:* Moss, Sidney P. ''Poe, Hiram Fuller, and the Duyckinck Circle.'' *American Book Collector*, 18 (1967): 8–18; *TPL,* xxv, 642–643, 662–663, 689–693, 696–697.

Fuller, [Sarah] Margaret [Ossoli]. (1810–1850). American author and editor. Of Poe's character, she confided to Elizabeth Barrett, "I think he really had no friend. I did not know him, though I saw and talked with him often, but he always seemed to me shrouded in an assumed character." She reviewed the 1845 edition of Poe's *Tales* in the New York *Daily Tribune*, finding them to be "a penetration into the causes of things which leads to original but credible results. Where the effects are fantastic, they are not unmeaningly so." Poe attacked her character and her association with the transcendentalists, but her opinion of Poe's artistry remained high. Reviewing *The Raven and Other Poems*, Fuller commented that his lines "breathe a passionate sadness, relieved sometimes by touches very lovely and tender." Poe's view of her literary ability is expressed in his portrait in "The Literati of New York City" in which he speaks of her style "as one of the very best with which I am acquainted" and quotes from her *Summer on the Lakes* as a demonstration of the fusion of "her literary and her conversational manner. . . . In spite of . . . her frequent unjustifiable Carlyleisms." *Text: CWP,* XV, 73–83. *Research:* Jones, L.C. "A Margaret Fuller Letter to Elizabeth Barrett Browning." *American Literature*, 9 (1937): 70–71; McNeal, Thomas H. "Poe's *Zenobia*: An Early Satire on Margaret Fuller." *Modern Language Quarterly*, 9 (1950): 215–226; Pollin, Burton R. "Poe on Margaret Fuller in 1845: An Unknown Caricature and Lampoon." *Women & Literature*, 5, no. 1 (1977): 47–50; Kimura, Haruko. "Margaret Fuller to Poe." In *Bungaku to America: Ohashi Kenzaburo Kyoju Kanreki Kinen Ranbunshu.* Tokyo: Nanundo, 1980, II, 7–27.

Furneaux, Lieutenant. English sailor and explorer. He accompanied Captain Cook on *The Resolution* and is mentioned in *The Narrative of Arthur Gordon Pym*. *Text: CWP,* III, 165–166.

G

G______, Lieutenant. Character in the short story ''The Gold-Bug.'' This army officer takes the scarabaeus from Legrand shortly after the latter finds it.

G______, The Minister. Character mentioned in the short story ''Metzengerstein.'' He is Baron Frederick Metzengerstein's father.

G______, Monsieur. Character in the short story ''The Purloined Letter.'' He is the bungling and baffled prefect of Parisian police. He also appears in ''The Mystery of Marie Rogêt'' and ''The Murders in the Rue Morgue.''

Gallagher, William Davis. (1808–1894). Author and compiler of *Selections from the Poetical Literature of the West* (1841), an anthology negatively reviewed by Poe. But in ''Autography,'' Poe declared, ''He has the true spirit, and will rise into a just distinction hereafter.'' *Text: CWP,* XV, 223. *Research: TPL,* xxv, 327–328.

Galt, William. (1755–1825). Wealthy Scottish ancestor of John Allan. His estate went to Allan upon his death in March 1825. *Research: TPL,* xxv; *PLL,* 20.

Garcio, Alfonzo. Character in the short story ''The Murders in the Rue Morgue.'' He is an undertaker who swears that he heard the murderer speaking English.

Garnett, James Mercer. (1770–1843). A contributor to *The Southern Literary Messenger*, he wrote under the pseudonym ''Oliver Oldschool'' and was one of the earliest and harshest critics of Poe. In 1835 he informed readers of *The Messenger* that Poe's writing ''has neither wit nor humor. . . . That he may be a 'scholar of the very highest grade' I will not question; but it is not always the best scholars that write best, or have the best taste and judgment.'' *Research: TPL,* xxv-xxvi.

Gauguin, Paul. (1848–1903). French postimpressionist artist. In his Tahitian memoir *Noa Noa*, Gauguin attributed the inspiration for his *Woman with Flower* to ''Ligeia.'' Recalling his early reading of Poe, he wrote: ''Do not get the notion of reading Edgar Allan Poe except in some very reassuring place.'' And on ''The Black Cat,'' ''Beware of reading Edgar A. Poe.'' *Research:* Gauguin, Paul. *The Writings of a Savage*, intro. Wayne Anderson; trans. Eleanor Levieux. New York: Viking Press, 1978.

Gellius, Aulus. (ca. 130–180). Roman writer. He compiled the *Noctes Atticæ* [Attic nights], a collection of excerpts from Greek and Latin authors. Poe mentions the work in *Pinakidia* and Gellius's name in the ridiculing review of *Paul Ulric*. *Text: CWP,* VIII, 204–205; XIV, 48.

"George Balcombe." A long and laudatory review of Nathaniel Beverley Tucker's novel appearing in *The Southern Literary Messenger* for January 1837. Poe explains that he has ''spoken at length of *George Balcombe*, because we are induced to regard it, upon the whole, as *the best* American novel.'' Its psychological intensity and interplay of characters remind Poe of Godwin's *Caleb Williams*. *Text: CWP,* IX, 243–265. *Research: LET,* I, 79, 187; *PJC,* 186–190.

George, Miles. Student acquaintance of Poe at the University of Virginia. He commented on Poe's temperament as ''very excitable and restless, at times wayward, melancholic and morose, but again—in his better moods, frolicksome, full of fun.'' *Research: TPL,* xxvi, 69–70.

"George P. Morris." Review of Morris's volume of poems appearing in *Burton's Gentleman's Magazine* for December 1839. The review was revised and reprinted in *The Southern Literary Messenger* for April 1849 with the title ''National Melodies of America. By George P. Morris, Esq.'' ''Morris is, very decidedly, our best writer of songs—and, in saying this, I mean to assign him a high rank as poet. For my own part, I would much rather have written the best *song* of a nation than its noblest *epic*.'' *Text: CWP,* X, 41–44.

"Georgia Scenes, Characters, Incidents, &c. In the First Half Century of the Republic." Review of Augustus Baldwin Longstreet's book of local sketches appearing in *The Southern Literary Messenger* for March 1836. Poe credits the author with a "penetrating understanding" of the southern character and admires the local humor he finds in such vignettes as "The Gander Pulling." Longstreet used two pseudonyms, "Baldwin" and "Hall." *Text: CWP,* VIII, 257–265. *Research: PJC,* 133.

Gérard de Nerval. (1805–1857). French poet whose life, which was marked by periods of mental derangement, and death under mysterious circumstances are often compared with Poe's. The motif of the double in *Aurélia* and *Les Chimères* invites a further comparison with Poe. *Research:* Lokke, Kari. *Gérard de Nerval: The Poet as Social Visionary.* Lexington, KY: French Forum Publishers, 1987, 14–15.

Gibbon, Edward. (1737–1794). English historian and author of *The Decline and Fall of the Roman Empire.* Gibbon's pessimistic view of history had some intellectual appeal for Poe, who discussed both his style and his theory of decline in "Literary Small Talk" and *Marginalia.* Although the terseness of Gibbon's style and "the peculiar construction of his sentences" were impediments to comprehension on a first reading, his greatness as a historian remained unquestioned. "In his endeavors to *crowd in* his vast stores of research, much of the artificial will, of course, be apparent; yet I cannot see that any other method would have answered as well. . . . It is his *indirectness* of observation, then, which forms the soul of the style of Gibbon, of which the apparently pompous phraseology is the body." *Text: CWP,* VIII, 224, 226–227; X, 2; XIV, 92–93; XVI, 14–17, 111. *Research:* Mabbott, T. O. "Poe's Word 'Porphyrogene.' " *Notes & Queries,* 177 (2 December 1939): 403; Whalen, Terence. "Correcting the Poe Canon: Beverley Tucker's Anecdote on Gibbon and Fox." *English Journal,* 82 (1993): 89–92.

Gibson, Thomas Ware. Poe's cadet roommate at West Point. He remarked on Poe's remarkable memory for reciting prose and verse. Concerning Poe's drinking, Gibson said, "I don't think he was ever intoxicated while at the Academy, but he had already acquired the more dangerous habit of constant drinking." Gibson published his recollections of Poe in *Harper's Magazine* for November 1867. *Research: TPL,* xxvi, 108–109; *PLL,* 46.

Gide, André. (1869–1951). French novelist and literary critic. Like other French writers, Gide became an ardent admirer of Poe and acknowledged him as the originator of "le monologue intérieur." As a young writer, Gide had been introduced to Poe in his correspondence with Paul Valéry and Paul Claudel. Gide's seminal study of Dostoevsky is relevant to his interest in Poe since he analyzes the Russian novelist's settings and characters in the context of perversity and self-torment. Like Poe's protagonists, Dostoevsky's characters are often "profoundly warped by humiliation" and "find satisfaction in the resultant degradation, loathsome though it be." *Research:* Rose, Marilyn Gaddis. " 'Emmanuèle'—'Morella': Gide's Poe Affinities.'' *Texas Studies in Language and Literature*, 5 (1963): 127–137.

Gifford, William. (1756–1826). English critic and editor of the *Quarterly Review*. Poe refers to the ''manifest injustice'' of his bitter criticism of young authors in the Outis correspondence. *Text: CWP,* XII, 84.

"The Gift: A Christmas and New Year's Present for 1836." Poe reviewed the 1836 number of *The Gift*, a popular annual issued by the Philadelphia publishers Cary and Hart in *The Southern Literary Messenger* for September 1835, paying special attention to the engravings. ''Never had Annual a brighter galaxy of illustrious literary names in its table of contents—and in no instance has any contributor fallen below his or her general reputation.'' Poe placed several of his tales in *The Gift*, among them ''William Wilson,'' ''Eleonora,'' ''The Pit and the Pendulum,'' ''The Purloined Letter,'' and a reprinting of ''MS. Found in a Bottle.'' *Text: CWP,* VIII, 50–51.

Gil Blas. Picaresque novel by Alain René Le Sage (1668–1747). Poe received a copy from John Allan. *Gil Blas* is mentioned in the short story ''The Angel of the Odd.'' In his scathing review of Morris Mattson's *Paul Ulric*, Poe implied that numerous specific details of the hero's escapades had been taken from *Gil Blas*. *Text: CWP,* II, 106; VIII, 196–197; X, 120; XI, 209. *Research: LET,* I, 40, 224, 232.

Gilfillan, George. (1813–1878). Nineteenth-century British literary critic. A Griswoldite, he contributed to the international character assassination of Poe by declaring in the *London Critic* of March 1854, ''His heart was as rotten as his conduct was infamous. Poe was a habitual drunkard, licentious, false, treacherous, and capable of everything that was mean, base, and malignant.'' *Research: TPL,* 675; *PLL,* 263.

Gill, William F. (1843–1882). Poe's first American biographer and author of *The Life of Edgar Allan Poe* (1877). Gill attempted to refute Griswold's vicious distortions. In ''Edgar Allan Poe and His Biographer: Rufus W. Griswold,'' Gill indicted Griswold and bitterly defended Poe against his falsifications including Griswold's charge that Poe was an alcoholic. In a gesture of grotesque respect that Poe himself might have appreciated, Gill acquired the bones of Virginia Clemm Poe in 1875 and kept them in a sort of reliquary under his bed. *Research: PLB,* 38–39.

Gillespie, William M. (1816–1868). Amateur writer and coeditor of the *New York World* whose profile is included in ''The Literati of New York City.'' He became professor of civil engineering at Union College, Schenectady, New York. Poe mentions his authorship of ''a neat volume entitled 'Rome as Seen by a New Yorker'—a good title to a good book.'' *Text: CWP,* XV, 19–20; XVI, 98. *Research: TPL,* xxvi; *MNR,* 495–496.

Glanvill, Joseph. (1636–1680). Mystic theologian and author of *Saducismus Triumphatus*, a work on witchcraft. The epigraph to ''Ligeia'' is supposedly taken from his works and refers to the power of the will to overcome death. *See:* ''Ligeia.'' *Text: CWP,* II, 225, 248, 253, 258. *Research: PLL,* 104.

Glendinning. Character in the short story ''William Wilson.'' He is ''a young parvenu nobleman'' who is being cheated at cards by Wilson when Wilson's double enters the room and exposes him.

Glenn, William J. (1822–1902). A Richmond acquaintance. He initiated Poe into the Sons of Temperance on 27 August 1849. *Research: TPL,* xxvi, 829.

Gliddon, Mr. Character in the short story ''Some Words with a Mummy.'' He translates the hieroglyphs on the mummy's coffin to mean ''Allamistakeo.''

Godey, Louis Antoine. (1804–1878). From 1830 to 1877, the editor and publisher of *Godey's Lady's Book*, a fashionable tea table periodical that catered to a vast female audience with its emphasis on fashion, morality, and profuse sentiment. Poe's editorial relations with Godey were reasonably amicable, although he did remark that ''Godey keeps almost as many ladies in his pay as the Grand Turk.'' His signature in ''Autography'' ''gives evidence of a fine taste, combined with an indefatigability which will ensure his permanent success in the world's affairs. No man has warmer friends or fewer enemies.'' *Text: CWP,* XV, 218. *Research: LTP,* 347, 349, 508, 564, 574; *TPL,* xxvi–xxvii, 348–349, 504–505, 648–649, 679–680, 702–703, 716–717; *PLL,* 194.

Godey's Lady's Book. Eloquent tea table periodical with a largely female readership. Although Poe sneered at its clientele and content, calling it a ''milliner's magazine,'' he made several contributions and was well paid. The issue for November 1845 reviewed Poe's tales, asserting that he was ''one of the most accomplished authors in America,'' exhibiting ''a skill in the 'building' of marvelous and grotesque stories which make the Arabian Nights seem tame and prosaic in comparison. We like a writer of this character and calibre. We are tired of being merely *satisfied*; and we like occasionally to be *astonished*.'' *Godey's Lady's Book* contains one of Poe's most controversial series of essays, ''The Literati of New York City.'' *See:* ''The Literati of New York City.'' *Research: PJC,* 354, 395; *TPL,* xxvi–xxvii.

Godwin, William. (1756–1836). English novelist and political philosopher. His novel *Things As They Are; or, The Adventures of Caleb Williams* is sometimes classified as the first detective novel since one of its characters probes deeply into the guilt of another. Thus, *Caleb Williams* is an important prototype of the psychological novel of crime and detection since it concentrates on the psychological bonding between criminal and victim, prefiguring many of the relationships Poe would develop a generation later, especially in those tales where the crime produces a desire for self-punishment. The influence of Godwin's novel may be clearly seen in both the Dupin stories and in the urge to commit the crime in order to confess it in "The Tell-Tale Heart" and "The Black Cat" and the psychodramatic struggle of the criminal and his conscience in "William Wilson." In a letter from Dickens to Poe on 6 March 1842, Dickens commented on the precise structure and careful character motivation in Godwin's novel of crime and punishment. In his review of Ainsworth's *Guy Fawkes*, Poe said of *Caleb Williams* that "we become at once absorbed in those details which so manifestly absorb his own soul. We read with the most breathless attention. We close the book with a real regret." *Text: CWP,* II, 154; IX, 265; X, 218–219; XI, 64; XIV, 189, 193; XVI, 48, 157. *Research:* Pollin, Burton. "Godwin and Poe." *DIP*, 107–127.

Goethe, Johann Wolfgang von. (1749–1832). German poet and novelist. He wrote *The Sufferings of Young Werther* and the dramatic poem *Faust*. Goethe is not mentioned in any of the tales or poems, an odd fact since Poe was drawn to German literature. His references to Goethe are noncommital, declaring in *Marginalia* that he is "not ashamed to say that I prefer even Voltaire to Goethe." *Text: CWP,* XI, 114; XII, 13–14; XVI, 117.

Gogol, Nicolai. (1809–1852). Russian novelist and author of the novel *Dead Souls* (1835). The two writers were almost contemporaneous. Both their lives and literary vision are often compared. Gogol's ghost story "The Cloak" could have been written by Poe himself. *Research:* Kaun, Alexander. "Poe and Gogol: A Comparison." *Slavonic and East European Review*, 15 (1937): 389–399; Stahlberg, Lawrence. "The Grotesque in Gogol and Poe." *Dissertation Abstracts International*, 38 (1978): 5449A–5450A (SUNY at Binghamton).

"The Gold-Bug." Short story by Poe published in two installments in the Philadelphia *Dollar Newspaper* of 21 and 28 June 1843. Poe had been given a $100 prize for the story. A tale of treasure hunting and deciphering of secret messages, the piece had an immediate success and became the most popular story written by Poe during his lifetime. Its cryptographer-hero, the reclusive William Legrand, lives alone on Sullivan's Island in the Harbor of Charleston, South Carolina. The story begins with the narrator's visit to Legrand and his old negro servant, Jupiter. Legrand has discovered a "scarabæus" or beetle "of a brilliant gold color" that Jupiter insists "is a goole-bug, solid, ebery bit of him, inside and all." The remarkable bug leads to an expedition into the hills of the island where the exploring party, including the narrator, soon unearths a treasure chest worth $1.5 million in "gold of antique date and of great variety" as well as precious stones and two complete skeletons apparently left behind by Captain Kidd. But finding the treasure is only the superficial half of the story. The remainder of the narrative is devoted to Legrand's explanation of his "methodical investigation of the affair" and his employment of the shrewd methods of the code-cracker to enable him to find the way to fabulous wealth. A small, dirty scrap of parchment on which Legrand has made a drawing of the bug is the treasure map that conceals the solution to the location. Traced faintly between the emblems of a death's head and a goat is a faint cryptic message that Legrand proceeds to solve as a substitution cipher, which discloses the exact location of the treasure. Once the cipher is broken, Legrand must then deal with the word code, a more difficult task than the simple decipherment. In making the final location, the Gold-Bug is used as a sort of surveyor's plumb bob to pinpoint the spot, which explains Legrand's crazy behavior of attaching it to a bit of whip cord that he twirled as the treasure hunters conducted their search. Although there is technically no crime to be solved, the story still involves many of the same qualities and attitudes to be found in Poe's detective tales. Like Dupin, Legrand's eccentric modes of detection coupled with his ratiocinative abilities enable him to crack the puzzle of the Gold-Bug. Both of these superior intellects surmount the "temporary paralysis" that impairs lesser minds who cannot synthesize reasoning and imagination. Because the narrator had thought Legrand to be mad, Legrand had "resolved to punish [him] quietly, in my own way, by a little bit of sober mystification." Perhaps the true treasure or the true gold yielded to Legrand is not Captain Kidd's buried booty but the satisfaction and gratification he gains in applying his mind to the conquest of an impossible enigma. For this reason the story ends without any reference to how the treasure will be enjoyed or even used by its discoverer. *Epigraph:* "What ho! what ho! This fellow is dancing mad!/ He hath been bitten by the Tarantula." Frederick Reynolds, *The Dramatist* (1789). (Poe's attribution, Arthur Murphy's *All in the Wrong*, is incorrect according to T. O. Mabbott.) *Text: MCW,* III, 799–847; *CWP,* V, 95–149. *Research:* Mabbott, T. O. "The Source of Poe's Motto for 'The Gold Bug.' " *Notes & Queries*, 198 (February 1953): 68; Goldhurst, William. "Edgar Allan Poe and the Conquest of Death." *New Orleans Review*, 2 (1969): 316–319; St. Armand, Barton L. "Poe's 'Sober Mystification': The Uses of Alchemy in 'The Gold Bug.' " *Poe Studies*, 4, no. 2 (1971): 1–7; Hennelly, Mark M. Jr. "Le Grand Captain Kidder and His Bogus Bug." *Studies in Short Fiction*, 17 (1980): 77–79; Williams, Michael. " 'The Language of the Cipher': Interpretation in the Gold-Bug." *American Literature*, 53 (1982): 646–660; Phillips, Elizabeth C. " 'The Right of Attendance': The Image of the Black Man in the Works of Poe and Two of His Contemporaries." In *No Fairer Land: Studies in Southern Literature before 1900*, ed. J. Lasley Dameron, James W. Mathews, and James H. Justus. Troy, NY: Whitston, 1986, 172–184; Kempton, Daniel. "The Gold/Goole/Ghoul Bug." *ESQ: A Journal of the American Renaissance*, 33 (1987): 1–19; Mathews, James W. "Legrand's Golden Vision: Meaning in 'The Gold Bug.' " *CEA Critic: An Official Journal of the College English Association*, 53, no. 3 (1991): 23–29; Toner, Jennifer DiLalla. "The 'Remarkable Effect' of 'Silly Words': Dialect and Signature in 'The Gold-Bug.' " *Arizona Quarterly*, 49 (1993): 1–20.

Goldsmith, Oliver. (1730–1774). English poet and novelist and author of *The Vicar of Wakefield.* Poe reviewed a reprinting of the novel in *Graham's Magazine* for January 1842. Poe apparently preferred the novelist to the poet, claiming twice that Goldsmith's lines "Man wants but little here below/ Nor wants that little long" were "stolen from [Edward] Young." *See:* "The Vicar of Wakefield, a Tale. By Oliver Goldsmith, M.B." *Text: CWP,* VIII, 41; XIV, 47–48; XVI, 76. *Research:* Dixon, Jeannie B. "Poe: A Borrowing from Goldsmith." *Notes & Queries,* 163 (12 November 1932): 350.

Goncourt, Edmond Louis Antoine Huot de, and Jules Alfred Hout de Goncourt. (1822–1896 and 1830–1870, respectively). French art critics and novelists much of whose work is fraternal collaboration. The Goncourt brothers were deeply impressed by Poe through reading him in the Baudelaire translations. They recognized as early as 1856 that Poe's originality, his decadence, and the rich fantasy life depicted in his fiction anticipated the fiction of the future that would "present all the revolutions of the soul in the sufferings of the body." *Research: PLL,* 268–269, 280–281.

Goodfellow, Charles. Character in the short story " 'Thou Art the Man.' " He is the alcoholic friend of Mr. Barnabas Shuttleworthy.

Gorgias of Leontini. (fl. 427 B.C.). Ancient Greek sophist and writer on rhetoric. In "The Man of the Crowd," the narrator refers mordantly to "the mad and flimsy rhetoric of Gorgias." *Text: CWP*, IV, 134.

Gould, Hannah Flagg. (1789–1865). Minor American children's poet whose mastery of the epigrammatic line was praised by Poe. Analyzing her signature in "Autography," Poe observed, "The literary style of one who writes thus is sure to be forcibly epigrammatic." *Text: CWP,* VIII, 202; XIII, 18; XV, 166, 196–197; XVI, 138–139. *Research: TPL,* 185, 211, 223, 231.

Gove, Mary Neal [Nichols]. (1810–1884). She attended Virginia Clemm Poe during her terminal illness. She was a novelist. Gove left an account of Virginia's dying days and the Poes' melancholy life at the Fordham cottage in the *Six Penny Magazine* for February 1863. Poe included a grateful portrait of her in "The Literati of New York City." *Text: CWP,* X, 197; XV, 61. *Research: LTP,* 569–571; *TPL,* xxvi, 607–608, 669–670, 685–686, 707–708.

Gowans, William. New York city bookseller. Poe, Virginia, and Maria Clemm shared a residence with Gowans at Sixth Avenue and Waverley Place beginning in February 1837. Gowans later wrote affectionately of both Poe and Virginia. He remembered Poe as "one of the most courteous, gentlemanly, and intelligent companions I have ever met, and I must say I never saw him in the least affected with liquor, nor even descend to any known vice." Of Virginia's appearance, he remarked that ''her eye could match that of any houri, and her face defy the genius of a Canova to imitate.'' *Research: TPL,* 242, 245; *PLL,* 92–93.

Graham, George Rex. (1813–1894). Philadelphia journal entrepreneur and founder of *Graham's Magazine*. He had interests in the *Saturday Evening Post* and *The Casket,* acquiring *Burton's Gentleman's Magazine* in 1840. He combined the various monthlies into *Graham's Magazine*, which began publication in December 1840. Graham was one of the few editorial authority figures in Poe's life with whom he did not openly feud. However, after Poe became the book reviewer for *Graham's* in February 1841, tensions increased, causing Poe to become mildly contemptuous of Graham's commercialism and parsimony. He grew resentful of his own $800 annual status at this ''nambypamby'' magazine. After Poe's death, Graham wrote and published in his magazine two defenses of Poe's art, ''The Late Edgar Poe'' (*Graham's*, March 1850) and ''The Genius and Characteristics of the Late Edgar Allan Poe'' (*Graham's*, February 1854), refuting the Griswold obituary's debasing claims. Poe possessed, in Graham's estimation, a ''management of the supernatural never attained or approached by any other writer.'' The brief remark about Graham in ''Autography'' says simply: ''For both of these journals he has written much and well.'' *Text: CWP,* XV, 213. *Research: PLB,* 14, 39; *TPL,* xxvi-xxvii; *MNR,* 162–163, 178–179.

Graham, William. Author of the pamphlet *The Prose Romances of Edgar A. Poe*, which also contained ''The Murders in the Rue Morgue'' and ''The Man That Was Used Up.'' The pamphlet was published privately in Philadelphia in July 1843. *Research: PLL,* 148.

Graham's Magazine. Began publication in December 1840 after Graham had combined *Burton's Gentleman's Magazine* and *The Casket*. Poe was hired as book review editor in February 1841 and remained at *Graham's* until April 1842. Although Poe's attitude toward *Graham's Magazine* was contemptuous—he derogated the subject matter as ''contemptible pictures, fashion plates, music and love tales''—he would also exploit his association with *Graham's* in his attempt to become America's preeminent arbiter of literary standards and taste. His many essays and reviews in *Graham's* established him as progenitor of American literary criticism, and his insistence that a literary work be read closely as a self-contained aesthetic entity anticipated the criteria of the New Criticism. His pieces for *Graham's* prompted George Bernard Shaw to call Poe ''the greatest journalistic critic of his time.'' In addition to criticism and reviews, Poe contributed tales and poetry to *Graham's* in steady profusion. Almost every number of *Graham's* contains a Poe story during his tenure there. *Research: PJC,* 249–328; *TPL,* xxvi–xxvii.

"Grammar of the English Language, in a Series of Letters, Addressed to Every American Youth. By Hugh A. Pue." Poe's savagely negative review of Pue's *Grammar* appeared in *Graham's Magazine* for July 1841. He referred to the primer as a "queer little book" and called the author a "nincompoop" whose own bad writing throughout furnishes "an analogy between ipecac and his grammar." *Text: CWP,* X, 167–171.

A Grand Turk from Stamboul. Character mentioned in the short story "Lionizing." He is a guest at the Prince of Wales's literary dinner and thinks that "the earth was supported by a sky-blue cow with an incalculable number of green horns."

Grattan, Henry. (1746–1820). Irish orator. Poe refers to his blustery eloquence in *Marginalia.* "He takes up too much time in the anteroom. He is never done with his introductions." The *Marginalia* entries indicate that Poe may have confused Henry Grattan with Thomas Colley Grattan. *Text: CWP,* XVI, 63, 140–141.

Grattan, Thomas Colley. (1792–1864). British diplomat and author of *Highways and By-ways; or, Tales of the Roadside, Picked Up in the French Provinces. By a Walking Gentleman.* The work was described as "[a] capital book, generally speaking, but Mr. Grattan has a bad habit—that of loitering in the road—of dallying and toying with his subjects." *Text: CWP,* XI, 223.

Graves, Sergeant Samuel "Bully." Poe's paid military substitute. Poe owed Graves $50 for filling out the term of his enlistment. *Research: TPL,* 90, 105; *PLL,* 48.

Gravina, Giovanni Vicenzo L'Abbate. (1664–1718). Italian critic and author of a treatise on tragedy, *Della Ragion Poetica.* Burton Pollin has pointed out the similarity between Gravina's title and Poe's treatise on metrics and scansion, "The Rationale of Verse." Gravina's statement that "If *any* music must imitate *any thing*, it were, undoubtedly, better that the imitation should be limited" is quoted several times by Poe. *Text: CWP,* X, 42–43; XIV, 274; XVI, 6, 29, 138. *Research: BRE,* 120.

Gray, Thomas. (1716–1771). English poet and member of the Graveyard School. Poe quotes lines from Gray's "The Bard" in *Pinakidia* and "Elegy Written in a Country Churchyard" in *Marginalia* with the appended suggestion that Gray was paraphrasing lines from Butler's *Hudibras* and Cary's translation of Dante. *Text: CWP,* XIV, 57–58; XVI, 75–76.

"Greek Song." Alternative title for the patriotic poem ''Hymn to Aristogeiton and Harmodius.'' *See:* ''Hymn to Aristogeitan and Harmodius. Translation from the Greek.''

Greeley, Horace. (1811–1872). Editor of the *New York Daily Tribune*. His loan of $50 that enabled Poe to purchase *The Broadway Journal* was never repaid. Greeley's signature in ''Autography'' indicates that ''[a]s a *belles-lettres* critic he is entitled to high respect.'' *Text: CWP,* XI, 224, 241; XIV, 179; XV, 250. *Research:* ''Greeley Pays Poe for Contributions to the Tribune with a Promissory Note.'' *Bruno's Weekly*, 4 March 1916, 526–528; Mabbott, T. O. ''Greeley's Estimate of Poe.'' *Autograph Album*, 1 (December 1933): 14–16, 61; *MNR,* 212–213, 275.

Greely. Character mentioned in the novel *The Narrative of Arthur Gordon Pym*. He is one of the mutinous sailors aboard the *Grampus* and is killed by Dirk Peters.

Greely, Frank. Character in *The Journal of Julius Rodman*. He is one of the five Greely brothers who participates in the exploring adventure.

Greely, John. Character in *The Journal of Julius Rodman*. He is the oldest of the five Greely brothers and one of the explorers.

Greely, Meredith. Character in *The Journal of Julius Rodman*. He is one of the five Greely brothers and an explorer.

Greely, Poindexter. Character in *The Journal of Julius Rodman*. He is one of the five Greely brothers and an explorer.

Greely, Robert. Character in *The Journal of Julius Rodman*. He is one of the five Greely brothers and an explorer.

Green, Charles. Character mentioned in the short story ''The Balloon Hoax.'' He is the scientist who invented the guide rope for use on the balloon.

Greenwich Street (number 130). Poe address in New York City where he resided in a boarding house in 1844.

Greenwich Street (number 154). Poe address in New York City where Poe resided in January 1845.

Grenouille, Prince de. Character in the short story ''Lionizing.''

Grey, Edward S. T. An alias sometimes used by Poe in his correspondence with Thomas Holley Chivers and others. *Research:* Pollin, Burton R. ''Poe as Edward S. T. Grey.'' *Ball State University Forum*, 14, no. 3 (1973): 44–46; *TPL*, 753–754; *MNR*, 273.

Grillparzer, Franz. (1791–1872). German dramatist. Discussing the reading of Mrs. Felicia Hemans, Poe mentions Grillparzer as one of her ''favorites among the minor German tragedians.'' *Text: CWP*, IX, 202.

Griswold, Rufus Wilmot. (1815–1857). Baptist clergyman and erstwhile friend of Poe. The author of a scurillous and infamous memoir of Poe, he was unfortunately selected by Poe himself to become his literary executor. He was on the staff of the Philadelphia *Daily Standard* and compiled *The Poets and Poetry of America* in 1842. In various public lectures and book reviews, Poe faulted Griswold's anthology, thus inviting Griswold's enmity. Griswold is also mocked in several tales as in ''The Angel of the Odd'' where the intoxicated narrator is made more stupid by reading Griswold's ''Curiosities.'' Griswold's abusive death notice for Poe published in the *New York Daily Tribune* in 1849 was later enlarged into his infamous ''Memoir'' attached to Griswold's 1850 edition of Poe's works. Griswold's slanderous characterization of Poe became the unofficial biographical record for the nineteenth century. His libelous obituary for Poe, published in the *New York Herald Tribune* for 9 October 1849, began a campaign of posthumous character assassination unequaled in the world of letters. Among other flagrant untruths, Griswold factualized such lies as Poe's expulsion from the University of Virginia, his desertion from the U.S. Army, his drug addiction, and his sexual aggressiveness toward John Allan's second wife to prove his main charge that Poe ''had no moral susceptibility.'' His ''Memoir of the Author'' introducing the 1850 edition of Poe's works established the fraudulent thesis that every one of Poe's depraved, homicidal, or suicidal characters were personal portraits. The autobiographical prevarication that Griswold promoted would dictate critical attitudes toward Poe well into the twentieth century. Analyzing Griswold's signature in ''Autography,'' Poe generously wrote that ''his knowledge of American literature, in all its details, is not exceeded by that of any man among us.'' *Text: CWP*, XV, 107, 121, 211, 215. *Research:* Campbell, Killis. ''The Poe-Griswold Controversy.'' *Publications of the Modern Language Association*, 34 (1919): 436–464; Neu, Jacob L. ''Rufus Wilmot Griswold.'' *University of Texas Studies in English*, 5 (1925): 101–165; McCusker, Honor. ''The Correspondence of R. W. Griswold.'' *More Books (Bulletin of the Boston Public Library)*, 16 (March–June 1941): 105–116, 152–156, 190–196, 286–289; Bayless, Joy. *Rufus Wilmot Griswold: Poe's Literary Executor*. Nashville, TN: Vanderbilt University Press, 1943; Cohen, B. Bernard, and Lucien A. Cohen. ''Poe and Griswold Once More.'' *American Literature*, 34 (1962): 97–101; *MNR*, 214.

Grosswigg. Character mentioned in the short story ''The Devil in the Belfry.'' He is an etymologist who has traced the derivation of the name of the borough of Vondervotteimittiss.

Gruff. Character in the short story "The Business Man." He is insulted and then sued for assault and battery by Peter Proffit.

Gruntundguzzell. Character mentioned in the short story "The Devil in the Belfry." He is cited as the author of the subcommentaries of Stuffundpuff's marginal notes on the source of the name of the borough of Vondervotteimittiss.

Gunner's Hall. Baltimore saloon. Poe was found drunk and delirious outside Gunner's Hall on election day, 3 October 1849.

Guy, Captain. Character in the novel *The Narrative of Arthur Gordon Pym.* He is skipper and part owner of the *Jane Guy*, the vessel that picks up Pym and Dirk Peters after the shipwreck of the *Grampus.*

"Guy Fawkes; or, The Gunpowder Treason. An Historical Romance. By William Harrison Ainsworth." Negative review of Ainsworth's historical novel appearing in *Graham's Magazine* for November 1841. The whole novel is an "admixture of pedantry, bombast, and rigmarole," "the plot is monstrously improbable," while "if ever, indeed, a novel were *less* than nothing, then that novel is 'Guy Fawkes.' " *Text: CWP,* X, 214–220. *Research: PJC,* 270–272.

H

Haines, Hiram. (1802–1841). Editor of various Petersburg, Virginia, newspapers: the *American Constellation*, *Th' Time o' Day*, and the *Virginia Star*. He was an early admirer and defender of Poe's work. *Research: TPL,* xxvii, 216–217.

Hale, David Emerson. (1814–1839). Fellow cadet at West Point. His mother was Sarah Josepha Hale, editor of *Godey's Lady's Book*. In a letter to his mother from West Point, he mentions that Poe "is thought a fellow of talent here." *Research: TPL,* xxvii, 114, 229.

Hale, Sarah Josepha. (1788–1879). Editor of the *Ladies' Magazine* and *Godey's Lady's Book*. She probably knew Poe casually in 1840. In "Autography" Poe's Joseph P. Q. Miller opined that her large handwriting "is indicative of a masculine understanding. . . . Mrs. Hale is well known for her masculine style of thought." *Text: CWP,* XV, 171, 203. *Research:* "When Edgar Allan Poe Wrote for 50 Cents a Page." New York *Times*, 28 January 1917, 14; *TPL,* xxvii.

Hall. Some of the sketches in *Georgia Scenes, Characters, Incidents, &c, in the First Half Century of the Republic* by Augustus Baldwin Longstreet bore the pseudonym "Hall." Others were pseudonymously signed "Baldwin." *See:* "Georgia Scenes, Characters, Incidents." *Text:* Ostrom, John W. "Two Unpublished Poe Letters." *Americana*, 36 (January 1942): 67–71; *CWP,* VIII, 259.

Halleck, Fitz-Greene. (1790–1867). American poet. Poe appealed to him for money when *The Broadway Journal* was in danger of going under. A portrait of Halleck is included in ''The Literati of New York City,'' and there is a short analysis of his handwriting in ''Autography,'' his signature revealing ''a free, mercantile hand, evinc[ing] a love for the graceful rather than for the picturesque.'' *See:* ''Alnwick Castle, with Other Poems.'' *Text: CWP,* XV, 49–56, 150–151, 189. *Research: LTP*, 335, 508, 542; *TPL,* xxvii.

Hammerhead, Marmaduke. Satiric name used for Poe by Dr. Thomas Dunn English in his novel *1844*, published in installments in the New York *Evening Mirror* through September and October 1846. English portrayed Poe as a surly and arrogant writer who ''never gets drunk more than five days a week.'' *See: Eighteen Forty Four.*

"Hans Phaall—A Tale." Original title and spelling of the short story ''The Unparalleled Adventure of One Hans Pfaall.'' The character's name was spelled variously in later printings and Poe's letters. *See:* ''The Unparalleled Adventure of One Hans Pfaall.''

Hansson, Ola. (1860–1925). Swedish poet and novelist. His high opinion of Poe is similar to that of Baudelaire and the symbolists. In an essay on Poe in *Kåiseier i mystik* (1889), he designated Poe ''[o]ne of the great maladies of mankind. His sickness is the sickness of beauty at its most sublime. Like most princes of culture, he is in one person the cloven trunk of madness and genius.'' *Research: PLL,* 282.

" 'The Happiest Day, the Happiest Hour.' " Poem by Poe in six quatrain stanzas first published in *Tamerlane and Other Poems* and in the 15 September 1827 number of *The North American, or, Weekly Journal of Politics, Science, and Literature*. Poe's brother, Henry Poe, had contributed the poem to *The North American* of 19 May 1827. Probably written while Poe was serving in the army, the juvenile poem is a self-pitying lament for the lost visions of youth and the ''highest hope of pride and power'' that ''have vanish'd long, alas!'' possibly reflecting as well his feelings of loss over Elmira Royster. *Text: MCW,* I, 80–82; *CWP,* VII, 20; Mabbott, T. O. ''Edgar Allan Poe: A Find.'' *Notes & Queries*, 150 (3 April 1926): 241.

The Harbinger. A journal published by the Brook Farm transcendentalist circle of West Roxbury, Massachusetts. The 12 July 1845 number contains Charles A. Dana's negative review of Poe's tales, although he attributes a certain power to them. ''It is the power of disease; there is no health about them.'' A review of *The Raven and Other Poems* by John S. Dwight in the 6 December 1845 number is similar in tone. *Research: PLB,* 204–206; *MNR,* 270, 300.

Hardy, Captain. Character in the short story ''The Oblong Box.'' He is captain of the packet ship *Independence*.

Hardy, Thomas. (1840–1928). English poet and novelist. Hardy had a high regard for Poe's style in both his tales and poetry. In Hardy's estimation, Poe was "the first to realise to the full the possibilities of the English language in thought and rhyme." Darker heroines such as Eustacia Vye in *The Return of the Native* point up Poe's influence in drawing mysterious characters, while short stories such as "The Three Strangers" have atmospheric touches of Poe-esque horror. *Research:* Fussell, D. H. "Do You Like Poe, Mr. Hardy?" *Modern Fiction Studies*, 27 (1981): 211–224.

Harker, Samuel. Editor of the Baltimore *Republican and Commercial Advertiser.* Poe noticed the content of White's *Southern Literary Messenger* for Harker's journal of 14 May, 13 June, and 10 July 1835. *Research: LET,* I, 115, 116; *TPL,* xxvii.

Harper & Brothers. James, John, Joseph, Fletcher. New York publishing house. It published Poe's *Narrative of Arthur Gordon Pym* but turned down *Tales of the Folio Club* and other submissions by Poe. *Research:* Wylie, John Cook. "Harper Records." *Bibliographical Society, University of Virginia*, 37, secretary news sheet (1957): 6; *TPL,* 192–193, 212–213; *PLL,* 106–107.

"Harper's Ferry." Unsigned article appearing in *Graham's Magazine* for February 1842. *Research:* Pollin, Burton. "Poe as Probable Author of 'Harper's Ferry.' " *American Literature*, 40 (1968): 164–178.

Harrington, Reverend Henry. Fanny Osgood's brother-in-law. He recalled Poe's passionate courtship of her following Virginia's death in 1846. *Research: MNR,* 496; *PLL,* 208.

Harrington, Sir John. (1561–1612). English poet, romancer, and author of the satire *The Metamorphosis of Ajax.* His name is mentioned in *Marginalia* with Cowley, Donne, and Carew. Since only the surname is used, Poe may have had in mind James Harrington (1611–1677), a cavalier songwriter. *Text: CWP,* X, 44; XVI, 139.

Harris, Alfred. Character in Poe's novel *The Narrative of Arthur Gordon Pym.* He is one of the sailors aboard the *Jane Guy* and is killed by the natives.

Harris, Joel Chandler. (1848–1908). American short story writer, local colorist, and creator of the Uncle Remus stories. In a review of Griswold's infamous biography, he called Poe "the great genius" and defended Poe against Griswold's prevarications, dismissing the Griswold memoir as "one of the most miserably gotten up affairs, perhaps, that ever intruded itself upon the reading public" with enough "nonsensical mediocrity, patronizing inferiority, and ridiculous envy in it to damn it forever in the mind of any reader of taste."

Research: Mabbott, Thomas Ollive. ''Joel Chandler Harris: A Debt to Poe.'' *Notes & Queries*, 166 (3 March 1934): 151–152; Bickley, R. Bruce, Jr. *Joel Chandler Harris.* Boston: Twayne; Twayne United States Authors Series Number (TUSAS) 308, 1978, 20, 21, 146.

Harrison, Gabriel. (1818–1902). New York artist and merchant. He knew Poe casually in New York City in 1844. He was also the president of the White Eagles Club, a political group for which Poe wrote a campaign song. *Research: TPL,* xxvii.

Harrison, J.[ames] A.[lbert]. (1848–1911). Poe biographer and editor. In 1902, he assembled and published *Life and Letters of Edgar Allan Poe* and later collected and edited *The Last Letters of Edgar Allan Poe to Sarah Helen Whitman* (1909). His seventeen-volume collection of *The Complete Works of Edgar Allan Poe* published in 1902 (Rpt. New York: AMS Press, 1965) became the standard edition. His two articles for *The Independent*, ''New Glimpses of Poe'' (6 September 1900) and ''A Poe Miscellany'' (1 November 1906), are important recollections and contributions to Poe correspondence. *Research:* Harrison, J. A., and Charlotte F. Dailey. ''Poe and Mrs. Whitman: New Light on a Romantic Episode.'' *Century*, 77 (January 1909): 439–452; O'Neill, Edward H. ''The Poe-Griswold-Harrison Texts of the 'Marginalia.' '' *American Literature*, 15 (1943): 238–250.

Harrison, William Henry. (1773–1841). General and ninth president of the United States. His military heroism may be the subject of Poe's satire in ''The Man That Was Used Up.'' On 26 June 1841, Poe wrote to F. W. Thomas regarding his political stance in the 1840 election that ''I battled with right good will for Harrison, when opportunity offered.'' *See:* ''The Man That Was Used Up.'' *Text: CWP,* IX, 23; IX, 122; XI, 221. *Research: LTP*, 381–382, 389, 396; *TPL,* xxvii, 295–296, 332–333.

Hassan. In a discussion of the etymology of the word *assassin* in *Pinakidia*, Poe suggests as a source the leader of this organization of murderous fanatics, ''Hassan.'' *Text: CWP,* XIV, 45.

Hatch & Dunning. Baltimore publishing firm. It published Poe's *Al Aaraaf, Tamerlane, and Minor Poems* in 1829. *Research: TPL,* 100–102.

"The Haunted Palace." Poem by Poe first published in the September 1839 number of *Burton's Gentleman's Magazine* when Poe incorporated it into ''The Fall of the House of Usher.'' The poem consists of six eight-line stanzas that are not arranged in any discernible pattern but that may relate thematically to the issues at work in the story, especially the approach of chaos and apocalyptic collapse. According to the narrator, the poem is Roderick Usher's composition centering on a king whose person and palace are endangered by sinister forces, ''evil things in robes of sorrow,/ [Who assail] the monarch's high estate.'' Other features of the poem such as the mad laughter, ''hideous throng,'' and ''pale door'' foreshadow the climax and collapse as well as Madeline's cadaverous return from her grave. In short, ''The Haunted Palace'' may be a symbolic encipherment of the tale's themes and singular effects. *See:* ''The Fall of the House of Usher.'' *Text: MCW,* I, 312–318; *CWP,* VII, 83–84. *Research:* Thomas, J. David. ''The Composition of Wilde's *The Harlot House.* '' *Modern Language Notes*, 65 (1950): 485–488; Mikami, Tadashi. ''An Essay on Poe's 'The Haunted Palace.' '' *Daito Bunka University Literature Department Bulletin* (Tokyo), 6 (1968): 23–34.

Havens, Benny. He owned a tavern at West Point that catered to the off-limits desires of the cadets. Poe frequented the Havens Tavern during his cadet days. *Research: PLL,* 44.

Hawk, Thomas. Character mentioned in the short story ''The Literary Life of Thingum Bob, Esq.'' Thingum Bob writes his savage reviews for the *Lollipop* under this nom de plume that is simply a pun on ''tomahawk.'' Poe himself acquired the name ''the tomahawk man'' for his ferocious manner of reviewing.

Hawkes, John. (1925–). American novelist. His novels *The Cannibal* (1949) and *Virginie: Her Two Lives* (1982) and, most particularly, the short novel *Travesty* (1976) are modernizations of Poe's settings, atmosphere, and frenzied characterizations. ''The spirit of Edgar Allan Poe is everywhere in *Travesty*, from the narrator in his death machine to the landscape of nightmare.'' Hawkes seems impelled by Poe's example in his ''monologues of desperate ratiocination, the narrator as psychopath, murderer, and artist. Hawkes and Poe are fellow travelers into the darkness.'' *Research:* Berryman, Charles. ''Hawkes and Poe: *Travesty.*'' *Modern Fiction Studies*, 29 (1983): 643–654.

Hawks, Dr. Francis Lister. (1798–1866). Editor of the religious quarterly *The New York Review,* to which Poe contributed. The brief sketch of his handwriting in ''Autography'' notes that ''his style, both as a writer and as a preacher, is characterized rather by perfect *fluency* than by any more lofty quality.'' *See:* ''Incidents of Travel in Egypt, Arabia Petræa, and the Holy Land.'' *Text: CWP,* XV, 205. *Research: TPL,* xxvii.

"The Hawks of Hawk-Hollow: A Tradition of Pennsylvania." Poe reviewed Robert Montgomery Bird's historical novel in *The Southern Literary Messenger* for December 1835. Poe's verdict was negative because he found the work ''by no means in the *best* manner of its illustrious author.'' He also found it to be a bad American imitation of Sir Walter Scott's less successful romances, ''a positive failure, and must take its place by the side of the Redgauntlets, the Monasteries, the Pirates, and the Saint Ronan's Wells.'' *Text: CWP,* VIII, 63–73. *Research: LET,* I, 101; *PJC,* 99–100.

Hawthorne, Julian. (1846–1934). American author and son of novelist Nathaniel Hawthorne. His short story ''My Adventures with Edgar Allan Poe,'' concerning an imaginary encounter with Poe, appeared in *Lippincott's Magazine*, 43 (1891): 240–246. *Research: PLB,* 40.

Hawthorne, Nathaniel. (1804–1864). American novelist and short story writer. Although the two writers never met, they did exchange letters and were deeply engaged by each other's fiction. Poe wrote a brief notice of Hawthorne's *Twice-Told Tales* for the April 1842 issue of *Graham's Magazine* and expanded his commentary in the May 1842 issue of *Graham's*. He again reviewed Hawthorne's work in revised form and under the title ''Tale-Writing'' in *Godey's Lady's Book* for November 1847. In a piece entitled ''Literary Intelligence'' published in the New York *Evening Mirror* of 6 February 1845, he expressed distress that *Twice-Told Tales* had gone out of print. In his ''Editorial Miscellany'' column in *The Broadway Journal* of 23 August 1845, Poe referred to Hawthorne as ''a prose poet, full of originality, beauty, and a refinement of style and conception.'' Although he did not favor allegory as a literary method, Poe was one of the first critics to acknowledge Hawthorne as a major American writer demonstrating ''more originality'' than Irving in his handling of American materials. What impressed Poe most was Hawthorne's command of the short story's form, his ability ''to carry out the fulness of his intention'' by placing the reader inside a fictional world where ''there are no external or extrinsic influences.'' Hawthorne's effective artistry confirmed many of the very points about composition, structure, and atmospheric depth of setting that Poe would declare to be imperative later in ''The Philosophy of Composition.'' Poe's judgment of Hawthorne was to prove prophetic for the American literary canon: ''Of Mr. Hawthorne's tales we would say, emphatically, that they belong to the very highest region of Art—and Art subservient to genius of a very lofty order.'' Even though Hawthorne usually avoided sensational gore in his stories, he could occasionally write in that vein as shown in one of Hawthorne's most Poe-esque tales, ''The White Old Maid.'' *See:* ''Tale-Writing—Nathaniel Hawthorne.'' *Text: CWP,* XI, 206; XIV, 75; XV, 3–4; XVI, 41. *Research:* Benson, Eugene. ''Poe and Hawthorne.'' *The Galaxy*, 6 (December 1868): 742–748; Miller, Harold P. ''Hawthorne Surveys His Contemporaries.'' *American Literature*, 12 (1940): 228–235; Marks, Alfred H. ''Two Rodericks and Two Worms: 'Egotism; or, The Bosom Serpent.' '' *Publications of the Modern Language Association*, 74 (1959): 607–612.

Hazlitt, William. (1778–1830). English essayist and critic. His literary life paralleled Poe's in several ways. He was independent and uncompromising in his criticism, holding to Romantic principles of composition and risking the admonition of those who equated literature with didacticism. And like Poe, Hazlitt would write literary criticism that was distinctly ahead of its time. Poe paid homage to Hazlitt in his review ''The Literary Remains of the Late William Hazlitt'' in *The Southern Literary Messenger* for September 1836. *See:* ''The

Literary Remains of the Late William Hazlitt.'' *Research:* Baker, Harry T. ''Poe and Hazlitt.'' *Nation*, 8 October 1908, 335.

Heath, James Ewell. (1792–1862). Original editor of *The Southern Literary Messenger*. He reviewed Poe's fiction in October 1839 and January 1840, noting Poe's artistic endowments, ''a taste classical and refined, an imagination affluent and splendid, . . . a singular capacity for minute and mathematical detail.'' His signature in ''Autography'' revealed ''his writings [to be] rather polished and graceful, than forcible or original.'' *Text: CWP*, XV, 241; *TPL*, xxviii, 147–149, 268–270.

Hédelin, François. [Abbé d'Aubignac]. (1604–1676). Homeric scholar mentioned in the short story ''Mystification.'' His belief in the multiple authorship of the Homeric epics is also the subject of a *Pinakidia* item. *Text: CWP*, IV, 109, 111; XIV, 44.

Hegel, Georg Wilhelm Friedrich. (1770–1831). German philosopher and logician. In *Marginalia*, Poe quotes Hegel's remark that '' 'Philosophy . . . is utterly useless and fruitless, and, *for this very reason*, is the sublimest of all pursuits, the most deserving attention, and the most worthy of our zeal,'' dismissing the remark as ''jargon'' in the manner of Tertullian. *Text: CWP*, XI, 136; XVI, 164.

Helen. Character in the poem ''To Helen.'' She is identified with Jane Stith Stanard.

Heliogabalus. [Elagabulus]. (201–222). Roman emperor. The transvestite emperor is mentioned in the short story ''Four Beasts in One; The Homo-cameleopard'' as ''a very notorious Roman emperor'' who instituted sun worship in the city and again in ''Mellonta Tauta.'' *Text: CWP*, II, 206; VI, 208.

Helvétius, Claude Arien. (1715–1771). Swiss philosopher and skeptical thinker. He is quoted in Poe's review of Bulwer's *Night and Morning* and in *Marginalia*. '' 'The men of sense,' says Helvétius, 'those idols of the unthinking, are very inferior to the men of passions. It is the strong passions which, rescuing us from sloth, can alone impart to us that continuous and earnest attention necessary to great intellectual efforts.' And Bulwer is, emphatically, one of the 'men of passions.' '' *Text: CWP*, X, 131; XVI, 158.

Hemans, Felicia Dorothea. (1793–1835). English poet extremely popular in both Great Britain and the United States for her pathetic and patriotic lyrics, the most famous of which is ''The boy stood on the burning deck'' from *Casabianca*. Poe compared her work with the themes and lines of Mrs. Sigourney, finding the American lady's verse to be so filled with mannered imitations of

Hemans so "as to give an almost ludicrous air of similitude to all articles of her composition." As a poet, Mrs. Hemans herself displays "an invincible inclination to apostrophize every object, in both moral and physical existence. . . . These were all, in Mrs. Hemans, mannerisms of a gross and inartificial nature." Hemans's "Hymn for Christmas" is quoted in *Marginalia* as an instance of the plagiarism of both her work and tone in the American annuals. *See:* Dodson, Richard W. *Text: CWP,* VIII, 124–126, 195–196; XV, 100; XVI, 141. *Research: PLB,* 77; *TPL,* 226–227.

Hemingway, Ernest. (1898–1961). American novelist. In *Green Hills of Africa* (1935), Hemingway credited Poe with technical expertise but little else: "Poe is a skillful writer. It is skillful, marvellously constructed, and it is dead." When he compared Faulkner to Poe, Hemingway told the critic Malcolm Cowley, "He is almost as much of a prick as Poe. But thank God for Poe and thank God for Faulkner." *Research:* Galinsky, Hans. "Beharrende Strukturzüge im Wandel eines Jahrhunderts amerikanischer Kurzgeschichte (darlegt an E. A. Poes 'The Masque of the Red Death' und Ernest Hemingways 'The Killers')." *Die Neueren Sprachen,* supplement III (1958): 5–45; Tarbox, Raymond. "Blank Hallucinations in the Fiction of Poe and Hemingway." *American Literature,* 24 (1967): 312–343; Pollin, Burton R. "Poe and Hemingway on Violence and Death." *English Studies,* 57 (1976): 139–142.

Henderson. Character mentioned in Poe's novel *The Narrative of Arthur Gordon Pym.* He is the first mate of the *Penguin* and rescues Pym and Augustus Barnard when their boat the *Ariel* is run down.

"Henry B. Hirst." A poet's profile included by Griswold in *The Poets and Poetry of America.* "His chief *sin* is imitativeness. He never writes anything which does not immediately put us in mind of something that we have seen better written before." *See:* Hirst, Henry Beck. *Text: CWP,* XIII, 209–213. *Research: LTP,* 421.

Henry, Caleb Sprague. (1804–1884). Educator, orator, essayist, and political journalist mentioned in "Autography." The signature revealed "a vacillating disposition with unsettled ideas of the beautiful. None of his epistles, in regard to their chirography, end as well as they begin." *Text: CWP,* XV, 197.

Henry, Francis, Earl of Bridgewater. (?–1829). Patron of the Royal Society of London. Poe discusses the bequest in his will for the preparation of various scientific papers known as the *Bridgewater Treatises. See:* "Animal and Vegetable Physiology, Considered with Reference to Natural Theology." *Text: CWP,* VIII, 206–209.

Henry, Patrick. (1736–1799). American statesman and orator. His reminiscences and powers as a speaker are briefly discussed in Poe's review of the

Reverend Francis L. Hawks's *Contributions to the Ecclesiastical History of the United States of America. Text: CWP,* VIII, 250. *Research: TPL,* 417.

Herbert, Henry William. (1807–1858). American dramatist, novelist, translator, and author of *Cromwell* and *Ringwood, the Rover.* He also edited the *American Monthly Magazine.* In ''Autography,'' Poe stated, ''His longer works evince much ability, although he is rarely entitled to be called original.'' *Text: CWP,* XV, 206. *Research: TPL,* 349, 431.

Herder, Johann Gottfried. (1744–1803). German poet and leader of the *Sturm und Drang* movement. His poem ''Stimmen der Völker in Liedern'' [''To speak of the people in songs''] is mentioned for its inspirational impact on the work of Felicia Hemans. *Text: CWP,* IX, 200; XI, 65.

Hermann, Johan. Character in the short story ''Mystification.'' He is a duelist and is as stupid as he is courageous.

Herodotus. (ca. 490–424 B.C.). Ancient Greek historian. Two references to Herodotus occur in *Pinakidia,* one involving his dating of the life of Queen Semiramis, the other, Herodotus's detailed description of the towers of the Temple of Belus. *Text: CWP,* XIV, 52, 65.

"The Heroine; or, The Adventures of Cherubina." Review of Eaton Stannard Barrett's bristling satire on gothic fiction appearing in *The Southern Literary Messenger* for December 1835. Barrett's antigothic novel ''is a book which should be upon the shelves of every well-appointed library.'' Poe especially appreciated Barrett's sarcastic wit, which he found ''positively inimitable.'' *Text: CWP,* VIII, 76–81. *Research:* Lewis, Paul. ''Laughing at Fear: Two Versions of the Mock Gothic.'' *Studies in Short Fiction,* 15 (1978): 411–414.

Herring, Elizabeth Poe. (1792–1822). Poe's aunt. Poe donated several poems to the album of her daughter, Elizabeth Rebecca Herring. *Research: TPL,* xxviii.

Herring, Elizabeth Rebecca. (1815–1889). Poe's cousin. She came to Fordham cottage during Virginia's last days in 1846. Poe wrote several acrostic poems for her. *See:* ''An Acrostic.'' ''Elizabeth.'' *Research: TPL,* xxviii.

Herring, Henry. (1791–1868). The husband of Poe's aunt Elizabeth ''Eliza'' Poe. He attended Poe's funeral in Baltimore on 8 October 1849. *Research: TPL,* xxviii.

Herron, James. Virginia engineer and inventor of the trellis track for railroads. In June 1842, Poe received a $20 gift from Herron. *Research: TPL,* xxviii.

Herschel, Sir John. (1792–1871). English astronomer and author of *The Outline of Astronomy.* In *Eureka,* Poe mentions a phrase in Herschel's writings in reference to star clusters, "a state of *progressive collapse,*" a negative convergence of stellar forces that related to *Eureka*'s central thesis of the universe's tendency to return to primal nothingness. *Text: CWP,* II, 104; VI, 100; XV, 127, 135; XVI, 297–300, 348, 352–353. *Research: PLB,* 87–88.

Hevelius, Johannes. (1611–1687). German astronomer who included a catalogue of stars in his *Prodromus astronomiæ* (1690). He is cited once in *Eureka* for his theory of the clarity of lunar light, that "the moon and its macula do not appear equally lucid, clear and perspicuous at all times, but are much brighter, purer, and more distinct at one time than another." *Text: CWP,* II, 96; XVI, 351–352.

Hewitt, John Hill. (1801–1890). Baltimore journalist and editor of the Baltimore *Saturday Visiter.* He condemned the obscurity of "Al Aaraaf" and made the scurillous claim that Poe was having an affair with his stepmother, Frances Keeling Allan. He was a competitor in the *Saturday Visiter*'s contest and entered a poem, "The Song of the Winds," that won the prize for poetry, thus angering Poe. He was insulted by Poe over the matter of the literary prize and retaliated by dealing Poe "a blow which staggered him, for I was physically his superior." *Research:* Starrett, Vincent. "A Poe Mystery Uncovered: The Lost *Minerva* Review of *Al Aaraaf.*" *Saturday Review of Literature,* 1 May 1943, 4–5, 25; Harwell, Richard B. "A Reputation by Reflection: John Hill Hewitt and Edgar Allan Poe." *Emory University Quarterly,* 3 (1947): 104–114.

Hewitt, Mary Elizabeth. (1818–1850). Amateur poet, bluestocking, and sister-in-law of a Poe foe, John Hill Hewitt. She knew Poe socially in New York City. He included a portrait of her in "The Literati of New York City" in which he cited several "forcible passages" from her poetry but added that her verse was "rather particularly than generally commendable. They lack unity, totality, ultimate effect." *Text: CWP,* XII, 254–259; XIII, 98–105; XV, 123–126; XVI, 38–39. *Research:* Williams, Stanley T. "New Letters About Poe." *Yale Review,* new series, 14 (1925): 755–773; Mabbott, T. O. "Letters from Mary E. Hewitt to Poe." In *A Christmas Book from the Department of English,* Hunter College of the City of New York. Brooklyn: Comet Press, 1937, 116–121; *TPL,* xxviii, 672–674; *MNR,* 383.

Heywood, Bardell. (1824–1899). Relative of Annie Richmond. He knew Poe casually from his visits to Lowell, Massachusetts. *Research:* Coburn, Frederick W. "Poe as Seen by the Brother of 'Annie.' " *New England Quarterly,* 16 (1943): 468–476; Freeman, Fred B., Jr. "Poe's Lowell Trips." *Poe Newsletter,* 4 (December 1971): 23–24; *TPL,* xxviii.

Heywood, Sarah H. (1829–1913). Sister of Bardell Heywood of Lowell, Massachusetts. She knew Poe from his visits to Annie Richmond and composed a memoir consulted by Gill and Ingram, Poe's early biographers. *Research: TPL,* xxviii.

Hicks, Absalom. Character mentioned in the novel *The Narrative of Arthur Gordon Pym.* He is a sailor aboard the *Grampus* who is murdered by Dirk Peters.

Higginson, Thomas Wentworth. (1823–1911). American critic, editor, and epistolary confidant of Emily Dickinson. Higginson never met Poe but was in the audience at the Boston Lyceum on 16 October 1845 to hear Poe's reading and recalled that "every syllable was accentuated with such delicacy, and sustained with such sweetness as I never heard equaled by other lips." He recalled Poe's face during his recitations of "Al Aaraaf" and "The Raven." "It was a face to rivet one's attention in any crowd; yet a face that no one would feel safe in loving." *Research: TPL,* xxviii, 577–578.

Hill, George Handel. (1809–1849). American actor and amateur poet known as "Yankee Hill" for his portrayal of folksy roles. In *Marginalia,* Poe charged Hill with plagiarizing his *The Ruins of Athens and Other Poems.* " *Text: CWP,* XI, 223; XVI, 143.

Hirst, Henry Beck. (1817–1874). Philadelphia poet who published a biographical essay on Poe in the 25 February and 4 March 1843 numbers of the Philadelphia *Saturday Museum.* Poe read law in Hirst's law office but could develop no interest in it. *See:* "The Coming of the Mammoth." *Text: CWP,* XII, 166–180; XV, 65, 269. *Research:* Minor, Benjamin Blake. "Who Wrote 'The Raven'—Poe or Hirst?" Richmond *Times,* 17 February 1895; *LTP,* 420–423; *TPL,* xxviii-xxix, 395–399.

"Historical Sketch; of the Second War between the United States of America and Great Britain, Declared by Act of Congress, the 18th of June, 1812, and Concluded by Peace, the 15th of February, 1815." Review of a historical monograph by Charles J. Ingersoll appearing in *The Broadway Journal* of 11 October 1845. Although Poe feels that the book "is rather a series of vivid pictures on the subject of the late war, than an Historical Sketch of it," he praises the work for its "honesty of narration" and "a plain, discerning and evidently faithful view of the events of the war." *Text: CWP,* XII, 252–254.

***The History of Ireland* (Volume I).** Work by Thomas Moore briefly noticed in *The Southern Literary Messenger* for June 1835. *Research: TPL,* 160.

"The History of Texas: Or the Emigrants', Farmers', and Politicians' Guide to the Character, Climate, Soil, and Productions of That Country; Geographically Arranged from Personal Observation and

Experience. By David B. Edward." Review of a book published in *The Southern Literary Messenger* for August 1836. Poe classifies the book as a "useful oddi[ty] . . . a valuable addition to our very small amount of accurate knowledge in regard to Texas." *Text: CWP,* IX, 78–79.

Hoffman, Charles Fenno. (1806–1884). American poet, New York City litterateur, and editor of the *Knickerbocker Magazine* and the *New York World* during 1847–1848. His verse was favored by Griswold in *The Poets and Poetry of America.* Poe noticed his *A Winter in the West,* by a New Yorker, in *The Southern Literary Messenger* for April 1835 but never reviewed the book. In his portrait of Hoffman in "The Literati of New York City" Poe belittles Griswold's praise for Hoffman's verse. "Whatever may be the merits of Mr. Hoffman as a poet, it may easily be seen that these merits have been put in the worst possible light by the indiscriminate and lavish approbation bestowed on them by Dr. Griswold in his 'Poets and Poetry of America.' " Hoffman's signature in "Autography" "fails in giving a correct idea of the general hand." *Text: CWP,* X, 44; XI, 223, 235, XI, 241; XV, 118–122, 250; XVI, 139. *Research: TPL,* xxix, 244–245.

Hoffman, David. (1784–1854). Lecturer and writer on the study of law and deportment of lawyers. His signature is analyzed in "Autography." "His style is terse, pungent, and otherwise excellent, although disfigured by a half comic half serious pedantry." *Text: CWP,* XV, 232. *Research: TPL,* 317.

Hoffmann, Ernst Theodor Amadeus. (1776–1822). German writer whose tales of grotesque fantasy are often mentioned as forerunners of Poe's work. His story "Das Majorat" [The entail] is an analogue to "The Fall of the House of Usher." Although Poe may have known of Hoffmann's writings, there is no direct allusion to the German dark romantic in his work. Various critics have substantiated the Hoffmann influence. *Research:* Cobb, Palmer. "Poe and Hoffmann." *South Atlantic Quarterly,* 8 (1909): 68–81; Kersten, Kurt. "E. A. Poe und E. Th. Hoffmann." *Fränkische Blätter für Geschichtsforschung und Heimatpflege,* 8, no. 3 (1955): 1–11; Vitt-Maucher, Gisela. "E.T.A. Hoffmann's 'Ritter Gluck' und E. A. Poe's 'The Man of the Crowd': Eine Gegenüberstellung." *German Quarterly,* 43 (1970): 35–46; Lloyd, Rosemary. "Sur Hoffmann, Poe et Baudelaire." *Bulletin Baudelairien,* 11, no. 2 (1976): 11–12; von der Lippe, George B. "The Figure of E.T.A. Hoffmann as *Doppelgänger* to Poe's Roderick Usher." *Modern Language Notes,* 92 (1977): 525–534.

Hogarth, William. (1697–1764). English painter and engraver best known for his series of social caricatures, *The Rake's Progress.* The narrator in "The Literary Life of Thingum Bob" agrees with Hogarth that genius "is but *diligence* after all." Certain decrepit characters in Poe such as the cadaverous gallery of "King Pest" have Hogarthian features. *Text: CWP,* VI, 26; X, 122.

Hogg, James. (1770–1835). Scottish novelist and creator of the novel of the double life *The Private Memoirs and Confessions of a Justified Sinner* (1824). In several obscure references, Poe might have used his name (spelled "Hog") to pun on Sir Francis Bacon in *Eureka*. "For many centuries, so great was the infatuation, about Hog especially, that a virtual stop was put to all thinking, properly so called." *Text: CWP,* XVI, 189–191, 195, 197.

Holden, Ezra. (1803–1846). Editor of the Philadelphia *Saturday Courier* and *Holden's Dollar Magazine*. His review of Poe's *Tales of the Grotesque and Arabesque* appeared there on 14 December 1839. In "Autography," Poe stated that his signature "indicates the frank and naive manner of his literary style—a style which not unfrequently flies off into whimsicalities." *Text: CWP,* XV, 212. *Research: TPL,* xxix.

Holmes, Dr. Oliver Wendell. (1809–1894). Professor of anatomy at Dartmouth College and, as he is profiled in "Autography," "the best of the humorous poets of the day." In December 1846, Poe wrote to Boston publisher William D. Ticknor, asking for a copy of Holmes's verse. Poe also agreed with Holmes that English is deficient in spondees and cited Holmes's line " 'Our grating English, whose Teutonic jar/ Shakes the rack'd axle of Art's rattling car.' " *Text: CWP,* XI, 126, 227; XV, 38, 256. *Research: TPL,* 675–676.

"Holy Eyes." Title of a poem included by Mabbott in his edition of the poems based on a tradition in the Houghton family that Poe planned and wrote such a poem for Marie Louise Shew. *Text: MCW,* I, 404–405.

Home Journal. New York City newspaper formerly the *National Press* and edited by Nathaniel P. Willis. The *Home Journal* reprinted "Ulalume: A Ballad" on 1 January 1848, printed Sarah Whitman's Valentine poem to Poe on 18 March 1848, and reprinted "For Annie" with a commentary by Willis on 28 April 1849. *Research: TPL,* 665–666, 674–677, 751–752, 799–800.

Homer. (ca. 900–800 B.C.). Greek epic poet and author of *The Iliad* and *The Odyssey*. Poe's familiarity with the Homeric epics is evidenced by observations on Homer's language in *Pinakidia.* He noted that the word, "Fortune does not appear once in the whole Iliad," and that, "There are about one thousand lines identical in the Iliad and Odyssey." Poe also showed an interest in the heroic apparatus of the epics, editions and versions of the poems in ancient times, and the meanings of specific lines. "In xviii, 192, of the Iliad, Achilles says none of the armor of the chieftains will fit him except the shield of Ajax: how then did his own armor fit Patroclus?" There are allusive references to Homer's epics in "The Man of the Crowd" (*Iliad* V, 127. Athene's removal of the haze from the eyes of Diomedes), and "The Imp of the Perverse" (the supernatural blow felt by the narrator recalls Apollo's striking of Patroclus) and "Shadow—A

Parable'' (where the multiple voices of the shadow recall the voice of Helen of Troy described in the *Odyssey*, IV, 277–279 where she speaks with many voices of the wives of the heroes). Poe also used various Homeric events as in his adaptation of Odysseus's encounter with the whirlpool Charybdis in Book XII of the *Odyssey* and the situation of the Norwegian fisherman in ''A Descent into the Maelström.'' *Text: CWP,* X, 43; XI, 148; XIV, 42; 44; 48; 53; 64; 66; 67; 246; XVI, 112. *Research: MCW,* II, 516; III, 1227.

Hood, Thomas. (1799–1845). English Romantic poet. Poe held Hood's verse in high regard but also considered his genius ''the result of vivid Fancy impelled, or controlled,—certainly tinctured, at all points, by hypochondriasis.'' In a review of Longfellow's ''The Waif'' in the New York *Evening Mirror* of 13–14 January 1845, Poe accused the poet James Aldrich of plagiarizing Hood's ''The Death-Bed.'' The charge brought immediate reaction from several Poe foes including Charles Briggs, who remarked in the 15 February 1845 number of *The Broadway Journal* that there was nothing ''sufficient to warrant the charge'' except ''the measure and subject which are certainly not peculiar to Hood.'' The ''Outis'' letter of 1 March 1845 in the New York *Evening Mirror* also refutes the charge of plagiarism. Poe defended his claim of Aldrich's theft of Hood's poem in several essays condemning plagiarism beginning with his ''Imitation—Plagiarism'' in the 15 February 1845 New York *Evening Mirror.* Plagiarism is a sin that ''involves the quintessence of meanness'' and is deadliest where found in prominent authors. Poe included discussions of Hood's ''Fair Ines,'' ''The Haunted House,'' and ''Bridge of Sighs'' in the text of ''The Poetic Principle,'' appraising Hood's verse to be ''powerfully ideal—imaginative.'' *See:* ''Wiley & Putnam's Library of Choice Reading, No. XVI. Prose and Verse. By Thomas Hood.'' *Text: CWP,* XII, 213–222; XIV, 283–287; XV, 62; XVI, 96. *Research: LET,* 332.

Hope, Thomas. (1770–1831). English novelist and travel writer. His oriental picaresque tale *Anastasius* (1819), gained Poe's praise as ''[t]hat most excellent and vivid (although somewhat immoral) series of Turkish paintings [which] left nothing farther to be expected, or even to be desired, in rich, bold, vigorous, and accurate delineation of the scenery, characters, manners, and peculiarities of the region to which its pages were devoted.'' *Text: CWP,* VIII, 223, 256–257.

"Hop-Frog." Short story by Poe first published in *The Flag of Our Union* of 17 March 1849 under the title ''Hop-Frog; Or, The Eight Chained Ourang-outangs.'' One certain source for Poe's fairytale of a court jester's revenge appeared in a passage quoted from the chronicles of the French medieval historian Jean Froissart in *The Broadway Journal* of 1 February 1845 that described a fire at the court of Charles VI. Unusual for Poe's normal working point of view, the tale is told through an innocent-eyed spectator, but it does resemble several other stories that focus on ingenious and well-deserved revenge as well as the human-into-beast motif. Three earlier stories in particular, ''The Cask of Amontillado,'' ''Four Beasts in One,'' and ''The System of Doctor Tarr and Professor Fether,'' have scenic and thematic connections with ''Hop-Frog,'' a story involving a preplanned and elaborately executed revenge for injuries suffered at the hands of fools. Humiliated and sadistically mocked by the King and his ministers, the crippled dwarf Hop-Frog devises a revenge that will literally make monkeys out of his tormentors and allow him to have the last laugh as he escapes from his captivity in the cruel court. To satisfy the King's craving for bizarre amusements, Hop-Frog provides ''something novel'' for the entertainment of the court, the ultimate prank as it were. Hop-Frog's suggestion is made just after the King has thrown wine into the face of the little dancer, Trippetta, Hop-Frog's fellow sufferer inside the palace. Hop-Frog proposes ''a capital diversion,'' a masquerade that has the King and his ministers put on tight-fitting costumes soaked with tar and covered with flax to make them look like ourangoutangs. At midnight, the eight ourangoutangs are suspended en masse from a chain attached to the chandelier, then set ablaze by the agile dwarf who now gives his final court performance and has the last laugh as he vanishes through a hole in the ceiling while ''[t]he eight corpses swung in their chains, a fetid, blackened, hideous, and indistinguishable mass.'' Because the tale relies so heavily on inversions of the human-beast and master-slave implications, it invites comparison with Melville's ''Benito Cereno.'' Whereas Hop-Frog (not his own name, but a name given to him by his masters) is enslaved and treated with brutal scorn, he is actually the heroic man, while the King, who thinks of himself as the paragon of civility, is really an animal. While Poe's fiction often resists political analyses, ''Hop-Frog'' might be a notable exception since the main character who is racially unspecified but deformed shares a fate in common with African slaves who likewise ''had been forcibly carried off from their respective homes'' and made to perform for their masters. Other parallels with the institution of slavery in nineteenth-century America are too pervasive to ignore. King and court view Hop-Frog's involuntary servitude as natural, just, and morally uncomplicated, while the survivors are ''horror-stricken'' by the ''fiery revenge'' that precedes the jester's flight to freedom. The narrator's closing observation that Hop-Frog and Trippetta ''effected their escape into their own country'' is an additional argument for a political reading of the fairytale. *Text: MCW,* III, 1343–1355; *CWP,* VI, 216–228. *Research:* Martin, Bruce K. ''Poe's 'Hop-Frog' and the Retreat from Comedy.'' *Studies in Short Fiction*, 10 (1973): 288–290; Pauly, Thomas H. '' 'Hop-Frog'—Is the Last Laugh Best?'' *Studies in Short Fiction*, 11 (1974): 307–309; Bachinger, Katrina. ''Together (or Not Together) Against Tyranny: Poe, Byron, and Napoleon Upside Down in 'Hop-Frog.' '' *Texas Studies in Language and Literature*, 33 (1991): 373–404.

"Hop-Frog; Or, The Eight Chained Ourangoutangs." Original title for the short story ''Hop Frog.'' *See:* ''Hop Frog.''

Hopkins, Charles. The first husband of Elizabeth Arnold Poe. He was an actor. *Research: PLL,* 2.

Hopkins, Reverend John Henry, Jr. (1820–1891). He summarized Poe's lecture on "The Universe" in the 4 February 1848 edition of the New York *Morning Express* and warned Marie Louise Shew against continuing her relationship with Poe lest she corrupt her religious faith through contact with his atheistic ideas, especially the dangerous pantheism of *Eureka. Research: TPL,* xxix, 745–746.

Hopkinson, Joseph. (1770–1842). Philadelphia judge and author of "Hail Columbia." In "Autography" Poe observed that his signature "evinc[ed] *indefatigability* of temperament." *Text: CWP,* XV, 162–163, 201. *Research: TPL,* xix.

Horace [Quintus Horatius Flaccus]. (65–8 B.C.). Roman poet. Poe includes a hypothetical scansion as Horace might have accomplished it of the First Ode ("Mæcenas atavis edite regibus") "when assured by the prosodists that he had no business to make any such division" in "The Rationale of Verse." *Text: CWP,* VIII, 45; XIV, 58, 171, 257–258; XVI, 47. *Research:* Pritchard, John Paul. "Horace and Edgar Allan Poe." *Classical Weekly,* 26 (6 March 1933): 129–133.

Horne, Richard Henry. (1803–1884). British poet, Poe correspondent, and author of the poem *Orion,* enthusiastically reviewed by Poe. *See:* "Orion." *Text: CWP,* XI, 244, 249–275; XIV, 233–244; XV, 124. *Research: PJC,* 339–344; *TPL,* xxix.

Horse, "A Gigantic and Fiery-Colored." Principal equine character in the short story "Metzengerstein." He is the agent of Count Berlifitzing's revenge.

"Horse-Shoe Robinson: A Tale of the Tory Ascendency." Review of an historical novel by John Pendleton Kennedy appearing in *The Southern Literary Messenger* for May 1835. Except for punctuation in the novel, Poe's comments were positive and laudatory. These volumes "will place Mr. Kennedy at once in the very first rank of American novelists." *Text: CWP,* VIII, 4–11. *Research: PLB,* 52; *LET,* I, 59–60; *PJC,* 80–83.

Horsley, Bishop Samuel. (1733–1806). English clergyman and Bishop of Rochester. His bitter remark on the law, "that the people have nothing to do with the laws but obey them," was cited by Poe in "Three Sundays in a Week" and again in "Fifty Suggestions." *Text: CWP,* IV, 230; XIV, 184. *Research: BRE,* 505.

"House of Furniture." Later title of the sketch "The Philosophy of Furniture." *See:* "The Philosophy of Furniture."

Housman, A.[lfred] E.[dward]. (1859–1936). English poet, critic, and classicist scholar. He expressed both an admiration and distaste for Poe's poetry, writing of ''The Haunted Palace'' in ''The Name and Nature of Poetry'' (1933) that it ''is one of Poe's best poems so long as we are content to swim in the sensations it evokes and only vaguely to apprehend the allegory. We are roused to discomfort, at least I am, when we begin to perceive how exact in detail the allegory is.'' *Research: PLL,* 111.

"How to Write a Blackwood Article." Short story in the form of a mock essay first published under the title ''The Psyche Zenobia'' in the Baltimore *American Museum* for November 1838. The same issue also printed ''The Scythe of Time'' (later entitled ''A Predicament''), which might be a sample of a model Blackwood article. The story appeared under the title ''How to Write a Blackwood Article'' in *The Broadway Journal* of 12 July 1845. Self-parody is certainly a strong possibility in this story, for Poe appears to mock some of his own in extreme situations and outré methods as well as the repetitive types and tenor of Blackwood's own horror offerings in a typical issue of the magazine. The narrator is Signora Psyche Zenobia who is heard from again in ''A Predicament.'' She is proud of her unusual name and resents the alias of ''Suky Snobbs'' pinned on her by the gossip Miss Tabitha Turnip. The ''How'' of writing the successful Blackwood article comes from Blackwood himself who discloses his editorial secrets in an interview with Signora Psyche Zenobia. Blackwood's advice is a mishmash of model passages from Schiller and Cervantes mixed in with Chinese and Chickasaw expressions. He urges her to throw in some ''nice Latin phrases'' and be sure to show off her Greek whether she knows the language or not. His parting gem of wisdom, when she comes to write stories of imminent horrible death, is: ''[T]hen only think of the sensations!''—a piece of advice that she follows to the letter in composing ''A Predicament.'' Analyzing the sensations during a fatal experience is also the formula applied by Poe himself in such tales as ''The Pit and the Pendulum'' and ''A Descent into the Maelström.'' *Epigraph:* '' 'In the name of the Prophet—figs!!'' James and Horace Smith, *Rejected Addresses: or The New Theatrum Poetarum* [other possible sources have been suggested]. *Texts: MCW,* II, 336–362; *CWP,* II, 269–282. *Research:* Taylor, Walter F. ''Israfel in Motley.'' *Sewanee Review*, 42 (1934): 330–340; Allen, Michael. *Poe and the British Magazine Tradition.* New York: Oxford University Press, 1969; McClary, Ben Harris. ''Poe's 'Turkish Fig Peddler.' '' *Poe Newsletter*, 2 (October 1969): 56.

Howard, Lieutenant J. Officer serving with Poe at Fort Moultrie. He assisted Poe in obtaining an early discharge from the army. *Research: TPL,* 84, 87, 90–91, 95–96.

Howells, William Dean. (1837–1920). American critic, novelist, and proponent of realism in literature. He mentioned Poe's tales of ratiocination in connection with the analytic qualities of Lincoln's mind in his biography of Lincoln. Howells told Emerson that he had once delighted in the cruel acuity of Poe's literary criticism. *Research:* Howells, William Dean. ''Edgar Allan Poe.'' *Harper's Weekly,* 16 January 1909, 12–13; *PLL,* 264.

Hoyle, Edmond. (1672–1769). Author of ''A Short Treatise on Whist,'' the authoritative rules book of the card game. Poe declared, ''If the popularity of a book be the measure of its worth, we should not be at once in condition to admit the inferiority of 'Newton's Principia' to 'Hoyle's Games.' '' The rules of Hoyle are also mentioned by the narrator in ''The Murders in the Rue Morgue'' as logical and comprehensible—hence, limited and suspect. *Text: CWP,* IV, 148; XI, 40.

Hoyt, Ralph. (1806–1878). American clergyman poet and author of *A Chaunt of Life and Other Poems.* There is a profile of Hoyt in ''The Literati of New York City.'' Poe thought many of the poems in Hoyt's collection full of ''rich imagination and exquisite pathos.'' *Text: CWP,* XII, 193–201; XV, 37–38. *Research: TPL,* 554, 641.

Hubner, Charles William. (1835–1929). Amateur man of letters. He attended Poe's funeral and wrote a reminiscence of the event. *Research: TPL,* xxix.

Hudson, Henry Norman. (1814–1886). Shakespearean scholar and lecturer. Poe met him after a Lyceum recitation in October 1845. In a letter to Evert A. Duyckinck dated 24 November 1845, Hudson claimed to be the author of an attack on Poe appearing in the *Boston Evening Transcript* of 18 October 1845. Hudson did aim occasional barbs at Poe, attacking his conduct after his Lyceum performance as ''utterly beneath the dignity of a gentleman; a disgrace to the name of literature.'' Poe mentions Hudson in connection with other ''Frogpondians'' in the editorial ''Boston and the Bostonians.'' There are several derogations of Hudson's abilities as a literary critic in *Marginalia.* ''No man living could say what it is Mr. Hudson proposes to demonstrate; and if the question were propounded to Mr. H. himself, we can fancy how particularly embarrassed he would be for a reply.'' *See:* ''Mr. Hudson.'' *Text: CWP,* XVI, 83–84, 90; XVI, 100. *Research: TPL,* xxix.

Hugo, Victor. (1802–1885). French novelist, dramatist, and author of *Les Misérables.* His controversial play *Hernani* (1830) is mentioned by Poe in ''The Masque of the Red Death'' in describing the ''glare and glitter'' of Prince Prospero's chambers. *Text: CWP,* IV, 259; X, 134, 136–37; XI, 26, 59; XVI, 172. *Research:* Mabbott, T. O. ''Another Source of Poe's Play, 'Politian.' '' *Notes & Queries,* 194 (June 1949): 279; Pollin, Burton. ''Victor Hugo and Poe.'' *DIP,* 1–23; Bandy, W. T. ''Hugo's View of Poe.'' *Revue de Littérature Comparée,* 49 (1975): 480–483; Breuer, Horst. ''E. A. Poe und Victor Hugo: Zur Quellenlage von Poes Erzählung.'' In *Theorie* *und Praxis im Erzählen des 19. und 20. Jahrhunderts: Studien zur englischen und amerikanischen Literatur zu Ehren von Willi Erzgräber.* Tübingen: Narr, 1986, 219–232.

"Human Magnetism; Its Claim to Dispassionate Inquiry. Being an Attempt to Show the Utility of Its Application for the Relief of Human Suffering. By W. Newnham." Review of a book on the hygienic and curative powers of magnetism appearing in *The Broadway Journal* of 5 April 1845. Although Poe ''disagree[s] with the author in some of the ideas of the curative effects of magnetism,'' he does not dispute ''in any degree, the prodigious importance of the mesmeric influence in surgical cases.'' *See:* Mesmerism. *Text: CWP,* XII, 121–123.

Human-Perfectibility Man. Character in ''Lionizing'' who attends the Prince of Wales's banquet and quotes all of the optimistic philosophers.

Humboldt, Friedrich Heinrich Alexander Baron von. (1769–1859). German mathematician and cosmologist. Poe dedicated *Eureka* to him and alluded to his ideas in several passages. *Text: CWP,* II, 67; XVI, 181–186.

Hume, David. (1711–1776). Scottish philosopher and religious skeptic. His intellectual skepticism is set against the intuitive positions of Joseph Hume (1777–1855) in *Eureka.* ''If the ability to conceive be taken as a criterion of Truth, then a truth to *David* Hume would very seldom be a truth to *Joe*; and ninety-nine hundredths of what is undeniable in Heaven would be demonstrable falsity upon Earth.'' *Text: CWP,* XI, 136; XVI, 193. *Research: PJC,* 21.

Hunt, Freeman. (1804–1858). A literary acquaintance of Poe who testified as a character witness in Poe's libel suit against Dr. Thomas Dunn English. Hunt had favorably reviewed *The Raven and Other Poems* in *The Merchant's Magazine*, which he published and edited. Poe included a portrait of Hunt in ''The Literati of New York City.'' Poe admired his tenaciousness and editorial fortitude. ''Having without aid put the magazine on a satisfactory footing as regards its circulation, he also without aid undertook its editorial and business conduct—from the first germ of the conception to the present moment having kept the whole undertaking within his own hands.'' *Text: CWP,* XV, 40–43. *Research:* Pollin, Burton R. ''Poe, Freeman Hunt, and Four Unrecorded Reviews of Poe's Works.'' *Texas Studies in Literature and Language*, 16 (1974): 305–313.

Hunt, Jedediah, Jr. (1815–1860). American editor with whom Poe corresponded on a single occasion when Hunt assailed Poe's critical theories in the Ithaca, New York, *National Archives* for 13 March 1845. *Research: TPL,* xxix, 518–519.

Hunt, John. Character mentioned in the novel *The Narrative of Arthur Gordon Pym.* He is a sailor on board the *Grampus.*

Hunt, Leigh [James Henry]. (1784–1859). English poet, essayist, and editor. As an essayist, Poe thought that his style resembled Hazlitt's but was inferior to it. ''Hunt has written many agreeable papers, but no great ones. His points will bear no steady examination.'' *See:* ''Wiley & Putnam's Library of Choice Reading, No. XX.'' *Text: CWP,* XI, 105; XII, 226, 237–238; XIII, 171; XIV, 220; XVI, 111.

Hunt, Wilson Price. (1783–1842). Chief agent of John Jacob Astor in the Pacific Fur Company. He is mentioned in ''Astoria.'' His published diary, ''A Sea Voyage from New York to the Columbia's Mouth,'' was consulted by Poe. *Text: CWP,* IX, 216–217.

Hunter, Robert Mercer Taliaferro. (1809–1887). A student who was acquainted with Poe at the University of Virginia. *Research: TPL,* xxv-xxvi.

Hunter, William. Poe's fellow student at Dr. Bransby's school at Stoke Newington. *Research: PLL,* 13.

Huxley, Aldous. (1894–1963). English novelist. He disliked Poe almost as much as he detested Shelley. Poe was guilty of ''incorrigibly bad taste'' and wrote an awkward ''walloping dactylic metre.'' Especially distressed by Poe's vulgarity and cheap sensationalism, Huxley inverted the high appraisal of Poe's French admirers: ''Baudelaire, Mallarmé, and Valéry are wrong and Poe is not one of our major poets.'' *Research:* Falk, Robert P. ''The Decline and Fall of the House of Usher.'' In *American Literature in Parody.* New York: Twayne, 1955, 105–125.

Huysmans, Joris-Karl. (1848–1907). French decadent writer. In his novel *À Rebours* [Against nature] (1884), Huysmans recognized the link running from Poe through Baudelaire to his own decadent dreams of odd and horrid beauty. Huysmans modeled his isolated aesthete protagonist Des Esseintes after ''the wise and wonderful Edgar Allan Poe,'' who ''better perhaps than anyone else, possessed those intimate affinities that could satisfy the requirements of Des Esseintes's mind.'' *Research:* Cevasco, G. A. ''*À Rebours* and Poe's Reputation in France.'' *Romance Notes*, 13 (1971): 255–261; Bandy, W. T. ''Huysmans and Poe.'' *Romance Notes*, 17 (1977): 270–271.

"Hymn." Poem first published as a song sung by Morella in the first printing of the story ''Morella'' and later published seperately as ''A Catholic Hymn'' in *The Broadway Journal* of 16 August 1845. In the short story ''Morella,'' the poem is a supplication to the Blessed Virgin by the heroine. Poe dropped it from later printings of ''Morella.'' The poem consists of twelve lines of rhyming couplets and is addressed to the Holy Virgin. The poem is unusual for Poe in its conventional beseeching of Mary's guidance and intercession when ''storms of Fate o'ercast.'' Unusual, too, is the poet's hopeful expression of a radiant future gained through Mary's succor. *See:* ''Morella.'' *Text: MCW,* I, 216–218.

"Hymn to Aristogeiton and Harmodius. Translation from the Greek." Patriotic poem to the Athenian warriors and freedom fighters and published as ''Greek Song'' under the signature P. in *The Southern Literary Messenger* for December 1835. ''Ye deliverers of Athens from shame!/ Ye avengers of Liberty's wrongs!'' Poe salutes these ''Beloved heroes'' whose souls reside on ''the isles of the blest . . . Where Achilles and Diomed rest.'' *Text: MCW,* I, 507.

"Hyperion: A Romance." Review of a narrative poem by Henry Wadsworth Longfellow appearing in *Burton's Gentleman's Magazine* for October 1839. Poe handles Longfellow roughly referring to the poem as a ''farrago'' and ''the grief of all true criticism.'' Although ''Hyperion'' has ''a profusion of rich thought,'' it lacks unity and is ''without design, without shape, without beginning, middle, or end. . . . We, therefore, dismiss his 'Hyperion' in brief.'' *Text: CWP,* X, 39–40. *Research: PJC,* 227.

I

"I Promessi Sposi, or The Betrothed Lovers; A Milanese Story of the Seventeenth Century." Review of the English translation of an Italian novel by Alessandro Manzoni appearing in *The Southern Literary Messenger* for May 1835. Poe liked Manzoni's historical romance but felt that it was imitative of Sir Walter Scott's *Waverley*. Poe also identified with the harsh deadline imposed by the publisher on the exploited translator. "The translation has many faults. We lament it the more, because they are obviously faults of haste. The translator, we fear, was hungry; a misfortune with which we know how to sympathize." *Text: CWP,* VIII, 12–19. *Research:* Holsapple, Cortell King. " 'The Masque of the Red Death' and *I Promessi Sposi*." *University of Texas Studies in English*, 18 (1938): 137–139.

Ianthe. Character in the poem "Al Aaraaf." She is an angelic creature who encourages her lover Angelo to be happy on the star Al Aaraaf.

Ide, Abijah Metcalf, Jr. (1825–1873). Amateur poet of South Attleborough, Massachusetts, and occasional Poe correspondent. Some of Ide's poems were published in the *Broadway Journal* in 1845. Several of these poems ("To Isidore," "Annette," "The Forest Reverie") were erroneously assigned to Poe by Ingram. *Research: MCW,* I, 509; *TPL,* xxix, 438–440.

"Ideals and Other Poems. By Algernon Henry Perkins." Review of a collection of poems appearing in *Graham's Magazine* for April 1842. Poe found most of the verse imitative of Longfellow, second rate, and commonplace.

''There is much poetry in his book, but none of a lofty order. . . . It has nothing, except its mechanical execution, to distinguish it from the multitudinous ephemera with which our national poetical press is now groaning.'' *Text: CWP,* XI, 114–115.

"Imitation." Poem by Poe first published in the collection *Tamerlane and Other Poems*, (1827). The poem is a twenty-line meditation in rhyming couplets in which the poet recalls his youth as a beautiful dream that contrasts sharply with a less-attractive present. At the poem's end, the poet attempts to reject his memories. ''And my worldly rest hath gone/ With a sigh as it passed on:/ I care not though it perish/ With a thought I then did cherish.'' *Text: MCW,* I, 75–76. *Research:* Ryan, John K. ''Growth of a Judgment.'' *Catholic Education Review*, 45 (February 1947): 85–96.

"Imitation—Plagiarism—Mr. Poe's Reply to the Letter of Outis—A Large Account of a Small Matter—A Voluminous History of the Little Longfellow War." A lengthy five-part defensive position paper on Poe's altercation with Longfellow and his accusation of plagiarism. Part one, ''A Reply to Outis,'' appeared in *The Broadway Journal* of 8 March 1845; part two, ''A Continuation of the Voluminous History of the Little Longfellow War—Mr. Poe's Further Reply to the Letter of Outis,'' ran on 15 March 1845; part three, ''A Reply to Outis,'' ran on 22 March; part four, ''A Reply to Outis,'' ran on 29 March; and part five, ''Postscript,'' ran on 5 April 1845. In the paper of 8 March Poe discussed plagiarism in general and observed, ''The attempt to *prove*, however, by reasoning *a priori*, that plagiarism cannot exist, is too good an idea on the part of Outis not to be a plagiarism in itself.'' In the paper of 15 March, Poe continued his attack on Outis's claim that the crime of literary theft does not exist by asking, ''Do I rightly comprehend Outis as demonstrating the impossibility of plagiarism where it *is* possible, by adducing instances of inevitable similarity where it is *not*?'' The third paper of 22 March reacts explicitly to Outis's comparison of Poe's ''The Raven'' with Bryant's ''The Dying Raven.'' ''When Outis, for example, picks out his eighteen coincidences . . . from a poem so long as The Raven in collation with a poem not forthcoming, and which may therefore, or anything anybody knows to the contrary, be as long as an infinite flock of ravens, he is merely putting himself into unnecessary trouble in getting together phantoms of arguments that can have no substance wherewith.'' In the fourth paper of 29 March, Poe offers parallel passages from Tennyson's ''The Death of the Old Year'' and Longfellow's ''Midnight Mass for the Dying Year'' as solid evidence of gross plagiarism. ''The fact of the matter is, that the friends of Mr. Longfellow, so far from undertaking to talk about my 'carping littleness' in charging Mr. Longfellow with imitation, should have given me credit, under the circumstances, for great moderation in charging him with imitation alone.'' The postscript of 5 April is conciliatory in tone, Poe writing, ''It should not be supposed that I feel myself individually aggrieved in the letter of Outis. . . . In replying to him, my design has been to place fairly and distinctly before the literary public certain principles of criticism for which I have been long contending.'' *See:* The Longfellow War; Outis. *Text: CWP,* XII, 41–106.

"The Imp of the Perverse." Short story first published in *Graham's Magazine* for July 1845 and reprinted in *The May-Flower for 1846.* The tale combines elements of confessional narrative and discursive essay, moving from an objective commentary on the human tendency to commit acts of perversity to a subjective outburst by the murderer-narrator whose perverse crimes have resulted in his ''tenanting this cell of the condemned.'' In essayist fashion, the narrator discourses scientifically on ''the spirit of the *Perverse*,'' asserting, ''We perpetrate them [i.e., perverse actions] merely because we feel that we should *not*. Beyond or behind this there is no intelligible principle.'' By demonstrating the discomforting psychological truth that human beings are often motivated by self-destructive impulses, ''The Imp of the Perverse'' posits a basis for understanding the irrational deeds of many Poe characters such as the impulsive murderers of ''The Tell-Tale Heart'' and ''The Black Cat.'' The imp-narrator makes it clear that the desire for self-punishment does not necessarily concern guilt or the need to receive justice from an authority figure. Instead, confession occurs when the criminal realizes the perverse pleasure involved in actively dooming himself; and the imp cannot be gratified until others are made fully aware of his crimes. Thus, the imp compels the criminal to publicize his perverse acts. As the narrator describes this irrepressible motive: ''Some invisible fiend, I thought, struck me with his broad palm upon the back. The long imprisoned secret burst forth from my soul.'' Biographically inclined critics have argued the connections between the tale and the many self-destructive choices Poe made throughout his life. Since perversity is one of the leading characteristics of Poe's interpersonal relationships, he might quickly agree with the narrator that ''I am one of the many uncounted victims of the Imp of the Perverse.'' Poe's biographers have accumulated overwhelming evidence of his perversity in his self-indulgence, his calculated collisions with authority figures, his alcoholic abuse and abusiveness, and his erratic treatment of others to the point where both friends and professional colleagues found him quite unbearable. One might extend the imp's forceful presence in Poe's own life to his slashing manner in book reviews, the drive to mutilate, to scarify, and to destroy literary foes for its own sake. The hegemony of the imp in the human makeup is confirmed in the work of writers strongly influenced by Poe's acknowledgment of the perverse in this tale. Certainly the ''longing of the soul to vex itself—to offer violence to its own nature—to do wrong for wrong's sake only'' drives and determines character behavior in the writings of Dostoevsky, Baudelaire, Kafka, Flannery O'Connor, and Joyce Carol Oates. *Text: MCW,* III, 1217–1227; *CWP,* VI, 145–153. *Research:* Kanjo, Eugene R. '' 'The Imp of the Perverse': Poe's Dark Comedy of Art and Death.'' *Poe Newsletter,* 2 (October 1969): 41–44; Spanier, Sandra Whipple. '' 'Nests of Boxes': Form, Sense, and Style in Poe's 'The Imp of the Perverse.' '' *Studies in Short Fiction,* 17 (1980): 307–

316; Brown, Arthur A. "Death and Telling in Poe's 'The Imp of the Perverse.' " *Studies in Short Fiction*, 31 (1994): 197–205.

"Impromptu—To Kate Carol." Unsigned four-line poem included by J. H. Whitty in his 1911 edition of *Poe's Complete Poems* and identified as the work of Poe by T. O. Mabbott. The lines first appeared in *The Broadway Journal* of 26 April 1845 and celebrated the poetic charms of Frances Sargent Osgood who sometimes used the pseudonym "Kate Carol." "When from your gems of thought I turn/ To those pure orbs, your heart to learn,/ I scarce know which to prize most high—/ The bright *i-dea*, or bright *dear-eye*." *Text: MCW,* I, 379–380. *Research:* Varner, John Grier. "Note on a Poem Attributed to Poe." *American Literature*, 8 (1936): 66–68.

" 'In Youth I Have Known One with Whom the Earth.' " Untitled poem by Poe first published in July 1827 in *Tamerlane and Other Poems*. The poem is in four octaves and is addressed to a mysterious "he . . . Whose fervid, flickering torch of life was lit/ From the sun and stars, whence he had drawn forth/ A passionate light such for his spirit was fit—" *See:* "Stanzas." *Text: MCW,* I, 76–78.

"Inaugural Address of the Reverend D. L. Carroll, D.D., President of Hampden Sidney College, Delivered on His Induction into That Office." Review of the address appearing in *The Southern Literary Messenger* for December 1835. Poe quotes several extracts and refers the reader to Carroll's remarks on "a subject too long overlooked, and too much neglected in all our schools. We refer to social qualities. On this subject the author's ideas are just and timely." *Text: CWP,* VIII, 116–117.

"Incidents of Travel in Central America, Etc. By John L. Stephens." Review of a book of travel sketches that Poe never received or read appearing in *Graham's Magazine* for August 1841. Poe considered Stephens to be deficient in profundity as a travel writer. Much of this review centers on Stephens's mistranslations of Hebrew in *Arabia Petræa*, but he is "not prepared to say that misunderstandings of this character will be found in the present 'Incidents of Travel.' . . . Here all is darkness. We have not yet received from the Messieurs Harper a copy of the book, and can only speak of its merits from general report and from the cursory perusal which has been afforded us by the politeness of a friend." *Text: CWP,* X, 178–181.

"Incidents of Travel in Egypt, Arabia Petræa, and the Holy Land." Archeological monograph and travelogue by John L. Stephens reviewed in *The New York Review* for October 1837. Poe had corresponded with Charles Anthon, asking him to translate several Hebrew quotations from the Old Testament since he was convinced while preparing the review that the book contained several inaccurate references. Poe respected Stephens's erudition and found the book to be "highly agreeable, interesting, and instructive," especially the sections dealing with the Holy Land. Poe did challenge the accuracy of some of the scriptural quotations in Hebrew and took exception to a few "misstatements" such as Stephens's locating of the place where Moses crossed the Red Sea. *Text: CWP,* X, 1–25.

"Infatuation." Satirical poem by Park Benjamin that Poe believed to be one of the best examples of the genre. "The poem is full of nerve, point, and terseness—the thrusts are dextrous and well aimed—and the versification peculiarly good of its kind." *See:* "Satirical Poems." *Text: CWP,* XII, 107–110; XIII, 165.

"The Infidel; or The Fall of Mexico, a Romance." Favorable review of a historical novel by Robert Montgomery Bird appearing in *The Southern Literary Messenger* for June 1835. The novel is a sequel to Bird's *Calavar; or The Knight of the Conquest.* "It is a work of great power. . . . We think the Infidel fully equal to its predecessor, and in some respects superior." *Text: CWP,* VIII, 32–37. *Research: PJC,* 85.

Ingram, James K. (fl. 1840). American novelist. Poe said of him in "Autography," "He appeals always to the tastes of the ultraromanticists . . . and thus is obnoxious to the charge of a certain cut-and-thrust, blue-fire melodramaticism." Poe perhaps had in mind Ingram's *Amelia Somers, the Orphan; or, The Buried Alive. Text: CWP,* XV, 188.

Ingram, John Henry. (1842–1916). Poe's first English biographer. Author of *Edgar Allan Poe: His Life, Letters and Opinions* (1874). He traced many Poe letters and corresponded extensively with Sarah Helen Whitman and Annie Richmond, enabling him capably to refute many of Griswold's venomous lies about Poe's relationships with women. The Ingram-Poe Collection is located in the Alderman Library at the University of Virginia, Charlottesville, Virginia. The Ingram-Whitman letters were published in 1979 as *Poe's Helen Remembers. Research:* Ticknor, Caroline. "Ingram—Discourager of Poe Biographers." *Bookman,* 44 (September 1916): 8–14; Wilson, James Southall. "Poe at the University of Virginia: Unpublished Letters from the Ingram Collection." *University of Virginia Alumni Bulletin,* 16, 3rd series (April 1923): 163–167; Miller, John Carl, comp. *John Henry Ingram's Poe Collection at the University of Virginia.* Charlottesville: University of Virginia Press, 1960; Hoffman, Paul Phillips, ed. *Guide to Microfilm Edition of John Henry Ingram's Poe Collection.* Charlottesville: University of Virginia Library, 1967; Miller, John Carl, "Poe's English Biographer." *BPB,* 1–18; Miller, John Carl. "John Henry Ingram Prepares to Write His Biography of Edgar Allan Poe." *BPB,* 235–244.

Inklings of Adventure. Book of sketches by Nathaniel Parker Willis reviewed by Poe in *The Southern Literary Messenger* for August 1836. This same number also included brief, untitled filler notices on an old play in ''Dodsley's Collection,'' on the power of the Inquisition, and Swift's ''Lilliputian Ode.'' There were also notes on ''The Battle of Lodi,'' ''The City of Sin,'' and ''MSS. of John Randolph.'' *Research: LET,* I, 99; *TPL,* 221.

Inman, Henry. (1801–1846). American portrait painter and engraver. He had done Fitz-Greene Halleck as well as Chief Justice Marshall. *Research: CWP,* XV, 56.

Insane Retreat at Utica New York. Throughout 1846, the rumor circulated that Poe had been confined to this mental institution. The *St. Louis Daily Reveillé* printed the insanity rumor on 12 April 1846 with the ''hope that this is not true; indeed, we feel assured that it is altogether an invention.'' Poe may have initiated stories of his insanity himself. *Research: TPL,* 633–634.

"Instinct Vs Reason—A Black Cat." Unsigned essay identified as Poe's work by Clarence Saunders Brigham and appearing in the Philadelphia newspaper *Alexander's Weekly Messenger* for 29 January 1840. The essay is a sort of tribute to the agility and intelligence of cats in general and to his cat Caterrina in particular. Poe has observed the skill of a black cat in opening doors and undoing latches, which confirms the premise of his article, ''that the boundary between instinct and reason is of a very shadowy nature. The black cat, in doing what she did, must have made use of all the perceptive and reflective faculties which we are in the habit of supposing the prescriptive qualities of reason alone.'' *Text: MCW,* II, 477–480. *Research:* Brigham, Clarence Saunders. ''Edgar Allan Poe's Contributions to *Alexander's Weekly Messenger.*'' *Proceedings of the American Antiquarian Society*, new series, 52 (April 1942): 45–124; Mairs, Nancy. ''Instinct vs. Reason: What Color of Cat? The Intuitive and Rational Modes in the Æsthetic Theories of Poe and Hawthorne.'' *Geolinguistics: Journal of the American Society of Geolinguistics*, 9, no. 1 (1979): 24–32.

"Introduction." Poem that introduces the poems in the 1831 volume *Poems by Edgar A. Poe* published by Elam Bliss. In subsequent printings the poem is entitled ''Romance.'' *See:* ''Romance.'' *Text: MCW,* I, 156–160.

"Irene." Original title of the poem ''The Sleeper.'' *See:* ''The Sleeper.''

Irene. Character in the poem ''The Sleeper.'' The poet hopes that Irene will rest peacefully. ''I pray to God that she may lie/ Forever with unopened eye,/ While the dim sheeted ghosts go by!'' ''Irene'' was also the first title of the poem ''The Sleeper'' when it appeared in the 1831 volume *Poems by Edgar A. Poe*. *See:* ''The Sleeper.''

Irving, Washington. (1783–1859). Leading American author of Poe's era whose work and reputation, Poe felt, were "much overrated and a nice distinction might be drawn between his just and his surreptitious and adventitious reputation." Irving was a constant presence and, to some extent, an influence on Poe's life and work. Irving's tone, style, and sense of humor are to be found in some of Poe's comic pieces such as "The Devil in the Belfry." The idea for the double story "William Wilson" was based partially on an article by Irving, "Unwritten Drama of Lord Byron." Irving's letters to Poe in the autumn of 1839 comment favorably albeit guardedly on "The Fall of the House of Usher." Poe would use Irving's comments to promote the sales of *Tales of the Grotesque and Arabesque*. Irving told Poe, "Its ["Usher's"] graphic effect is powerful," but he liked "William Wilson" better because it was simpler. Poe reviewed Irving's work favorably on several occasions and included an analysis of his signature in "Autography," noting that it revealed "an eye deficient in a due sense of the *picturesque*." *See:* "Astoria; or, Anecdotes of an Enterprise Beyond the Rocky Mountains," "The Crayon Miscellany No. II. " *Text: CWP,* XV, 153–154. *Research:* Watts, Charles H., II. "Poe, Irving, and *The Southern Literary Messenger*." *American Literature*, 27 (1955): 249–251; St. Armand, Barton Levi. "Some Poe Debts to Irving's *Alhambra*." *Poe Studies* 10 (1977): 42.

Isabel. Character in the poem "Fairy Land." She and the narrator observe the starlit fairyland until many threatening moons blot out the starlight.

"The Island of the Fay." Short story published in *Graham's Magazine* for June 1841 and again in *The Broadway Journal* of 4 October 1845. This sketch was specifically designed to accompany the issue's steel engraving frontispiece by John Sartain, "The Island of the Fay." Not so much a short story as a prose poem reverie on the magnificence of natural scenery in its opening scenes, the story is atypical of Poe in its serene vision of nature and nearly transcendental appreciation of God's artistry in "nature's holy plan." The narrator, a lonely wanderer of the type of Chateaubriand's René, is deeply moved by "the dark valleys, and the gray rocks, and the waters that silently smile, and the forests that sigh in uneasy slumbers, and the proud watchful mountains that look down upon all." But these edenic rhapsodies cease abruptly when the narrator comes upon the eastern end of the island of the race of fay, which he finds "whelmed in the blackest shade." The landscape suddenly becomes haunted as he spies "the form of one of those very fays about whom I had been pondering as it made its way slowly into the darkness from out the light at the western end of the island. . . . [H]er shadow fell from her, and was swallowed up in the dark water, making its blackness more black." The dark mood and even the syntax are strikingly similar to the sinking of the House of Usher into the blackness of the tarn as the narrator's paradise dissolves into a dream of despair with the fay's disappearance "into the region of the ebony flood—and that she issued thence at all I cannot say, for darkness fell over all things, and I beheld her magical figure no more.'' The spiritualization of nature symbolized by the presence of the earth's last fay becomes a reflection, perhaps even an extension, of the narrator's failed quest for natural beauty. Like all living things, her natural beauty is transitory and her short life span inspires the narrator to view her as the emblem of a cruel transience that holds sway over both the natural and the supernatural world. *Epigraph:* ''Nullus enim locus sine genio est'' [No place is without its genius]. Servius, Commentary on *The Æneid. Text: MCW,* II, 597–606; *CWP,* IV, 193–199. *Research:* Miller, F. DeWolfe. ''The Basis for Poe's 'The Island of the Fay.' '' *American Literature*, 14 (1942): 135–140; Ljungquist, Kent. ''Poe's 'Island of the Fay': The Passing of Fairyland.'' *Studies in Short Fiction*, 14 (1977): 265–271.

"Israfel." Poem in eight stanzas of five, six, seven, and eight lines first appearing in April 1831 in Elam Bliss's edition of *Poems by Edgar A. Poe* and later published in *The Southern Literary Messenger* for August 1836. In the Koran, Israfel is an angel gifted with sublime voice and thus becomes Poe's emblem of the ideal poet. Singing in heaven, the angel Israfel captivates his audience through his sublime voice which causes ''the stars [to] be mute.'' The earth-bound poet longs to use his voice in the celestial realm because only there can poetry and song attain perfect beauty. The poem's essence is contained in its two final stanzas, which are reminiscent of Keats's ''Ode to a Nightingale'' as the poet moves from ethereal ecstasy to a melancholy dwelling on the painful separation of mortal longing from higher beauty. Unlike Israfel, the earthly poet is condemned to reside in ''a world of sweets and sours; . . . The shadow of thy perfect bliss/ Is the sunshine of ours.'' Held in thrall by the lower world of mutable objects and appalling time, the poet dreams of changing places with Israfel in his poetic paradise. Were such a transposition possible, Israfel ''would not sing so wildly well'' when chained to earth, while the poet once freed from ''mortal melodies'' would strike ''a bolder note'' upon his ''lyre within the sky.'' *Text: MCW,* I, 173–179; *CWP,* VII, 47–48; *Research:* Werner, William L. ''Poe's Israfel.'' *Explicator*, 2 (April 1944): item 44; ''Israfel in the Laboratory.'' *Times Literary Supplement*, 7 October 1949, 648; St. Armand, Barton Levi. ''Poe's Unnecessary Angel: 'Israfel' Reconsidered.'' In *Ruined Eden of the Present: Hawthorne, Melville, Poe*, ed. G. R. Thompson, Virgil L. Lokke, and Chester E. Eisinger. West Lafayette, IN: Purdue University Press, 1981, 283–302.

The Italian-Sketch Book. Book noticed by Poe in *The Southern Literary Messenger* for June 1835. *Research: TPL,* 160.

J

Jacinta. Character in the drama *Politian.* She is Lalage's maid, then Alessandra's maid.

James, G.[eorge] P.[ayne] R.[ainsford]. (1799–1860). English historical novelist and short story writer. Poe found his ''multitudinous novels'' readable but inferior to Scott. ''Had Sir Walter Scott never existed, and Waverley never been written, we would not, of course, award Mr. J. the merit of being the first to blend history, even successfully, with fiction.'' *See:* ''Lives of the Cardinal de Richelieu, Count Oxenstiern, Count Olivarez, and Cardinal Mazarin.'' *Text: CWP,* IX, 168–170; X, 132; X, 207; XIV, 171.

James, Henry. (1843–1916). American novelist and short story writer. James maintained an ambivalent outlook on Poe, stating, on the one hand, that ''[a]n enthusiasm for Poe is the mark of a decidedly primitive stage of reflection'' and, on the other hand, that Poe ''had the advantage of being a man of genius, and his intelligence was frequently great.'' In his autobiography, *A Small Boy and Others*, James mentions that as a child he had been fascinated by Poe's strange elegiac poems and brooding tales of horror. Poe is directly mentioned in James's preface to ''The Altar of the Dead'' and *The Golden Bowl* and is allusively present in many of James's own tales of terror and ghost stories including ''Owen Wingrave,'' ''The Turn of the Screw,'' ''De Grey: A Romance,'' ''The Jolly Corner,'' and ''Sir Edmund Orme.'' *Research:* Pollin, Burton R. ''Poe and Henry James: A Changing Relationship.'' *Yearbook of English Studies*, 3 (1973): 232–242; Tintner, Adeline R. ''Poe's 'The Spectacles' and James' 'Glasses.' ''

Poe Studies, 9 (1976): 53–54; Tintner, Adeline R. ''James Corrects Poe: The Appropriation of *Pym* in *The Golden Bowl.*'' *American Transcendental Quarterly*, 37 (1978): 87–91; Nettels, Elsa. ''Poe and James on the Art of Fiction.'' *Poe Studies*, 13 (1980): 4–8; Brown, Christopher. ''Poe's 'Masque' and *The Portrait of a Lady*.'' *Poe Studies*, 14, no. 1 (1981): 6–7; Tintner, Adeline. ''Facing the 'Alter Ego': Edgar Allan Poe's Influence on Henry James.'' *AB Bookman Weekly*, 12 January 1987, 105–109; Gargano, James W. ''Henry James and the Question of Poe's Maturity.'' In *Poe and His Times: The Artist and His Milieu*, ed. B. F. Fisher IV. Baltimore: Edgar Allan Poe Society, 1990, 247–255.

Jefferson, Thomas. (1743–1826). Third president of the United States, author, scientist, statesman, and philosopher. An essay by William Kirkland on ''The Tyranny of Public Opinion in the United States'' ''demonstrates the truth of Jefferson's assertion, that in this country, which has set the world an example of physical liberty, the inquisition of popular sentiment overrules in practice the freedom asserted in theory by the laws.'' *Text: CWP,* IV, 12, 17, 19; VIII, 250; IX, 214; XI, 238; XV, 24. *Research:* Schick, Joseph S. ''Poe and Jefferson.'' *Virginia Magazine of History and Biography*, 54 (October 1946): 316–320; Jacobs, Robert D. ''Poe among the Virginians.'' *Virginia Magazine of History and Biography*, 67 (January 1959): 30–48; McLaughlin, Jack. ''Jefferson, Poe, and Ossian.'' *Eighteenth-Century Studies*, 26 (1993): 627–634.

Johnson, Dr. Samuel. (1709–1784). English essayist, critic, lexicographer, and arbiter of neoclassicism. In his review of Charles Richardson's *New Dictionary of the English Language*, Poe expressed his respect for Johnson as a lexicographer, but in the Johnson references in *Marginalia*, he corrected several of the great doctor's errors in his pronouncements on literature. *Text: CWP,* VIII, 204; IX, 104–105; X, 43; XIV, 41, 94; XVI, 40, 98, 175. *Research: PJC,* 20, 84, 169, 231–232, 371; Jeffrey, David K. ''The Johnsonian Influence: *Rasselas* and 'The Domain of Arnheim.' '' *Poe Newsletter*, 3 (1970): 26–29.

Johnston, Edward William. Journalist associated with *The Southern Literary Messenger* who attempted to find an English publisher for Poe's *Tales of the Folio Club*. His article in the August 1831 number of *The Southern Review* advocated the necessity for American writers to imitate English literary models. *Research: TPL,* xxx.

Jones, John Beauchamp. (1810–1866). Editor of the Baltimore *Saturday Visiter* from May 1840 to November 1841. He contributed to *Burton's Gentleman's Magazine* during Poe's editorial tenure. In his ''Autography'' analysis, Poe mentions him as ''the author of a series of papers of high merit . . . and entitled 'Wild Western Scenes.' '' *Text: CWP,* XV, 235. *Research: TPL,* xxx, 266–267.

Jones, Robert. A character in and the narrator of the short story "Lionizing." He is a large-nosed expert on nosology whose reputation is destroyed when he shoots off the nose of the Elector of Bluddennuff.

Jones, Timothy. Fellow cadet of Poe at West Point. He thought Poe to be a remarkable student but "certainly given to extreme dissipation." *Research: TPL,* 106–109.

Jones, William Alfred. (1817–1900). In *The Broadway Journal* of 20 September 1845 while summarizing the contents of the *Democratic Review* for September 1845, Poe contemptuously smashed Jones's essay "American Humor" as "insufferable" and "a nuisance." He was further critical of Jones's adulation of Charles F. Briggs, in Poe's words, "a vulgar driveller." *Text: CWP,* XIII, 193. *Research:* TPL, xxx, 570–572.

Jonson, Ben[jamin]. (1572–1637). English dramatist and author of *Volpone; or, The Fox.* A Jonson couplet is quoted in "The Drake-Halleck Review." *Text: CWP,* VIII, 294; IX, 91.

"Joseph Rushbrook; or, The Poacher. By Captain Marryatt." Review of a novel appearing in *Graham's Magazine* for September 1841. Because he felt that Marryatt catered to public tastelessness, Poe's opinion of Marryatt as a writer was negative in the extreme. "His books are essentially 'mediocre.' His ideas are the common property of the mob, and have been their common property time out of mind." As for *Joseph Rushbrook* in particular, "it deserves little more than an announcement. . . . Its English is excessively slovenly. Its events are monstrously improbable. There is no adaptation of parts about it. The truth is, it is a pitiable production." *Text: CWP,* X, 197–202. *Research: PJC,* 268–269.

Josephus, Flavius. (37–93). Ancient Jewish historian. His *History of the Jewish War* and depictions of the lost Jerusalem may have inspired "The City in the Sea." *Text: CWP,* XIV, 1, 55; *Research: PLL,* 52.

"Journal—By Frances Anne Butler." Review of the theatrical reminiscences of the English actress Fanny Kemble (1809–1893) appearing in *The Southern Literary Messenger* for May 1835. Poe was struck by "the vivacity of its style, the frequent occurrence of beautiful descriptions, of just and forcible observations, and many sound views of the condition of society in this country" but also criticized "the dictatorial manner of the writer. A female, and a young one too, cannot speak with the self-confidence which marks this book." *Text: CWP,* VIII, 19–31.

The Journal of Julius Rodman, Being an Account of the First Passage across the Rocky Mountains of North America Ever Achieved by Civilized Man. Unfinished serialized novel published in six installments in *Burton's Gentleman's Magazine* beginning in the January 1840 number and terminated by Poe after the sixth installment in the June 1840 number after Burton had discharged Poe. In June 1840, Poe had responded to Burton's letter of dismissal by refusing to continue the series. An inferior adventure story, *The Journal* is a fictional account of the first crossing of the Rocky Mountains in 1792 by the English adventurer Julius Rodman and a party of companions. To provide a factual atmosphere, Poe plundered details from Irving's *Astoria* and the *Journals* of Lewis and Clark. The novel begins with Rodman lost in the wilderness and seeking refuge from ''the unknown,'' then tediously sinks into geographical description and minutiae of landscape, flora, and fauna. Poe had obviously lost all interest in the story even before the break with Burton. *Text: CWP,* IV, 9–101; *The Imaginary Voyages: The Journal of Julius Rodman*, ed. Burton Pollin. Boston: G. K. Hall, 1981, 507–653. *Research:* Crawford, Polly Pearl. ''Lewis and Clark's Expedition as a Source for Poe's 'Journal of Julius Rodman.' '' *University of Texas Studies in English*, 12 (1932): 158–170; Turner, H. Arlin. ''Another Source of Poe's *Julius Rodman.*'' *American Literature*, 8 (1936): 69–70; Levine, Stuart G. ''Poe's *Julius Rodman*: Judaism, Plagiarism, and the Wild West.'' *Midwest Quarterly* (1960): 245–259; Teunissen, John J., and Evelyn J. Hinz. ''Poe's *Journal of Julius Rodman* as Parody.'' *Nineteenth Century Fiction*, 27 (1972): 317–338; Saxena, M. C. ''Evident Rapture: Poe's *Journal of Julius Rodman* as Western Narrative.'' *Indian Journal of American Studies*, 7, no. 1 (1977): 41–53; Mainville, Stephen. ''Language and the Void: Gothic Landscapes in the Frontiers of Edgar Allan Poe.'' *Genre*, 14 (1981): 347–362; Weissberg, Liliane. ''Editing Adventures: Writing the Text of *Julius Rodman.*'' *Modern Fiction Studies*, 33 (1987): 413–430.

Jovius, Paulus. [Paolo Giovio]. (1483–1552). Italian historian who wrote Latin histories. His ''pen of gold'' and ''pen of iron'' are mentioned in *Marginalia* and in the prospectus for *The Stylus*. *See: The Stylus. Text: CWP,* XVI, 168.

Joyce, James. (1882–1941). Irish novelist and short story writer. Joyce mentions Poe in *Dubliners*, *Ulysses*, and *Finnegan's Wake*. In an essay on James Clarence Mangan (1902) Joyce called Poe ''the high priest of most modern schools.'' Joyce's use of ''life preserving coffins'' in *Ulysses* achieves the same admixture of horror and humor attained by Poe in ''The Premature Burial.'' *Research:* Kronegger, M. E. ''Joyce's Debt to Poe and the French Symbolists.'' *Revue de Littérature Comparée*, 39 (1965): 243–254; *PLL,* 293–294.

Joyeuse, Madame. Character in the short story ''The System of Doctor Tarr and Professor Fether.''

"Judge Story's Discourse on Chief-Justice Marshall. Binney's Eulogium." A brief notice of two eulogies in *The Southern Literary Messenger* for December 1835. Together with *Binney's Eulogium*, Poe noticed a discourse on Chief Justice Marshall and promised a more extended piece in a subsequent issue of *The Messenger*. *Text: CWP,* VIII, 114–115.

Jules, the Canadian. Character in the unfinished novella *The Journal of Julius Rodman*. He is Rodman's Canadian interpreter and has a narrow escape from an attacking bear.

Juniper. Character mentioned in "How to Write a Blackwood Article." Juniper is Signora Psyche Zenobia's pet baboon.

Junot, M. Pierre. Character in the novella *The Journal of Julius Rodman*. He is a neighbor who accompanies Rodman on his journey.

Jupiter. Character in the short story "The Gold-Bug." He is the old black servant of William Legrand. Although wary of Legrand's excursion, he is devoted to his master and helps in the digging that reveal's Captain Kidd's treasure.

K

Kafka, Franz. (1883–1924). Czechoslovakian novelist and short story writer. The psychological and temperamental similarity of the two writers is noteworthy. Kafka might have been commenting on himself when he said of his American soul mate: "He was a poor devil who had no defenses against the world. So he fled into drunkenness. Imagination served him only as a crutch. He wrote tales of mystery to make himself at home in the world. That's perfectly natural. Imagination has fewer pitfalls than reality has. . . . I know his way of escape and his dreamer's face." Like Poe's victims, Kafka's characters often find themselves trapped in an absurd world they can neither control nor comprehend. The menacing shadow of authority in *The Trial*, the strange distortions of reality in "The Metamorphosis," mechanized torture in "In the Penal Colony," the grotesque plight of the artist in "A Hunger Artist," and the dark comedy of existence in many of his stories all bear the impression of Poe on Kafka's imagination. Further close parallels between Poe and Kafka are to be seen in their concern with how a sensitive artistic being can survive in a merciless mercantile environment that values neither art nor the artist along with their frequent strategy of merging horror and humor in their highly factual fantasies of transformation and public dying. *Research:* Hofrichter, Laura. "From Poe to Kafka." *University of Toronto Quarterly*, 29 (1960): 405–419; Lyons, Nathan. "Kafka and Poe—and Hope." *Minnesota Review*, 5 (1965): 158–168; Francavilla, Joseph Vincent. "Double Voice and Double Vision: Edgar Allan Poe and Franz Kafka." *Dissertation Abstracts International*, 49 (1988): 1138A (SUNY at Buffalo).

Kant, Immanuel. (1724–1804). German philosopher. Poe mentions Kant's *Critique of Pure Reason* in the short story "How to Write a Blackwood Article" and Kant's metaphysics in a satiric context in "Bon-Bon." *Research:* Omans, Glen A. " 'Intellect, Taste, and Moral Sense': Poe's Debt to Immanuel Kant." *Studies in the American Renaissance*, (1980): 123–128; Dayan, Joan. "Poe, Locke, and Kant." In *Poe and His Times: The Artist and His Milieu*, ed. B. F. Fisher IV. Baltimore: Edgar Allan Poe Society, 1990, 30–44.

Kate. Character in the short story "Three Sundays in a Week." She is the betrothed of the narrator, Bobby.

Kean, Edmund. (1789–1833). English actor. He excelled in Shakespearean roles. Poe quoted Felicia Hemans's admiring remark: "Of Kean, she said that 'seeing him act was like reading Shakespeare by flashes of lightning.' " *Text: CWP,* VIII, 321; IX, 199.

Keats, John. (1795–1821). English Romantic poet. Many Poe poems show the strong influence of Keats and, more particularly, the quintessential Keatsian notion of a beautiful bond between love and death. In "Ode to a Nightingale," Keats's poet, like Poe's ideal poet, is "half in love with easeful death." Poe's regard for Keats is heard in a statement in one of the Longfellow reviews. "Of the poets who have appeared most fully instinct with the principles now developed, we may mention *Keats* as the most remarkable. He is the sole British poet who has never erred in his themes. Beauty is always his aim." Both early and throughout his poetic career, Poe was drawn to the moods, material, and musicality of Keats's lines and began the short story "The Duc de L'Omelette" with a reference to Keats's death at the hand of a hostile reviewer: "Keats fell by a criticism." *See:* "Ballads and Other Poems." *Research:* Perry, Marvin B., Jr. "Keats and Poe." In *English Studies in Honor of James Southall Wilson*. Richmond: William Byrd Press, 1951, 45–52; *PLB,* 79, 148; *LET,* 257–258.

Keese, John. (1805–1856). American author, anthologist, and editor of *The Opal*. Poe commented favorably on his *Poets of America* and his edition of *The Poetical Writings of Mrs. Elizabeth Oakes Smith*. *Text: CWP,* XI, 149–150; XII, 228; XIII, 78. *Research: TPL,* xxx, 534–535.

Keith, Dr. Alexander. (1791–1880). Biblical scholar mentioned in Poe's review of "Arabia Petræa" and *Marginalia* for his work "upon the literal fulfilment of Biblical prophecies." His book *Evidence of the Truth of the Christian Religion Derived from the Literal Fulfilment of Prophecy* was consulted by Poe during the writing of *The Narrative of Arthur Gordon Pym*. *Text: CWP,* X, 9–17, 82–84, 179–180; XVI, 63–66. *Research: BRE*, 220.

Kempelen, Baron Wolfgang von. (1734–1804). Inventor of the chess playing robot or intelligent machine discussed in "Maelzel's Chess-Player." *Text: CWP,* XIV, 21, 27–29, 35.

Kennedy, John Pendleton. (1795–1870). Baltimore lawyer and amateur man of letters. He was a friend and literary patron of Poe who recognized Poe's genius as well as his psychological disparities. He judged Poe's prize story for the *Baltimore Saturday Visiter*, "MS. Found in a Bottle." Of the polarities in Poe's personality Kennedy remarked: "I have never known, nor heard of anyone, whose life so curiously illustrated that twofold existence of the spiritual and the carnal disputing the control of the man, which has often been made the theme of fiction. He was debauched by the most grovelling appetites and exalted by the richest conceptions of genius." Poe included an analysis of Kennedy's character through his signature in "Autography" noting that Kennedy had "the eye of a painter, more especially in regard to the picturesque—to have refined tastes generally—to be exquisitely alive to the proprieties of life—to possess energy, decision, and great talent—to have a penchant also for the *bizarre*." *Text: CWP,* XV, 155, 184–185. *Research:* Bohner, Charles H. "The Poe-Kennedy Friendship." *Pennsylvania Magazine of History and Biography*, 82 (April 1958): 220–222; *PJC,* 80–83.

Kepler, Johannes. (1571–1630). German astronomer who adduced laws on planetary motion. Poe wrote: "Great intellects *guess* well. The laws of Kepler were, professedly, *guesses*." And again in *Eureka*, Poe attributed Kepler's arrival at these laws not to deduction or induction but to scientific intuition. "Yes!—these vital laws Kepler *guessed*—that is to say, he *imagined* them." *Text: CWP,* VI, 205; XIV, 187; XVI, 196–197. *Research: LET,* II, 380; *PJC,* 415–416.

Kettell, Samuel. (1800–1855). An anthologist who compiled *Specimens of American Poetry*, dismissed by Poe as a mediocre and unrepresentative array of doggerel. "The 'specimens' of Kettell were specimens of nothing but the ignorance and ill taste of the compiler." *Text: CWP,* XI, 149–150. *Research: TPL,* 101, 512.

The King. Unnamed royal character in the short story "Hop-Frog." He keeps the crippled dwarf Hop-Frog as his court fool.

King, Henry, Bishop of Chichester. (1592–1669). Poe took the motto for "The Assignation" from his poem "Exequy on the Death of His Wife" and elsewhere accused Longfellow of plagiarizing from these lines. *Text: CWP,* II, 124; XII, 103.

"King Pest the First. A Tale Containing an Allegory." Short story first published in *The Southern Literary Messenger* for September 1835. In *Tales of the Grotesque and Arabesque* it was entitled "King Pest." A revision of the story was printed in *The Broadway Journal* of 18 October 1845 and signed pseudonymously by "Littleton Barry." The tale is one of Poe's cleverest gothic emetics, an admixture of nauseous humor and horror. Readers have also identified specific literary and political satire in the ''allegory'' in its allusions to Disraeli's *Vivian Grey* (1826) and the rowdy corruption of the Andrew Jackson administration. Set in one of the plague years during the reign of Edward III (1327–1377), the tale graphs the adventures of a pair of pub-crawling seamen, the lanky Legs and the dumpy Hugh Tarpaulin, Poe's version of Mutt and Jeff. Skipping their bar bill at the Jolly Tar alehouse, they flee the angry landlady and stray into that district of London where the pest ban is in effect, a metropolitan mortuary where ''the whole mass of forbidden buildings was, at length, enveloped in terror as in a shroud . . . leaving the entire vast circuit of the prohibited district to gloom, silence, pestilence, and death.'' Fleeing down a putrid labyrinth of streets, the pair must literally crawl over the carcasses of plague victims (''it was by no means seldom that the hand fell upon a skeleton or rested upon a more fleshy corpse'') until they stagger against a door that proves to be an undertaker's shop. The shop holds the family court of King Pest, the monarch of death and disease, the rotting royal presence surrounded by a company of six cadaverous relatives in various stages of decay. The gothic unites with the comic in such a way as to disgust and amuse by its excess. The narrator lingers over each decomposing courtier, coming finally to a description of the king and queen of pestdom. For the treason of violating the privacy of King Pest and his family, Legs and Tarpaulin are sentenced to '' 'be tied neck and heels together and duly drowned as rebels in yon hogshead of October beer!' '' When Queen Pest carries out this sentence on Tarpaulin, Legs is moved to topple ''the fatal hogshead full of October ale and Hugh Tarpaulin.'' The result is a ''deluge of liquor'' that drowns the entire pest family court or, in the case of the fat lady in the shroud and Hugh Tarpaulin, floats them toward the next pub, the ''Free and Easy,'' and presumably the next drunken adventure. Comic execution by alcohol and cadaverous farce link the story to ''The Cask of Amontillado'' and ''The Angel of the Odd.'' *Epigraph:* ''The gods do bear and well allow in kings/ The things which they abhor in rascal roots.'' Thomas Norton and Thomas Sackville, *Gorboduc*. *Text: MCW*, II, 238–255; *CWP*, II, 168–184. *Research:* Goldhurst, William. ''Poe's Mutiple King Pest: A Source Study.'' *Tulane Studies in English*, 20 (1972): 107–121; Lucas, Mary. ''Poe's Theatre: 'King Pest' and 'Hop-Frog.' '' *Journal of the Short Story in English*, 14 (1990): 25–40.

King, Stephen Edwin. (1947–). American novelist and leading modern horror story writer. King responds to the example and work of Poe on a variety of levels in his fiction, inspired by Poe's explorations of the collective and personal unconscious, an inner gothic landscape that is inaccessible to straightforward realism but made visible through Poe's mastery of horror art. Several dimensions of Poe's horror art are to be seen in King's recreating of an unsafe and mind-threatening American culture. For example, strong textual echoes of two enclosure stories, ''The Masque of the Red Death'' and ''The Fall of the House of Usher,'' inform King's novel *The Shining* (1977) and deepen the terrifying claustrophobic atmosphere that envelops the doomed family. *The Shining* also reflects the bizarre opulence to be found in many Poe settings, right down to a specific detail from ''The Masque of the Red Death,'' the ebony clock. Direct allusions to Poe's tale compel a comparison between Prince Prospero and Jack Torrance and their respective fates. In King's more recent fiction such as the 1992 novel *Gerald's Game*, ''The Raven'' becomes his means for creating an intertextual parallel linking the plight of the novel's self-tormented heroine to Poe's melancholy narrator. The presence of Poe's plotting is assertive in many King pieces. The horrific ''circumscription of space'' in ''The Pit and the Pendulum'' is converted into a similar lethal predicament in King's story ''The Ledge.'' In the short stories ''Dolan's Cadillac'' and ''The Doctor's Case'' King has consciously superimposed Poe's plotline upon his own material. Finally, Poe's theme of the revenge of the artist upon an uncaring and insensitive world is to be seen in King's ''The Monkey'' and ''Battleground.'' *Research:* Magistrale, Anthony. *Stephen King, the Second Decade: Danse Macabre to the Dark Half.* New York: Twayne; TUSAS 599, 1992, 38, 44, 58, 65, 87, 89, 145, 150; Pollin, Burton R. ''Stephen King's Fiction and the Heritage of Poe.'' *Journal of the Fantastic in the Arts*, 5, no. 4 (1993): 2–25.

Kingsbridge Road and 192nd Street. Location of the two-story cottage atop Fordham Hill. There Edgar and Virginia Poe took up occupancy in May 1846.

Kipling, Rudyard. (1865–1936). English poet and novelist. Many of his characters and tales register the influence of Poe on Kipling's imagination as well as his fondness for the morbid supernatural. ''My own personal debt to Poe,'' Kipling once declared, ''is a heavy one.'' Poe's ability to evoke terror through physical and psychological description deeply impressed Kipling, who often depicted things unnatural, preternatural, or supernatural residing in the natural world. Among Kipling's stories that register a ''personal debt'' to Poe are ''The Phantom Rickshaw,'' ''Bimi,'' ''The Tomb of His Ancestors,'' and ''In the House of Suddhoo.'' *Research:* Smith, Mr. ''Poe and Kipling.'' *Literary Digest, International Book Review*, 4 (September 1926): 623.

Kircher, Athanasias. (1602–1680). Commentator on whirlpools and sea vortexes cited in ''A Descent into the Maelström.'' *Text: CWP,* II, 232.

Kirkland, Caroline Matilda. (1801–1864). New York literary lady and editor of the *Union Magazine*. She rejected ''Ulalume'' for publication. In his ''The Literati of New York City,'' Poe's portrait of her is quite complimentary, especially in her handling of western scenes and pioneer character. ''Unquestionably, she is one of our best writers, has a province of her own, and in that province has few equals. Her most noticeable trait is a certain *freshness* of style, seemingly drawn, as her subjects in general, from the west.'' *Text: CWP,* XV, 84–88. *Research: TPL,* xxx.

Kirkland, William. (1800–1846). American essayist and journalist. Poe included a profile of Kirkland in "The Literati of New York City," singling out his articles "The Tyranny of Public Opinion in the United States" and "The West, the Paradise of the Poor" as especially valuable. *Text: CWP,* XV, 23–24. *Research: TPL,* xxx.

Kissam, Mr. Character mentioned in "Von Kempelen and His Discovery" who claimed to have discovered the invention before Von Kempelen.

Knickerbocker Magazine. New York journal edited by Lewis Gaylord Clark, a Poe foe. The review of *The Narrative of Arthur Gordon Pym* in the issue for August 1838 is severe but artistically fair: "There are a great many tough stories in this book, told in a loose and slip-shod style. . . . The work is one of much interest with all its defects, not the least of which is, that it is too liberally stuffed with 'horrid circumstance of blood and battle.' " The issue for November 1846 contained a satiric poem mocking Poe in "Epitaph on a Modern 'Critic.' 'P'OH PUDOR!" "Here ARISTARCHUS lies, (nay, never smile,)/ Cold as his muse, and stiffer than his style;/ But whether BACCHUS or MINERVA claims/The crusty critic, all conjecture shames;/ Nor shall the world know which the mortal sin,/ Excessive genius or excessive gin." *See:* Clark, Lewis Gaylord. *Research: PLB,* 128–131; *PJC,* 132, 136, 210, 236; *TPL,* 669.

Knowles, [James] Sheridan. (1784–1862). American novelist, elocutionist, and playwright mentioned in the essay "The American Drama." He wrote *The Hunchback* and *Caius Gracchus.* "The most successful of the more immediate modern playwrights has been Sheridan Knowles and to play Sheridan Knowles seems to be the highest ambition of our writers for the stage." *Text: CWP,* XIII, 36, 53.

Koliades, Constantine [Jean Baptiste Lechevalier]. (1752–1836). French classical scholar mentioned in *Pinakidia* for writing a "book to prove that Homer and Ulysses were one and the same." *Text: CWP,* XIV, 67.

Koran. Poe's familiarity with the holy book of Islam is borne out by the several references to and usages of the Koran in both the prose and poetry. The blue cow that supports the earth is mentioned in "The Thousand-and-Second Tale of Scheherazade"; the angel Israfel whose musical voice in the Koran proclaims the day of resurrection is Poe's emblem for the poet in the poem "Israfel"; and the name of the star of paradise, Al Aaraaf, in the poem of that title is taken from the Koran where Al Aaraaf is the name of the wall barrier separating paradise from Eblis or Hell where those who have died await Allah's permission to enter paradise.

Körner, Karl Theodor. (1791–1813). German patriotic poet. His ''Sword Song'' is mentioned in Poe's review of Longfellow's *Ballads and Other Poems*. *Text: CWP,* XI, 65, 80.

Kreutzenstern, Captain. Russian navigator and oceanic explorer mentioned along with Captain Lisiausky in chapter sixteen of *The Narrative of Arthur Gordon Pym*. *Text: CWP,* III, 167–168.

Kroutaplenttey. Character mentioned in the short story ''The Devil in the Belfry.'' He has traced the origin of the name of the borough of Vondervotteimittiss.

L

La Bruyère, Jean de. (1645–1696). French character writer. The epigraph for ''The Man of the Crowd'' is taken from his writings. Discussing the talents of the writer of ''Georgia Scenes,'' Poe noted, ''Of geese and ganders he is the La Bruyère.'' *Text: CWP,* IV, 134; VIII, 258.

La Harpe, Jean François de. (1739–1803). French critic and defender of Racine's tragic dramas. He is mentioned once in *Marginalia* as having ''done little more than strict justice to the fine taste and precise finish of Racine.'' *Text: CWP,* XVI, 32.

La Seine, Pierre. [Pietro Lasena]. (1590–1636). French critic and Homeric commentator. He is mentioned in ''Never Bet the Devil Your Head'' and *Pinakidia* on the subject of temperance. *Text: CWP,* IV, 213; XIV, 64.

Lackobreath. Character in and narrator of the short story ''Loss of Breath.'' He suddenly loses his breath while verbally abusing his wife.

Lackobreath, Mrs. Character in the short story ''Loss of Breath'' and the wife of the narrator.

Lady Fortunato. Character mentioned in the short story ''The Cask of Amontillado.'' She awaits Fortunato at their palazzo.

Lafayette, Marie Joseph Paul Yves Roch Gilbert du Motier, Marquis de. (1757–1834). French general and hero of the American Revolution and friend of Poe's patriotic grandfather, "General" David Poe. Poe saw Lafayette on his visit to Richmond in October 1824 while on parade in Capitol Square as a member of a volunteer company of riflemen in Lafayette's honorary bodyguard. *Research: LET,* I, 44, 45, 92; *MNR,* 25.

"Lafitte: The Pirate of the Gulf." Review of a historical novel by Professor Joseph H. Ingraham appearing in *The Southern Literary Messenger* for August 1836. Poe summarizes the novel at length, criticizes the syntax, orthography, and typography, and finds the portrayal of the pirate hero unsatisfactory. He "is a weak, a vacillating villain, a fratricide, a cowardly cut-throat. . . . Yet he is never mentioned but with evident respect." *Text: CWP,* IX, 106–116.

Lafourcade, Mademoiselle Victorine. Character in "The Premature Burial." She is the subject of one of the case studies of premature interment.

"The Lake." Poem first published in *Tamerlane and Other Poems* in June 1827. In the collection *Al Aaraaf, Tamerlane, and Minor Poems* the poem was entitled "The Lake—To—" and revised to appear in the annual *The Missionary Memorial* for 1846. Here we have Poe's version of Thoreau's Walden experience in the lyric's celebration of solitude, meditation on self, and reverie inspired by water. By the isolated "wild lake" ringed by tall pines the narrator experiences exquisite pleasure in a "terror [that] was not fright, but a tremulous delight." As is the case with so many of Poe's poems, the contemplative union of beauty and death is not so much a morbid imagining as it is central and necessary to the poet's desire to transcend all material banality, to locate the beauty behind or within the terror, and to regard dying as a step toward the beauty beyond. Although the poet finds that "Death was in that poisonous wave," the terror of the lone lake points the way to hidden paradises of the imagination. Made wise by loneliness, death, and terror, the "solitary soul" of the poet discovers that it "could make an Eden of that dim lake." Mabbott called "The Lake" "the best of Poe's early poems. It comes last in his first volume, and even in its first form shows maturity and power." *Text: MCW,* 82–86; *CWP,* VII, 21. *Research:* Morrison, Robert. "Poe's 'The Lake: To—' " *Explicator*, 7 (December 1848): item 22; Franklin, Rosemary F. "Poe and *The Awakening*." *Mississippi Quarterly*, 47 (1993–1994): 47–57.

Lalage. Character in Poe's drama *Politian*. Loved by Politian, she suffers humiliation at the hands of Count Castiglione, prompting Politian's revenge.

Lalande, Madame Eugénie. Character in the short story "The Spectacles." The great-great-grandmother of Napoleon Buonaparte Froissart, she fools him into proposing marriage.

Lalande, Madame Stephanie. Character in the short story "The Spectacles." She becomes Madame Eugénie Lalande's substitute at the altar when Napoleon Buonaparte Simpson recognizes that his poor eyesight has led him to propose marriage to his own great-great-grandmother.

Lamartine, Alphonse Prat de. (1798–1869). French Romantic poet. Poe compared his verse and sense of "ideal composition" to that of Longfellow and Moore in several reviews. *Text: CWP,* VIII, 138–139; X, 25, 69, 136–137; XI, 65; XVI, 27. *Research: LET,* 379.

Lamb, Charles. [pseud. Elia]. (1775–1834). English critic and essayist. Poe considered Lamb to be a fine stylist with "a vivid originality of manner and expression." *Text: CWP,* VIII, 320; XI, 60, 105; XV, 67.

Landor, Mr. Character in the short story "Landor's Cottage." The narrator describes him as civil and cordial, but is more interested in "the arrangement of the dwelling . . . than the personal appearance of the tenant."

Landor, William. Occasional pseudonym of Horace Binney Wallace, American novelist and contributor to various periodicals. In "Autography," Poe wrote of his signature, "The whole is strongly indicative of his literary qualities. He is an elaborately careful, stiff, and pedantic writer, with much affectation and great talent." *See:* Wallace, Horace Binney. *Text: CWP,* XV, 198.

"Landor's Cottage. A Pendant to 'The Domain of Arnheim.'" Short story or sketch appearing in *The Flag of Our Union* of 9 June 1849. During the summer, the narrator takes a walking tour of the Hudson River counties of New York State. Following no particular path among a maze of paths, he wanders into a gorge where he is overwhelmed by the luxuriant beauty of the natural world. "Everywhere was variety in uniformity." As the sun sets, the narrator notices a cottage on a loop of land in a lovely lake. "Its marvellous *effect* lay altogether in its artistic arrangement *as a picture*. I could have fancied, while I looked at it, that some eminent landscape-painter had built it with his brush." Surveying the cottage and its surroundings, he is convinced that a fine artist with an acute eye for form and detail must have superintended the overall effect. Entering with his dog Ponto, he is greeted by a dark-eyed young woman named Annie and ushered into the parlor to meet Mr. Landor himself whose "keenest sense of combined novelty and propriety" has given perfect artistic balance to the neat and graceful cottage and the sublime natural scenery. The sketch contains a reference to William Beckford's *Vathek* and a pen portrait of Annie Richmond. There is also a direct reference to the landscape painter Salvator Rosa and allusive references to the painters of the Hudson River School, Thomas Cole and Asher Durand. *Text: MCW,* III, 1325–1343; *CWP,* VI, 255–271. *Research:* Rosenfeld, Alvin. "Description in Poe's 'Landor's Cottage.'" *Studies in Short Fiction,*

4 (1967): 264–266; Dayan, Joan. ''The Road to Landor's Cottage: Poe's Landscape of Effect.'' *University of Mississippi Studies in English*, 3 (1982): 136–154; Rainwater, Catherine. ''Poe's Landscape Tales and the 'Picturesque' Tradition.'' *Southern Literary Journal*, 16, no. 2 (1984): 30–43.

"The Landscape Garden." Short story or sketch first published in Snowden's *Ladies' Companion for October 1842* and in a revised version in *The Broadway Journal* of 20 September 1845. The story was retitled ''The Domain of Arnheim'' in an expanded version published in The *Columbian Magazine* for March 1847. *Epigraph:* ''The garden like a lady fair was cut,/ That lay as if she slumbered in delight,/ And to the open skies her eyes did shut;/ The azure fields of heaven were 'sembled right/ In a large round set with flow'rs of light;/ The flowers de luce and the round sparks of dew/ That hung upon their azure leaves did show/ Like twinkling stars that sparkle in the evening blue.'' Giles Fletcher the younger, ''Christ's Victorie on Earth.'' *See:* ''The Domain of Arnheim, or the Landscape Garden.'' *Text: MCW,* II, 700–713; *CWP,* VI, 176–186. *Research:* Hess, Jeffry A. ''Sources and Æsthetics of Poe's Landscape Fiction.'' *American Quarterly*, 22 (1970): 177–189.

Lane, Thomas Henry. (1815–1900). New York customs man and publisher of the New York *Aristidean*. Poe obtained $40 from him in return for a half interest in *The Broadway Journal* in November 1845. *Research: TPL,* xxx-xxxi.

Langtree, S. D. Critic and editor of the Georgetown *Metropolitan* and *Democratic Review*. He is characterized in ''Autography'' as ''just, bold and acute, while his prose compositions generally, evince the man of talent and taste.'' *Text: CWP,* XI, 82–83, 85; XV, 232.

Laplace, Ma'm'selle. Character in the short story ''The System of Doctor Tarr and Professor Fether.'' She is one of the lunatics who attends the mad banquet.

Laplace, Marquis Charles de. (1749–1827). French physicist and astronomer. Poe frequently refers to ''the sagacity of Laplace'' and ''the Nebular Cosmogony of Laplace'' throughout *Eureka*. *Text: CWP,* XVI, 223, 245, 252, 256, 260–262. *Research: TPL,* 723–724.

Lasalle, General. Salvational figure in ''The Pit and the Pendulum.'' He is the French general whose rescuing arm saves the narrator at the climax of the tale.

Latin Hymn. Untitled mock anthem found in the text of the short story ''Four Beasts in One.'' *See:* ''Four Beasts in One; The Homo-Cameleopard.'' *Text: MCW,* I, 218–219.

Latrobe, John Hazelhurst Boneval. (1803–1891). He judged Poe's prize-winning story ''MS. Found in a Bottle'' in the *Baltimore Saturday Visiter*. He described Poe's apparel as that of a man in black. "He was dressed in black, and his frock-coat was buttoned to the throat, where it met the black stock, then almost universally worn. Not a particle of white was visible." *Text: CWP,* VIII, 111–114. *Research: TPL,* xxxi, 129–130.

Lauvrière, Émile. Poe biographer. He was among the first to study Poe's life from a psychoanalytic perspective. Author of *Edgar Poe, sa vie et son oeuvre: Étude de psychologie pathologique* (1904).

Lauzanne, Jacques. Character in the novella *The Journal of Julius Rodman.* He accompanies Rodman on his journey and dies of a snakebite.

Lawrence, D. H. (1885–1930). English novelist, short story writer, and poet. In 1923, Lawrence published *Studies in Classic American Literature*, a landmark monograph that insisted upon the self-destructive nature of American literary art in Poe and all of his contemporaries, all of them obsessed with the "disintegration processes" of the psyche. Applied to Poe, Lawrence's thesis concludes that his "tales need to have been written . . . because the old white psyche has to be gradually broken down before anything else can come to pass." Love throughout Poe is the vehicle whereby he explores and portrays all the extremes of psychopathological behavior. Centering on "Ligeia" and "The Fall of the House of Usher," Lawrence argued that Madeline and Ligeia were transformed into vampires and drained of life by their respective male counterparts. "To try to know any living being is to try to suck the life out of that being. . . . It is the temptation of the vampire fiend, is this knowledge." For Lawrence, such illicit incest-lust between Roderick and Madeline Usher and the narrator's drive "to know" Ligeia to the point of her death parallel the more overt examples of the hate-love that motivates many Poe characters. Lawrence was among the first Poe critics to realize that his fiction deals with subconscious urges, declaring that Poe "was an adventurer into the vaults and cellars and horrible underground passages of the human soul." *Research:* Lawrence, D. H. "Edgar Allan Poe." In *Classic American Literature.* New York: Doubleday, 1951, 73–92.

Lawson, James. (1799–1880). Poe's collection of profiles "The Literati of New York City" contains a short portrait of Lawson, author of *Giordano, a Tragedy* (1832). Poe appears to know very little about his literary endeavors as marked by the brief generalization that Lawson is one of the "few men of letters [to] have more ardently at heart the welfare of American letters." *Text: CWP,* XV, 83–84. *Research: TPL,* 612, 640, 657.

Lawson, Mary L. (fl. 1840). Minor American poet whose "nearly faultless poem," "The Haunted Heart" is quoted by Poe in his review of Griswold's *Poets and Poetry of America. Text: CWP,* XI, 232–233.

Le Blanc, Monsieur. Character in the short story ''The Mystery of Marie Rogêt.'' He is the proprietor of the perfume shop where Marie Rogêt was employed prior to her murder.

Le Bon, Adolphe. Character in the short story ''Murders in the Rue Morgue.'' He accompanied Madame L'Espanaye to her residence with the 4,000 francs and is wrongly accused of the murders, then exonerated by Dupin.

Lea & Blanchard. Philadelphia publishing firm. The house issued Poe's *Tales of the Grotesque and Arabesque* in 1839.

Lea, Isaac. (1792–1886). Philadelphia publisher of the house of Carey, Lea & Carey. Lea assisted Poe in the preparation of *The Conchologist's First Book. Research: TPL,* xix, xxxi.

Lee, Zaccheus Collins. (1805–1859). A classmate of Poe at the University of Virginia. He attended Poe's funeral on 8 October 1849. *Research: TPL,* xxxi.

Legaré, Hugh Swinton. (1797–1843). South Carolina politician, journalist, and contributor to the periodicals. In ''Autography,'' Poe mentions, ''He contributed many articles of high merit to the 'Southern Review' and has a wide reputation for scholarship and talent.'' *Text: CWP,* XV, 215. *Research: TPL,* xxx.

"Legends of a Log Cabin. By a Western Man." Review appearing in *The Southern Literary Messenger* for December 1835. Poe thought ''The Hunter's Vow'' to be the best of the seven tales. ''We recommend the volume to the attention of our readers. It is excellently gotten up.'' *Text: CWP,* VIII, 120–121.

Legrand, William. Character in the short story ''The Gold-Bug.'' He discovers a coded message that leads him to the burial place of Captain Kidd's treasure.

Legs. Character in the short story ''King Pest.'' With his drinking companion, Hugh Tarpaulin, he meets King Pest and his family court during the London plague.

Leibnitz, Gottfried Wilhelm. (1646–1716). German mathematician and philosopher. Poe criticized him along with Locke for misapprehending the function of memory and found his scientific speculations to be debased by his ethical speculations. In *Marginalia*, Poe refers to him as ''[t]hat Leibnitz, who was fond of interweaving even his mathematical, with ethical speculations, making a medley rather to be wondered at than understood.'' *Text: CWP,* II, 126; IV, 134; IX, 65; XII, 165; XVI, 25, 46, 223–224.

Leicester, Earl of. Character in Politian's title *Politian.*

"Lenore." Poem first published in James Russell Lowell's *The Pioneer* for February 1843. In its earliest version, it was entitled ''A Pæan'' and published in Elam Bliss's edition of Poe's *Poems* in April 1831. Originally consisting of eleven balladic stanzas, the poem was revised by Poe several times, with the first extensive revision appearing in *The Pioneer* where it was retitled ''Lenore.'' In a version published in *The Broadway Journal* of 16 August 1845, the poem was compressed into three stanzas with an interstanzaic rhyme scheme. The resulting lengthening of the lines perhaps reflected Poe's desire to repeat the metrical success of ''The Raven.'' Told from the point of view of the grieving lover, Guy De Vere, this dirge resembles ''Annabel Lee'' in that it is a lamentation for a young woman whose death is welcomed, and perhaps caused, by a ''slanderous tongue/ That did to death the innocence that died, and died so young.'' Defeating her persecutors—also a callous family as in ''Annabel Lee''—Lenore ascends in death ''From grief and groan, to a golden throne, beside the King of Heaven.'' Whereas ''Annabel Lee'' stresses the deathless love between the narrator and the maiden, ''Lenore'' places its emphasis on the culpability of her persecutors, those ''fiends below,'' and her eventual triumph over the grave. By the poem's fourth stanza, the narrator has ceased to mourn and instead celebrates the victory of beauty over ''the damned Earth.'' '' 'No dirge will I upraise,/ But waft the angel on her flight with a pæan of old days!' '' *See:* ''A Pæan.'' *Text: MCW,* I, 330–339; *CWP,* VII, 753–754. *Research:* Broderick, John C. ''Poe's Revisions of 'Lenore.' '' *American Literature*, 35 (1964): 504–510; Pollin, Burton R. ''Poe and Frances Osgood, as Linked Through 'Lenore.' *Mississippi Quarterly*, 46 (1993): 185–197.

Lenore. Dead character appearing in two poems, ''The Raven'' and ''Lenore.'' She is the dead beloved in each case.

Leslie, Eliza. (1787–1858). Philadelphia author of juvenile stories including the very popular *Amelia, or a Young Lady of Vicissitudes* (1848). From an analysis of her signature in ''Autography'' Poe deduced ''that Miss L. regards rather *the effect of her writings as a whole* than the polishing of their constituent parts.'' *Text: CWP,* VIII, 50–51, 292; XV, 152, 198–199. *Research: TPL,* 142–143, 171–172.

L'Espanaye, Madame. Character mentioned in the short story ''The Murders in the Rue Morgue.'' She is one of the murder victims. Her case is mentioned in ''The Mystery of Marie Rogêt.''

L'Espanaye, Mademoiselle Camille. Character mentioned in the short story ''The Murders in the Rue Morgue.'' The police discover her corpse wedged into a chimney. Her case is mentioned in ''The Mystery of Marie Rogêt.''

"Letter to B.______." First written to the publisher of *Poems* (1831), Elam Bliss, as "Letter to Mr.______ ______: Dear B____" and printed as a preface to the collection, then published in *The Southern Literary Messenger* for July 1836 as "Letter to B. ______." This epistolary essay marks Poe's early effort to establish himself as critic and theorist of American literature. The letter shows the strong influence of Coleridge's ideas on Poe's critical principles and suggests that Poe had probably read the *Biographia Literaria* by 1829 and was particularly impressed by Coleridge's dictum that "the fancy combines, the imagination creates." Poe acknowledges the vital worth of Coleridge's premise that the poem's "immediate object [is] pleasure, not truth." If the poem is made beautifully, the truth will follow from its beauty. As he would later insist in "The Poetic Principle," poetic pleasure arises by virtue of the musical qualities inherent in the poem itself. "Music, when combined with a pleasurable idea, is poetry; music without the idea is simply music; the idea without the music is prose from its very definitiveness." *Text: CWP,* VII, xxv. *Research: PJC,* 35; O'Neill, James. "A Closer Source for the Goths in Poe's 'Letter to B.______.' " *Poe Studies*, 12 (1979): 19–20.

"Letter to Mr.______ ______: Dear B____." *See:* "Letter to B.______."

"Letters, Conversations, and Recollections of S. T. Coleridge." Review of Harper's edition of Coleridge's correspondence appearing in *The Southern Literary Messenger* for June 1836. "In the volume now before us, we behold the heart, as in his own works we have beheld the mind, of the man." Poe also laments the fact that "the *Biographia Literaria* here mentioned in the foot note has never been republished in America." *Text: CWP,* IX, 51–52.

"Letters Descriptive of the Virginia Springs. The Roads Leading Thereto and the Doings Thereat. Collected, Corrected, Annotated, and Edited by Peregrine Prolix." Review of a book by Peregine Prolix [Philip H. Nichelin] appearing in *The Southern Literary Messenger* for August 1836. "The volume is a very small one—a duodecimo of about 100 pages—but is replete with information of the most useful and the most enticing nature to the tourist." *Text: CWP,* IX, 79–80.

"Letters of Eliza Wilkinson, During the Invasion and Possession of Charleston, S.C. by the British, in the Revolutionary War." Poe devoted a *Marginalia* entry to this book, a sort of miniature review. Poe judged the letters "silly. . . . The only supposable merit in the compilation is that dogged air of truth with which the fair authoress relates the lamentable story of her misadventures." *Text: CWP,* XVI, 51–52. *Research: BRE*, 199.

"Letters to Young Ladies. By Mrs. L. H. Sigourney." Review of the second edition of an epistolary collection appearing in *The Southern Literary Messenger* for July 1836. Poe refers to the excellence of the twelve letters "so redolent of the pious, the graceful, the lofty, and the poetical mind from which it issues." *Text: CWP,* IX, 64–66.

Lewis, Captain Meriwether. (1774–1809). American explorer and partner in the Lewis and Clark Expedition of 1803. He is mentioned at length in *The Journal of Julius Rodman* and in Poe's review of Irving's "Astoria." *Text: CWP,* IV, 18–21; IX, 212, 228.

Lewis, Sarah Anna. (1824–1880). Amateur poet who knew Poe at the Fordham cottage after Virginia's death. She apparently gave Poe the sum of $100 in return for his writing of a laudatory review of her work. Griswold included "Estelle Anna Lewis," Poe's biocritical essay that concluded that "all critical opinion must agree in assigning her a high, if not the very highest rank among the poetesses of her land." Griswold's papers also contained the unpublished notice "Memorandum by Poe in the Griswold Collection Relating to Mrs. E. A. Lewis—'Stella.' " *See:* "Annabel Lee;" "The Child of the Sea and Other Poems." *Text: CWP,* XI, 59–60; XIII, 155–165, 225–226. *Research:* Ingram, John H. "Edgar Allan Poe and 'Stella.' " *Albany Review*, 1 (1907): 417–423; Ostrom, John W. "Poe's Manuscript Letter to Stella Lewis—Recently Located." *Poe Newsletter*, 2 (April 1969): 36–37. *TPL,* xxxi, 678–679, 709–711, 753–754, 803–804, 811–812.

Lieber, Professor Francis. (1800–1872). Professor of history and political economy at the College of South Carolina. He wrote *A Journal of a Residence in Greece* and an essay cited as worthy by Poe in his "Autography" sketch of Lieber, "Essay on International Copyright." In general, his handwriting exhibits "vivacity and energy of thought." *Text: CWP,* VIII, 162–168; XV, 170–171, 202. *Research:* "New Letter of Edgar Allan Poe." *Emerson Society Quarterly*, 61 (2nd Q 1968): 51–53; *TPL,* 212–213.

"Life and Literary Remains of L. E. L. By Laman Blanchard." Review of a biography of the poet Miss Landon appearing in *Graham's Magazine* for August 1841. Poe regarded her as one of the "loftiest of the female poets of the present generation" and placed her together with Mrs. Norton and Felicia Hemans "in one glorious trio." *Text: CWP,* X, 195.

"The Life and Surprising Adventures of Robinson Crusoe, of York, Mariner: With a Biographical Account of Defoe. Illustrated with Fifty Characteristic Cuts, from Drawings by William Harvey, Esq. and Engraved by Adams." Review of Harper's reprint of Defoe's novel appearing in *The Southern Literary Messenger* for January 1836. Poe praises the elegance of the edition and rhapsodizes on his own first reading experience of the novel. "How fondly do we recur, in memory, to those enchanted days of our boyhood when we first learned to grow serious over Robinson Crusoe! . . . Indeed the author of Crusoe must have possessed, above all other faculties, what has been termed the faculty of *identification*—that dominion exercised by volition over imagination which enables the mind to lose its own, in a fictitious, individuality.'' *See:* Defoe, Daniel. *Text: CWP,* VIII, 169–173.

"Life in Death." First title for the short story ''The Oval Portrait.'' *See:* ''The Oval Portrait.''

"A Life of George Washington, in Latin Prose: By Francis Glass." Review of the biography edited by J. N. Reynolds appearing in *The Southern Literary Messenger* for December 1835. Poe is impressed by ''the *Washingtonii Vita*'' as well as Reynolds's preface. ''We really can call to mind, at this moment, no modern Latin composition whatever much superior to the *Washintonii Vita* of Mr. Glass.'' *Text: CWP,* VIII, 103–107.

"Life of Petrarch. By Thomas Campbell." Review of a biography appearing in *Graham's Magazine* for September 1841. Poe criticized the biography's ''*Slovenliness of style*'' and ''the want of comprehensive analysis of the poet's character, and of the age in which he lived.'' Part of Poe's negativity may arise from his disregard for Petrarch to whom he refers as ''the pertinacious sonneteer. Grace and tenderness we grant him; but these qualities are surely insufficient to establish his poetical apotheosis.'' *Text: CWP,* X, 202–206.

"A Life of Washington. By James K. Paulding." Review of a biography appearing in *The Southern Literary Messenger* for May 1836. Poe praised both the content and the style and recommended ''the immediate introduction of his book into every respectable academy in the land.'' *Text: CWP,* IX, 13–16.

"Life on the Lakes: Being Tales and Sketches Collected During a Trip to the Pictured Rocks of Lake Superior. By the Author of 'Legends of a Log Cabin.' " Negative review appearing in *The Southern Literary Messenger* for July 1836. Poe disapproved of the title and thought the lithographs ''abominable in every respect. . . . In the manner of the narrative, too, there is a rawness, a certain air of foppery and ill-sustained pretension—a species of abrupt, frisky, and self-complacent Paul Ulricism, which will cause nine-tenths of the well educated men who take up the book, to throw it aside in disgust.'' *See:* ''Paul Ulric.'' *Text: CWP,* IX, 77–78.

"Ligeia." Short story first published in the Baltimore *American Museum* for September 1838. This first printing of the tale did not include the poem ''The Conqueror Worm'' which would appear for the first time when the story was published in the *New York World* of 15 February 1845 and *The Broadway Journal* of 27 September 1845. One of Poe's best-known ''love'' stories and designated by him as a favorite, ''Ligeia'' features three prototypical Poe themes: the death of a mysteriously beautiful woman, the psychological instability of a bereaved narrator, and a cadaverous resurrection. The opening paragraphs of the story are devoted entirely to the narrator's veneration of the Lady Ligeia after his ironic admission that he cannot "remember how, when, or even precisely where, [he] first became acquainted with" her. Her physical beauty is itemized in voluptuous detail with a concentration on her strange, large eyes, but it is Ligeia's beauty of mind—she is his intellectual superior in all respects—that the narrator finds most attractive. "I was sufficiently aware of her infinite supremacy to resign myself, with a child-like confidence, to her guidance through the chaotic world of metaphysical investigation at which I was most busily occupied during the early years of our marriage." The core of Ligeia's philosophy, which is purportedly adapted from the mystic theologian Joseph Glanvill, holds that the will is stronger than death or decay. If the passionate will for life is sufficiently vigorous, then the mind, soul, and the body itself can conquer the ravages of time and disease. Ligeia's theory of psychic and physical survival is soon tested as she succumbs to a fatal illness while the narrator degenerates into "a bounden slave in the trammels of opium." Just prior to her death, Ligeia asks her husband to recite a verse composed by herself, "The Conqueror Worm," whose content seems to express her dread of the grave's finality and, more particularly, of bodily decomposition, thus negating her doctrine of the potency of the will to forestall death. As to why the narrator takes a second wife, the blond and conventionally beautiful Lady Rowena Trevanion of Tremaine, no clear explanation is offered. In every physical and mental aspect, she is Ligeia's opposite, a fact that so irritates the narrator that many readers have implicated him in her strange illness and death. The narrator's insistence that the poisonous droplets within the goblet of Rowena emanate "from some invisible spring in the atmosphere of the room" and his failure to warn his second wife about her imminent danger cannot be explained. Rowena's death, it seems, is a necessary prelude for the unfolding of the last act of "this hideous drama of revivification." Exercising colossal, postmortem willpower, Ligeia will now inhabit and gradually displace Rowena's body with her own, using the dying blond as a means of reanimation. The cadaverous climax offers neither an explanation for this occurrence nor a clear picture of the emotional state of the narrator. As numerous commentators have noted, the reader is left with many options—perhaps too many—concerning Ligeia's return. Has the narrator finally succeeded in validating Ligeia's theory of willpower by using his own will to summon her back to life? Or has Poe written an orthodox supernatural climax to a Germanic thriller that depicts the victory of evil in the figure of the dark, demonic lady? Or is this a special variety of the vampire legend that sees the creature feed off the soul of a sleeping beauty instead of her blood? Or are we dealing with the narrator's unexpressed intellectual jealousy of his first wife and his sexual frustration with his second wife? Or finally and most perplexing, is the rebirth of Ligeia an instance of genuine supernatural survival or the diseased hallucination of a hopeless addict to opium whose mind has imagined both wives into existence in one of the bizarrest cases of bigamy ever recorded? Does the narrator's final mental state reflect a crazed victim's horror or a bereaved lover's rapture? The multiplicity of interpretation is most evident in the story's climactic final paragraph. During the corpse vigil, he has noticed that "the hues of life flushed up with unwonted energy within the countenance," but the phenomenon does not frighten him in the least. "I trembled not—I stirred not—but gazed upon the apparition." Upon recognizing that it is his dark-haired Ligeia under the unraveling "ghastly cerements" the narrator shrieks in excited delight over his accomplishment. No other horror tale by Poe combines such simplicity of plot with such equivocal complexity of meaning. *Epigraph:* "And the will therein lieth, which dieth not. Who knoweth the mysteries of the will, with its vigor? For God is but a great will pervading all things by nature of its intentness. Man doth not yield himself to the angels, nor unto death utterly, save only through the weakness of his feeble will." Source unknown (Poe attributed falsely to Joseph Glanvill). *Text: MCW,* II, 305–334; *CWP,* II, 248–268. *Research:* Basler, Roy R. "The Interpretation of 'Ligeia.' " *College English*, 5 (1944): 363–372; Griffith, Clark. "Poe's 'Ligeia' and the English Romantics." *University of Toronto Quarterly*, 24 (1954): 8–25; Schroeter, James. "A Misreading of Poe's 'Ligeia.' " *Publications of the Modern Language Association*, 76 (1961): 397–406; Gargano, James W. "Poe's 'Ligeia': Dream and Destruction." *College English*, 23 (1962): 337–342; Lauber, John. " 'Ligeia' and Its Critics: A Plea for Literalism." *Studies in Short Fiction*, 4 (1966): 28–33; Thompson, G. R. " 'Proper Evidences of Madness': American Gothic and the Interpretation of 'Ligeia.' " *ESQ: A Journal of the American Renaissance*, 18 (1972): 30–49; Matheson, Terence J. "The Multiple Murders in 'Ligeia': A New Look at Poe's Narrator." *Canadian Review of American Studies*, 13 (1982): 279–289; Bieganowski, Ronald. "The Self-Consuming Narrator in Poe's 'Ligeia" and 'Usher.' " *American Literature*, 60 (1988): 175–187; McEntee, Grace. "Remembering Ligeia." *Studies in American Fiction*, 20 (1992): 75–83; Kennedy, J. Gerald. "Poe, 'Ligeia,' and the Problem of Dying Women." In *New Essays on Poe's Major Tales*, ed. Kenneth Silverman. Cambridge: Cambridge University Press, 1993, 113–129.

"The Light-House." Short story left unfinished and unpublished at his death. Because of the setting on the Norwegian seacoast, Mabbott suggests that the story was "planned as a companion piece to 'A Descent into the Maelström.' " The finished portion of the story consists of three diary entries by the narrator for 1 January, 2 January, and 3 January of the year 1796. The narrator has taken up his duties as lighthouse keeper with his dog Neptune out of a compulsive desire to be alone. He writes in the log for 2 January: "I have passed this day in a species of ecstasy that I find it impossible to describe. My passion for solitude could scarcely have been more thoroughly gratified." This absolute bliss of self-sequestration is followed by the narrator's description of the strength of the tower. "No mere sea, though, could accomplish anything with this solid iron-riveted wall." If this is to be a typical Poe tale, the double bliss of solitude and security will shortly be aborted by some terribly natural disaster or sinister human encroachment. *Text: MCW,* III, 1388–1392. *Research:* Mabbott, T. O. "Poe's Tale, 'The Light House.' " *Notes & Queries*, 182 (25 April 1942): 226–227.

Lillo, George. (1693–1739). English dramatist. His domestic tragedy, *The London Merchant, or the History of George Barnwell* (1731) aroused Poe's critical animosity. " 'George Barnwell' is applauded for its 'moral'—that is to say, for the impressiveness with which it conveys the *truth* that dissipation leads to crime and crime to punishment; but we are at a loss to understand how this truth, or how any truth can be conveyed by that which is itself confessedly a lie. . . . *It is not in the power of any fiction to inculcate any truth.*" *Text: CWP,* XIII, 112–113.

Lily, William. (1468–1522). English grammarian. His work on Latin syntax is mentioned once in "The Rationale of Verse." *Text: CWP,* XIV, 212.

"Lines on Ale." Nonauthenticated drinking song in eight lines printed by T. O. Mabbott in his edition of the poems. According to Mabbott, the "Lines on Ale" were written by Poe at the Washington Tavern in Lowell, Massachusetts, in 1848 as he fortified himself prior to a public lecture. The text is as follows: "Fill with mingled cream and amber,/ I will drain that glass again./ Such hilarious visions clamber/ Through the chamber of my brain—/ Quaintest thoughts—queerest fancies/ Come to life and fade away;/ What care I how time advances?/ I am drinking ale today." *Text: MCW,* I, 449–450. *Research:* Mabbott, T. O. "Newly-Identified Verses by Poe." *Notes & Queries*, 177 (29 July 1939): 77–78.

"Lines on Joe Locke." Satiric poem recalled by his West Point classmate Thomas W. Gibson. Poe wrote a series of comic poems that he shared with his fellow cadets about instructors at the United States Military Academy. Locke was one officer who inspired Poe's mordant attention. Mabbott included the eight-line mock encomium among the fugitive pieces. *See:* Locke, Lieutenant Joseph Lorenzo. *Text: MCW,* I, 150–151.

"Lines Written in an Album." Poem first published under this title in *The Southern Literary Messenger* for September 1835. *See:* "To Elizabeth."

Linnæus, Carl. (1707–1778). Swedish botantist who developed modern botantical nomenclature. Poe cites him once in *Pinakidia* in connection with Theophrastus who "anticipated the sexual system of Linnæus." *Text: CWP,* XIV, 42.

"The Linwoods; or, 'Sixty Years Since' in America." Review of Miss Sedgwick's novel appearing in *The Southern Literary Messenger* for December 1835. Poe read the novel with "real pleasure" and "recommend[ed] *The Linwoods* to all persons of taste. But let none others touch it." *Text: CWP,* VIII, 94–100.

"Lionizing." Short story by Poe published in *The Southern Literary Messenger* for May 1835. This comic tale is the burlesque account of a literary banquet attended by one Robert Jones, eminent and expert nosologist, citizen of the city of Fum-Fudge. Kicked out of his home by his father after declaring his intention of following his nose and becoming a nosologist, Jones determines upon a literary career as a nosey pamphleteer. In an artist's studio he encounters a gallery of eccentric men and women and is invited to dine with the Prince of Wales, apparently to gather material for his pamphlet on nosology. The tale edges toward a satire on the egotistic business of becoming a literary lion in Jones's recitation of the guest list at the Prince of Wales's banquet. Coming to his own name, he explains the vulgar craft of lionizing. ''There was myself. I spoke of myself;—of myself, of myself;—of Nosology, of my pamphlet, and of myself. I turned up my nose and I spoke of myself.'' After shooting off the nose of the Elector of Bluddennuff, Jones returns home to his father to inquire about the deeper meaning of his adventures as a nosologist and is informed that ''in Fum-Fudge the greatness of a lion is in proportion to the size of his proboscis'' and is satisfied with this absurd moral for success in the literary arena. The character names, comic subject matter, and violent absurdities are borrowed almost verbatim from Laurence Sterne's *Tristram Shandy*. *Epigraph:* ''______all people went/ Upon their ten toes in wild wonderment.'' Bishop Joseph Hall, *Satires* (approximated by Poe). *Text: MCW,* II, 169–187; *CWP,* II, 35–41. *Research:* Arnold, John. ''Poe's 'Lionizing': The Wound and the Bawdry.'' *Literature and Psychology*, 17 (1967): 52–54; Thompson, G. R. ''On the Nose—Further Speculations on the Sources and Meaning of Poe's 'Lionizing.' '' *Studies in Short Fiction*, 6 (1968): 94–97.

"Lion-izing. A Tale." The short story was originally published under this title. *See:* ''Lionizing.''

Lippard, George. (1822–1854). Philadelphia urban Gothic novelist and editor of various journals including *The Quaker City* and *The Citizen Soldier*. He admired Poe's work and befriended him in July 1849 when Poe was desperate for money to get to Richmond. Lippard's moving death notice for Poe was published in *The Quaker City* for 20 October 1849. Saluting Poe's genius, he put tersely what many others felt about Griswold's vicious dealings with Poe, calling him ''a respectable jackal.'' In the November 1843 number of *The Citizen Soldier*, Lippard had written of *The Narrative of Arthur Gordon Pym* that Poe's adventure novel contained ''perceptive and descriptive powers that rival De Foe, combined with an analytical depth of reasoning in no manner inferior to Godwin or Brockden Brown.'' *Research: LET,* I, 242–243; II, 455, 456; De Grazia, Emilio. ''Poe's Devoted Democrat, George Lippard.'' *Poe Studies*, 6, no. 1 (1973): 6–8; *PLL,* 259–260.

"Literary Intelligence." Item appearing in the *New York Evening Mirror* of 6 February 1845. Poe decries the fact that Hawthorne's *Twice-Told Tales* has gone out of print.

"The Literary Life of Thingum Bob, Esq. Late Editor of the 'Goosetherumfoodle' by Himself." Unsigned short story originally appearing in *The Southern Literary Messenger* for December 1844 and republished in *The Broadway Journal* of 26 July 1845. Poe revised the tale for *The Broadway Journal* version in order to direct several sarcastic barbs at his enemy Lewis Gaylord Clark. In an article on Poe for *Graham's Magazine* for February 1845, "Our Contributors, No. XVII: Edgar Allan Poe," Lowell identified Poe as the author of the anonymous short story. A satire on magazine editors, hacks, and quill drivers, the story takes the form of a bogus biography of the poet-plagiarist Thingum Bob who has "resolved at once to become a great man" by his pen and stands as a good example of Poe's ability to transform the daily drudgery of the magazine trade into successful parody. In relating his success saga, Thingum Bob never misses the opportunity to extol his literary virtues, trumpet his successes, and promote his intelligence, which extends to stealing lines from Shakespeare and Milton to adorn his work. He soars to literary fame in the journals with the publication of his two-line ode, "The Oil-of-Bob," and is offered the position of Thomas H. Hawk by Mr. Crab, publisher of the *Lollipop*. The role of Thomas H. Hawk, Tommy Hawk, or "Tomahawk" is suited to Thingum Bob's skills since it permits him to cut up literary adversaries by savage reviewing or "tomahawking." Finally, Thingum Bob succeeds in the magazine world where Poe himself had failed by launching a megamagazine of his own, *Rowdy-Dow, Lollipop, Hum-Drum, and Goosetherumfoodle*. Poe satirizes the journals of his day but also appears to attack the readers of these magazines for their capricious, mediocre, and self-serving pretensions. In Thingum Bob's speech on literary fame in the final paragraphs of the story, Poe lowers the mask of satire to speak candidly of his own experiences in the periodical world as well as the frustration that he frequently felt over its vulgar standards and cheap dealings with contributors. "After all, what is it?—this indescribable something which men will persist in terming 'genius'? I agree with Buffon—with Hogarth—it is but *diligence* after all. Look at *me*!—how I labored—how I toiled—how I wrote! Ye Gods, did I *not* write? I knew not the word 'ease.' " The story has obvious connections with "How to Write a Blackwood Article" and "Magazine-Writing—Peter Snook." *Text: MCW,* III, 1124–1149; *CWP,* VI, 1–27. *Research:* Whipple, William. "Poe, Clark, and 'Thingum Bob.' " *American Literature*, 29 (1957): 312–316; Pollin, Burton R. "Poe's Dr. Ollapod." *American Literature*, 42 (1970): 80–82.

"The Literary Remains of the Late William Hazlitt, with a Notice of his Life by his Son, and Thoughts on his Genius and Writings, By E. L. Bulwer, M. P. and Mr. Sergeant Talfourd." Poe reviewed a memorial volume compiled by Bulwer and Mr. Sergeant Talfourd in *The Southern Literary Messenger* for September 1836. *Text: CWP,* IX, 140–146.

"Literary Small Talk." Article appearing in *The American Museum* for January–February 1839. The essay consists of various critiques of Edward Gibbon's

Decline and Fall of the Roman Empire and begins with an exposé of the historical flaws of Bulwer's novel *The Last Days of Pompeii*. Poe was particularly impatient with Gibbon's ponderous style in his monumental history. "It is his *indirectness* of observation, then, which forms the soul of the style of Gibbon, of which the apparently pompous phraseology is the body." *Text: CWP,* XIV, 90–100.

"Literary Theft." An unsigned paragraph article appearing in *The Spy* (Columbia, Pennsylvania) attributed to Poe by T. O. Mabbott. *Research:* Spannuth, Joseph E., and Thomas Ollive Mabbott, *Doings of Gotham: Poe's Contributions to "The Columbia Spy."* Pottsville, PA: Jacob E. Spannuth, 1929.

"The Literati of New York City." Thirty-eight sketches and biographical profiles of literary friends, enemies, acquaintances, and other literary people published in several numbers of *Godey's Lady's Book* from May through October 1846. Drawing upon his own reviews and critical notices, Poe used these occasions to write a column commenting on the condition of American letters. His tone ranged from the complimentary to the scathingly insulting. He praised certain New York writers such as the poets Anna Cora Mowatt and Fanny Osgood but devastated Griswold's *The Poets and Poetry of America*, accused Longfellow of plagiarism, and directed satiric barbs at the New England transcendentalists. Not content to limit his biographical exposés to their literary character, Poe frequently evaluated their physical appearance, mental properties, habits of fashion and dress, education, financial status, and general standing in the community. Of Charles F. Briggs, Poe's former partner at *The Broadway Journal*, Poe wrote "Mr. Briggs has never composed in his life three consecutive sentences of grammatical English. He is grossly uneducated." Of Margaret Fuller's face and lips, Poe felt the need to inform his readers that she "habitually uplifts herself, conveying the impression of a sneer." Poe's column was enormously popular, fomenting both criticism and delight among readers in New York and Boston. Unable to keep up with demand, Godey reprinted Poe's first installment in the same issue that contained the second series, *Godey's Lady's Book* for June 1846, and further offered to buy back from subscribers any and all copies of the May number for resale. Several New York newspapers censured Poe for his intrusions into private lives. Poe eventually concluded the series because "people insisted on considering them elaborate criticisms when I had no other design than critical gossip." Among those literati featured over the life of the series were Nathaniel P. Willis, William M. Gillespie, Richard Adams Locke, William Kirkland, Charles Anthon, Freeman Hunt, Laughton Osborn, and Piero Maroncelli. Poe used the third installment to assassinate the character of his enemy Dr. Thomas Dunn English, attacking his grammatical ineptitude and reminding his readers that he had recently given English a beating "which he will remember to the day of his death." *Text: CWP,* XV, 1–137. *Research: PLB,*

112–114; Moss, Sidney. *Poe's Major Crisis: His Libel Suit and New York's Literary World.* Durham, NC: Duke University Press, 1970.

Little Lame Old Gentleman. Satanic character in the short story "Never Bet the Devil Your Head." He wears odd black clothes and inhabits the "nook of the frame of the bridge" that Toby Dammit crosses.

Little Snake. Character in the novella *The Journal of Julius Rodman.* He is a native American chief who befriends Rodman.

Littleton Barry. A Poe pseudonym. *See:* Barry, Lyttleton.

"Lives of the Cardinal de Richelieu, Count Oxenstiern, Count Olivarez, and Cardinal Mazarin. By G. P. R. James." Review of several biographies by James appearing in *The Southern Literary Messenger* for October 1836. Poe evaluates G. P. R. James as a novelist, calling him "an indifferent imitator" of Scott. Only the concluding paragraph of the review comments on the biographies. "Of the volumes now before us we are enabled to speak more favorably—yet not in a tone of high commendation. . . . What is done, however, is done with more than the author's usual ability." *Text: CWP,* IX, 168–170.

"Lives of the Necromancers: Or An Account of the Most Eminent Persons in Successive Ages, Who Have Claimed for Themselves, or to Whom Have Been Imputed by Others, the Exercise of Magical Power." Review of the Harper reprint of William Godwin's collection of biographical portraits of alchemists, sorcerers, and necromancers appearing in *The Southern Literary Messenger* for December 1835. "His compilation is an invaluable work, evincing much labor and research, and full of absorbing interest. . . . The pen which wrote Caleb Williams, should never for a moment be idle." *Text: CWP,* VIII, 92–94.

Livy. [Titus Livius]. (59 B.C.–A.D. 17). Ancient Roman historian. He is on the devil's menu in "Bon-Bon" and is mentioned once in *Marginalia.* "I believe that Hannibal passed into Italy over the Pennine Alps; and if Livy were living now, I could demonstrate this fact even to him." *Text: CWP,* II, 142; IX, 193; XVI, 5.

Lobelia Cardinalis. A flower "commonly called *the Indian Bright*" mentioned in Poe's review of "Ups and Downs in the Life of a Distressed Gentleman." *Text: CWP,* IX, 31.

Locke, Jane Ermina. (1805–1859). Amateur poet of Lowell, Massachusetts. Her relationship with Poe began in December 1846 when she sent him her poem "An Invocation to Suffering Genius," a lament for Poe's situation. She arranged for Poe's Lowell lecture of 10 July 1848, "The Poets and Poetry of America." Like several other women who had been enamored of Poe, her desire turned to animosity when he did not reciprocate her feelings, and she turned her talents to ruining the relationship between Poe and Annie Richmond. *Research:* Reilly, John Edward. "Ermina's Gales: The Poems Jane Locke Devoted to Poe." In *Papers on Poe: Essays in Honor of John Ward Ostrom*, ed. Richard P. Veler. Springfield, OH: Chantry Music Press, Wittenberg University, 1978, 206–220; *TPL,* xxxi, 739–741.

Locke, John. (1632–1704). English philosopher and epistemologist. In "Morella," the narrator comments, "That identity which is termed personal, Mr. Locke, I think, truly defines to consist in the saneness of a rational being." *Text: CWP,* II, 29; IX, 65. *Research:* Sandler, S. Gerald. "Poe's Indebtedness to Locke's *An Essay concerning Human Understanding.*" *Boston University Studies in English*, 5 (1961): 107–121; Thompson, G. R. "Locke, Kant, and Gothic Fiction: A Further Word on the Indeterminism of Poe's 'Usher.' " *Studies in Short Fiction*, 26 (1989): 547–550.

Locke, Lieutenant Joseph Lorenzo. (1808–1864). Instructor in military tactics while Poe was a cadet at the United States Military Academy. Poe regarded him as a ridiculous martinet and mocked his vanity in the one surviving example of Poe's West Point verse. "John Locke is a notable name/Joe Locke is a greater." *Research: TPL,* xxxi-xxxii, 108–109.

Locke, Richard Adams. (1800–1871). New York City journalist. His "Moon-Hoax" appearing in the *New York Sun* in August 1835 under the title "Great Astronomical Discoveries, Lately Made by Sir John Herschel" attracted Poe's attention since Poe believed that his balloon story, "The Unparalleled Adventure of One Hans Pfaall," had inspired Locke's charade. Poe included a profile of Locke in "The Literati of New York City," giving a history of *The Sun* and recognizing Locke's journalistic acumen. "His prose style is noticeable for its concision, luminousness, completeness. . . . Like most men of true imagination, Mr. Locke is a seemingly paradoxical compound of coolness and excitability." His signature is included in "Autography" for the "unquestionable genius" of his "Moon Hoax." "As an editor—as a political writer—as a writer in general—we think that he has scarcely a superior in America." *Text: CWP,* XV, 126–137, 259–260. *Research:* Ingram, John H. "The Lunar Hoax." *Athenæum*, 19 August 1876, 241–242; *TPL,* xxxii, 166, 249–250, 619–620.

Lofland, Dr. John. (1798–1849). Amateur poet. He was a casual acquaintance of Poe in Baltimore. *Research: TPL,* xxxii.

Long, George. Professor of ancient languages at the University of Virginia during Poe's residency. *Research: TPL,* 68, 73.

Longfellow, Henry Wadsworth. (1807–1882). American poet. He was often the undeserving target of Poe's furious charges of literary larceny but never replied to Poe's several attacks on him for plagiarism. Longfellow praised Poe after his death and attributed Poe's charges to "a sensitive nature chafed by some indefinite sense of wrong." Poe's "Autography" anecdote reiterates the charge of plagiarism. "His good qualities are all of the highest order, while his sins are chiefly those of affectation and imitation—an imitation sometimes verging upon downright theft." *See:* "Imitation—Plagiarism—Mr. Poe's Reply to the Letter of Outis"; The Longfellow War; *Text: CWP,* XI, 227, 239, 241; XII, 10–11; XIV, 258; XV, 4, 49–50, 191–192; XVI, 72, 79–81, 97, 132.

The Longfellow War. In February 1840, Poe accused Longfellow of plagiarizing his poem "Midnight Mass for the Dying Year" from Tennyson's "Death of the Old Year" and also claimed that Longfellow had lifted "The Beleaguered City" from Poe's "The Haunted Palace." Other assaults by Poe included the accusation that Longfellow had stolen the ideas for his *Spanish Student* from Poe's play *Politian.* Poe found some occasion to berate Longfellow in nearly every issue of *The Broadway Journal* throughout the winter and spring of 1845. It is also possible that Poe concocted the correspondence of "Outis" to perpetuate his war against Longfellow. As is typical of Poe's negative critical mode, he assailed Longfellow's personality, insisting that he would not have achieved the slightest reputation "without the adventitious influence of his social position as Professor of Modern Languages and Belles Lettres at HARVARD, and an access of this influence by marriage to an heiress." None of Poe's charges of plagiarism have any textual foundation. Perhaps Poe himself came to realize his unmotivated contumaciousness, for in May 1841 in a letter to Longfellow, Poe told the poet that his genius had inspired him and called Longfellow "unquestionably the best poet in America." George Rex Graham suggested that Poe's ambivalence could be attributed to Poe's jealousy over Longfellow's reputation and the fact that he had made poetry financially advantageous. "Your wealth," he told Longfellow, "is sufficient to settle your damnation so far as Mr. Poe may be presumed capable of effecting it." *See:* "Imitation—Plagiarism—Mr. Poe's Reply to the Letter of Outis"; *Research: PLB,* 156–182; Piacentino, Edward J. "The Poe-Longfellow Plagiarism Controversy: A New Critical Notice in the *Southern Chronicle.*" *Mississippi Quarterly,* 42 (1989): 173–182.

Longinus. (213–273). Greek rhetorician, philosopher, and author of a treatise *On the Sublime.* Poe cites him once in *Pinakidia*: "Longinus calls pompous and inflated thoughts 'reveries of Jupiter.' " *Text: CWP,* XIV, 60. *Research:* Rosenthal, M. L. "Hurrah for Longinus! Lyric Structure and Inductive Analysis." *Southern Review,* 25 (1989): 30–51.

Lord, William Wilberforce. (1819–1907). Amateur poet named "the American Milton" when his collection of *Poems* appeared in 1845. The collection was blasted by Poe in *The Broadway Journal* of 24 May 1845. *Text: CWP,* IV, 22; XV, 76; XVI, 103–104, 150–151. *Research:* Schwartzstein, Leonard. "Poe's Criticism of William W. Lord. *Notes & Queries*, 100, new series 2 (July 1955): 312; *TPL,* xxxii, 534–535.

"Loss of Breath: A Tale Neither in Nor Out of 'Blackwood.' " Short story first appearing under the title "A Decided Loss" in the Philadelphia *Saturday Courier* of 10 November 1832. The title "Loss of Breath, a Tale à la Blackwood" was used when the story was printed in *The Southern Literary Messenger* for September 1835 and was signed by "Lyttleton Barry." Mr. Lackobreath's vicious verbal assault on his new and apparently unfaithful wife causes him suddenly to lose his breath, this interruption in his vocal powers possibly connected with a lapse of sexual virility since he happens to grow short of breath on his nuptial night. Mr. Lackobreath spends the remainder of the narrative literally trying to catch his breath in a series of absurd travels that blend the slapstick and the macabre. On one occasion Lackobreath's lack of breath causes a surgeon to pronounce him dead, and he is partially eviscerated despite his "most furious contortions." He escapes from this autopsy-in-progress by leaping from a window into a hangman's passing cart and is soon on his way to the gallows where he is promptly hanged. Later he finds himself "interred in a public vault" and gropes through "numerous coffins," prying them open and "speculat[ing] about the mortality within." One coffin contains the corpse of Mr. Windenough, alleged lover of Lackobreath's wife. When the corpse energetically revives, Lackobreath is convinced "that the breath so fortunately caught by the gentleman (whom I soon recognized as my neighbor Windenough) was, in fact, the identical expiration mislaid by myself in the conversation with my wife." The verbally powerless Lackobreath must now attempt to recapture his lost breath from the verbally potent Windenough, his wife's purported lover. The story's lack of an ending and ridiculous edge dull the potential for Poe's treatment of the importance of language and the consequences of its misuse. The theme of sexual impotency as argued by one Poe critic, Daniel Hoffman, thus loses its comic force in the mishandled ending after Lackobreath and Windenough escape from the sepulchre together. Some of the events of Poe's tale parallel E.T.A. Hoffmann's comic saga of a man who loses his shadow, "A New Year's Eve Adventure," as well as Adelbert von Chamisso's shadow-trading hero Peter Schlemihl. *Epigraph:* "O breathe not, &c." Thomas Moore, "O breathe not his name" in *Irish Melodies. Text: MCW,* II, 51–81; *CWP,* II, 151–167. *Research:* Bachinger, Katrina E. "Towards a New Era in Poe Studies: The Case for a Byronic Interpretation of Poe's Tales Illustrated by 'A Decided Loss' and 'Bon-Bon.' " In *A Salzburg Miscellany: English and American Studies 1964–1984*, ed. Wilfried Haslauer. Salzburg, Austria: Institut für Anglistik & Amerikanstik, University of Salzburg, 1984, I, 37–54; Abdoo, Sherlyn. "Poe's 'Loss of Breath' and the Problem of Writing." In *The Elemental Passions of the Soul: Poetics of the Elements in the Human Condition*, ed. Anna-Teresa Tymieniecka. Dordrecht, South Africa: Kluwer, 1992, 581–594.

"The Lost Pleiad; And Other Poems. By T. H. Chivers, M.D." Favorable review of Thomas Holly Chivers's poetry appearing in *The Broadway Journal* of 2 August 1845. ''Many of the pieces in the volume before us possess merit of a very lofty—if not the loftiest order.'' *Text: CWP,* XII, 201–206.

Loud, John. Philadelphia piano manufacturer who came into contact with Poe in August 1849. He offered Poe $100 for editing his wife's verse, having noted Poe's praise for Marguerite St. Leon Loud in ''Autography.'' *Research: TPL,* xxxii, 828–830.

Loud, Marguerite St. Leon. (1800–1889). Philadelphia poet. Her poems had been praised by Poe in ''Autography,'' especially ''a truly beautiful little poem entitled 'The Dream of the Lonely Isle.' '' *Text: CWP,* XV, 230 *Research: TPL,* xxxii, 828–830.

Lovecraft, H.[oward] P.[hillips]. (1890–1937). American supernatural fiction writer and gothic fantasist. Tales such as ''The Outsider,'' ''The Dunwich Horror,'' and ''The Rats in the Walls'' show Poe's influence on Lovecraft's style and his vision of horror. Both the horror art and the short lives of the two writers are frequently compared by critics. Lovecraft said of Poe, ''Whatever his limitations, Poe did that which no one else ever did or could have done; and to him we owe the modern horror-story in its final and perfected state. . . . Poe studied the human mind rather than the usages of Gothic fiction.'' *Research:* Lovecraft, H. P. ''Edgar Allan Poe.'' In *Supernatural Horror in Literature*, ed. E. F. Bleiler. New York: Dover Publications, 1973, 52–59; Taylor, John. ''Poe, Lovecraft, and the Monologue.'' *Topic* (Washington and Jefferson College), 31 (1977): 52–62; Estren, Mark James. ''Horrors within and without; A Psychoanalytic Study of Edgar Allan Poe and Howard Phillips Lovecraft.'' *Dissertation Abstracts International*, 39 (1978): 1565A (SUNY at Buffalo); Bloch, Robert. ''Poe and Lovecraft.'' In *H. P. Lovecraft: Four Decades of Criticism*, ed. S. T. Joshi. Athens: Ohio University Press, 1980, 158–160; Buchanan, Carl. '' 'The Outsider' as an Homage to Poe.'' *Lovecraft Studies*, 31 (1994): 12–14.

Lowell, James Russell. (1819–1891). American poet and essayist and founder-editor of the Boston monthly *The Pioneer*. He met Poe only once in May 1845. His evaluative essay in *Graham's Magazine* used the phrase ''æsthetically deficient'' and suggested that Poe ignored the ''ethics of art,'' but he also accorded Poe a place in the American literary canon. ''Mr. Poe has attained an individual eminence in our literature, which he will keep.'' Lowell aided Poe in January 1845 in obtaining an editorial appointment to *The Broadway Journal*. Lowell's signature in ''Autography'' shows ''the vigor of his imagination—a faculty to be first considered in all criticism upon poetry. . . . His ear for rhythm, nevertheless, is imperfect, and he is very far from possessing the artistic ability of either Longfellow, Bryant, Halleck, Sprague, or Pierpont.'' *See:* ''A Fable for Critics.'' *Text: CWP,* XI, 65, 68, 125–126, 241, 243–249; XIII, 165–175; XV, 92, 239–

240; XVI, 69, 145. *Research:* Cauthen, Irby B., Jr. "Lowell on Poe: An Unpublished Comment, 1879." *American Literature*, 24 (1952): 230–233; *PJC*, 396–397.

Lucan. [Marcus Annæus Lucanus]. (39–65). Roman poet and author of *Pharsalia*. In *Marginalia*, Poe accuses Tasso of stealing from Lucan. Lucan is also mentioned in "How to Write a Blackwood Article" and furnishes one of the epigraphs for "A Tale of Jerusalem." *Text: CWP*, II, 280; XIV, 59; XVI, 75.

Luchesi. Character mentioned in the short story "The Cask of Amontillado." He is a wine expert who "cannot tell Amontillado from Sherry" and is the object of Fortunato's scorn.

Lucian. (120–?). Greek writer and author of *Dialogues of the Gods* and *Dialogues of the Dead* whose cynical vigor Poe admired. His satiric observations are cited in *Marginalia* and "Fifty Suggestions." *Text: CWP*, IV, 138; XIV, 175; XVI, 12.

Lucretius. [Titus Lucretius Carus]. (99–55 B.C.). Roman poet and author of *De Rerum natura* [*On the nature of things*]. Poe quotes Lucretius in *Pinakidia*, *Marginalia*, and his review of Griswold's *The Poets and Poetry of America*. *Text: CWP*, XI, 233; XIV, 70; XVI, 77. *Research:* Driskell, Daniel. "Lucretius and 'The City in the Sea.' " *Poe Newsletter*, 5, no. 2 (1972): 54–55.

"Ludwig." Pseudonym occasionally employed by Rufus Griswold. "The 'Ludwig' Article," Griswold's damaging obituary for Poe, was printed in the New York *Daily Tribune* of 9 October 1849. With this piece, Griswold began the process of exacting posthumous revenge against Poe, depicting him as a mentally unstable misanthrope who "had few or no friends." *Research: PLB*, 80, 121, 125, 155.

Lugné, Aurélian-François. (1869–1940). French actor and director. He was so obsessed with Poe's personality and writing that he became known as "Lugné-Poe." *Research: PLL*, 329.

Lummis, Colonel William. Mrs. Elizabeth Ellet's brother. She dispatched him to retrieve her letters from Poe. *See:* Ellet, Elizabeth Fries. *Research: TPL*, 623, 648.

Lunt, George. (1803–1883). American poet described by Poe in "Autography" as "a poet of much vigor of style and massiveness of thought. He delights in the grand, rather than in the beautiful." He was the author of *The Grave of Byron, with Other Poems*. *Text: CWP*, XV, 216. *Research: TPL*, 211, 445.

Luther, Martin. (1483–1546). German theological reformer. He is mentioned twice in *Pinakidia*. With gusto, Poe quoted Luther's characterization of Henry VIII upon acquiring the title ''Defender of the Faith'': '' 'a pig, an ass, a dunghill, the spawn of an adder, a basilisk, a lying buffoon dressed in a king's robes, a mad fool with a frothy mouth and a whorish face.' '' *Text: CWP,* XIV, 49, 66.

Lynch, Anne Charlotte. (1815–1891). Hostess and Poe acquaintance in New York in 1845. ''He was soon off her guest list because of her disapproval of Poe's contemptuous treatment of Elizabeth Fries Ellet.'' Poe's profile of her in ''The Literati of New York City'' is laudatory, singling out her poems ''Bones in the Desert,'' Farewell to Ole Bull,'' ''The Ideal,'' and ''The Ideal Found'' for their ''elevation of sentiment'' and ''energy of expression.'' *Text: CWP,* XI, 159; XV, 116–118. *Research: TPL,* xxxii, 536–537, 718–719.

Lyttleton, George, First Baron Lord. (1709–1773). English politician and author of *Dialogues of the Dead* (1760). Poe mentions his dialogues in *Pinakidia. Text: CWP,* XIV, 56.

Lytton, Edward George Earle Lytton Bulwer-. (1803–1873). English historical novelist and the subject of several reviews and much comment by Poe. The summation of Bulwer Lytton's artistic strengths and weaknesses in *Marginalia* was stern but fair: ''As a novelist, then, Bulwer is far more than respectable; although *generally* inferior to Scott, Godwin, d'Israeli, Miss Burney, Sue, Dumas, Dickens. . . . As a dramatist, he deserves more credit, although he receives less.'' Poe also negatively reviewed the poetry of Lytton in a notice in *The Broadway Journal* of 8 February 1845. *See:* ''Night and Morning.'' *Text: CWP,* V, 156, 202; IX, 168, 205; X, 47, 150; XI, 60; XIV, 189; XV, 81; XVI, 31, 40, 42–43, 109–110, 157–159. *Research:* Pollin, Burton. ''Bulwer Lytton and 'The Tell-Tale Heart.' '' *American Notes & Queries*, 4 (1965): 7–9; Spies, George H. ''Edgar Allan Poe's Changing Critical Evaluation of the Novels of Edward Bulwer-Lytton.'' *Kyushu American Literature* (Fukuoka, Japan), 17 (1976): 1–6.

M

Mabbott, Thomas Ollive. (1898–1968). Eminent scholar who devoted his academic life to the study of Poe and the reprinting of ignored Poe works. With the assistance of his wife, Maureen C. Mabbott, he edited the definitive twentieth century edition of Poe, *Collected Works of Edgar Allan Poe*, and was engaged in this project at his death. Mabbott also devoted much scholarly effort to locating and verifying Poe's unsigned work in various periodicals. *See:* "Literary Theft." *Research:* Dameron, J. Lasley. "Thomas Ollive Mabbott on the Canon of Poe's Reviews." *Poe Studies*, 5, no. 2 (1972): 56–57; Moldenhauer, Joseph J. "Mabbott's Poe and Questions of Copy-Text." *Poe Studies*, 11 (1978): 41–46.

Macaulay, Thomas Babington. (1800–1859). English historian and essayist. Poe reviewed his work and admired the "critical learning" that lay behind his analytic and stylistic powers as a critic. *See:* "About Critics and Criticism." *Research: PLB,* 82; *PJC,* 362–363.

Machiavelli, Nicolo. (1469–1527). Florentine statesman and author of *The Prince*. Poe refers to Machiavelli's thefts from Plutarch in the introduction to *Pinakidia* but never discusses his political theories. *Text: CWP,* X, 47; XIV, 39.

Mackenzie, Lieutenant Alexander Slidell. (1803–1848). American naval officer, author of *A Year in Spain* and *An American in England*, and commanding officer of the Brig-of-War *Somers* during the mutiny of December 1841. In "Autography" Poe noted sneeringly, "Both these books abound in racy description, but are chiefly remarkable for their gross deficiencies in grammatical construction.'' *Text: CWP,* VIII, 214–222; IX, 1–13, 83–84; XV, 201–202.

Mackenzie, John Hamilton. Son of William Mackenzie. He became the guardian of Rosalie Poe after his father's death and knew Poe well enough to share his memories with Susan Archer Weiss Talley who included them in her *Home Life of Poe* (1907). *Research: TPL,* xxxiii, xxxix.

Mackenzie, Thomas Gilliat. (1821–1867). Occasional Poe correspondent. Poe corresponded with him concerning the subscription list for *The Southern Literary Messenger. Research:* Miller, John C. ''A Poe Letter Re-Presented.'' *American Literature,* 35 (1963): 359–361; *TPL,* xxxiii, 401, 411.

Mackenzie, William. (1775–1829). Richmond merchant who adopted and cared for Rosalie Poe after the death of her mother. He and his wife, Jane Scott Mackenzie, had ten children of their own. *Research: TPL,* xxxiii.

Mackintosh, Sir James. (1765–1832). Author of *The History of the Revolution in England in 1688* (1834). His work and speeches were noticed by Poe in ''The Edinburgh Review, No. CXXIV, for July 1835.'' *Text: CWP,* VIII, 82–83.

Macrobius. [Ambrosius Theodosius]. (early fifth century A.D.). Roman author of a commentary on *Cicero's Dream of Scipio.* His imprecation or curse ''by which the Romans believed whole towns could be demolished and armies defeated'' is quoted in *Pinakidia. Text: CWP,* XIV, 48.

"Madrid in 1835. Sketches of the Metropolis of Spain and Its Inhabitants, and of Society and Manners in the Peninsula." Review of travel sketches ''By a Resident Officer'' appearing in *The Southern Literary Messenger* for October 1836. ''The manner of the narrative is singularly *à la Trollope.* . . . The author deals freely and en connoisseur, with the Ministry, the Monasteries, the Clergy and their influence, with Prisons, Beggars, Hospitals, and Convents.'' *Text: CWP,* IX, 157–158.

"Maelzel's Chess-Player." Article appearing in *The Southern Literary Messenger* for April 1836. The title refers to a pseudomechanical device employed by a traveling confidence man named Maelzel to perpetrate a hoax. Maelzel activated an automaton seated at a chessboard. Once activated, the robot chess player in Turkish costume would proceed automatically to defeat all human opponents. Poe exposes the hoax by observing that the chess player played each game with his left arm only. Using deductive methodology to explain his conclusions in seventeen sequential points leading to the discovery of the hoax, Poe anticipated the crime-solving formula he would again apply in the character of

C. Auguste Dupin in the detective tales. Poe's interest in calculating machines, computer androids, and automata is noteworthy throughout the essay. *Text: CWP,* XIV, 6–37. *Research:* Panek, Leroy L. " 'Maelzel's Chess-Player,' Poe's First Detective Mistake." *American Literature*, 48 (1976): 370–372; Irwin, John T. "Handedness and the Self: Poe's Chess Player." *Arizona Quarterly*, 45 (1989): 1–28.

"Magazine Writing—Peter Snook." Article appearing in *The Southern Literary Messenger* for October 1836 and republished in *The Broadway Journal* of 7 June 1845. Speaking of the poor condition of magazine writing in America, Poe maintains that "we are behind the age in a very important branch of literature" and "lamentably deficient, not only in invention proper, but in that which is, more strictly, *art*." As opposed to French and English periodicals with their diverse subject matter and variety of lively styles, American magazine writing paid poorly and failed to attain the artistic fulfillment of "the true magazine spirit." Poe traced these shortcomings to the absence of copyright laws protecting foreign authorship; American magazine publishers freely pirated British work, thus bypassing the need to compensate American writers. Much of the essay is devoted to James Forbes Dalton's story "Peter Snook," which is cited and summarized by Poe as an example of the artistic superiority of material in British and French magazines as contrasted with the mediocrity of fiction in American periodicals. Poe's complaints were assailed by Lewis Gaylord Clark in the "Editor's Table" column of the *Knickerbocker Magazine* for July 1845. *Text: CWP,* XIV, 73–89. *Research: PLB,* 99–100.

Maginn, William. (1793–1842). He was the author of a gothic tale of horrible enclosure, "The Man in the Bell," appearing in *Blackwood's Magazine* for November 1821. Poe mentions Maginn in "How to Write a Blackwood Article." Maginn's tale of auditory torture may have served as a source for Poe's "The Pit and the Pendulum" and "The Devil in the Belfry." *Text: CWP,* II, 274. *Research:* Wilt, Napier. "Poe's Attitude toward His Tales; A New Document." *Modern Philology*, 25 (1927): 101–105.

Magritte, René François-Ghislain. (1898–1967). French surrealist painter. He pictorialized the surreal qualities of Poe in such works as *The Castle of the Pyrenees. Research:* Robinson, Fred Miller. "The Wizard Proprieties of Poe and Magritte." *Word and Image: A Journal of Verbal/Visual Inquiry*, 3 (1987): 156–161.

Magruder, Allan. Fellow cadet and acquaintance of Poe at the United States Military Academy. He recalled Poe as a "devourer of books" but an indifferent cadet. *Research: PLL,* 46.

"Mahmoud." Review of an anonymous collection of Turkish sketches appearing in *The Southern Literary Messenger* for March 1836. Poe believed that the work derived from Thomas Hope's novel *Anastasius* (1819) and was inferior to "that most excellent and vivid (although somewhat immoral) series of Turkish paintings." *Text: CWP,* VIII, 256–257.

Maillard, Monsieur. Character in the short story "The System of Doctor Tarr and Professor Fether." He is the former superintendent of the Maison de Santé, or madhouse. He goes insane.

Main and Fifth Streets. A Poe address in Richmond. *See:* Moldavia.

Maiter-di-dauns, Mounseer, Count A. Goose, Look-aisy. The little Frenchman who wears his hand in a sling in the short story "Why the Little Frenchman Wears His Hand in a Sling."

Malherbe, François de. (1555–1628). French poet. His epigram on St. Catherine is mentioned in *Pinakidia. Text: CWP,* XIV, 61.

Mallarmé, Stéfane [Étienne]. (1842–1898). French poet. With Mallarmé's encouragement, the poets of the French symbolist movement adopted Poe as their patron saint. Mallarmé remarked that Poe had taught him to eliminate all chance from poetry and to calculate the semantic and aural impact of every word during the act of composition. Mallarmé's memorial sonnet, "Le Tombeau d'Edgar Poe," was written for the 1876 remembrance at Poe's gravesite. The poem is an encomium to the transcendent artist whose grasp of beauty has transformed him into an angelic figure rising above the trials of mortal existence. The symbol of the angel as a deification of the artist was important to the symbolists, representing both artistic transcendence and immortality. Mallarmé reiterated the view of Poe put forward by Baudelaire: that he was a tortured genius doomed by that very isolated genius to special greatness. Poe's art was the product of suffering and sacrifice accomplished in the face of the world's ignorance and vulgarity. *Research:* Alexander, Jean. "Poe's 'For Annie' and Mallarmé's *Nuit d'Idumée.*" *Modern Language Notes*, 77 (1962): 534–536; *Two Mementoes from the Poe-Ingram Collection: An Anniversary Keepsake for Members of the Bibliographical Society of the University of Virginia 1946–1971.* Charlottesville: Bibliographical Society of the University of Virginia, 1971.

"The Man of the Crowd." Short story first appearing in *Burton's Gentleman's Magazine* for December 1840 and *The Casket* for December 1840. Because Graham had acquired *Burton's Gentleman's Magazine*, the issue in which the story appeared was headed "*Graham's Magazine.*" The tale is unusual in that there are no named characters in this vignette of urban anonymity. And contrary to the enclosed condition of much of Poe's fiction, the characters have total freedom of movement. Sitting in a London coffee house window seat, the nameless narrator amuses himself by observing a busy street scene, fascinated by the anonymity of the persons passing, "the tumultuous sea of human heads." He is especially drawn to those individuals bearing the marks of poverty and despair, the loneliest and most miserable members of the lonely crowd. Poe's sense of urban scenery is reminiscent of Hogarth and Dickens and anticipates the grim street world of Dostoevsky's city novels. The action of the story is deliberately minimal. Because of his look "of supreme despair," one individual man amidst the crowd rivets the attention of the narrator to the point where he decides to leave the coffee house and follow the stranger on his night journey through the London streets to satisfy "a craving desire to keep the man in view—to know more of him." It is never clear why this other nameless character so haunts and possesses the narrator, but the implication is that he represents some secret side or shadow self of the narrator. But unlike the clear-cut theme of the double in "William Wilson," there is never any direct confrontation of the two selves. Their separation even when they are together as the two hesitate in front of "one of the palaces of the fiend, Gin" is appropriate to this tale of incommunication and existential loneliness. The moment of potential human contact, recognition, and sharing is missed or denied, for after overtaking the man of the crowd, the narrator "gazed at him steadfastedly in the face. He noticed me not, but resumed his solemn walk, while I ceasing to follow, remained absorbed in contemplation." Is the narrator in some obscure and half-understood way condemning himself when he aborts the relationship? " 'This old man,' I said at length, 'is the type and genius of deep crime. . . . It will be in vain to follow; for I shall learn no more of him, nor of his deeds." By implication, the narrator experiences an uncanny and unspoken feeling of having met himself and no longer desires to deepen the relationship. The lost brother shall remain lost both geographically and spiritually as the terror of this Poe tale penetrates to the anxiety and guilt endemic to modern urban life. *Epigraph:* "Ce grand malheur, de ne pouvoir être seul" [That great evil, to be unable to be alone]. Jean de La Bruyère, *Les Caractéres. Text: MCW,* II, 505–518; *CWP,* IV, 134–145. *Research:* Shelden, Pamela J. "Poe's Urban Nightmare: 'The Man of the Crowd' and the Gothic Tale." *Studies in the Humanities* (Indiana, PA), 4, no. 2 (1975): 31–35; Mazurek, Ray. "Art, Ambiguity, and the Artist in Poe's 'The Man of the Crowd.' " *Poe Studies*, 12 (1979): 25–28; Grunes, Dennis. "Fraternal Hopes Dashed: Poe's 'The Man of the Crowd.' " *College Language Association Journal*, 25 (1982): 348–358; Keogh, J. G. "The Crowd as No Man's Land: Gas-Light and Poe's Symbolist Effects." *Antigonish Review*, 58 (1984): 19–31; Elbert, Monika M. " 'The Man of the Crowd' and the Man outside the Crowd: Poe's Narrator and the Democratic Reader." *Modern Language Studies*, 21, no. 4 (1991): 16–30.

"The Man That Was Used Up. A Tale of the Late Bugaboo and Kickapoo Campaign." Short story first published in *Burton's Gentleman's Magazine* for August 1839, then slightly revised for publication in *Tales of the Grotesque and Arabesque*, and revised again when it appeared in *The Broadway Journal* of 9 August 1845. The tale is often regarded as a satiric allegory on American political and military fame because the sham general who comes apart piece by piece and then reconstructs himself is associated with William Henry Harrison, hero of the Battles of Tippecanoe and the Thames and ninth president of the United States who would be "used up" after only thirty-one days in office. To the narrator, Brevet Brigadier-General John A.B.C. Smith appears to be "one of the *most* remarkable men of the age" with a "high reputation for courage." He also appears to be a magnificent physical specimen with "a mouth utterly unequalled," "large and lustrous" eyes, and a "countenance of the marble Apollo." This hero of the Bugaboo and Kickapoo campaign seems to be a cultural icon of splendid national vigor, and the fact that he discourses constantly on "the rapid march of mechanical invention . . . the most wonderful—the most ingenious—the most useful—mechanical contrivances" places him in the narrator's eyes in the vanguard of progressive civilization. Yet there is something suspiciously fake about Smith that causes the narrator to seek further information about the great man. Deciding to pay Smith an unexpected visit at his home, the narrator enters a chamber to find no Smith but instead "a large and exceedingly odd looking bundle of something which lay close by [his] feet on the floor." When the bundle begins to talk, the narrator begins to realize Smith's charade as a single leg emerges from the bundle and begins to draw on a stocking. His physical appearance, like his grandiloquent statements about progress and his great victories over the lesser breeds, is utterly without substance. Item by item with the assistance of his negro valet, Pompey, Smith now assembles himself in the presence of the narrator. A wig, chest, arms, glass eye, and false teeth are pieced together until finally the handsome general takes shape once again. The amazed narrator now takes his leave "with a perfect understanding of the true state of affairs." Even though Smith is nothing, he is able to dupe his public into the deluded belief that he is everything. Poe's satire reflects his antidemocratic inclinations and contempt for the American masses who repeat the crime of allowing themselves to be fooled by slick men of the people who are devoid of substance. The role of the slave Pompey remains curious, for it is through the black man's assistance that the general is able to construct his successful illusion of heroic dignity. Could Poe have been commenting in a subtle way on the part that slavery played in maintaining the illusion of southern heroic manhood? *Epigraph:* "Pleurez, pleurez, mes yeux, et fondez-vous en eau!/ La moitié de ma vie a mis l'autre au tombeau" [Weep, weep, my eyes! It is no time to laugh/For half myself has buried the other half]. Pierre Corneille, *Le Cid. Text: MCW,* II, 376–392; *CWP,* III, 259–272. *Research:* Wetzel, George. "The Source of Poe's 'The Man That Was Used Up.' " *Notes & Queries*, 198 (January 1953): 38; Pry, Elmer L. "A Folklore Source for 'The Man That Was Used Up.' " *Poe Studies*, 8 (1975): 46; Curran, Robert T. "The Fashionable Thirties: Poe's Satire in 'The Man That Was Used Up.' " *Markham Review*, 8 (1978): 14–20; Alekna, Richard A. " 'The Man That Was Used Up': Further Notes on Poe's Satirical Targets." *Poe Studies*, 12 (1979): 36; Rougé, Bertrand. "La Pratique des corps limites chez Poe: La Vérité sur le cas de 'The Man That Was Used Up.' " *Poétique*, 15 (1984): 473–488; Mead, Joan Tyler. "Poe's 'The Man That Was Used Up': Another Bugaboo Campaign." *Studies in Short Fiction*, 23 (1986): 281–286.

Manasseh ben Israel, Rabbi. (1604–1657). Poe refers to his book, *The Hopes of Israel* (1650) in *Pinakidia*. *Text: CWP,* XIV, 45.

Manchester, Edwin. Providence daguerreotypist. He made a daguerreotype of Poe shortly after his November 1848 suicide attempt. *Research: PLL,* 232.

Mancur, John Henry. (1774–1850). Minor English novelist and imitator of Scott. His *The Palais Royal* is mentioned for its laboriousness in *Marginalia*. *Text: CWP,* XVI, 71.

Manet, Édouard. (1832–1883). French impressionist painter. He made three studies of Poe in the 1870s. *Research:* Cauthen, I. B., Jr. ''Another Mallarmé-Manet Bookplate for Poe's 'Raven.' '' *Poe Studies*, 5, no. 2 (1972): 56; St. Armand, Barton Levi. ''A Mallarmé-Manet Bookplate in Providence.'' *Poe Studies*, 11 (1978): 15; Forestier, Louis. ''Autour de trois livres illustrés: Manet, Cros, Mallarmé, Poe.'' In *Tradition et Modernité: Mélanges offerts à Maciej Zurowski*, ed. Henryk Chudak, Zbigniew Naliwajek, Zdzislaw Rylko, and Joanna Zurowska. Warsaw, Poland: University de Varsovie, 1991, 95–103.

Mann, Captain. Character mentioned in the short story ''The Man That Was Used Up.'' He fights a duel with Brigadier General John A.B.C. Smith.

Mann, Thomas. (1875–1955) German novelist. He praised Poe's ''William Wilson'' when comparing it to Dostoevsky's *The Double* in his essay ''Dostoevsky within Limits.'' *Research: PLL,* 287.

Manor House School. Poe attended the school at Stoke Newington while with the Allans in England between 1817 and 1820.

"Marginal Notes—No.1: A Sequel to the 'Marginalia' of the 'Democratic Review.' " *See:* Marginalia.

"Marginal Notes—No.2." *See:* Marginalia.

Marginalia. A series of reflective comments and short paragraph essays on random subjects. Some of the marginalia are miniature literary reviews. Others are sarcastic or despondent in tone and reminiscent of the cynical observations of La Rouchefoucauld and Ambrose Bierce in *The Devil's Dictionary* or Twain in *Letters from the Earth*. Still others are pseudointellectual gibberish, all quite deliberate on Poe's part. Publication was intermittent and scattered through several periodicals. The first installment was published in the *Democratic Review* for September 1844 with a preface by Poe that T. O. Mabbott included in his edition of the *Tales and Sketches* ''since it is itself fiction.'' The second installment appeared in the *Democratic Review* for December 1844. *Godey's Lady's*

Book for August 1845 printed ''Marginal Notes—No. 1: A Sequel to the 'Marginalia' of the 'Democratic Review.' '' *Godey's Lady's Book* for September 1845 printed ''Marginal Notes—No. 2.'' More ''Marginalia'' appeared in *Graham's Magazine* for March 1846, in the *Democratic Review* for April 1846, in the *Democratic Review* for July 1846, in *Graham's Magazine* for November 1846, in *Graham's Magazine* for December 1846, in *Graham's Magazine* for January 1848, in *Graham's Magazine* for February 1848, and in *Graham's Magazine* for March 1848. Five installments of *Marginalia* appeared in the April, May, June, July, and September numbers of *The Southern Literary Messenger* for 1849. In his preface, Poe indicated that the underlying feature of the *Marginalia* would be a prevalent spirit of nonsense. ''It may be as well to observe, however, that just as the goodness of your true pun is in direct ratio of its intolerability, so is nonsense the essential sense of the Marginal Note.'' Along with practical subjects such as the purposes of women's purses and mordant aphorisms on the human condition, many of the marginalia concern the art of poetry and the art of literary criticism. Poetry subdues and transmutes passion. True poetry is always creative, never merely descriptive. The Alexandrine line is metrically capable of both speed and slow pace. Poetic art cannot and should not imitate actuality. ''Shelley is the most fatiguing of poets. Yet he wearies in saying too little rather than too much.'' ''In Tennyson, poetic inconsistency attained its extreme . . . leading him first to condemn, and secondly to investigate his early manner, and finally to winnow, from its magnificent elements, the truest and purest of all poetical styles.'' The highest form of criticism will ''look *less* at merit and *more* at demerit. . . . Now, it is the business of the critic so to soar that he shall *see the sun*, even though its orb be far below the ordinary horizon.'' A platonic conception forms the basis for the definition of art in a June 1849 marginalium. ''Were I called on to define, very briefly, the term 'Art,' I should call it 'the reproduction of what the Senses perceive in Nature through the veil of the soul.' The mere imitation, however accurate, of what is in Nature, entitles no man to the sacred name of 'Artist.' . . . I have mentioned 'the veil of the soul.' Something of the kind appears indispensable in Art.'' Poe's misanthropic pessimism, a major mood throughout the *Marginalia*, is occasionally tempered by remarking, ''It is only the philosophical lynxeye that, through the indignity-mist of Man's life, can still discern the dignity of man.'' *Text: MCW*, III, 1112–1118; Pollin, Burton R., ed. *Marginalia, the Brevities: Collected Writings of Edgar Allan Poe*. New York: Gordian Press, 1985, 107–423; *CWP*, XVI, 1–178. *Research:* O'Neill, E. H. ''The Poe-Griswold-Harrison Texts of the *Marginalia*.'' *American Literature*, 15 (1943): 238–250; Weissberg, Liliane. ''Von Naturalienkabinett zur Ästhetik der Moderne: Zu den Marginalien Edgar Allan Poes.'' In *Die Erfindung der Natur: Max Ernst, Paul Klee, Wols und das surreale Universum*. Freiburg, Germany: Rombach, 1984, 89–96; Cappello, Mary. '' 'Berenice' and Poe's *Marginalia*: Adversaria of Memory.'' *New Orleans Review*, 17, no. 4 (1990): 54–65.

Marmontel, Jean F. (1723–1799). French author and contributor to *The Encyclopedia*. Poe found his observations on drama questionable. ''Marmontel in his 'Encyclopédie,' roundly declares that there is not a single comedy in the language worth reading; and the usual error on this subject has probably found its origin in his ignorance.'' *Text: CWP,* XII, 223.

Maroncelli, Piero. (1795–1846). Exiled Italian poet living in America. Maroncelli's profile is included in ''The Literati of New York City.'' Poe further mentions his ''Essay on the Classic and Romantic Schools.'' ''There is at least some scholarship and some originality in this essay.'' *Text: CWP,* XV, 43–44. *Research:* Lograsso, A. H. ''Poe's Piero Maroncelli.'' *Publications of the Modern Language Association,* 58 (1943): 780–789; *LET,* II, 316, 317; *TPL,* 638, 641.

Marshall, John. (1755–1835). American chief justice of the Supreme Court. His signature is included in ''Autography.'' ''The whole air of the MS. in its utter simplicity, is strikingly indicative of the man.'' *Text: CWP,* XV, 157. *Research: LET,* I, 65–66.

Marston, John. (1575–1634). English dramatist. In ''Loss of Breath,'' the narrator recalls a line from his play *The Malcontent. Text: CWP,* II, 161.

Martin, John. (1789–1854). English painter of fantastic dreamscapes. His work inspired Sartain's engraving for Poe's short story ''The Island of the Fay.'' *Research: TPL,* 285.

Martineau, Harriet. (1802–1876). English author and social reformer. She is discussed in relation to the curative powers of mesmerism. *See:* ''Human Magnetism; Its Claim to Dispassionate Inquiry.'' *Text: CWP,* XII, 123.

Marvell, Andrew. (1621–1678). English poet. Poe praised Marvell's ''The Maiden Lamenting for Her Fawn'' as verse ''of the very *loftiest order*. It is positively crowded with *nature* and with *pathos*.'' *Text:CWP,* IX, 100–103; XII, 143–146. *Research: PLB,* 79.

Marx, Issacher. Character in the short story ''The Facts in the Case of M. Valdemar.'' This is Valdemar's pen name.

Mason, Monck. Character in the short story, ''The Balloon Hoax.'' He is one of the balloon *Victoria*'s pilots.

"The Masque [Mask] of the Red Death." Short story first appearing in *Graham's Magazine* for May 1842 and reprinted in the Lowell, Massachusetts, *Literary Souvenir* of 4 June 1842 with the title ''The *Mask* of the Red Death.'' A revised version appeared in *The Broadway Journal* of 19 July 1845 with the title altered to ''The *Masque* of the Red Death.'' The tale's unity of horror arises out of the stark realization that ''Death conquers all,'' a fact that must be learned by those who attempt to shut it out. The artistry of the tale is due in no small measure to its economy of language. Of the pestilence called simply ''The Red Death,'' the narrator avers that ''Blood was its Avatar and its seal—the redness and the horror of blood.'' It is possible, although not provable, that the narrator is none other than this avatar, the Red Death himself. Prince Prospero, a wealthy, powerful, and self-indulgent ruler, has sought safety from the raging plague within a secluded abbey with his ''thousand hale and light-hearted friends. . . . All these and security were within. Without was the 'Red Death.' . . . The external world could take care of itself.'' Named after Shakespeare's godlike creator of his own private and inviolable world in *The Tempest*, Prospero also closely resembles William Beckford's sensuous and selfish caliph, Vathek, in his decadent behavior, lavish indulgences, and proud seclusion from the suffering masses of humanity. And like Beckford's Vathek, Prince Prospero has established an exclusive and enclosed world of pleasure and perpetual revelry consisting of seven profusely decorated and multicolored chambers of delight to please the senses of himself and his retinue even as the plague rages outside the abbey walls. ''There were buffoons, there were improvisatori, there were ballet-dancers, there were musicians, there was Beauty, there was wine. All these and security were within.'' The pleasure palace's seven chambers correspond to the seven ages of man and, ironically, to the seven stages of deadly sin culminating in the worst of the sins, pride. The chambers are connected by a serpentine corridor running from east to west to track the movement of the sun. The westernmost chamber is decorated entirely in black and holds a giant ebony clock at whose chiming ''it was observed that the giddiest grew pale.'' When Prince Prospero gives a lavish masquerade ball at the height of the plague, an uninvited guest appears wearing a mask and costume ''resembling the countenance of a stiffened corpse.'' When the furious Prince Prospero pursues and confronts the masked figure within the black chamber for his failure to unmask at midnight, the figure wheels upon him, felling the Prince in his tracks and dooming all of the revelers in a grisly apocalypse. ''One by one dropped the revellers in the blood-bedewed halls of their revel.'' The final paragraph of the story contains seven pulsating clauses, each commencing with ''and,'' a clock-like peal of doom. The theme of devastating time, so pronounced in so many of Poe's tales of horror, is linked to the prospect of ubiquitous decay and futility of life in the Red Death's ''dominion over all.'' Even though Poe denied the didactic as a legitimate motive for art, ''The Mask of the Red Death'' is a didactic masterpiece in its implied assertion of two stern morals: It is futile and fatal for the artist to attempt to create a purely imaginative realm beyond the strictures of reality; the wages of sin is death especially when that sin is the sort of pride that sets itself apart from humanity. *Text: MCW,* II, 667–678; *CWP,* IV, 250–258. *Research:* Roppolo, Joseph. ''Meaning and 'The Masque of the Red Death.' '' *Tulane Studies in English*, 13 (1963): 59–69; Vanderbilt, Kermit. ''Art and Nature in 'The Masque of the Red Death.' '' *Nineteenth Century Fiction*, 22 (1968): 379–389; Goodwin, Sarah Webster. ''Poe's 'Masque of the Red Death' and the Dance of Death.''

In *Medievalism in American Culture: Special Studies*, ed. Bernard Rosenthal, Paul E. Szarmach, and Leslie J. Workman. Binghamton, NY: Center for Medieval & Early Renaissance Studies, 1987, 17–28; Cassuto, Leonard. ''The Coy Reaper: Unmasque-ing the Red Death.'' *Studies in Short Fiction*, 25 (1988): 317–320; Zapf, Hubert. ''Entropic Imagination in Poe's 'The Masque of the Red Death.' '' *College Literature*, 16 (1989): 211–218.

"Master Humphrey's Clock. By Charles Dickens." Review appearing in *Graham's Magazine* for May 1841 and included with Poe's review of ''The Old Curiosity Shop and Other Tales.'' Poe criticized the publisher's confusing arrangement of the novel with the stories. ''We plainly see that it with the design of intimating the *entireness* of the volume now before us, that '*The Old Curiosity Shop, and Other Tales*,'' has been made not only the primary and main title, but the name of the whole publication as indicated by the back. This may be quite fair in trade, but is morally wrong not the less.'' *See:* ''The Old Curiosity Shop, and Other Tales.'' *Text: CWP,* X, 142–148.

The Mastiff. Cordial canine in the short story ''Landor's Cottage.'' ''He not only shut his mouth and wagged his tail, but absolutely offered me his paw—afterward extending his civilities to Ponto.''

Mathews, Cornelius. (1817–1899). New York author, literary friend of Evert A. Duyckinck, and editor of the monthly magazine *Arcturus*. Poe knew him in New York and listed his best works in ''Autography.'' ''He is the author of 'Puffer Hopkins,' a clever satirical tale somewhat given to excess in caricature, and also of the well-written retrospective criticisms which appear in his magazine.'' Mathews's epic poem *Wakondah* was severely reviewed by Poe, but his *Big Abel and Little Manhattan* earned Poe's approbation. *See:* ''Wakondah, The Master of Life. A Poem.'' *Text: CWP,* XV, 249. *Research: PJC,* 275, 283; *TPL,* xxxiii.

Matisse, Henri Émile Benoît. (1869–1954). French artist. His etching of Poe done in 1932 is called *Le Tombeau d'Edgar Poe*. *Research: PLL,* 334.

Matthias, Benjamin. Editor of the Philadelphia *Saturday Chronicle* to which, according to the entry for his signature in ''Autography,'' ''he has furnished much entertaining and instructive matter.'' Poe may have been familiar with his *Rules of Order: A Manual for Conducting Business in Town and Ward Meetings*. *Text: CWP,* XV, 212.

Maturin, Charles Robert. (1782–1824). Irish gothic novelist who gained international fame for his *Melmoth the Wanderer*. The influence of Maturin's gothic style on Poe's idiom of terror has never been sufficiently studied. Poe's remark on *Melmoth the Wanderer* in his review of Cockton's *Stanley Thorn* (''the devil in 'Melmoth' plots and counterplots through three octavo volumes for the entrapment of one or two souls, while any common devil would have demolished one or two thousand'') is not a complete indicator of Poe's debt to Maturin. *Text: CWP,* VII, xxxvii; XI, 13. *Research: LET,* II, 316; Swann, Charles. ''Poe and Maturin—A Possible Debt.'' *Notes & Queries*, 37 (1990): 424–425.

"Maury's Navigation." Review of a nautical text appearing in *The Southern Literary Messenger* of June 1836. The manual's ''style is concise without being obscure. The diagrams are selected with taste, and the engraving and typography, especially that of the tables, are worthy of the highest praise.'' *Text: CWP,* IX, 48–50.

Mavis, Martin Van Buren, "The Poughkeepsie Seer." Character mentioned in the letter prologue to the short story ''Mellonta Tauta.'' He is the translator of the ''odd-looking manuscript'' that the narrator has found ''in a jug floating in the *Mare Tenebrarum.*''

"May Queen Ode." Unpublished poem written for a Richmond schoolgirl in 1836. It was included in Whitty's second edition of *The Complete Poems* (1917) and in Mabbott's edition of the *Poems*. The five lines have much lyric charm: ''Fairies guard the Queen of May,/ Let her reign in Peace and Honor—/ Every blessing be upon her;/ May her future pathway lie/ All beneath a smiling sky.'' *Text: MCW,* I, 302.

McCabe, Dr. John Collins. (1810–1875). Amateur poet of Richmond. Poe published several of his pieces while editing *The Southern Literary Messenger* and included his signature in ''Autography.'' *Text: CWP,* XV, 231. *Research: TPL,* xxxii, 192, 242.

McHenry, Dr. James. (1785–1845). American poet and historical novelist. In ''Autography,'' Poe defended his poem *The Antediluvians* from the unjust attacks of hostile reviewers and referred to McHenry's poem as ''the only tolerable American epic.'' *Text: CWP,* XV, 258. *Research: PLB,* 64–67; *PJC,* 65.

McIntosh, Maria Jane. (1803–1878). Casual acquaintance and writer of children's stories under her pen name ''Aunt Kitty.'' She acted as informal go-between in introducing Poe to Sarah Helen Whitman. *Research: LET,* II, 375, 376; *TPL,* xxxiii, 754–755.

McJilton, John N. (1805–1875). Contributor to *The Southern Literary Messenger.* Poe corresponded with him about ciphers and included his signature in ''Autography.'' As editor of the *Baltimore Athenaeum and Young Men's Paper*, McJilton also praised Poe's early story writing, declaring of ''Hans Pfaall'' and other stories that, ''He writes with a bold free hand and is irresistibly interesting. *Research: TPL,* xxxiii, 170, 337–338, 362–363.

McMakin, Andrew. An editor of the Philadelphia *Saturday Courier* and poet. His signature in "Autography" shows the clarity and grace of his poems. Poe had probably seen his *Panorama and Views of Philadelphia and Its Vicinity* (1838). *Text: CWP,* XV, 229. *Research: TPL,* xxix; 441; 718.

McMichael, Morton. (1807–1879). American poet and journalist. He reviewed *Tales of the Grotesque and Arabesque* in *Godey's Lady's Book* for January 1840. His rave review cited in particular Poe's expert sense of the comically absurd. In general, the collection contained "some of the most vivid scenes of the wild and wonderful which can be found in English literature." Poe returned the compliment in "Autography," writing, "As a poet, he has produced some remarkably vigorous things. We have seldom seen a finer composition than a certain celebrated 'Monody.' " *Text: CWP,* XV, 224. *Research: TPL,* xxxiii.

Mechanics Row, Wilkes Street, Baltimore. A Poe address. Poe resided here briefly when he lived in Baltimore in May 1831.

Mellen, Grenville. (1799–1841). A Portland, Maine, judge and amateur poet. From his signature in "Autography," he is described as "a man of excessive sensibility amounting nearly to disease—of unbounded ambition, greatly interfered with by frequent moods of doubt and depression, and by unsettled ideas of the beautiful." Poe might have read his *Requiem for the Marquis de Lafayette* (1834). *Text: CWP,* XV, 167–168, 186. *Research: TPL,* 208, 211, 231.

"Mellonta Tauta." Short story first published in *Godey's Lady's Book* for February 1849. Under the title "A Remarkable Letter," a portion of the futuristic fantasy appeared in *Eureka*. The title signifies that "These things are imminent." The utopian antiscientific fantasy is set in the year 2848 and cast in the form of a fake scientific report. The frame device is a letter from Poe to the editor of *Godey's Lady's Book* describing an enclosed odd-looking manuscript found "tightly corked up in a jug floating in the *Mare Tenebrarum*" that Poe "hopes the editor will comprehend rather more distinctly than I do myself." The manuscript details the voyage of the hot air balloon *Skylark* in the form of a ship's log with the first entry dated April 1, 2848, April Fool's Day,—with the emphasis upon hot air, windiness, and bluster. Much of the story reflects Poe's pessimistic politics and aversion to democracy, calling it "a very admirable form of government—for dogs" and referring acerbically to the central tenets of the Declaration of Independence as "the queerest idea conceivable, viz: that all men are born free and equal—this in the very teeth of the laws of *gradation* so vividly impressed upon all things both in the moral and physical universe." In addition to satirizing democratic institutions and berating mobocracy, the *Skylark*'s passengers, Pundit and Pundita, revel in a great deal of intellectual nonsense and pseudoscientific persiflage. They cite from the researches of "the Hindoo Aries Tottle" and his disciples "one Neuclid and one

Cant'' and confuse Sir Francis Bacon with James Hogg in a muddled explication of a posteriori logic. Portions of ''Mellonta Tauta'' reappeared in *Eureka*, conveying the strong suggestion that the cosmology, like the hot air of the balloon story, was itself almost entirely a pseudoscientific hoax. *See:* ''A Remarkable Letter.'' *Text: MCW,* III, 1289–1309; *CWP,* VI, 197–215. *Research:* Pollin, Burton R. ''Politics and History in Poe's 'Mellonta Tauta': Two Allusions Explained.'' *Studies in Short Fiction*, 8 (1971): 627–631.

Melville, Herman. (1819–1891). American novelist, poet, and short story writer. Although diverse in their rendering of the American experience, the two writers are nearly parallel in their perception of ''the power of blackness'' that lies at the center of that experience. Several critics have suggested that the character of Bulkington in Melville's *Moby Dick* is a profile of Poe. There are many Poe-esque qualities in Melville's novel *Pierre; or, the Ambiguities* and the sinister descriptions in Melville's tale of fraudulent appearances, *Benito Cereno*, also evoke Poe's gothic dreamscapes. Melville's library did have the 1859 edition of *The Works of the Late Edgar Allan Poe*. *Research:* Beaver, Harold. ''Poe and Melville: Appendix II.'' In *The Narrative of Arthur Gordon Pym*. Baltimore: Penguin Books, 1975, 278–281; Eisiminger, Sterling. ''Melville's Small Debt to Poe.'' *American Notes & Queries*, 15 (1977): 70–71; Hollister, Michael. ''Melville's Gam with Poe in *Moby Dick*: Bulkington and Pym.'' *Studies in the Novel*, 21 (1989): 279–291.

"A Memoir of the Reverend John H. Rice, D.D. First Professor of Christian Theology in Union Theological Seminary, Virginia." A neutral review of a memoir by William Maxwell appearing in *The Southern Literary Messenger* for December 1835. By citing Rice's letters, the memoirist allows ''the subject of the Memoir to tell, in a great measure, his own story in his own words.'' *Text: CWP,* VIII, 101–102.

"Memoirs and Letters of Madame Malibran. By the Countess de Merlin." Review of the memoirs and letters of the opera singer Maria Felicia Garcia (Madame Malibran) appearing in *Burton's Gentleman's Magazine* for May 1840. ''The merely private anecdotes related in these volumes of the sensitive and vivacious woman are very entertaining and strongly characteristic.'' *Text: CWP,* X, 91–96.

"Memoirs of an American Lady. With Sketches of Manners and Scenery in America, as They Existed Previous to the Revolution." Review of a book by Anne Grant appearing in *The Southern Literary Messenger* for July 1836. ''The book is full of good things; and as a memorial of the epoch immediately preceding our Revolution, is invaluable. . . . In Albany and New York it will possess a local interest of no common character.'' *Text: CWP,* IX, 70–71.

"Memoirs of Lucian Bonaparte, (Prince of Canino,) Written by Himself." Review of the English translation of the memoirs appearing in *The Southern Literary Messenger* for October 1836. Although the volume is of "deep interest" for the light it casts on politics and history, it is stylistically flawed by "affectations," "*Tacitus-ism*," and "indiscriminate elevation of tone." *Text: CWP,* IX, 155–156.

"Memorandum by Poe in the Griswold Collection Relating to Mrs. E. A. Lewis—'Stella.' " This unpublished notice was included by Harrison in *The Complete Works.* "The poems of Mrs. Lewis, generally, are distinguished by a fluent *abandon* of style and thought, throughout all which the strictest precision of language is observed." *Text: CWP,* XIII, 225–226.

"Memorials of Mrs. Hemans, with Illustrations of Her Literary Character from Her Private Correspondence. By Henry F. Chorley." Review of a book on the English poet Felicia Dorothea Hemans appearing in *The Southern Literary Messenger* for October 1836. Poe views the memorialist as "one of the most brilliant of the literary stars of England," while the memorial is written in such a way that "no shadow of vanity or affectation could be discerned in either the Memorialist or his subject." *Text: CWP,* IX, 195–204.

Menander. (343–291 B.C.). Ancient Greek comic dramatist. In *Marginalia*, Poe refers to the Roman dramatist Terence as "Menander and nothing beyond." In "Bon-Bon," Menander tastes exactly the same as Terence to the devil's palate. *Text: CWP,* II, 142; XVI, 72.

Mencken, H.[enry] L.[ouis]. (1880–1956). American journalist, wit, iconoclast, and cultural historian. Mencken's essay "The Mystery of Poe" appeared in *The Nation* of 17 March 1926. In reviewing Joseph Wood Krutch's biography *Edgar Allan Poe: A Study in Genius*, the essay attacked narrowminded American attitudes about the role of the artist in society and asserted Mencken's view that Poe's alcoholism in no way detracted from his genius, a genius missed or misunderstood by the culturally shallow American audience. But Mencken could also be Mencken as when he wrote of Poe's female characterizations: "Women stirred him only when they were in decay, and even then they did not stir his hormones. His heroines all suffer from phagocytolysis, and he approaches them on his knees." Mencken also wrote a biographical piece on "Poe's Start in Life" appearing in *The Chicago Sunday Tribune* of 1 March 1925, *The National Letters, Prejudices: Second Series*, 1920, and a brief piece on the outrageous shabbiness of the Poe memorial in the Presbyterian churchyard in Baltimore. "He was planted, as I have said, in a Presbyterian church-yard, among generations of honest believers in infant damnation, but the officiating clergyman was a Methodist. . . . And so he rests: thrust among Presbyterians by a Methodist and formally damned by a Baptist [Rufus W. Griswold]." Mencken regarded

Poe as "the lonely artist, . . . a man of so forceful habit of mind . . . of prodigal and arresting originality" and a pioneer in the art of literary criticism. "You will find in 'The Poetic Principle' what is perhaps the clearest statement of this new and sounder concept of beauty than has ever been made—certainly it is clearer than any ever made by a Frenchman." *Research:* Goldberg, Isaac. "Poe and Mencken, a Literary Divertisement." *Stratford Monthly*, 1, new series (May 1924): 137–145; Boynton, Percy Holmes. "Mr. Mencken Does His Bit." *The Challenge of Modern Criticism*. Chicago: Chicago University Press, 1951, 29–46; Babcock, Merton C. "The Wizards of Baltimore: Poe and Mencken." *Texas Quarterly*, 13, no. 3 (1970): 110–115.

Mentoni, Marquesa Aphrodite. Character in the short story "The Assignation." She is the beautiful mother and wife who agrees to a suicide pact with her former lover after he rescues her baby from a Venetian canal.

Mentoni, Marquese. Character mentioned in the short story "The Assignation." He is a "satyr-like figure." The name probably derives from the villain of Mrs. Radcliffe's *Mysteries of Udolpho*, Signor Montoni.

"Mephistopheles in England, or the Confessions of a Prime Minister." Review of a book by R. F. Williams appearing in *The Southern Literary Messenger* for September 1835. Poe compared the author's political satire unfavorably against Byron's "English Bards and Scotch Reviewers." "The most glaring defect, however, is its utter want of *keeping*. It appears, moreover, to have no just object or end." *Text: CWP,* VIII, 42–43. *Research: PJC,* 89.

"Mercedes of Castile." Review of James Fenimore Cooper's historical romance appearing in *Graham's Magazine* for January 1841. Poe opened his review with an onslaught against Cooper. "As a history this work is invaluable; as a novel, it is well nigh worthless. . . . We can neither disguise from ourselves, nor from our readers, that it is, if possible, the worst *novel* ever penned by Mr. Cooper. A hasty sketch of the plot will fully sustain our assertion." *Text: CWP,* X, 96–99.

Mercier, Sébastien Louis. (1740–1814). French dramatist. His futuristic fantasy *L'An 2440* [The Year 2440] is mentioned in *Pinakidia* and *Marginalia*. *Text: CWP,* XIV, 56; XVI, 36.

Merry, Felix. *See:* Duyckinck, Evert Augustus.

Mesmer, Friedrich Antoine. (1734–1815). German physician who experimented with hypnotic trance in the treatment of patients. Poe's interest in mesmeric or hypnotic phenomena is to be seen in several short stories. In "Some Words with a Mummy," Count Allamistakeo refers to "the manoeuvres of

Mesmer'' and his ''contemptible tricks.'' *See:* ''The Facts in the Case of M. Valdemar''; ''Mesmeric Revelation.''

"Mesmeric Revelation." Short story first published in the *Columbian Magazine* for August 1844 and reprinted in the Philadelphia *Saturday Museum* of 31 August 1844. To Poe's dismay, the story was also printed as a serious scientific report in *The American Phrenological Journal* for September 1845, the editors not realizing the possibility of a hoax and taking his fiction for fact. The tale explores postmortem survival during hypnotic trance, a situation dramatized elsewhere for its horror potential in the short stories. The story takes the form of the mesmerist's scientific experiment on Mr. Vankirk, who is put under and then interviewed by the mesmerist narrator called P. While under hypnosis, Vankirk responds to a series of questions put to him by P. on the nature of God, the materiality of deity, postmortem survival, and other metaphysical matters. Several of Vankirk's answers to these queries would be developed by Poe later in *Eureka*, particularly Vankirk's response that '' 'God, with all the powers attributed to spirit, is but the perfection of matter. . . . These gradations of matter increase in rarity or fineness, until we arrive at matter *unparticled*—without particles—indivisible—one.' '' Vankirk's dialogue with P. from beyond life terminates suddenly in his death when P. attempts to restore him to consciousness. Having experienced a mesmeric revelation induced by ''keenly refined perception'' on the other side during the trance, Vankirk apparently declines to return by opting to remain in this ideal state of being and smiles blissfully as he expires. The unexpected death of Vankirk leaves the alarmed and frustrated P. without a firm and definite answer to his curiosity about the soul's immortality or any control over his subject's condition. Like Hawthorne's tales of immoral experimentation on human subjects, Poe's ambiguous treatment of theoretical science makes a statement on the perils of research for research's sake. *See:* ''The Facts in the Case of M. Valdemar.'' *Text: MCW,* III, 1024–1042; *CWP,* V, 241–254. *Research:* Stern, Madeleine B. ''Poe: 'The Mental Temperament' for Phrenologists.'' *American Literature*, 40 (1968): 155–163; *PJC,* 410–412.

Mesmerism. The techniques and procedures of hypnosis developed by the German physician F. A. Mesmer (1734–1815). Poe remained intrigued by mesmerism throughout his life and often wrote on the subject in fiction and fact. The intermediate state between life and death held an obvious fascination for him as shown in the short stories ''Some Words with a Mummy,'' ''Mesmeric Revelation,'' and ''The Facts in the Case of M. Valdemar,'' as well as his reviews of books on the subject. In a letter of 10 July 1844 to Thomas Holly Chivers, he detailed the philosophic value of his story ''Mesmeric Revelation'' to his own position on the nature of God. Poe's own mesmeric characters are always depicted as ''in articulo mortis,'' that is, able to communicate in the death state. Other characters such as the cataleptic Madeline Usher exhibit mesmeric traits. *See:* ''Human Magnetism; Its Claim to Dispassionate Inquiry.'' *Research:*

Lind, S. E. ''Poe and Mesmerism.'' *Publications of the Modern Language Association*, 62 (1947): 1077–1094; Carlson, Eric W. ''Charles Poyen Brings Mesmerism to America.'' *Journal of the History of Medicine and Allied Science*, 15 (1960): 121–132; Petersen, Pam. ''Mesmerism, Popular Science, and Poe.'' In *Proceedings of the Sixth National Convention of the Popular Culture Association, Chicago Illinois, April 22–24*, 1976, ed. Michael T. Marsden. Bowling Green, OH: Bowling Green State University Popular Press, 1976, 251–262.

"The Messenger Star." Poe gave the poem ''Al Aaraaf'' this title in one of his public recitations. *See:* Cushing, Caleb.

"Metzengerstein; A Tale in Imitation of the German." Short story first appearing in the Philadelphia *Saturday Courier* of 14 January 1832 and reprinted in *The Southern Literary Messenger* for January 1836. Some commentators have suggested that Poe might have been lampooning as well as imitating Germanic gothicism and *schauerromantic* excesses in this early tale of fantastic supernatural revenge. One of Poe's most orthodox gothic thrillers, it features many of the devices that have characterized the gothic genre from their first appearance in Horace Walpole's *The Castle of Otranto* (1764): internecine family rivalry and sensational death; cryptic and foreboding prophecies; two horrible conflagrations; two dark and brooding Hungarian castles containing secret histories of sin and obsession; animated tapestry; and an atmosphere that is heavy with the dreamscape of unfolding nightmare. The rhetoric of supernatural gothic catastrophe is also obvious from the tale's opening sentence: ''Horror and fatality have been stalking abroad in all ages.'' To these orthodox gothic features Poe added the theme of metempsychosis, or equine metempsychosis, since the psychic transmigration here is from human into horse. The hero-villain of the tale is the Baron Frederick Metzengerstein, ''a petty Caligula,'' who sets fire to the stables of Castle Berlifitzing, destroying his rival who is burned to death trying to save his horses. Out of the flaming stables emerges a single mysterious horse, an equine reincarnation of the murdered Berlifitzing bearing the owner's initials, W.V.B., on its forehead. The fire seems to be the fulfillment of an ancient prophecy that dooms the house of Berlifitzing, although the prophecy proves to be both false and backwards: ''A lofty name shall have a fearful fall when, as the rider over his horse, the mortality of Metzengerstein shall triumph over the immortality of Berlifitzing.'' When the Berlifitzing horse is brought to him, the Baron soon develops ''a perverse attachment to his lately acquired charger'' that is almost sodomic, ''an attachment which seemed to attain new strength from every fresh example of the animal's ferocious and demonlike propensities.'' The strange stallion with its ''human-looking eye'' now begins to exert its control over the Baron. Figuratively, the horse now rides the man in a reversal of power roles, a relationship that might suggest Baron Metzengerstein's repressed awareness of his guilt in the killing of Berlifitzing or an odd fulfillment of the prophecy of doom in reverse. ''One tempestuous night,'' a second conflagration demolishes the Palace Metzengerstein, the fiery crash of the battlements accompanied by the horrifying spectacle of ''a steed, bearing an unbonneted and disordered rider'' who shrieks so loudly in agony that ''his lacerated lips . . . were bitten through and through in the intensity of terror.'' Bearing the hysterical and unwilling rider to his death, the demonic horse charges into the flaming Castle Metzengerstein and is seen once more at the climax as a ''colossal figure'' rising triumphantly over the funeral pyre of the wicked Baron. Since this story is one of the earliest of the horror tales, commentators have been interested in the critical question of how serious Poe was with the gothic usages at his disposal at this point in his writing career. Is the tale to be categorized as a spoof on the Germanic shocker or a hoaxing of the most horrific type of hair-raising and money-making short gothic thriller so prevalent in the magazines of the period? Whether it is a burlesque or a ''serious imitation of the German'' as the subtitle proclaims, ''Metzengerstein'' confirms Poe's early and permanent attraction to the ways and means of gothic fiction. *Epigraph:* ''Pestis eram vivus—moriens tua mors ero.'' [Living I have been your plague—dying I shall be your death]. Martin Luther in a letter to the pope. *Text: MCW,* II, 15–31; *CWP,* II, 185–196. *Research:* Thompson, G. R. ''Poe's 'Flawed' Gothic: Absurdist Techniques in 'Metzengerstein' and the Courier Satires.'' *Emerson Society Quarterly* (supplement), 60 (1970): 35–58; Fisher, Benjamin Franklin, IV. ''Poe's 'Metzengerstein': Not a Hoax.'' *American Literature*, 42 (1971): 487–494; Hirsch, David H. ''Poe's 'Metzengerstein' as a Tale of the Subconscious.'' *University of Mississippi Studies in English*, 3 (1982): 40–52.

Metzengerstein, Baron Frederick. Character in the short story ''Metzengerstein.'' He is the wicked baron who burns the stables of Castle Berlifitzing.

Metzengerstein, Lady Mary. Character in the short story ''Metzengerstein.'' She is Baron Frederick Metzengerstein's mother who dies shortly after her husband's death.

Michaelangelo. [Buonarotti]. (1475–1564). Florentine sculptor, painter, and poet. Discussing Hawthorne, Poe quotes Michaelangelo's couplet: ''The best of artists does not have a concept, that the marble block does not circumscribe.'' *Text: CWP,* II, 119; XI, 84, 90; XVI, 43. *Research: LET,* I, 19, 261.

Mignaud, Jules. Character in the short story ''The Murders in the Rue Morgue.'' He is a banker who confirms that Madame L'Espanaye made a withdrawal three days prior to her death.

Military Service. Poe served in the United States Army from May 1827 to April 1829 and had various postings that included Fort Moultrie, Charleston, South Carolina, Fortress Monroe, Virginia, and Fort Independence in Boston Harbor. He was also a cadet at West Point from July 1830 until his court martial and dismissal in February 1831. *Research:* Allan, Carlisle. ''Cadet Edgar Allan Poe,

USA.'' American Mercury, 29 (August 1933): 446–455; Helfers, M. C. ''The Legendary Edgar Allan Poe.'' *Assembly* (West Point), 27 (1969): 6–7; Russell, J. Thomas. *Edgar Allan Poe: The Army Years. USMA Library Bulletin No. 10*, foreword by Egon A. Weiss. West Point, NY: United States Military Academy, 1972; Cameron, Kenneth Walter. ''Young Poe and the Army—Victorian Editing.'' *American Transcendental Quarterly*, 20, supplement part 4 (Fall 1973): 154–182; Oelke, Karl E. ''Poe at West Point—A Revaluation.'' *Poe Studies*, 6, no. 1 (1973): 1–6.

Mill, James. (1773–1836). Political economist and utilitarian philosopher. His views were the object of scrutiny and criticism in *Marginalia* and *Eureka*. *Text: CWP,* XVI, 1, 38, 70, 193–194.

Mill, John Stuart. (1806–1873). Political writer and utilitarian thinker. He is mentioned in ''Mellonta Tauta.'' *Research: PJC,* 112, 358.

Miller, Dr. James Henry. (1788–1853). One of the judges for the *Baltimore Saturday Visiter* who awarded the $50 prize to Poe for his ''MS. Found in a Bottle.'' *Research: TPL,* xxxiii, 129–130, 132–133, 167–169.

Miller, Joseph [various middle initials]. The autographer and collector of signatures who brings the letters of various prominent individuals to Poe's editorial offices and offers them for publication. ''The package handed us by Mr. M. we inspected with a great deal of pleasure. . . . We print them verbatim, and with facsimiles of the signatures, in compliance with our friend's suggestion.'' *See:* ''Autography.'' *Text: CWP,* XV, 139–144.

Milton, John. (1608–1674). English poet. Poe read Milton early in life and often cited or quoted his poetry and political tracts. Additional evidence of Miltonic grandeur of theme, diction, and style may be heard in the ''Nicean barks'' of ''To Helen'' and the epigraph to ''Miscellaneous Poems'' in the *Tamerlane* volume. *Paradise Lost* is mentioned in ''The Poetic Principle'' and favorably commented on in the review of Griswold's edition of *The Prose Works of John Milton* in *The Broadway Journal* of 27 September 1845. The name of the heroine of ''Ligeia'' may derive from a character in Milton's *Comus*: ''And fair Ligea's golden comb'' (line 880). In *Pinakidia*, Poe comments on ''[t]he noble simile of Milton, of Satan with the rising sun in the first book of 'Paradise Lost' '' and suggests that the famous oxymoron from *Paradise Lost*, ''darkness visible,'' was taken from Spenser's line ''a little gloaming light much like a shade.'' Poe was fascinated by Milton's dignity of versification and sonorous language, although he also felt that *Paradise Lost* was marred by length. *See:* ''The Prose Works of John Milton, with a Biographical Introduction by Rufus Wilmot Griswold.'' *Text: CWP,* VII, 27; IX, 273, 277, 290; X, 190; XI, 84, 242; XII, 102, 244–247; XIII, 86, 151; XIV, 47, 53–54, 57; XVI, 26, 74–76. *Research:* Durham, Frank M. ''A Possible Relationship between Poe's 'To Helen' and Milton's Paradise Lost, Book IV.'' *American Literature*, 16 (1945): 340–343; *PLB,* 64, 202; *PJC,* 156, 169, 170;

Gerber, Gerald E. "Milton and Poe's 'Modern Woman.' " *Poe Newsletter*, 3 (1970): 25–26; Ka, Eimei. "The Influence of *Paradise Lost* on Poe's 'Al Aaraaf.' " *Sophia English Studies*, 3 (1978): 30–44.

Minor, Benjamin Blake. (1818–1905). Editor of *The Southern Literary Messenger*. He received and printed a revised version of "The Raven" in March 1845. *Research: TPL,* xxxiii.

Mirabeau, Gabriel Honoré Riquetti Comte de. (1749–1791). French statesman noted for shrewd eloquence. In *Pinakidia*, Poe commented on these qualities: "Mirabeau, I fancy, acquired his wonderful tact at foreseeing and meeting *contingencies*, during his residence in the stronghold of *If*." *Text: CWP,* XIV, 171; XVI, 166.

Misquash. Character mentioned in *The Journal of Julius Rodman*. He is Chief Waukerassah's son who joins Julius Rodman for part of the journey.

Mitchell, Dr. John Kearsley. (1793–1858). A Poe family physician who attended them in Philadelphia. He was also a songwriter and received a mention in "Autography." "He has also given the world a volume of poems, of which the longest was remarkable for an old-fashioned polish and vigor of versification." *Text: CWP,* XV, 220–221. *Research: TPL,* xxxiv.

M'Kay, Alexander. He was employed by Astor in the Pacific Fur Company and discussed by Poe in "Astoria." *Text: CWP*: IX, 215–219.

M'Lellan, Robert. One of the partners in Astor's Pacific Fur Company. *Text: CWP,* IX, 225–226.

Mob. Character mentioned in the short story "Some Words with a Mummy." He is a tyrant who rules thirteen Egyptian provinces.

A Modern Platonist. Character mentioned in the short story "Lionizing." He is one of the intellectuals who attend the Prince of Wales's dinner party.

Moissart, Mademoiselle. Character mentioned in the short story "The Spectacles." She is the daughter of Madame Eugénie Lalande.

Moldavia. The large house purchased by John Allan in 1825, it was also a Poe address. It was the family home of the Allans where Poe spent his boyhood and where he lived prior to his entrance at the University of Virginia. It stood on the southeast corner of Main and Fifth Streets in Richmond. *Research: MNR,* 28, 46, 59–60.

Moliere. [Jean Baptiste Pocquelin]. (1622–1673). French comic dramatist. He is mentioned only once by Poe, somewhat disparagingly. ''For one Fouqué there are fifty Molieres.'' *Text: CWP,* XI, 89–90.

Moneypenny, Dr. Character mentioned in the short story ''How to Write a Blackwood Article.'' He is an acronymist, ''[a] vulgar man . . . but he's deep'' and one of the members of The Society for the Diffusion of Useful Knowledge.

Monk. Character in the unpublished drama *Politian*. He is Lady Lalage's religious adviser. His icon is not the crucifix, but a cross-handled dagger.

Montani, Alberto. Character mentioned in the short story ''The Murders in the Rue Morgue.'' He is a confectioner who testifies that he heard the killer speaking Russian.

Montesquieu, Charles Louis de Secondat de. (1689–1755). French political philosopher and author of *The Spirit of the Laws*. Poe mentions his *Persian Letters* as an admirable source for other oriental travel tales. *Text: CWP,* XIV, 41; XVI, 40.

Montfleury, Zacharie Jacob. (1600–1667). French actor and author who is said to have died while playing Orestes in Racine's *Andromache*. He is cited in Poe's footnote in the short story ''Duc de L'Omelette'' where a speech from hell from his *Parnasse Réformé* is quoted and mentioned again in *Marginalia.* Poe may have confused him with his dramatist son, Antoine Jacob Montfleury (1640–1685). *Text: CWP,* II, 197; XVI, 74.

Montgomery, James. (1771–1854). Minor English poet. Poe briefly mentions his *A Poet's Portfolio; or Minor Poems* in a summary of the contents of *The Edinburgh Review* for July 1835. *Text: CWP,* VIII, 88–89.

Montgomery, Robert. (1807–1855). English religious poet known as ''Hell Fire Montgomery'' and author of ''The Omnipresence of the Deity.'' His work was damned by Poe in *Marginalia*. *Text: CWP,* XVI, 4–5, 44.

Montresor. Character in the short story ''The Cask of Amontillado.'' He narrates the account of the revenge he takes on his enemy Fortunato.

Moore, Marianne. (1887–1972). American poet. She stated on several occasions that ''she had been influenced by Poe's prose.'' Her poem ''The Steeple-Jack'' shows the rhythmic influence of ''The Raven.'' *Research: PLL,* 332.

Moore, Thomas. (1779–1852). Irish poet and author of oriental tales in verse, *Lalla Rookh*. Poe considered *Lalla Rookh* a brilliant work and Moore ''the most skilful literary artist of his day,—perhaps of any day,—a man who stands in the singular and really wonderful predicament of being undervalued on account of the profusion with which he has scattered about him his good things.'' Poe reviewed his *History of Ireland* in *The Southern Literary Messenger* for June 1835 and *Alciphron: A Poem* in *Burton's Gentleman's Magazine* for January 1840. Less than a month before his death, Poe left behind a copy of Moore's *Irish Melodies* in the office of the physician Dr. John Carter. Moore's *Irish Melodies* furnished the epigraph for the short story ''Loss of Breath.'' *See:* ''Alciphron: A Poem'' *Research: PJC,* 234–243.

Moran, Dr. John. Physician who attended Poe in his final hours in Baltimore's Washington College Hospital. The doctor reported that Poe shouted for the explorer Reynolds before dying at 5 A.M. on 7 October 1849. The exact medical cause of Poe's death remains a subject for debate and was certainly a combination of several factors, each related to alcoholic poisoning. Various biographers have suggested hypoglycemia, a low blood sugar condition aggravated by liver disease, as the main cause. *See:* Reynolds, Jeremiah. *Research:* Bandy, W. T. ''Dr. Moran and the Poe-Reynolds Myth.'' *Myths and Reality: The Mysterious Mr. Poe,* ed. B. F. Fisher IV. Baltimore: Edgar Allan Poe Society, 1987, 26–36; *TPL,* 845–847.

More, Sir Thomas. (1478–1535). English statesman and martyr. He was the author of the *Utopia.* A reference to his laughter on the scaffold as he faced death occurs in ''The Assignation.'' *Text: CWP,* II, 117. *Research:* Pitcher, Edward W. R. '' 'To Die Laughing': Poe's Allusion to Sir Thomas More in 'The Assignation.' '' *Studies in Short Fiction,* 23 (1986): 197–200.

Moreau, Pierre. Character in the short story ''The Murders in the Rue Morgue.'' He is a Parisian tobacconist who testifies that Madame L'Espanaye has been one of his customers.

Morella. The name of two characters in the short story ''Morella.'' *Research:* Gargano, James W. ''Poe's Morella: A Note on Her Name.'' *American Literature,* 47 (1975): 259–264.

"Morella." Short story first published in *The Southern Literary Messenger* for April 1835 and reprinted in *Burton's Gentleman's Magazine* for November 1839. The poem ''A Catholic Hymn'' was also incorporated into the story's text. The tale involves the obsessive theme of psychic survival and return in bringing a woman back from death. The central theme of passionate longing for immortality, especially in a woman who is less flesh and blood than etherealized being, is carried over from ''Morella'' to its sister story, ''Ligeia.'' The narrator of ''Morella'' who ''never spoke of passion nor thought of love . . . the fires were not of Eros'' grows weary of Morella while she is alive, the basis for this weariness and revulsion apparently the narrator's hatred of her physical and intellectual vitality. Morella appears to sense the narrator's "consuming desire for the moment of [her] decease" and, when she dies in childbirth, delivers a deathbed commandment in the form of a poetic couplet that is as much a curse as it is a prophecy. Vowing to return, she predicts that he will love her in death as passionately as he had hated her in life. " 'The days have never been when thou couldst love me—but her whom in life thou didst abhor, in death thou shalt adore." A female child, born simultaneously with the death of the mother, becomes the reincarnated embodiment of Morella. While the narrator loves his nameless daughter, he is unable to separate her identity from the detested mother. At her baptism, the narrator impulsively whispers Morella's name to the priest and suffers an immediate spasm of fear and guilt over his choice of name. "What fiend spoke from the recesses of my soul, when, amid those dim aisles, and in the silence of the night, I whispered within the ears of the holy man the syllables—Morella?" Suddenly the child convulses and dies as Morella's posthumous vow is kept and she responds to the deadly christening with the whispered " 'I am here.' " When the narrator inters the dead child in the ancestral vault, he finds no charnel traces at all in the empty tomb of his wife. The two Morellas have taken their revenge upon the bereft husband and father. The dead Morella's reanimation through the body of her daughter might be read as a victory for the poetic imagination (her final words are a poem) over the narrator's guilt, emotional confusion, and failure to love. *Epigraph:* "Itself—alone by itself—eternally one and single." Plato, *Symposium* (Greek text translated by Poe). *Text: MCW,* II, 221–237; *CWP,* II, 27–34. *Research:* Neale, Walter G. "The Source of Poe's 'Morella.' " *American Literature*, 9 (1937): 237–239; Richmond, Lee J. "Edgar Allan Poe's 'Morella': Vampire of Volition." *Studies in Short Fiction*, 9 (1972): 93–95; Bickman, Martin. "Animatopoeia: Morella as Siren of the Self." *Poe Studies*, 8 (1975): 29–32. Fukuchi, Curtis. "Repression and Guilt in Poe's 'Morella.' " *Studies in Short Fiction*, 24 (1987): 149–154; *TPL,* 151.

Morning Express. New York City newspaper that carried a brief notice of Poe's illness on 15 December 1846 and Virginia's terminal "consumption" along with an appeal for assistance. "We are sorry to mention the fact that they [Poe and Virginia] are so far reduced as to be barely able to obtain the necessaries of life. This is, indeed, a hard lot, and we do hope that the friends and admirers of Mr. Poe will come promptly to his assistance in his bitterest hour of need." A death notice for Virginia appeared in the *Morning Express* of 2 February 1847. *Research: TPL,* 672–676, 719–723, 742–743.

"Morning on the Wissahiccon." Travel sketch by Poe better known under the title "The Elk." *See:* "The Elk." *Text: MCW,* III, 860–867; *CWP,* V, 156–162.

Morning Telegraph. New York City newspaper that carried the querelous "Reply to Mr. Poe" by Dr. Thomas Dunn English on 23 June 1846. English impugned Poe's financial and intellectual honesty and called him a drunkard "thoroughly unprincipled, base and depraved . . . not alone an assassin in morals, but a quack in literature.'' *See:* English, Dr. Thomas Dunn.

Morphine, Dr. Character in the short story ''A Predicament.'' Poe used the name as an alternative for Dr. Ollapod. *Research: MCW,* II, 362.

Morrell, Captain Benjamin. Author of *Narrative of Four Voyages to the South Seas and Pacific, 1822–1831* (1832), one of Poe's sources for *The Narrative of Arthur Gordon Pym. Text: CWP,* III, 164, 168–170.

Morris, George Pope. (1802–1864). Editor of the New York *Evening Mirror* and the *National Press: A Journal for Home*. Poe admired his work and allotted him an entry in ''Autography.'' *Text: CWP,* XV, 221; *PJC,* 230–234; *TPL,* xxxiv.

Morris, Robert. (1809–1874). Editor of *The Pennsylvania Inquirer*. His poetry was recognized by Poe in ''Autography'' and ''The Quacks of Helicon: A Satire.'' *Text: CWP,* XI, 224, 242; XV, 211.

"Mosses from an Old Manse." Short story collection by Nathaniel Hawthorne reviewed negatively by Poe. Poe devoted five pages of his lengthy review published in *Godey's Lady's Book* for November 1847 to Hawthorne's collection of short stories and modified his enthusiasm shown earlier for *Twice-Told Tales*. Although Poe allows that the stories ''rivet the attention,'' he faults Hawthorne for a lack of passion and a tendency to rely on the ''abstract ideas'' of allegory. The rancor of this second review of Hawthorne might be explained in terms of Poe's vendetta against the New England writers. For more than three years, Hawthorne had been living at the Old Manse in Concord, Massachusetts, Ralph Waldo Emerson's home. In Poe's mind, such a residency aligned Hawthorne with the transcendentalist circle and, more particularly, with such journals as *The Dial* and *The North American Review*, both inimical to Poe and his work. For the wrong reasons, Poe in his review berated Hawthorne for such associations. ''Let him mend his pen, get a bottle of visible ink, come out from the Old Manse, cut Mr. Alcott, hang (if possible) the editor of 'The Dial,' and throw out of the window to the pigs all his odd numbers of the North American Review.'' *See:* ''Tale-Writing—Nathaniel Hawthorne.''

Motherwell, William. (1797–1835). Scottish poet. His *Minstrelsy, Ancient and Modern* (1827) was cited by Poe as one of Longfellow's unacknowledged sources, yet another charge of plagiarism denied by Longfellow in a letter to *Graham's Magazine* for May 1845. *Text: CWP,* XII, 93–95; XIV, 291. *Research: PLB,* 161, 162, 174, 175.

Mott, Valentine. (1785–1865). Physician at the New York University School of Medicine. At the request of Marie Louise Shew, who was of the opinion that

Poe was suffering from a brain lesion, Mott examined Poe. Mott apparently confirmed Mrs. Shew's diagnosis, but performed no treatment. Although never medically confirmed, the presence of a brain lesion might explain Poe's intensifying hallucinations and mental instability during 1848 and 1849. *Research: TPL,* xxxiv; 694; *MNR,* 329.

Motte, Madame de la. She was a member of Queen Marie Antoinette's court at Versailles and forged a letter from the queen to obtain a diamond necklace from a German jeweller at court, one Boehmer. Poe discussed her character and intrigue at length in his review of Wraxall's ''Posthumous Memoirs of His Own Time.'' *Text: CWP,* IX, 179–183.

"A Moving Chapter." The first of three unsigned sketches published in the Philadelphia *Public Ledger* of 17 July 1844. T. O. Mabbott included it in his edition of Poe's *Tales and Sketches.* ''A Moving Chapter'' is Poe's witty description of the omnibus, its special comforts and conveniences, and its clear superiority to the stagecoach. ''A wet umbrella and a dirty dog are useful in a full omnibus. When you enter and leave, tread upon the company's toes; it hurts their feelings, but yet makes an impression.'' *See:* ''Desultory Notes on Cats''; ''A Moving Chapter Continued.'' *Text: MCW,* III, 1088–1091. *Research:* Spannuth, Jacob E. *Doings of Gotham: Poe's Contributions to the Columbia Spy.* Pottsville, PA: Jacob E. Spannuth, 1929, 79–91.

"A Moving Chapter Continued." The second of three unsigned sketches published in the Philadelphia *Public Ledger* of 18 July 1844. T. O. Mabbott included it in his edition of Poe's *Tales and Sketches.* Poe continued his discourse on the omnibus with a mock etymology of the word *cab* and remarks on ''the manners which one should practice in a cab.'' As for the origins of the word itself, ''[t]he derivation of the word *cab* is not quite certain. According to Dr. Lumberskull, of Gutt-stuffin University, the word comes from the lately discovered antidiluvian Arabic. In that language *caba* means *go-ahead*—hence a cab, a thing for going ahead.'' *Text: MCW,* III, 1091–1095.

Mowatt, Anna Cora. (1819–1870). Playwright, socialite, and author of the comedy *Fashion* (1845). Poe reviewed the play in a lengthy essay in his portrait of her in ''The Literati of New York City.'' *See:* ''Prospects of the Drama.—Mrs. Mowatt's Comedy.'' *Text: CWP,* XV, 27–32. *Research:* Barnes, Eric W. *The Lady of ''Fashion'': The Life and the Theatre of Anna Cora Mowatt.* New York: Scribner's, 1954; *PJC,* 377–378; Hutchisson, James M. ''Poe, Anna Cora Mowatt, and T. Tennyson Twinkle.'' *Studies in the American Renaissance,* (1993): 245–254.

Moyamensing Prison. Philadelphia penal facility where Poe was detained for public drunkenness in July 1849. Poe's biographers note the first onset of delirium tremens during this incarceration. *Research: TPL,* 812.

Mozart, Wolfgang Amadeus. (1756–1791). Austrian composer and musical prodigy. Poe quotes his deathbed remark in *Marginalia* that he " 'began to see what *may* be done in music.' " *Text: CWP,* XVI, 171.

"Mr. Griswold and the Poets." Review of Rufus Griswold's anthology *The Female Poets of America* with incidental remarks on Griswold's earlier anthology, *The Poets and Poetry of America*, appearing in the *Boston Miscellany* for November 1842. In July 1842, Griswold had commissioned Poe to write the review in the belief that "the name of Poe—gratuitously furnished—might be of some consequence." Having paid Poe for writing it Griswold expected unqualified praise, but was disappointed with Poe's reservations. Griswold even considered withholding the review but ultimately decided to print it in a Boston periodical "lest Poe should think I had prevented its publication." Mutual antipathy between the two would deepen from this point on. Poe's review was especially critical of many of Griswold's critical assertions and displeased with the consigning of his own work to the rear of the volume. Griswold's high regard for the New England poets was yet another source of irritation. Griswold's anthology of female poets included selections from ninety-five examples from Ann Bradstreet to Helen Irving (Miss Anna H. Phillips) and won Poe's praise for being "a man not more of taste than—shall we say it?—courage. The most skilful merely, of those [female poets] just mentioned are Mrs. Osgood, Miss Lynch, and Mrs. Signourney. The most imaginative are Miss Cary, Mrs. Osgood, Miss Talley, and Miss Fuller. The most accomplished are Mrs. Ellet, Mrs. Eames, Mrs. Lewis, Mrs. Whitman, and Mrs. Oakes Smith. The most popular are Mrs. Osgood, Mrs. Oakes Smith, and Miss Hooper." *See:* "The Poets and Poetry of America, with an Historical Introduction. By Rufus Wilmot Griswold." *Text: CWP,* XI, 147–160. *Research: PJC,* 330–331.

"Mr. Hudson." Negative notice of a public lecture given at the Society Library on Shakespeare's *King Lear*. The short review appeared in *The Broadway Journal* of 13 December 1845. The lecturer displayed "want of concentration—want of consecutiveness—want of definite purpose" and "an elocution that would disgrace a pig, and an odd species of gesticulation of which a baboon would have excellent reason to be ashamed." *Text: CWP,* XIII, 26–27.

"Mrs. R. S. Nichols." Review of the poem "An Address of the Carriers of the Cincinnati *Daily American Republican* to Its Patrons, for January, 1845" appearing in *The Broadway Journal* of 22 March 1845. Poe quotes the poem in full and praises her "well-cultivated ear." *Text: CWP,* XII, 110–111.

"MS. Found in a Bottle." Prize-winning short story published in the *Baltimore Saturday Visiter* of 19 October 1833. In setting, characterization, and situation, the story has connections with two later sea tales, *The Narrative of Arthur Gordon Pym* and "A Descent into the Maelström." Told in the first person, the narrative recounts a shipwreck and the narrator's strange voyage of discovery aboard a second ship, a sort of haunted mansion gone to sea and manned by a spectral crew of ancient mariners, "their shriveled skins rattl[ing] in the wind; their voices . . . low, tremulous, and broken; their eyes glisten[ing] with the rheum of years; and their gray hairs stream[ing] terribly in the tempest." The ship's mysterious journey southward (a kind of global descent) propelled by an unknown current that pulls it toward the South Pole itself is recorded by the narrator in his journal up to the final plunge and disappearance of the ship into an immense whirlpool that carries the narrator to a desired death. Earlier, he has written in his journal about the opportunity for knowledge in such a self-destructive moment. "Yet a curiosity to penetrate the mysteries of these awful regions, predominates even over my despair, and will reconcile me to the most hideous aspect of death. It is evident that we are hurrying onward to some exciting knowledge—some never-to-be-imparted secret, whose attainment is destruction." Leaving behind a manuscript account in a bottle, the posthumous narrator willingly and eagerly goes down with *The Discovery* in quest of that secret. Like Arthur Gordon Pym and the descending voyager of "A Descent into the Maelström," the narrator submits to the force of the whirlpool and chooses death over life in return for ultimate insight. The journey of the aesthetic hero in these seafaring narratives is much more than a fatal geographical excursion. The descent represents the elective affinity of the soul toward self-negation and a paradoxical moment of creative self-destruction. The whirlpool intervenes as the necessary matrix of terror and beauty between the real and the imaginary or the mundane and the eternal. Although the manuscript that floats ashore for the reader's perusal never discloses the precise nature of the "exciting knowledge," its account is "an expression more of the eagerness of hope than of the apathy of despair," and as such, the heroic example of the narrator summons future explorers of the mysterious world of beauty to follow him over the edge. *Epigraph:* "Qui n'a a plus qu'un moment à vivre/ N'a plus rien à dissimuler" [He who has but a moment to live, has no longer anything to dissemble]. Philippe Quinault, *Atys. See:* "A Descent into the Maelström." *Text: MCW,* II, 130–148; *CWP,* II, 1–15. *Research:* French, John C. "Poe and the Baltimore *Saturday Visiter.*" *Modern Language Notes*, 33 (1918): 257–267; Stauffer, Donald Barlow. "The Two Styles of Poe's 'MS. Found in a Bottle.' " *Style*, 1 (spring 1967): 107–120; Pollin, Burton. "Poe's Use of Material from Bernadin de Saint-Pierre's *Études.*" *Romance Notes*, 12 (1971): 1–8; Hoffman, Steven K. "Sailing into the Self: Jung, Poe, and 'MS. Found in a Bottle.' " *Tennessee Studies in Literature*, 26 (1981): 66–74; Scharnhorst, Gary. "Another Night-Sea Journey: Poe's 'MS. Found in a Bottle.' " *Studies in Short Fiction*, 22 (1985): 203–208; Smith, Don G. "Shelley's *Frankenstein*: A Possible Source for Poe's 'MS. Found in a Bottle.' " *Poe Studies*, 25, nos. 1–2 (1992): 37–38.

Mumblethumb, Mr. Character mentioned in the short story "The Literary Life of Thingum Bob, Esq." He is paid fifty cents for his "Monody in a Mud-Puddle."

"The Murders in the Rue Morgue." Short story first published in *Graham's Magazine* for April 1841. A first French translation without any acknowledgment of Poe's authorship appeared in *La Quotidienne* of 11, 12, and 13 June 1846. There are several sources for the tale that indicate Poe's reading as well as his fascination with violent urban crime. *Burton's Gentleman's Magazine* for October 1838 serialized an article on the "Unpublished Passages in the Life of Vidocq, the French Minister of Police." The public exhibition of an orangutan (ourang outang) at the Masonic Hall in Philadelphia during August and September 1839 inspired Poe to sensationalize the animal in his detective story. The narrative features the personality of the consummate analyst and student of crime, C. Auguste Dupin, Western literature's first famous detective. While he uses logic in reaching his solutions, Dupin is no mere cold logician, and his principles of observation and detection resemble Poe's own keen eye for detail. Dupin believes that "there is such a thing as being too profound. Truth is not always in a well. In fact, as regards the more important knowledge, I do believe that she is invariably superficial. . . . By undue profundity we perplex and enfeeble thought." With the fumbling assistance of the narrator who plays the part of straight man, Dupin is able to solve a horrifying double murder that has the Parisian police baffled. He applies his imaginative and deductive skills to the contradictory testimony of many witnesses who heard the murders being committed and is able to conclude with swift accuracy that the two female victims were savagely killed by an ourang outang on the loose from its keeper, a French sailor. Since no witness agrees with any other on the language spoken by the murderer, Dupin quickly eliminates the possibility that the crime was committed by a human speaker. He further notices various aspects of the crime scene overlooked by the police such as the fact that one of the nails supposedly securing a locked window from the inside is broken and that only an agile beast or a creature of superhuman strength could have climbed into the apartment by means of a lightning rod and window shutters. Armed with such information and energized by "the wild fervor, and the vivid freshness of imagination," Dupin is capable of leaps of logic beyond the laborious methods of the police. Faced with the unusual circumstances of the crime, the police are confused because they assume a human perpetrator and a human motive. Dupin, on the other hand, operates on the theory that the extraordinary always manifests itself in the ordinary. Such deviations from the normal stimulate Dupin's imaginative capacities and enable him to conceptualize a scenario for the crime that has never before occurred. The Poe scholar T. O. Mabbott referred to the story as "a great literary monument. It may not be the first detective story, but it is the first story deliberately written as such to attain worldwide popularity." *Epigraph:* "What song the Syrens sang, or what name Achilles assumed when he hid himself among women, although puzzling questions, are not beyond *all* conjecture." Sir Thomas Browne, *Hydriotaphia* [Urn burial]. *Text: MCW,* II, 521–574; *CWP,* IV, 146–192. *Research:* Bandy, W. T. "Who Was Monsieur Dupin?" *Publications of the Modern Language Association*, 79 (1964): 509–510; Wilbur, Richard. "The Poe Mystery Case."

New York Review of Books, 13 July 1967, 16, 25–28; Bronzwaer, W. ''Deixis as a Structuring Device in Narrative Discourse: An Analysis of Poe's 'The Murders in the Rue Morgue.' '' *English Studies*, 56 (1975): 345–359; Lemay, J. A. Leo. ''The Psychology of 'The Murders in the Rue Morgue.' '' *American Literature*, 54 (1982): 165–188; Conger, Syndy M. ''Another Secret of the Rue Morgue: Poe's Transformation of the Geisterseher Motif.'' *Studies in Short Fiction*, 24 (1987): 9–14; Martin, Terry J. ''Detection, Imagination, and the Introduction to 'The Murders in the Rue Morgue.' '' *Modern Language Studies*, 19 (1989): 31–45; Cresswell, Catherine J. ''Poe's Philosophy of Æsthetics and Ratiocination: Compositions of Death in 'The Murders in the Rue Morgue.' '' In *The Cunning Craft: Original Essays on Detective Fiction and Contemporary Literary Theory*, ed. Ronald G. Walker, June M. Frazer, David R. Anderson. Macomb: Western Illinois University Press, 1990, 38–54; Ritter, Erich H. ''Ratiocination about an Ape: A Poeto-Logical Investigation of a Murder.'' *Orbis Litterarum*, 46 (1991): 65–86; Irwin, John T. ''Reading Poe's Mind: Politics, Mathematics, and the Association of Ideas in 'The Murders in the Rue Morgue.' '' *American Literary History*, 4 (1992): 187–206.

Murdoch, James Edward. (1811–1893). American actor. He performed ''The Raven'' at *The Broadway Journal* offices in February 1845. *Research: TPL,* xxxiv, 500.

Murray, Lindley. (1745–1826). English grammarian sometimes called ''the Father of English Grammar.'' His *English Grammar* (1795) is cited by Poe in ''The Rationale of Verse'' and elsewhere. *Text: CWP,* VIII, 60; XI, 225; XIV, 212.

Musæus, Johann Karl August. (1735–1787). German author of supernatural tales. In *Marginalia*, Poe compared his fairytale, ''Libussa'' with Motte Fouqué's *Undine*. *Text: CWP,* XVI, 117.

Muset, Isidore. Character in the short story ''The Murders in the Rue Morgue.'' He is the gendarme who first investigates the murders and gives testimony.

"The Musiad or Ninead, by Diabolus." Anonymous literary satire published in Baltimore in 1830. Poe is mockingly referred to as the man who ''smil'd at reason, laughed at law'' because of his attack on cold logic and hard science in ''Sonnet—To Science.'' *Research: TPL,* 103; *PLL,* 43.

The Mysteries of Paris. Criminal romance novel by Eugène Sue published in 1842. In *Marginalia*, his attitude toward the novel was mixed. ''I have just finished 'The Mysteries of Paris'—a work of unquestionable power—a museum of novel and ingenious incident—a paradox of childish folly and consummate skill.'' Poe also reviewed the novel in *Graham's Magazine* for January 1844. The review was unsigned but attributed to Poe by Mabbott. *See:* Sue, Eugène.

Text: CWP, XVI, 104–109. *Research:* Mabbott, Thomas O. ''Newly Identified Reviews by Edgar Poe.'' *Notes & Queries,* 163 (17 December 1932): 441.

"Mysterious Star." Poem of twenty-nine lines included by Mabbott in his edition of the *Poems* as verse substituted by Poe for the first fifteen lines of ''Al Aaraaf'' in the 1831 volume *Poems by Edgar A. Poe*. The star symbolizes the higher poetic world of supernal beauty toward which the poet directs all his hopes and energies: ''Thy world has not the dross of ours,/ . . . Little—oh! little dwells in thee/ Like unto what on earth we see.'' *Text: MCW,* I, 159–160.

"The Mystery of Marie Rogêt. A Sequel to 'The Murders in the Rue Morgue.' " Short story first serialized in three parts in *Snowden's Ladies' Companion* beginning in November 1842, continuing in the December 1842 number, and concluding in the February 1843 number. This long tale should probably be classified as a novella rather than a short story. The details were based upon an actual and unsolved crime, the murder of Miss Mary Cecilia Rogers whose corpse was found in the Hudson River on 28 July 1841. Inspired by the sensational details, Poe reworked it into a whodunit, which permitted the reappearance of his detective, now the Chevalier C. Auguste Dupin. Poe also transferred the American murder to Paris and changed the criminal circumstances to fit a French venue. The cigar store saleslady, Mary Rogers, became Marie Rogêt. After being missing for four days, her mutilated body is found in the Seine. The Parisian police who had shunned his assistance in the Rue Morgue cases now ask for Dupin's help in solving the murder of Marie Rogêt, a young girl employed in a perfume shop. As had the New York City newspapers, the Parisian press has seized the opportunity to sensationalize the crime, filling their columns with inane solutions, all duly exposed by Dupin. He observes, ''We should bear in mind that, in general, it is the object of our newspapers rather to create a sensation—to make a point—than to further the cause of truth.'' According to Dupin, truth is also not well served by the courts and formal hearings. ''I would here observe that very much of what is rejected as evidence by a court, is the best evidence to the intellect.'' Applying the same mental principles that enabled him to solve the double murders in the Rue Morgue, Dupin reconstructs the murderer's frame of mind and pieces together the facts of this ''ordinary, although an atrocious, instance of crime.'' What is more, he does so without ever leaving the confines of his study. Armed with his intuitive skills, he gains the necessary information and clues from the numerous conflicting newspaper accounts to discern a pattern that will explain the facts in the case of Marie Rogêt and break through the journalistic distortions. For example, Dupin deduces that because a cloth belt was fastened around her waist, the body had been dragged to the river. She was not mauled and murdered by a gang, as the press has suggested, but by a single slayer still at large, probably by a secret lover yet to be identified, who had dumped the corpse from a boat, then set the boat adrift to confuse the police. The story concludes without a brilliant revelation of the truth by Dupin as he urges that a search be undertaken to find "the lonely assassin['s]" boat. "This boat shall guide us, with a rapidity which will surprise even ourselves, to him who employed it in the midnight of the fatal Sabbath. Corroboration will rise upon corroboration, and the murderer will be traced." Despite Dupin's confidence, his role in this tale of detection remains weaker and far less satisfying than his analytic brilliance in "The Murders in the Rue Morgue" and "The Purloined Letter." Of special interest in the publication history of the story is Poe's revision of the story in the 1845 edition of the *Tales*. When the New York *Daily Tribune* of 18 November 1842 suggested that Mary Rogers had died from an abortion operation, Poe changed the details of the story to make the murderer "a young physician, who undertook to procure for her a premature delivery." *Epigraph:* "Es giebt eine Reihe idealischer Begebenheiten, die der Wirklichkeit parallel lauft. Selten fallen sie zusammen. Menchen und Züfalle modificeren gewöhnlich die idealische Begebenheit, so dass sie unvollkommen erscheint, und Ihre Folgen gleichfalls unvollkommen sind. So bei der Reformation; statt des Protestantismus kam das Lutherthum hervor." [Poe's translation: There are ideal series of events which run parallel with the real ones. They rarely coincide. Men and circumstances generally modify the ideal train of events, so that it seems imperfect, and its consequences are equally imperfect. Thus with the Reformation; instead of Protestantism came Lutheranism.] Quotation from Novalis, *Moralische Ansichten*, taken by Poe from Sarah Austin's *Fragments from German Prose Writers*. *Text: MCW,* III, 715–788; *CWP,* V, 1–66. *Research:* Wimsatt, W. K. "Poe and 'The Mystery of Marie Rogêt.' " *Publications of the Modern Language Association*, 61 (1941): 230–248; Walsh, John. *Poe the Detective: The Curious Circumstances Behind "The Mystery of Marie Rogêt."* New Brunswick, NJ: Rutgers University Press, 1968; *TPL,* 386; Roth, Martin. "The Mysteries of 'The Mystery of Marie Rogêt.' " *Poe Studies*, 22, no. 2 (1989): 27–34.

The Mystery of St. Denis. A miracle play mentioned in *Pinakidia*. After decapitation, the Saint "takes his head under his arm and walks off the stage in all the dignity of martyrdom." *Text: CWP,* XIV, 52.

"Mystification." Short story first appearing under the title "Von Jung, the Mystific" in the New York *American Monthly Magazine* for June 1837 and entitled "Von Jung" when it was published in *Tales of the Grotesque and Arabesque*. A revised version with the title "Mystification" appeared in *The Broadway Journal* of 27 December 1845. The narrator's clever and intellectual friend Baron Ritzner Von Jung visits him at the university and finds himself one evening engaged in a vigorous discussion of the gentlemanly benefits and pleasures of dueling. Aware of the Baron's total contempt for the duello, the narrator is amazed by the Baron's brilliant discourse on the subject "with an ardor, an eloquence, an impressiveness, and an affectionateness of manner, which elicited the warmest enthusiasm from his hearers in general." One of the gentleman duelists, Johan Hermann, sneeringly belittles the Baron Von Jung's knowledge of the subject, ending with the insult, " 'I would say, sir, that your opinions are not the opinions to be expected from a gentleman.' " By such provocation, the proud young lout hopes to force Von Jung into a duel. Like Fortunato in his vanity over his connoisseurship in wines, Hermann regards himself as the leading expert on duels and dueling, a reputation compromised by the Baron's command of the subject. "But it was upon his minute acquaintance with the *etiquette* of the duello, and the *nicety* of his sense of honor, that he most especially prided himself." While the Baron's revenge on the fool is not as elaborate or deadly as that of Montresor on Fortunato, it is equally just and clever. He first responds to the insult by hurling a decanter of wine at Hermann's reflection in the mirror in order to perplex his antagonist. Unable to decide whether or not wine thrown into a reflected face is a proper challenge, he retires to his rooms to examine all of the books that he has on dueling etiquette in his large library. In pompous triumph, he believes he has found an answer in a tome "written in barbarous Latin" and entitled *Duella Lex Scripta, et non; aliterque.* A letter of challenge is sent, and the Baron replies, inflicting yet a second humiliation on the fool. As the Baron reveals, the great treatise on dueling, the *Duella Lex Scripta*, is "framed so as to present to the ear all the outward signs of intelligibility, and even of profundity, while in fact not a shadow of meaning existed." When the second and third words of the sentences are omitted alternately, the treatise when read aloud "proved to be a most horribly absurd account of a duel between two baboons." Hermann's stupidity and pomposity make it impossible for him to admit that the book is nonsense. He would rather die a thousand deaths than acknowledge his foolishness. In the tale, a sort of duel of wits is fought without the loser's awareness that he has been neatly and fatally wounded. *Epigraph:* "Slid, if these be your 'passados' and 'montantes,' I'll have none o'them." Ben Jonson, *Every Man in His Humour. Texts: MCW,* II, 291–305; *CWP,* IV, 102–113. *Research:* Pollin, Burton R. "Poe's 'Mystification': Its Source in Fay's *Norman Leslie.*" *Mississippi Quarterly*, 25 (1972): 111–130.

Mythology. Poe's knowledge of classical mythology is reflected in the numerous references to mythological characters and places in his writings. He made stylistic use of mythology in many instances as in the reference to the Procrustean bed in "The Purloined Letter," Æolus in "Eleonora," Artemis in "Lionizing," Cerberus and Charon in "Bon-Bon," Halcyon and Naiad in "Berenice," Lotophagi in "Never Bet the Devil Your Head," Niobe in "The Assignation," Orion and the sirens in "The Murders in the Rue Morgue," Pallas Athena in "The Raven," Phlegethon in "A Descent into the Maelström," Psyche in "Ulalume," the satyrs in "The Assignation" and "The Fall of the House of Usher," the Cumæan Sybil in "Silence—A Fable," and Zephyr in "Loss of Breath." Homer's Helen, a figure of deadly beauty, becomes the inspiration for Poe's "To Helen," in which Poe refers to her "Naiad airs," the spirits that occupied waters and lakes. In the poem's final stanza, Helen is compared to

Psyche, the Greek myth's personification of the soul. Poe intended his mythological allusions to enrich a character's attributes or to invoke a special atmosphere or setting. Poe was also familiar with Jacob Bryant's *A New System or an Analysis of Ancient Mythology*. *See:* Bryant, Jacob.

N

Nabokov, Vladimir. (1899–1977). Russian-American short story writer and novelist. His admiration for Poe is evident throughout the novel *Lolita* (1955), originally entitled *The Kingdom by the Sea*. His story ''A Forgotten Poet'' (1944) is a retelling of Poe's struggle for artistic immortality, and there are repeated echoes of Poe's poetry throughout the novel *Bend Sinister*. *Research:* Campbell, Felicia F. ''A Princedom by the Sea.'' *Lock Haven Review*, 10 (1968): 30–46; Clark, George P. ''A Further Word on Poe and *Lolita*.'' *Poe Newsletter*, 3 (December 1970): 39; Goldhurst, William, Alfred Appel, Jr., and George P. Clark. ''Three Observations on 'Amontillado' and *Lolita*.'' *Poe Studies*, 5, no. 2 (1972): 51; Le Clair, Thomas. ''Poe's Pym and Nabokov's *Pale Fire*.'' *Notes on Contemporary Literature*, 3, no. 2 (1973): 2–3; Maddox, Lucy B. ''Necrophilia in Lolita.'' *Centennial Review*, 26 (1982): 361–374; Peterson, Dale. E. ''Nabokov and the Poe-etics of Composition.'' *Slavic and East European Journal*, 33 (1989): 95–107; *PLL*, 301–302.

The Narrative of Arthur Gordon Pym of Nantucket. Poe's only novel first published in full by Harper in July 1838. The novel was partially published in installments in the January and February 1837 numbers of *The Southern Literary Messenger*. The full title is: *The Narrative of Arthur Gordon Pym of Nantucket. Comprising the Details of a Mutiny and Atrocious Butchery on Board the American Brig, Grampus, on Her Way to the South Seas, in the Month of June, 1827. With an Account of the Recapture of the Vessel by the Survivers; Their Shipwreck and Subsequent Horrible Sufferings from Famine; Their Deliverance by Means of the British Schooner Jane Guy; The Brief Cruise of This Latter Vessel in the Antarctic Ocean; Her Capture, and the Massacre of Her*

Crew among a Group of Islands in the Eighty-fourth Parallel of Southern Latitude; Together with the Incredible Adventures and Discoveries Still Farther South to Which That Distressing Calamity Gave Rise. The work shows the strong impression made on Poe's imagination by Captain John Symmes's *Theory of Concentric Spheres* (1826), which had theorized that the earth is "hollow, habitable, and widely open about the poles." The Symmes thesis of a south polar region that was hot and concave coupled with the mania for polar exploration following the Weddell expedition of 1823 encouraged Poe to attempt a novel-length thriller that would convey his hero to the very ends of the earth. Poe further planned to have him arrive at the antarctican continent and pole before any other explorer. To give his journey an air of realism, Poe extracted many details from contemporary travelogues such as Benjamin Morrell's *Narrative of Four Voyages to the South Seas and Pacific, 1822–1831*. Like the other two tales in Poe's saltwater trilogy, "MS. Found in a Bottle" and "A Descent into the Maelström," *The Narrative of Arthur Gordon Pym* attempts to merge scientific thought and theory with the motif of the fatal voyage. The novel's deceptive title and its format of diary and logbook entries underscore Poe's strategy of creating an artful and factual documentary similar to the methods of Defoe and Swift in their imaginary voyages. The preface is a further assurance to the reader that the work is a factual account of real and recent travels. The structure of the novel is highly episodic with the dangerous sea journey itself as the sole unifying feature. Thus, the work is less a novel than a series of action scenes showing characters in crisis interrelated solely by the device of the voyage itself. If Poe had any unity of plot or single conception of effect in mind, these artistic goals were never fully realized in a loose narrative that is crammed with exciting and horrific events in sequence but without consequence. With its mysterious and much-debated ending and its confluence of strange and life-threatening events, it is possible to understand the narrative in terms of a gothic novel gone afloat. Poe globalizes the central setting of all gothic fiction, the confining castle, by sending his hero on a downward journey of hemispheric dimensions and having him grope his way toward freedom from this enlarged underworld of mutiny, butchery, premature entombment, cannibalism, cadaverous encounter, and mass death. The ordeal once reserved for the maiden in flight now becomes the pattern of Pym's existence enroute toward an absolute south of no return. Aboard the boats and ships *Ariel*, *Grampus*, *Jane Guy*, and a canoe, he experiences nearly every form of gothic shock including suffocating confinement within "a labyrinth of lumber," shipwreck highlighted by a cannibal feast, the feeding of his companion, Augustus Barnard, to the sharks, an unnatural avalanche on the forbidden island of Tsalal (or "Last Land"), suicidal longings to plunge or fall, secret writing, and at the climax, an encounter with a gigantic snow image as he sails "beyond the veil" of reality over a torrid polar sea without a single particle of ice and into the yawning abyss of total whiteness. The mounting intensity of these fantastic occurrences and the enigmatic beauty and serenity of the ending indicate that Pym's voyage conveys him to the outskirts of the domain of Israfel that is ''out of SPACE,— Out of TIME,'' into a visionary white place of cosmic bliss and beauty undisturbed and untouched by earthly reality. In the course of this journey, Pym is transformed from mere adventurer (his Nantucket self) into poet and artist (his polar self). Both ''the fever called living'' and the nightmare of memory are left behind as the narrative changes from conventional gothic shocker to Eurekan parable of discovery. Once one of the most neglected of Poe's tales, *The Narrative of Arthur Gordon Pym* has enjoyed a prolonged renaissance of inquiry since W. H. Auden included it and praised it in his 1950 edition of Poe's stories. Many critics have presented intriguing and ingenious interpretations of the novel's final scene, but currently no Pymologist has produced a totally satisfactory explication of the great and final whiteness and the colossal figure of white. *See: Knickerbocker Magazine*; Peters, Dirk; ''Report on the Committee of Naval Affairs.'' *Text: The Imaginary Voyages: The Narrative of Arthur Gordon Pym*, ed. Burton Pollin. Boston: G. K. Hall, 1981, 1–363. *CWP,* III, 1–245. *Research:* Bezanson, Walter E. ''The Troubled Sleep of Arthur Gordon Pym.'' In *Essays in Literary History Presented to J. Milton French*, ed. Rudolf Kirk and C. F. Main. New Brunswick, NJ: Rutgers University Press, 1960, 149–175; Fiedler, Leslie A. ''The Blackness of Darkness: E. A. Poe and the Development of the Gothic.'' In *Love and Death in the American Novel.* New York: Criterion, 1960, 370–382; Frank, Frederick S. ''Polarized Gothic: An Annotated Bibliography of Poe's *Narrative of Arthur Gordon Pym.*'' *Bulletin of Bibliography*, 38 (1981): 117–127; Rosenzweig, Paul. '' 'Dust within the Rock': The Phantasm of Meaning in *The Narrative of Arthur Gordon Pym.*'' *Studies in the Novel*, 14 (1982): 137–151; Billy, Ted. ''Providence and Chaos in *The Narrative of Arthur 'Goddin' Pym.*'' *Journal of Evolutionary Psychology*, 9, nos. 1–2 (1989): 126–133; Miecznikowski, Cynthia. ''End(ings) and Mean(ing)s in *The Narrative of Arthur Gordon Pym* and *Eureka.*'' *Studies in Short Fiction*, 27 (1990): 55–64; Kopley, Richard, ed. *Poe's ''Pym'': Critical Explorations*. Durham, NC: Duke University Press, 1992; Kennedy, J. Gerald. *The Narrative of Arthur Gordon Pym and the Abyss of Interpretation.* New York: Twayne, 1995.

Narrators. Although lacking names, many of Poe's narrators are major characters in his works both as observers and as participants. Among those tales related by nameless narrators are ''The Fall of the House of Usher,'' ''The Sphinx,'' ''The Tell-Tale Heart,'' ''Ligeia'' (the narrator has a name but cannot remember it), ''MS. Found in a Bottle,'' ''The Murders in the Rue Morgue,'' ''The Mystery of Marie Rogêt,'' ''The Pit and the Pendulum,'' ''The Masque of the Red Death,'' ''Mystification,'' and ''The Man That Was Used Up.'' Poe criticism has often called attention to the reliability or lack thereof of individual Poe narrators. The traditionally assumed maleness of certain unnamed narrators has also come under scrutiny by feminist criticism. *See:* ''The Tell-Tale Heart.'' *Research:* Gargano, James W. ''The Question of Poe's Narrators.'' *College English*, 25 (1963): 177–181.

"National Melodies of America By George P. Morris, Esq." Revised review of George P. Morris's poetry appearing in *The Southern Literary Messenger* for April 1849. *See:* ''George P. Morris.'' *Research: PJC,* 230–234.

"Nature and Art." Editorial appearing in the New York *Evening Mirror* of 17 January 1845. Poe replied to a piece defending James Russell Lowell appearing in the New York *Daily Tribune* of 15 January 1845 and reprinted in the *Weekly Mirror* of 25 January 1845. "There being then no dispute about Mr. L.'s meaning, we object that, in Letters, he improperly distinguishes nature from art." *Text: TPL,* 489.

Neal, John Clay. (1793–1876). American poet and novelist. He admired and defended Poe, once writing of him, "If the young author now before us should fulfil his destiny, he will be foremost in the rank of real poets." Poe mentions Neal in the opening paragraph of his satiric sketch, "Diddling." An analysis of Neal's signature is included in "Autography." "Any one, from Mr. Neal's penmanship, might suppose his mind to be what it really is—excessively flighty and irregular, but active and energetic." *Text: CWP,* V, 210; XI, 110, 206; XII, 66, 154; XV, 45–46, 115, 154–155, 204; XVI, 152. *Research:* Lease, Benjamin. "John Neal and Edgar Allan Poe." *Poe Studies*, 7 (1974): 38–41; *TPL,* xxxiv, 97–101.

Neal, Joseph Clay. (1807–1847). American contributor to the periodicals and author of *Charcoal Sketches*. In "Autography" Poe charged him with tasteless repetitiousness. "To dub the author of these 'Charcoal Sketches' (which are really very excellent police reports) with title of 'the American Boz' is either outrageous nonsense or malevolent irony." *Text: CWP,* X, 206–207; XV, 199–200, 229. *Research: TPL,* xxxiv, 267–268, 279–80.

"Ned Myers, Edited by James Fenimore Cooper." Book reviewed by Poe in *Graham's Magazine* for January 1844. *Research:* Mabbott, T. O. "Newly-Identified Reviews by Edgar Allan Poe." *Notes & Queries*, 163 (17 December 1932): 441. *Research: TPL,* 446.

Neptune. Canine character mentioned in the novella *The Journal of Julius Rodman*. Neptune is also the name of the lighthouse keeper's dog in the unfinished story "The Light-House."

Nesace. Character in the poem "Al Aaraaf." She lives on the star Al Aaraaf and represents a type of ideal beauty.

"Never Bet the Devil Your Head." Short story first appearing under the title "Never Bet Your Head: A Moral Tale" in *Graham's Magazine* for September 1841. The revised version used the title "Never Bet the Devil Your Head" and appeared in *The Broadway Journal* of 16 August 1845. This story of a satanic encounter contains much topical literary satire of a personal nature in Poe's mockery of the nebulous circumlocutions of transcendentalism and his resentment at being negatively reviewed by *The Dial*, a transcendentalist journal. The narrator, an anonymous author who has been accused by his literary colleagues of never having written a moral tale, "offer[s] the sad history appended,—a history about whose obvious moral there can be no question whatever." The sad history is the saga of the narrator's deceased friend, Toby Dammit, a man doomed to ruin by his unrestrained behavior, which includes "cursing and swearing, and . . . backing his assertions by bets." When the narrator attempts to cure him of his wagering compulsion, Toby Dammit "offer[s] to bet the Devil his head that I would not venture to try that experiment again." But when Dammit bets on anything—and he bets on everything—he always bets his head to the Devil, an expression that is particularly annoying to the narrator. "I began not to like it at all. Mr. Dammit's soul was in a perilous state. I resolved to bring all my eloquence into play to save it." Dammit's conversation and conduct are so bizarre that the narrator can only muse that he is somehow infected with transcendentalism, the New England disease. "I am not well enough versed, however, in the diagnosis of this disease to speak with decision upon the point; and unhappily there were none of my friends of the *Dial* present." Out on a walk with Dammit, the two come to a bridge and turnstile that he immediately bets that he can avoid by leaping over it. The narrator puns heavily on the term "style" in asserting that Toby Dammit lacks sufficient transcendental style to make any such stylistic leap. After all, even the narrator's friend, Mr. Thomas Carlyle, might encounter difficulties with such a leap of style. The narrator now notices a little lame old gentleman stationed inconspicuously in "a nook of the framework of the bridge." He is dressed in shabby black and mutters "Ahem" as he shakes hands with Toby Dammit to seal the wager recently and rashly made. "Wait here, till I take my place by the stile," he tells Dammit, "so that I may see whether you go over it handsomely, and transcendentally, and don't omit any flourishes of the pigeon-wing." As the narrator watches in horror, Dammit soars high in the air and falls to the ground, losing the bet and losing his head to the comic little fiend who "limp[s] off at the top of his speed, having caught and wrapped up in his apron something that fell heavily into it from the darkness of the arch just over the turnstile." Having paid for Dammit's funeral and billed the transcendentalists for same, the narrator gets no reimbursement from them and in retaliation "had Mr. Dammit dug up at once, and sold him for dog's meat." *Text: MCW,* II, 619–634; *CWP,* IV, 213–226. *Research:* Glassheim, Eliot. "A Dogged Interpretation of 'Never Bet the Devil Your Head.'" *Poe Newsletter*, 2 (October 1969): 44–45.

"Never Bet Your Head: A Moral Tale." Original title of the short story "Never Bet the Devil Your Head." *See:* "Never Bet the Devil Your Head."

"New and Compendious Latin Grammar; With Appropriate Exercises, Analytical and Synthetical. For the Use of Primary Schools, Academies, and Colleges. By Bayard R. Hall." A positive review of a Latin primer appearing in *The Southern Literary Messenger* for October 1836. "It is free from every species of empiricism, and, following the good old track as far as that track can be judiciously followed, admits of no royal road to the acquisition of Latin. The arrangement is lucid and succinct. . . . Yet nothing of consequence to the student is omitted.'' *Text: CWP,* IX, 166–167.

"A New and Comprehensive Gazetteer of Virginia, and the District of Columbia: Containing a Copious Collection of Geographical, Statistical, Political, Commercial, Religious, Moral, and Miscellaneous Information, Collected and Compiled from the Most Respectable, and Chiefly from Original Sources; by Joseph Martin." Review of a book of facts appearing in *The Southern Literary Messenger* for February 1836. Poe recommends it as ''a work of great utility and importance'' but also urges that some statistical inaccuracies be corrected in further editions. *Text: CWP,* VIII, 211–214.

"The New Comedy by Mrs. Mowatt." A lengthy review of Mrs. Anna Cora Mowatt's play *Fashion* appearing in two installments of *The Broadway Journal* of 29 March and 5 April 1845. Poe attended the comedy's opening on 26 March 1845 and saw additional performances. Poe's appraisal is mildly favorable since the dialogue is ''spirited, generally terse, and well seasoned at points with sarcasm of much power,'' but her play also has all the flaws of the modern drama in general. *See:* ''Prospects of the Drama.—Mrs. Mowatt's Comedy.'' *Text: CWP,* XII, 112–121.

"New Dictionary of the English Language: By Charles Richardson." Review of a reference work appearing in *The Southern Literary Messenger* for August 1836. Poe paraphrases Richardson's prospectus, discusses Dr. Johnson's *Dictionary* and the grammatical system of Horne Tooke, and concludes by ''heartily recommending the work of Mr. Richardson to the attention of the readers. It embraces, we think, every desideration in an English Dictionary.'' *Text: CWP,* IX, 103–106.

"A New Theoretical and Practical Treatise on Navigation." *See:* ''Maury's Navigation.''

Newton, Sir Isaac. (1642–1727). English mathematician, physicist, and philosopher. Poe referred to him as ''the prophetic Newton'' and in several places in *Eureka* discussed the relevance of Newton's theory of gravity to his own view of the universal return to original unity. ''Thus it will be seen, also, that the establishment of my propositions would involve no *necessity* of modification in the terms of the Newtonian definition of gravity. . . . I can only declare that, with an irresistible intuition, I perceive Unity to have been the source of the observed phænomena of the Newtonian gravitation.'' *Text: CWP,* VI, 98, 205; XI, 40; XIV, 192; XVI, 40, 212–215, 221–224, 231, 239, 260–263, 279, 324. *Research: PJC,* 23, 416.

Nichol, Dr. John Pringle. (1804–1859). Astronomer and author of *The Architecture of the Heavens*. In *Eureka*, Poe discusses his work with telescopes, nebulae, and his thesis concerning the cosmos's simplicity of design. *Text: CWP,* XII, 165; XVI, 222–223, 262, 297–298.

Nichols, Mrs. Rebecca Shepard Reed. (1819–1903). Cincinnati poet and a contributor to various magazines and annuals mentioned once by Poe in "Autography." In June 1844, Poe wrote to Lewis J. Cist that "I have long admired her writings," a reference to her collection *Bernice; or, The Curse of Minna and Other Poems*. *Text: CWP,* XV, 258–259. *Research: TPL,* 464.

Nichols, Thomas Low. (1815–1901). American journalist and radical reformer. He wrote an account of the balloon hoax episode in his *Forty Years of American Life: 1821–1861*. *See:* "The Balloon Hoax." *Research:* Falk, Doris V. "Thomas Low Nichols, Poe, and 'The Balloon Hoax.' " *Poe Studies*, 5, no. 2 (1972): 48–49. *Research: TPL,* xxxvi.

Niebuhr, Barthold Georg. (1776–1831). German historian and writer of Roman and Byzantine history. *See:* "Reminiscences of an Intercourse with Mr. Niebuhr." *Text: CWP,* VIII, 162–168, 227; X, 22.

Nietzsche, Friedrich. (1844–1900). German philosopher. He expressed his opinion of Poe in *Beyond Good and Evil* (1886) and *The Will to Power* (1901), linking him with Byron and Musset. All three writers have "souls in which they usually try to conceal some fracture; often taking revenge with their works for some inner contamination." *Research: PLL,* 270.

"Night and Morning: A Novel." A long review of Bulwer's novel appearing in *Graham's Magazine* for April 1841. Poe used the review as an occasion for digressing on the art of fiction particularly from the standpoint of the necessity for plot and story length. Poe credits Bulwer's attempt to render a perfect plot but also says of plot itself, "Some of the finest fictions in the world have neglected it altogether. . . . But in the book before us *much* is sacrificed for its sake and everything is rendered subservient to its purposes." Although Bulwer is not "a bad stylist," his English "is grossly defective—turgid, involved, and ungrammatical." Poe ends his mixed review with a mixed judgment of *Night and Morning* by declaring, "In pathos, humour, and verisimilitude he is unequal to Dickens," but the novel is "not [Bulwer's] worst." *Text: CWP,* X, 114–133. *Research: PJC,* 250–255.

Noah, Major Mordecai Manuel. (1785–1851). Editor of the *Evening Star* and the *Sunday Times and Messenger*. He testified on Poe's behalf as a character witness in Poe's libel suit against Dr. Thomas Dunn English. His signature in "Autography'' displays ''an air of the quizzical, and the devil-may-care.'' *Text: CWP,* XIII, 10–11; XV, 171–172, 207. *Research: TPL,* xxxiv, 581–582, 688–689.

"Noble Deeds of a Woman." Review of an anonymous work appearing in *The Southern Literary Messenger* for February 1836. Poe approved of the book's anecdotal organization. ''But be the 'Noble Deeds of a Woman' English or American, we recommend them heartily to public attention.'' *Text: CWP,* VIII, 238.

Norfolk Southern Argus. This newspaper covered and commented on Poe's ''Poetic Principle'' lecture of 14 September 1849, calling it ''chaste and classic in its style of composition, smooth and graceful in its delivery.'' *Research: TPL,* 835.

"Norman Leslie; A Tale of the Present Times." Novel by Theodore Sedgwick Fay attacked by Poe in a lengthy and savage review appearing in *The Southern Literary Messenger* for December 1835. Poe began the review with caustic vigor, writing, ''This is *the* book—*the* book *par excellence*—the book bepuffed, beplastered, and be-*Mirrored*,'' and proceeded to excoriate the novel with such judgments as ''[t]he characters *have no character*,'' ''Mr. Fay's *style* . . . is unworthy of a schoolboy,'' and ''the plot . . . is a monstrous piece of absurdity and incongruity.'' *Text: CWP,* VIII, 51–62. *Research:* Moss, Sidney. ''Poe and the *Norman Leslie* Incident.'' *American Literature*, 25 (1953): 293–306; *PLB,* 42–46; *LET,* I, 101, 102, 103; *PJC,* 97–98; Pollin, Burton R. ''Poe's 'Mystification': Its Source in Fay's *Norman Leslie*.'' *Mississippi Quarterly*, 25 (1972): 111–130.

North Amity Street (number 203). A Poe address in Baltimore and referred to in modern travel guides as ''the Poe House.'' He resided here with Maria Clemm, Virginia, and Virginia's grandmother from 1832 to 1835.

North Seventh Street (number 234). A Poe address in Philadelphia where Poe resided in the spring of 1843.

Norton, Mrs. Caroline. (1808–1877). Minor English poet. Poe felt that her poetry showed imagination and wit and compared her favorably with Felicia Hemans. *Text: CWP,* X, 196; XI, 275; XVI, 54.

"Notes upon English Verse." A first version of the critical essay ''The Rationale of Verse'' published in *The Pioneer* for March 1843. The essay included a single line of verse described by Poe as ''a perfect English hexameter formed upon the model of the Greek.'' Mabbott included the line in his edition of Poe's poems. ''Man is a complex, compound, compost, yet is he God-born.'' *See:* ''The Rationale of Verse.'' *Text: MCW,* I, 339; *CWP,* XIV, 209–265.

"A Notice of William Cullen Bryant." Review of Bryant's verse appearing in *Burton's Gentleman's Magazine* for May 1840. Poe furnished a short biographical profile and explained "[w]hy his 'Thanatopsis' has been so widely received and quoted as his finest production. . . . A graceful simplicity is the chief feature of this poem,—simplicity both of design and execution. . . . But breathings of a high ideality are also observable, which render the lines distinctive." *Text: CWP,* X, 85–91.

"Notices of the 'Messenger.'" Poe replied to his critics by making "selections from the notices received" in an article appearing in *The Southern Literary Messenger Supplement* for July 1836. To the "Newbern (North Carolina) Spectator—a general dissenter from all favorable opinions of our Magazine," Poe wittily replied that the opinions expressed in *The Messenger* "are open to the comments and censures of even the most diminutive things in creation—of the very Newbern Spectators of the land. If the editor of this little paper does not behave himself we will positively publish his verses." *Text: CWP,* VIII, 333–340.

"Notices of the War of 1812. By John Armstrong." Review of "Notices" by the former secretary of war appearing in *The Southern Literary Messenger* of June 1836. They are "a valuable addition to our history, and to our historical literature—embracing a variety of details which should not have been so long kept from the cognizance of the public." *Text: CWP,* IX, 22–23.

Novalis [Friedrich von Hardenberg]. (1772–1801). German Romantic poet mentioned by Poe in the dream excursion story "A Tale of the Ragged Mountains." Poe also refers to Novalis as among those German writers most admired by Felicia Hemans. *Text: CWP,* IX, 202; XI, 5; XVI, 98–99.

Nu-Nu. Character in the novel *The Narrative of Arthur Gordon Pym.* He is a native who accompanies Pym in his boat as they approach the great white chasm.

"Nuts to Crack: Or Quips, Quotes, Anecdote and Facete of Oxford and Cambridge Scholars. By the Author of Facetiæ Cantabrigiensis." Review of an intellectual's joke book appearing in *The Southern Literary Messenger* for December 1835. "Never was there a better thing for whiling away a few loose or unappropriated half hours—that is to say in the hands of a reader who is imbued with a love of classical whimsicality." *Text: CWP,* VIII, 90–91.

O

Oates, Joyce Carol. (1938–). American novelist and short story writer. Oates's entire literary output shows a strong fascination with Poe's major themes of perversity, revenge, tormented guilt, and psychosexual violence. In the ''Afterword'' to her short story collection *Haunted: Tales of the Grotesque*, Oates explicitly acknowledges her debt to Poe: ''Who has not been influenced by Poe?—however obliquely, indirectly; however the influence, absorbed in adolescence or even in childhood, would seem to be far behind us.'' Almost every story in Oates's collection *Nightside* has an analogue among Poe's tales and one story in particular, ''The Dungeon,'' is a line-by-line transcription of Poe's ''The Pit and the Pendulum.'' Oates's story titles in *Nightside*, ''The Dungeon,'' ''Bloodstains,'' ''Exile,'' ''Fatal Woman,'' and ''Further Confessions'' immediately recall Poe. *Research:* Oates, Joyce Carol. ''Wonderlands.'' *Georgia Review*, 38 (1984): 487–506; Egan, James. '' 'Romance of a Darksome Type': Versions of the Fantastic in the Novels of Joyce Carol Oates.'' *Studies in Weird Fiction*, 7 (1990): 12–21.

"The Oblong Box." Short story first published in *Godey's Lady's Book* for September 1844 and republished in *The Broadway Journal* of 13 December 1845. The tale involves a mystery at sea and the disillusionment of an overly curious narrator who ''like[s] to be precise.'' The narrator embarks upon a voyage from Charleston to New York aboard the packet ship *Independence* commanded by Captain Hardy. Among his fellow passengers are his artist friend, Cornelius Wyatt, and Wyatt's wife and two sisters. When the narrator notices that they occupy an extra stateroom and that Mrs. Wyatt is closely veiled and seldom accompanies her husband anywhere on the ship, he becomes inquisitive. His curiosity is further aroused by the placement of an oblong box ''six feet in length by two and a half in breadth'' in Wyatt's stateroom. Although the box's very dimensions suggest a coffin, the narrator assumes that it contains a copy of Leonardo's *Last Supper*, which Wyatt is smuggling into New York. When the sounds of hammering, prying, and sobbing are heard in Wyatt's cabin, the narrator assumes that he has ''opened his oblong box, in order to feast his eyes on the pictorial treasure within.'' When the *Independence* goes down in a hurricane, Cornelius Wyatt madly returns to the sinking ship to retrieve his oblong box. As the survivors watch in horror ''both body and box were in the sea—disappearing suddenly, at once and forever.'' Left with the annoying dilemma of what the oblong box contained, the narrator is later enlightened by Captain Hardy, who explains that Wyatt was conveying ''the corpse of his adored wife'' to her mother in Albany. The Captain himself had participated in the concealment in order not to alarm the other passengers. Chagrined by his wrong assumptions and realizing that he was perhaps the only passenger who could not recognize a coffin, he berates himself for having ''too careless, too impulsive, and too inquisitive a temperament.'' Although Poe often inveighed against ''the heresy of the didactic'' in literature, this tale does draw a moral; as the prying narrator confesses to his shame, pride of observation often blinds the observer. *Text: MCW,* III, 919–935; *CWP,* V, 274–298. *Research:* Vierra, Clifford Carley. ''Poe's 'Oblong Box': Factual Origins.'' *Modern Language Notes*, 74 (1959): 693–695; Goldhurst, William. ''Self-Reflective Fiction by Poe: Three Tales.'' *Modern Language Studies*, 16, no. 3 (1986): 4–14; McMullen, Bonnie Shannon. ''Lifting the Lid on Poe's 'Oblong Box.' '' *Studies in American Fiction*, 23 (1995): 203–214.

O'Bumper, Bibulus. Character in the short story ''Lionizing.'' He is an expert on wine and one of the guests at the Prince of Wales's literary dinner.

Occidente, Maria del. [Maria Gowan Brooks]. (1794–1845). American poet and dramatist who wrote under the name ''Maria of the West.'' Poe attributed ''passion, enthusiasm, and abandon'' to her verses. *Text: CWP,* XI, 275; XIII, 156, 225; XVI, 54.

O'Connor, Flannery. (1925–1964). American novelist and short story writer. Her fusion of the grotesque and horrible with the comic and ludicrous is frequently compared to Poe's artistry. In a letter of 28 August 1955 to ''A,'' O'Connor stated that early in her career she experienced an extensive ''Edgar Allan Poe period which lasted for years and consisted chiefly in a volume called *The Humorous Tales of E. A. Poe*. . . . This is an influence I would rather not think about.'' O'Connor's disclaimer notwithstanding, it is hardly possible to read any of her Georgia gothic tales and novels without finding the southern-bred Poe's influence and inspiration a deeply ingrained feature of both her style and themes. Poe's admixture of comic horror is the defining element in such stories as ''Good Country People,'' ''A Good Man Is Hard to Find,'' ''A Late

Encounter with the Enemy," "A Stroke of Good Fortune," "Parker's Back," and "Everything That Rises Must Converge." Although the specific Christian cosmology that dramatically informs O'Connor's world in absent in Poe's, both writers place their characters in extreme or lethal situations that are often resolved by decisive violent actions that give way to antivisionary moments or distorted epiphanies. *Research:* Montgomery, Marion. "Of Cloaks and Hats and Doublings in Poe and Flannery O'Connor." *South Carolina Review*, 11, no. 1 (1978): 60–69.

Odenheimer. Character in the short story "The Murders in the Rue Morgue." He is a restaurateur who does not speak French but had heard shouts in French when he passed the house during the time of the murders.

O'Grandison, Sir Pathrick Barronitt. Character and narrator in the short story "Why the Little Frenchman Wears His Hand in a Sling."

"Oh, Tempora! Oh, Mores!" Unpublished early poem surviving in transcription possessed by Poe's sister Rosalie. It was printed in the Richmond *Southern Opinion* of 7 March 1868 and later as a newly discovered Poe poem in *No Name Magazine* for October 1889. The poem is an imitation of Pope's biting couplets in "Epistle to Dr. Arbuthnot." "Ah growl, say you, my friend, and pray at what?/ Why, really, sir, I almost had forgot—/ But damn it, sir, I deem it a disgrace/ That things should stare us boldly in the face,/ And daily strut the street with bows and scrapes,/ Who would be men by imitating apes." *Text: MCW,* I, 8–13. *Research:* Hubbell, J. B. " 'Oh, Tempora! Oh, Mores!' " A Juvenile Poem by Edgar Allan Poe." In *Elizabethan Studies and Other Essays in Honor of George F. Reynolds*, *University of Colorado Studies* (series B), *Studies in the Humanities*, 2, no. 4 (1945): 314–321.

Oinos. (1). One of the cosmic voices or angelic intelligences in the short story "The Power of Words." Newly arrived in the heavens from "the fair earth which lately perished," Oinos receives instruction from Agathos on the power of words to create a universe.

Oinos. (2). Character in the short story "Shadow—A Parable." He is the posthumous narrator of the story.

"The Old Curiosity Shop, and Other Tales. By Charles Dickens." Review of the Dickens novel appearing in *Graham's Magazine* for May 1841. Poe admired Dickens's control of characterization but thought the death of Little Nell too painful to permit a second reading. "In the instances of Nelly, the grandfather, the Sexton, and the man of the furnace, the force of the creative intellect could scarcely have been engaged with nobler material, and the result is that these personages belong to the most august regions of the *Ideal.*" Poe also compared Dickens's realist artistry to the false and strained realism of

Bulwer. ''Mr. Bulwer, through art, has almost created a genius. Mr. Dickens, through genius, has perfected a standard from which Art itself will derive its essence, its rules.'' *Text: CWP,* X, 142–155. *Research: PJC,* 255–257.

"Old English Poetry.—The Book of Gems. Edited by S. C. Hall." A second review of an anthology of English poetry appearing in *The Broadway Journal* of 17 May 1845. Poe took exception to some of the selections, saying, ''There are long passages now before us, of the most despicable trash, with no merit whatever, beyond that of their antiquity.'' But he did note with approval the inclusion of George Wither's ''The Shepherd's Hunting'' and Marvell's ''Maiden Lamenting for her Fawn.'' *See:* ''The Book of Gems.'' *Text: CWP,* XII, 139–146.

Old Nick. Character mentioned in the short story ''The Devil in the Belfry.''

The Old Swede. Character mentioned in the short story ''MS. Found in a Bottle.'' He is one of the sailors aboard the shipwrecked merchantman.

"The Old World and the New: Or a Journal of Reflections and Observations Made on a Tour in Europe. By the Reverend Orville Dewey." Review of a book appearing in *The Southern Literary Messenger* for August 1836. Poe cannot recommend the travel book to all readers because he feels that ''we would be doing our conscience a great wrong in recommending the work before us as a whole. Here is some amusement—great liberality—much excellent sense—a high spirit of sound morality and genuine philanthropy; but indeed very little of either novelty or profundity.'' *Text: CWP,* IX, 80–82.

Oldeb. Character in ''The Tale of the Ragged Mountains.'' Oldeb is Augustus Bedloe's alterego.

Ollapod, Dr. Character mentioned in the short story ''A Predicament.''

O'Neill, Eugene. (1888–1953). American playwright. O'Neill expressed a deep personal identification with Poe. The structural and stylistic influence of Poe is perhaps most evident in O'Neill's one-act plays such as *Where the Cross Is Made.* The brooding atmosphere of family decline and decay in *Long Day's Journey into Night* further recalls Poe. The early play *Gold* uses details of entrapment from *The Narrative of Arthur Gordon Pym. Research:* Sheaffer, Louis. *O'Neill: Son and Playwright.* Boston: Little, Brown, 1968; Goldhurst, William. ''Misled by a Box: Variations on a Theme from Poe.'' *Clues,* 3 (1982): 31–37; Robinson, Lennox.

"*Beyond the Horizon* versus *Gold*." In *Eugene O'Neill's Critics: Voices from Abroad*, ed. Horst Frenz and Susan Tuck. Carbondale: Southern Illinois University Press, 1984, 11–15.

Oppodeldoc. Character in the short story "The Literary Life of Thingum Bob, Esq." It is the pen name used by Thingum Bob to sign his plagiarized poems.

"Oracles from the Poets." Book of poetic excerpts by Caroline Gilman briefly noticed by Poe in the *Broadway Journal" of 11 October 1845. Research: TPL,* 575.

"Oration on the Life and Character of the Rev. Joseph Caldwell, D.D. Late President of the University of North Carolina." Review of a pamphlet by Walter Anderson appearing in *The Southern Literary Messenge*r for December 1835. "The tone of feeling pervading the oration is quite characteristic of its author—ardent—affectionate—consistent." *Text: CWP,* VIII, 102–103.

"Orion: An Epic Poem in Three Books. By R. H. Horne." Review of Richard Henry Horne's narrative poem appearing in *Graham's Magazine* for March 1844. Having previously admired Horne's tragedy *Gregory the Seventh*, Poe concentrated on the "multitudinous beauties" and metrical command of *Orion* in his lengthy review. "It is our deliberate opinion that, in all that regards the loftiest and holiest attributes of the true Poetry, 'Orion' has never been excelled." Poe also used the review as an occasion for stating his poetric principle "that the origin of Poetry lies in a thirst for a wilder Beauty than Earth supplies—that Poetry itself is the imperfect effort to quench this immortal thirst by novel combinations of beautiful forms." *Text: CWP,* XI, 249–275. *Research: LET,* I, 245, 246, 302; *PJC,* 339–345.

Orndoff. Character mentioned in the unfinished and unpublished short story "The Light-House." He has apparently asked the narrator to accompany him to the lighthouse and has been denied.

Osborn, Laughton. (1809–1878). Amateur novelist. He knew Poe casually in New York. Poe drew a profile of Osborn in "The Literati of New York City" in which he lauded his novels, especially *The Adventures of Jeremy Levis*, "in one volume, a kind of medley of fact, fiction, satire, criticism and novel philosophy. It is a dashing, reckless *brochure*, brimful of talent and audacity." *See:* "Confessions of a Poet." *Text: CWP,* VIII, 2–3; XIII, 165, 168; XV, 44–49, 151–152. *Research: TPL,* xxxiv-xxxv, 151–155.

Osgood, Frances [Fanny] Sargent. (1811–1850). Sentimental poet and one of the ladies in Poe's life. Poe made her acquaintance in March 1845. Poe had a high regard for her as "a worshipper of beauty." Their friendship was purely aesthetic and welcomed by Virginia. Poe's enraptured praise of her work indicates that he felt she had all those qualities of imagination that he cherished in his own verse, "a true imagination, with a 'movement' or energy." On her deathbed in 1850, she described her first encounter with Poe as having "a peculiar and irresistible charm in the chivalric, graceful, and almost tender reverence with which he invariably approached all women who won his respect." In his affectionate portrait of her in "The Literati of New York City," Poe praised her collection *A Wreath of Wild Flowers from New England* by printing several extracts and summed up her character as follows: "Her character is daguerreotyped in her works—reading the one we know the other. She is ardent, sensitive, impulsive; the very soul of truth and honor; a worshipper of the beautiful, with a heart so radically artless as to seem abundant in art—universally respected, admired and beloved." *Text: CWP,* XI, 159–160, 241; XIII, 17–26, 105–25, 188–193; XV, 90, 94–105; XVI, 144. *Research:* Didier, Eugene L. "Poe's Female Friends." *Chatauquan*, 15 (September 1892): 723–729; Jones, Buford, and Kent Ljungquist. "Poe, Mrs. Osgood, and 'Annabel Lee.' " *Studies in the American Renaissance* (1983): 275–280; *TPL,* xxxv; De Jong, Mary G. "Lines from a Partly Published Drama: The Romance of Frances Sargent Osgood and Edgar Allan Poe." In *Patrons and Protegées: Gender, Friendship, and Writing in Nineteenth Century America*, ed. Shirley Marchalonis. New Brunswick, NJ: Rutgers University Press, 1994, 31–58.

Osgood, Samuel. Estranged husband of Frances Osgood. He painted Poe's portrait in 1845. *Research: PLL,* 174.

O'Sullivan, John Louis. (1813–1895). Editor of the *Democratic Review* and advocate of an American literature that was culturally distinct and original. He published several Poe pieces. *Research: TPL,* xxxv, 260, 587.

Otis, James Frederick. (1808–1867). Casual Poe correspondent. He contributed several suggestive signatures to Poe's "Autography" where his signature indicates "that his prose and poetry are equally good; but he writes too much and too hurriedly to write invariably well." *Text: CWP,* XV, 243. *Research:* Thomas, Dwight. "James F. Otis and 'Autography': A New Poe Correspondent." *Poe Studies*, 8 (June 1975): 12–15; *TPL,* xxxv, 210–211.

O'Trump, Mrs. Kathleen. Character in the short story "The Man That Was Used Up." She is a widow who gives a soirée attended by the narrator.

"Our Amateur Poets, No. I.—Flaccus." Review of the poetry of "a Mr. ———Ward" appearing in *Graham's Magazine* for March 1843. Poe found the poems in the collection that was "entitled, somewhat affectedly, 'Pasaic, a Group of Poems Touching That River: With Other Musings by Flaccus' " to be not "altogether destitute of merit." But moving forward into the review, Poe became increasingly negative and "fairly wearied with this absurd theme. *Who* calls Mr. Ward a poet? He is a second-rate, or a third-rate, or perhaps a ninety-ninth rated poetaster.'' *Text: CWP,* XI, 160–174.

"Our Amateur Poets, No. III. William Ellery Channing." Review of Channing's verse appearing in *Graham's Magazine* for August 1843. With bitter gusto, Poe compared Channing unfavorably against Tennyson, writing of the poems that he ''appears to have been inoculated, at the same moment, with *virus* from Tennyson and Carlyle.'' Most of the review is in this sarcastic vein as in this statement in the first paragraph: ''His book contains about sixty-three things, which he calls poems, and which he no doubt seriously supposes so to be. They are full of all kinds of mistakes, of which the most important is that of their having been printed at all.'' *Text: CWP,* XI, 174–190.

"Our Contributors, No. VIII.—Fitz-Greene Halleck." Review of the verse of Fitz-Greene Halleck appearing in *Graham's Magazine* for September 1843. As he had previously in *The Southern Literary Messenger*, Poe found most of Halleck's verse rhymically defective and lacking in ideality, which he demonstrated by scanning lines from one of Halleck's best poems in Poe's estimation, ''Fanny.'' The poem, '' 'Marco Bozzaris' is by far the best of the poems of Halleck. It is not very highly ideal, but is skillfully constructed, abounds in the true lyrical spirit, and, with slight exception, is admirably versified.'' *See:* ''Alnwick Castle, with Other Poems. By Fitz-Greene Halleck'' *Text: CWP,* XI, 190–204.

"Our Island of Dreams." Poem by Sarah Helen Whitman concerning her agonized decision not to marry Poe and their permanent separation. *Research: PLL,* 236.

"Our Magazine Literature." Article signed ''L.'' appearing in the *New York World* of 11 March 1843 and sometimes attributed to Poe but probably not by him. *Research: PLB,* 93, 95, 96; *TPL,* xvii.

Outis. Journalistic pseudonym of the writer of articles defending Longfellow against Poe's charges of plagiarism. The name means ''Nobody.'' Some Poe scholars have contended, solely on the basis of internal evidence, that ''Outis'' was Poe himself. *See:* ''Imitation—Plagiarism—Mr. Poe's Reply to the Letter of Outis''; ''Outis Papers.'' *Research:* Campbell, Killis. ''Who Was 'Outis'?'' *University of Texas Studies in English*, 8 (1928): 107–109; Pollin, Burton R. ''Poe as the Author of the 'Outis' Letter and 'The Bird of the Dream.' '' *Poe Studies*, 20 (1987): 10–15; Ljungquist, Kent, and Buford Jones, ''The Identity of 'Outis': A Further Chapter in the Poe-Longfellow War.'' *American Literature*, 60 (1988): 402–415.

"Outis Papers." Series of letters concocted under the signature ''Outis,'' an anonymous journalist, who took up Longfellow's cause against Poe's attacks and leveled the satiric charge that Poe's ''The Raven'' was a pilfered poem.

Poe replied in a five-part series of articles in *The Broadway Journal*. *Text: CWP,* XII, 41–106. *See:* "Imitation—Plagiarism—Mr. Poe's Reply to the Letter of Outis"; "Outis."

"Outre-Mer." Longfellow poem noticed briefly by Poe in *The Southern Literary Messenger* for June 1835. *Research: TPL,* 160.

"The Oval Portrait." Short story first published in *Graham's Magazine* for April 1842 under the title "Life in Death." A revised version using the title "The Oval Portrait" appeared in *The Broadway Journal* of 26 April 1845. The tale contains a rare reference to the English gothic novelist Mrs. Ann Radcliffe. The wounded narrator who seeks refuge in a gloomy château refers to his sanctuary as one "of those piles of commingled gloom and grandeur which have long frowned among the Apennines, not less in fact than in the fancy of Mrs. Radcliffe." To recover from his wound, the narrator convalesces in a remote turret of the château where he is much taken by the paintings that adorn the walls, especially the oval portrait of "a young girl just ripening into womanhood." As he contemplates the painting's beauty, he slowly realizes that the portrait's entrancing effect lies in "an absolute lifelikeness of expression, which, at first startling, finally confounded, subdued, and appalled me." Feeling that something horrible must lurk in the portrait's beauty, the narrator takes up and reads a volume at his bedside that describes the paintings and their histories. The concluding paragraph of the story is an account describing the making of the oval portrait. The beautiful woman who sat for the portrait was deeply in love with the artist, a passionate, studious, austere, wild, and moody man whose first and only love was his art. As she posed for many months he "took a fervid and burning pleasure in his task, and wrought day and night to depict her who so loved him, yet who grew daily more dispirited and weak. The tints which he spread upon the canvas were drawn from the cheeks of her who sat beside him." The horror inherent in the portrait's beauty lies in the artist's draining of the life force of his subject and its transfer to the cold canvas. The lifelikeness of the vital colors reveals a portrait almost literally painted in blood. Poe's alternate portrait of the artist as vampire can be compared with Hawthorne's similarly destructive artist figures in such tales as "The Artist of the Beautiful." A closer parallel with Hawthorne is the similarity of "The Oval Portrait" to "The Birthmark." The artists in both tales—Hawthorne's Aylmer and Poe's unnamed painter—willingly sacrifice their subjects in the pursuit of artistic perfection. In each case the female subjects ironically participate in their own destruction in their devotion to the artist. The woman in the oval portrait "smiled on and still on, uncomplainingly. The subdued horror of the observer's situation can further be related to the same murderous conditions in Browning's "My Last Duchess." *Text: MCW,* II, 659–667; *CWP,* IV, 245–249. *Research:* Gross, Seymour. "Poe's Revision of 'The Oval Portrait.' " *Modern Language Notes*, 74 (1959): 16–20; Hafley, James. "Malice in Wonderland." *Arizona Quarterly*, 15 (1959): 5–12; Thompson, Gary

R. ''Dramatic Irony in 'The Oval Portrait.' '' *English Language Notes*, 6 (1968): 107–114; Twitchell, James. ''Poe's 'Oval Portrait' and the Vampire Motif.'' *Studies in Short Fiction*, 14 (1977): 387–393; Scheick, William J. ''The Geometric Structure of Poe's 'The Oval Portrait.' '' *Poe Studies*, 11 (1978): 6–8; Lecercle, Ann. ''L'Inscription du regard.'' In *Du Fantastique en littérature: Figures et figurations: Eléments pour une poétique du fantastique sur quelques exemples anglo-saxons*, ed. Max Duperray. Aix-en-Provence: University de Provence, 1990, 77–93.

Ovid. [Publius Ovidius Naso]. (43 B.C.–A.D. 18). Roman poet and author of the *Ars Amatoria* and *Metamorphoses*. Ovid is quoted as a metrical example of the use of spondees in Latin hexameter in Poe's review of Griswold's *Poets and Poetry of America* and is on the devil's menu in ''Bon-Bon.'' '' 'But they want *flavor*, these Romans. One fat Greek is worth a dozen of them.'' *Text: CWP*, XI, 233; XVI, 77.

P

P. Character and narrator in the short story ''Mesmeric Revelation.'' He places Mr. Vankirk in a trance and questions him about the nature of the soul and the afterlife.

P——. Character in the short story ''The Facts in the Case of M. Valdemar.'' He is the narrator and the hypnotist who conducts the postmortem experiment on Valdemar.

P., Mr. Character mentioned in the short story ''Mystification.'' He is Johan Hermann's second who delivers the challenge to the Baron Ritzner Von Jung.

Pabodie, William Jewett. (1815–1870). Providence littérateur and acquaintance of Poe at the home of Sarah Helen Whitman. He advised her against her ''hasty and imprudent'' decision to marry Poe. *Research: TPL,* xxxv, 772–780.

"A Pæan." Poem first published in Elam Bliss's edition of Poe's *Poems* in April 1831 and in *The Southern Literary Messenger* for January 1836. Later variant versions bore the title ''Lenore.'' *See:* ''Lenore.'' *Text: MCW,* I, 204–207.

Paine, Thomas. (1737–1809). American political pamphleteer and author of *The Age of Reason*. Poe mentions Paine's book in *Marginalia*. *Text: CWP,* XVI, 12.

"Palæstine." Unsigned article (signed ''P.'') appearing in *The Southern Literary Messenger* for February 1836. Poe gives the geography, history of conquest, principal towns and cities, and other facts about the Holy Land. Poe's name is attached to the article in the issue's table of contents. *Text: CWP,* XIV, 1–5.

Palfrey, John Gorham. An editor of *The North American Review*. His signature as harshly analyzed in ''Autography'' displays ''a total deficiency in the sense of the beautiful. . . . forceless, graceless, tawdry, vacillating and unpicturesque. . . . It will not do to place any dependence upon his wisdom or upon his taste.'' *Text: CWP,* XV, 208.

Paradox, Sir Positive. Character in the short story ''Lionizing.'' He is one of the guests at the Prince of Wales's literary dinner.

"Paris and the Parisians in 1835. By Frances Trollope." Review of a book appearing in *The Southern Literary Messenger* for May 1836. Poe dismisses Mrs. Trollope's political views but recommends ''*Paris and the Parisians* to all lovers of fine writing, and vivacious humor. It is impossible not to be highly amused with the book.'' *Text: CWP,* IX, 17–22. *Research: TPL,* 208.

Parker, Archbishop Matthew. (1504–1575). English churchman. His 1564 version of the *Psalms* is mentioned in *Pinakidia*. *Text: CWP,* XIV, 71.

Parker, Richard. Character in the novel *The Narrative of Arthur Gordon Pym*. After the shipwreck, he suggests that one of the survivors be killed and cannibalized so that the others might live and becomes the first victim of his suggestion.

Parrhasius. (fl. 400 B.C.). Ancient Greek artist. His work is compared against another Greek artist, Zeuxis, in *Marginalia*. *Text: CWP,* XI, 84; XVI, 164.

Parsons, Alan. (1949–). English rock musician and producer. With the assistance of lyricist Eric Woolfson, 200 musicians and the rock group called ''The Alan Parsons Project,'' he produced an album entitled *Tales of Mystery and Imagination* (1975), which consisted of music inspired by several of Poe's tales and poems. Some of the tracks are instrumental renditions, combining electric guitars and synthesizers, while others create electronically simulated voices that recite various passages and lines from the short stories and poems. *Research:* Colin Larkin, ed. *The Guinness Encyclopedia of Popular Music*. Middlesex, UK; Guiness Publishing, 1981, I, 3189–3190.

"The Partisan: A Tale of the Revolution." Review of a historical novel of the American Revolution in the Carolinas by William Gilmore Simms appearing in *The Southern Literary Messenger* for January 1836. Poe's notice is mixed. He finds the novel formless and Simms's English "shockingly bad." "In spite, however, of its manifest and manifold blunders and impertinences, 'The Partisan' is no ordinary work. Its historical details are replete with interest." *Text: CWP,* VIII, 143–158. *Research:* Ridgely, J. V. *William Gilmore Simms.* New York: Twayne, 1962, pp. 93–94; *PJC,* 118–120; *PLL,* 184–196.

"Pasaic, a Group of Poems Touching That River: With Other Musings, by Flaccus." *See:* "Our Amateur Poets, No. I. Flaccus." *Text: CWP,* XI, 161.

Pascal, Blaise. (1623–1662). French philosopher and mathematician. Poe quotes from his *Pensées* in the short story "The Colloquy of Monos and Una." Poe quotes his definition of the universe in *Eureka*: " 'It is a sphere,' he says, 'of which the centre is everywhere, the circumference, nowhere.' " *Text: CWP,* IV, 204; XVI, 204.

Pasta, Giuditta. [Maria Costanza]. (1797–1865). Italian opera singer. "Pasta was everything which mere art could effect—always correct, always graceful. But, being compact of art, she was invariably the same." *Text: CWP,* X, 93.

Patten, Lieutenant George Washington. (1808–1882). Author of various cavalry and infantry tactical manuals and minor American poet included under "Various Authors" in Griswold's *The Poets and Poetry of America,* "thereby throwing openly the charge of their incompetency to sustain the name of Poets." *Text: CWP,* XI, 241.

Patterson, Edward Horton Norton. (1828–?). The young and wealthy editor of the Illinois weekly, *The Oquawka Spectator.* He approached Poe by letter on 18 December 1848 with an offer of editorship of a national magazine to be financed by Patterson. Poe responded enthusiastically, but the project was never begun, and the two men never met. *Research:* McElroy, M. D. "Poe's Last Partner: E. H. N. Patterson of Oquawka, Illinois." *Papers on Language and Literature,* 7 (1971): 252–271; *TPL,* xxxv-xxxvi, 803–809; *PLL,* 242–243.

Patterson, Mr. Character mentioned in *The Narrative of Arthur Gordon Pym.*

"Paul Ulric; or, The Adventures of an Enthusiast." Novel by Morris Mattson reviewed negatively by Poe in *The Southern Literary Messenger* for January 1836. This is one of Poe's nastiest reviews. He begins: "In itself, the book before us is too purely imbecile to merit an extended critique—but as a portion of our daily literary food—as an American work published by the Harpers—as one of the class of absurdities with an inundation of which our country is grievously threatened—we shall have no hesitation, and shall spare no pains, in exposing fully before the public eye its four hundred and forty-three pages of utter folly, bombast, and inanity.'' *Text: CWP,* VIII, 178–205. *Research: PLB,* 43–44; 77–78; *LET,* 101; *PJC,* 122–124.

Paulding, James Kirke. (1778–1860). American man of letters and editor of the humor magazine *Salamagundi* with Washington Irving. He followed Poe's career with approval, offering him advice about successful writing and attempting to assist him in securing a publisher for the tales. In a letter to Thomas Willis White of 2 January 1846, Paulding informed the editor of *The Southern Literary Messenger*, ''Your publication is decidedly superior to any Periodical in the United States, and Mr. Poe is decidedly the best of all our going writers.'' In ''Autography,'' Poe wrote of Paulding, ''No correct notion of Mr. Paulding's literary peculiarities could be obtained from an inspection of his MS.'' *See:* ''A Life of Washington. By James K. Paulding.'' *Text: CWP,* VIII, 223, 338; IX, 13–16; XI, 16; XIII, 16; XV, 51, 115, 146–147, 186. *Research: TPL,* 184.

Peabody, William Bourn Oliver. (1799–1847). Author and orator identified in ''Autography'' as a writer of light verse ''known chiefly to the readers of our light literature, and much more familiarly to Northern than to Southern readers.'' His *Catechism for the Use of Children* (1824) was widely used. *Text: CWP,* XV, 252.

Pedder, James. (1775–1859). Children's author. He knew and befriended Poe in Philadelphia in 1838. Pedder had also developed a plan to extract sugar from beet roots, a scheme discussed by Poe in a short untitled article in *Alexander's Weekly Messenger* for December 1839. *Research:* Mabbott, T. O. ''Poe's Essay on the Beet Root.'' *Notes & Queries*, 167 (15 December 1934): 420; *TPL,* 282.

Pedro. Character in the short story ''The Oval Portrait.'' He is the narrator's valet.

"Pencil Sketches (Second Series)." Book by Eliza Leslie briefly noticed by Poe in *The Southern Literary Messenger* for June 1835. *Research: TPL,* 160.

The Penn Magazine. Journal project planned and projected by Poe in 1840. He envisioned a literary journal of high quality to be edited by himself and sought financial and artistic backing from George R. Graham, John Neal, and others. In May of 1840, Poe prepared and circulated a prospectus to various newspapers. Published in the *Saturday Evening Post* of 6 June 1840, the prospectus declared, ''Its aim, chiefly, shall be to please; and this through means of versatility, originality, and pungency. It must not be supposed, however, that the intention is never to be serious. There is a species of grave writing, of which the spirit is novelty and vigor, and the immediate object the enkindling of the imagination. In such productions, belonging to the loftiest regions of literature, the journal shall abound.'' After Poe altered the name of his magazine to *The Stylus* in February 1843, the project was abandoned when Poe failed to interest enough necessary subscribers and Thomas Clarke of the Philadelphia *Saturday Museum* withdrew his support. *See: The Stylus. Research:* Webb, Howard W. ''Contributions to Poe's *Penn Magazine.*'' *Notes & Queries*, 203 (December 1958): 447–448; *PLB,* 90–91; *TPL,* 298–303; 304–307; 316–318.

Pennifeather, Mr. Character in the short story, '' 'Thou Art the Man.' '' He is the nephew of Mr. Barnabas Shuttleworthy and is the prime suspect in the murder of his uncle.

Perry, Edgar A. Poe's United States Army alias. He enlisted in Battery H, First Artillery under this name on 26 May 1827. On 31 October 1827, Poe's unit was posted to Fort Moultrie, Charleston, South Carolina; then to Fortress Monroe, Virginia, in December 1838. Poe was discharged from the army on 15 April 1829. *See:* Military Service. *Research: LTP*, 167, 171, 195.

Pest, Queen. Cadaverous character in the short story ''King Pest.'' She seizes Hugh Tarpaulin and hurls him into a huge puncheon of October ale.

Pest-iferous, Arch Duke. Character in the short story ''King Pest.'' He is one of the company of six rotting relatives of King Pest.

Pest-ilential, The Duke. Character in the short story ''King Pest.'' He is one of the company of six rotting relatives of King Pest.

Pest the First, King. Character in the short story ''King Pest.'' He is the ruler of plague and death. '' 'Know then that in these dominions I am monarch, and here rule with undivided empire under the title of ''King Pest the First.'' ' ''

"Peter Pendulum. The Business Man." Short story first published under this title in *Burton's Gentleman's Magazine* for February 1840 and later published under the title ''The Business Man.'' *See:* ''The Business Man.''

Peters, Dirk. Character in the novel *The Narrative of Arthur Gordon Pym.* He is a halfbreed who sometimes acts as Pym's dark guardian and savior. Peters's role in Poe's novel has been compared to Queequeg in *Moby Dick* and Jim in *Huckleberry Finn*, the young white man befriended and protected by the dark-skinned guardian.

Peterson, Charles Jacobs. (1819–1887). An assistant editor of *Graham's Magazine*. His assumption of Poe's editorial responsibilities while Poe was ill precipitated Poe's resignation. There is a vague description of his character in ''Autography'' noting that his handwriting ''when unhurried, is a very good one—clear, weighty, and picturesque; but when carelessly written is illegible. *Text: CWP,* XI, 224; XV, 235. *Research: TPL,* xxxvi, 320–321; 367–368.

Peterson, Mr. Character mentioned in the novel *The Narrative of Arthur Gordon Pym.* He is Arthur Gordon Pym's grandfather. The name is mentioned again to identify a Londoner.

Petrarch, Francesco. (1304–1374). Italian sonneteer. In *Pinakidia,* Poe emphatically denied that Petrarch was the father of the sonnet. ''The Italian sonnet can be traced back as far as the year 1200. Petrarch was not born until 1304.'' *Text: CWP,* XIV, 54, 56–57.

Pfaall, Grettel. Wife of the balloonist Hans Pfaall in ''The Unparalleled Adventure of One Hans Pfall.''

Pfaall, Hans. Character in the short story ''The Unparalleled Adventure of One Hans Pfaall.'' He is the intrepid balloonist.

Phantasy-Pieces. In 1842, Poe planned a three-volume collection of his tales under this title, but the project never saw publication. *Research: TPL,* 370–371.

Philadelphia Saturday News. Philadelphia newspaper noticed by Poe in *The Southern Literary Messenger. Research: TPL,* 219; Kopley, Richard. *Edgar Allan Poe and the Philadelphia Saturday News.* Baltimore: Enoch Pratt Free Library and Edgar Allan Poe Society and Library of the University of Baltimore, 1991.

Phillips, Anna H. [Helen Irving]. (fl. 1840). American poet included by Griswold in *The Female Poets of America.* Poe saw her work in the annual, *The Floral Wreath and the Ladies' Wreath. Text: CWP,* XI, 159.

"The Philosophy of Composition." Critical essay appearing in *Graham's Magazine* for April 1846. The essay is one of the central texts in Poe criticism and sets forth many of his theoretical convictions concerning the creative process. The piece also offers an analytic profile of the conception and inception of ''The Raven,'' precipitating much debate among literary historians over the reliability of Poe's account of the compositional process. In the making of ''The Raven,'' brevity of execution and precise planning of the desired effect are imperative to the aesthetic success of the poem. The artist must have the climax or denouement in mind from the very beginning of the compositional process and avoid lengthiness. Lengthiness in any poem leads to destruction of impression and diminution of effect. ''If any literary work is too long to be read at one sitting, we must be content to dispense with the immensely important effect derivable from unity of impression—for, if two sittings be required, the affairs of the world interfere, and every thing like totality is at once destroyed.'' Poe further states "that Beauty is the sole legitimate province of the poem," that if the poet creates beautifully, the truth of such beauty will follow from the evocation of this primary quality. Poe's discussion of the enclosed locale or setting of "The Raven" is applicable to the conditions he prefers in the narrow spaces of the horror tales. "It has always appeared to me that a close *circumscription of space* is absolutely necessary to the effect of insulated incident." As a rationalized manifesto of his artistic theories, "The Philosophy of Composition" assumes a place beside Sidney's "Defense of Poesy" and Shelley's "Defense of Poetry" in the library of critical theory. *See:* "The Poetic Principle." *Text: CWP,* XIV, 193–208. *Research:* Colby, Robert A. "Poe's Philosophy of Composition." *University of Kansas City Review*, 20 (1954): 211–214; Burke, Kenneth. "The Principle of Composition." *Poetry*, 99 (October 1961): 46–53.

"The Philosophy of Furniture." Essay and sketch appearing in *Burton's Gentleman's Magazine* for May 1840. Revised and retitled "House of Furniture," it reappeared in *The Broadway Journal* of 3 May 1845. Written in the manner of an "Elia essay" (Charles Lamb), the sketch is a witty disquisition on national differences in interior decorating and overdecorating. The perversion of taste and confused substitution of size and cost for true beauty and taste in American furnishing are the direct result of our vulgar belief in "an aristocracy of dollars, the display of wealth here to take the place and perform the office of the heraldic display in monarchial countries." Other nations, too, fall far beneath the supremacy of English restraint and tasteful proportion. "In Spain they are all curtains—a nation of hangmen." Turkish carpets are nothing more than "taste in its dying agonies." The American "rage for glitter has led us to the exaggerated employment of mirrors." The sketch terminates with a description of a model apartment in which the furniture is an exact philosophical expression of graceful and unpretentious beauty and tone. *Text: MCW,* II, 494–504; *CWP,* XIV, 101–109. *Research:* Sherman, G. W. "Poe and the Panopticon." *Poe Studies*, 14, no. 2 (1981): 31.

"Philothea: A Romance." Review of a novel of ancient Athens by Mrs. Child appearing in *The Southern Literary Messenger* for September 1836. Poe gives an appreciative summary of the plot and closes the review by suggesting that "Philothea might be introduced advantageously into our female academies. Its purity of thought and lofty morality are unexceptionable. It would prove an effectual aid in the study of Greek antiquity, with whose spirit it is wonderfully imbued." *Text: CWP,* IX, 146–155.

"Phrenology, and the Moral Influence of Phrenology: Arranged for General Study, and the Purposes of Education, from the First Published Works of Gall and Spurzheim, to the Latest Discoveries of the Present Period. By Mrs. L. Miles." Review of a scientific treatise appearing in *The Southern Literary Messenger* for March 1836. Poe took a serious interest in phrenology, its medical uses, and its value as a science, noting that ''as a science, [it] ranks among the most important which can engage the attention of thinking beings.'' He was especially interested in Miles's chapter on the relationship between skull contours and the mental quality of combativeness, a character faculty that he would explore in ''The Imp of the Perverse'' and several other stories. The concentrated description of the cranium of Roderick Usher also reflects Poe's phrenological interests. Poe observes that ''a skull which is large, which is elevated or high above the ears, and in which the head is well developed and thrown forward, so as to be nearly perpendicular with its base, may be presumed to lodge a brain of greater power.'' *Text: CWP,* VIII, 252–255. *Research:* Hungerford, Edward. ''Poe and Phrenology.'' *American Literature*, 2 (1930): 209–213; *PJC,* 131–132; Stauffer, Donald B. ''Poe as Phrenologist: The Example of Monsieur Dupin.'' In *Papers on Poe: Essays in Honor of John Ward Ostrom*, ed. Richard P. Veler. Springfield, OH: Chantry Music Press at Wittenberg University, 1972, 113–125.

The Physician of the Family. Minor character in the short story ''The Fall of the House of Usher.'' His face wears ''a mingled expression of low cunning and perplexity'' when the narrator passes him on the staircase as he ascends to Usher's apartments.

"The Pic Nic Papers. By Various Hands, Edited by Charles Dickens." Review of a miscellany of articles by Dickens, Thomas Moore, W. H. Ainsworth, G. P. R. James, and others appearing in *Graham's Magazine* for November 1841. Poe challenged the crass commercial use of Dickens's name and the misuse of ''Pickwick'' in the title and further condemned the contents as even beneath hack work standards. ''These 'Pic Nic Papers' are very great trash, although written by very clever men. Their general merit, in our opinion, is below that of the mere *make-weight* of our commonest newspapers and magazines.'' Only ''The Lamplighter's Story,'' a tale by Dickens, escaped Poe's denunciation. *Text: CWP,* X, 206–209. *Research: PJC,* 269–270.

Pierpont, Reverend John. (1785–1866). American poet. In ''Autography'' Poe praised ''His 'Airs of Palestine' [which] is distinguished by the sweetness and vigor of its versification, and the grace of its sentiments.'' *Text: CWP,* XV, 192–193, 239.

Pike, Albert. (1809–1891). Amateur poet and journalist mentioned once with lavish praise in ''Autography.'' ''He is the most classic of our poets in the best sense of the term. . . . Upon the whole, there are few of our native writers to whom we consider him inferior.'' *Text: CWP,* XV, 257–258.

Pike, Major Zebulon Montgomery. (1779–1813). American army officer, explorer, and author of *Account of Expeditions to the Sources of the Mississippi* *and through the Western Parts of Louisiana*. He is mentioned in *The Journal of Julius Rodman*. *Text: CWP,* IV, 19.

Pilau, Madame. Character mentioned in the short story "The Imp of the Perverse." Her murder by the device of a poisoned candle gives the narrator the idea for carrying out his crime.

Pinakidia. Article appearing in *The Southern Literary Messenger* for August 1836 containing 173 one- or two-sentence random observations on miscellaneous subjects, most of these eccentric, obscure, or arcane. The Greek title means "tablets," an anthology, or more loosely, a grab bag. Poe himself referred to *Pinakidia* as a "heterogeneous farrago," "a confused mass of marginal notes." The eccentric content may show the influence of Poe's reading in Sir Thomas Browne and Laurence Sterne. The items deal with linguistic enigmas and textual mysteries in Greek and Hebrew classics, the history of plagiarism, and esoterica of all sorts. Thus, Poe reports to his readers, "The word . . . Fortune does not appear once in the whole Iliad," that "The Song of Solomon" "does not, like every other sacred book, contain even the name of the deity," that "Attrogs, a fruit common in Palestine, is supposed to have been 'the forbidden.' " and that "[t]he heathen poets are mentioned three times in the New Testament. Aratus in the seventeenth chapter of Acts—Menander in the fifteenth chapter of 1 Corinthians—also Epimenides." Perhaps the strangest item amidst this bizarre array of irrelevance is Poe's comment on the manliness of Venus: "Servius on Virgil's Æneid speaks of a bearded Venus. The poet Calvus in Macrobius speaks of Venus as masculine." *Text:* Pollin, Burton R., ed. *Pinakidia, the Brevities*. New York: Gordian Press, 1985, 1–172; *CWP,* XIV, 38–72. *Research: TPL,* 221–222, 233; *MNR,* 116.

Pinckney, Edward Coote. (1802–1828). Poet acquaintance of Poe's brother Henry and composer of "A Health," a lyric much admired by Poe. Discussing "A Health" in "The Poetic Principle," Poe called it "a poem . . . full of brilliancy and spirit. . . . It was the misfortune of Mr. Pinckney to have been born too far south. Had he been a New Englander, it is probable that he would have been ranked as the first of American lyricists." *Text: CWP,* XIV, 280–281; XVI, 143. *Research: TPL,* xxxvi, 328–329.

Pindar of Thebes. (522–448 B.C.). Greek lyric poet and writer of odes. Poe expressed no view of his verse but does call him a liar in "A Few Words about Brainard," repeating the charge in *Marginalia*: "Pindar says he 'saw' Archilochus, who died ages before the former was born." *Text: CWP,* X, 203; XI, 20, 174; XIII, 15; XIV, 53; XVI, 170.

Pinxit. Character mentioned in the short story "Loss of Breath." He is an illustrator who attends the hanging of the narrator and sketches the event.

The Pioneer. Short-lived periodical edited by James Russell Lowell. Poe's "The Tell-Tale Heart" was published here. *Research: TPL,* 394.

"The Pirate." Short story by Poe's brother, Henry Poe, published in *The North American* of 27 October 1827. The tale contains hints and echoes of Poe's love affair with Elmira Royster. *Research: PLL,* 34.

Pirouette, Mrs. Character in the short story "The Man That Was Used Up." She attends the soirée at Mrs. O'Trump's.

Pisistratus. (605–527 B.C.). Ancient Athenian politician. He is numbered by the devil in "Bon-Bon" among those without a soul and mentioned in *Pinakidia* for his collection of the *Iliad. Text: CWP,* II, 144; XIV, 66.

"The Pit and the Pendulum." Short story by Poe first published in *The Gift: A Christmas and New Year's Present, MDCCCXLIII* (1843) and revised for publication in *The Broadway Journal* of 17 May 1845. One of the great horror stories of the world, the tale has been variously interpreted. To early Poe critics, it depicted the quintessential gothic situation of a victim's architectural entrapment and imminent horrible death. To psychoanalytic interpreters, its symbolic content pointed to the great antagonisms and absences in Poe's sad life, the authoritarian paternal threat above and the maternal void below that compel the victim to desire death. The story has also been read as the ultimate existential allegory of an anguished consciousness confronted by nothingness in a senseless universe whose shape and direction can never be ascertained, a dramatization of John Paul Sartre's being and nothingness. Modern critics have tended to dismiss any possibility that the tale is Poe's brilliant condensation of a popular type of gothic novel, the monastic shocker, or tale of inquisitorial fiendishness and ingenious cruelty. If read as a reduction of this kind of horror novel, the victim simply becomes a desperate voice, not some emblem for the soul in political, psychological, or existential distress. Except for the salvational figure of General Lasalle, no characters in the story are named. The nameless victim is condemned by nameless Inquisitors in Toledo to a slow and timely death concocted by the dark fathers who consign the son to the black dungeon depths for a crime that is never disclosed. Stylistically, the tale is marked by a series of repetitive metronymic sentences whose cadence echoes the descending arc of the pendulum. "I was sick—sick unto the death with that long agony." "Down—steadily down it crept. Down—certainly, relentlessly down! Down—still unceasingly—still inevitably down!" Buried in the indeterminate depths, the victim is at first free to grope about; he attempts to measure his cell and to determine its shape. By chance or accident, he falls on the hem of his robe, this fortunate fall foreshadowing his miraculous delivery since his head "although seemingly at less elevation than the chin, touched nothing." The fall had saved him from a plunge into the pit. After "a sleep like that of death," he awakens to find himself tied face upward on a wooden frame. The cell is now illuminated and he can see and hear a huge pendulum overhead as it ''perceptibly descended'' toward his exposed breast. His strategy under stress is to lie absolutely still and permit hordes of rats to gnaw away the bandage or surcingle that fastens him to the frame. Just as he had luckily fallen before going over the brink of the pit, so now he liberates himself from the blade in a foreshadowing of his final deliverance. No sooner free from the ''hellish machine'' of time, he is alarmed to find the walls of his prison growing hot and contracting into a flattening diamond shape with the pit at the center. Like another victim of the diminishing circle, the narrator of ''A Descent into the Maelström,'' the Pit narrator saves himself by disregarding life and rushing to the ''deadly brink.'' At this fatal point, the redeeming hand of God in the person of General Lasalle stretches forth to catch the fainting, falling victim in an act of absurd salvation. But the improbable and some would say contrived but timely denouement is entirely consistent with the laws of survival operative in the closed space of the story. Whether or not the story can be understood as a portrait of the artist in extremis or a profound parable of the human condition, it cannot be denied that its ''theme is alienation; [its] plot survival; its character, anxiety personified'' (Stephen Mooney, ''Poe's Gothic Wasteland''). *Epigraph:* ''Impia tortorum longas hic turba furores/ Sanguinis innocui, non satiata, aluit./ Sospite nunc patria, fracto nunc funeris antro,/ Mors ubi dira fuit, vita salusque patent'' [Here the wicked mob, unappeased, long cherished a hatred of innocent blood. Now that the fatherland is saved, and the cave of death demolished; where grim death has been, life and health appear]. Poe's source, an inscription on the gates of a market erected on the site of the Jacobin Club House in Paris, is conjectural. *Text: MCW,* II, 678–700; *CWP,* V, 67–87. *Research:* Clark, David L. ''The Source of Poe's 'The Pit and the Pendulum.' '' *Modern Language Notes*, 44 (1929): 349–356; Mooney, Stephen L. ''Poe's Gothic Wasteland.'' *Sewanee Review*, 70 (1962): 261–283; Hirsch, David H. ''The Pit and the Apocalypse.'' *Sewanee Review*, 76 (1968): 632–652; Robinson, Douglas. ''Trapped in the Text: 'The Pit and the Pendulum.' '' *Journal of the Short Story in English*, 7 (1986): 63–75; Malloy, Jeanne M. ''Apocalyptic Imagery and the Fragmentation of the Psyche: 'The Pit and the Pendulum.' '' *Nineteenth Century Fiction*, 46 (1991): 82–95.

"Plato contra Atheos—Plato against the Atheists; or The Tenth Book of the Dialogue on Laws, Accompanied with Critical Notes, and Followed by Extended Dissertations on Some of the Main Points of the Platonic Philosophy and Theology Especially as Compared with the Holy Scriptures, by Tayler Lewis." Review of a philosophical study appearing in *The Broadway Journal* of 21 June 1845. Poe provides a synopsis of the Tenth Book and is critical of Lewis's anti-Baconian commentary as well as his failure to furnish a translation to accompany the Greek text. *Text: CWP,* XII, 162–166.

Plato of Athens. (428–348 B.C.). Greek philosopher whose work takes the form of dialogues with Socrates as the principal speaker. Poe's references to Plato and Platonic idealism are numerous. He was attracted to Platonic idealism's central tenet of the unity of the good, the true, and the beautiful and showed his knowledge of the dialogues and "the ingenuity of the Platonian intellect" in his review "Plato contra Atheos." Plato is also mentioned in "Morella" and "Bon-Bon." *See:* "Plato contra Atheos." *Text: CWP,* II, 27, 126, 131, 139, 142; IV, 204; V, 210; VIII, 203, 205; IX, 146; XII, 162–166; XIII, 212; XIV, 44; XV, 170; XVI, 163, 279. *Research: PJC,* 307–308; Soew, Gora. "From Plato to Coleridge: The Influence of the Platonic Tradition, on Poe's Critical Essays, Tales, and Poems." *Dissertation Abstracts International*, 47 (1986): 902A (Oklahoma State University).

"A Pleasant Peregrination through the Prettiest Parts of Pennsylvania. Performed by Peregrine Prolix." Review of travel letters appearing in *The Southern Literary Messenger* for June 1836. Poe approved of the "exceedingly witty-pedantic style" and the traveler's clever ramblings. "It is very certain that *Peregrine Prolix* is a misnomer, that his book is a very excellent thing, and that the Preface is not the worse part of it." *Text: CWP,* IX, 36–43.

Plutarch. (46–120). Ancient Greek biographer who wrote *Parallel Lives of the Noble Greeks and Romans*. Poe refers to "the luminousness of Plutarch" in *Marginalia* and in *Pinakidia* attributes "all the erroneous opinions on the subject of the old Greek comedy to Plutarch's comparison between Aristophanes and Menander." *Text: CWP,* XIV, 39, 62; XVI, 7.

Pluto. Feline character in the short story "The Black Cat." Pluto is the first cat owned by the narrator and is mutilated and hanged.

Poe, Amelia. (1809–?). Neilson Poe's twin sister and Poe's cousin. *Research: TPL,* xxxvii, 6.

Poe, Amelia Fitzgerald. (1833–1913). Neilson Poe's daughter. She gave her impressions of Poe to the biographers John Ingram and George Woodberry. *Research: TPL,* xxxviii.

Poe, David, Jr. (1784?-1811). Poe's father. He married Eliza Arnold Hopkins in April 1806, displeasing his father by marrying an actress. Drawn to the theater rather than the world of business, he joined Eliza on stage and tour but could not equal or even complement her theatrical talents. Deserting his wife and children, David Poe vanished in July 1811. On stage, he played a variety of melodramatic roles satisfactorily but was artistically inferior to Elizabeth. He lacked stage presence and frequently failed in major and minor Shakespearean roles. The couple often performed together in melodramatic crowd pleasers, as when they were seen in New York on 6 September 1809 in Matthew Gregory "Monk" Lewis's gothic play *The Castle Spectre*. No firm record of the place and date of David Poe's death exists. His unexplained disappearance left a permanent psychic scar on Poe's character. Biographer Jeffrey Meyers observes, "From his father Edgar inherited family pride, incongruous gentility, histrionic habits, a volatile temperament, sensitivity to criticism, self-pity, instability, a perverse self-destructive tendency and an Irish weakness for drink." *Research:* "A Note on David Poe as Actor." *Publisher's Weekly*, 21 June 1930, 3041–3042. *LTP*, 20, 70, 116, 163, 262; *TPL,* xxxvi-xxxvii, 3–5; *MNR,* 1, 3–7; *PLL,* 3–7, 189.

Poe, David, Sr. (1742–1816). Paternal grandfather of Edgar Allan Poe. During the American Revolution, he was assistant deputy quartermaster general for Baltimore. Thus, he was known as "General" Poe to friends and family. *Research: TPL,* xxxvi, 5–7.

Poe, Edgar Allan. (1809–1849). American poet, short story writer, journalist, and critic born 19 January 1809, at Carver Street near Boston Common, and died on 7 October 1849 at the Washington Hospital in Baltimore. For the special circumstances of Poe's life, death, and art, see the following studies. *See:* Bibliography; Collections; Correspondence and Correspondents; Cryptography; Military Service; Portraits and Daguerreotypes of Poe. *Research:* On alcohol and Poe: Bruce, Philip A. "Was Poe a Drunkard?" *South Atlantic Quarterly*, XI (January 1912): 3–21; Bittner, William. "Poe and the 'Invisible Demon.' " *Georgia Review*, 17 (1963): 134–138; Roth, Marty. "The Unquenchable Thirst of Edgar Allan Poe." *Dionysos: The Literature and Addiction TriQuarterly*, 3, no. 3 (1992): 3–16; Croghan, Melissa Irwin. "Alcohol and Art in Nineteenth Century American Fiction: Studies of Poe and Stowe." *Dissertation Abstracts International*, 53 (1993): 3905A–3906A (University of Pennsylvania). On cinematic treatments of Poe's tales and poems: Clarens, Carlos. *An Illustrated History of the Horror Films*. New York: G. P. Putnam, 1967. On the death of Poe: Stern, Philip Van Doren. "The Strange Death of Edgar Allan Poe." *Saturday Review of Literature*, 15 October 1949, 8–9, 28–30; Groves, B. Cowan. "The Death of Poe: The Case for Hypoglycemia." *RE: Artes Liberales*, 5, no. 2 (1979): 7–19; Bandy, W. T. "Two Notes on Poe's Death." *Poe Studies*, 14, no. 2 (1981): 32. On fictional portrayals of Poe: Dedmond, Francis B. "Poe in Drama, Fiction, and Poetry." *Bulletin of Bibliography*, 21 (1954): 107–114. On the international reading and reception of Poe: Carlson, Eric W. "Edgar Allan Poe in Romania, 1963–1983." *Bulletin of Bibliography*, 44 (1987): 75–81. On Poe's love affairs: Benton, Richard P. "Friends and Enemies: Women in the Life of Edgar Allan Poe." In *Myths and Reality: The Mysterious Mr. Poe*, ed. B. F. Fisher IV. Baltimore: Edgar Allan Poe Society, 1987, 1–25. On monuments, memorials, and Poe museums: Krainik, Clifford. "The Sir Moses Ezekiel Statue of Edgar Allan Poe in Baltimore." *Myths and Reality: The Mysterious Mr. Poe*, ed. B. F. Fisher IV. Baltimore: Edgar Allan Poe Society, 1987, 48–58. On music, dance, and Poe: Evans, Mary Garretson. *Music and Edgar Allan Poe: A Bibliographical Study*. Baltimore: Johns Hopkins Press, 1931. On parodies and satires of Poe: Clark, Lewis Gaylord. "Epitaph on a Modern 'Critic.' " *PLB,* 118. On Poe pedagogy and classroom presentation: Haviland, Thomas P. "Readings in Poe," *Emerson Society Quarterly*, 31 (2nd Q 1963): 32–34; Jacobs, Robert D. "Poe as a Literary Critic; A Teaching." *Emerson Society Quarterly*, 31 (2nd Q 1963): 7–11. On special and peculiar biographical facts: Garnett, R. S. "The Mystery of Edgar Allan Poe." *Blackwood's Magazine*, 227 (February 1930): 235–248. On translations of Poe: Bandy, William T. ''Were the Russians the First to Translate Poe?'' *American Literature*, 31 (1960): 479–480.

Poe, Eliza[beth] Arnold. (1787–1811). Poe's mother. She was a superb actress and thespian prodigy as a child. Only one portrait exists, an oval miniature. She excelled on the stage as a vocalist and in a variety of comic and tragic roles including the Shakespearean heroines Juliet, Cordelia, and Ophelia. She was married first to the actor Charles Hopkins, then to wayward actor David Poe, Jr. In destitute extremes, she died in Richmond of tuberculosis at the age of twenty-four on 8 December 1811. According to biographer Jeffrey Meyers, ''Poe inherited his mother's precocity, talent, imagination, dedication to art and courage in adversity as well as the indelible image of a beautiful dying young woman. He would also share her itinerant way of life, her impoverished existence and her dreary death.'' *Research: LTP*, 3, 5–9; Hubbell, Jay B. ''Poe's Mother, with a Note on John Allan.'' *William and Mary Quarterly*, 21 (1941): 250–254; Zimmerman, Elena. ''Tragic Ingenue: Memories of Elizabeth Arnold Poe.'' In *No Fairer Land: Studies in Southern Literature before 1900*, ed. J. Lasley Dameron, James W. Mathews, and James H. Justus. Troy, NY: Whitston, 1986, 124–143; *TPL*, xxxvii, 3–10; *MNR*, 1–9; *PLL*, 2–7; 60–61.

Poe, Elizabeth Cairnes. (1756–1835). Poe's paternal grandmother and wife of ''General'' Poe. She was taken in by her daughter, Maria Clemm. Her death in July 1835 intensified Maria Clemm's destitution because with her death an annuity ceased. *Research: TPL*, xx-xxi, 5–7.

Poe, George, Jr. (1778–1864). Son of Poe's paternal granduncle and first cousin of his father, David Poe, Jr. A prominent Baltimore banker and businessman, he avoided all contact with his erratic and constantly impoverished cousin. He was approached by David Poe for financial assistance in February 1809, a request that he apparently denied. *Research: MNR*, 6.

Poe, George, Sr. (1744–1823). Poe's paternal grand uncle. *See:* Clemm, Harriet Poe. *Research: TPL*, xxxvii.

Poe, Harriet. (1785–1815). First wife of William Clemm, Jr. and Maria Clemm's first cousin. *See:* Clemm, Harriet Poe.

Poe, James Mosher. (1812–1885). Poe's cousin, the son of Jacob and Bridget Poe. *Research: TPL*, xxxvii.

Poe, Josephine Emily Clemm. (1808–1889). She was the wife of Neilson Poe and his first cousin. A half sister of Virginia Clemm Poe. *Research: TPL*, xxxviii.

Poe, Neilson. (1809–1884). Poe's second cousin. Poe referred to him as his ''bitterest enemy'' and regarded him as a rival for Virginia Clemm's affection. At various times, he was a journalist, publisher, editor, and lawyer and associated with the *Baltimore Chronicle*. He did attend Poe's funeral on 8 October 1849 and the Poe memorial tribute of 17 November 1875. *See:* Poe, Josephine Emily Clemm. *Research: PLL,* 43, 72, 109, 186, 252.

"Poe on Headley and Channing." Two posthumously published samples of Poe's savage reviewing style appearing in *The Southern Literary Messenger* for October 1850. *See:* ''Our Amateur Poets, No. III. William Ellery Channing''; ''The Sacred Mountains by T. J. Headley.'' *Text: CWP,* XIII, 202–209.

Poe, Rosalie. (1810–1874). Poe's sister. She was adopted by and lived with the Mackenzies of Baltimore. Poe had only occasional contact with her throughout his lifetime, mainly during his Richmond visits. No letters between Poe and Rosalie survive. *Research:* Miller, John Carl. ''Rosalie Poe Begs for Help.'' *BPB*, 58–64; *TPL,* xxxvii-xxxix, 61–62, 749–750, 841–842.

Poe, Virginia Eliza Clemm. (1822–1847). Poe's sickly wife and also his first cousin. They were married in Richmond on 16 May 1836. Virginia died of tubercular consumption at the Fordham cottage on 30 January 1847. Poe's letter to Virginia of 12 June 1846 is the single surviving letter. *Research: LTP*, 203–206, 579–581; Rein, David M. ''Poe and Virginia Clemm.'' *Bucknell Review*, 7 (1958): 207–216; *TPL,* xx-xxi, 207–208, 244–245, 456–457, 672–678; *MNR,* 300–304, *PLL,* 207–208.

Poe, William. (1755–1804). Poe's granduncle and brother of ''General'' Poe. His son, William Poe (1802–?), corresponded with Poe. *Research: TPL,* xxxix, 165–166.

Poe, William Henry Leonard. (1807–1831). ''Henry'' Poe was the elder brother of Edgar Allan Poe. After his mother's death, he was raised by his grandparents, David Poe, Sr., and Elizabeth Cairnes Poe. He wrote sentimental verse and short fiction, made sea voyages, corresponded with his brother, and died on 1 August 1831 probably of tuberculosis. His character has been connected with Arthur Gordon Pym's friend, Augustus Barnard, in *The Narrative of Arthur Gordon Pym.* There are temperamental resemblances between the brothers. Henry was ''a thin, dark eyed young man who . . . shared Edgar's dreamy Romanticism, morbid melancholy, wild streak and weakness for liquor'' but lacked his brother's ''compelling genius.'' *See:* ''The Pirate.'' *Research:* Allen, Hervey, and Thomas Ollive Mabbott. *Poe's Brother: The Poetry of William Henry Leonard Poe.* New York: Doran, 1926; *TPL,* xxxviii.

Poems by Edgar A. Poe. Poe's third book of verse dedicated to ''The U.S. Corps of Cadets'' and published by Elam Bliss of New York in April 1831. The poems in the work are: ''Romance,'' ''To Helen,'' ''The Doomed City,'' ''Fairy Land,'' ''Irene,'' ''A Pæan,'' The Valley Nis,'' ''Al Aaraaf,'' and ''Tamerlane.'' Poe received $170 in payment, with much of the money raised by seventy-five cent subscriptions of the cadets. *Research:* Campbell, Killis. ''Bibliographical Note.'' In *Poems, by Edgar Allan Poe. Reproduced from the edition of 1831. Facsimile Text Society Number 35.* New York: Columbia University Press, 1936, 1–8; Reilly, John E. ''Poe's 'Introduction, XXXI-XXXIV.' '' *Explicator,* 20 (September 1961): item 8.

"Poems. By Frances S. Osgood." Review appearing in *The Broadway Journal* of 13 December 1845. Poe credits her verse with ''[a] happy refinement—an exquisite instinct of the pure—the delicate—the graceful—[which] gives a charm inexpressible to everything which flows from her pen.'' He quotes in full ''The Spirit of Poetry,'' ''She Loves Him Yet,'' ''Aspirations,'' ''Lenore,'' and ''A Song'' as examples of her concentrated and sustained sublimity. A lengthened version of the review appeared in *Godey's Lady's Book* for March 1846. *Text: CWP,* XIII, 17–26, 105–125, 188–193. *Research: TPL,* 604–606.

"Poems by James Russell Lowell." Review of Lowell's verse appearing in *Graham's Magazine* for March 1844. Although Poe pointed out that ''Mr. Lowell is, in some measure, infected with the poetical conventionalities of the day,'' he admired many of the poems in the collection and singled out ''Legend of Brittany'' as a sublime example of Lowell's poetical powers. ''The defects observable in the 'Legend of Brittany' are, chiefly, consequent upon the error of *didacticism.*'' *Text: CWP,* XI, 243–249. *Research: PJC,* 396–397.

"Poems—by Miss H. F. Gould." Review of the third edition of her poems appearing in *The Southern Literary Messenger* for January 1836. Although Poe criticizes her ''flippancy of the metre,'' he generally approves of her poetic skill and cites her poem ''The Dying Storm'' as a forceful example of her command of the muse. *Text: CWP,* VIII, 135–138. *Research: PJC,* 104.

"Poems, by William Cullen Bryant." (1). Review of Bryant's verse published in *The Southern Literary Messenger* for January 1835. Poe salutes his ''great intellectual power,'' his ''deep and sacred communings with the world of poetry,'' and regrets that Bryant's ''muse has languished probably for want of that due encouragement, which to our shame as a nation be it spoken, has never been awarded to that department of native literature.'' *Text: CWP,* VIII, 1–2. *Research: PJC,* 192–208.

"Poems by William Cullen Bryant." (2). Review of the fourth edition of Bryant's poems appearing in *The Southern Literary Messenger* for January 1837.

Poe comments extensively on Bryant's poem ''The Ages,'' concentrating on the poem's metrics, and concludes the long review with an encomium to Bryant. ''In regard to his proper rank among American poets there should be no question whatever. Few—at least few who are fairly before the public, have more than shallow claims to a rivalry with the author of Thanatopsis.'' *Text:* CWP, IX, 268–305. *Research: PJC,* 192–208, 388–389.

"Poems. By William W.[ilberforce] Lord." A scathing review of a collection of poems appearing in *The Broadway Journal* of 24 May 1845. Poe chose a number of Lord's poems for exuberant tomahawking, accusing him of disfigurations of language, metrical stupidity, and outright plagiarism. ''The fact is, the only remarkable things about Mr. Lord's compositions are their remarkable conceit, ignorance, impudence, platitude, stupidity, and bombast.'' *Text: CWP,* XII, 146–161.

"The Poems of Alfred Tennyson." Review of Tennyson's verses appearing in *Graham's Magazine* for September 1842. Poe is appreciative of Tennyson, but not lavishly so. Although he ''frequently exhibits a rare sense of the beautiful,'' Poe does not see in his verse ''proofs of an original mind. . . . That Tennyson has genius cannot be denied, but his works have too little of many qualities, especially of manliness, to be long popular.'' *Text: CWP,* XI, 127–131; *PJC,* 362–364, 388–390.

"Poems of John G. C. Brainard." Collection of poems reviewed in *Graham's Magazine* for February 1842. *See:* ''A Few Words About Brainard.''

"Poems; Translated and Original. By Mrs. E. F. Ellet." Review of her poetry appearing in *The Southern Literary Messenger* for January 1836. Poe comments on her abilities as translator since many of the poems in the collection were her renderings of Schiller, Lamartine, and others. ''Of the original poems, which form the greater part of the volume, we have hardly been able to form an opinion, during the cursory perusal we have given them. Some of them have merit.'' *Text: CWP,* VIII, 122–142. *Research: PJC,* 67.

"Poe's Addenda to Eureka." *See: Eureka.*

"The Poetic Principle." Critical statement concerning Poe's poetics and theory of verse and, together with ''The Rationale of Verse'' and ''The Philosophy of Composition,'' a central text in Poe's criticism. Poe used the title for several lectures on 20 December 1848 in Providence, 17 and 24 August 1849 in Richmond, and 14 September in Norfolk. He once lost this lecture and other documents in a Philadelphia train station in June 1849. The critical manifesto appeared posthumously in the *Home Journal* of 31 August 1850 and *Sartain's Union Magazine* for October 1850. The lecture/critical essay includes illustrative poems by Longfellow, Bryant, Shelley, Willis, Thomas Moore, Byron, Hood, and Tennyson. Poe denounces the "epic mania" of lengthiness and wordiness in poetry and rejects the notion that poetry must serve a moral end, referring to the ethical motive in poetry as "the heresy of *The Didactic*." He insists that the sole raison d'être of the poem ought to be its aesthetic essence, for poetry's only subject and object ought to be "*The Rhythmical Creation of Beauty*. Its sole arbiter is Taste. With the Intellect or with the Conscience it has only collateral relations. Unless incidentally, it has no concern whatever either with Duty or with Truth." He cites William Cullen Bryant's lyric "June" and the final song from Tennyson's "The Princess" as examples of the attainment of "Supernal Beauty" and "an elevating excitement of the Soul." Poe's poetic principle, then, rests solely on an aesthetic perception of the artist as maker of beautiful things whose existence is justified by the perfection of their beauty. This late essay is a fuller expression of the young Poe's assertion in the preface to *Tamerlane*, "With me poetry has not been a purpose, but a passion; and the passion should be held in reverence." *Text: CWP,* XIV, 266–292. *Research:* Thorpe, Dwayne. "The Limits of Flight: Poe and the Poetic Principle." *Topic* (Washington and Jefferson College), 16, no. 30 (1976): 68–80; Hovey, Kenneth Allan. "Critical Provincialism: Poe's Poetic Principle in Antebellum Context." *American Quarterly*, 39 (1987): 341–354.

"Poetical Remains of the Late Lucretia Maria Davidson. Collected and Arranged by Her Mother, with a Biography by Miss Sedgwick." Review of a biographical obituary appearing in *Graham's Magazine* for December 1841. Poe had previously reviewed Irving's memorial biography of her sister, Margaret Miller Davidson. "Margaret, we think, has left the better poems—certainly the more precocious; while Lucretia evinces more unequivocally the soul of the poet." *See:* "The Biography and Poetical Remains of the Late Margaret Miller Davidson." *Text: CWP,* X, 221–226. *Research: PJC,* 267–268.

"Poetical Writings of Mrs. Elizabeth Oakes Smith." A generous review of the poet better known as "Mrs. Seba Smith" appearing in *The Broadway Journal* of 23 August 1845 and printed again in *Godey's Lady's Book* for December 1845. Poe discusses the merits and flaws of three poems, "The Sinless Child," "The Acorn," and "The Water," finding this last poem to be the object of literary theft by Longfellow in his "Rain in Summer." *Text: CWP,* XII, 228–233; XIII, 78–93. *Research: PJC,* 263.

"Poetry." This unpublished poem was one of Poe's first poems discovered by Hervey Allen among the papers of Ellis and Allan in the Library of Congress. The two-line poem was reprinted by Mabbott. "Last Night, with many cares and toils oppress'd,/ Weary, I laid me on a couch to rest." *Text: MCW,* I, 5–6.

"Poetry of America." Lecture delivered by Poe on 21 November 1843. He attacked the selective content of Griswold's anthology *The Poets and Poetry of America*. *Research: TPL,* 441.

"The Poetry of Life. By Sarah Stickney." Review of her studies of poetry appearing in *The Southern Literary Messenger* for January 1836. Poe's opinion is mixed since he feels that she has "a keen relish for the minor forms of poetic excellence" but is "insufficiently alive to the *delicacies* of the beautiful—unable fully to appreciate the *energies* of the sublime. . . . Miss Stickney should immediately burn her copy of Shelley—it is to her capacities a sealed book." *Text: CWP,* VIII, 173–177.

"The Poetry of Rufus Dawes—A Retrospective Criticism." Negative and scathing review of a Poe foe published in *Graham's Magazine* for October 1842. "His poems have not been condemned, only because they have never been read." Poe dismantles Dawes's "Geraldine," "Athenia of Damascus," and *Miscellaneous Poems*, writing of "Geraldine" that "it is a mere mass of irrevelevancy, amid the mad farrago of which we detect with difficulty even the faintest vestige of a narrative, and where the continuous lapse from impertinence to impertinence is seldom justified by any shadow of appositiveness or even of the commonest relation." *Text: CWP,* XI, 131–147. *Research: PJC,* 331–333.

"The Poets and Poetry of America. With an Historical Introduction." Review of the third edition of Griswold's anthology appearing in the Philadelphia *Saturday Museum* of 28 January 1843. In the *Collected Works*, James Harrison assigned this review to Poe, but it was actually written by Henry B. Hirst. As the excoriating style of the review shows, Hirst apparently tried to emulate Poe's aptitude with the literary tomahawk. Poets omitted by Griswold should be "gratified at their non-appearance in the volume before us, for if ever such a thing as literary ruin existed, or exists, nine-tenths of the *Poets* (!) of America are ruined forever by the praise of Mr. Griswold!" *See:* "Mr. Griswold and the Poets." *Text: CWP,* XI, 220–243. *Research: TPL,* 395.

"The Poets and Poetry of America, with an Historical Introduction. By Rufus Wilmot Griswold." Laudatory review of a one-volume anthology of American poetry compiled by Rufus Wilmot Griswold and appearing in *Graham's Magazine* for June 1842. Poe judged it "the best Collection of American Poets that has yet been made . . . superior to any former collection of the American Poets, whether we regard its size, its completeness, or the taste displayed in the selections." Poe singled out two minor flaws: Griswold's undue favoritism in the selections toward the New England writers; his inclusion of too few poems by younger poets, especially James Russell Lowell and Oliver Wendell Holmes. The short story "Never Bet the Devil Your Head," contains a less-than-complimentary reference to Griswold's collection. *See:* "Mr. Griswold and the Poets." *Text: CWP,* XI, 124–126, 153–156, 220–243. *Research: PJC,* 330–331.

Poitiaux, Catherine Elizabeth. Poe's childhood companion and Frances Allan's godchild. She left a memorial poem, "Lines on the Death of Edgar A. Poe," based on her memories of his visit to her home in August 1849. *Research: TPL,* xxxix, 829–830.

Politian. Unfinished drama by Poe published in *The Southern Literary Messenger* for December 1835 and January 1836 and in *The Raven and Other Poems* in 1845. Written in stilted blank verse, the play is based on the facts of the Beauchamp-Sharp murder case. Poe's only play also has literary roots in the Elizabethan and Jacobean revenge tragedies of Webster, Chapman, Tourneur, and Ford. The play is a rhetorical and theatrical failure throughout and one of the least interesting works in the Poe canon. Even T. O. Mabbott's modern edition of 1923 did little to raise its esteem with Poe scholars. In Poe's adaptation of the Beauchamp-Sharp case, the characters are lifeless facsimiles of a typical revenge tragedy cast. The seducer, Castiglione, his victim, the orphaned ward of his father, Lalage, and Politian, the Earl of Leicester, are transcriptions of the principals in the murder case. When Castiglione becomes engaged to his cousin Alessandra after seducing Lalage, she swears revenge and employs Politian, newly come to Rome from England, as the the instrument of retribution. Although he loves Lalage, Politian is unable to carry out her murderous request and retires to the Colosseum to meditate. Lalage joins him amidst the ruins and urges him to keep his promise even as Castiglione prepares to marry Alessandra. The drama aborts as Politian departs apparently to perform the revenge. The text of the play includes the poem "The Coliseum." *See:* Beauchamp-Sharp Murder Case. *Text: MCW,* I, 241–298; *CWP,* VII, 59–79. *Research:* Jackson, David K. "Prose Run Mad: An Early Criticism of Poe's Politian." In *Poe and His Times: The Artist and His Milieu,* ed. B. F. Fisher IV. Baltimore: Edgar Allan Poe Society, 1990, 88–93; *PLL,* 76–77.

Poliziano, Angelo Ambrogino. (1454–1494). Italian lyric poet. One of his love stanzas is quoted in *Pinakidia.* Poe anglicized the name to become the "Politian" of his unfinished tragedy. *Text: CWP,* II, 120; XIV, 65.

Pollin, Burton. (1916–). An important and industrious twentieth-century Poe scholar. Many of his articles deal with contemporary reviews of Poe's writings, with the identification of unsigned material, and with Poe's variegated sources. Pollin's computer-generated *Dictionary of Names and Titles in Poe's Collected Works* (1968) is a valuable concordance and indispensable finding list. His *Discoveries in Poe* studies Poe's literary relationship with Victor Hugo, Mary Shelley, and William Godwin, and the important reference work *Images of Poe's*

Works: A Comprehensive Descriptive Catalogue of Illustrations is the best guide to pictorial renditions of the tales and poems.

Polybius. (204–122 B.C.). Greek historian who wrote Roman history. Like so many other ancient authors, he appears on the devil's menu in "Bon-Bon." *Text: CWP,* II, 142.

Polyglott, Delphinus. Character in the short story "Lionizing." He is one of the guests at the Prince of Wales's literary banquet and informs the other guests of "what had become of the eighty-three lost tragedies of Æschylus."

Pompey. (1). Character in the short stories "A Predicament" and "How to Write a Blackwood Article." He is Signora Psyche Zenobia's negro servant. He is "three feet in height."

Pompey. (2). Canine character in the short story "The Business Man." He is Peter Proffit's dog.

Pompey. (3). Character in the short story "The Man That Was Used Up." He is Brigadier General John A.B.C. Smith's negro valet and assists in putting the general together.

Pompey. [Gnæus Pompeius]. (106–48 B.C.). Roman general and triumvir with Caesar and Crassus in the first triumvirate. He is mentioned in "A Tale of Jerusalem" as "the Roman Pompey who is now impiously besieging the city of the Most High." *Text: CWP,* II, 214–215, 217.

Ponnonner, Doctor. Character in the short story "Some Words with a Mummy." Proposes to unravel the mummy and is kicked out of the window by the reanimated remains.

Ponto. Canine character in the short story "Landor's Cottage." He shakes paws with Mr. Landor's guardian mastiff.

Pope, Alexander. (1688–1744). English poet and satirist. Like Pope, Poe savored literary controversy and maintained running battles with a large group of adversaries. Pope is mentioned in "The Quacks of Helicon." *Pinakidia*, "The Rationale of Verse," and *Marginalia*. Some readers have noted a strong parallel between the concluding line of Pope's *Dunciad* and the final sentence of "The Masque of the Red Death." Pope's *Dunciad*: "Thy hand, great Anarch! lets the curtain fall;/ And universal Darkness buries All." "The Masque": "And Darkness and Decay and the Red Death held illimitable dominion over all." *Text: CWP,* IX, 273–274; X, 68, 141, 183; XIV, 47, 56, 58, 223, 224, 223; XVI, 32, 75–76, 154. *Research: PLB,* 75, 148; *LET,* I, 78; *PJC,* 156, 257; *PLL,* 135.

Porphyry. (272–305). Greek scholar and philosopher of neoplatonism. In *Pinakidia*, Poe paraphrased his monotheistic view that all earth deities and demigods were one in the same. "Vesta, Rhea, Ceres, Themis, Priapus, Proserpina, Bacchus, Attis, Adonis, Silenus and the Satyrs [were] one in the same." *Text: CWP,* II, 38; XIV, 51.

Portraits and Daguerreotypes of Poe. Several daguerreotypes or photographs, watercolor, and oil paintings of Poe were taken or drawn at different stages of his life. The several portraits made of Poe depict a variety of facial appearances. The most important and most frequently seen portraits and daguerreotypes of Poe are a watercolor miniature of Poe at thirty-seven by John A. McDougall, the 1845 oil portrait by Samuel S. Osgood, several daguerreotypes taken in Providence in 1848 known as the "Ultima Thule" and "Whitman" daguerreotypes, a daguerreotype taken in Lowell, Massachusetts, the "Stella" daguerreotype showing Poe in Napoleonic pose, the "Annie" daguerreotype with Poe wearing a faint sneer, the "Pratt" daguerreotype of September 1849, a watercolor by A. C. Smith, and a steel engraving by Welch & Walter made to accompany Lowell's article on Poe in *Graham's Magazine*. *See:* Manchester, Edwin. *Research:* Uchida, Ichigoro. "A Study on the Portraits and Daguerreotypes of Edgar Allan Poe." In *Collected Essays by the Members of the Faculty.* (Kyoritsu Women's Junior College) (1971): 19–38; Uchida, Ichigoro. "The Daguerreotypes of Edgar Allan Poe Taken in New England in 1848." *Collected Essays by the Members of the Faculty* (Kyoritsu Women's Junior College), 25 (1982): 1–15; Uchida, Ichigoro. "Edgar Allan Poe's Portraits in His Philadelphia Days, 1838–1844." *Collected Essays by the Members of the Faculty* (Kyoritsu Women's Junior College), 29 (1986): 1–14; Ichigoro, Uchida. "The Two Portraits of Edgar Allan Poe by Gabriel Harrison." *Collected Essays by the Members of the Faculty* (Kyoritsu Women's Junior College), 31 (1988): 33–46; Deas, Michael. *The Portraits and Daguerreotypes of Edgar Allan Poe.* Charlottesville: Virginia University Press, 1989; *PLL,* 166–167; 232–233.

"Posthumous Memoirs of His Own Time by Sir N.W. Wraxall." Review of a book on the Regency and George IV appearing in *The Southern Literary Messenger* for October 1836. "Altogether, these 'Posthumous Memoirs' afford a rich fund of entertainment—and in especial to the lovers of political gossip we most heartily recommend their perusal." *Text: CWP,* IX, 174–184.

"The Posthumous Papers of the Pickwick Club: Containing a Faithful Record of the Perambulations, Perils, Travels, Adventures, and Sporting Transactions of the Corresponding Members." Review of Dickens's novel appearing in *The Southern Literary Messenger* for November 1836. "The author possesses nearly every desirable quality in a writer of fiction. . . . We can only express our opinion that his general powers as a prose writer are equalled by few." *Text: CWP,* IX, 205. *Research: PJC,* 269.

Pound, Ezra. (1885–1972). American poet and translator. In several essays on Poe, Pound challenged the exaltation of Poe by Mallarmé and Baudelaire and criticized the absurdity of the Poe cult by dismantling Mallarmé's translation of "The Raven" ("et le corbeau dit jamais plus"). "After Whitman," Pound conceded, Poe was "the best [poet] America has produced. Personally I think an ambition to write as well as Poe is a low one." *Research:* Pound, Ezra. "The Renaissance." In *Literary Essays*, introduction by T. S. Eliot. Norfolk, CT: New Directions, 1954, 218; *PLL,* 275–276.

Power, Anna Marsh. Sarah Helen Whitman's strong-willed mother. She vehemently opposed her daughter's engagement to Poe. *Research: TPL,* xlviii, 766–768.

"The Power of Words." Short story by Poe first published in the *Democratic Review* for June 1845 and again in *The Broadway Journal* of 25 October 1845. The form of the story is a philosophic dialogue between the two "angelic intelligences," Agathos (from Agathon, a tragic poet of ancient Athens) and Oinos. Oinos has newly arrived in the heavens from "the fair earth which lately perished" and queries the wise Agathos on the nature of matter, knowledge, and God's creative role in uniting matter with spirit and endowing it with life force. While they converse, the two undertake a cosmic voyage with Agathos instructing Oinos as they rise to worlds as yet uncreated. "We will leave to the left the loud harmony of the Pleiades, and swoop outward from the throne into the starry meadows beyond Orion." To Oinos's inquiry, " 'Then all motion, of whatever nature, creates?' " Agathos speaks lyrically of the divine power of words as the primum mobile of all things. Some 300 years before, Agathos had spoken into existence or endowed with original form the "wild star" at which the cosmic voyagers have arrived at the conclusion of the dialogue. The mysticism of the dialogue recalls Blake's lines "To see the world in a grain of sand, or heaven in a wild flower" and anticipates ideas expressed in *Eureka* about the poet as maker of universes through his divine power of words. *Text: MCW,* III, 1210–1217; *CWP,* VI, 139–144. *Research:* Michael, John. "Narration and Reflection: The Search for Grounds in Poe's 'The Power of Words' and 'The Domain of Arnheim.' " *Arizona Quarterly*, 45 (1989): 1–22.

"Powhatan: A Metrical Romance in Seven Cantos. By Seba Smith." Review of a narrative poem appearing in *Graham's Magazine* for July 1841. Poe's denunciation is scorching and severe: "In truth, a more absurdly flat affair—for flat is the only epithet which applies in this case—was never before paraded to the world with so grotesque an air of bombast and assumption." *Text: CWP,* X, 162–167. *Research: PJC,* 263.

Pratt, Captain. Character in the short story "Three Sundays in a Week." He is one of the "naval acquaintances" of Kate.

"A Predicament." Short story first published under the title ''The Scythe of Time'' in the Baltimore *American Museum* for November 1838. The story was published as ''A Predicament'' in the *Broadway Journal* of 12 July 1845. Horror and hilarity are combined to achieve gruesome buffoonery in this parody of lethal entrapment and extravagant victimization. The menace of the clock and mutilation by the force of time, themes that are portrayed seriously in ''The Pit and the Pendulum'' and ''The Masque of the Red Death,'' are treated comically in the gradual guillotining of the victim in ''A Predicament.'' The narrator, Signora Psyche Zenobia, and her traveling companions, the three-foot-high negro Pompey and her poodle Diana, arrive in the goodly city of Edina (Edinburgh). The compulsion of Signora Psyche Zenobia's life is the climbing of towers, turrets, steeples, pinnacles—architectural apexes of any type. Noticing a ''Gothic cathedral—vast, venerable, and with a tall steeple which towered into the sky,'' she yields to her toweromania, ''the uncontrollable desire to ascend the giddy pinnacle.'' Reaching the belfry, the toweromaniac stands on the shoulders of Pompey and extends her head out of the convenient aperture of the great clock face to obtain a superior view of the inferior world below. But the Signora should have watched the time (5:25 in the afternoon) because doing so would have freed her from the predicament that now arises, ''for the huge, glittering, scimitar-like minute hand of the clock had, in the course of its hourly revolution, descended upon my neck. There was, I knew, not a second to be lost.'' Now follows a calm, analytic, and ''disembodied'' description of her own gradual decapitation. To pass the time, she recites from Cervantes, Ariosto, and Schiller, watches one of her dislodged eyes stare up at her from the gutter below, and continues to talk on even after the head has been separated from the body since this occasion provides an opportunity for discoursing on the dichotomy of body and soul. The prisoner in ''The Pit and the Pendulum'' escapes the descending blade at the last moment, but no such lucky salvation will extricate Signora Psyche Zenobia from her curious chronometric fate. The headless torso's final words, ''What now remains for the unhappy Signora Psyche Zenobia?—Alas nothing! I have done,'' suggest Poe's brilliant play on the headless babbler in a private tower of babble. *Text: MCW,* II, 347–357; *CWP,* II, 283–295. *Research:* Mooney, Stephen LeRoy. ''The Comic in Poe's Fiction.'' *American Literature*, 33 (1962): 433–441; Lewis, Paul. ''Laughing at Fear: Two Versions of the Mock Gothic.'' *Studies in Short Fiction*, 15 (1978): 411–414.

"A Prediction." Unpublished cosmological speculation included by Harrison and Mabbott in their editions of Poe's works. The prediction deals with the origins of the solar system and its eventual contraction and collapse. Poe was excited by the discovery of the planet Neptune in 1846 and offered his ''opinion as to the origin of the satellites . . . that these came, not from vapor sent off in volcanic burnings and by simple diffusion under the solar rays, but from rings of it which were left in the inter-planetary spaces, after the precipitation of the primaries.'' *Text: MCW,* III, 1319–1323; *CWP,* XVI, 337–339.

"Preface and Introduction to 'The Conchologist's First Book by Thomas Wyatt.' " Poe's contribution to the ancillary matter of this scientific text published in April 1839 defines *conchologist* and argues the need for a close study of the field. "So far from admitting the venerable error even now partially existing to the discredit of Conchology, we should not hesitate to acknowledge, that while few branches of Natural History are more direct, *very few* are of more adventitious importance." *Text: See: The Conchologist's First Book. Text: CWP,* XIV, 95–100.

"Preface [to *Tamerlane and Other Poems*]." Foreword to Poe's first collection of poetry. "The greater part of the poems which compose this little volume, were written in the year 1821–2, when the author had not completed his fourteenth year." *See: Tamerlane and Other Poems. Research: TPL,* 81.

The Prefect of Police. Character mentioned in the short story "The Murders in the Rue Morgue." He is embarrassed by Dupin's simian solution to the murders and suggests that Dupin should mind his own business.

"The Premature Burial." Short story first published in the Philadelphia *Dollar Newspaper* of 31 July 1844 and reprinted in *The Broadway Journal* of 14 June 1845. The story commences with several authentic case studies of live burial whereby "the lethargy which had been mistaken for death" had resulted in this horrible situation. The final case study is the personal history of the narrator whose cataleptic trance and "condition of semi-syncope" are mistaken for death and cause his premature burial. In spite of the precautions he has taken to avoid this hideous predicament including the remodeling of the family vault to permit escape, he awakens from his trance to find that they "had buried me as a dog—nailed up in some common coffin—and thrust deep, deep, and forever, into some ordinary and nameless grave." The powerful and tactile horror of the story is undermined by the meretricious ending. The narrator had been squeezed into a tight berth aboard a sloop on the James River and only imagined the burial. Having nearly frightened himself to death, the narrator uses the experience to become a new man. "I dismissed forever my charnal apprehensions, and with them vanished the cataleptic disorder, of which, perhaps, they had been less the consequence than the cause." *Text: MCW,* III, 953–972; *CWP,* V, 255–273. *Research:* Bandy, W. T. "A Source of Poe's 'The Premature Burial.' " *American Literature*, 19 (1947): 167–168; Kennedy, J. Gerald. "Poe and Magazine Writing on Premature Burial." *Studies in the American Renaissance*, (1977): 165–178; Engel, Leonard W. "Claustrophobia, the Gothic Enclosure, and Poe." *Clues*, 10 (1989): 107–117.

Presbyterian Cemetery, Baltimore. Poe was interred here on 8 October 1849. *Research: TPL,* 847–848.

Prescott, W.[illiam] H.[ickling]. (1796–1859). American historian and author of *The History of the Conquest of Mexico* and *The History of the Conquest of Peru.* In his review of von Raumer's *America and the American People*, Poe uses Prescott as a prime example of the underpaid writer exploited by American publishers. *Text: CWP,* XIII, 15; XIV, 180. *Research: TPL,* 562, 605.

The President of Fum-Fudge University. Character in the short story ''Lionizing.'' He is one of the guests at the Prince of Wales's literary dinner party.

Preston, John L. T. (?–1890). Fellow student with Poe at Clarke's school. His recollection of young Poe discloses his impulsiveness and rather reckless athletic ability in running, swimming, and boxing. His father, Colonel James Patton Preston (1774–1843), recommended Poe for appointment to the United States Military Academy. *Research: TPL,* xxxix.

Preston, Mr. Character in the short story ''William Wilson.'' William Wilson meets Glendinning in Mr. Preston's Oxford chambers.

Price, Richard. (1723–1791). English clergyman and ardent defender of the perfectibility of humankind. The human-perfectibility man at the Prince of Wales's banquet in ''Lionizing'' quotes Price. *Text: CWP,* II, 38; IV, 259.

Priestley, Joseph. (1733–1804). English chemist and moral philosopher who advocated the happiness of the majority. He is quoted by the human-perfectibility man at the Prince of Wales's banquet in ''Lionizing.'' *Text: CWP,* II, 38; IV, 259.

Proffit, Peter. Character in the short story ''The Business Man,'' apparently the name of the businessman.

"The Prose Works of John Milton, with a Biographical Introduction by Rufus Wilmot Griswold." Review of Griswold's edition of Milton's prose appearing in *The Broadway Journal* of 27 September 1845. Poe praised the editing of Griswold in bringing out the first American edition of Milton's works but found the biographical introduction slightly marred by Griswold's biases. ''Dr. Griswold's Introduction is, nevertheless, well written, and well adapted to its purposes. At points, however, it may be thought extravagant or dogmatic. We have no patience with the initial sneer at Bacon, as 'the meanest of mankind.' '' *Text: CWP,* XII, 244–247. *Research: PJC,* 156, 169, 170.

"Prospects of the Drama.—Mrs. Mowatt's Comedy." A continuation of Poe's review of her play *Fashion* appearing in *The Broadway Journal* of 5 April 1845. Poe thought that *Fashion* could stand as an elevating example of American dramatic art. ''We are delighted to find, in the reception of Mrs. Mowatt's comedy, the clearest indications of a revival of the American drama. . . . As an absolutely necessary condition of its existence this play may usher in a thorough remodification of the theatrical *physique*.'' *See:* ''The New Comedy by Mrs. Mowatt.'' *Text: CWP,* XII, 124–129. *Research: PJC,* 377–378.

Prospero, Prince. Character in the short story ''The Masque of the Red Death.'' He provides his courtiers with a gala masked ball during the plague but cannot keep death off his guest list.

Protogenes. (?–300 B.C.). Ancient Greek painter. In *Marginalia*, Poe mentions Apelles's insult that his painting was '' 'too natural.' '' *Text:* CWP, XVI, 173.

Proust, Marcel. (1871–1922). French novelist and author of *Remembrance of Things Past.* As a devoted reader of Poe, he showed an appreciation for the aesthetic perspective in the Parisian tales ''The Purloined Letter'' and ''The Murders in the Rue Morgue.'' Poe sought to arrive at the beautiful through evocation and an elimination of moral motives in his art. *Research:* Stone, Edward. ''The Paving Stones of Paris: Psychometry from Poe to Proust.'' *American Quarterly,* 5, no. 2 (1953): 121–131; Fraisse, Luc. ''Méthode de composition: Marcel Proust Lecteur d'Edgar Poe.'' *Revue des Lettres Modernes,* 1067–1072 (1992): 35–82.

Psalemoun. Character mentioned in *The Narrative of Arthur Gordon Pym.*

Psyche. Character in the poem ''Ulalume.'' She accompanies the narrator as he roams in the ''ghoul-haunted woodland of Weir.''

"The Psyche Zenobia." Original title of the short story ''How to Write a Blackwood Article.'' *See:* ''How to Write a Blackwood Article.''

Ptolemy. [Ptolemy Chennos of Hephestion]. (second century A.D.). Greek astronomer, mathematician, and geographer. He compiled the *Almagest.* His epicyclic theory of the lunar month is mentioned in *Marginalia.* His name is also referred to by the narrator of ''Berenice'' in connection with the lethal ''touch of the flower called Asphodel.'' *Text: CWP,* II, 21; XVI, 187–188.

Puckle, James. (1667–1724). English author of *The Club, or a Dialogue between Father and Son* (*or Gray Cap for a Green Head*), a book of axioms quoted frequently by Poe in *Marginalia. Text: CWP,* XI, 15; XIV, 172; XVI, 12, 87.

Pückler-Muskau, Prince Hermann Ludwig Heinrich, Fürst von. (1785–1871). German travel and landscape gardening writer. Poe used his *Tour in England, Ireland, and France* as a source for details in his ''The Domain of Arnheim'' and ''The Landscape Garden.'' *Text: CWP,* IV, 262; VI, 179.

Pulci, Luigi. (1432–1484). Florentine satiric poet and humanist. In *Pinakidia*, Poe notes that ''Pulci, 'the sire of half-serious rhyme,' has a passage expressly alluding to the western continent.'' *Text: CWP,* XIV, 53.

Pundit. Character in the short story ''Mellonta Tauta.'' He is a passenger aboard the balloon *Skylark* and responsible for much of the gossipy scientific nonsense in Pundita's bottled-up letter to the world.

Pundita. Character mentioned in the short story ''Mellonta Tauta.'' The fake log of the balloon *Skylark* is signed ''Pundita.''

Purgstall, Countess. [Jane A. Cranstoun]. (1771–1835). Poe refers to her in his review of *Skimmings; or A Winter at Schloss Hanfeld in Lower Styria* as a source figure for Scott's heroine, Diana Vernon, in *Rob Roy*. *Text: CWP,* IX, 171–173.

"The Purloined Letter." Short story first published in the annual *The Gift: A Christmas, New Year, and Birthday Present, MDCCCXLV* (1845, published in September 1844). An abridgement of the story appeared in *Chambers's Edinburgh Journal* of 30 November 1844. The tale features the superb and superior inductive and intuitive powers of C. Auguste Dupin, but it is also a story of revenge and poetic justice since the purloiner of the letter, Minister D.______, ''at Vienna once, did me an evil turn, which I told him, quite good-humoredly, that I should remember.'' The narrator and Dupin are discussing the previous cases of the murders in the Rue Morgue and Marie Rogêt when they are visited by Monsieur G.______, Prefect of the Parisian police. A scheming government minister, Minister D.______, has purloined a letter from the royal apartments. The contents of the letter ''give its holder a certain power in a certain quarter where such power is immediately valuable.'' Having vainly searched everywhere within Minister D.______'s rooms, the Prefect has now come to Dupin for advice and assistance. Dupin advises a search of the premises, knowing full well that the policeman's methods will again turn up nothing, thus providing Dupin with the opportunity of cracking the case. When the Prefect revisits Dupin a month later, he is astonished to find the detective in possession of the stolen letter, which he has somehow located and extracted from Minister D.______'s apartments. He pays the reward of 50,000 francs and rushes off with the letter, leaving Dupin to explain to the narrator at leisure just how he did it. Dupin takes the occasion to explicate his methods of solution, which involve simplicity and a poetic logic that is superior to the inferior mathematical thoroughness of the police. Dupin was also able to place himself inside the mind of the criminal, whom he knows to be ''both mathematician and poet.'' The letter had not been concealed at all but left brazenly in the open on a card rack where it was overlooked by the zealous investigators. Wearing green spectacles to conceal his eye movements, Dupin had gone to Minister D.______'s apartments and retrieved the letter by a ruse, then replaced it with a facsimile containing a mocking message to D——, a quotation in French aptly chosen from Crébillon's revenge play *Atrée*. Like another skilled and clever revenger, Montresor, in "The Cask of Amontillado," C. Auguste Dupin relishes the outwitting of his injurious victim. *Epigraph:* "Nil sapientiæ odiosius acumine nimio" [Nothing is more hateful to wisdom than too much cunning]. Seneca (specific source of the epigraph unknown). *Text: MCW,* III, 972–997; *CWP,* VI, 28–52. *Research:* Haycraft, Howard. "Poe's 'Purloined Letter.' " *Papers of the Bibliographical Society of America*, 56 (1962): 486–487; Babener, Liahna K. "The Shadow's Shadow: The Motif of the Double in Edgar Allan Poe's 'The Purloined Letter.' " *Mystery and Detection Annual*, 1 (1972): 21–22; Bellei, Sergio L. P. " 'The Purloined Letter': A Theory of Perception." *Poe Studies*, 9 (1976): 40–44; Holland, Norman N. "Re-Covering 'The Purloined Letter': Reading as a Personal Transaction." In *The Reader in the Text:* Essays on Audience and Interpretation, ed. Susan R. Suleiman and Inge Crosman. Princeton: Princeton University Press, 1980, 350–370; Muller, John P., and William J. Richardson. "Lacan's Seminars on 'The Purloined Letter': Map of the Text." In *The Purloined Poe: Lacan, Derrida, and Psychoanalytic Reading*. Baltimore: Johns Hopkins University Press, 1988, 77–82; Blythe, Hal, and Charlie Sweet. "The Reader as Poe's Ultimate Dupe in 'The Purloined Letter.' " *Studies in Short Fiction*, 26 (1989): 311–315; Muckley, Peter A. "The Radicalness of These Differences: Reading 'The Purloined Letter.' " *University of Mississippi Studies in English*, 8 (1990): 227–242; Schweizer, Harold. "Nothing and Narrative 'Twilighting' in 'The Purloined Letter.' " *Literature & Psychology*, 37 (1991): 63–69.

Putnam, George Palmer. (1814–1872). New York publisher. Impressed by the verisimilitude of *The Narrative of Arthur Gordon Pym*, he brought out an English edition in August 1838. In 1848, Poe asked Putman to print 50,000 copies of *Eureka*; 500 were printed. *Research: TPL,* xxxix-xl, 762–763, 803–804.

Q

"The Quacks of Helicon—A Satire." Review of Lambert A. Wilmer's satiric poem "The Quacks of Helicon," published in *Graham's Magazine* for August 1841. Poe was generally delighted with Wilmer's assault on literary imbecility, comparing the satire favorably with "the full spirit of the polish and of the pungency of Dryden" and the "abortive" satire of Byron in *English Bards and Scotch Reviewers*. Only "the sin of indiscriminate censure" and the imitative tone of some of the bitterest verses mar Wilmer's work. Poe also used the review as an occasion for condemning the "system of puffery" or intellectually dishonest reviewing so prevalent in American journals as well as the smug self-deceit of literary coteries and cliques. "As a literary people, we are one vast perambulating humbug." *See:* Wilmer, Lambert. *Text: CWP,* X, 182–195. *Research: PLB,* 33–35, 60–61, 145–146; *PJC,* 263–264.

Quarles Pamphlet. Anonymous pamphlet once ascribed to Poe. It responds defensively to Dickens's critique of American life in his *American Notes*. Poe had used the pseudonym "Quarles" for the poem "The Raven" in *The American Review* for February 1845.

Quevedo Villegas, Francisco Gomez de. (1580–1645). Spanish satiric poet. Poe quotes lines from his sonnet "Rome in Ruins" in his review "Poems; Translated and Original. By Mrs. E. F. Ellet." *Text: CWP,* VIII, 138, 140.

Quintilian. [Marcus Fabius Quintilianus]. (35–100). Ancient Roman rhetorician. Poe included a quip from his writings in *Pinakidia.* ''Quintilian mentions a pedant who taught obscurity, and who was wont to say to his scholars, 'This is excellent—I do not understand it myself.' '' Poe linked the pedant's comment with Emerson's style in ''Autography.'' *Text: CWP,* XIV, 61; XV, 260.

R

Rabelais, François. (1494–1553). French satiric author. Poe refers to his *Gargantua* in "The Quacks of Helicon—A Satire" and has his character M. Ernest Valdemar make a Polish translation of Rabelais's *Gargantua*. Poe characterized the King in "Hop-Frog" as a man who "would have preferred Rabelais' 'Gargantua' to the 'Zadig' of Voltaire." *Text: CWP,* VI, 155, 216; IX, 273; X, 39, 194; XI, 25; XIV, 170, 217, 230; XV, 27. *Research:* Angioletti, Giovanni Battista. "Rabelais e Poe rivoluzionari." *Mondo*, 6 (12 January 1954): 9.

Rachmaninoff, Sergei. (1873–1943). Russian composer. He wrote a choral symphony based on Poe's poem "The Bells." *Research:* Evans, May Garretson. *Music and Edgar Allan Poe: A Bibliographical Study*. Baltimore: Johns Hopkins Press, 1939.

Racine, Jean. (1639–1699). French tragic dramatist. Poe regarded him as a writer of "fine taste and precise finish" but also charged him with plagiarizing scenes from Seneca in *Pinakidia*. *Text: CWP,* XIV, 41, 63; XVI, 32.

Radcliffe, Ann. (1764–1824). English gothic novelist. She wrote *The Romance of the Forest*, *The Mysteries of Udolpho*, *The Italian*, and other gothic novels. She is mentioned by name in "The Oval Portrait" in the wounded narrator's description of the château. In an essay entitled "Tale Writers" appearing in *The Daily National Intelligencer* of 30 August 1845, Rufus Griswold connected Poe directly with the art of Mrs. Radcliffe. "GEORGE WALKER, ANN RADCLIFFE, MARIA ROCHE could alarm with dire chimeras, could lead their characters into difficulties and perils—but they extricated them so clumsily as to destroy every impression of *reality*. Mr. POE's scenes all seem to be actual.'' *Text: CWP,* IV, 245. *Research:* Whitt, Celia. ''Poe and *The Mysteries of Udolpho.*'' *University of Texas Studies in English,* 17 (1937): 124–131; *PLB,* 78; *PJC,* 175; Lecercle, Ann. ''L'Inscription du regard.'' *Du Fantastique en littérature: Figures et figurations: Eléments pour une poétique du fantastique sur quelques exemples anglo-saxons.* Aix-en-Provence: University of Provence, 1990, 77–93.

"Raising the Wind; or, Diddling Considered as One of the Exact Sciences." First title of the short story ''Diddling Considered as One of the Exact Sciences.'' *See:* ''Diddling Considered as One of the Exact Sciences.''

"The Rambler in North America, 1832–1833. By Charles Joseph Latrobe." Favorable review of the epistolary reminiscences of an English missionary appearing in *The Southern Literary Messenger* for December 1835. Poe recommends the book as ''the best on America yet published. Mr. Latrobe is a scholar, a man of intellect and a gentleman.'' Latrobe had accompanied Irving on his tour of the prairies and dedicated his book to Irving. *Text: CWP,* VIII, 111–114.

Ranke, Leopold von. (1795–1886). German historian. In discussing Macaulay, Poe mentions his *History of the Popes. Text: CWP,* X, 158; XIV, 191.

Raphael. [Raffaello Sanzio]. (1483–1520). Italian painter. In ''The Duc de L'Omelette,'' Satan informs the Duc when showing him his infernal chambers that ''Rafael has beheld them! Yes, Rafael has been here.'' *Text: CWP,* II, 200; VIII, 52; IX, 18; XIV, 57; XIV, 185.

"The Rationale of Verse." Critical essay published in *The Southern Literary Messenger* for October–November 1848. This essay might be called Poe's ''Poetics'' since it is a treatise on poetic meter and poetic form. In his edition of Poe's *Poems,* Mabbott included the various metrical specimens contained in the essay. Poe stressed the importance of repetition, parallelism, and refrain, elements that are salient in many of his poems and particularly prominent in ''The Raven,'' a poem that is in many ways a stylistic model for the principles set forth in ''The Rationale of Verse.'' Poe emphasized the application of formal poetics in achieving totality of effect whereby the poem communicates its essence through carefully orchestrated metrical and stanzaic proportions. Without proportion, there could be no unity. Poe maintained, ''Verse originates in the human enjoyment of equality, fitness. Its idea embraces those of similarity, proportion, identity, repetition, adaption.'' Consequently, a long poem always remained a contradiction in terms for Poe since any totality of effect or pleasure in proportion could not be sustained through several reading sessions. *Text: CWP,*

XIV, 209–265; *MCW,* I, 392–396. *Research:* Stovall, Floyd. *The Poems of Edgar Allan Poe.* Charlottesville: Virginia University Press, 1965, 222–223.

Raumer, Friedrich Ludwig Georg von. (1781–1873). German historian whose works were reviewed by Poe. *See:* "America and the American People"; "England in 1835." *Text: CWP,* IX, 53–64; IX, 76; XIII, 13–16; XIV, 42; XVI, 35.

"The Raven." Poe's most famous poem appeared in the New York *Evening Mirror* of 29 January 1845 and again in the *American Review* for February 1845 under the title "The Raven— by Quarles." Subsequent printings and public performances of the poem throughout Poe's lifetime were numerous. Consisting of eighteen six-line stanzas and an unvaried rhyme scheme of ABCBBB, the poem is almost synonymous with the name of Poe and was often the subject of his own critical commentaries on the art of poetry. In fact, Poe was sometimes called "The Raven," and he often cited the poem in theoretical discussions of the art of poetry such as "The Philosophy of Composition" and "The Rationale of Verse." The poem itself can be read as a versified short story of a sinister nocturnal visit to a bereaved lover—or misread as a parody of these circumstances, as one obtuse modern critic has done. Why would Poe parody one of his most cherished themes, the death of a beautiful woman? Like the short stories, the distinguishing feature of the poem is the voice of the poet-narrator, which operates on a level somewhere between the conversational and vernacular and an epic/tragic loftiness. The poem also commences as a monologue, then becomes a reflective dialogue with the intrusive bird. On a "midnight dreary," the poet "ponders weak and weary" out of sorrow for the lost Lenore. As he nurtures his melancholy, his isolation is interrupted by the raven whose mission seems to be to intensify the misery of the poet as it refuses his command to "leave my loneliness unbroken!—quit the bust above my door!" The bust is that of Pallas Athena, goddess of wisdom, in this case the wisdom of death, which cannot be expelled or denied. A colloquy between bird and poet now ensues with each of the mourner's frustrated queries provoking a single-word response from the night visitor, "Nevermore." The demonic qualities of the bird are concentrated in its burning glance and repeated universal negative. The raven, therefore, embodies the poet-narrator's own Promethean inclinations toward self-torment. The Raven's inexorable series of "Nevermores" forces the narrator's mood from initial bemusement, to anger, to a deep and permanent sense of despair. At poem's end, he appears to find a genuine pleasure in the gloom afforded by the bird's presence within his chamber and, by extension, within his soul. "The Raven" has no climax, not even a frustrated resolution of the situation by violence as in the short stories "The Tell-Tale Heart" and "Berenice." In fact, the final "Nevermore" is not spoken by the raven but is the utterance of the desolate and defeated poet-narrator. *Text: MCW,* I, 350–374; *CWP,* VII, 94–100. *Research:* Forsythe, Robert S. "Poe's 'Nevermore': A Note." *American Literature,* 7 (1936): 439–452; Merivale, Patricia. "The Raven and the Bust of

Pallas: Classical Artifacts and the Gothic Tale.'' *Publications of the Modern Language Association*, 89 (1974): 960–966; Bachinger, Katrina. '' 'A Fit Horror': Edgar Allan Poe's 'The Raven.' '' In *Studies in Nineteenth Century Literature*. Salzburg, Austria: Institute für Anglistik & Amerikanistik, University of Salzburg, 1979, 48–60; Mabbott, Maureen Cobb. ''Reading 'The Raven.' '' *University of Mississippi Studies in English*, 3 (1982): 96–101; Gerber, Gerald E. ''Epes Sargent and 'The Raven.' '' *Poe Studies*, 19 (June 1986): 24; Pribek, Thomas. '' 'The Raven' and the Madness of Poe's Student.'' *Journal of Evolutionary Psychology*, 7, nos. 1–2 (1986): 22–24; Eddings, Dennis W. ''Theme and Parody in 'The Raven.' '' In *Poe and His Times: The Artist and His Milieu*,'' ed. B. F. Fisher IV. Baltimore: Edgar Allan Poe Society, 1990, 209–217; Person, Leland S., Jr. ''Poe's Composition of Philosophy: Reading and Writing 'The Raven.' '' *Arizona Quarterly,* 46 (1990): 1–15.

The Raven. The bird night visitor that torments the narrator in the poem ''The Raven.'' By the poem's end, the raven is the dominant figure in the poet's life.

The Raven and Other Poems. Collection of verse published by Wiley & Putnam in November 1845 and dedicated to Elizabeth Barrett. Poe's ''preface'' belittled his own worth as a poet with American readers. ''I think nothing in this volume of much value to the public.'' *Research: MNR,* 299.

"The Raven—by Quarles." Title used by Poe for the poem ''The Raven'' when it appeared in the *American Review*, February 1845 *See:* ''The Raven.''

Read, Thomas Buchanan. (1822–1872). American poet remembered for ''Sheridan's Ride.'' In *Marginalia*, Poe calls him ''one of our truest poets. . . . His most distinctive features are, first, 'tenderness,' or subdued passion, and secondly, fancy. His sin is imitativeness.'' *Text: CWP,* XVI, 144–145.

The Red Death. Character in the short story ''The Masque of the Red Death.'' He is the spectral embodiment of the plague itself and the uninvited guest at Prince Prospero's final fête.

Redfield, J. S. (1810–1888). The New York publisher who brought out Griswold's edition of Poe's *Works*. *Research: BPB*, 102.

Reid, Mayne. (1818–1883). Irish novelist and Philadelphian friend of Poe as well as drinking companion. Of Poe's low tolerance for alcohol, Reid commented in his memoir that ''a single glass . . . used to affect him so much that he was hardly any longer responsible for his actions.'' Reid recalled his friend Poe in ''A Dead Man Defended: Being Some Reminiscences of the Poet Poe'' in the journal *Onward* for April 1869. *Research: PLL,* 60, 142.

"A Remarkable Letter." A shortened epistolary version of the futuristic fantasy included in the text of *Eureka*. *See:* ''Mellonta Tauta.'' *Text: MCW,* III, 1310–1319.

"Reminiscences of an Intercourse with Mr. Niebuhr, the Historian, During a Residence with Him in Rome, in the Years 1822 and 1823. By Francis Lieber." Review of the work and character of the classical historian appearing in *The Southern Literary Messenger* for January 1836. ''Dr. Francis Lieber himself is well known to the American public as the editor of the Encylopedia Americana. . . . Niebuhr's noble nature is, herein, rendered hardly more apparent than the mingled simplicity and enthusiasm of his biographer.'' *Text: CWP,* VIII, 162–168. *Research: TPL,* 212–213.

Reni, Guido. (1575–1642). Italian portrait painter. He is mentioned in ''The Assignation'' in the description of the stranger's chambers.

"Reply to Mr. English and Others." After *Godey's Lady's Book* refused to publish Poe's rejoinder to Dr. Thomas Dunn English's character assault on him, Poe paid ten dollars to the Philadelphia newspaper, *Spirit of the Times*, to print his irate ''Reply to Mr. English and Others'' in the issue of 10 July 1846. Poe denounces all of English's charges as ''oozing from the filthy lips of which a lie is the only natural language.'' *See: Spirit of the Times. Research: TPL,* 652.

"Reply to Mr. Poe." Riposte to Poe's attack on him by Dr. Thomas Dunn English appearing in the New York *Morning Telegraph* of 23 June 1847. English followed up his physical battering of Poe with a verbal pummeling by blasting Poe as ''unprincipled, base, depraved, silly, vain, and ignorant.'' *See:* Ellet, Elizabeth Fries; English, Dr. Thomas Dunn.

"Reply to Mr. Poe's Rejoinder." A second irate defense by Dr. Thomas Dunn English appearing in the New York *Evening Mirror* of 13 July 1846. English taunted Poe for public drunkenness and dared him to bring the libel suit that Poe had threatened to bring. *See:* English, Dr. Thomas Dunn.

"Report of the Committee on Naval Affairs, to Whom Were Referred Memorials from Sundry Citizens of Connecticut Interested in the Whale Fishing, Praying That an Exploring Expedition Be Fitted Out to the Pacific Ocean and South Seas. March 21, 1836." Review appearing in *The Southern Literary Messenger* for August 1836. Poe praises the efforts of the explorer Jeremiah N. Reynolds and argues that it is a national duty to carry out such expeditions. ''We possess, as a people, the mental elasticity which liberal institutions inspire, and a treasury which can afford to remunerate scientific research. Ought we not, therefore, to be foremost in the race of philanthropic discovery, in every department embraced by this comprehensive term?'' *See: The Narrative of Arthur Gordon Pym*; Reynolds, Jeremiah. *Text: CWP,* IX, 84–90.

"A Reviewer Reviewed." Incomplete manuscript acquired by Griswold after Poe's death and published in the *New York Journal* of 15 March 1896. T. O. Mabbott believed ''It has enough of the element of fiction in it to justify its collection among the Tales and Sketches.'' Poe probably intended to have it published in *Graham's Magazine* and used the pseudonym ''Walter G. Bowen.'' In the piece, Poe playfully reviews himself with obvious delight in the contrived situation. ''With Mr. Poe's general *style* no great fault can be justly found. He has the rare merit of distinctness and simplicity, and can be forcible enough on occasion; but as he has a most unmannerly habit of picking flaws in the grammar of other people, I feel justified in showing him that he is far from being immaculate himself.'' *Epigraph:* ''As we rode along the valley we saw a herd of asses on the top of one of the mountains—how they viewed and reviewed us.'' Laurence Sterne, *Tristram Shandy* (attributed by Poe to ''Letter from France''). *Text: MCW,* III, 1377–1388. *Research: TPL,* 671.

Reynolds, Frederic Mansel. (?–1850). English dramatist and author of ''the morbid Godwinian novel'' *Miserrimus*, which Poe referred to as ''a very powerful fiction.'' In *Marginalia*, Poe again praised the work but confused Frederic M. Reynolds with the writer of Victorian ''bloods,'' G. W. M. Reynolds. *Text: CWP,* XIII, 93, 95; XVI, 62–63, 142. *Research: DIP*, 190–205; *BRE,* 217.

Reynolds, Jeremiah. (1799–1858). American navigator and explorer who advocated the exploration of the South Polar region. His ''Address on the Subject of a Surveying and Exploring Expedition to the Pacific Ocean and South Seas'' (1836) is a main source for Poe's novel *The Narrative of Arthur Gordon Pym.* Poe reviewed Reynolds's address in *The Southern Literary Messenger* for January 1837. Poe included a very brief analysis of Reynolds's signature in ''Autography,'' mentioning his shameful exclusion from the South Polar Expedition he had promulgated and organized. While delirious and dying, Poe is said to have shouted Reynolds's name repeatedly. *See:* Moran, Dr. John. *Text: CWP,* XV, 159, 243–244. *Research: LET,* I, 272, 273; *TPL,* xl; *MNR,* 435.

"Rhymes of Travel." In *Marginalia*, Poe reacted to a notice of Bayard Taylor's book of verse in which he defended Taylor against the patronizing tone of the reviewer. *Text: CWP,* XVI, 145–148.

Rice, Sara Sigourney. Poe defender and advocate who organized the first memorial ceremony for him in Baltimore in 1875. She also solicited memorial encomia from Whittier, Bryant, Longfellow, Tennyson, and Swinburne, compiling these testimonials of genius into a keepsake. *Research: PLL,* 264–265.

Richardson, Charles. (1775–1865). English lexicographer noticed by Poe. *See:* "A New Dictionary of the English Language." *Text: CWP,* IX, 103–106.

Richmond Compiler. This newspaper assailed the severity of Poe's reviews. He responded in a letter to the editor. *Research:* Pollin, Burton R. "The *Richmond Compiler* and Poe in 1845: Two Hostile Notices." *Poe Studies,* 18, no. 1 (1985): 6–7; *TPL,* 41–42, 45–46, 152–155, 173–174, 200–203, 220–226.

Richmond Daily Republican. The paper covered Poe's lectures on "The Poetic Principle" in August 1849 and commented that these were "one of the richest intellectual treats we have ever had the good fortune to hear." *Research: TPL,* 820–821, 825–826.

Richmond, Nancy Locke Heywood ["Annie"]. (1820–1898). One of the married women in Poe's life. She met Poe at his Lowell Lecture on American poets on 10 July 1848. Poe's relationship with her was emotionally and intellectually intense, as his letters to her verify. She shared Poe's love letters with the English biographer John Henry Ingram, who published them without her permission. Poe continued to court her even during his passionate affair with Sarah Helen Whitman in 1848 and informed her of his suicide attempt by laudanum on 5 November 1848. Poe celebrated her beauty in several stories and poems. *See:* "The Domain of Arnheim"; "For Annie"; "Landor's Cottage." *Research:* Rede, Kenneth. "Poe's Annie: Leaves from Lonesome Years." *American Collector,* 4 (April 1927): 21–28; Miller, John Carl. "Annie Richmond's Trust Is Betrayed." *BPB,* 146–194; *TPL,* xl, 740–742, 807–810.

Ricketts, Mr. Character mentioned in *The Narrative of Arthur Gordon Pym.* He is Pym's schoolmaster, "a gentleman with only one arm, and of eccentric manners."

"Rienzi, The Last of the Tribunes." Review of a historical novel by Bulwer appearing in *The Southern Literary Messenger* for February 1836. The review is a lavish tribute to Bulwer whom Poe regards as in the first rank of all living novelists. "There *may* be men now living who possess the power of Bulwer—but it is quite evident that very few have made that power so palpably manifest. . . . He is unsurpassed by any writer living or dead. . . . As Rienzi is the last, so it is the best of Bulwer." *Text: CWP,* VIII, 222–229. *Research:* Piacentino, Edward J. "An Error in Poe's Review of *Rienzi.*" *American Notes & Queries,* 1 (1988): 136–137. *Research: PJC,* 122–124.

Riley, James Whitcomb. (1849–1916). American (Indiana) poet known as the "Hoosier Poet." His poem "Leonainie" imitated Poe's lyrics and hoaxed the tone of "Lenore" and others. *Research:* Wallace, Alfred Russel. "The 'Leonainie' Problem." *Fortnightly Review,* 75 (April 1904): 706–711; Wallace, Alfred Russel. *Edgar Allan Poe: A Series of Seventeen Letters concerning Poe's Scientific Erudition in Eureka and His Authorship of Leonainie.* New York: Union Square Bookshop, 1930.

Rilke, Rainer Marie. (1875–1926). German poet. He thought highly of Poe's artistic daring in the penetration and exploration of dangerous but fascinating inner worlds, writing of Poe's prisons and enclosures, "Most people learn to know only a corner of their room, a place by the window, a strip of floor on which they walk up and down. Thus they have a certain security. And yet that dangerous insecurity is so much more human which drives the prisoners in Poe's stories to feel out the shapes of their horrible dungeons and not be strangers to the unspeakable terror of their abodes." *Research: PLL,* 270–271.

Rimbaud, Arthur [Jean]. (1854–1891). French poet. He came to Poe through the Baudelaire translations and was especially drawn toward Poe's depictions of the wonders and horrors of the multiple self. Poe's influence is seen in such poems as "Vowels" (1871) and "A Season in Hell." *Research: PLL,* 286.

Ritchie, Leitch. (1800–1865). English travel and romance writer reviewed by Poe. *See:* "Russia and the Russians." *Text: CWP,* IX, 75–76; X, 207–209.

Rocchietti, Joseph. (1854–1891). American Historian. His book, *Why a National Literature Cannot Flourish in the United States* was vigorously condemned by Poe in a short notice appearing in *The Broadway Journal* of 8 February 1845. *Research: TPL,* 501.

Rochefoucauld, François de la. (1613–1680). French philosopher and writer of maxims. Poe was familiar with his *Maximes* (1665). Dupin refers to Rouchefoucauld disparagingly in "The Purloined Letter" as a writer of "spurious profundity." *Text: CWP,* VI, 41; VIII, 58; X, 47.

Rodman, James E. Character in the novella *The Journal of Julius Rodman.*

Rodman, Jane. Character in the novella *The Journal of Julius Rodman.*

Rodman, Julius. Principal character in the novella *The Journal of Julius Rodman.*

Rogers, Hartman. Character mentioned in *The Narrative of Arthur Gordon Pym.* He is one of the *Grampus* survivors and a member of the Cook's party.

Rogers, Miss Mary C. Her corpse was found in the Hudson River in July 1841. The unsolved murder became the foundation for Poe's "The Mystery of Marie Rogêt." *See:* "The Mystery of Marie Rogêt." *Research: TPL,* 336–337; 385–387.

Rogêt, Estelle. Character in the long short story "The Mystery of Marie Rogêt." She is the murdered girl's mother.

Rogêt, Marie. Character in the short story "The Mystery of Marie Roget." She is the murder victim.

Roget, Dr. Peter Mark. (1779–1869). Compiler of *Thesaurus of English Words and Phrases* and secretary of the Royal Society. He wrote a scientific text reviewed by Poe. *See:* "Animal and Vegetable Physiology." *Text: CWP,* VIII, 210.

Rohan, Prince René Edouard Louis de. (1734–1803). Austrian nobleman who was ambassador to the French court during the reign of Louis XVI. His profile appears in Poe's review of Wraxall's *Posthumous Memoirs of His Own Time. Text: CWP,* IX, 179–183.

"Romance." Poem first printed in *Al Aaraaf, Tamerlane, and Minor Poems* in December 1829 and called "Preface" in that volume. In variant form, it appeared as "Introduction" in the 1831 volume *Poems by Edgar A. Poe.* Reprinted under the title "Romance" in the Philadelphia *Saturday Museum* of 25 February 1843 and *The Broadway Journal* of 30 August 1845. This lyric poem in two stanzas indicates Poe's special affinity with Keats's view that the world of mundane things imposes itself to disrupt the imaginative flights of the poet and mar the visionary experience. Like Keats in "The Ode to a Nightingale," Poe depicts the spirit of romance as an exotic bird "far down within some shadowy lake." The bird inspires the poet, but only briefly, since the "tumult" of the world intervenes to "shake the very heaven on high" and distract the poet from the dream of beauty. "Romance" also invites autobiographical readings since Poe began his career as a poet dedicated to beauty but often deferred this dedication to compose fiction out of financial necessity. *Text: MCW,* 127–129, 156–159; *CWP,* VII, 40. *Research:* Lavin, Audrey. "A Birder's Re-Reading of Poe's 'Romance.' " *University of Mississippi Studies in English,* 9 (1991): 199–204.

Ronald, Mr. E. Character mentioned in *The Narrative of Arthur Gordon Pym.* He runs an academy attended by young Arthur Gordon Pym.

Ross, Emmet. Character mentioned in *The Narrative of Arthur Gordon Pym.* A New Bedford relation of Pym.

Ross, Mr. Character mentioned in *The Narrative of Arthur Gordon Pym.* He is a New Bedford relation of Pym.

Ross, Robert. Character mentioned in *The Narrative of Arthur Gordon Pym.* A New Bedford relation of Pym.

Rossetti, Dante Gabriel. (1828–1882). English painter and poet and leader of the pre-Raphaelite movement. His youthful poem ''The Blessed Damozel'' was strongly influenced by Poe's ''The Raven.'' Having noted ''that Poe had done the utmost it was possible to do with the grief of the lover on earth,'' Rossetti ''reverse[d] the condition, and g[a]ve utterance to the yearning of the loved one in heaven.'' *Research:* Mabbott, Thomas Ollive. ''Echoes of Poe in Rossetti's 'Beryl Song.' '' *Notes & Queries*, 168 (2 February 1935): 77; *PLL*, 289.

Rousseau, Jean-Jacques. (1712–1778). French philosopher and author of *The Social Contract* and *Confessions*. Poe mentions Rousseau in several short stories, quoting from his *Nouvelle Héloise* in the final sentence of ''The Murders in the Rue Morgue.'' *Text: CWP,* II, 152, 356; IV, 192; XI, 165; XIV, 180; XV, 120. *Research:* Suther, Judith D. ''Rousseau, Poe, and the Idea of Progress.'' *Papers on Language and Literature*, 12 (1976): 469–475.

Rowson, Susan Haswell. (1762–1824). American novelist and author of *Charlotte Temple*. Her novel is mentioned favorably in Poe's review of *Barnaby Rudge*. *Text: CWP,* XI, 40.

Rubadub, Professor. Character in ''The Unparalleled Adventure of One Hans Pfaall.'' Vice president of the Rotterdam College of Astronomy who receives Pfaall's letter from the skies.

Rumgudgeon. Character in the short story ''Three Sundays in a Week.'' He is the granduncle of the narrator, Bobby.

"Russia and the Russians; or, A Journey to St. Petersburg and Moscow, through Courland and Livonia; with Characteristic Sketches of the People. By Leitch Ritchie." Review of a travelogue appearing in *The Southern Literary Messenger* for July 1836. Poe approved of both the book's elegant appearance and Ritchie's writing skill. ''His Russia and the Russians has all the spirit and vigor of romance. It is full of every species of entertainment, and will prove in America as it has in England, one of the most popular books of the season.'' *Text: CWP,* IX, 75–76.

S

Sabretash, Captain Arthur. Character mentioned in the short story ''Some Words with a Mummy.'' He provides the mummy for the midnight unwrapping session.

"The Sacred Mountains: By T. J. Headley." Posthumous review published by *The Southern Literary Messenger* for October 1850 under the title ''Poe on Headley and Channing.'' This specimen piece was inserted by Harrison in the *Complete Works* to demonstrate ''that tomahawk-style of criticism of which the author was so great a master.'' Poe buried his tomahawk deep in Headley's literary skull when he wrote: '' 'Quack' is a word that sounds well only in the mouth of a duck; and upon our honor we feel a scruple in using it:—nevertheless the truth should be told; and the simple fact is, that the author of the 'Sacred Mountains' is the Autocrat of all the Quacks.'' *Text: CWP,* XIII, 202–209. *Research: PLB,* 80.

"Sacred Philosophy of the Seasons, Illustrating the Perfections of God in the Phenomena of the Year. By the Rev. Henry Duncan." Review of a theological tract appearing in *Burton's Gentleman's Magazine* for March 1840. Poe finds the book ''especially well adapted to those educational purposes for which the volumes are designed.'' *Text: CWP,* X, 81–85.

Sade, Abbé Jacques François Paul Aldonce de. (1705–1778). Author of *The Life of Petrarch.* According to Poe, ''He was unquestionably the most accomplished foreigner who wrote on the affairs of Italy in the fourteenth century.'' *Text: CWP,* X, 203–204.

The Sailor. Character in the short story ''The Murders in the Rue Morgue.'' He is the owner of the murderous Orang-Outang.

St. Eustache, Jacques. Character in the short story ''The Mystery of Marie Rogêt.'' He is the murdered girl's betrothed. He dies of an overdose of laudanum.

St. Louis Daily Reveillé. This newspaper carried rumors of Poe's insanity. The issue of 12 April 1846 reported that ''A rumor is in circulation in New York, to the effect that Mr. Edgar A. Poe, the poet and author, has become deranged, and his friends are about to place him under the charge of Dr. Brigham, of the Insane Retreat at Utica [New York].'' *Research: LET,* II, 318, 324, 327; *TPL,* 633–634; *MNR,* 268, 301, 307.

Sallust. [Gaius Sallustius Crispus]. (86–35 B.C.). Roman historian. He wrote *The Jurguthine War*, a history. Poe quotes his definition of a king in *Pinakidia*: ''To do with impunity whatever one fancies is to be a king.'' Compared with Carlyle, Sallust's ''obscurity, his unusuality of expression, and his Laconism . . . bore the impress of his genius.'' *Text: CWP,* XIV, 66; XV, 180; XVI, 37, 122.

Salsafette, Ma'm'selle Eugènie. Character in the short story ''The System of Doctor Tarr and Professor Fether.'' She ''wished to dress herself, always, by getting outside instead of inside her clothes.''

Sand, George. [Baronne Lucile Dupin]. [Armandine Aurore Dudevant]. (1804–1876). French novelist. In ''Byron and Miss. Chaworth,'' Poe characterized George Sand as ''a woman who intersperses many an admirable sentiment amid a chaos of the most shameless and altogether objectionable fiction.'' *Text: CWP,* X, 134, 136–137; XIV, 150.

Sanderson, Professor John. (1783–1844). Professor of Greek and Latin in the High School of Philadelphia and author of a series of letters, *The American in Paris*. Poe included a short sketch of Sanderson in ''Autography,'' remarking on his ''ease and vivacity of style, with occasional profundity of observation.'' *Text: CWP,* XV, 196.

Sappho of Lesbos. (ca. 590 B.C.). Greek love poet often referred to in classical studies as ''the tenth muse,'' or the first and greatest love poetess. Poe refers to her death in ''Al Aaraaf.'' *Text: CWP,* VII, 24.

Sargent, Epes. (1813–1880). Boston poet and dramatist profiled in ''The Literati of New York City'' and in ''Autography.'' He wrote *Velasco, a Tragedy*, based on the life of El Cid, which Poe compared against Mrs. Mowatt's play *Fashion*. ''His prose is not quite so meritorious as his poetry. He writes 'easily,' and is apt at burlesque and sarcasm—both rather broad than original.'' *Text: CWP*, XV, 91–93, 252–253. *Research:* Gerber, Gerald E. ''Epes Sargent and 'The Raven.' '' *Poe Studies*, 19 (1986): 24; *TPL*, xl, 744–745.

Sartain, John. (1808–1897). Engraver whom Poe met in Philadelphia in 1838. The two men worked together and respected one another's art at *Burton's Gentleman's Magazine* and *Graham's Magazine*. In his ''Reminiscences of a Very Old Man'' (1899) Sartain gives a vivid account of Poe's alcoholic frenzies in the delirium tremens stage. *Text: CWP*, VIII, 102. *Research:* Tuerk, Richard. ''John Sartain and E. A. Poe.'' *Poe Studies*, 4, no. 2 (1971): 21–22.

Sartain's Union Magazine. Philadelphia journal begun in January 1849. It published posthumously Poe's ''The Bells,'' ''Annabel Lee,'' and ''The Poetic Principle.'' *Research: TPL*, xl-xli, 752–753, 793–797.

"Satirical Poems." Critical essay appearing in *The Broadway Journal* of 15 March 1845. Poe claims that ''in verse we are scarcely so much satirists, as subjects for satire. . . . We have really nothing to show a foreigner as a specimen of our satirical abilities done into verse.'' *See:* ''Infatuation.'' *Text: CWP*, XII, 107–110.

Saturday Courier. Philadelphia periodical that published several of Poe's first stories in 1832, among these ''Metzengerstein,'' ''The Duke de L'Omelette,'' and ''A Tale of Jerusalem.'' *Research:* Varner, John Greer. *Facsimile Reproductions of the ''Philadelphia Saturday Courier.''* Charlottesville: University of Virginia, 1933.

Saturday Evening Post. Philadelphia journal to which Poe contributed reviews and the story ''The Black Cat.'' In the issue of 14 March 1846, Poe is charged with plagiarizing *The Conchologist's First Book* from *The Text-Book of Conchology*, by Capt. Thomas Brown. The *Saturday Evening Post* also carried a brief notice of the destitution and illness of both Virginia and Edgar Poe, but the notice expressed neither sympathy nor any appeal for assistance. *Research: TPL*, 76–77, 274–275, 292–293, 361–362, 629–630.

"Saul, A Mystery." Review of a work by Arthur Coxe. *See:* ''Coxe's Saul.'' *Text: CWP*, XII, 243–244.

Sawyer, Annie. Lowell, Massachusetts, schoolteacher. Poe occasionally corresponded with her. The letters were printed in the *New England Quarterly* in September 1943. *Research: TPL,* xxviii, 809–810.

"Scenes from an Unpublished Drama." *See: Politian. Text: CWP,* VII, 194.

"Scenes from Politian; An Unpublished Drama." Poe's only play. *See: Politian. Text: CWP,* VII, 59–79.

Scheherazade. Character in the short story ''The Thousand-and-Second Tale of Scheherazade.

Schiller, Johann Christoph Friedrich von. (1759–1805). German poet and dramatist. He is mentioned in Poe's ''Memorials of Mrs. Hemans'' and misidentified in the mottos for several short stories. Schiller's lyric ''The Song of the Bell'' is an obvious source for Poe's ''The Bells.'' *Text: CWP,* II, 279, 295; VI, 155; VIII, 138; IX, 202, 204. *Research:* Cameron, Kenneth W. ''Poe's 'Bells' and Schiller's 'Das Lied von der Glocke.' '' *Emerson Society Quarterly*, 19 (2nd Q 1960): 37.

Schlegel, Augustus Wilhelm von. (1767–1845). German romantic critic and translator of Shakespeare. Poe was attracted to Schlegel's emphasis upon unity or ''totality of interest'' as vital to the artistic success of a work. *Text: CWP,* VIII, 126; XI, 79, 250. *Research:* Lubell, Albert J. ''Poe and A.W. Schlegel.'' *Journal of English and Germanic Philology*, 52 (1953): 1–12; *PJC,* 90, 114, 115–116, 250–251; Wittmann, Carola Elfriede. ''Schlegelian Tales in Early Nineteenth Century American Literature.'' *Dissertation Abstracts International*, 51 (1991): 3735A–3736A (University of Washington).

Schlegel, Karl Wilhelm Friedrich von. (1772–1829). German Romantic critic. Poe mentions him in connection with the artistic views of his brother, Augustus Wilhelm. *Text: CWP,* XI, 5; XVI, 117. *Research: PJC,* 297.

Schroeter, Johann Hieronymus. (1745–1816). German astronomer mentioned in the unpublished notes to *Eureka*. Poe knew his *Observations of the Great Comet of 1807*. *Text: CWP,* XVI, 348, 352–354.

Scissors. Character mentioned in the short story ''Loss of Breath.'' He is the author of a treatise upon ''the nature and origin of subterranean noises.''

Scott, Sir Walter. (1771–1832). English historical novelist. A devoted reader of Scott, Poe called *The Bride of Lammermoor* ''that most pure, perfect, and radiant gem of fictitious literature'' and often used Scott's genius in the field of the historical novel as a criterion against which to measure the success or the failure of other historical novelists in his reviews, noting at one point that Bulwer was ''altogether inferior.'' *Text: CWP,* VIII, 63–65, 73, 223, 235; IX, 123, 168–169, 199, 202–203; X, 132; XII, 190; XVI, 83, 157. *Research:* Moore, John Robert. ''Poe, Scott, and 'The Murders in the Rue Morgue.' '' *American Literature*, 8 (1936): 52–58; Moore, John Robert. ''Poe's Reading of *Anne of Geierstein.*'' *American Literature*, 22 (1951): 493–496; Newlin, Paul A. ''Scott's Influence on Poe's Grotesque and Arabesque Tales.'' *American Transcendental Quarterly*, 2 (1969): 9–12; Ringe, Donald A. ''Poe's Debt to Scott in 'The Pit and the Pendulum.' '' *English Language Notes*, 18 (1981): 281–283.

"The Scythe of Time." Original title of the short story ''A Predicament.'' *See:* ''A Predicament.''

The Seaman's Friend. Book by Richard Henry Dana, Jr., reviewed by Poe in *Graham's Magazine* for December 1841. *Research: TPL,* 351.

"Secret Writing." (1). Poe received a cryptogram from F. W. Thomas in response to his essay ''A Few Words on Secret Writing.'' The addendum in *Graham's Magazine* for August 1841 prints the cryptogram with Poe's offer for a one-year's free subscription ''to any person who shall solve it with the key.'' *See:* ''A Few Words on Secret Writing.'' *Text: CWP,* XIV, 133–137.

"Secret Writing." (2). In this addendum in *Graham's Magazine* for October 1841, Poe comments on a cryptogram submitted to him in August by a subscriber under the ''nom de guerre of Timotheus Whakemwell.'' Poe not only solved the cryptogram but penetrated the true identity of Whakemwell to be his Baltimore friend Mr. J. N. McJilton. *Text: CWP,* XIV, 138–140.

"Secret Writing." (3). More reaction to Poe's essay on cryptography appeared in *Graham's Magazine* for December 1841. Poe discussed the formation of hieroglyphic cyphers and commented on the general value of cryptography as a practical science. ''Cryptography is, indeed, not only a topic of mere curiosity but is of general interest, as furnishing an excellent exercise for mental discipline, and of high practical importance on various occasions'' to statesmen, generals, scholars, travelers, and lovers. *Text:* CWP, XIV, 140–149.

Sedgwick, Miss Catherine Maria. (1789–1867). Massachusetts poet and historical novelist. She was active in reform causes. Poe summarized her work in his sketch of her in ''The Literati of New York City'' and concluded, ''She is an author of marked talent, but by no means of such decided genius as would entitle her to that precedence among our female writers which . . . *seems* to be yielded her by the voice of the public.'' Poe wrote of her handwriting in ''Autography'' that it reflected ''strong common sense, and a scorn of superfluous ornament,'' both features of her literary style. *Text: CWP,* XV, 108–113, 149–150, 204–205. *Research: TPL,* 185–186, 434–435.

Seetzen, Ulrich Jasper. (1767–1811). German explorer and archeologist mentioned in Poe's review of Stephens's *Arabia Petræa*. Poe had read his *Travels through Syria, Palestine, Phoenicia, and the Trans-Jordan*. *Text: CWP,* X, 2, 14–16.

"Select Orations of Cicero: With an English Commentary, and Historical, Geographical, and Legal Indexes. By Charles Anthon." Review of scholarly commentaries by the Jay Professor of Ancient Literature at Columbia College, appearing in *The Southern Literary Messenger* for January 1837. Poe respected this classicist and his work, writing, ''As a critic and commentator, Professor Anthon must be regarded with the highest consideration. . . . He has dared to throw aside the pedant, and look *en homme du monde* upon some of the most valued of the literary monuments of antiquity.'' *See:* Anthon, Charles. *Text: CWP,* IX, 266–268.

Seneca, Lucius Annaeus. (A.D. ?–65). Roman philosopher and dramatist. His learning is cited in *Pinakidia* and *Marginalia*. *Text: CWP,* X, 47; XIV, 41, 44, 64; XVI, 47, 72.

The Seven Ministers. Characters in the short story ''Hop-Frog.'' They are the King's counselors who are burned alive in their ourangoutang costumes.

Seymour. Character in the novel *The Narrative of Arthur Gordon Pym*. He is the ship's murderous black cook.

"Shadow—A Parable." Short story published in *The Southern Literary Messenger* for September 1835. This tale of revels during plague time is a miniature version of Poe's ''Masque of the Red Death'' and has connections with another plague story, ''King Pest.'' Additionally, the tone and construction are highly reminiscent of Hawthorne's style of ghost story. The postmortem narrator, Oinos, who has ''long since gone into the region of shadows,'' addresses his parable to the living as one who speaks for the multitudes of the dead. During the plague year of 794 in the city of Ptolemais, seven revellers have taken refuge from the pestilence in a strong chamber with a door of brass. There they drink deeply and sing the songs of Anacreon, ''although the purple wine reminded us of blood.'' There is also an eighth reveller present at the gala, the corpse of young Zoilus, enshrouded and ''distorted with the plague.'' Like the Red Death, the uninvited ghostly guest in shadowy form appears to deliver an epitaph to bliss, security, and life. Oinos recalls the horror of the shadow's voice tones, ''not the tones of any one being, but of a multitude of beings,'' a choric salutation from beyond the curtain of death. Apparently, only the now-dead Oinos realizes that the shadow is a phantom of "many thousand departed friends" who ate, drank, and were merry but were, like the cadaverous guest Zoilus, mere shadows without substance. Poe again seems to have transformed some famous Shakespearean lines from *Macbeth*, "Life's but a walking shadow," into the eerie situation of the story. *Epigraph:* "Yea! though I walk through the valley of the *Shadow*." Psalm 23. *Text: MCW,* II, 187–192; *CWP,* II, 147–150. *Research:* Pollin, Burton R. "Poe's 'Shadow' as a Source for His 'The Masque of the Red Death.' " *Studies in Short Fiction*, 6 (1968): 104–107; De Falco, Joseph. "The Sources of Terror in Poe's 'Shadow—A Parable.' " *Studies in Short Fiction*, 6 (1969): 643–649; Williams, Michael. "Poe's 'Shadow—A Parable' and the Problem of Language." *American Literature*, 57 (1985): 622–632.

Shakespeare, William. (1564–1616). English dramatist. Frequent allusions to Shakespeare's plays and sonnets occur throughout Poe. The narrator's phrase "of worms, of tombs, of epitaphs" in "The Premature Burial" is from *Richard the Second*, II.ii.45. Richard the Third's murderous dismissal "So much for Buckingham" is spoken by Bullet-head in "X-ing a Paragrab." "But the figure in question had out-Heroded Herod" in "The Masque of the Red Death" is based on Hamlet's advice to the players in *Hamlet*, III.ii.14. The line "Satisfying your eyes with the memorials and the things of fame that most renown this city" in "Four Beasts in One" is spoken by Sebastian in *Twelfth Night*, III.iii.22–24. Thingum Bob's inaccurate plagiarisms "ministers saying grace" and "goblin damned" come from *Hamlet*, I.iv.39–40. Poe often restaged brutal, violent, and ridiculous incidents from Shakespeare's plays as in the short story "King Pest" where the drunken sailor, Hugh Tarpaulin, is drowned in a cask of October ale, thus recalling the murder of the Duke of Clarence in the Tower in *Richard the Third*, I.iv. Elsewhere, Poe uses Shakespearean allusions to deepen and enrich the meanings of his own fiction. A major instance is the character of Prospero and the setting he occupies in "The Masque of the Red Death." Shakespeare's Prospero controls and rules over a magical world immune to the threat of outside civilization. Poe's Prospero ironically attempts to turn the interior of the abbey into a safe zone of eternal magic and frolic separated from the contaminated world without. The Shakespearean allusiveness of the tale extends beyond Prospero's character and name to the very title of the story itself, taken from Caliban's curse uttered against his master in I.ii.364: "the red plague rid you." Poe also displays his interest in *The Tempest* in naming the boat in which Augustus and Pym take their wild midnight sail the *Ariel*. *See:* "Wiley & Putnam's Library of Choice Reading, No. VII; The Characters of Shakespeare. by William Hazlitt." *Text: CWP*. II, 205, 362; V, 243; VI, 1, 189; VII, 32, 63; VIII, 93, 99, 189, 235; IX, 25, 29, 30, 47, 91, 197, 199; X, 63; XI, 242; XII, 127, 180, 186, 211, 226–228, 261; XIII, 47, 197; XIV, 162; XV, 110; XVI, 35, 42, 83, 100, 110, 172. *Research:* Campbell, Killis. "Poe's Reading: Addenda and Corrigenda." *University of Texas Studies in English*, 7 (1927): 175–180; *LET,* I, 32, 190, II, 436; McIlvaine, Robert. "A Shakespearean Echo in 'The Tell-Tale Heart.' " *American Notes & Queries*, 15 (1976): 38–40; Pollin, Burton R. "The Self-Destructive Fall: A Theme from Shakespeare Used in *Pym* and 'The Imp of the Perverse.' " *Études Anglaises*, 29 (1976): 199–202; Cheney, Patrick. "Poe's Use of *The Tempest* and the Bible in 'The Masque of the Red Death.' " *English Language Notes*, 20, nos. 3–4 (1983): 31–39; Pollin, Burton R. "Shakespeare in the Works of Edgar Allan Poe." *Studies in the American Renaissance* (1985): 157–186; Candran, K. Narayana. "Poe's Use of *Macbeth* in 'The Masque of the Red Death.' " *Papers on Language and Literature*, 29 (1993): 236–240.

Shaw, George Bernard. (1856–1950). Irish playwright. He called Poe "the greatest journalistic critic of his time" and accused American critics of ignoring or misunderstanding Poe's genius in the two areas of criticism and original fiction. *Research:* Shaw, George Bernard. "Edgar Allan Poe." In *Pen Portraits and Reviews*. London: Constable, 1932, 220–236.

Shelley, Percy Bysshe. (1792–1822). English Romantic poet. Among those poems of Shelley most admired by Poe, verse in which "an Ideality in a wonderful degree" is prominent, are *Queen Mab*, "Hymn to Intellectual Beauty," and "The Sensitive Plant." Poe's review "The Drama of Exile, and Other Poems" contains a tribute to Shelley's high order of genius. "If ever poet sang (as a bird sings)—impulsively, earnestly, with utter abandonment—to himself solely—and for mere joy of his own song—that poet was the author of the Sensitive Plant. . . . With such a man, to imitate was out of the question; it would have answered no purpose—for he spoke to his own spirit alone. . . . He was therefore profoundly original. . . . He had no *affectations*." *Text: CWP,* IV, 269; VIII, 176–177, 283, 299–301; IX, 299; X, 63–66; XI, 65; XII, 32–35; XIV, 269–270; XVI, 4, 148–150. *Research:* Routh, James. "Notes on the Sources of Poe's Poetry: Coleridge, Keats, Shelley." *Modern Language Notes*, 29 (1914): 72–75; Laser, Marvin. "The Growth and Structure of Poe's Concept of Beauty." *Journal of English Literary History*, 15 (1948): 69–84; *PLB,* 79; *LET,* I, 32, 207, 257–258; 332.

Shelton, Elmira Royster. (1810–1888). Poe's love affair with her began in 1825 when she was fifteen years old. Her father rejected him as a future son-in-law, and Elmira married Alexander B. Shelton in December 1828. In the final year of his life, Poe proposed to the rich widow, who privately agreed to marriage even though she would have to relinquish most of the income from her copious estate. She provided the early Poe biographer Edward V. Valentine with a vivid memory profile before her death, remarking, "I married another man, but the love of my life was Edgar Poe. I never loved anyone else." *Research:* Dietz, Frieda Meredith. "Poe's First and Final Love." *The Southern Literary Messenger*, 5 (March 1943): 38–47; Rein, David M. "Poe and Mrs. Shelton." *American Literature*, 28 (1956): 225–227; *TPL,* xli; *MNR,* 425–428, 430–433; *PLL,* 248–251.

"Sheppard Lee." Review of Robert Montgomery Bird's novel appearing in *The Southern Literary Messenger* for September 1836. Poe was interested in the novel's metempsychotic themes in Bird's antislavery sentiments, descriptions of slave insurrections, and the hero's displacement from his own body. Poe's opinion of the novel is mixed. He finds it "an original in American Belle Lettres at least," but "some fault may be found with the conception of metempsychosis which is the basis of the narrative. . . . The hero, very awkwardly, partially loses, and partially does not lose, his identity, at each transmigration." *Text: CWP,* IX, 126–139. *Research: PJC,* 173–174.

Sheridan, Mrs. Frances. (1724–1766). English novelist. Poe refers to her *History of Nourjahad* (1767) in comparing Ligeia's eyes to "the Gazelle eyes of the tribe of Nourjahad." *Text: CWP,* II, 251.

Shew, Marie Louise [Houghton]. (?–1877). She nursed Virginia Clemm Poe without pay during her terminal illness. Poe showed his gratitude by writing a poem for her, "The Beloved Physician." Poe was romantically involved with her to the extent of writing valentine poems to her such as "To M. L. S.______." He referred to her in a letter as "an angel to my forlorn and darkened nature." *See:* "The Bells"; "To M. L. S.______." *Research:* Ingram, John H. "Edgar Allan Poe's Last Poem 'The Beloved Physician.' " *Bookman*, 28 (January 1909): 452–454; Miller, John Carl. "Mary Louise Shew Houghton Leads and Misleads Poe's Biographer." *BPB*, 88–145; *TPL,* xli.

Shuttleworthy, Mr. Barnabas. Character in the short story " 'Thou Art the Man.' " He is the man missing from Rattleborough.

Sidney, Sir Philip. (1554–1586). English poet, scholar, and courtier. Poe cites Sidney's *Arcadia* and *Astrophil and Stella* sonnet sequence. His essay on poetic theory, "The Defence of Poesy," foreshadows many of Poe's ideas about the theory and practice of the art. Poe shared Sidney's nonmimetic notion that the true poet never imitates nature but creates a new or higher nature. *Text: CWP,* XI, 36, 81; XII, 102; XIV, 54; XVI, 72–73.

Sigourney, Lydia Huntley. (1791–1865). Hartford, Connecticut, poet and contributor to *The Southern Literary Messenger*. Poe commented on her signature in "Autography" and reviewed *Zinzendorff, and Other Poems*. "Were one to form an estimate of the character of Mrs. Sigourney's compositions from the character of her handwriting, the estimate would not be far from the truth. Freedom, dignity, precision, and grace of thought, without abrupt or startling transitions, might be attributed to her." *See:* "Zinzendorff, and Other Poems." *Text: CWP,* XV, 145–146, 187. *Research: PJC,* 104–116; *TPL,* xli–xlii, 209–210.

"Silence—A Fable." Short story by Poe first published in the *Baltimore Book* in 1838 under the title "Siope—A Fable." The tale was included in *Tales of the Grotesque and Arabesque* again under the title "Siope," then printed in *The Broadway Journal* of 6 September 1845 as "Silence—A Fable." The story is a kind of exercise in dream fantasy in which Poe locates the Byronic hero in an opium-induced De Quinceyesque dreamscape. The strange and wild reverie is recited by a Demon to the deceased auditor (''that fable which the Demon told me as he sat by my side in the shadow of the tomb'') and involves the Demon's narcoleptic recollection of his strange experience on the banks of the river Zaire in Libya. The Demon's narrative is accompanied by his touch as he places his hand upon the auditor's head and apparently keeps it there during the recitation. Wandering through rainstorms of blood and oozy beds of poisonous water lilies, the Demon had followed the beacon of a crimson moon until he came to a dark rock bearing the inscription ''DESOLATION.'' Atop the rock in a toga stands a silent figure in the posture of Byron's Childe Harold, ''his brow lofty with thought, his eye wild with care.'' The Demon ''read[s] the fables of sorrow, and weariness, and disgust with mankind, and a longing after solitude'' in the sad, silent face. At this point, the Demon's strange narrative takes up the refrain ''But the night waned and he sat upon the rock.'' The Demon grows furious with the enigmatic figure of silence when suddenly ''the moon ceased to totter up its pathway to heaven'' and the inscription changes from ''DESOLATION'' to ''SILENCE.'' The mysterious figure moves to the edge of the rock, listens intently, shudders, and hastens away. The Demon remains concealed in the morass of sick and toxic flowers, never communicating his presence to the man atop the rock. The meaning of the fable remains cryptic. At the end within the auditor's tomb, the Demon laughs and curses the auditor because ''I could not laugh with the Demon,'' thus suggesting that the fable that the Demon has told is merely a malicious prank. *Epigraph:* ''The mountain pinnacles slumber; valleys, crags, and caves *are silent*.'' Alcman in Apollonius's *Homeric Lexicon* (Greek text translated by Poe). *Text: MCW,* II, 192–200; *CWP,* II, 220–224. *Research:* Claudel, Alice M. ''What Has Poe's 'Silence—A Fable' to Say?'' *Ball State University Forum*, 10 (1969): 66–70; Fisher, Benjamin Franklin IV. ''The Power of Words in Poe's 'Silence.' '' *Library Chronicle*, 41 (1976): 56–72.

"Silence—A Sonnet." Poem first published in the Philadelphia *Saturday Courier* of 4 January 1840. The poem was later revised and published under the title ''Sonnet—Silence'' in *The Broadway Journal* of 26 July 1845 and published under this title in *The Raven and Other Poems* in 1845. The poem is a meditation on two types of silence: the silence that attends the demise of the body; and the incorporeal silence that is presumably produced by the death of the soul. Poe implies that to ''meet his shadow/ That haunteth the lone regions where hath trod/ No foot of man'' is certain to involve the nothingness that lies beyond comprehension. *Text: MCW,* I, 320–323; *CWP,* VII, 201. *Research: LET,* I, 126–127.

Silius Italicus. (25–101). Roman poet. In *Pinakidia*, Poe quotes several of his lines as an example of ultimate sublimity. *Text: CWP,* II, 280; XIV, 59, 262.

Simeon the Pharisee. Character in the short story ''A Tale of Jerusalem.'' He belongs to the sect called ''Dashers,'' those who deliberately lacerate their feet by dashing.

Simms. Character mentioned in *The Narrative of Arthur Gordon Pym.*

Simms, William Gilmore. (1806–1870). American novelist and editor. Like many other writers who had received severe treatment by Poe, the reviewer, Simms could still acknowledge Poe's genius as both a short story writer and a poet. ''His scheme of poem requires that his reader shall surrender himself to influences of pure imagination.'' Simms reviewed *The Raven and Other Poems* for the *Southern Patriot* of 2 March 1846. From Simms's signature in ''Autography'' Poe deduced that he ''possess[ed] the eye of a painter.'' *See:* ''The Partisan: A Tale of the Revolution''; ''Sheppard Lee.'' *Text: CWP,* VIII, 143–158, 202; IX, 126–139; X, 49–56; XI, 206; XII, 247–250; XIII, 93–97, 153; XIV, 75; XV, 119, 168, 193; XVI, 41, 59–62. *Research: LET,* I, 105, 185; Turner, Arlin. ''Poe and Simms: Friendly Critics, Sometimes Friends.'' In *Papers on Poe: Essays in Honor of John Ward Ostrom*, ed. Richard P. Veler. Springfield, OH: Chantry Music Press at Wittenberg University, 1972, 140–160.

Simpson, Adolphus. Character mentioned in the short story ''The Spectacles.''

Simpson, Napoleon Buonaparte [also Froissart]. Character and narrator of the short story ''The Spectacles.''

Sinavate, Mr. Theodore. Character in the short story ''The Man That Was Used Up.'' He is a friend of the narrator who gives him evasive answers about Smith's character.

Sinbad the Sailor. *Arabian Nights* adventurer whose tale of the vermin-bearing sea monster is recited by the Queen in ''The Thousand-and-Second Tale of Scheherazade.''

"Siope—A Fable. *See:* ''Silence—A Fable.''

Sismondi, Léonard. (1773–1842). French historian who wrote Italian history. In his review of Bulwer's *Rienzi*, Poe claimed that his works were not history but merely ''a tissue of dates and details.'' *Text: CWP,* VIII, 224, 226.

Sitwell, Edith. (1887–1964). English poet. She paid homage to Poe's genius in the preface to *The American Genius* (1951) by calling him the sole American poet prior to Whitman whose work was not ''bad and imitative of English poetry.'' *Research: PLL,* 326.

Sixth Avenue and Waverley Place. In New York City. Poe lived here briefly in February 1837.

"Sketches of Conspicuous Living Characters of France. Translated by R. M. Walsh." Review of a translation from the French of biographical profiles of literary and political worthies including Thiers, Chateaubriand, Lamartine, Hugo, George Sand, and the Duke de Broglie appearing in *Graham's Magazine* for April 1841. Poe enjoyed the anecdotes rendered in translation but found the translation itself ''in some respects, not very well done. Too little care has been taken in rendering the French idioms by English equivalents.'' *Text: CWP,* X, 133–139. *Research: PJC,* 78, 209.

"Sketches of History, Life and Manners in the West. By James Hall." Review appearing in *The Southern Literary Messenger* for December 1835. ''To those who are at all acquainted with Mr. Hall's writings, it is superfluous to say that the book is well written. Wild romance and exciting adventure form its staple.'' *Text: CWP,* VIII, 108–109.

"Sketches of Switzerland. By an American, Part Second." Review of James Fenimore Cooper's book appearing in *The Southern Literary Messenger* for October 1836. Cooper ''imparts a narrative interest to his journey; and, being an American, yet intimately conversant with all the beauties of the Old World, he looks at Switzerland with a more instructed eye than the mass of travellers. . . . The present volumes strike us as more entertaining upon the whole than those which preceded them.'' *Text: CWP,* IX, 162–164.

"Skimmings; Or a Winter at Schloss Hainfeld in Lower Styria. By Captain Basil Hall." Review of a journal of excursions and Hall's sojourn with the Countess Purgstall appearing in *The Southern Literary Messenger* for October 1836. Countess Purgstall had influenced the literary character of Sir Walter Scott. Hall's ''reminiscences of Sir Walter form, possibly, the most interesting portions of Schloss Hainfield. . . . Captain Hall is no ordinary writer. This justice must be done him.'' *See:* Purgstall, Countess. *Text: CWP,* IX, 170–174.

"Slavery in the United States. By J. K. Paulding." Review appearing in *The Southern Literary Messenger* for April 1836. Poe reviewed Paulding's book only minimally, using the review to state his own theories about the morality of slavery as an institution. He indirectly answered Paulding's depiction of the institution by maintaining that a beneficial moral relationship existed between master and slave and was the normal state of affairs in the South. ''We speak of the moral influences flowing from the relation of master and slave, and the moral feelings engendered and cultivated by it.'' Included in the same review are Poe's observations on slavery from the southern point of view. *See:* ''The South Vindicated from the Treason and Fanaticism of the Northern Abolitionists.'' *Text:*

CWP, VIII, 265–275. *Research:* Rosenthal, Bernard. ''Poe, Slavery, and the *Southern Literary Messenger.*'' *Poe Studies*, 7 (1974): 29–38.

"The Sleeper." Poem first published in the Philadelphia *Saturday Chronicle* of 22 May 1841. The first title of ''The Sleeper'' was ''Irene'' when the poem appeared in Elam Bliss's April 1831 edition of Poe's *Poems.* The poem underwent several significant revisions by Poe and shows an evolving text as it changed from the seventy-four lines of the 1831 version to the sixty lines of the poem as published in the 1845 volume *The Raven and Other Poems.* The poem is another celebration of the dream state and its link to the freedom that Poe often associates with death. Like the psychic landscapes of ''Fairy Land,'' ''The Valley of Unrest,'' and ''The City in the Sea,'' the poem's geography of the mind is deeply evocative. Its haunting imagery of ''opiate vapour,'' ''rosemary nod[ding] upon the grave,'' and ''the lily loll[ing] upon the wave'' expresses the bliss of death and the hope that Irene's sleep will be restful and deep. *Text: MCW,* I, 179–189; *CWP,* VII, 51–52. *See:* Irene. *Research:* T. O. Mabbott. ''Poe's 'The Sleeper' Again.'' *American Literature*, 21 (1949): 339–340; *LET,* I, 258, 332.

Slidell, Lieutenant. *See:* Mackenzie, Lieutenant Alexander Slidell.

Slyass, Mr. Character mentioned in the short story ''The Literary Life of Thingum Bob, Esq.'' He is the author of an ''inimitable paper on 'Pigs.' ''

Smith, A. C. In 1843, this Philadelphia artist painted a watercolor portrait of Poe. *Research: TPL,* 446, 490.

Smith, Brevet Brigadier-General A. B. C. Character in the short story ''The Man That Was Used Up.'' He looks solid and handsome but really consists of removable artificial parts.

Smith, Elizabeth. [Mrs. Henry Arnold]. Poe's maternal grandmother and an actress at Covent Garden Theater, London. She brought her daughter Elizabeth to the United States in 1795. *Research: LTP*, 4–6.

Smith, Elizabeth Oakes. (1806–1893). Amateur poet and bluestocking. She knew Poe in New York and left a description of him in her autobiography. Her husband, Seba Smith, was a well-known political satirist. *Research: TPL,* xlii, 534–535; Ljungquist, Kent. ''Elizabeth Oakes Smith on Poe: A Chapter in the Recovery of His Nineteenth Century Reputation.'' In *Poe and His Times: The Artist and His Milieu*, ed. Benjamin Franklin Fisher IV. Baltimore: Edgar Allan Poe Society, 1990, 235–246.

Smith, John. Character in the short story ''X-ing a Paragrab.'' He is the rival editor of the *Alexander-the-Great-o-Nopolis Gazette*.

Smith, Richard Penn. (1799–1854). Amateur Philadelphia playwright and author of the tragedy *Caius Marius*. He knew Poe casually through William Burton. Poe lists his chief dramatic works in "Autography" but admits that he "is not sufficiently cognisant of any of these works to speak with decision respecting their merits." *Text: CWP,* XV, 255–256. *Research: TPL,* xlii.

Smith, Seba. (1792–1868). American author. He wrote *Letters of Major Jack Downing* and *Powhatan, a Metrical Romance*. In "Autography," Poe comments, "These were very clever productions; coarse, but full of fun, wit, sarcasm, and sense." Poe included Jack Downing's "good, honest, sensible hand" in "Autography." *Text: CWP,* X, 162–167; XI, 241; XV, 200, 238–239. *Research: PJC,* 263.

Smith, Thomas. Character in the short story "Lionizing."

Smith, Thomas S. (1798–1873). Philadelphia Collector of Customs. He was approached by Poe in 1842 for a position in the customs house but ignored his application. *Research: TPL,* xlii, 378–380, 383–384.

Smitherton, Captain. Character in "Three Sundays in a Week." He is one of the "naval acquaintances" of Kate.

Smollett, Tobias George. (1721–1771). English novelist and author of *The Expedition of Humphry Clinker*. Poe had read and savored Smollett's ugly and abusive characterizations in *Roderick Random* and had also responded to his nasty and scatological energies. Poe vilified his old enemy Charles Briggs by writing that he "carries the simplicity of Smollett to insipidity, and his picturesque low-life is made to degenerate into sheer vulgarity." *Text: CWP,* X, 168; XI, 14, 90; XV, 20–21; XVI, 62. *Research: PLB,* 241.

Snap. Character in the short story "The Business Man." When seen by the narrator at the exchange, he deliberately steps on Snap's toe.

Snob. Character in the short story "The Literary Life of Thingum Bob, Esq." Thingum Bob signs his two-line ode "The Oil-of-Bob" with this name.

Snobbs, Suky. (1). Character in the short story "How to Write a Blackwood Article." This is the name given to Signora Psyche Zenobia by her enemies.

Snobbs, Suky. (2). Character in the short story "A Predicament."

Snodgrass, Joseph Evans. (1813–1880). Medical doctor, editor of the Baltimore monthly *The American Museum* and the *Baltimore Saturday Visiter*, and frequent Poe correspondent. Snodgrass attended to Poe's final hours of alcoholic agony in the streets of Baltimore and wrote a detailed if moralizing account of Poe's death from drink in the *New York Woman's Temperance Paper*. Snodgrass also attended Poe's funeral and noted the crudity of Poe's coffin. In ''Autography,'' Poe wrote ''We like his prose much better than his poetry.'' *Text: CWP,* XV, 222. *Research:* I, *LET,* 125, 127, 152; *PLL,* 253–254.

So-And-So, Marquis of. Character mentioned in the short story ''Lionizing.''

Socrates. (ca. 470–399 B.C.). Greek philosopher and principal character in Plato's *Dialogues*. Poe mentions Socrates in ''The Assignation'' and *Marginalia* but does not discuss his ideas. *Text: CWP,* II, 118; VIII, 203; XI, 189–190; XVI, 43. *Research: LET,* I, 261.

"Some Account of Stonehenge, The Giant's Dance, A Druidical Ruin in England." Article appearing in *Burton's Gentleman's Magazine* for June 1840. Poe carefully and clearly described the layout of the outer and inner circles but was equally careful about proposing any theory about the builders or their purposes. ''To behold this 'wonder of Britain' it should be viewed with an artist's eye, and contemplated by an intellect stored with antiquarian and historical knowledge.'' *Text: CWP,* XIV, 110–113.

"Some Ancient Greek Authors." Anonymous essay appearing in *The Southern Literary Messenger* for April 1836 and assigned to Poe by Benjamin Blake Minor, Killis Campbell, and other Poe scholars. *Research:* Jackson, David K. '' 'Some Ancient Greek Authors': A Work of Poe.'' *Notes & Queries*, 166 (26 May 1934): 368.

"Some Passages in the Life of a Lion." Alternate title for the short story ''Lionizing.'' *See:* ''Lionizing.''

"Some Secrets of the Magazine Prison-House." Essay appearing in *The Broadway Journal* of 15 February 1845. The subject is the need for an international copyright law since it is ''nearly impossible to attain anything from the booksellers in the way of remuneration for literary labor.'' Poe relates the case history of ''your true poor devil author'' who is cheated and defrauded by unscrupulous magazine publishers. ''Why (since pay they must) do they not pay with good grace, and promptly? Were we in an ill humor at this moment, we could a tale unfold which would erect the hair on the head of Shylock.'' *Text: MCW,* III, 1205–1210; *CWP,* XIV, 160–163. *Research: PLL,* 138.

"Some Words with a Mummy." Short story first published in *The American Review: A Whig Journal* for April 1845 and reprinted in *The Broadway Journal* of 1 November 1845. The tale is a clever mock serious exposé of Galvanic experimentation with dead tissue as well as a satire on scientific, political, and sartorial progress. Retiring early from what appears to be a severe hangover from the previous day, the narrator is summoned by a note from Doctor Ponnonner to attend the unwrapping of a mummy at his home ''at eleven to-night.'' The group proceeds to unpack three anthropoid encasements to reveal the mummy itself where they find ''the flesh in excellent preservation, with no perceptible odor.'' Because it is so well preserved, they decide to attach a battery or ''Voltaic pile'' to the mummy in an attempt at reanimation. With the electrodes attached to the tip of its nose, the mummy becomes *in articulo mortis*, ''address[ing] them in very capital Egyptian,'' denouncing them all for violating its 5,050 year sleep. The scientists cannot resist the opportunity of interrogating the mummy, and their seminar becomes a kind of debate between the ancients and the moderns to determine which civilization is the more advanced and superior. To each example of modern scientific superiority, the mummy replies with a sneer, and when the conversation turns to the virtues of democracy, the mummy, echoing the words of the Brobdingnagian King in Swift's *Gulliver's Travels*, refers to this inferior form of government as ''the most odious and insupportable despotism that was ever heard of upon the face of the earth.'' But only the narrator is convinced by the mummy's words and departs after noticing ''the poor mummy's mortification'' over one of Doctor Ponnonner's inane examples of modern superiority, the manufacture of Ponnonner's lozenges and Brandreth's pills. Thoroughly sick of scientific achievement and modern democracy, the narrator will ''just step over to Ponnonner's and get embalmed for a couple of hundred years.'' If ''Ligeia'' is ''the hideous drama of revivification,'' this tale is a burlesque counterpart of that same drama. *Text: MCW,* III, 1175–1201; *CWP,* VI, 116–137. *Research:* Campbell, Killis. ''The Source of Poe's 'Some Words with a Mummy.' '' *Nation*, 23 June 1910, 625–626; Pollin, Burton R. ''Poe's 'Some Words with a Mummy' Reconsidered.'' *Emerson Society Quarterly*, 60 (fall 1970): 60–67; Williams, Michael. ''The Voice in the Text: Poe's 'Some Words with a Mummy.' '' *Poe Studies*, 16 (1983): 1–4; Long, David A. ''Poe's Political Identity: A Mummy Unswathed.'' *Poe Studies*, 23, no. 1 (1990): 1–22.

"Song" ("I saw thee on thy bridal day."). Poem first printed in *Tamerlane and Other Poems* in June 1827 under the title ''To ______ ______'' and based on his melancholy memory of the marriage of his youthful sweetheart, Sarah Elmira Royster, to another man, although it is not certain that she is the bride of the poem. The poet regrets the marriage of his beloved to another, but there is also a twist on this Wertheresque theme insofar as he expresses some spitefulness in the implied hope that she may live to regret her choice. *Text: MCW,* I, 65–66; *CWP,* VII, 106.

Song of Triumph. Untitled poem found in the text of the short story ''Four Beasts in One; The Homo-Cameleopard.'' In mocking fashion, it celebrates the divinity of King Epimanes: ''There is none but Epimanes/ No—there is none!/

So tear down the temples/ And put out the sun!'' *See:* ''Four Beasts in One.'' *Text: MCW,* I, 220.

"The Songs of Our Land, and Other Poems. By Mary E. Hewitt." Review of Hewitt's poems appearing in *The Broadway Journal* of 25 October 1845 and reprinted in *Godey's Lady's Book* for February 1846. Poe found ''God Bless the Mariner'' and ''Alone'' much to his taste and referred favorably to ''the author's poetic fervor, classicism of taste, and keen appreciation of the morally as well as the physically beautiful.'' *Text: CWP,* XII, 254–256; XIII, 98–105.

"Sonnet." Poe's first title for the poem ''An Enigma.'' *See:* ''An Enigma.''

"Sonnet—Silence." *See:* ''Silence—A Sonnet.

"Sonnet—To Science." Poem first appeared as in *Al Aaraaf, Tamerlane, and Minor Poems* by Edgar A. Poe in December 1829 and was used as an introduction to the collection. The sonnet levels a romantic protest against frigid empiricism and scientific rationalism, arguing that the beautiful mysteries that had once been the province of myth, magic, and artistic creativity have been defiled by science. Even the authority of the poet has been undermined: ''Why preyest thou thus upon the poet's heart[?]'' In the sestet, the verbs *dragged, driven,* and *torn* highlight the aggressive and intrusive nature of science in Western culture, while the characterization of science as a ''Vulture, whose wings are dull realities'' is a prophetic anticipation of a modern empiricism that would feed upon and dominate not only Poe's generation but those to follow. The sonnet's attitude toward science can be compared with e.e. cummings's poem ''O sweet spontaneous earth.'' *Text: MCW,* 90–92; *CWP,* VII, 22. *Research:* Holt, Palmer C. ''Notes on Poe's 'To Science,' 'To Helen,' and 'Ulalume.' '' *Bulletin of the New York Public Library,* 63 (October 1959): 568–570; Voss, James. ''Poetry and Mythic Thought: A Structural Approach to the Love Sonnet and to Poe's 'Sonnet—To Science.' '' *Edda: Nordisk for Litteraturforsking* (1978): 271–292.

Sons of Temperance. Poe became a member of the Richmond chapter of this antidrinking organization on 27 August 1849, probably to impress the wealthy widow Elmira Shelton whom he was courting and hoped to marry. *Research:* Moore, Rayburn S. ''A Note on Poe and the Sons of Temperance.'' *American Literature,* 30 (1958): 359–361.

Sophocles. (497–405 B.C.). Ancient Greek tragic playwright. Poe ranked Sophocles below Aeschylus (''Euripides and Sophocles were merely echoes of Æschylus'') and considered the *Antigone* overrated by criticism. ''About the Antigone . . . there seems to me a certain baldness, the result of inexperience in art.'' *See:* ''The Antigone at Palmo's.'' *Text: CWP,* VIII, 43–47; XII, 4, 13, 130–135; XIV, 62; XVI, 72, 119, 174.

Souciet, Pere Étienne. (1671–1744). Astronomer and historian of ancient China. His treatise on coins and medals is mentioned in *Pinakidia*. *Text: CWP,* XIV, 69–70.

South Barracks (number 28). Poe address where he lived while he was a cadet at West Point.

"The South Vindicated from the Treason and Fanaticism of the Northern Abolitionists." Review appearing in *The Southern Literary Messenger* for April 1836 as the second part of his review of Paulding's *Slavery in the United States.* Poe took a prosouthern point of view of the morality of the institution when he wrote that ''in continuing to command the services of their slaves, they violate no law divine or human. . . . Society in the South will derive much more of good than of evil from this much abused and partially-considered institution.'' *Text: CWP,* VIII, 265–275.

The Southern Literary Messenger. Monthly literary periodical based in Richmond and published by Thomas Willis White. Poe joined the staff of the magazine as critic and contributing editor from August 1835 to January 1837. His involvement with *The Messenger* began early in 1835 when Poe wrote to White offering suggestions about how the magazine might be improved and circulation increased. White was sufficently impressed to encourage Poe, who began publishing tales and book reviews in quantity. Between March and November 1835 there appeared ''Berenice,'' ''King Pest,'' and five installments of the drama *Politian.* In August 1835, Poe joined the staff as a salaried staff member and eventually became *The Messenger*'s editor from mid-1836 to January 1837 when the relationship with White deteriorated. Poe left the magazine, calling White an ''illiterate and vulgar, although well-meaning man.'' Poe's accomplishments as editor included an expansion and sophistication of the book review section and the emergence of his own prominence as a literary critic to be respected and feared. During Poe's tenure as editor, *The Messenger*'s circulation rose from 500 to 3,500, making it one of America's most popular and influential literary journals. But during his editorship, Poe's salary never rose above the original $10 per week for which he was originally contracted. Low salaries would become a permanent pattern of Poe's magazine career as well as a source of bitterness even as he struggled to elevate the practice of literary criticism. *Research:* Jackson, David K. *Poe and The Southern Literary Messenger*, with a foreword by J. H. Whitty. Richmond, VA: Press of the Dietz Printing Company, 1934; *PLB,* 76–79; *PJC,* 61–72, 94–207.

Southey, Robert. (1774–1843). English poet. Poe mentions his epic poem *Thalaba* respectfully but expresses no strong opinion about his verse in the several references to Southey in his reviews. *Text: CWP,* VIII, 48–49; IX, 66–69, 73–74; X, 174, 223–225; XI, 13, 159; XIII, 197–199. *Research: PLB,* 78; Pollin, Burton

R. ''Southey's *Curse of Kehama* in Poe's 'City in the Sea.' '' *Wordsworth Circle*, 7 (1976): 101–106.

"Spain Revisited." Review of a travel book by Lieutenant Slidell appearing in *The Southern Literary Messenger* for May 1836. Although Poe objected to the artificiality of the book's dedicatory epistle, he found the book itself to be superior to the average travelogue. ''*Spain Revisited*, although we cannot think it at all equal to the *American in England* for picturesque description (which we suppose to be the forte of Lieutenant Slidell) yet greatly surpasses in this respect most of the books of modern travels with which we now usually meet.'' Poe repeated this judgment of Lieutenant Slidell's literary abilities in ''Autography,'' crediting him with ''close observation in detail—a habit which, when well regulated, as in the case of Lieut. Slidell, tends greatly to vigor of style.'' *Text: CWP,* IX, 1–13; XV, 169. *Research: LET,* I, 101.

"The Spanish Student." Poetic drama by Longfellow. Poe's evaluation is included in his review ''The American Drama.'' Poe's scathing review criticizes Longfellow mercilessly, attacking his plagiaristic tendencies (which Poe invents). ''The play is a poor composition with some fine poetical passages.'' Graham paid Poe $30 for the review, assuring Longfellow that it would be withheld from publication. Graham later used the threat of publication as a means of coercing Longfellow to contribute to *Graham's Magazine*. *See:* ''The American Drama.'' *Text: CWP,* XIII, 54–73. *Research: LET,* I, 238, 258; *PJC,* 385.

Sparks, Jared. (1789–1866). Professor of history at Harvard. His signature is described in ''Autography'' as ''written by a man who was very busy among a great pile of books and papers.'' *Text: CWP,* XV, 164–165, 214.

Spear, Thomas G. (fl. 1830). Minor American poet. In ''Autography,'' Poe wrote, ''His productions have been much admired, and are distinguished for pathos and grace.'' But his signature is ''too clerky for our taste.'' Poe was probably referring to his *Sylvan Scenes, and Other Poems* (1838). *Text: CWP,* XV, 210–211.

"The Spectacles." Short story first published in the Philadelphia *Dollar Newspaper* for 27 March 1844 and the next year in the London newspaper *Lloyd's Entertaining Journal* of 3 May 1845. Not a tale of terror but an optical comedy in which the eyes most certainly do *not* have it. The dismantling climax also is comparable to ''The Man That Was Used Up'' when the object of the narrator's affection reveals herself by tearing off her wig and other false items. The narrator is a highly romantic young man, Napoleon Buonaparte Simpson, whose sole physical drawback is weak eyes. But he refuses to wear glasses since spectacles would mar his handsomeness. He accompanies his friend Talbot to the Paris opera and is there struck by ''the form divine'' of a female figure in one of the boxes, the beautiful widow Madame Eugénie Lalande. A flirtation follows as she returns Simpson's "burning gaze" and "allows her bright eyes to set fully and steadily upon his own." All of the classic symptoms of love at first sight seem to be in effect. Passionate letters flow between the two and Buonaparte is particularly charmed by Madame Lalande's rendition of an aria from Bellini's *Otello* at a musical soirée. To Simpson's passionate proposal, she makes a small demand, a "little boon," that he will abandon his vain affectation about no eyeglasses and wear spectacles for her sake. Simpson's eyes are opened when, upon putting on his specs, he receives a full horrific shock when the real Madame Laland comes into repulsive focus. "Was that—was that—was that rouge? And were those—and were those—were those wrinkles, upon the visage of Eugénie Lalande? What—what—what had become of her teeth?" To compound the fool's humiliation, this eighty-two-year-old spectacularly ugly specimen is Simpson's great-great-grandmother. She had concocted the plot to punish Simpson for his vanity and imprudence and to demonstrate to him the emptiness of the romantic cliché that "love is blind." The arch comedy of the story resembles the type of wit found in Gogol's tales such as "The Nose." *Text: MCW,* III, 883–919; *CWP,* V, 177–209. *Research:* Mooney, Stephen L. "The Comic in Poe's Fiction." *American Literature*, 33 (1962): 433–441; Pollin, Burton R. " 'The Spectacles' of Poe—Sources and Significance." *American Literature*, 37 (1965): 187–190; Salzburg, Joel. "Preposition and Meaning in Poe's 'The Spectacles.' " *Poe Newsletter*, 3, no. 1 (1970): 21.

Spenser, Edmund. (1552–1599). English poet and author of *The Færie Queene*. Poe criticized and amended Spenser's punctuation in "Fifty Suggestions XLIII." *Text: CWP,* XIV, 53, 184. *Research:* Baker, Christopher. "Spenser and 'The City in the Sea.' " *Poe Newsletter*, 5 (December 1972): 55.

"The Sphinx." Short story first published in *Arthur's Ladies' Magazine* for January 1846 and reprinted in *The American Keepsake for 1851.* The frame device involves plague since "the dread reign of cholera in New York" has made the narrator take refuge with an unnamed relative at his pleasant country cottage on the banks of the upper Hudson. The tale also has some resemblances to "The Fall of the House of Usher" since the narrator has fallen "into a condition of abnormal gloom" and his host, like Roderick Usher, has "a richly philosophical intellect" and a magnificent library. Musing over one of these books, the narrator gazes upon a distant hill of the river bank there to behold "some living monster of hideous conformation" with scales, seventy-foot trunk, and the insignia of the death's head covering "nearly the whole surface of its breast." The narrator and his host have often discussed the power of omens, with the narrator taking the position of passionate believer, and the host taking the view of scientific skeptic. The monster now in his view must be a confirmation of the power of omens, perhaps "an omen of my death, or, worse, as the forerunner of an attack of mania." When informed of the narrator's vision, the rational host takes from the bookcase a manual of lepidoptery and reads aloud a description of the genus *Sphinx* of the family of Crepuscularia, a rare species of butterfly also called the Death's-headed Sphinx. The narrator has been victimized by his own overwrought imagination, which has magnified a harmless insect into an ominous monster. In its study of contrastive personalities—the rational skeptic and the mystical believer—the tale reverses the relationship of Roderick Usher and his pragmatic and skeptical guest. *Text: MCW,* III, 1245–1251; *CWP,* VI, 238–244. *Research:* Elmar, Schenkel. ''Disease and Vision: Perspectives on Poe's 'The Sphinx.' '' *Studies in American Fiction*, 13 (1985): 97–102; Goldhurst, William. ''Self-Reflective Fiction by Poe: Three Tales.'' *Modern Fiction Studies*, 16, no. 3 (1986): 4–14.

Spirit of the Times. Philadelphia journal. It published a prospectus for Poe's projected *Penn Magazine*. In the July 1846 issue, in his ''Reply to Mr. English,'' Poe angrily denounced Dr. Thomas Dunn English's character assassination in the New York *Morning Telegraph* for 23 June 1846. This piece is one of Poe's ugliest character assaults in its comparison of English's face to a ''Barnum baboon.'' *Research: TPL,* 295–296, 407–409, 447–448.

"Spirits of the Dead." Poem first published as ''Visit of the Dead'' in *Tamerlane and Other Poems* in June 1827 and as ''Spirits of the Dead'' in *Al Aaraaf, Tamerlane, and Minor Poems* in December 1829. The five stanzas describe a graveyard reverie in which the narrator, one of the spirits of the dead, advises the visitor at his tombstone to ''Be silent in that solitude,/ Which is not loneliness—for then/ The spirits of the dead who stood/ In life before thee are again/ In death around thee—and their will/ Shall overshadow thee: be still.'' *Text: MCW,* I, 70–73; *CWP,* VII, 13.

"Spiritual Song." Fragmentary poem discovered and given a title by the editor of his poetry, J. H. Whitty, in *The Complete Poems of Edgar Allan Poe* (1911). Mabbott included the three-line fragment in his edition of the poems. They read: ''Hark, echo!—Hark, echo!/ 'Tis the sound/ Of Archangels, in happiness wrapped.'' *Text: MCW,* I, 303–304.

Sprague, Charles. (1791–1875). Boston poet sometimes considered to be a member of the Graveyard School. Poe provides an unflattering portrait of him in ''Autography.'' ''His 'Shakespeare Ode,' upon which his high reputation mainly depended, is quite a *second-hand* affair—with no merit whatever beyond that of a polished and vigorous versification. Its imitation of 'Collins' Ode to the Passions' is obvious. Its allegorical conduct is mawkish, *passé*, and absurd.'' *Text: CWP,* XV, 248–249. *Research: PJC,* 255; *TPL,* 323, 337, 338, 355, 447, 508, 510, 513.

Squibalittle, Mrs. Character mentioned in the short story "The Literary Life of Thingum Bob, Esq." She is one of the contributors to the *Lollipop*.

Staël, Anne Louise Germaine Madame de. (1766–1817). French essayist, cultural historian, social critic, and novelist. Poe refers to the influence of her feminist novel *Corinne* on Felicia Hemans and other women writers. Madame de Staël is mentioned in the short story "Lionizing." *Text: CWP*, II, 38; IV, 271; VI, 188; IX, 202.

Stanard, Jane Stith Craig. (1793–1824). Richmond lady and one of Poe's first loves, "the first purely ideal love of my soul." She was the inspiration for the first poem "To Helen" and died at the age of thirty-one after going mad. Her tender graciousness toward Poe might have provided him with the sort of maternal love that his life lacked. After her death on 28 April 1824, Poe frequently visited her grave. *See:* "To Helen." *Research: PLL*, 17, 20, 103, 229.

Stanard, Robert Craig. (1814–1857). Poe's junior and classmate at William Burke's school. He befriended Poe by introducing him to his mother, Jane Stith Stanard. *Research: TPL*, xliii.

"Stanley Thorn. By Henry Cockton." Negative review of a novel appearing in *Graham's Magazine* for January 1842. Poe thought the novel's characters were weak imitations of Fielding, Smollett, and Dickens and belittled the author by referring to him as "Mr. Bogton" throughout the review. "He is a consummate plagiarist; and, in our opinion, nothing more despicable exists. . . . Who so dull as to give Mr. Bogton any more credit for these things than we give the buffoon for the *role* which he has committed to memory?" *Text: CWP*, XI, 10–15. *Research: PJC*, 280.

"Stanzas." Untitled poem appearing in *Tamerlane and Other Poems* in 1827. The title "Stanzas" was assigned in the edition of Poe's *Works* published by Stedman and Woodberry. The poem is a further example of Poe's attempt to depict beauty in terms of metaphors of luminosity, in this instance, a "wild light" that infuses the world and provides a flash of illuminating insight "hid from us in life—but common . . . to awake us." The poem bears close comparison with Emily Dickinson's "A Certain Slant of Light." *See:* " 'In Youth I Have Known One with Whom the Earth.' " *Text: MCW*, I, 76–78; *CWP*, VII, 153. *Research: PEP*, 116.

"Stanzas. To F. S. O." ("Lady! I would that verse of mine"). Poem signed "P." written to Frances Sargent Osgood appearing in *Graham's Magazine* for December 1845. Poe's title was simply "Stanzas." J. H. Whitty's edition of *The Complete Poems* contained the note that Mrs. Osgood had added "To F.

S. O.'' to the title in her own copy of *Graham's Magazine*. *Text: MCW,* I, 385–386.

Stapleton, Mr. Edward. Character in ''The Premature Burial.'' He is one of several case studies of premature interment.

Starr, Mary. (1816–1877). Philadelphia lady who was romantically involved with Poe briefly in Baltimore in 1834. She also knew the Poes in New York City and attended Virginia's funeral on 2 February 1847. Her recollections of Poe appeared in *Harper's* for March 1889 in an article, ''Poe's Mary,'' written by her nephew Augustus Van Cleef. In his edition of the *Poems*, T. O. Mabbott lists a lost poem ''[To Mary Starr''] that he felt must still exist even though he failed to locate any printing. Van Cleef related that his aunt had told him that the poem's contents were ''very severe, and spoke of fickleness and inconstancy.'' *Research: MCW,* I, 232–233; *TPL,* xliii.

Stedman, Mrs. E. Clementine. (fl. 1835). Poet who, according to the remarks on her signature in ''Autography,'' was ''among the best of the contributors to 'Graham's Magazine.' '' *Text: CWP,* IX, 241; XV, 245.

Stedman, Edmund Clarence. (1833–1908). Poe biographer and author of ''Memoir,'' *Edgar Allan Poe*. (1881). In collaboration with G. E. Woodberry, Stedman compiled an edition of Poe's works in ten volumes (Chicago: Stone & Kimball, 1894–1896). *Research:* Scholnick, Robert J. ''In Defense of Beauty: Stedman and the Recognition of Poe in America, 1880–1910.'' In *Poe and His Times: The Artist and His Milieu*, ed. B. F. Fisher IV. Baltimore: Edgar Allan Poe Society, 1990, 256–276.

Steen, Jan. (1626–1679). Dutch painter. Poe used the example of Steen to reinforce his view that beauty, not truth, is the goal of art. ''If truth is the highest aim of either Painting or Poesy, then Jan Steen was a greater artist than Angelo. . . . For one Angelo there are five hundred Jan Steens.'' *Text: CWP,* II, 39; XI, 84, 90.

Stephens, Ann Sophia. (1813–1836). Historical novelist and an editor of *Snowden's Lady's Companion* ''to which she has contributed many articles of merit and popularity.'' Poe included her portrait in ''The Literati of New York City'' and her signature in ''Autography,'' describing her as one who has ''written much and well'' for several periodicals. *Text: CWP,* XV, 56–58, 246. *Research: TPL,* 211, 349, 351, 359, 647, 686.

Stephens, John Lloyd. (1805–1852). American travel book writer and archeologist. He wrote *Incidents of Travel in Egypt* and *Incidents of Travel in Yucatan*. *See:* ''Incidents of Travel in Central America;'' ''Incidents of Travel in

Egypt.'' *Text: CWP,* X, 1–25, 83, 178–181; XVI, 63. *Research: LET,* I, 179, II, 313, 316; *TPL,* xxvii, 244–245, 337–338.

Sterne, Laurence. (1713–1768). English novelist and author of *Tristram Shandy.* Poe's placement of the nonsensical and the absurd in both his comic and his serious tales shows his appreciation of Sterne's irrational comedy. The eccentricities of the characters in the cast of ''Lionizing'' are almost verbatim transcriptions of *Tristram Shandy*'s bizarre cast. *Text: CWP,* IX, 67; XIV, 38; XVI, 30, 145. *Research: PLB,* 133.

Stevenson, Andrew. (1793–1824). Richmond congressman. His letter of 6 May 1829 recommended Poe for appointment to the United States Military Academy at West Point. *Research: TPL,* xliii.

Stevenson, Robert Louis. (1850–1894). English novelist and short story writer. He created ''The Strange Case of Dr. Jekyll and Mr. Hyde'' (1886). Stevenson held partially negative views of Poe, expressing disgust for the subject matter but acknowledging Poe's technical brilliance. ''He who could write 'King Pest' has ceased to be a human being.'' Despite his distaste for Poe, Stevenson's work still shows the mark of Poe's influence, which he was quick to admit. In writing *Treasure Island* (1883), ''I broke into the gallery of Mr. Poe.'' His ghoulish story ''The Body-Snatcher'' ''suggests the dangers of premature *dis*-interment, the thin partition between life and death, [and] the gruesome contrast between the physical and spiritual aspects of man.'' Some critics have argued that ''Jekyll and Hyde'' ought to be read as a detective tale in the mode of Poe's tales of detection. In the absence of a Dupin figure, the novella's secret crime is discovered by the reader and Jekyll's colleagues. *Research:* Campbell, Killis. ''Poe, Stevenson, and Béranger.'' *The Dial,* 16 November 1909, 374–375; Stevenson, Robert Louis. ''The Works of Edgar Allan Poe.'' In *The Works of Robert Louis Stevenson.* New York: Charles Scribner's Sons, 1925, XXIV, 107–118; *PLL,* 160.

Stilleto, Don. Character in the short story ''Lionizing.'' He witnesses Robert Jones's challenge to the Elector of Bluddenuff.

Stockton, Thomas Hewlings. (1808–1868). Amateur poet and hymnologist. According to the ''Autography'' entry, he ''has written many pieces of fine poetry, and has lately distinguished himself as the editor of the 'Christian World.' '' *Text: CWP,* XV, 225.

Stockton, William Telfair. (1812–1869). Fellow cadet at West Point. In later life, he was the author of hunting stories under the title *Dog and Gun. Research: TPL,* xliii.

Stoddard, Richard Henry. (1825–1903). Poe editor and biographer. His memoir, "Life of Poe," was attached to his edition of *The Works of Edgar Allan Poe* (New York: A. C. Armstrong, 1884). He was the author of a poem, "Ode on a Grecian Flute," submitted to Poe when he was editor of *The Broadway Journal*. Poe claimed to have "mislaid" the contribution. Stoddard retaliated for this insult in the poem "Miserrimus." *Research:* Pollin, Burton. "Poe as 'Miserrimus.' " *DIP*, 190–205; Pollin, Burton R. "Stoddard's Elegiac Sonnet on Poe." *Poe Studies*, 19 (1986): 32–34; Reilly, John E. "Preuss and Stoddard on Poe." *Poe Studies*, 25, nos. 1–2 (1992): 38–39.

Stoke Newington, England. Poe's English boarding school. He recalled the place in the short story "William Wilson." *Research:* Chase, Lewis. "Poe's School at Stoke Newington." *Athenæum*, 4606 (June 1916): 294; *MNR*, 17–18, 23–24.

Stone, William Leete. (1792–1844). Editor of the New York *Commerical Advertiser*. He became one of Poe's journalistic enemies when he attacked Poe's harsh reviews in *The Southern Literary Messenger*. Poe included Stone's signature in "Autography" but wrote that "no precise opinion can be had of Mr. Stone's literary style." Poe thought much of his work "absurd" as accurately reflected in his signature in "Autography," "heavy and sprawling, resembling his mental character in a species of utter unmeaningness, which lies like the nightmare, upon his autograph." *See:* "Ups and Downs in the Life of a Distressed Gentleman." *Text: CWP,* XV, 173, 213–214. *Research: PLB,* 51–52.

Story, Judge Joseph. (1779–1845). Massachusetts jurist mentioned in "Autography." "His chirography is a noble one—bold, clear, massive, and deliberate, betokening in the most unequivocal manner all the characteristics of his intellect." *Text: CWP,* XV, 158–159, 242.

Strabo. (63 B.C.–A.D. 23). Ancient Greek geographer. In *Marginalia*, Poe notes the skepticism of "this philosopher [which] must be regarded as one of the most remarkable anomalies on record." *Text: CWP,* XIV, 66; XVI, 92.

Street, Alfred Billings. (1811–1881). Poet of the periodicals who composed nature verse much in the manner of William Cullen Bryant. Poe included a list of his finer poems in "Autography" and noted that "He has made Mr. Bryant his model, and in all Mr. Bryant's good points would be nearly his equal, were it not for the sad and too perceptible strain of imitation." *Text: CWP,* XV, 254. *Research: TPL,* 607.

"Street Paving." Article appearing in *The Broadway Journal* of 19 April 1845. Poe gives a technical description of Roman road making as well as a brief history of the macadamizing process and the alternative use of wooden paving. To solve the problem of deteriorating surfaces in New York, he suggests the use of ''Kyanized wooden pavement.'' ''The preservative agent employed was that of corrosive sublimate—the Bi-Chloride of Mercury. Let a pound of sublimate be dissolved in fifteen or sixteen gallons of water, and a piece of wood (not decayed) be immersed for seventy-two hours in the solution, and the wood *cannot afterward be rotted.* An instantaneous mineralization can be effected.'' *See:* ''Why Not Try a Mineralized Pavement?'' *Text: CWP,* XIV, 164–169. *Research: TPL,* 526.

Stubbs. Character in the short story ''The Spectacles.'' He is Talbot's footman and is pestered by the narrator, Simpson.

Stuffundpuff. Character mentioned in the short story ''The Devil in the Belfry.'' His autograph is cited as a source for the name of the borough of Vondervotteimittiss.

The Stylus. Literary journal planned and projected by Poe in 1843, ''a journal wherein may be found, at all times, upon all subjects within its legitimate reach, a sincere and a fearless opinion.'' He began a partnership with Thomas Clarke, the Philadelphia publisher, but the venture failed when no subscribers were forthcoming. *See:* Clarke, Thomas. *Research: LTP,* 450–453; Pollin, Burton. ''Poe's Iron Pen.'' *DIP,* 206–229; *TPL,* 394–396, 398–399; *MNR,* 191–195.

"A Succession of Sundays." Original title for the short story ''Three Sundays in a Week.'' *See:* ''Three Sundays in a Week.''

Sue, Eugène. (1804–1857). French novelist. Poe had read his novel *Le Juif errant* [The wandering Jew] and mentioned the novel in a note in the short story ''The Domain of Arnheim.'' In a 1,500-word review of the novel in manuscript, Poe attacked Sue's book on grounds of length and disunity of effect. *See: The Mysteries of Paris. Text: CWP,* VI, 179; XVI, 104–109, 157. *Research: LET,* I, 305; Pollin, Burton R. ''The Living Writers of America: A Manuscript by E. A. Poe.'' *Studies in the American Renaissance* (1991): 151–211.

Sully, Robert Matthew. (1803–1855). Nephew of the painter Thomas Sully. He knew Poe casually as a fellow student at Joseph H. Clarke's school and in later life. *Research: TPL,* xliv.

Sully, Thomas. (1783–1872). American portrait painter. Poe mentions his striking style of portraiture in ''The Oval Portrait.'' Sully painted a portrait of Poe in 1839. *Research: TPL,* xliv, 84.

Sulpicius. [Servius Sulpicius Rufus]. (105–43 B.C.). Roman jurist. In *Pinakidia,* Poe accused Tasso of ''literary robbery'' from a letter of Sulpicius to Cicero. *Text: CWP,* XIV, 59–60; XVI, 75, 606.

The Sun. New York City newspaper. It published Poe's most successful public hoodwinking, "The Balloon Hoax," on 13 April 1844. *See:* "The Balloon Hoax."

The Swan Tavern. Richmond boarding hotel where Poe lived in the summer of 1849.

Swedenborg, Emmanuel. (1688–1772). Swedish philosopher, mystic, and visionary. *Concerning Heaven and its Wonders, and Concerning Hell; From Things Heard and Seen* of Swedenborg is one of the volumes in Usher's library. Poe also mentioned "the Swedenborians" in connection with the veracity of his story "Mesmeric Revelation." *Text: CWP,* III, 287; XVI, 71. *Research: TPL,* 468–556, 587, 748, 752.

Swift, Jonathan. (1667–1745). English satirist and author of *Gulliver's Travels*. Although Poe's writings contain no direct discussion of Swift's satiric genius, he obviously admired Swift's misanthropic energy. In his review of Horne's *Orion*, Poe coined the adverb "Laputically" (from Laputa in Book III of *Gulliver's Travels*) to describe a "great work of progress that never progresses." *Text: CWP,* II, 349; V, 211; VIII, 328; IX, 273; X, 184; XI, 252; XIV, 230; XV, 27, 88; XVI, 94. *Research: LET,* 232; Pollin, Burton R. "Dean Swift in the Works of Poe." *Notes & Queries*, 20 (1973): 244–246; *PLL,* 313–314.

Swinburne, Algernon Charles. (1837–1909). English poet. He often berated Americans for failing "to show public reverence" for Poe. *Research:* Swinburne, Algernon. *Letters Chiefly Concerning Edgar Allan Poe from Algernon Charles Swinburne to John H. Ingram.* London: Printed for private circulation, 1910; *PLL,* 265.

"The Swiss Bell-Ringers." Short unsigned article appearing in the New York *Evening Mirror* of 10 October 1844 and ascribed to Poe by T. O. Mabbott in his edition of the *Tales and Sketches*. With tongue in cheek, Poe's paragraph declares that the bell ringers are an automaton group activated by electric current. He is "firmly convinced that they are ingenious pieces of mechanism, contrived on the principle of Maelzel's Automaton Trumpeter and Piano-forte player (exhibited here some years ago), but made so much more perfect and effective by the application to them of the same power which operates in the *Electro-Magnetic* Telegraph, but which should be called *Electro-Tintinnabulic*." *Text: MCW,* III, 1118–1120.

"The Swiss Heiress; or, The Bride of Destiny—A Tale." Novel reviewed negatively in *The Southern Literary Messenger* for October 1836. Poe provides a sarcastic summary of the complicated plot after warning the reader that the novel "should be read by all who have nothing better to do." He ends the review: "and now, in the name of 'fate, foreknowledge and free will,' we solemnly consign it to the fire." *Text: CWP,* IX, 185–191.

Symons, Arthur. (1865–1945). English essayist, poet, and critic. He wrote four essays on Poe and discussed Poe in his study *The Symbolist Movement in Literature* (1899). *Research:* Dameron, J. Lasley. "Arthur Symons on Poe's 'The Fall of the House of Usher.' " *Poe Studies*, 9 (1976): 46–49; *PLL*, 275.

"A Synopsis of Natural History; Embracing the Natural History of Animals, with Human and Animal General Physiology, Botany, Vegetable Physiology, and Geology." Review of Thomas Wyatt's English translation of C. Lemmonnier's scientific text appearing in *Burton's Gentleman's Magazine* for July 1839. Poe recommends it as a textbook for American schools. "The whole work does credit to all parties, and should be patronized." *Text: CWP,* X, 26–27.

"The System of Doctor Tarr and Professor Fether." Short story published in *Graham's Magazine* for November 1845. The narrator, a rather slow-witted but morbidly curious young man, and his companion are touring the south of France when the urge to visit a private madhouse, or Maison de Santé, takes possession of him. Through the friend, the narrator gains an introduction to Monsieur Maillard, superintendent of the santitarium. The description of the narrator's approach to the madhouse is almost a verbatim rewriting of the opening paragraph of "The Fall of the House of Usher." It reads: "Through this dank and gloomy wood we rode some two miles, when the Maison de Santé came in view. It was a fantastic château, much dilapidated, and indeed scarcely tenantable through age and neglect. Its aspect inspired me with absolute dread, and, checking my horse, I half resolved to turn back." Superintendent Maillard welcomes the narrator and agrees to give him the grand tour, although his "system of soothing," which had permitted the inmates free rein, has had to be abandoned "to return to the old usages." Maillard is the quintessence of rationality, sanity, decorum, and self-control—or so he seems to the narrator. Throughout the story, he drops blunt hints of his own madness, all of which are missed by the narrator. The highpoint of the narrator's tour is a lavish banquet attended by thirty guests bedecked in finery and feasting on a "profusion that was absolutely barbaric." Each guest comments with great gusto on the particular lunacies of the patients, and one lady begins to remove her clothes to demonstrate the nudity psychosis of Ma'm'selle Salsafette—that the only way that one could get inside one's clothes was to get outside of them. The mad banquet comes to a climax, "a sort of pandemonium in petto," when all the guests laugh, shout, jest, and "perpetrate a thousand absurdities" while wine flows and the fiddles shriek. Amid the mad uproar the windows of the hall are shattered by the entry of what the narrator takes to be "a perfect army of chimpanzees, ourangoutangs, or big black baboons." The simian army consists of the ten keepers who have been overpowered by the maniacs, then tarred, feathered, and incarcerated in underground cells. The system of Doctor Tarr and Professor Fether appears to have worked to perfection, with the mad now in authority and the sane now monkified. *Text: MCW,* III, 997–1024; *CWP,* VI, 53–77. *Research:* Drabeck, Bernard A. " 'Tarr and Fether': Poe and Abolitionism." *American Transcendental Quarterly*, 17 (1972): 177–184; Johansen, Ib. "The Madness of the Text: Deconstruction of Narrative Logic in 'Usher,' 'Berenice,' 'Doctor Tarr and Professor Fether.' " *Poe Studies*, 22 (1989): 1–9.

T

T., Miss Tabitha. Character in the short story "The Man That Was Used Up." The narrator sits next to her during Drummummupp's sermon.

Tacitus. (55–117). Roman historian. His histories are praised for "concision" in *Pinakidia* and *Marginalia*. *Text: CWP,* III, 269; VII, 231; IX, 156, 193; XIV, 3–5, 49, 69; XVI, 2. *Research: LET,* 5; Arms, George. "Tacitus and Those Goths in 'Letter to B——.'" *Poe Studies*, 13 (1980): 37.

Taglioni, Maria. (1804–1884). Italian ballet dancer mentioned in "Fifty Suggestions," "Loss of Breath," and *Marginalia*. *Text: CWP,* II, 360; X, 91; XIV, 179; XVI, 44.

Talbot, Mr. Character in the short story "The Spectacles."

"A Tale of Jerusalem." Short story published in the Philadelphia *Saturday Courier* for 9 June 1832 and in *The Southern Literary Messenger* for March 1836. A revised version also appeared in *The Broadway Journal* of 20 September 1845. Events take place on the tenth day of the month of Thammuz in the year 3941 as the Roman army of Pompey besieges the Holy City. A trio of pious Jews, Abel-Phittim, Buzi-Ben-Levi, and Simeon the Pharisee, lower a tribute basket from the temple wall laden with the shekels of the tabernacle. They hope and expect to receive in return from the Romans below a sacrificial lamb or ram and believe that such is what they have as they pull up the basket through a heavy mist. " 'The Lord hath softened their hearts to place therein a beast of good weight!' '' But Romans will be Romans, especially during a siege, and as the basket emerges from the mist ''a low grunt betrayed to their perception a *hog* of no common size.'' Only another swine can repay the swine below as the three Jews release their hold on the basket, causing the ''emancipated porker [to tumble] headlong among the Philistines.'' The comic naming and farcical ending render the tale one of Poe's best light pieces of historical fantasy. *Epigraph:* ''Intonsos rigidam in frontem ascendere canos/ Passus erat______a bristly bore'' [He let his uncut gray hair stand on end]. Lucan's *Pharsalia. Text: MCW,* II, 41–51; *CWP,* II, 214. *Research:* Varner, J. G. ''Poe's 'Tale of Jerusalem' and The Talmud.'' *American Book Collector*, 6 (February 1935): 56–57.

"A Tale of the Ragged Mountains." Short story published in *Godey's Lady's Book* for April 1844 and again in *The Broadway Journal* of 29 November 1845. The story reflects Poe's interest in mesmeric experimentation and metempsychotic transfer. The setting is the mountain range near Charlottesville, Virginia. Suffering from neuralgia, the tale's narrator, Augustus Bedloe, submits to Dr. Templeton's mesmeric therapy. On a walking excursion over the Ragged Mountains on an Indian Summer day, Bedloe descends into a chasm in the wilderness and experiences a drug-induced visionary transfer. He is transported backward in time to the city of Benares during the Warren Hastings rebellion of 1780 and is killed there by an arrow through the temple. When he relates his strange experience to the mesmerist, Templeton, he is shown a portrait of Templeton's friend Oldeb, his exact double and the officer who was killed by the arrow in the streets of Benares during the Hastings uprising. This carefully crafted tale illustrates Poe's ability to obliterate or blur those states of mind usually considered to be categorically separate such as waking and sleep, thereby questioning material notions of reality. *Text: MCW,* III, 935–953; *CWP,* V, 163–176. *Research:* Thompson, G. R. ''Is Poe's 'A Tale of the Ragged Mountains' a Hoax?'' *Studies in Short Fiction*, 6 (1969): 454–460; Isani, Mukhtar Ali. ''Some Sources of Poe's 'A Tale of the Ragged Mountains.' '' *Poe Studies*, 5, no. 2 (1972): 38–40; Friederich, Reinhard H. ''Necessary Inadequacies: Poe's 'Tale of the Ragged Mountains' and Borges' 'South.' '' *Journal of Narrative Technique*, 12 (1982): 155–166; Horn, Andrew. ''Poe and the Tory Tradition: The Fear of Jacquerie in ''A Tale of the Ragged Mountains.' '' *ESQ: A Journal of the American Renaissance*, 29 (1983): 25–30; Kopley, Richard. ''Poe's Pym-esque 'A Tale of the Ragged Mountains.' '' In *Poe and His Times: The Artist and His Milieu*, ed. B. F. Fisher IV. Baltimore: Edgar Allan Poe Society, 1990, 167–177.

"Tales and Sketches. By Miss Sedgwick." Review appearing in *The Southern Literary Messenger* for January 1836. Poe has read most of the pieces in the volume and been ''enamoured of their pervading spirit of mingled chivalry and pathos.'' Poe had favorably reviewed her novel *The Linwoods* in the December 1835 number of *The Southern Literary Messenger. Text: CWP,* VIII, 160–162.

Tales by Edgar A. Poe. Collection of twelve stories published by Wiley and Putnam in June 1845. The volume was part of the publisher's ''Library of

American Books'' and contained ''The Gold-Bug,'' ''The Black Cat,'' ''Mesmeric Revelation,'' ''Lionizing,'' ''The Fall of the House of Usher,'' ''A Descent into the Maelström,'' ''The Colloquy of Monos and Una,'' ''The Conversation of Eiros and Charmion,'' ''The Murders in the Rue Morgue,'' ''The Mystery of Marie Rogêt,'' ''The Purloined Letter,'' and ''The Man of the Crowd.'' *Research: TPL,* 540–541.

Tales of the Folio Club. A proposed anthology of short fiction compiled by Poe consisting of eleven pieces alleged to be the work of eleven ''Dunderhead'' members of a literary club. Rejected for publication by Harper, Carey & Lea, and other publishers, the collection never saw light. The literary activities of the Folio Club were described to the Philadelphia publisher Harrison Hall in a letter of 2 September 1836. *See:* Dunderheads. *Research:* Mabbott, T. O. ''On Poe's 'Tales of the Folio Club.' '' *Sewanee Review*, 36 (1928): 171–176; *LET,* 53, 55, 103–104; Hammond, Alexander. ''A Reconstruction of Poe's 1833 *Tales of the Folio Club.*'' *Poe Newsletter*, 5 (December 1972): 25–32; Hammond, Alexander. ''Further Notes on Poe's Folio Club Tales.'' *Poe Studies*, 8 (1975): 38–42; Hammond, Alexander. ''Edgar Allan Poe's *Tales of the Folio Club*: The Evolution of a Lost Book.'' *Library Chronicle*, 41 (1976): 13–43; Richard, Claude (Mark L. Mitchell, trans.). ''The Tales of the Folio Club and the Vocation of Edgar Allan Poe as Humorist.'' *University of Mississippi Studies in English*, 8 (1990): 185–199.

Tales of the Grotesque and Arabesque. Collection of Poe's stories in two volumes published by Lea & Blanchard on 4 December 1839 and dedicated to Colonel William Drayton, Poe's commanding officer while he was stationed at Fort Moultrie. Poe's short ''preface'' is a reply to those critics who had accused him of '' 'Germanism' and gloom. . . . If in many of my productions terror has been the thesis, I maintain that terror is not of Germany, but of the soul,—that I have deduced this terror only from its legitimate sources, and urged it only to its legitimate results.'' Volume I contained fourteen stories: ''Morella,'' ''Lionizing,'' ''William Wilson,'' ''The Man That Was Used Up,'' ''The Fall of the House of Usher,'' ''The Duc de L'Omelette,'' ''MS. Found in a Bottle,'' ''Bon-Bon,'' ''Shadow,'' ''The Devil in the Belfry,'' ''Ligeia,'' ''King Pest,'' and ''The Signora Psyche Zenobia'' with ''The Scythe of Time.'' Volume II contained eleven stories, several retitled: ''Epimanes'' (''Four Beasts in One; The Homo-Cameleopard''), ''Siope'' (''Silence—A Fable''), ''Hans Phaall'' (''The Unparalleled Adventure of One Hans Pfaall''), ''A Tale of Jerusalem,'' ''Von Jung'' (''Mystification''), ''Loss of Breath,'' ''Metzengerstein,'' ''Berenice,'' ''Why the Little Frenchman Wears His Hand in a Sling,'' ''The Visionary'' (''The Assignation''), and ''The Conversation of Eiros and Charmion.'' *Research:* Charvat, William. ''A Note (on the Publication of) Poe's *Tales of the Grotesque and Arabesque*.'' *Publisher's Weekly*, 23 November 1946: 2957–2958.

"Tales of the Peerage and the Peasantry, Edited by Lady Dacre." Review of a collection of short stories appearing in *The Southern Literary Mes-*

senger for December 1835. The three tales are: "Winifred, Countess of Nithsdale," "The Hampshire Cottage," and "Blanche." "There can be no doubt that Lady Dacre is a writer of infinite genius, possessing greater felicity of expression . . . than any of her female contemporaries." *Text: CWP,* VIII, 74–75. *Research: PJC,* 100.

"Tale-Writing—Nathaniel Hawthorne—Twice-Told Tales. By Nathaniel Hawthorne." A double review of Nathaniel Hawthorne's volume of short stories appearing in *Graham's Magazine* for April and May 1842. Poe recognized Hawthorne "as the example, *par excellence*, in this country, of the privately admired and publicly unappreciated man of genius," although Hawthorne's art was marred by his insistent use of allegory, which Poe regards as "metaphor run-mad." The review contains Poe's argument for the artistic superiority of the short story to longer types of fiction. Hawthorne's short stories furnished superlative examples of the power of brevity, singularity of effect, and "true unity." Ranking the "brief prose tale" just beneath the poem as the ideal artistic medium for "the purposes of ambitious genius," Poe attributed to the short story "the immense benefit of *totality*. . . . In the brief tale . . . the author is enabled to carry out his full design without interruption. During the hour of perusal, the soul of the reader is at the writer's control." Among those Hawthorne tales that Poe believed to demonstrate these artistic criteria are "The Hollow of the Three Hills," "The Minister's Black Veil," "Wakefield," and "The White Old Maid." Other stories such as "Sights from a Steeple," "The Haunted Mind," and "The Sister Years" struck Poe not as brief prose fiction at all but as "pure essays." *See:* Hawthorne, Nathaniel; "Tale-Writing—Nathaniel Hawthorne—Twice-Told Tales. . . . Mosses from an Old Manse." *Text: CWP,* XI, 102–104. *Research: PJC,* 317–328; Evans, Walter. "Poe's Revisions in His Reviews of Hawthorne's *Twice-Told Tales*." *Papers of the Bibliographical Society of America*, 66 (1972): 407–419; McAndrews, Carleen. "Edgar Allan Poe's Hawthorne Criticism: An Addition." *Nathaniel Hawthorne Review*, 18 (1992): 21.

"Tale-Writing—Nathaniel Hawthorne—Twice-Told Tales. By Nathaniel Hawthorne. James Munroe & Co., Boston. 1842.—Mosses From an Old Manse. By Nathaniel Hawthorne. Wiley & Putnam, New York. 1846." A revised and expanded version of the review of Hawthorne's tales appearing in *Graham's Magazine* for April and May 1842, this later review appeared in *Godey's Lady's Book* for November 1847. Poe repeated his general view of Hawthorne that "he evinces extraordinary genius, having no rival either in America or elsewhere," but concluded that "he is peculiar and not original. . . . He is infinitely too fond of allegory, and can never hope for popularity so long as he persists in it." Poe also used the review as an occasion for delivering numerous literary opinions on the writing of William Gilmore Simms, John Neal, Charles W. Webber, Ludwig Tieck, and others. Of Bunyan's *The Pilgrim's Progress*, Poe remarked that it "is a ludicrously over-rated book . . . but the pleasure derivable from it, in any sense, will be found in the direct ratio of the reader's capacity to smother its true purpose.'' *See:* Hawthorne, Nathaniel. *Text: CWP,* XIII, 141–155. *Research:* McKeithan, D. M. ''Poe and the Second Edition of Hawthorne's Twice-Told Tales.'' *Nathaniel Hawthorne Journal* (1974): 257–269.

Talfourd, Sir Thomas Noon. [Sergeant Talfourd]. (1795–1854). English jurist, poet, and playwright. Poe was familiar with his popular play *The Athenian Captive. See:* ''The Literary Remains of the Late William Hazlitt.'' *Text: CWP,* IX, 144–145; XV, 92. *Research: TPL,* 227, 346.

Talley, Susan Archer (Weiss). (1822–1917). An amateur Richmond poet, she was acquainted with Poe late in his life and published a memoir of him in *Scribner's Monthly* for March 1878. Her book *Home Life of Poe* (1907) gives a vivid account of his final days but also contains material considered unverifiable rumor. *Research: TPL,* xliv; *PLL,* 243–249.

"Tamerlane." Poem first printed in *Tamerlane and Other Poems* in June 1827. Poe reduced the poem from its original 403 lines to 223 lines when it was published in *Al Aaraaf, Tamerlane, and Minor Poems.* The poem laments the gap separating simple childhood values from the demands of the adult world. The poet recognizes that he has sacrificed ''The loveliness of loving well'' to achieve worldly fame. Poe dramatizes the conflict in the figure of the dying Mongol conqueror, Tamerlane, who pines for the love of a peasant girl. ''I was ambitious—have ye known its fiery passion?'' Having sacrificed the best part of himself in quest ''of power and pride,'' he would now perform a kind of penance for his tragic choice and trade ''A kingdom for a broken heart.'' *Text: MCW,* I, 22–64; *CWP,* VII, 127–139. *Research:* Linz, Franz. ''Poe's 'Tamerlane,' Shakespeare, Keats, and Emily Dickinson.'' *Literaturwissenschaftliches Jahrbuch im Auftrage der Görres-Gesellschaft,* 29 (1988): 323–325.

Tamerlane and Other Poems. By a Bostonian. Poe's first published poetry. In July 1827, fifty copies of the forty-page pamphlet were published by Calvin F. S. Thomas at Poe's own expense. The poems in the volume are ''Tamerlane,'' ''Fugitive Pieces,'' ''To——— ———.'' (''I saw thee on thy bridal day''), ''Dreams,'' ''Visit of the Dead,'' ''Evening Star,'' ''Imitation,'' ''The Lake,'' and three titleless poems, '' 'In youth I Have Known One with Whom the Earth,' '' '' 'A Wilder'd Being from My Birth,' '' and '' 'The Happiest Day, The Happiest Hour.' '' One critic has suggested that ''Tamerlane is meant to be an allegory of Poe's poetic ambition and disappointed love for Elmira Royster.'' *Research:* Wegelin, Oscar. ''The Printer of Poe's *Tamerlane.*'' *New York Historical Society Quarterly Bulletin,* 24 (January 1940): 23–25; *PLL,* 33–35.

Tarpaulin, Hugh. Character in the short story ''King Pest.''

Tasistro, "Count" Louis Fitzgerald. (1807–1868). American critic, actor, and editor of *The Expositor.* His journal is described in ''Autography'' as ''a critical journal of high merit in many respects, although somewhat given to verbiage.'' A review of Poe's *Tales* appearing in the *New-York Mirror* of 28 December 1839 is by Tasistro. *Text: CWP,* XV, 217, 236, 244. *Research: LET,* 212, 213, 316; Tasistro, Louis Fitzgerald. ''A Notice of Poe's Tales.'' In *The Recognition of Edgar Allan Poe: Selected Criticism since 1829*, ed. Eric Carlson. Ann Arbor: Michigan University Press, 1966, 4–5; *TPL,* 284; Bandy, W. T. ''Poe and Tasistro.'' *Poe Studies*, 23, no. 2 (1990): 37–40.

Tasso, Torquato. (1544–1595). Italian poet and author of the epic *Jerusalem Delivered.* While a student in the Italian class of Professor George Blaettermann at the University of Virginia, Poe translated some lines from Tasso and accused Longfellow of literary theft from Tasso in *Marginalia. Text: CWP,* XI, 114; XIV, 44, 59; XV, 87, 237; XVI, 74; *MCW,* I, 13.

Tate, Allen. (1899–1979). American poet and critic. He wrote several influential essays on Poe as a forerunner of the modern existential consciousness, pointing out that Poe's central subject was ''dehumanized man, alone in the world and thus dead to it.'' *Research:* Tate, Allen. ''Our Cousin, Mr. Poe.'' *Partisan Review*, 16 (1949): 1207–1217; Tate, Allen. ''Three Commentaries: Poe, James, and Joyce.'' *Sewanee Review*, 58 (1950): 1–15; Tate, Allen. ''The Angelic Imagination: Poe and the Power of Words.'' *Kenyon Review*, 14 (1952): 455–475; Tate, Allen. ''The Poetry of Edgar Allan Poe.'' *Sewanee Review*, 76 (1968): 214–225; *PJC,* 300, 315, 432, 448.

Tattle, Mr. Character in the short story ''The Man That Was Used Up.''

Taylor, Bayard. (1825–1878). American poet. Poe defended his *Rhymes of Travel* at some length in *Marginalia*, calling attention to the ''grandeur'' of the poetry and denouncing a reviewer. ''My very soul revolts at *such* efforts, (as the one I refer to,) to depreciate *such* poems as Mr. Taylor's.'' *Text: CWP,* XVI, 145–148, 176. *Research: TPL,* xliv, 738, 744, 789.

"The Tell-Tale Heart." Short story published in the Boston *Pioneer* for January 1843 and reprinted in the *Dollar Newspaper* of 25 January 1843. The epigraph from Longfellow's ''Psalm of Life'' appeared only in the first version of the story and was dropped in later printings. A revised version appeared in *The Broadway Journal* of 23 August 1845. In this homicidal monologue, the nameless narrator, who begins the account by declaring total sanity, recalls in detail how he killed an ''old man'' who resided with him in a dilapidated old house. He was driven to the deed by the annoying and accusing eye of the old man, which happened to be ''open—wide, wide open'' when the narrator had stealthily entered the old man's bedchamber one night apparently to spy on the sleeper. Discovering that one of the old man's eyes is ''wide, wide open'' the narrator is suddenly infuriated and, in a savage burlesque of nursery routine, puts the old man to bed for the final time by tipping the bed over on him and smothering him. He then meticulously dismembers the body, hiding the pieces under the floor planking. But soon the pulsations of the old man's heart assail the ears of the murderer, causing him to scream out his guilt to the police and to point out the location of the victim, this confession apparently caused not by regret but by the unbearably painful ringing in his ears of a stentorian heartbeat. In this ultimate gothic story of the self entrapped within a cerebral maze of half-understood impulses, the body deprives the mind of choice, and the narrator is compelled to ''scream or die.'' He ends where he begins as a prisoner of space and time confined to the dark dungeon of his own base drives. Critics have generally regarded the narrator as male, but since the sex of the speaker is indeterminate, there is no reason why the narrator could not be a woman whose whole life has been a confinement to an old dark house. Such an incarceration would be the classic situation of the gothic heroine, although in this case, passive suffering erupts into violence. *Epigraph:* ''Art is long and Time is fleeting,/ And our hearts, though stout and brave,/ Still, like muffled drums, are beating/ Funeral marches to the grave.'' Henry Wadsworth Longfellow, ''A Psalm of Life.'' *Text: MCW,* III, 789–799; *CWP,* V, 88–94. *Research:* Robinson, E. Arthur. ''Poe's 'Tell-Tale Heart.' '' *Nineteenth Century Fiction*, 19 (1965): 369–378; Tucker, D. '' 'The Tell-Tale Heart' and the 'Evil Eye.' '' *Southern Literary Journal*, 13, no. 2 (1981): 92–98; Witherington, Paul. ''The Accomplice in 'The Tell-Tale Heart.' '' *Studies in Short Fiction*, 22 (1985): 471–475; Rajan, Gita. ''A Feminist Rereading of Poe's 'The Tell-Tale Heart.' '' *Papers on Language and Literature*, 24 (1988): 283–300; Gauer, Denis. '' 'The Tell-Tale Heart de Poe': Angoisse et stratégie littéraire.'' *Revue Française d'Études Américaines*, 14 (1989): 395–406.

Tem-pest, Duke. Cadaverous character in the short story ''King Pest.'' He is one of the company of six rotting relatives of the mouldering monarch.

Templeton, Doctor. Character in ''The Tale of the Ragged Mountains.'' He is a physician and mesmerist who treats Augustus Bedloe by inducing hypnotic sleep.

"Ten Thousand a Year. By the Author of 'The Diary of a London Physician.' " Review of a ''periodical novel'' by Dr. Samuel Warren appearing in *Graham's Magazine* for November 1841. Poe was severe in his dismissal of the book as worthless, calling it ''shamefully ill written. Its mere English is disgraceful to an L.L.D.—would be disgraceful to the simplest tyro in rhetoric.'' Further at fault was the novel's lengthy and tedious moralizing. ''Two thirds of the whole novel might have been omitted with advantage.'' *Text: CWP,* X, 210–212. *Research: PJC,* 272.

Tennyson, Alfred Lord. (1809–1892). English poet. He was singled out by Poe for special praise. ''I am profoundly excited by music and by some poems—those by Tennyson especially—whom, with Keats, Shelley, Coleridge (occasionally) and a few others of like thought and expression, I regard as the sole poets.'' *See:* ''Alfred Tennyson.'' *Research: LET,* I, 246–247, 253, 257; *PJC,* 362–364, 388–390; Joseph, Gerhard J. ''Poe and Tennyson.'' *Publications of the Modern Language Association*, 88 (1973): 418–428; Meyers, Terry L. ''An Interview with Tennyson on Poe.'' *Tennyson Research Bulletin*, 2 (1975): 167–168; Jones, Denis H. ''Two Influences on Tennyson.'' *Tennyson Research Bulletin*, 2 (1976): 214.

Terence. [Publius Terentius Afer]. (190–159 B.C.). Roman comic dramatist. He is on the devil's menu in ''Bon-Bon.'' In *Marginalia*, Poe refers to Terence as ''Menander and nothing beyond.'' *Text: CWP,* II, 142; IX, 193; XVI, 72.

Tertullian. [Quintus Septimius Florens Tertullianus]. (ca. 160–ca. 230). Latin church father. Poe's epigraph in ''Berenice'' is taken from his writings. The ''paradox of Tertullian,'' that the resurrection of Christ is certain because it is impossible, is cited in *Marginalia*. *Text: CWP,* II, 21; IV, 139; XVI, 90, 164, 169.

Teufel. Character in the short story ''The Devil in the Belfry.''

Thayer, Colonel Sylvanus. Commandant of cadets during Poe's residence at the United States Military Academy. After his dismissal from the academy, Poe approached Colonel Thayer, seeking his assistance to help him obtain a commission in the Polish army to join the struggle against Russian tyranny, Poe's notion of a Byronic gesture. *Research: PLL,* 43, 44.

Theocritus of Syracuse. (ca. 310–250 B.C.). Ancient Greek pastoral poet. When tasted by the devil in ''Bon-Bon,'' ''Virgilius had a strong twang of Theocritus.'' *Text: CWP,* II, 142.

Theology, Theologus. Character in the short story ''Lionizing.'' He is a guest at the Prince of Wales's literary dinner

Theophrastus. (ca. 372–ca. 287 B.C.). Greek philosopher and character writer. Poe comments in *Pinakidia* that ''Theophrastus, in his botanical works, anticipated the sexual system of Linnæus.'' *Text: CWP,* II, 39; VIII, 258; XIV, 42.

Thingum. Character in the short story ''The Literary Life of Thingum Bob, Esq.''

Thirteenth and East Main Streets. A Poe address in Richmond and the location of the firm of Ellis & Allan in the port and warehouse district of the city. Poe lived here after being taken in by the Allans in 1812.

This-and-That, Earl of. Character mentioned in the short story "Lionizing." He flirts with the Duchess of Bless-My-Soul in the artist's studio.

Thomas, Calvin Frederick Stephen. (1808–1876). Boston printer and publisher. He brought out Poe's first collection of verse, *Tamerlane and Other Poems*, in 1827. *Research: TPL,* xliv, 80–81.

Thomas, Creed. (1812–1889). Classmate of Poe at William Burke's school. *Research: TPL,* xliv, 56–57.

Thomas, Dylan. (1914–1953). English (Welsh) poet. His short life and the circumstances of his death are sometimes compared with Poe's career as a *poet maudit*. In his correspondence, Thomas commented on Poe's theme of the death of a beautiful woman. "The most beautiful thing in the world to Poe was a woman dead. . . . To love a dead woman does not appear to me to be unnecessarily unhealthy, but it is a love too onesided to be pure." *Research: PLL,* 103.

Thomas, Edward J. One of Poe's many enemies in New York in 1845. His romantic interest in Frances S. Osgood brought him into conflict with Poe. *Research: TPL,* xliv, 539–540, 647–648.

Thomas, Frederick William. (1806–1866). Poe correspondent and lifelong friend. He attempted to interest Poe in a position with the government and used his influence through Robert Tyler, the president's son, to procure Poe a place in the Philadelphia Customs House. Thomas remained a lifelong Poe correspondent after meeting Poe in May 1840. In "Autography," Poe referred to his novel *Clinton Bradshaw* as "remarkable for a frank, unscrupulous portraiture of men and things, in high life and low." Thomas's papers contained "Recollections of Edgar A. Poe," an intimate friend's documentary. *See:* Whitty, J.[ames] H. *Text: CWP,* XI, 223, 240; XIV, 133; XV, 209–210. *Research: TPL,* xliv-xlv.

Thompson, John Reuben. (1823–1873). Editor of *The Southern Literary Messenger*. He encountered Poe in the Alhambra Saloon in Richmond in 1848 "mounted on a marble table-top, declaiming passages from *Eureka*." *Research: TPL,* xlv, 788–789, 808–809, 819–820.

Thompson, Mr. Character mentioned in the short story "The Man That Was Used Up." The narrator is erroneously addressed by this name by Brevet Brigadier-General John A.B.C. Smith.

Thomson, Charles West. (1798–1879). Poet mentioned by Poe in ''Autography.'' ''Mr. Thomson has written many short poems, and some of them possess merit. They are characterised by tenderness and grace.'' *Text: CWP,* XI, 241–242; XV, 226. *Research:* Mabbott, T. O. ''An Unpublished Letter to Poe.'' *Notes & Queries*, 174 (28 May 1938): 385; *TPL,* xlv, 789–790, 819–820.

Thornton, Andrew. Character in the short story *The Journal of Julius Rodman.*

" 'Thou Art the Man.' " Short story first published in *Godey's Lady's Book* for November 1844. The tale is a clever murder mystery and story of revenge with the narrator providing both the just revenge and the ingenious solution to the crime. When Mr. Barnabas Shuttleworthy, a wealthy citizen of Rattleborough, mysteriously disappears on the way to a bank in a nearby city, all clues of foul play point to his nephew, Mr. Pennifeather. These clues, a bloody knife, shirt, and bullet all belonging to Pennifeather, are so heavy and obvious that the Dupinesque narrator knows immediately that they are false. The murderer is surely Shuttleworthy's friend, good old Charley Goodfellow, but how can he be exposed and brought to justice with young Pennifeather convicted and awaiting the gallows? Using Dupin's logical skills and Montresor's techniques of entrapment, the narrator lures Goodfellow with a fake letter promising a double boxed shipment of the fine wine Château Margaux. The box holding the wine will contain instead the recovered corpse of Shuttleworthy rigged with a whalebone spring device to make the body sit up at the proper moment. At the climax of a drunken party given by Goodfellow, the wine box is opened ''and, at the same instant, there sprang up into the sitting position, directly facing the host, the bruised, bloody, and nearly putrid corpse of the murdered Mr. Shuttleworthy himself.'' The cadaver's accusing gaze followed by the words ''Thou art the man'' cause the instant death of the murderer, Goodfellow. Having carefully arranged all the details of the revenge, the narrator had exercised his ''ventriloquial abilities'' to make the corpse seem to utter the death sentence. The story has connections with the Dupin stories and other tales of revenge, especially ''The Cask of Amontillado.'' The bloody corpse at the banquet indicates Poe's way of adapting a Shakespearean moment, in this case, the appearance of the murdered Banquo at Macbeth's table, to his own preconceived effect. *Text: MCW,* III, 1042–1060; *CWP,* V, 290–309. *Research:* Cecil, L. Moffitt. ''Poe's Wine List.'' *Poe Newsletter*, 5 (December 1972): 41–42; Rougé, Bertrand. ''Irony and Ventriloquism: Notes toward an Interpretation of Edgar Allan Poe's 'Thou Art the Man.' '' In *Interface: Essays on History, Myth, and Art in American Literature*, ed. Daniel Royot. Montpellier, France: Publications de la Recherche, Université Paul Valéry, 1985, 21–30.

"Thoughts on His Intellectual Character." *See:* Hazlitt, William; ''The Literary Remains of the Late William Hazlitt.'' *Text: CWP,* IX, 144–145.

"Thoughts on the Religious State of the Country; With Reasons for Preferring Episcopacy." Review of a religious tract by the Reverend Calvin Colton appearing in *The Southern Literary Messenger* for June 1836. Although Poe criticized the style of the work as ''excessively faulty—even uncouth,'' he recommended the tract to ''all classes of the Christian community who admire perspicuity, liberality, frankness, and unprejudiced inquiry.'' *Text: CWP,* IX, 33–36.

"A Thousand, a Thousand, a Thousand." A mock war song. *See:* ''Four Beasts in One.'' *Text: CWP,* II, 209.

"The Thousand-and-Second Tale of Scheherazade." Short story first published in *The Broadway Journal* of 25 October 1845 and in *Godey's Lady's Book* for February 1845. The thousand-and-second is the final and, as it turns out, fatal tale and has come down to the narrator by way of the ancient authority of the ''Tellmenow Isitsöornot,'' a text that recites the true history of the vizier's daughter who preserved her life each night by leaving a wondrous tale unfinished for her homicidal royal husband. On night 1,002, Scheherazade regaled the king with another saga of Sinbad the sailor wherein he rode upon the back of a seamonster from strange land to strange land. The king grows progressively impatient and annoyed with the mounting absurdities of her narrative as his increasingly irate interjections show, passing from ''Humph'' to ''Pooh'' to ''Pshaw'' to ''Stuff'' to ''Nonsense'' to ''Twattle'' to ''Ridiculous'' to ''Absurd'' to ''Preposterous'' to ''Stop!'' when Scheherazade describes a land where female beauty is measured by the size of camel humps on women's backs. ''I can't stand that, and I won't. You have already given me a dreadful headache with your lies. You might as well get up and be throttled.'' In this story of exaggerated storytelling, Poe plays with the notion of any audience's large but limited tolerance for exotic fantasy. The elaborate footnoting adorning the tale provides modern scientific verification for nearly every one of Scheherazade's wild, impossible, and grotesque events and locales. *Epigraph:* ''Truth is stranger than fiction.'' Traditional adage. *Text: MCW,* III, 1149–1174; *CWP,* VI, 78–102. *Research:* Denuccio, Jerome D. ''Fact, Fiction, Fatality: Poe's 'The Thousand-and-Second Tale of Scheherazade.' '' *Studies in Short Fiction*, 27 (1990): 365–370.

"Three Sundays in a Week." Short story by Poe originally entitled ''A Succession of Sundays.'' It was first published under this title in the Philadelphia *Saturday Evening Post* of 27 November 1841 and under the current title in *The Broadway Journal* of 10 May 1845. The story is not a tale of terror but a parlor piece. It also has strong autobiographical overtones since the woman whom the narrator, Bobby, wishes to marry is his cousin. Bobby seeks permission from his granduncle Rumgudgeon, a ''hard-hearted, dunder-headed, obstinate, rusty, crusty, musty, fusty old savage,'' and is informed that he can marry his fifteen-year-old daughter Kate ''when three Sundays come together in a week.'' The lovers' dilemma created by the curmudgeonly uncle, whose character carries overtones of John Allan, is resolved when two ''naval acquaintances'' of Kate, Captains Pratt and Smitherton, visit the household on Sunday and resolve the problem. Abetted by Kate, the sea captains deliberately start a friendly argument over what day of the week it is. Since Captain Smitherton has sailed east around the world, Captain Pratt has sailed west around the earth, and Kate has remained at home with her father, it would seem that ''three Sundays have come together in a week'' since one captain lost a day, while the other gained one. ''With [Smitherton], yesterday was Sunday, with [Kate], to-day is Sunday, and thus, with Pratt, tomorrow will be Sunday.'' Entrapped by this stroke of circumnavigatory logic, Uncle Rumgudgeon surrenders Kate to his nephew. ''Three Sundays in a row! I'll go, and take Dubble L. Dee's opinion upon that.'' *Text: MCW,* II, 648–659; *CWP,* IV, 227–235. *Research:* Cherry, Fannye N. ''The Source of Poe's 'Three Sundays in a Week.' '' *American Literature*, 2 (1930): 332–335; Taylor, Archer. ''Poe's Dr. Lardner and 'Three Sundays in a Week.' '' *American Notes & Queries*, 3 (1944): 153–155; Roth, Martin. ''Poe's 'Three Sundays in a Week.' '' *Sphinx*, 4, no. 4 (1985): 258–267.

Tickell, Thomas. (1686–1740). English poet and translator of *The Iliad.* His verse is quoted in *Pinakidia.* In *Marginalia*, Poe comments that ''Macaulay . . . overrates Tickell'' and accuses Tickell of plagiarizing his lines from Boileau. *Text: CWP,* XIV, 58; XVI, 47, 77.

Tieck, Johann Ludwig. (1773–1853). German fantasy writer. Poe compared Tieck's style to Hawthorne's. Tieck's novel *Journey into the Blue Distance* (1834) is one of the titles in Usher's library. Several modern critics have argued for various parallels of style, subject matter, and situation between the tales of Poe and Tieck. *Text: CWP,* III, 287; IV, 102; IX, 202; XIII, 144–145; XVI, 42. *Research:* Zeydel, Edwin H. ''Edgar Allan Poe's Contacts with German as Seen in his Relations with Ludwig Tieck.'' In *Studies in German Literature of the Nineteenth and Twentieth Centuries: Festshrift for Frederic E. Coenen*, ed. Siegfried Mews. Chapel Hill: North Carolina University Press, 1970, 47–54; Lewis, Paul. ''The Intellectual Functions of Gothic Fiction: Poe's 'Ligeia' and Tieck's 'Wake Not the Dead.' '' *Comparative Literature Studies*, 16 (1979): 207–221.

Tiger. Canine character in the novel *The Narrative of Arthur Gordon Pym.* He is Pym's dog and is in the dark hold of the *Grampus* when Pym awakens to find some sort of monster on his chest.

Tintontintino, Signor. Character in the short story ''Lionizing.'' He is an art expert and one of the guests at the Prince of Wales's literary dinner.

"To ———." ("I heed not that my earthly lot"). Variant text of the poem ''To M ——.'' *See:* ''To M ——.'' *Text: MCW,* I, 137.

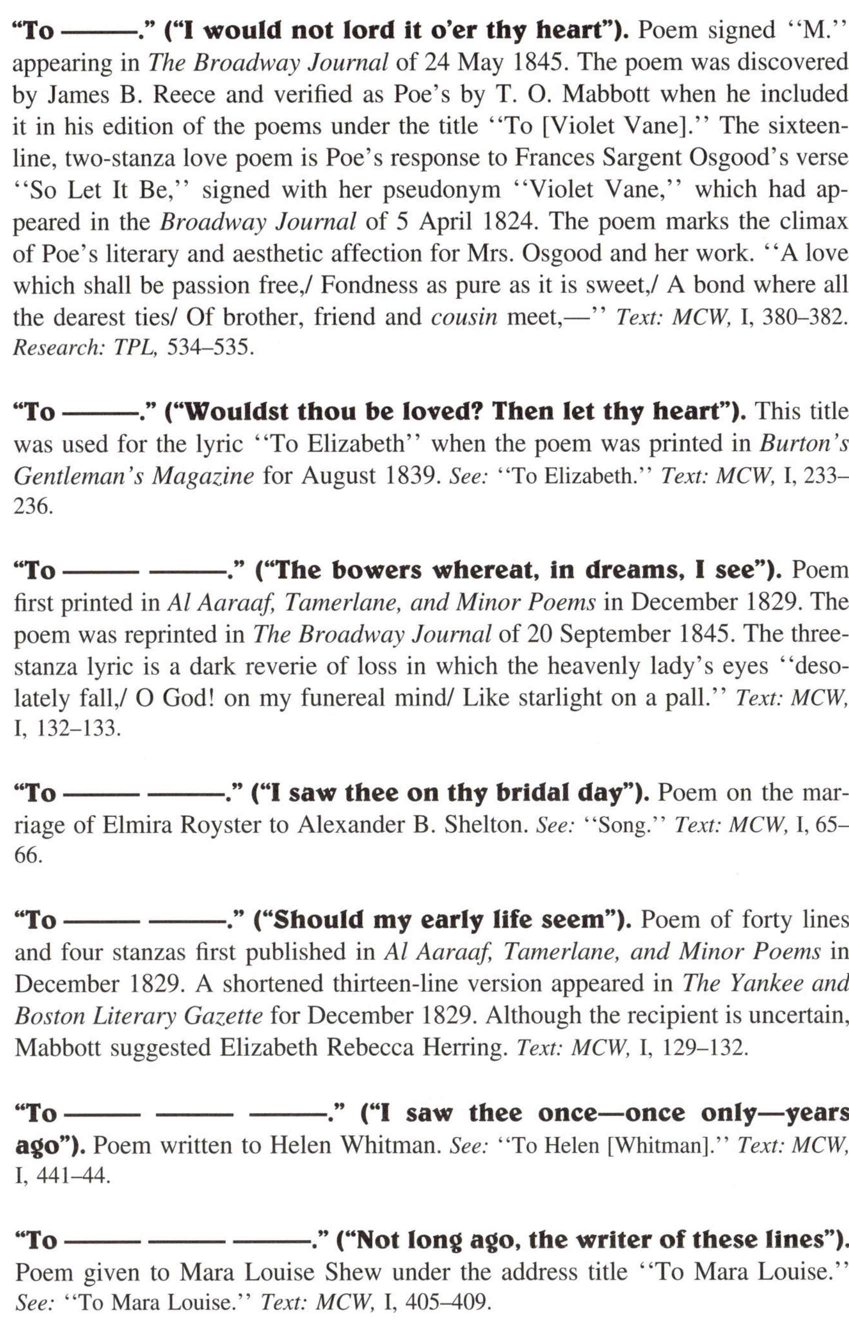

"To ———." ("I would not lord it o'er thy heart"). Poem signed ''M.'' appearing in *The Broadway Journal* of 24 May 1845. The poem was discovered by James B. Reece and verified as Poe's by T. O. Mabbott when he included it in his edition of the poems under the title ''To [Violet Vane].'' The sixteen-line, two-stanza love poem is Poe's response to Frances Sargent Osgood's verse ''So Let It Be,'' signed with her pseudonym ''Violet Vane,'' which had appeared in the *Broadway Journal* of 5 April 1824. The poem marks the climax of Poe's literary and aesthetic affection for Mrs. Osgood and her work. ''A love which shall be passion free,/ Fondness as pure as it is sweet,/ A bond where all the dearest ties/ Of brother, friend and *cousin* meet,—'' *Text: MCW,* I, 380–382. *Research: TPL,* 534–535.

"To ———." ("Wouldst thou be loved? Then let thy heart"). This title was used for the lyric ''To Elizabeth'' when the poem was printed in *Burton's Gentleman's Magazine* for August 1839. *See:* ''To Elizabeth.'' *Text: MCW,* I, 233–236.

"To ——— ———." ("The bowers whereat, in dreams, I see"). Poem first printed in *Al Aaraaf, Tamerlane, and Minor Poems* in December 1829. The poem was reprinted in *The Broadway Journal* of 20 September 1845. The three-stanza lyric is a dark reverie of loss in which the heavenly lady's eyes ''desolately fall,/ O God! on my funereal mind/ Like starlight on a pall.'' *Text: MCW,* I, 132–133.

"To ——— ———." ("I saw thee on thy bridal day"). Poem on the marriage of Elmira Royster to Alexander B. Shelton. *See:* ''Song.'' *Text: MCW,* I, 65–66.

"To ——— ———." ("Should my early life seem"). Poem of forty lines and four stanzas first published in *Al Aaraaf, Tamerlane, and Minor Poems* in December 1829. A shortened thirteen-line version appeared in *The Yankee and Boston Literary Gazette* for December 1829. Although the recipient is uncertain, Mabbott suggested Elizabeth Rebecca Herring. *Text: MCW,* I, 129–132.

"To ——— ——— ———." ("I saw thee once—once only—years ago"). Poem written to Helen Whitman. *See:* ''To Helen [Whitman].'' *Text: MCW,* I, 441–44.

"To ——— ——— ———." ("Not long ago, the writer of these lines"). Poem given to Mara Louise Shew under the address title ''To Mara Louise.'' *See:* ''To Mara Louise.'' *Text: MCW,* I, 405–409.

"To ——— ——— ———." ("Sleep on, sleep on, another hour—"). Poem addressed to an anonymous lady first printed in the *Baltimore Saturday*

Visiter of 11 May 1833 and signed "Tamerlane." The five-stanza lullaby implores her to "Sleep on, some fairy dream/ Perchance is woven in thy sleep—/ But, O, thy spirit, calm, serene,/ Must wake to weep." *Text: MCW,* I, 223–224. *Research:* French, John C. "Poe and the Baltimore *Saturday Visiter.*" *Modern Language Notes*, 33 (1918): 257–267.

"To Elizabeth." ("Would'st thou be loved? Then let thy heart"). Poem written for his cousin Elizabeth Rebecca Herring and inscribed by Poe in her album in 1833. The poem was published in *The Southern Literary Messenger* for September 1835 and written to Eliza White, daughter of the magazine's owner. When it was reprinted in *Burton's Gentleman's Magazine* for August 1839, it was addressed to no lady in particular. Later versions of the lyric were dedicated to Frances S. Osgood. *See:* "To F____s S. O____d." *Text: MCW,* I, 233–236.

"To F ____." ("Beloved, amid the earnest woes"). Poem written to Frances Sargent Osgood and published under various titles. It appeared under the title "To F ____" in *The Broadway Journal* of 26 April 1845 and as a four-line tribute in *The Broadway Journal* of 6 September 1845. *See:* "To Frances"; "To Mary"; "To One Departed." *Text: MCW,* I, 236–237.

"To F____s S. O____d." ("Thou wouldst be loved?—then let thy heart"). Poem written to Frances S. Osgood first published under this title in *The Raven and Other Poems* and in *The Lover's Gift* for 1848. *See:* "To Elizabeth."

"To Frances." Later title used for the poem "To F ____." *See:* "To F ____."

"To Helen." ("Helen, thy beauty is to me"). The first of two poems with this title, written for Jane Stith Stannard. The poem first appeared in *Poems by Edgar A. Poe* and was reprinted in *The Southern Literary Messenger* for March 1836. With "The Raven," it remains Poe's most popular recitation piece. The Helen of the poem symbolizes the peace, serenity, ideal beauty, and divine form associated with the art of antiquity, all a solace for "The weary, way-worn wanderer" to whom Helen brings sublime peace of mind from his painful travels "On desperate seas long wont to roam." *Text: MCW,* I, 163–171; *CWP,* VII, 46. *Research:* Baum, Paull F. "Poe's 'To Helen.' " *Modern Language Notes*, 64 (1949): 289–297; Walker, Warren S. "Poe's 'To Helen.' " *Modern Language Notes*, 72 (1957): 491–492; Gargano, James W. "Poe's 'To Helen.' " *Modern Language Notes*, 75 (1960): 652–653.

"To Helen [Whitman]." ("I saw thee once—once only—years ago"). The second of two poems with this title, written for Sarah Helen Whitman. It was first published in the *Union Magazine* for November 1848 under the title "To ______ ______ ______." When Poe first saw Sarah Helen Whitman on

21 September 1848 he beheld "Helen—my Helen—the Helen of a thousand dreams—she whose visionary lips had so often lingered upon my own in the divine trance of passion." *Text: MCW,* I, 441–449; *CWP,* VII, 107–109.

"To Her Whose Name Is Written Below." Heading for Poe's poem "A Valentine" addressed to Frances S. Osgood and appearing in the New York *Evening Mirror* of 21 February 1846. *See:* "A Valentine."

"To Ianthe in Heaven." Poem first printed under this title in *Burton's Gentleman's Magazine* for July 1839. *See:* "To One in Paradise."

"To Isaac Lea." Four-line poem contained in a letter to the publisher Isaac Lea. Mabbott dated the poem at May 1829. The "cause" mentioned in the two-couplet quatrain is the writing of poetry itself. "It was my choice or chance or curse/ To adopt the cause for better or worse/ And with my worldly goods and wit/ And soul and body worship it." *Text: MCW,* I, 147.

"To M ——." ("Oh! I care not that my earthly lot"). Poem originally entitled "Alone" first appearing in *Al Aaraaf, Tamerlane, and Minor Poems* in December 1829. In five quatrains, the poet-narrator's voice from the grave speaks to the woman who treads on his grave. "But that, while I am dead yet alive/ I cannot be, lady, alone." *Text: MCW,* I, 135–138.

"To M. L. S. ——." Valentine poem given by Poe to Marie Louise Shew and published in the *Home Journal* of 13 March 1847. In a single stanza of eighteen lines, Poe expresses his deep gratitude to her for the care given to Virginia Poe in her final illness, especially "the seraphic glancing of thine eyes." *Text: MCW,* I, 399–401; *CWP,* VII, 101.

"To Margaret." Unpublished poem identified by T. O. Mabbott and contained in holographic form in the album of Margaret Bassett in September 1827. The poem is a pastiche of lines from Milton, Cowper, Shakespeare, and Pope. Hamlet's third soliloquy becomes "To write? To scribble? Nonsense and no more?" *Text: MCW,* I, 14–16; *TPL,* 82.

"To Marie Louise." ("Not long ago, the writer of these lines"). Valentine poem sent to Marie Louise Shew in February 1848 and published under the title "To —— —— ——" in the *Columbian Lady's and Gentleman's Magazine* for March 1848. *Text: MCW,* I, 405–409.

"To Mary." Poem by Poe written for Miss Mary Winfree and first published in *The Southern Literary Messenger* for July 1835 and printed as "To One Departed" in *Graham's Magazine* for March 1842. Poe converted the title "To

F____'' when he became romantically involved with Frances Sargent Osgood in 1845. *See:* ''To F ____''; ''To One Departed.''*Text: MCW,* I, 236–237.

"To Mary Starr." A lost poem described by Mabbott in his edition of the poetry. *See:* Starr, Mary. *Research: MCW,* I, 232.

"To Miss Louise Olivia Hunter." Unpublished valentine poem. In manuscript, the poem is dated by Poe as written on 14 February 1847. A fifteen-line poem on disappointed love, it contains the interesting lines: ''While on dreams relying,/ I am spelled by art.'' *Text: MCW,* I, 396–399. *Research:* McLean, Sydney R. ''Poeana I. A Valentine.'' *Colophon*, new series I, (autumn 1935): 183–187; *TPL,* 625.

"To My Mother." Sonnet first published in *The Flag of Our Union* of 7 July 1849 and in the annual *Leaflets of Memory for 1850.* The sonnet pays tribute to Maria Poe Clemm who was both Poe's aunt and mother-in-law. His real mother is referred to in lines 9 and 10: ''My mother—my own mother, who died early,/ Was but the mother of myself.'' *Text: MCW,* I, 465–468; *CWP,* VII, 116.

"To Octavia." Youthful nine-line unpublished poem written for the album of Octavia Walton in March 1827. The poem's title was assigned by T. O. Mabbott. Poe expressed his love in the quatrain. ''But Octavia, do not strive to rob/ My heart, of all that soothes its pain/ The mournful hope that every throb/ Will make it break for thee!'' *Text: MCW,* I, 16–17. *Research: TPL,* 79.

"To One Beloved." Alternative title for a poem by Poe entitled ''To One in Paradise.'' The poem was entitled ''To One Beloved'' when it appeared in the *Saturday Evening Post* of 9 January 1841. *See:* ''To One in Paradise.''

"To One Departed." This poem is a revised version of ''To Mary'' and first appeared under this title in *Graham's Magazine* for March 1842. *See:* ''To Mary.''

"To One in Paradise." Poem by Poe originally included with the short story ''The Visionary'' in *The Southern Literary Messenger* for July 1835 and in *The Lady's Book* for January 1834. Later titles include ''To Ianthe in Heaven,'' ''To One Beloved,'' and ''To One Departed.'' *See:* ''The Assignation''; ''To Ianthe in Heaven.'' *Text: MCW,* I, 211–216; *CWP,* VII, 86. *Research:* Basler, Roy P. ''Byronism in Poe's 'To One in Paradise.' '' *American Literature*, 9 (1937): 232–236.

"To the River _____." Poem first published in *Al Aaraaf, Tamerlane, and Minor Poems* in December 1829. The poem was frequently reprinted in various periodicals including *Burton's Gentleman's Magazine* for August 1839, the Philadelphia *Saturday Museum* of 4 March 1843, and *The Broadway Journal* of 6

September 1845. The serene lyric of fourteen lines celebrates the river's containment of the poet's beloved. ''For in his heart, as in thy stream,/ Her image deeply lies.'' Mabbott claimed that Poe wanted the reader to think of the River Po in Italy by way of an unstated pun. *Text: MCW,* I, 133–135; *CWP,* VII, 42. *Research:* Mabbott, T. O. ''Poe's 'To the River.' '' *Explicator*, 3 (June 1945): query 21; Pollin, Burton. ''Poe and the River.'' *DIP*, 144–165.

"To Zante." Poem by Poe first appearing in *The Southern Literary Messenger* for January 1837. It is a Shakespearean sonnet that rhapsodizes on the beauties of the island of that name. ''Fair isle, that from the fairest of all flowers,/ Thy gentlest of all gentle names dost take!/ How many memories of what radiant hours/ At sight of thee and thine at once awake.'' *Text: MCW,* I, 310–312; *CWP,* VII, 197. *Research:* Pollin, Burton. ''Poe's 'Sonnet to Zante': Sources and Associations.'' *DIP*, 91–106.

Toby. Character mentioned in the novella *The Journal of Julius Rodman*. This black man is ''as ugly an old gentleman as ever spoke—having all the peculiar features of his race.''

"Tom O'Bedlam's Song." Used by Poe as an epigraph for ''The Unparalleled Adventure of One Hans Pfaall.'' The line ''With a burning spear and a horse of air'' also suggests the supernatural climax of ''Metzengerstein.''

Tomlin, John. (1806–1850). Amateur journalist, regular Poe correspondent, and backer of *The Penn Magazine* and *The Stylus*. Tomlin was a an avocational letter writer who corresponded with all of the literary notables of his day. Together with Poe, he received replies to his letters from Longfellow, Tennyson, Dickens, and others, publishing these under the pen name ''Joe Bottom'' in a series of pieces called ''The Autobiography of a Monomaniac.'' The ''Autography'' entry mentions his excellent contributions to *Burton's Gentleman's* and *Graham's Magazine* ''and to several of the Southern and Western Journals.'' *Text: CWP,* XV, 231. *Research: TPL,* xlv, 309–310, 353–354, 383–385, 422–423, 434–436.

Tooke, John Horne. (1736–1812). English philologist. In his review of Charles Richardson's *A New Dictionary of the English Language*, Poe called Tooke ''the greatest of all philosophical grammarians, and whose developments of an entirely novel theory of language have excited the most profound interest and respect in the minds of all who think.'' *Text: CWP,* IX, 105; XVI, 3.

Too-Wit. Character in *The Narrative of Arthur Gordon Pym*. He is a treacherous native chieftain.

"Tortesa, the Usurer: A Play. By N. P. Willis." Review of Nathaniel Parker Willis's drama appearing in *Burton's Gentleman's Magazine* for August 1839. Poe declared the drama to be "by far the best play from the pen of an American author" and continued his review in this lavish mood, citing the drama's "naturalness, truthfulness" and "conception of character" and crediting Willis with amending nature through his art. "Mr. Willis has not lost sight of the important consideration that the perfection of the dramatic, as well as of plastic skill, is found not in the imitation of Nature, but in the artistical adjustment and amplification of her features." *See:* "The American Drama." *Text: CWP,* X, 27–30. *Research: PLB,* 154; *LET,* 116, 119, 417; *PJC,* 221–222, 382–383.

Touch-and-Go Bullet-head. Character in the short story "X-ing a Paragrab."

Touch-Me-Not, His Royal Highness of. Character mentioned in the short story "Lionizing." He is seen in the artist's studio.

"The Tower of London." Review of William Harrison Ainsworth's historical novel appearing in *Graham's Magazine* for March 1841. Poe judges the novel to be "utterly destitute of every ingredient requisite to a good romance. . . . The 'Tower of London' is, at once, forced and uninteresting. It is such a novel as sets one involuntarily to nodding." *Text: CWP,* X, 110–111.

Town, Charles H. (fl. 1840). His 1843 translation for Harper of Eugene Sue's *Mysteries of Paris* was criticized as flawed by Poe in *Marginalia. Text: CWP,* XVI, 105–107.

Townshend, Chauncey Hare. (1798–1868). English poet, painter, and student of mesmerism. Poe referred admiringly to his book, *Facts in Mesmerism* in *Marginalia. Text: CWP,* XII, 123, XVI, 115. *Research: BRE,* 304.

Tracle, Misthress. The "purty widdy" who is ogled by the little Frenchman who wears his hand in a sling in the short story "Why the Little Frenchman Wears His Hand in a Sling."

"Traits of American Life. By Mrs. Sarah J. Hale." Review appearing in *The Southern Literary Messenger* for December 1835. Poe lists the fourteen pieces and singles out "The Silver Mine" as "perhaps, the best of the whole—but they are all written with grace and spirit, and form a volume of exceeding interest." *Text: CWP,* VIII, 117–118.

Trevanion, Lady Rowena of Tremaine. Character in the short story "Ligeia." She is the narrator's second wife.

Trippetta. Character in the short story ''Hop-Frog.'' She is retained by the King as a court dancer and is ''a young girl very little less dwarfish than [Hop-Frog] himself.''

Trotter, Mrs. Character in the short story ''Diddling.'' She is the fictitious wife in one of the case studies on how to diddle successfully.

Trumbull, John. (1750–1831). American poet and author of the satire *M'Fingal, a Modern Epic Poem* condemned by Poe in ''The Quacks of Helicon'' as a ''clumsy poem.'' *Text: CWP,* X, 182; XIII, 165; XV, 47. *Research: TPL,* 517.

Tsalemon. Character mentioned in *The Narrative of Arthur Gordon Pym.*

Tucker, Nathaniel Beverley. (1784–1851). American southern jurist, novelist, and contributor to *The Southern Literary Messenger*. Poe reviewed his novel *George Balcombe* (1836). Tucker's handwriting in ''Autography'' suggested that he ''is more given to vituperation for the mere sake of *point* or pungency than is altogether consonant with his character as a judge.'' *See:* ''George Balcombe.'' *Text: CWP,* VIII, 243–244, 246–247; IX, 243–265; XV, 195–196; XVI, 142. *Research:* Wilson, James Southall. ''Unpublished Letters of Edgar Allan Poe.'' *Century*, 108 (March 1924): 34–59; *PJC,* 96–120.

Tuckerman, Henry Theodore. (1813–1871). Editor of the *Boston Miscellany* from which position he rejected ''The Tell-Tale Heart.'' Poe included him in ''Autography'' as an example of literary dullness. ''He is a correct writer so far as mere English is concerned, but an insufferably tedious and dull one.'' *Text: CWP,* VII, 110; XV, 217. *Research: TPL,* xlvi, 388–389, 548–549.

Tupper, Martin Farquhar. (1810–1889). Reviewer for the *London Literary Gazette*. He noticed Poe's *Tales* enthusiastically in the issue of 31 January 1846. *Research: TPL,* xlvi, 607–608.

Turgenev, Ivan Sergievich. (1818–1883). Russian novelist and short story writer. His reading of Poe is evident in the short story ''Klara Milich,'' which he called in a letter ''a semi-fantastic story in the manner of Poe.'' *Research:* Turjan, Marietta. ''Turgenev i Edgar Po.'' *Studia Slavica Academiæ Scientiarum Hungaricæ*, 19 (1973): 407–415; Seeley, Frank F. *Turgenev: A Reading of His Fiction.* Cambridge: Cambridge University Press, 1991, 325.

Turnip, Miss Tabitha. Character mentioned in the short story ''How to Write a Blackwood Article.'' She is the gossip who misreports Signora Psyche Zenobia's name to be Suky Snobbs.

Turtle Bay, 47th Street, at East River. A Poe address in New York City where he resided in the spring of 1846 from February to May.

Twain, Mark. [Samuel Langhorne Clemens]. (1835–1910). American novelist and humorist. Of Poe, Twain wrote: ''To me his prose is unreadable—like Jane Austen's. No, there is a difference. I could read his prose on salary, but not Jane's.'' A recent critic comments: ''Familiar with Poe's stories from an early date, Mark Twain recognized a corresponding spirit and a parallel vision'' in his ''portraying [of] existence as a lonely, absurd drifting in a dead universe.'' *Research:* Kennedy, Susan Ann. ''Mark Twain and Edgar Allan Poe: The Development of the Grotesque Absurd.'' *Dissertation Abstracts International*, 39 (1977): 1785A (Arizona State University); Kemper, Steven E. ''Poe, Twain, and Limburger Cheese.'' *Mark Twain Journal*, 21 (1981–1982): 13–14.

"Twice-Told Tales. By Nathaniel Hawthorne." (1). Review appearing in *Graham's Magazine* in April 1842. Poe used the review as an occasion for designating the short story ''as affording the best prose opportunity for display of the highest talent. It has peculiar advantages which the novel does not admit.'' Of Hawthorne's own fine talent as a short story writer, Poe wrote that ''the style of Mr. Hawthorne is purity itself. His *tone* is singularly effective—wild, plaintive, thoughtful, and in full accordance with his themes.'' Poe singled out Hawthorne's ''The Hollow of the Three Hills,'' ''The Minister's Black Veil,'' ''Wakefield,'' ''Mr. Higginbotham's Catastrophe,'' ''Fancy's Show-Box,'' ''Dr. Heidegger's Experiment,'' ''David Swan,'' ''The Wedding Knell'' and ''The White Old Maid'' as among the best. *Text:* CWP, XI, 102–104.

"Twice-Told Tales. By Nathaniel Hawthorne." (2). A second review of Hawthorne's collection of stories appearing in *Graham's Magazine* in May 1842. This review contains Poe's famous formula for the success of short fiction by the creation of a ''preconceived effect.'' ''If wise, he [the artist] has not fashioned his thoughts to accommodate his incidents; but having conceived, with deliberate care, a certain unique or single *effect* to be wrought out, he then invents such incidents—he then combines such events as may aid him in establishing this preconceived effect. If his very initial sentence tend not to the outbringing of this effect, then he has failed in his first step.'' Poe expanded his commentary on those tales he had singled out in the April 1842 review and closed the review with the suggestion that Hawthorne had plagiarized from ''William Wilson'' in his story ''Howe's Masquerade.'' *Text:* CWP, XI, 104–113. *See:* ''Twice-Told Tales. By Nathaniel Hawthorne.'' (1).

Tyler, John. (1790–1862). Tenth president of the United States. In March 1843 Poe traveled to Washington to seek an appointment in the Tyler administration. *Research: LET,* I, 170–172, 227; *TPL,* xliv, 332–334.

Tyler, Robert. (1816–1877). Son of President Tyler and casual acquaintance of Poe's friend Frederick W. Thomas. Poe sought a U.S. Customs House appointment in 1841 through these connections but was unsuccessful. *Research: LET,* 212, 228; *TPL,* xliv-xlvi; *MNR,* 188–189; 194–195.

U

Ugo. Character in the drama *Politian.* He is one of the Di Broglio family servants.

Ulalume. Character in the poem ''Ulalume.'' She is the bereaved poet-narrator's lost beloved.

"Ulalume: A Ballad." The poem is a ballad in nine stanzas first printed unsigned in *The American Review* for December 1847 and reprinted in the *Home Journal* of 1 January 1848. The first printing contained a tenth stanza later omitted. On a dark night ''in the lonesome October,'' the poet makes an excursion with Psyche, his soul, through ''the ghoul-haunted woodland of Weir,'' which is bordered by ''the dank tarn of Auber.'' The purpose of the journey is not clear at first, but it bears some relationship to the death of the narrator's beloved exactly one year ago (''Ah, night of all nights in the year!''). Enroute, the narrator reveals to Psyche that he is drawn to the moon goddess Astarte, symbol of sexual fertility and carnal passion, but when they behold ''Astarte's bediamoned crescent'' in the sky, Psyche grows apprehensive and warns the narrator, '' 'Sadly this star I mistrust.' '' So as not to violate the memory of his beloved, whose name is not yet disclosed, Psyche would have the narrator resist the attractions of the flesh represented by Astarte. But the narrator assures her that ''this tremulous light . . . we safely may trust to its gleaming'' and pacifies her fears for the loss of his soul by a kiss. It is only when the two are abruptly ''stopped by the door of a tomb'' that the narrator realizes both where and why he has made this midnight voyage on the anniversary of Ulalume's death. It is

Psyche who first speaks her forgotten name to the narrator: " 'Ulalume—Ulalume—'Tis the vault of thy lost Ulalume!' " His higher love now remembered and his grief renewed, the poet experiences a sort of dark epiphany and grasps fully the choice between remembrance and forgetfulness as well as between the love of the flesh and the love of the spirit. The journey now becomes a quest for knowledge achieved as the narrator recognizes the place, "Well know[s], now, this dank tarn of Auber, This ghoul-haunted woodland of Weir." Poe, the despiser of allegory, may well have written in "Ulalume" the ultimate private allegory of his own conflict of mind after Virginia's death over whether he should seek the love of another woman or remain united to her memory. It is, after all, the poet's own soul that guides him to his true love and insists that he remain faithful to her. Most appropriately, there is no return from the tomb at the end of the ballad. *Text: MCW,* I, 409–423; *CWP,* VII, 102–105. *Research:* Miller, James E., Jr. " 'Ulalume' Resurrected." *Philological Quarterly*, 34 (1955): 197–205; Mulqueen, James E. "The Meaning of Poe's 'Ulalume.' " *American Transcendental Quarterly*, 1 (1969): 27–30; Omans, Glen. "Poe's 'Ulalume': Drama of the Solipsistic Self." In *Papers on Poe: Essays in Honor of John Ward Ostrom*, ed. Richard P. Veler. Springfield, OH: Chantry Music Press at Wittenberg University, 1972, 62–73; Robinson, David. " 'Ulalume': The Ghouls and the Critics." *Poe Studies*, 8 (1975): 8–10.

Una. Character in the short story "The Colloquy of Monos and Una."

Unamuno, Miguel de. (1864–1936). Spanish existential philosopher, dramatist, poet, and novelist. His short novels *The Marquis of Lumbria*, *Nothing Less Than a Man*, and *Mist* contain Poe-esque incident, setting and characterization. *Research:* Inge, M. Thomas, and Gloria Downing. "Unamuno and Poe." *Poe Newsletter*, 3 (1970): 35–36.

"Undine: A Miniature Romance; From the German of Baron de la Motte Fouqué." Review published in *Burton's Gentleman's Magazine* for September 1839 of a translation appearing in *Colman's Library of Romance*. Poe gives a detailed summary of the romance and faults the work because it "does not afford the fairest field to the romanticist—does not appertain to the higher regions of ideality." Poe also used the review as an occasion for extending his attack on allegory. Undine "has too close an affinity to that most indefensible species of writing." *Text: CWP,* X, 30–39. *Research: PJC,* 223–226.

"The Universe." Title of Poe's public lecture based on his cosmology *Eureka: An Essay on the Material and Spiritual Universe*. *See: Eureka.*

University of Virginia. Charlottesville institution of higher learning where Poe studied in 1826. Its founder, Thomas Jefferson, died on 4 July 1826, while Poe was in residence. Poe concentrated on ancient and modern languages attending lectures on Greek, Latin, French, Spanish, and Italian. He translated

Tasso and demonstrated great fluency in reading and reciting the Latin classics including Cicero, Horace, and Juvenal. Poe also participated in the diversions and dissipations of student life. Several biographers have repeated the tradition that Poe's nickname was "Guffy" and that he had once broad-jumped twenty-one and one half feet. *See:* "West Range Number 13." *Research:* Luck, John Jennings. "Poe and the University of Virginia." *University of Virginia Magazine*, 69 (January 1909): 204–209; Alderman, Edwin A. "Edgar Allan Poe and the University of Virginia." *Virginia Quarterly Review*, 1 (1925): 78–84; Stovall, Floyd. "Edgar Poe and the University of Virginia." *Virginia Quarterly Review*, 43 (1967): 297–317.

"The Unparalleled Adventure of One Hans Pfaall." Short story by Poe published under the title "Hans Phaall—A Tale" in *The Southern Literary Messenger* for June 1835. Poe used a variety of spellings in referring to his balloonist hero as "Phaal," "Phaall," and "Pfaall." Modern reprintings use the title selected by Poe in 1842 for *Phantasy-Pieces* (never published), "The Unparalleled Adventure of One Hans Pfaall." Poe's hoaxing story exploits the mania for international balloon flight by delivering a lengthy fake news bulletin from Rotterdam, a city "in a high state of philosophical excitement" over the recent landing of a balloon piloted by a munchkin aeronaut. This odd UFO is made out of filthy newspapers, resembles a huge fool's cap turned upside down, and is adorned with a large tassel and tinkling sheepbells. The pilot bears a letter to the president and vice president of the Rotterdam College of Astronomy. The letter describes Pfaall's adventures during the five years since his departure from Rotterdam, including the secret scientific process by which he had built the craft after his discovery of a gas thirty-seven times lighter than hydrogen. His adventures have involved him in explosions, crash landings, lunar forays, and polar voyages including the North Pole itself. But the city fathers are skeptical because Hans Pfaall, like Rip Van Winkle before him, might just have vanished to escape his nagging wife, Vrow Grettel Pfaall, who always regarded him as a wastrel and a windbag. Furthermore, as Professor Rubadub and Mynheer Superbus von Underduk note, Pfaall and his companions have recently been seen in a local tavern. The sham big story is substantiated by absurdly learned footnotes and allusions to the ascent record of balloon meisters Gay-Lussac and Biot. *See:* "The Balloon Hoax." *Text:* The *Imaginary Voyages: The Unparalleled Adventure of One Hans Pfaal*, ed. Burton Pollin. Boston: G. K. Hall, 1981, 365–506; *CWP*, II, 42–103. *Research:* Gravely, William H., Jr. "A Note on the Composition of Poe's Hans Pfaal.' " *Poe Newsletter*, 3, no. 1 (1970): 2–5; Ketterer, David. "Poe's Use of the Hoax and the Unity of 'Hans Phaall.' " *Criticism*, 13 (1971): 377–385; Pollin, Burton. "Hans Pfaall: A False Variant of the Phallic Fallacy." *Mississippi Quarterly*, 31 (1978): 519–527; Bennett, Maurice T. "Edgar Allan Poe and the Literary Tradition of Lunar Speculation." *Science-Fiction Studies*, 10 (1983): 137–147; Bennett, Maurice J. " 'Visionary Wings': Art and Metaphysics in Edgar Allan Poe's 'Hans Pfaall.' " In *Poe and His Times: The Artist and His Milieu*, ed. B. F. Fisher IV. Baltimore: Edgar Allan Poe Society, 1990, 76–87; Brody, Selma B. "The Source and Significance of Poe's Use of Axote in "Hans Pfaall.' " *Science Fiction Studies*, 17 (1990): 60–63.

Unterduk, Mynheer Superbus von. Character in ''The Unparalleled Adventure of One Hans Pfaall.''

"Ups and Downs in the Life of a Distressed Gentleman." Novel by W. L. Stone reviewed negatively by Poe in *The Southern Literary Messenger* for June 1836. Poe took his time with the cutting of the author's throat, beginning with the assertion that the book was ''a public imposition'' and ending with the slash, ''It is written . . . by Col. Stone of the New York Commercial Advertiser, and should have been printed among the quack advertisements in a space corner of his paper.'' *Text: CWP,* IX, 24–33. *Research: PLB,* 51–52; *LET,* I, 101, 103; *PJC,* 161–162.

Ure, Andrew. (1778–1857). English economist. His book *The Philosophy of Manufactures: or an Exposition of the Scientific, Moral, and Commercial Economy of the Factory System of Great Britain* was briefly noticed by Poe in his summary of the contents of ''The Edinburgh Review, No. CXXIV, for July 1835.'' *Text: CWP,* VIII, 88.

Usher, Luke Noble. Actor companion of Eliza Poe. Usher cared for Edgar and Rosalie during Eliza's terminal illness in 1811. The Poe scholar T. O. Mabbott commented on the name's possible connection with the brother and sister in ''The Fall of the House of Usher'' in view of the fact that the actor's children, James Campbell Usher and Agnes Pye Usher, were neurasthenics. *Research:* Mabbott, T. O. ''Poe's 'The Fall of the House of Usher.' '' *Explicator*, 15 (November 1956): item 7; *MNR,* 5.

Usher, Madeline. Character in the short story ''The Fall of the House of Usher.'' She is Roderick Usher's twin sister and is prematurely interred.

Usher, Roderick. Main character in the short story ''The Fall of the House of Usher'' and the master of the crumbling mansion.

Ussher, Archbishop James. (1581–1656). Irish church historian. Poe refers to the ''purloining'' of his Irish histories in *Pinakidia. Text: CWP,* XIV, 52.

V

Vachieras [Vaqueiras], Rambaud de. (1155–1207). Spanish troubadour poet. Poe mentions him in relation to Dante in *Pinakidia.* ''Dante left a poem in three languages—Latin, Provençal, and Italian. Vachieras left one in five.'' *Text: CWP,* XIV, 43.

Valdemar, M. Ernest. Character in the short story ''The Facts in the Case of M. Valdemar.'' He is the subject of the mesmerist's experiment. Valdemar is an author, the compiler under the pen name Issachar Marx of the ''Bibliotheca Forensica.''

Valence. Character mentioned in the short story ''The Mystery of Marie Rogêt.'' He is an employee at Madame Deluc's restaurant.

"A Valentine." A twenty-one line acrostic poem by Poe composed on Valentine's eve 13 February 1846 for Frances Sargent Osgood and first published in the New York *Evening Mirror* of 21 February 1846 under the heading ''To Her Whose Name Is Written Below.'' A revised version appeared in *The Flag of Our Union* of 3 March 1849. The poem is an additional demonstration of Poe's obsession with the mechanics of versification and fascination with puzzles and cryptograms. The acrostic format constitutes the subject matter since the woman's name, mispelled in the first version, is encrypted within the twenty lines. *Text: MCW,* I, 386–391; *CWP,* VII, 115. *Research:* Mabbott, T. O. ''Allusion to a Spanish Joke in Poe's 'A Valentine.' '' *Notes & Queries*, 169 (14 September 1935): 189.

Valentine, Ann Moore. (1787–1850). Sister of Frances Keeling Valentine Allan. Poe refers to her as ''Miss Nancy'' in his letters to Allan. *Research: TPL,* xl, xlvi, 24–27.

Valentine, Edward V. (1838–1930). Richmond relative of the Allans who possessed some Poe letters. Reminiscences of Poe appear in his diary. *Research: TPL,* xl, xlvi.

Valéry, Paul. (1871–1945). French poet. In a 1930 essay ''The Position of Baudelaire,'' he literally enshrined Poe's originality and genius and was especially adulatory about Poe's accomplishments in *Eureka.* For Valéry, Poe was the paragon of artists, ''[t]he only writer without any fault. He never makes a false move. He creates form out of the void. . . . All his work manifests on every page an intelligence which is to be observed to the same degree in no other literary career.'' Poe is ''a demon of lucidity, a psychologist of the exceptional.'' Valéry's adoration of Poe has puzzled critics such as Aldous Huxley and T. S. Eliot, but Valéry's opinion of Poe is characteristic of the ''French Face'' of the American writer. *Research:* Quinn, Patrick F. *The French Face of Edgar Allan Poe.* Carbondale, IL: Southern Illinois University Press, 1957; Virtanen, Reino. ''Allusions to Poe's Poetic Theory in Valéry's *Cahiers.*'' In *Poetic Theory/Poetic Practice: Papers of the Midwest Modern Language Association,* ed. Robert Scholes. Iowa City, IA: Midwest Modern Language Association, 1969, 113–120; Ospina-Gracés de Fonseca, Helena. ''Paul Valéry et Edgar Poe: L'influence de la théorie poétique de Poe chez Valéry.'' In *Anales del Departmento de Lenguas Modernas, Universidad de Costa Rica,* ed. K. H. Mann. San José: Universidad de Costa Rica, 1972, 3–13; Ghali, Samir. ''La Portée d'Edgar Poe sur las pensée et l'oeuvre de Paul Valéry.'' *Publications of the Arkansas Philological Association,* 2, no. 2 (1976): 33–40; Vines, Lois. ''Dupin-Teste: Poe's Direct Influence on Valéry.'' *French Forum,* 2 (1977): 147–159; Vines, Lois Davis. *Valéry and Poe: A Literary Legacy.* New York: New York University Press, 1992.

"The Valley Nis." Poem Poe printed for the first time in Elam Bliss's edition of *Poems by Edgar A. Poe* in April 1831. Its later title is ''The Valley of Unrest.'' *See:* ''The Valley of Unrest.'' *Text: MCW,* I, 189–196; *CWP,* VII, 115.

"The Valley of Unrest." Poem first published under the title ''The Valley Nis'' and published in a revised version as ''The Valley of Unrest'' in *The American Review* for April 1845. Like ''The City in the Sea,'' the poem is a strongly evocative mood piece relying upon surreal and unearthly imagery to project the landscape of a visionary experience. The valley is now a place where ''Nothing there is motionless,'' but it was not always so. Once it was a ''silent dell'' until the inhabitants chose to go ''unto the wars,'' naively trusting their fate ''to the mild-eyed stars.'' The destruction has transformed the valley into the haunted place beheld by the poet, a brooding terrain where lilies weep and clouds are driven by invisible forces. The valley's supernatural restlessness is a fitting memorial for the ''nameless grave'' that is the end of war. *Text: MCW,* I,

189–196; *CWP,* VII, 55. *Research:* Basler, Roy P. "On Poe's 'The Valley of Unrest.' " *Explicator*, 5 (December 1946): item 25; Bledsoe, Thomas F. "On Poe's 'Valley of Unrest.' " *Modern Language Notes*, 61 (1946): 91–92; Kiehl, James M. "The Valley of Unrest: A Major Metaphor in the Poetry of Edgar Allan Poe." *Thoth*, 5 (winter 1964): 45–52.

Vankirk, Mr. Character in the short story "Mesmeric Revelation." He is hypnotized by the narrator.

Varro, Marcus Tarentius. (116–27 B.C.). Roman historian and philologist. In *Pinakidia*, Poe cites his three epochs of human history, "the uncertain," "the fabulous," and "the historical." *Text: CWP,* XIV, 65.

Vere, Guy De. Character in the poem "Lenore." He is the grieving lover of Lenore.

Vergil. [Publius Vergilius Maro]. (70–19 B.C.). Roman author of *The Æneid.* The *Æneid* is mentioned in "The Purloined Letter" by Dupin who refers to the "facilus descensus Averni" or "easy descent to Avernus." Other references to Vergil occur in *Pinakidia* and *Marginalia. Text: CWP,* II, 142; XI, 82; XIII, 48; XIV, 43; XVI, 35, 47.

Verne, Jules. (1828–1905). French novelist and science fiction pioneer. He showed his debt to Poe by writing a sequel to *The Narrative of Arthur Gordon Pym, Le sphinx des glaces* [The sphinx of the ice fields] (1897). In his 1864 essay, "Poe et ses oeuvres" [Poe and his works], Verne recognized the genius of Poe's tales of the sea and balloon flight. Verne's *Voyage au centre de la terre* [Journey to the center of the earth] as well as other science fiction fantastic voyages register his respect for Poe as a pioneer in this field of writing. *Research:* Sprout, Monique. "The Influence of Poe on Jules Verne." *Revue de Littérature Comparée*, 41 (1967): 37–53; Beaver, Harold, ed. "Appendix I: Jules Verne, *Le Sphinx des Glaces, Verne's Sequel to* The Narrative of Arthur Gordon Pym of Nantucket." Baltimore: Penguin Books, 1975, 282–311; Desvignes, Lucette. "De Poe à Jules Verne et du mystère au gouffre." In *Travaux compartistes*, ed. Lucette Desvignes. Saint Etienne: Centre d'Etudes Compar. ed de Recherche sur l'Expression Dramatique, 1978, 155–162; Ponnau, Gwenhaël. "Edgar Poe et Jules Verne: Le Statut de la science dans la littérature fantastique et dans la littérature science-fiction." In *Mythes, Images, Representations*, ed. Jean-Marie Grassin. Paris: Didier, 1982, 359–367; Zanger, Jules. "Poe's Endless Voyage: *The Narrative of Arthur Gordon Pym.*" *Papers on Language and Literature*, 22 (1986): 276–283; Di Maio, Mariella. "Jules Verne et le voyage au second degré ou un avatar d'Edgar Poe." *Romantisme: Revue du Dix-Neuvième Siècle*, 19 (1990): 100–109; Meakin, David. "Like Poles Attracting: Intertextual Magnetism in Poe, Verne, and Gracq." *Modern Language Review*, 88 (1993): 599–611; *PLL,* 328.

Verplanck, Gulian Crommelin. (1786–1870). New York politician, lecturer, and pamphleteer. Poe included Verplanck's profile in ''The Literati of New York City'' and said of his signature in ''Autography'' that ''his orations, reviews, and other compositions all evince the cultivated belles-lettres scholar, and man of intellect and taste.'' *Text: CWP,* XV, 39–40. *Research: LET,* II, 313, 316; *TPL,* 638, 641.

"The Vicar of Wakefield, a Tale. By Oliver Goldsmith, M.B. Illustrated With Numerous Engravings. With an Account of the Author's Life and Writings. By J. Aikin, M.D." Review of a reprinting of the Oliver Goldsmith novel appearing in *Graham's Magazine* for 1842. ''The memoir by Dr. Aikin is highly interesting, and embodies in a pleasing narrative, (with little intermixture of criticism upon what no longer requires it,) all that is, or need be known of Oliver Goldsmith.'' *Text: CWP,* XI, 8–10.

Vidocq, François-Eugène. (1775–1857). French policeman and detective. He is mentioned in ''The Murders in the Rue Morgue.'' Poe had probably read *Unpublished Passages in the Life of Vidocq* (a translation signed J.M.B.) appearing in *Burton's Gentleman's Magazine* from September 1838 to May 1839. *Text: CWP,* IV, 166. *Research:* Ousby, Ian V. K. '' 'The Murders in the Rue Morgue' and 'Doctor D'Arsac.' '' *Poe Newsletter*, 5 (1972): 52.

Vigènere, Blaise de. (1523–1596). French chronicler and cryptographer. Poe mentions his treatise on ciphers, *Tracté des chiffres, ou secretes manieries d'escrire* (1586), and his polyalphabetic encipherment table in ''Secret Writing.'' *Text: CWP,* XIV, 132.

"The Visionary—A Tale." Title first used for the short story ''The Assignation.'' *See:* ''The Assignation.''

"Visit of the Dead." Original title of the poem ''Spirits of the Dead.'' *See:* ''Spirits of the Dead.''

"Visits to Remarkable Places, Battle-Fields, Cathedrals, Castles, etc. By W. Howitt." Review of a travel guide appearing in *Graham's Magazine* for March 1841. Volume II of the work took up ''The Rural Life of England.'' Poe was especially approving of Howitt's description of gypsies and a chapter entitled ''A Day-dream at Tintagel'' wherein ''[t]he old castle of King Arthur seems once more to lift its massy battlements.'' *Text: CWP,* X, 112–114.

"Voices of the Night." Review of a book of verse by Henry Wadsworth Longfellow appearing in *Burton's Gentleman's Magazine* for February 1840. Poe's review continues his war with Longfellow with the accusation that the poem ''Midnight Mass for the Dying Year'' is plagiarized from Tennyson's

''The Death of the Old Year.'' Poe does praise Longfellow's ''Hymn to the Night'' but finds the poems in the collection ''singularly deficient in all those important faculties which give artistical power, and without which never was immortality effected.'' *Text: CWP,* X, 71–80. *Research: PJC,* 353.

Voissart, Victor. Character in the short story ''The Spectacles.''

Voltaire. [François Marie Arouet]. (1694–1778). French philosopher and novelist. There are four references to Voltaire in *Marginalia*, each one reflecting Poe's distrust of his rationalism. Voltaire is also mentioned in ''Bon-Bon'' and ''The Thousand-and-Second Tale of Scheherazade,'' which contains a quotation from *Contes Moreaux*. T. O. Mabbott traced the origin of Poe's detective Monsieur Dupin to ''the philosophic protagonist of Voltaire's *Zadig*—a story in which the hero describes a dog he has never seen.'' *Text: CWP,* II, 145, 178–179; VII, 30, 94; XVI, 6, 45, 74, 95, 117. *Research:* Allen, Mozelle Scaff. ''Poe's Debt to Voltaire.'' *University of Texas Studies in English*, 15 (1935): 63–75; *LET,* II, 379; *MCW,* II, 521.

Von Jung, Baron Ritzner. Character in the short story ''Mystification.'' Although he detests the practice of dueling, he is well informed about it.

"Von Jung, the Mystific." First title of the short story ''Mystification,'' which appeared under this title in the *American Monthly Magazine* for June 1847. *See:* ''Mystification.''

Von Kempelen. Character in the short story ''Von Kempelen and His Discovery.'' He is also mentioned in ''Maelzel's Chess-Player.''

"Von Kempelen and His Discovery." Short story appearing in *The Flag of Our Union* of 14 April 1849. The tale mocks the appetite for gold touched off by the California discoveries and their sensationalizing in the press. Plagiarizing Sir Humphrey Davy's chemical diary, the chemist or alchemist, Von Kempelen of Bremen, has discovered the philosopher's stone, which enables him to transmute lead into gold. The process makes lead the more preferred, hence, the more valuable metal. ''Gold now is, or at least soon will be (for it cannot be supposed that Von Kempelen can long retain his secret), of no greater value than lead, and of far inferior value to silver. The announcement of the discovery six months ago would have had material influence in regard to the settlement of California.'' *Text: MCW,* III, 1355–1367; *CWP,* VI, 245–254. *Research:* Weissbuch, Ted N. ''Edgar Allan Poe: Hoaxer in the American Tradition.'' *New York Historical Society Quarterly Bulletin*, 45 (1961): 291–309; Hall, Thomas. ''Poe's Use of a Source: Davy's Chemical Researches and 'Von Kempelen and His Discovery.' '' *Poe Newsletter*, 1 (October 1968): 28; Pollin, Burton. ''Poe in 'Von Kempelen and His Discovery.' '' *DIP*, 166–189.

Vondel. Joost von den. (1587–1679). Dutch dramatist. His play *The Deliverance of the Children of Israel* is mentioned in *Pinakidia*. *Text: CWP,* XIV, 53.

Voyage of the U.S. Frigate Potomac. Book briefly noticed by Poe in *The Southern Literary Messenger* for June 1835. *Research: TPL,* 160.

Vredenburgh, Peter. Character mentioned in *The Narrative of Arthur Gordon Pym*.

W., The Mail-Robber. Character mentioned in the short story ''Loss of Breath.'' Mr. Lackobreath takes his place by mistake when he escapes from the hangman's cart enroute to the gallows.

"Wakondah; The Master of Life, A Poem." A viciously negative review of a narrative poem, a thirty-four stanza Indian saga, by Cornelius Mathews appearing in *Graham's Magazine* for February 1842. Poe quoted extensively from the poem and followed up with the slash, ''Let us endeavor to translate this gibberish, by way of ascertaining its import, if possible.'' The review is filled with similar sarcasms. Warming to his task, Poe declared, '' 'Wakondah,' then, from beginning to end is trash. With the trivial exceptions which we shall designate, it has *no* merit whatsoever. . . . a mere jumble of incongruous nonsense . . . this trumpery declamation, this maudlin sentiment, this metaphor run-mad, this twaddling verbiage, this halting and doggerel rhythm, this unintelligible rant and cant!'' *Text: CWP,* XI, 25–38. *Research: LET,* I, 245; *PJC,* 283–288.

Wallace, Horace Binney. [pseud. William Landor]. (1817–1852). Amateur author and contributor to *Graham's Magazine*. *See:* Landor, William. *Text: CWP,* V, 33; XV, 198. *Research:* Hatvary, George E. ''Poe, Griswold, and Wallace.'' *Mid-Hudson Language Studies*, 4 (1981): 83–94; *TPL,* xlvi, 335.

Wallace, William Ross. (1819–1881). Kentucky-born poet who knew Poe in New York City. Poe recited the newly published ''Raven'' to Wallace in a New York City street. *Text: CWP,* XI, 241; XVI, 175–177. *Research: PLL,* 143, 164.

Wallis, Dr. John. Cryptographer mentioned in ''Secret Writing'' (3) and ''Autography.'' *Text: CWP,* XIV, 147; XV, 181.

Walpole, Horace. (1717–1797). English art connoisseur, dilettante, and author of *The Castle of Otranto*, the first English gothic novel. Poe cites Walpole several times in *Marginalia* and refers to him as a man of erudition elsewhere. There is one direct allusion to *The Castle of Otranto* in his discussion of the tale ''Castle Dismal'' in the review of William Gilmore Simms's short stories in *The Wigwam and the Cabin.* Several critics have proposed that the supernatural gothicism of the first gothic novel was a definite inspirational model for ''Metzengerstein'' and that certain events, particularly the collapse of the mansion in ''The Fall of the House of Usher,'' are modeled on the supernatural climax of Walpole's work. *Text: CWP,* X, 47; XII, 48; XVI, 60, 144, 168. *Research:* King, Lucille. ''Notes on Poe's Sources.'' *University of Texas Studies in English,* 10 (1930):128–134; *MCW,* II, 15–17.

Walsh, Robert M. (1784–1859). Editor of the *American Quarterly Review* and professor of English at the University of Pennsylvania. In May 1829, Poe sought his advice concerning his poetry. Poe included his signature in ''Autography,'' remarking on its ''dictatorial'' traits. *Text: CWP,* VIII, 321–329; X, 133–139; XIV, 134–135; XV, 144–145, 187–188. *Research: TPL,* xlvi-xlvii, 92–93.

Walter, Cornelia Wells. (1815–1898). Editor of the *Boston Evening Transcript* and one of Poe's most formidable literary foes. She hostilely reviewed Poe's public recitations at Boston's Odeon Theater. Poe replied to her criticism in *The Broadway Journal* of 22 November 1845. *See:* ''Boston and the Bostonians.'' *Text: CWP,* XII, 104; XIII, 6, 8–9, 10–12. *Research:* Scott, W. T. ''New England's Newspaper World.'' *Saturday Review of Literature*, 22 May 1943, 19–20; *TPL,* 579–580; Prown, Katherine Hemple. ''The Cavalier and the Syren: Edgar Allan Poe, Cornelia Wells Walter, and the Boston Lyceum Incident.'' *New England Quarterly*, 66 (1993): 110–123.

Walton, Octavia. She was the daughter of George Walton, Secretary of West Florida. Poe composed a poem for her album in May 1827. *See:* ''To Octavia.'' *Research: MCW,* I, 16, 62, 539; *TPL,* 79.

Ward, Robert Plumer. (1765–1846). English critic and novelist. He is cited and censured in *Marginalia* for his lavish praise of Bulwer's *Tremaine. Text: CWP,* XVI, 156–157.

Ward, Thomas. (1807–1873). Amateur poet derided by Poe in ''Our Amateur Poets No. 1—Flaccus'' in *Graham's Magazine* for March 1843. *See:* ''Our Amateur Poets, No. I—Flaccus.'' *Text: CWP,* XI, 160–174. *Research: PLB,* 93; *TPL,* xlvii.

Ware, Professor Henry. (1794–1843). American clergyman, temperance lecturer, and poet mentioned once in "Autography" as the author of "some very excellent poetry" and known best for his religious writings, particularly the pamphlet "Formation of the Christian Character." *Text: CWP,* XV, 251–252.

Warren, Dr. Samuel. (1807–1877). Author of *Passages from the Diary of a London Physician. See:* "Ten Thousand a Year." *Text: CWP,* IX, 205; X, 210. *Research: TPL,* 344.

Washington College Hospital. Poe was taken here on 3 October 1849 after being found half drunk and unconscious in the streets of Baltimore. *Research: PLL,* 254–255.

Waterman, Catherine Harbeson. [Catherine H. Esling]. (1812–?). American poet. Of her handwriting in "Autography" Poe observed, "She deserves *nearly* all the commendation which she has received." *Text: CWP,* XI, 241; XV, 206.

Waters, John. [pseud. Henry Cary]. *See:* Cary, Henry. *Text: CWP,* XV, 67; XVI, 94–95.

"Watkins Tottle and Other Sketches, Illustrative of Every-Day Life, and Every-Day People." Review of a work by Dickens appearing in *The Southern Literary Messenger* for June 1836. Poe lists the titles of the "Sketches by Boz" in the volume and singles out "The Black Veil" as "distinct in character from all the rest—an act of stirring tragedy and evincing lofty powers in the writer." *Text: CWP,* IX, 45–48. *Research: PJC,* 162–164.

Watson, Henry Cood. (1818–1875). Music critic for *The Broadway Journal* during Poe's tenure on the staff. *Research: TPL,* xlvii.

Waukerassah, Chief. Character mentioned in *The Journal of Julius Rodman.*

Waverley Place at Sixth Avenue. A Poe address in New York City. With Virginia and Maria Clemm, he shared a residence with the Gowanses here in February 1837.

Webb, James Watson. (1802–1884). Publisher of the New York *Morning Courier.* He assisted the Poes during their destitute residence at the Fordham cottage. *Research: TPL,* xlvii, 120–121.

Webbe, Cornelius. (fl. 1830). English comic essayist and friend of Keats. Of *The Man about Town,* his collection of essays, Poe wrote: "*Cornelius Webbe* is one of the best of that numerous school of extravaganzists who sprang from the ruins of [Charles] Lamb.'' *Text: CWP,* XVI, 39.

Webber, Charles Wilkins. (1819–1856). American author-adventurer and writer of tales of the Wild West. In a review of Hawthorne's *Twice-Told Tales,* Poe mentions Webber's western thriller story ''Jack Long; or, The Shot in the Eye'' as ''[o]ne of the happiest and best sustained tales I have seen.'' *Text: CWP,* XIII, 142, 154. *Research:* Marovitz, Sanford E. ''Poe's Reception of C. W. Webber's Gothic Western, 'Jack Long; or, The Shot in the Eye.' '' *Poe Studies,* 4, no. 1 (1971): 11–13.

Webster, Noah. (1758–1853). American lexicographer and compiler of *The American Dictionary of the English Language* (1828). In one of the ''Fifty Suggestions,'' Poe suggested, ''In his great Dictionary, Webster seems to have had an idea of being more English than the English.'' *Text: CWP,* IX, 106; XIV, 185.

Weddell, Captain James. (1787–1834). English South Polar explorer and navigator whose 1823 approach to the Antarctic continent is mentioned several times in *The Narrative of Arthur Gordon Pym.* He published *A Voyage toward the South Pole Performed in the Years 1822–24* (1825). *Text: CWP,* III, 163, 168, 171.

Weir, Robert. Drawing instructor at West Point. The line in ''Ulalume,'' ''the ghoul-haunted woodland of Weir'' refers to his eerie landscapes. *Research:* Leary, Lewis. ''Poe's 'Ulalume.' '' *Explicator,* 6 (February 1948); item 25; *PLL,* 45, 211.

Weiss, Susan Archer Talley. (1822–1917). Richmond poet. *See:* Talley, Susan Archer Weiss. *Research: PLL,* 243–249.

Welby, Amelia Ball. (1819–1852). American poet praised by Poe in *Marginalia* and elsewhere. Poe wrote of her work, ''As for our *poetesses* (an absurd but necessary word), none of them approach her.'' *Text: CWP,* XI, 157; XIII, 18, 125, 192; XVI, 54–59. *Research: PJC,* 346–348.

Weld, Horatio Hastings. (1811–1888). Editor of the New York *Tatler, Brother Jonathan,* and *Dollar Magazine, a Monthly Gazette of Current Literature, Music, and Art.* Poe included his signature in ''Autography'' with an approving comment on his editorials which are ''usually well written.'' *Text: CWP,* XV, 229. *Research: TPL,* 338.

Wells, H.[erbert] G.[eorge]. (1866–1946). English novelist and science fiction writer. Poe's influence on Wells was both inspirational and textual. Discussing the composition of *The War of the Worlds* (1898) and *The First Men* *in the Moon* (1901), he noted that "Poe's *Narrative of A. Gordon Pym* tells what a very intelligent mind could imagine about the south polar regions a century ago." *Research:* Rainwater, Catherine. "H. G. Wells's Re-Vision of Poe: *The Undying Fire* and *Mr. Blettsworthy on Rampole Island.*" *English Literature in Transition*, 30 (1987): 423–436; *PLL,* 329.

Wertenbaker, William. (1797–1882). Student and later librarian at the University of Virginia during Poe's student residency. He commented upon Poe's compulsive gambling and other features of his character in a memoir published in the November–December 1868 issue of the *Virginia University Magazine. Research: TPL,* xlvii, 75–76.

West Point. Site of the United States Military Academy on the upper Hudson River. Poe entered West Point as a cadet on 20 June 1830 and was court-martialed and dismissed for deliberate neglect of duty on 6 March 1831, leaving the Academy on 19 February 1831. *See:* Military Service.

West Range Number 13. A Poe address. The room in which Poe lived at the University of Virginia. It was one of 109 dormitory rooms of Jefferson's designed campus and is preserved today in its 1826 condition as a Poe memorial. *Research:* Stovall, Floyd. "Poe and the University of Virginia." *Virginia Quarterly Review*, 43 (1967): 297–317.

Wetmore, Prosper Montgomery. (1798–1876). Prominent soldier poet whose collection *The Battle of Lexington with Other Fugitive Poems* (1830) was mentioned favorably by Poe in his profile of the general in "The Literati of New York City." In "Autography," Wetmore's "clerky flourishes indicate a love of the beautiful with an undue straining for effect—qualities which are distinctly traceable in his poetic efforts." *Text: CWP,* XV, 88–89, 251. *Research: LET,* II, 316, 317; *TPL,* 657.

Whipple, Edwin Percy. (1819–1886). Literary critic mocked in "Autography" and presented as a negative example of sound critical principles in Poe's posthumous essay "About Critics and Criticism." Poe and Whipple were sworn literary enemies. *Text: CWP,* XII, 180–184; XIII, 193–202. *Research:* Gerber, Gerald E. "E. P. Whipple Attacks Poe: A New Review." *American Literature*, 53 (1981): 110–113.

White, Charles Erskine. *See:* Osborn, Laughton. *Text: CWP,* XVI, 151–152.

White, Eliza. Daughter of Thomas Willis White. Poe wrote a poem for her in 1835. She was a guest at the wedding of Poe and Virginia. *Research: TPL,* xlviii.

White, Henry Kirke. (1785–1806). Precocious English poet mentioned once by Poe in his review of the poetry of Lucretia Maria Davidson. *Text: CWP,* X, 224.

White, Thomas Willis. (1788–1843). Founder and publisher of *The Southern Literary Messenger.* His relationship to Poe was cordial at first, but Poe's erratic habits soon caused difficulties and the two went through a series of dismissals and rehirings. White thought Poe highly talented but "rather dissipated,—and therefore I can place very little reliance upon him." In August 1835, White hired Poe as assistant editor but discharged him for drinking on 3 January 1837. *Research: TPL,* xlvii-xlviii, 139–141, 147–148, 182–185, 401–402.

Whitman, Sarah Helen Power. (1803–1878). Providence, Rhode Island widowed poet and one of the women in Poe's life, especially during 1848, the year before his death, when Poe proposed to her in Providence's Swan Point Cemetery, and they became engaged. An avid reader of Poe before their meeting, she was probably the most intellectually sophisticated of all of Poe's late-in-life poetic mistresses. The relationship was initiated by her playfully flirtatious poem "To Edgar A. Poe" delivered on 14 February 1848. "Oh, thou grim and ancient Raven,/ From the night's Plutonian shore,/ Oft, in dreams, thy ghostly pinions/ Wave and flutter round my door." Her poem to Poe, "Arcturus," is in a more serious vein: "Hast thou not stooped from heaven, fair star! To be/ So near me in this hour of agony?—" Their romance reached a pinnacle when she became engaged to Poe, but she terminated it on 23 December 1848 when Poe's drinking alarmed her. Although she never saw Poe again, she remained intellectually faithful to him after his death, defending his genius in *Edgar Poe and His Critics* (1860) and sharing her high regard for the man and his art with John Henry Ingram. *See:* "To Helen [Whitman]." *Text: CWP,* XI, 159–160. *Research: LTP,* 624–625; Vincent, H. P. "A Sarah Helen Whitman Letter about Edgar Allan Poe." *American Literature,* 13 (1941): 162–167; Bliss, Carey S. "Poe and Sarah Helen Whitman." *Book Collector,* 12 (winter 1963): 490; Rosenfeld, Alvin. "Wilkins Updike to Sarah Helen Whitman: Two New Letters." *Rhode Island History,* 15 (October 1966): 97–109; Reilly, John E. "Sarah Helen Whitman as a Critic of Poe." *University of Mississippi Studies in English,* 3 (1982): 120–127.

Whitman, Walt. (1819–1892). American poet. He first knew Poe from a single chance meeting at the offices of *The Broadway Journal* in November 1845. Whitman was the only major poet to attend the 1875 memorial celebration. Whitman's often-quoted assessment of Poe's cold brilliance appears in *Specimen Days* where Poe is placed "among the electric lights of imaginative literature, brilliant and dazzling, but with no heat." In the *Washington Star* of 18 November 1875 Whitman evaluated Poe's art and importance to American letters, admitting his "distaste for Poe's writings" but also admitting his changed and elevated view of Poe twenty-six years after his death. "Poe's genius has yet conquered a special recognition for itself, and I too have come to fully admit it, and appreciate it and him.'' *Research:* Silver, Rollo G. ''A Note about Whitman's Essay on Poe.'' *American Literature*, 6 (1935): 435–436; Hindus, Milton. ''Whitman and Poe: A Note.'' *Walt Whitman Newsletter*, 3 (March 1957): 5–6; Tanasoca, Donald. ''Poe and Whitman.'' *Walt Whitman Birthplace Bulletin*, 2 (April 1959): 3–7; 2 (July 1959): 6–11; Spencer, Benjamin T. '' 'Beautiful Blood and Beautiful Brain': Whitman and Poe.'' *Emerson Society Quarterly* (2nd Q 1964): 45–49; Long, John C. ''The Scene at the Sickbed: Poe, Hawthorne, and Whitman: The Clinic as Discourse in Tales and Poems of Morbid Psychic.'' *University of Hartford Studies in Literature: A Journal of Interdisciplinary Criticism*, 21 (1989): 21–37.

Whittier, John Greenleaf. (1807–1892). American poet. In ''Autography,'' Poe assessed his poetic abilities severely and was ''not disposed'' to place Whittier ''in the very front rank of American poets. . . . Mr. Whittier is a fine versifier. . . . but in taste, and especially in *imagination*, which Coleridge has justly styled the *soul* of all poetry, he is ever remarkably deficient. His themes are *never* to our liking.'' *Text: CWP,* XV, 245. *Research: LTP*, 346, 536; *TPL,* 338, 455, 774.

Whitty, J.[ames] H. Editor of Poe's poetry. He identified and included some unsigned poems in his edition of Poe's poetry with a ''Memoir,'' *The Complete Poems of Edgar Allan Poe; collected, edited, and arranged with memoir, textual notes and bibliography* (Boston and New York: Houghton Mifflin, 1911).

"Why a National Literature Cannot Flourish in the United States." A book by Joseph Rocchietti negatively reviewed by Poe in *The Broadway Journal* of 8 February 1845. *Research: TPL,* 501.

"Why Not Try a Mineralized Pavement?" Editorial appearing in the New York *Evening Mirror* of 8 February 1845. *See:* ''Street Paving.'' *Research: TPL,* 501.

"Why the Little Frenchman Wears His Hand in a Sling." Short story by Poe published initially in the first volume of *Tales of the Grotesque and Arabesque* in December 1839 and reprinted several times in periodicals during Poe's lifetime, for instance, *The Broadway Journal* of 6 September 1845. The story is a comic monologue written in brogue. The narrator, Sir Pathrick O'Grandison, Barronitt, recalls his rival love affair with the ''purty widdy Misthress Tracle'' and how his courtship was challenged by ''the little ould furrener Frinchman as lived over the way,'' Mounseer, the Count, A Goose, Look-aisyh, Maiter-di-dauns. The rival suitors decide to plead their cases to Misthress Tracle to ''see now whither it's your swate silf, or whither it's Mounseer Maiter-di-dauns, that Misthress Tracle is head and ears in love wid.'' What follows is a three-way tête-à-tête aboard Misthress Tracle's ''sofy'' with much secretive hand holding and amorous ''squazing of flippers.'' When Sir Pathrick receives a subtle return squeeze, he assumes that the field of Venus belongs to him. But when the desirable widow rises and departs the room, he discovers that the hand he has been holding so passionately belongs to the little Frenchman. ''If it wasn't his spalpeeny little paw that I had hould of in my own. I gived it such a nate little broth of a squaze, as made it all up into a raspberry jam.'' The little Frenchman's hand permanently hidden in the sling, then, is the crushed flipper given him by a crushed lover. The sofa scene in the story with Madame wedged between the groping fingers of the Frenchman and the Irishman recalls the erotic comedy of Laurence Sterne's *Sentimental Journey through France and Italy*. T. O. Mabbott called the tale ''a mere comic anecdote, and almost the slightest story that Poe ever wrote.'' *Text: MCW,* II, 462–471; *CWP,* IV, 114–121. *Research: TPL,* 568–569; *MNR,* 15; *PLL,* 10.

Wieland, Christoph Martin. (1733–1813). German poet, dramatist, and novelist. He was the author of *Agathon* and *Oberon*, both works known to Poe. Wieland's *Private History of Peregrinus Proteus the Philosopher* is quoted in *Marginalia*. *Text: CWP,* XI, 99; XVI, 161.

Wilbur, Richard. (1921–). American poet and critic. His landmark essay ''The House of Poe'' was first delivered as a lecture at the Library of Congress in 1959. Wilbur read Poe's fiction and poetry as artistic parables of transcendence or the failure to transcend the limits of the physical world. Enclosures in Poe's work signified the entrapment of the poetic soul and its struggle to escape into a world of pure beauty and intuitive finality. *Research:* Wilbur, Richard. ''The House of Poe.'' In *The Recognition of Edgar Allan Poe*, ed. Eric Carlson. Ann Arbor: Michigan University Press, 1966, 254–277.

Wilde, Oscar Fingal O'Flahertie Wills. (1854–1900). Irish novelist, dramatist, poet, and wit. He called Poe ''this marvellous lord of rhythmic expression.'' His novel *The Picture of Dorian Gray* and various short stories such as ''The Birthday of the Infanta'' were influenced by Poe. *Research:* Thomas, J. David. ''The Composition of Wilde's 'The Harlot House.' '' *Modern Language Notes*, 65 (1950): 485–488.

Wilde, Richard Henry. (1789–1847). Georgia politician and inferior poet. In ''Autography'' Poe disposes of Wilde's poetry as follows: ''Upon the whole it is hardly worth quarreling about. Far better verses are to be found in every second newspaper we take up.'' Poe may have had in mind Wilde's *Hesperia, a Poem*. *Text: CWP,* XV, 236.

"A Wilder'd being from my birth." Untitled poem which first appeared in *Tamerlane and Other Poems*. Later versions dropped this opening line and gave the poem the title "A Dream." *See:* "A Dream;" *Tamerlane and Other Poems. Research: MCW,* I, 80.

Wiley & Putnam. New York publishing house. It issued Poe's *Tales* in June 1845, followed by *The Raven and Other Poems* in November 1845.

"Wiley & Putnam's Library of American Books, No. IV. The Wigwam and the Cabin. By William Gilmore Simms." A review of Simms's tales written for the annuals appearing in *The Broadway Journal* of 4 October 1845. The review also appeared in *Godey's Lady's Book* for January 1846. Poe liked everything in the collection, calling it "one of the most interesting numbers of the Library yet published—and decidedly the most American of the American books." Of the stories, "Murder Will Out" is "the best ghost-story we ever read." The review is noteworthy for its mention of Walpole's *Castle of Otranto* in connection with Simms's "Castle Dismal," called by Poe "one of the most original fictions ever penned." *Text: CWP,* XII, 247–250; XIII, 93–97. *Research: PLB,* 105.

"Wiley & Putnam's Library of Choice Reading, No. XVII. The Characters of Shakespeare, By William Hazlitt." Favorable review appearing in *The Broadway Journal* of 16 August 1845. Hazlitt's dramatic criticism, while differing from his own sense of criticism, is "brilliant, epigrammatic, startling, paradoxical, and suggestive, rather than accurate, luminous, or profound." The review also contains Poe's central view of Shakespeare's empathic identification with his characters. "He felt it through his marvellous power of identification with humanity at large. . . . He wrote of Hamlet as if Hamlet he were." *Text: CWP,* XII, 226–228.

"Wiley & Putnam's Library of Choice Reading, No. XVI. Prose and Verse. By Thomas Hood." A review of a collection of Hood's poetry appearing in *The Broadway Journal* in three installments of 9 August 1845, 23 August 1845 (No. XIX), and 30 August 1845 (No. XIX). Poe strongly objected to the editor's clumsy puns on Hood's surname and might have been writing about his own work when he wrote of Hood that "His true province—that is to say the field in which he is distinctive—is a kind of border land between the Fancy and the Fantasy—but in this region he reigns supreme." Poe also repeated his view that Hood's poetic genius was "certainly tinctured, at all points, by hypochondriasis." *See:* Hood, Thomas. *Text: CWP,* XII, 213–222.

"Wiley & Putnam's Library of Choice Reading, No. XIX. Prose and Verse. By Thomas Hood. Part II." The second part of a review of Hood's works appearing in *The Broadway Journal* of 23 August 1845. Poe judged "The Bridge of Sighs" to be "the finest written by Hood" and called attention to the hypochondriasis that impelled "The Song of the Shirt." *See:* Hood, Thomas. *Text: CWP,* XII, 233–234.

"Wiley & Putnam's Library of Choice Reading, No. XIX. Prose and Verse. By Thomas Hood. Part III." The third part of a review of Hood's works appearing in *The Broadway Journal* of 30 August 1845. Poe singled out the poem "The Haunted House," designating it "a masterpiece of its kind and a perfect specimen of unity of effect." "The strength of the poet is put forth in the invention of traits in keeping with the ideas of crime, abandonment, and ghostly visitation. Every legitimate art is brought in to aid in conveying the intended effects." *See:* Hood, Thomas. *Text: CWP,* XII, 235–237.

"Wiley & Putnam's Library of Choice Reading, No. XX. The Indicator and Companion. By Leigh Hunt. Part II." A review of Hunt's essays appearing in *The Broadway Journal* of 30 August 1845. Poe's opinion of Hunt as a writer was severely critical. "As a rambling essayist he has too little of the raw material. As a critic he is merely saucy, or lackadaisical, or falsely enthusiastic, or at best pointedly conceited." And as an imaginative writer, "The highest literary quality of Hunt is a secondary or tertiary grade of Fancy." *Text: CWP,* XII, 237–238.

"Wiley & Putnam's Library of Choice Reading, No. XXI. Genius and Character of Burns. By Professor Wilson." Review of a study of the Scottish poet appearing in the *Broadway Journal* of 6 September 1845. Poe begins the notice with a mock tribute to the professor's erudition, then undercuts it with his real opinion of the professor's scholarship. "He is no analyst. He is ignorant of the machinery of his own thoughts and the thoughts of other men." *Text: CWP,* XII, 239–241.

"William Cullen Bryant." Critical essay appearing in *Godey's Lady's Book* for April 1846. Poe discusses the underestimation of Bryant's poetic genius. "Mr. Bryant has genius, and that of a marked character, but it has been overlooked by the modern schools, because deficient in those externals which have become in a measure symbolical of those schools." The essay also contains Poe's commentary on "The Ages," a long poem in Spenserian stanzas, as well as his view that "Thanatopsis" "owes the extent of its celebrity to its nearly absolute freedom from *defect.*" The review concludes with a detailed description of Bryant's physique. *Text: CWP,* XIII, 125–141.

"William Wilson." Short story first published in the annual *The Gift: A Christmas and New Year's Present for 1840* (published in mid-1839) and reprinted in *Burton's Gentleman's Magazine* for October 1839. The 1840 issue of *The Gift* had already appeared in 1839. The theme of the double life or secret sharer occurs in several Poe stories but is given its most formal expression in "William

Wilson.'' Details of the story's setting also derive from Poe's English schooldays. The narrator, the first of two characters named William Wilson, recalls the annoying presence in his life of a mysterious twin or exact physical double who has haunted him since his schooldays. The two Wilsons are identical in bodily appearance only; otherwise, they are moral and intellectual opposites. The first Wilson is by temperament a perverted and dissolute character who is given to every vice and vicious pleasure. Sadistic and scheming, he is especially fond of tyrannizing over others. The second Wilson constantly calls him to account, warns him against his evil ways, and always seems to appear to interfere with his perverse pleasures at the critical moment of attainment. At Dr. Bransby's school, Eton, Oxford, throughout Europe, and finally in Rome, the angelic Wilson figure stalks his satanic brother to thwart his degenerate schemes. In Rome, the malicious Wilson has planned to seduce the Duchess di Broglio, but his moral shadow intervenes, an interruption that precipitates a furious attack upon his other self and the murder of the doppelgänger. ''In an absolute frenzy of wrath, I turned at once upon him who had thus interrupted me, and seized him violently by the collar . . . and thus, getting him at mercy, plunged my sword, with brute ferocity, repeatedly through and through his bosom.'' As the double dies, he pronounces judgment on the first Wilson: ''You have conquered. . . . Yet henceforward art thou also dead.'' Since the dying guardian angel utters the tale's final words, the effect of the deed of self-slaughter on the criminal Wilson remains ambiguous. In any event, he has liberated himself from all constraints of conscience and can now pursue his predatory career with total license. The psychological skill of Poe's presentation of the dual personality bears comparison with later versions of the double theme, Dostoevsky's ''The Double'' and Conrad's ''The Secret Sharer.'' *Epigraph:* ''What say of it? What say of CONSCIENCE grim,/ That spectre in my path.'' William Chamberlayne, *Love's Victory* (attributed incorrectly by Poe to Chamberlayne's *Pharonnida*, but corrected by T. O. Mabbott). *Text: MCW*, II, 422–451; *CWP*, III, 299–325. *Research:* Rothwell, Kenneth S. ''Source for the Motto to Poe's 'William Wilson.' '' *Modern Language Notes*, 74 (1959): 297; Walsh, Thomas F. ''The Other William Wilson.'' *American Transcendental Quarterly*, 10 (1971): 17–25; Carlson, Eric W. '' 'William Wilson': The Double as Primal Self.'' *Topic* (Washington and Jefferson College), 16, no. 30 (1976): 35–40; Sullivan, Ruth. ''William Wilson's Double.'' *Studies in Romanticism*, 15 (1976): 253–263; Hubbs, Valentine C. ''The Struggle of the Wills in Poe's 'William Wilson.' '' *Studies in American Fiction*, 1 (1983): 73–79; Engel, Leonard W. ''Identity and Enclosure in Edgar Allan Poe's 'William Wilson.' '' *College Language Association Journal*, 29 (1985): 91–99; Joswick, Thomas. ''Who's Master in the House of Poe? A Reading of 'William Wilson.' '' *Criticism*, 30 (1988): 225–251; Ware, Tracy. ''The Two Stories of 'William Wilson.' '' *Studies in Short Fiction*, 26 (1989): 43–48.

Williams, William Carlos. (1883–1963). American poet and critic. He took a positive view of Poe's contribution to American literature in his essay ''Edgar Allan Poe'' in *The American Grain*. ''Poe gives the sense for the first time in America, that literature is *serious*.'' *Research: PLL*, 275, 332.

Willis, Nathaniel Parker. (1806–1867). Editor of the New York *Evening Mirror* and *American Monthly Magazine*. He befriended Poe in New York and provided him with the position of "paragrapher," a sort of assistant editor, at the *Evening Mirror* in 1844. Willis championed Poe after his death by refuting the attacks of Griswold and others in the *Home Journal* of 20 October 1849 and 30 October 1858. Poe included a sketch of Willis in "The Literati of New York City" and an analysis of his signature in "Autography." *See:* "Tortesa, the Usurer." *Text: CWP,* XV, 9–18, 165, 190. *Research:* Benton, Richard P. "The Works of N. P. Willis as a Catalyst of Poe's Criticism." *American Literature*, 39 (1967): 315–325; *PJC,* 171–172, 221–222, 365–373; Cameron, Kenneth Walter. "A Late Defence of Poe by N. P. Willis." *American Transcendental Quarterly*, 36 (1977): 69–74.

Wilmer, Lambert. (1805–1863). Baltimore journalist and litterateur. He was a friend to both Poe brothers, Edgar and Henry, and wrote a dramatic poem, *Merlin*, based on Poe's affair with Elmira Royster. He described Poe as intellectually industrious since he always seemed to be hard at work when in Wilmer's company but added elsewhere that his work habits were "excessively slothful, and wonderfully industrious—by fits." Wilmer published "Recollections of Edgar A. Poe" in 1866. His signature in "Autography" provoked this advice to him from Poe: " 'Hold to the right way,' despising the yelping of the small dogs of our literature." *See:* "The Quacks of Helicon—A Satire." *Text: CWP,* XV, 228. *Research: PLL,* 259–260.

Wilson. Character mentioned in *The Narrative of Arthur Gordon Pym.*

Wilson, Edmund. (1895–1972). American literary critic. Writing on Poe the critic, in *The Nation*, Wilson commented, "His literary articles and lectures surely constitute the most remarkable body of criticism ever produced in the United States." *Research:* Wilson, Edmund. "Poe as a Literary Critic," *Nation*, 31 October 1942, 452–453; Wilson, Edmund. "Poe at Home and Abroad." In *Shores of Light*. New York: Farrar, Straus and Young, 1952, 179–190.

Wilson, Professor John. [pseud. Christopher North]. (1785–1854). English literary critic and editor of *Blackwood's Magazine*. *See:* "Wiley & Putnam's Library of Choice Reading. No. XXI. Genius and Character of Burns." *Text: CWP,* VIII, 259; XII, 84, 239–241; XV, 258. *Research: TPL,* xlix, 574–576.

Wimble, Will the Undertaker. Character mentioned in the short story "King Pest." His establishment contains King Pest and his royal pest court enthroned on coffins.

Windenough, Mr. Character in the short story "Loss of Breath." He has sent some billets-doux to Lackobreath's wife and is later discovered in a coffin and seized by the nose by Lackobreath.

Winfree, Miss Mary. Young woman of Chesterfield, Virginia and friend of Elmira Shelton. After meeting her in 1834, Poe composed the poem ''To Mary'' for her. *See:* ''To Mary.'' *Research: MCW,* I, 136, 236, 545; *TPL,* 143.

Wirt, William. (1772–1834). United States Attorney General. Poe knew him briefly in Baltimore in 1829 and sought his opinion of the early poems. In ''Autography'' Poe noted that although ''the writing is black, strong, clear, and very neat'' that it is ''upon the whole, little in accordance with Mr. W.'s compositions.'' *Text: CWP,* XV, 157–158; Davis, Richard B. ''Poe and William Wirt.'' *American Literature*, 16 (1944): 212–220.

Wither, George. (1588–1667). English poet. Poe quotes his stanzas, ''The Shepherd's Hunting,'' in his review of *The Book of Gems*. *Text: CWP,* IX, 98; XII, 142.

Wolf. Canine character in the short story ''The Gold-Bug.'' He is William Legrand's Newfoundland dog.

Wolfe, Thomas. (1900–1938). American novelist and author of *Look Homeward Angel.* In *The Hills Beyond*, Wolfe commented on the dark and solitary nature of American literary art. ''It seems to me that all American writing of the first mark has had in it a quality of darkness and of night—I mention Poe, Hawthorne, Melville, Whitman (most decidedly), Mark Twain, and Sherwood Anderson.'' Of his particular bond with Poe, Wolfe wrote ''Everything, all or nothing, the most trivial incidents, the most casual words, can in an instant strip me of my armor, palsy my hand, constrict my heart with frozen horror, and fill my bowels with the gray substance of shuddering impotence.'' Wolfe's stylistic and thematic connections with Poe remain to be traced. *Research:* Cargill, Oscar. ''Gargantua Fills His Skin.'' In *Thomas Wolfe: Three Decades of Criticism*, ed. Leslie A. Field. New York: New York University Press, 1968, 4–5; Rubin, Larry. ''An Echo of Poe in *Of Time and the River*.'' *Poe Newsletter*, 3 (1970): 38–39.

Wolff, Oskar Ludwig Bernhard. (1799–1851). German translator and collector of Volkslieder and ballads. He also compiled an encyclopedia of German literature. Poe accused Longfellow of borrowing from Wolff's translations during the Longfellow War. *Text: CWP,* XII, 95–96. *See:* Longfellow War.

Wollstonecraft [Godwin], Mary. (1759–1797). The mother of Mary Shelley and author of *A Vindication of the Rights of Woman* is mentioned once by Poe in the opening paragraph of his review of Elizabeth Barrett's *The Drama of Exile, and Other Poems*. *Text*: *CWP,* XII, 1.

Woodberry, George E.[dward]. (1855–1930). Poe biographer and editor. He was the author of *The Life of Edgar Allan Poe, Personal and Literary, with His Chief Correspondence with Men of Letters* (1885).

Woods, John W. Baltimore printer who issued Poe's *Al Aaraaf, Tamerlane, and Minor Poems* in 1829. *Research: TPL,* xlix, 157–158.

Woodworth, Samuel. (1785–1842). American journalist, dramatist, songwriter, and editor of the *New York Weekly Mirror.* Poe objected that he was subordinately classified by Griswold under "Various Authors" in *The Poets and Poetry of America. Text: CWP,* XI, 241.

Wordsworth, William. (1770–1850). English romantic poet. Poe considered Wordsworth to be a fine poet whose lines lost their beauty wherever his didacticism intruded. He quoted respectfully from Wordsworth's poetry in his reviews of Bryant and Drake-Halleck. Elsewhere he refers to "the misplaced didacticism of Wordsworth" and "the out-of-place didacticism of Wordsworth." Wordsworth's poem "She Dwelt Among the Untrodden Ways" is quoted several times for its pure beauty unsullied by didacticism of any kind. *Text: CWP,* VIII, 135, 317–318; IX, 203, 276; XI, 12, 202, 235; XII, 140; XV, 55; XVI, 100, 150. *Research: PLB,* 64; Hinden, Michael. "Poe's Debt to Wordsworth: A Reading of 'Stanzas.'" *Studies in Romanticism,* 8 (1969): 109–120; *PJC,* 35–58.

"The Works of Lord Bolingbroke, with a Life Prepared Expressly for This Edition, Containing Additional Information Relative to His Personal and Private Character." Review of the four volumes of Bolingbroke's works appearing in *Graham's Magazine* for July 1841. Poe considered the philosophical essays in the four volumes "comparatively valueless, and inferior, both in style and matter, to the political tracts." But he admired Bolingbroke's genius as a public speaker, comparing his oratorical abilities to Cicero. As for the biographical preface to the collection, Poe savagely dismissed it as a "ragged, piebald piece of composition. . . . If ever a man deserved a horsepond, it is the inditer of this biography." *Text: CWP*, X, 171–174.

Worth, Colonel William Jenkins. (1794–1849). Poe's commanding officer at Fortress Monroe. He had been commandant of cadets at West Point. Poe asked and received his recommendation for appointment to the Military Academy. *Research: PLL,* 348.

Wotton, Sir Henry. (1586–1639). English poet mentioned in the review of *The Book of Gems*. Poe thinks the lavish praise given to his verse "On His Mistress, the Queen of Bohemia" is grossly exaggerated. *Text: CWP,* IX, 96–97; XII, 141.

"A Would-Be Crichton." A marginalia anecdote on ''a flippant pretender to universal acquirement—a would-be Crichton'' included by Mabbott in his edition of Poe's *Tales and Sketches.* James Crichton was a seventeenth-century intellectual, wit, adventurer, and man of many physical and mental accomplishments. *Text: MCW,* III, 1323–1325.

"A Wreath of Wild Flowers from New England." Generally favorable review of the poetry of Frances Sargent Osgood appearing in *Godey's Lady's Book* for March 1846. In Poe's estimation, she possesses ''deep feeling and exquisite taste.'' Much of the review is devoted to ''Elfrida, a Dramatic Poem in Five Acts,'' a work that contains some fine poetic flourishes, but ''as a drama, [Poe finds] Elfrida faulty in the extreme.'' *Text: CWP,* XIII, 105–125.

Wright, Richard. (1908–1960). American novelist, short story writer, and author of *Native Son.* Wright discovered Poe early in his career and acknowledged his debt in an article in the *Saturday Review* for June 1940, ''How Bigger Was Born.'' Wright's *Native Son* often crosses over into the realm of the horror tale where Poe's influence is specifically apparent in both scenic construction and language. When the novel's protagonist, Bigger Thomas, is interrogated about the missing heiress, Mary Dalton (whom he has murdered), a white cat leaps on his shoulder and perches there in a transcription of the exposure of the murderer in Poe's ''The Black Cat.'' Wright shared with Poe an interest in probing the mental processes of the criminal mind as well as an appreciation for the range of extremes present in that type of mind. Like Poe's homicidal narrators, Wright's Bigger Thomas experiences an initial euphoria and relief after the killing that dissipates into obsessional guilt intensified by the recurrent nightmare of the victim's severed head. Wright's subterranean urban gothic tale ''The Man That Lived Underground'' and ''The Man Who Killed a Shadow'' yield further evidence of Poe's pervasive presence in his imagination. *Research:* Fabre, Michel. ''Black Cat and White Cat: Richard Wright's Debt to Edgar Allan Poe,'' *Poe Studies,* 4, no. 2 (1971): 17–19; Prior, Linda T. ''A Further Word on Richard Wright's Use of Poe in *Native Son.*'' *Poe Studies,* 5, no. 2 (1972): 52–53; Gross, Seymour. ''*Native Son* and 'The Murders in the Rue Morgue': An Addendum.'' *Poe Studies,* 8 (1975): 23; Sisney, Mary F. ''The Power and Horror of Whiteness: Wright and Ellison Respond to Poe.'' *College Language Association Journal,* 29 (1985): 82–90.

"Writings of Charles Sprague." Review of the collected poems appearing in *Graham's Magazine* for May 1841. Poe ranks the poem ''The Shakespeare Ode'' ''the best of them,'' compared to those poems such as ''Lines on the Death of M. S. C.,'' which falter because they ''evince little ideality.'' *Text: CWP,* X, 139–142.

"Wyandotté, or The Hutted Knoll." Review of a novel of the American Revolution by James Fenimore Cooper appearing in *Graham's Magazine* for

November 1843. To Poe, both the disunified plotting and the prolix style are the "most unaccountable faults" of the book. "In general, there is quite too much colloquy for the purpose of manifesting character, and too little for explanation of motive." But Poe adds, "The negroes are, without exception, admirably drawn. The Indian, Wyandotté, however, is the great feature of the book, and is, in every respect, equal to the previous Indian creations of the author." *Text: CWP,* XI, 205–220.

Wyatt, Cornelius. Character in the short story "The Oblong Box." He is a passenger aboard the packet ship *Independence* and keeps a mysterious oblong box in his stateroom.

Wyatt, Marian. Character in the short story "The Oblong Box." She is the sister of the artist Cornelius Wyatt.

Wyatt, Mrs. W. Character in the short story "The Oblong Box." She is supposedly the wife of Cornelius Wyatt, but revelations after the shipwreck prove otherwise.

Wyatt, Thomas. Author of the *Manual of Conchology* (1838) and *A Synopsis of Natural History* (1839). Poe received $50 from Wyatt for coauthoring *The Conchologist's First Book*, but precisely how much actual writing Poe did is questionable. *See: The Conchologist's First Book. Research: LET,* I, 225, II, 343; Moldenhauer, Joseph J. "Beyond the Tamarind Tree: A New Poe Letter." *American Literature*, 42 (1971): 468–477; *TPL,* xlix-l, 260–261.

X

Xenophon. (431–355 B.C.). Ancient Greek historian. Xenophon's campaign history, *The Anabasis*, is mentioned as a necessary component of the classical curriculum in Poe's review of ''An Address Delivered Before the Students of William and Mary.'' *Text: CWP,* IX, 193.

"X-ing a Paragrab." Short story by Poe published in *The Flag of Our Union* of 12 May 1849. The story has the quality of hack work about it or journalist's boilerplate. The fiery editor, Mr. Touch-and-go Bullet-head, goes west to establish a newspaper in the city of Alexander-the-Great-o-nopolis where he soon clashes with the rival paper of John Smith, the Nopolis Gazette. A literary war ensues, and an editorial by Smith mocks Bullet-head's overuse of letter O's. Bullet-head responds by composing a paragraph containing ''the beautiful vowel—the emblem of Eternity'' no less than 175 times. Smith is OOOed to death by Bullet-head's paragraph—or would be, were it not for the fact that in setting it up the printer runs out of O's and has to substitute X's. The published result is the X-ed paragrab, an explosion of gibberish that rouses the populace to riot and ''a general rush to Bullet-head's residence, for the purpose of riding him on a rail.'' But discreetly, Bullet-head has vanished from the city leaving behind an ''X-cellent joke'' and an ''X-ample to posterity.'' In this late story with its mechanical humor, Poe may have expressly intended to deride the pointlessness of his own countless wars in print with various editors. *Text: MCW,* III, 1367–1376; *CWP,* VI, 229–237. *Research:* Perkins, Leroy, and Joseph A. Dupras. ''Mystery and Meaning in Poe's 'X-ing a Paragrab.' '' *Studies in Short Fiction*, 27 (1990): 489–494; Sirvent, Michel. ''Lettres volées. Métareprésentation et lipogramme chez E. A. Poe et G. Perel.'' *Littérature*, 83 (1991): 12–30.

Y

Yarrington, Martha. She operated a boarding house in Richmond where the wedding of Edgar and Virginia took place on 16 May 1836. *Research: TPL,* xxv, 174–175, 207.

Yeadon, Richard. William Gilmore Simms's novel *The Partisan* is dedicated to him. Poe included the dedication in his review of the novel. *Text: CWP,* VIII, 143–145.

"A Year in Spain. By a Young American." Review of the third edition of a book by Lieutenant Slidell appearing in *The Southern Literary Messenger* for August 1836. "The book has a vigorous interest—has received a great deal of commendation—and deserves it." *Text: CWP,* IX, 83–84.

Yeats, William Butler. (1865–1939). Irish poet. Although he thought most of Poe's writings "vulgar and commonplace" as well as too reliant upon "an appeal to the nerves by tawdry physical affrightments," he did admire a few of the lyrics. Yeats's ambivalence resurfaced in his statement that Poe was "certainly the greatest of American poets, and always and for all lands a great lyric poet." Yeats's lifelong preoccupation with the occult and the supernatural as shown in his "Supernatural Songs" links the two writers. *Research: PJC,* 155; *PLL,* 273–274.

Young, Edward. (1683–1765). English poet and author of *Night Thoughts on Life, Death, and Immortality*. Poe refers to Young in "The Premature Burial" and quotes a Young line, "Man wants but little, nor that little long," in *Pinak-*

idia and *Marginalia*. Young is also mentioned in connection with the morbid beauty of William Cullen Bryant's verse. *Text: CWP,* V, 273; IX, 283, 305; XIII, 130; XIV, 47–48, 64; XVI, 76. *Research: PJC,* 257.

"The Young Wife's Book; A Manual of Moral, Religious, and Domestic Duties." Review of a manual of conduct appearing in *The Southern Literary Messenger* for January 1836. Poe enjoyed the manual's ''mingled amusement and instruction'' but is disappointed that the work is unsigned. ''It may be taken for granted that every reader, in perusing a book, feels some solicitude to know, for example, *who wrote it*; or (if this information be not attainable,) at least *where it was written*.'' *Text: CWP,* VIII, 158–160.

Z

Zaïat, Ebn. [Abou Giafar Mohammed ben Abdalmalek ben Abban]. (d. 218). Arabian poet and grammarian. Poe assigned the epigraph of ''Berenice'' to him. *Text: CWP,* II, 16, 26.

"Zanoni, a Novel." Review of a novel on Rosicrucian themes and the evil eye by Bulwer appearing in *Graham's Magazine* for June 1842. Poe continued his assault on Bulwer. The plot is ''grossly defective,'' the writing is ''inflated, often bombastic,'' the characters have no ''individuality,'' and ''the author has erred in calling his book a Novel. . . . Through every line, the author looks out, like Snug the joiner, to tell you he is there.'' *Text: CWP,* XI, 115–123. *Research: LET,* I, 202.

Zanthe. Character in the poem ''Al Aaraaf.'' After Nesace returns to her halls, ''She paus'd and panted, Zanthe.''

Zenobia, Signora Psyche. Character in and narrator of the short stories ''How to Write a Blackwood Article'' and ''A Predicament.''

Zeuxis. (ca. 400 B.C.). Ancient Greek painter. He did a portrait of Helen for the Temple of Hera. Discussing realism and mere imitation of nature in the arts in *Marginalia*, Poe refers to the famous anecdote about his painting of grapes that rendered them edible to the naked eye. *Text: CWP,* XI, 84; XVI, 164.

"Zinzendorff, and Other Poems. By Mrs. L. H. Sigourney." Review of a verse collection by Lydia Huntley Sigourney appearing in *The Southern Literary Messenger* for January 1836. Poe objected to her work as lacking in unity and much too imitative of Felicia Hemans but found the versification of ''Zinzendorff'' ''particularly good—always sweet—occasionally energetic.'' Mrs. Sigourney's verse was reviewed together with the poetic work of Miss H. F. Gould and Mrs. E. F. Ellet. *See:* ''Poems—By Miss H. F. Gould;'' ''Poems; Translated and Original. By Mrs. E. F. Ellet.'' *Text: CWP,* VIII, 122–135. *Research: LET,* I, 90; *PJC,* 104–116.

Zoilus. The corpse-guest and plague victim in attendance at the drinking party in the short story ''Shadow—A Parable.''

Bibliography

EDITIONS OF COLLECTED AND INDIVIDUAL WORKS

Poe, Edgar Allan. *The Works of the Late Edgar Allan Poe*. 4 vols., ed. Rufus Wilmot Griswold. New York: Redfield, 1850–1856.

———. *The Works of Edgar Allan Poe*. 10 vols., eds. Edmund Clarence Stedman and George Edward Woodberry. Chicago: Stone & Kimball, 1894–1896.

———. *The Complete Tales and Poems of Edgar Allan Poe*, ed. Hervey Allen. Modern Library. New York: Random House, 1938; Rpt. New York: Vintage/Random House, 1975.

———. *Selected Writings of Edgar Allan Poe*, ed. Edward H. Davidson. Riverside Edition. Boston: Houghton Mifflin, 1956.

———. *Edgar Allan Poe: Selected Writings*, ed. David Galloway. Baltimore: Penguin Books, 1967.

———. *Portable Poe*, ed. Philip V. Stern. New York: Viking/Penguin, 1977.

———. *Selections from the Critical Writings of Edgar Allan Poe*, ed. F. C. Prescott. New York: Gordian Press, 1981.

———. *Essays and Reviews*, ed. G. R. Thompson. New York: Library of America, 1984.

———. *Collected Writings of Edgar Allan Poe*. 4 vols., ed. Burton R. Pollin. Boston: Twayne, 1981 (volume I); New York: Gordian Press, 1985–1986 (volumes II, III, IV).

———. *The Complete Stories*. New York: Everyman's Library/Alfred A. Knopf, 1992.

See also under "Abbreviations": *BRE*, *CWP*, *MCW*, *PEP*.

BIOGRAPHIES AND BIOCRITICAL STUDIES

Bittner, William. *Poe: A Biography*. Boston and Toronto: Atlantic Monthly Press, 1962.

Dow, Dorothy. *Dark Glory*. New York: Farrar & Rinehart, 1931.

Haining, Peter, ed. *The Edgar Allan Poe Scrapbook: Articles, Essays, Letters, Anecdotes, Photographs, and Memorabilia about the Legendary American Genius*. New York: Schocken Books, 1978.

Krutch, Joseph Wood. *Edgar Allan Poe: A Study in Genius*. New York: Alfred A. Knopf, 1926.

Lindsay, Philip. *The Haunted Man: A Portrait of Edgar Allan Poe*. London: Hutchinson, 1953.

Mankowitz, Wolf. *The Extraordinary Mr. Poe*: A Biography of Edgar Allan Poe. London: Weidenfeld & Nicolson, 1978.

Miller, John Carl, ed. *Poe's Helen Remembers*. Charlottesville: University of Virginia Press, 1979.

Phillips, Mary Elizabeth. *Edgar Allan Poe: The Man*. Chicago and Philadelphia: John C. Winston, 1926.

Pope-Hennessy, Una. *Edgar Allan Poe: A Critical Biography*. London: Macmillan, 1934; Rpt. New York: Haskell House, 1969.

Porges, Irwin. *Edgar Allan Poe*. New York and Philadelphia: Chilton Books, 1963.

Quinn, Arthur Hobson. *Edgar Allan Poe: A Critical Biography*. New York: Appleton-Century-Crofts, 1941; Rpt. New York: Cooper Square Publishers, 1969.

Shanks, Edward. *Edgar Allan Poe*. London: Macmillan, 1937.

Sinclair, David. *Edgar Allan Poe*. Totowa, NJ: Rowman & Littlefield, 1978.

Stoddard, Richard Henry. "Life of Poe." In *The Works of Edgar Allan Poe*. 6 vols. New York: A. C. Armstrong, 1884, I, 1–200.

Symons, Julian. *The Tell-Tale Heart: The Life and Works of Edgar Allan Poe*. New York: Harper & Row, 1978.

Wagenknecht, Edward. *Edgar Allan Poe: The Man behind the Legend*. New York: Oxford University Press, 1963.

Walter, Georges. *Edgar Poe*. Paris: Flammarion, 1991.

Winwar, Frances. *The Haunted Palace: The Life of Edgar Allan Poe*. New York: Harper, 1959.

See also under "Abbreviations": *BPB*, *LET*, *LTP*, *MNR*, *PLL*, *TPL*.

BIBLIOGRAPHIES, CONCORDANCES, SYNOPSES, CATALOGUES, AND OTHER REFERENCE SOURCES

Argersinger, Jana L., and Steven Gregg. "Subject Index to 'International Poe Bibliography': Poe Scholarship and Criticism, 1983–1988." *Poe Studies*, 24, nos. 1–2 (1991): 1–48.

Booth, Bradford Allen, and Claude E. Jones. *A Concordance of the Poetical Works of Edgar Allan Poe*. Baltimore: Johns Hopkins Press, 1941.

"Current Poe Bibliography" and "International Poe Bibliography" in the journal *Poe Studies*, Washington State University, Pullman, WA. [*Poe Studies* began as *Poe Newsletter* (1968–1970), then was renamed *Poe Studies* in 1971].

Dameron, J. Lasley, and Irby B. Cauthen, Jr. *Edgar Allan Poe: A Bibliography of Criticism: 1827–1967*. Charlottesville: University of Virginia Press, 1974.

Dameron, J. Lasley, and Louis Charles Stagg. *An Index to Poe's Critical Vocabulary*. Hartford, CT: Transcendental Books, 1966.

Dedmond, Francis B. ''A Checklist of Poe's Works in Book Form Published in the British Isles.'' *Bulletin of Bibliography*, 21 (1953): 16–20.

———. ''Poe in Drama, Fiction, and Poetry.'' *Bulletin of Bibliography*, 21 (1954): 107–114.

Gale, Robert L. *Plots and Characters in the Fiction and Poetry of Edgar Allan Poe*. Hamden, CT: Archon, 1970.

Hammond, J. R. *An Edgar Allan Poe Companion*. New York: Barnes & Noble, 1981.

Heartman, Charles F., and James R. Canny. *A Bibliography of First Printings of the Writings of Edgar Allan Poe*. Hattiesburg, MS: Book Farm, 1943.

Hubbell, Jay B. ''Poe.'' In *Eight American Authors: A Review of Research and Criticism*, ed. Floyd Stovall. New York: Modern Language Association, 1956, 1–46; Rpt. ed. James L. Woodress. New York: W. W. Norton, 1971.

Hull, William Doyle, II. ''A Canon of the Critical Works of Edgar Allan Poe.'' Ph.D. dissertation, University of Virginia, 1941.

Hyneman, Esther F. *Edgar Allan Poe: An Annotated Bibliography of Books and Articles in English, 1827–1973*. Boston: G. K. Hall, 1974.

Ljungquist, Kent P. ''Edgar Allan Poe.'' In *Facts on File: Bibliography of American Fiction through 1865*, ed. Kent P. Ljungquist. New York: Facts on File; A Manly Book, 1994, 200–208.

Marrs, Robert L. '' 'The Fall of the House of Usher': A Checklist of Criticism since 1960.'' *Poe Studies*, 5 (1972): 23–24.

Moldenhauer, Joseph. *A Descriptive Catalogue of Edgar Allan Poe Manuscripts in the Humanities Research Center Library*. Austin: Texas University Press, 1973.

''Poe.'' In *American Literary Scholarhip/An Annual*. Durham, NC: Duke University Press, 1963–1965. [Compiled by various editors annually under the categories ''Bibliographical, Textual,'' ''Biographical Work,'' ''Books, Parts of Books, Poems, Tales, Sources, Influence.'']

Pollin, Burton R. ''Music and Edgar Allan Poe: A Second Annotated Checklist.'' *Poe Studies*, 15, no. 1 (1982): 7–13.

———. *Word Index to Poe's Fiction*. New York: Gordian Press, 1982.

———. *Images of Poe's Works: A Comprehensive Descriptive Catalogue of Illustrations*. Westport, CT: Greenwood Press, 1989.

Quinn, Arthur H., and Richard H. Hart. Edgar Allan Poe: *Letters and Documents in the Enoch Pratt Free Library*. New York: Scholars' Facsimiles and Reprints, 1941.

Robbins, J. Albert. *Checklist of Edgar Allan Poe*. Columbus, OH: Charles E. Merrill, 1969.

Robertson, John W. *Bibliography of the Writings of Edgar A. Poe*. 2 vols. San Francisco: Russian Hill Private Press, 1934; Rpt. New York: Kraus Reprint, 1969.

———. ''Poe: A Bibliographic Study.'' In *Edgar A. Poe: A Study*. San Francisco: Bruce Brough, 1921; Rpt. New York: Haskell House, 1970.

Wiley, Elizabeth. *Concordance to the Poetry of Edgar Allan Poe*. Selinsgrove, PA: Susquehanna University Press, 1989.

See also under ''Abbreviations'': *DNT*.

SELECTED GENERAL CRITICAL STUDIES

Abel, Darrel. ''Edgar Poe: A Centennial Estimate.'' *University of Kansas City Review*, 16 (1949): 77–96.

Asselineau, Roger. *Edgar Allan Poe: University of Minnesota Pamphlets on American Writers*. Minneapolis: University of Minnesota Press, 1970.

Bleiler, E. F. "Edgar Allan Poe, 1809–1849." *Supernatural Fiction Writers*. 2 vols. New York: Charles Scribner's, 1985, II, 697–705.

Bloom, Clive. *Reading Poe, Reading Freud: The Romantic Imagination in Crisis*. New York: St. Martin's Press, 1988.

Braddy, Haldeen. *Glorious Incense: The Fulfillment of Edgar Allan Poe*. Metuchen, NJ: Scarecrow Press, 1952; Rpt. Port Washington, NY: Kennikat Press, 1968.

Buranelli, Vincent. *Edgar Allan Poe*. Boston: Twayne, 1977.

Campbell, Killis. *The Mind of Poe and Other Studies*. Cambridge, MA: Harvard University Press, 1933.

Clarke, Graham, ed. *Edgar Allan Poe Critical Assessments, I: Life and Works; II: Poe in the Nineteenth Century; III: Poe the Writer: Poems, Criticism and Short Stories; IV: Poe in the Twentieth Century*. East Sussex, United Kingdom: Helm Information, 1991.

Davidson, Edward H. *Poe, a Critical Study*. Cambridge, MA: Belknap Press of Harvard University, 1957.

Dayan, Joan. *Fables of Mind: An Inquiry into Poe's Fiction*. New York: Oxford University Press, 1987.

Fagin, N. Bryllian. *The Histrionic Mr. Poe*. Baltimore: Johns Hopkins University Press, 1949.

Garrison, Joseph M., Jr. "The Function of Terror in the Work of Edgar Allan Poe." *American Quarterly*, 18 (1966): 136–150.

Halliburton, David. *Edgar Allan Poe: A Phenomenological View*. Princeton, NJ: Princeton University Press, 1973.

Hoffman, Daniel. *Poe Poe Poe Poe Poe Poe Poe*. New York: Doubleday, 1972.

Kennedy, J. Gerald. *Poe, Death and the Life of Writing*. New Haven, CT: Yale University Press, 1987.

Ketterer, David. *Edgar Allan Poe: Life, Work, and Criticism*. Fredericton, New Brunswick, Canada: York University Press, 1989.

Knapp, Bettina. *Edgar Allan Poe*. New York: Frederick Ungar, 1984.

Lawson, Lewis A. "Poe's Conception of the Grotesque." *Mississippi Quarterly*, 19 (1966): 200–205.

Lee, A. Robert. *Edgar Allan Poe: The Design of Order*. Totowa, NJ: Barnes & Noble, 1987.

Levin, Harry. "Journey to the End of Night" and "Notes from Underground." In *The Power of Blackness: Hawthorne, Poe, Melville*. New York: Vintage, 1960, 101–164.

Levine, Stuart. *Edgar Poe: Seer and Craftsman*. Deland, FL: Everett/Edwards, 1972.

Matthiessen, F. O. "Poe." *Sewanee Review*, 54 (1946): 175–205.

May, Charles E. *Edgar Allan Poe: A Study of the Short Fiction*. Boston: Twayne, 1991.

Phillips, Elizabeth. *Edgar Allan Poe: An American Imagination*. Port Washington, NY: Kennikat Press, 1979.

Rosenheim, Shawn, and Steven Rachman, eds. *The American Face of Edgar Allan Poe*. Baltimore: Johns Hopkins University Press, 1995.

Stoehr, Taylor. "Unspeakable Horror in Poe." *South Atlantic Quarterly*, 78 (1979): 317–332.

Williams, Michael J. *A World of Words: Language and Displacement in the Fiction of Edgar Allan Poe*. Durham, NC: Duke University Press, 1988.
Wuletich-Brinberg, Sybil. *Poe: The Rationale of the Uncanny*. New York and Bern: Peter Lang, 1988.

See also under ''Abbreviations'': *DIP*.

SELECTED SPECIALIZED CRITICAL STUDIES

Alexander, Jean, ed. *Affidavits of Genius: Edgar Allan Poe and the French Critics, 1847–1924*. Port Washington, NY: Kennikat Press, 1971.
Allen, Michael. *Poe and the British Magazine Tradition*. New York: Oxford University Press, 1969.
Bailey, J. O. ''Poe's Palestine.'' *American Literature*, 13 (1941): 44–58.
Cabale, Dean William. ''Appropriating Poe: Problems in American Literary History.'' *Dissertation Abstracts International*, 53 (1992): 1912A (SUNY at Stony Brook).
Cooke, John Estren. *Poe as a Literary Critic*. Baltimore: Johns Hopkins University Press, 1946.
Dayan, Joan. ''Amorous Bondage: Poe, Ladies, and Slaves.'' *American Literature*, 66 (1994): 239–273.
Dean, John. ''Poe and the Popular Culture of His Day.'' *Journal of American Culture*, 10 (1987): 35–40.
Forrest, William M. *Biblical Allusions in Poe*. New York: Macmillan, 1926.
Foust, R. E. ''Aesthetician of Simultaneity: E. A. Poe and Modern Literary Theory.'' *South Atlantic Review*, 46, no. 2 (1981): 17–25.
Hale, Brian Patrick. ''To Touch the Stars: The Neo-Classicism of Edgar Allan Poe.'' *Dissertation Abstracts International*, 54 (1994): 2578A (University of South Carolina).
Kesterton, David B., ed. *Critics on Poe*. Coral Gables, FL: Miami University Press, 1973.
Ketterer, David. *The Rationale of Deception in Poe*. Baton Rouge: Louisiana State University Press, 1979.
Lévy, Maurice. ''Poe and the Gothic Tradition.'' *ESQ: A Journal of the American Renaissance*, 18 (1972): 19–28. [Translated by Richard Henry Haswell].
Ljungquist, Kent P. ''Uses of the Daemon in Selected Works of Edgar Allan Poe.'' *Interpretations*, 12 (1980): 31–39.
Mainville, Stephen. ''Language and the Void: Gothic Landscapes in the Frontiers of Edgar Allan Poe.'' *Genre*, 14 (1981): 347–362.
McGill, Meredith L. ''Poe's Plagiarisms: Literary Property and the Authorial Self in Antebellum America.'' *Dissertation Abstracts International*, 55 (1994): 567A (Johns Hopkins).
Miller, Perry. *The Raven and the Whale*. New York: Harcourt, Brace, 1956.
Mooney, Stephen L. ''Poe's Gothic Wasteland.'' *Sewanee Review*, 70 (1972): 261–283.
Moss, Sidney P. *Poe's Major Crisis: His Libel Suit and New York's Literary World*. Durham, NC: Duke University Press, 1970.
Norman, Emma K. ''Poe's Knowledge of Latin.'' *American Literature*, 6 (1934): 72–77.
Parks, Edd Winfield. *Edgar Allan Poe as Literary Critic*. Athens: Georgia University Press, 1964.

Person, Leland S., Jr. "Poe's Fiction: Women and the Subversion of Masculine Form." In *Aesthetic Headaches: Women and a Masculine Poetics in Poe, Hawthorne, Melville*. Athens: Georgia University Press, 1988, 19–47, 180–182.

Reilly, John E. *The Image of Poe in American Poetry*. Baltimore: Enoch Pratt Free Library, Edgar Allan Poe Society, and the Library of the University of Baltimore, 1976.

Saliba, David R. *A Psychology of Fear: The Nightmare Formula of Edgar Allan Poe*. Lanham, MD: University Press of America, 1980.

Smith, Ronald L. *Poe in the Media: Screen, Songs, and Spoken Word Recordings*. New York: Garland Publishing, 1990.

Thompson, G. R. *Poe's Fiction: Romantic Irony in the Gothic Tales*. Madison: Wisconsin University Press, 1973.

———. *Circumscribed Eden of Dreams: Dream Vision and Nightmare in Poe's Early Poetry*. Baltimore: Edgar Allan Poe Society, 1984.

Walker, I. M. *Edgar Allan Poe: The Critical Heritage*. London and New York: Routledge and Kegan Paul, 1986.

Weissberg, Liliane. "The Heart of the Letter: Allegory in Edgar Allan Poe." *Dissertation Abstracts International*, 45 (1984): 515A–516A (Harvard University).

Wilbur, Richard. "Poe and the Art of Suggestion." *University of Mississippi Studies in English*, 3 (1982): 1–13.

See also under "Abbreviations": *PJC, PLB*.

SELECTED INFLUENCE STUDIES

Anderson, Carl L. *Poe in Northlight: The Scandanavian Response to His Life and Works*. Durham, NC: Duke University Press, 1973.

Bandy, William T. *The Influence and Reputation of Edgar Allan Poe in Europe*. Baltimore: F. T. Cimino, 1962. [Lecture to the Edgar Allan Poe Society in October 1959].

Benson, Adolph B. "Scandanavian References in the Works of Poe." *Journal of English and Germanic Philology*, 40 (1941): 73–90.

Cambiaire, Célestin Pierre. *The Influence of Edgar Allan Poe in France*. New York: G. E. Stechert, 1927.

Carlson, Thomas C. "The Reception of Edgar Allan Poe in Romania." *Mississippi Quarterly*, 38 (1985): 441–446.

———. "Edgar Allan Poe in Romania, 1963–1983," *Bulletin of Bibliography*, 44 (1987): 75–81.

Dorset, Gerald. *An Aristocrat of the Intellect*. London: Hornsey Printers, 1959.

Englelkirk, John Eugene. *Edgar Allan Poe in Hispanic Literature*. New York: Instituto de las Españas en los Estados Unidos, 1934; Rpt. New York: Russell & Russell, 1972.

Grossman, John Delaney. *Edgar Allan Poe in Russia: A Study in Legend and Literary Influence*. Wirzburg, Germany: Jal Verlag, 1973.

Hoffmann, Gerhard. "Edgar Allan Poe and German Literature." In *American-German Literary Interrelations in the Nineteenth Century*, ed. Christoph Wecker. Munich: Germany; Fink, 1983, 52–104.

Smith, Charles Alphonso. *Edgar Allan Poe: How to Know Him*. Indianapolis, IN: Bobbs-Merrill, 1921.

Index of Critics, Editors, and Acquaintances

Page numbers in **bold type** refer to main entries in the encyclopedia.

Index of Authors, Artists, and Titles

Poe titles and page numbers for main entries appear in **bold type**.

Index of Themes, Subjects, and Characters

Poe characters and page numbers for main entries appear in **bold** type. Places where Poe lived appear in *italic* type. Cross references may refer to any of the three indexes in the encyclopedia.

About the Authors

FREDERICK S. FRANK is Professor Emeritus of English at Allegheny College. He has published articles in journals such as *Bulletin of Bibliography*, *American Transcendental Quarterly*, and *Extrapolation*. His books include *Through the Pale Door: A Guide to and Through the American Gothic* (Greenwood, 1990).

ANTHONY MAGISTRALE is Professor of English at the University of Vermont. His publications include *The Dark Descent: Essays Defining Stephen King's Horrorscape* (Greenwood, 1992).

ISBN 0-313-27768-0
90000>
EAN
9 780313 277689
HARDCOVER BAR CODE